W9-AZO-585

**Price Theory
and Applications**

Price Theory and

Jack Hirshleifer

University of California, Los Angeles

Applications

Prentice-Hall, Inc., Englewood Cliffs, New Jersey

Library of Congress Cataloging in Publication Data

HIRSHLEIFER, JACK.
   Price theory and applications.

   Includes index.
    1. Microeconomics. I. Title.
HB171.5.H66   330   75-6800
ISBN 0-13-699645-0

Price Theory and Applications
Jack Hirshleifer

© 1976 by Prentice-Hall, Inc., Englewood Cliffs, N.J.

All rights reserved.
No part of this book may be reproduced
in any form or by any means
without permission in writing from the publisher.

Printed in the United States of America

10 9 8 7 6 5 4 3 2 1

Prentice-Hall International, Inc., London
Prentice-Hall of Australia, Pty. Ltd., Sydney
Prentice-Hall of Canada, Ltd., Toronto
Prentice-Hall of India Private Limited, New Delhi
Prentice-Hall of Japan, Inc., Tokyo
Prentice-Hall of Southeast Asia (Pte.) Ltd., Singapore

Contents

One
Introduction

Two
Preference, Consumption, and Demand

Three
Equilibrium and Exchange

Four
The Firm and the Industry

Five
Factor Markets, Distribution, and Intertemporal Analysis

Six
Political Economy

Preface

Price theory—the set of principles governing the production, exchange, and consumption of goods and services—is the heart of economics and the key to its application in the world of affairs.

The student's desire to obtain command of price theory beyond the level of the elementary course may have arisen from any of a number of motives. He or she may simply be interested in personal financial advancement, an entirely legitimate aim. ("There are few ways in which a man can be more innocently employed than in getting money."—Dr. Samuel Johnson, 1775.) The impulse may be ideological, stemming from commitment to reform or revolution, or alternatively to defense against reformist or revolutionary attacks. (And there will be those choosing to acquire more information before deciding whether it is dismantling or reforming or defending that is called for!) Finally, some students may be motivated by purely scientific aims, and simply want better knowledge of what makes things tick.

All three of these motivations—personal political, and scientific,—are entirely valid. But even for those whose primary interest is in the instrumental use of economic knowledge rather than in knowledge for its own sake, scientific understanding is an essential prerequisite. In this regard there are two, somewhat opposed, pedagogical problems.

On the one hand, the introductory treatment that aroused the student's interest is likely to have been largely descriptive and institutional. But in economic *analysis* the recital of facts such as the date of the Sherman Act or the capitals of the Federal Reserve districts plays essentially zero role. The student must therefore shift gears to cope with a much more abstract subject matter.

But on the other hand, economics is *not* a branch of mathematics, a body of theorems deducible from given postulates. Unfortunately, one sometimes encounters intellectually muscle-bound theorists, overtrained virtuosos who may be knowledgeable about Frobenius matrices and conditions of multidimensional dynamic stability, but are at a loss to explain why vegetables are cheaper after the harvest than before. *Economics is a science designed to ex-*

plain the nature of the real world. Consequently, it is not only duller but fundamentally misleading to present "theory" in the absence of "application." *Theory is justified only by its power of application.* The intent here is to keep the integration of theory and application always before the student.

Such an integration poses, however, a difficult—indeed, perhaps an impossible—problem for any single text. Real applications tend to be complex, almost always raising surprisingly subtle issues. Applications should properly be presented as case studies, extensively described. Lack of space has unavoidably dictated placing predominant emphasis upon exposition and elucidation of the theory itself. But a noticeable feature of this book is the dozens of brief discussions of real-world "Examples," designed both to display the relevance of the theory and to provide some expository change of pace. In addition, a number of applied topics—such as import quotas, the negative income tax, rationing, subsidy versus voucher support for education, monopolistic suppression of inventions, and investment in human capital—are discussed in more extended fashion.

A peculiarly difficult problem is posed by the variety of backgrounds and of degrees of effort that students can bring to bear. Some students will already have taken a full-year basic economics course and additional applied-area studies before approaching intermediate theory; others may have no more than a single-semester "elements" course as background. In some cases the previous courses may have been demanding, in other cases perhaps too easy. As for the price theory course itself, some colleges cover it in a single term while others may devote an entire year. A price theory course offered by a graduate school of business or of public administration will encounter students already mature, with considerable experience of the world. But the book should also remain accessible to undergraduates at the sophomore level. Apart from use as text in a course, the book ought to be capable of serving as general reference and guide for later study and review.

It is evidently impossible to meet all these requirements. The particular compromise adopted here is as follows: First of all, and taken as a whole, *this is not a minimal book.* The intent was to build a growth potential into the book that would match the student's later deepening understanding of economics. *But it is not absolutely necessary to take the book as a whole.* A number of more difficult or ancillary topics, not essential for logical continuity, are relegated to special optional starred sections or sub-sections within chapters. Omitting some or all of these will help meet time pressure. Finally, a book-within-the-book exists in the form of the series marked CORE CHAPTERS (Chapters 1 through 5, 7, 9 through 11, 14, and 15) that can serve as the basis for a course under more severe time constraints.

Some specific innovations in textual coverage may be mentioned.

1. Traditional intermediate texts are silent or evasive on the price-theoretic underpinnings of *money.* In Chapter 8, the analysis of exchange as an actual (and therefore costly) economic activity provides the foundation for understanding the function of a monetary commodity. Similar reasoning serves in Chapter 9 to explain the existence of the business firm as another institution called into being by the costliness of exchange.

2. The traditional topic of "monopolistic competition" is presented here as only one instance of a more general issue—*variation of product.* Topics covered under this heading include optimal product assortment and equilibrium level of quality. Product variation can of course emerge from monopolistic, competitive, and other market structures apart from the special case of monopolistic competition.

3. Chapter 16 is devoted to the topic of intertemporal choice, leading to a theory of investment and saving decisions. This is a helpful bridge to macroeconomics, and also to the business-finance literature.

4. After a treatment of traditional welfare economics in Chapter 17 ("The Theory of Economic Policy"), Chapter 18 provides a *positive* analysis of government. The apparatus of the state is treated as consisting of human agents responding to motivations of individual advantage. Government is shown to be an institutional alternative to the market, but one whose functioning and performance are still analyzable by economic techniques. More generally, market and non-market institutions are seen to be differentiated not by "higher" or "lower" motivations, but by the rules governing the processes of human interaction.

One point always in contention is the appropriate mathematical level for a book like this one. The choice was adopted here of eschewing calculus techniques—except in marked "mathematical footnotes" and in the appendix on equations of general equilibrium. But the delta (Δ) notation employed in the definitions of "marginal" concepts will be naturally interpretable in differential or derivative terms by the student equipped with calculus. No use is made of integrals or matrices. The instructor should, of course, warn serious students that further command of college mathematics is a necessity for study of economics beyond the intermediate level.

Whether a proper balance has been struck between coverage and simplicity, between theory and application, between technical accuracy and suggestive exposition, only the reader can judge. The author will be grateful for guidance on this point from instructors and students, as well as for specific corrections where errors appear.

ACKNOWLEDGMENTS

Thanks are due to a considerable number of colleagues who have reviewed or commented upon portions of this text at various stages. I would like to mention especially Professors Robert Dorfman (Harvard), Ross Eckert (U.S.C.), David L. McNicol (Pennsylvania), Edwin Mills (Princeton), R. Charles Moyer (University of Houston), and Lloyd M. Valentine (University of Cincinnati). None bears any responsibility for remaining errors or omissions. My research assistant, Charles Knoeber, developed most of the examples used in the text and also suggested many of the questions which follow each chapter.

**Price Theory
and Applications**

One

Introduction

Chapter 1
The Nature and
Scope of Economics

1. A ECONOMICS AS A SOCIAL SCIENCE

Economic philosophy, economic history and scholarship, and economic persuasion are all respectable intellectual activities. But this book is an introduction to economics as a *science*: as a body of analytical models (theories) that yield verifiable implications about the real world.

1. A. 1 Is Economics Scientific?

Economics claims to be a social science. That it concerns behavior in human society no one will deny. But can it be a science? Cynics cite two important pieces of evidence to the contrary: (1) On any issue one can find economists on either side of the argument; indeed, they always seem to disagree. (2) If economics were really a science, economists would be able to predict commercial and financial affairs and so should be (but visibly are not) all rich! Each of these contentions is worthy of serious attention.

As to arguments among economists, individuals disagree in all aspects of life—and in science as well. To mention only a few great scientific debates: In astronomy the geocentric model of Ptolemy was opposed by the newer heliocentric model of Copernicus; in chemistry Priestley supported the phlogiston theory of combustion while Lavoisier propounded the oxidation theory; and in biology the creationism of earlier naturalists was countered by Darwin's theory of evolution. It is not universal agreement, but rather the willingness to consider evidence that signals the scientific approach. For Galileo's opponents to disagree with him about Jupiter's moons was not unscientific of itself; what was unscientific was their refusal to look through his telescope and see. An inspection of economic texts and journals will reveal that current great issues, whether it be the monetarist vs. fiscalist hypotheses in macroeconomics, or the determinants of labor's share in distribution theory, or the effectiveness of centralized planning versus *laissez faire* for achieving economic growth, are under continous scientific evaluation. Failure to arrive at a general scientific consensus[1] may be due to the complexity of the problem or to the incompetence of the investigators, but there will always be unresolved issues in any living science.

Are there, however, any *resolved* issues in economics? This book will highlight a great many, in the area of price theory or microeconomics. (For some comments on *macro*economics, see Section D below.) There is little remaining disagreement on essentials of such topics as the impact of taxes or subsidies upon prices and outputs, the implications for consumers of competitive vs. monopolistic market structures, the effects of reducing tariffs, etc.

Observers often exaggerate not only the extent of disagreement among economists, but also the degree to which the natural sciences (sometimes miscalled the "exact" sciences) have mastered their respective fields of inquiry. Few topics have been so well studied as strength of materials in applied physics. Yet engineers, after going through their calculations, commonly add on a huge safety factor (50% or even 100%) before undertaking construction of a bridge or a dam. And even so, bridges still collapse and dams wash away. If economists predicting the rate of inflation were permitted as wide a safety factor as engineers, they would rarely go astray!

[1]*Scientific* consensus need not imply general agreement as to *policy*, however. See the discussion of "Normative versus Positive Analysis" below.

Example 1.1
Hydrology
versus
Economics

In 1955 the Board of Water Supply of New York City projected that the city's future rate of water use would reach 1320 MGD (million gallons per day) as of 1960, rising further to 1500 MGD by 1970. "Safe yield" (a hydrologic concept supposedly representing a reliable minimum supply) from existing water sources was pegged at 1550 MGD throughout. With only a thin safety margin (1550 − 1500 = 50 MGD) anticipated as remaining by 1970, the Board of Water Supply decided to acquire a new water source to come into service before that date.

A team of economists reviewed this decision in 1960. They concluded that the Board's projections of water use were much too high; the economists' prediction was that actual water use in New York City would surely not reach 1500 MGD by 1970, if ever. Since the "safe yield" supposedly guaranteed by hydrologic science already equalled 1550 MGD, the economists concluded that provision of a new supply was not warranted.

After 1960, the economists' predictions about actual use were borne out. Water consumption in New York City stabilized well below 1300 MGD, far under the Board's projected rate of 1500 MGD, and never came anywhere near the supposed "safe yield" of 1550 MGD. So all should have been well. Instead, the city was hit by a catastrophic water shortage. What had happened? Throughout the early 1960's the *actual* yield of water sources was far, far below the hydrologists' alleged "safe yield." Incredibly, the actual water yield remained below 1200 MGD in almost every year for half a decade. The projections of the social sciences thus proved to be immensely more reliable than those of one of the vaunted natural sciences.[2]

Comment: In making policy recommendations, the economist may be in a position of having to evaluate the reliability of other sciences as well as his own.

[2]For a discussion, see J. Hirshleifer and J. W. Milliman, "Urban Water Supply: A Second Look," *American Economic Review*, v. 57 (May 1967), pp. 169–78.

What about the charge that their own poverty disproves the economists' scientific claims? To this several answers, not all mutually consistent, are commonly offered. It is sometimes argued that a scientific knowledge of economics ought *not* to be expected to lead to financial success: Would a comprehension of the aerodynamic equations governing the motion of spheroidal missiles have helped Henry Aaron beat Babe Ruth's home-run record? This argument should not be pressed too far, however. After all, what is the use of economics (or of aerodynamic knowledge for that matter) if it does not lead to *some* practical result? In the case of economics this usefulness is surely in the understanding of observable market phenomena, which ought to be convertible at least to some extent into higher cash income. While the general run of people can hardly be expected to match the achievements of geniuses like Henry Aaron in his field or J. Paul Getty in his, there ought to be some observable effect of economics training upon income. And indeed, to some degree, there is!

Example 1. 2
Salaries

The Table below shows 1968 salaries for teachers in different professions (fields of study).

1968 Salaries by Profession

Profession by Rank	1968 Median Salary
Economics	$15,000
Statistics	14,900
Physics	14,000
Chemistry	13,500
Psychology	13,200
Mathematics	13,000
Biology	13,000
Earth Science	12,900
Anthropology	12,700

1968 Salaries by Profession (Continued)

Profession by Rank	1968 Median Salary
Sociology	12,000
Linguistics	11,500
Agriculture	11,000
All Professions	13,200

Source: G. Schachter, B. Cohen, and H. Goldstein, "The Demand and Supply of Teachers of Economics 1969–70," *The American Economist*, v. 16 (Spring 1972), pp. 126–27.

Comment: These salary data cover only *teachers* and thus are not conclusive for ranking the incomes of *all* practitioners of the different disciplines. But since (as we shall see in Chapter 14) employers of teachers must compete against all other possible employers of trained professionals, differential earnings in teaching are a fairly reliable guide to relative income status in general.

Nevertheless, the data in the Example do not suffice to prove that it is *the economics training* that leads to the higher incomes reported. There are other possible explanations of income differentials. One might be that economics is so unpleasant that its practitioners must be offered added financial compensation—rather like sewage workers or executioners. More self-gratifying to economists, however, is the idea that the higher salaries they earn are only normal rewards for those exceptional talents necessary to understand economics in the first place.

1. A. 2   Relation to Other Social Disciplines

Economics is not the only social science. Boundaries between different sciences are generally indistinct, which is usually a healthy intellectual situation since the modes of attack of different disciplines can then compete over the bordering territories. It is useful to think of economics as having a *core area* as base, plus outlying extensions into the domains more usually associated with other disciplines. The core area of economics is a limited range of human activity: that characterized by *rational behavior* on the part of individuals, interacting upon one another through a particular social mechanism, *the market*.

Rational behavior is nothing more than *action well-suited to achieve your goals*, within your limitations and capacities. Everyone behaves irrationally to some extent (out of passion, thoughtlessness, mental defect, or just plain perverseness), and some to such a great degree that they are institutionalized for their own or others' protection. In view of the prevalence of irrationality, how can rationality be postulated in economics? Clearly, only to the extent that the assumption works in providing usable predictions of social phenomena. Rational behavior is systematic and purposive, whereas irrational behavior tends to be unpredictable and erratic. Since it is the aggregate behavior of a great number of individuals that determines social results, the cumulative effect of even a limited degree of rationality tends to dominate over the unsystematic irrational elements. Predictions of social phenomena in terms of rational responses do tend to work, often in surprising ways (see, for example, the data on bank robbery below). And yet economics as a science is not irrevocably wedded to the rationality postulate. When an alternative that proves more usable for predictive purposes comes along, it will be adopted instead.

Example 1. 3
Psychotic Yes,
but Stupid No ![3]

With 44 female psychotics (primarily schizophrenics) as experimental subjects, the psychologists T. Ayllon and N. H. Arzin studied responsiveness of patients in a mental institution to changes in systems of reward for services. Prior to the beginning of the experiment patients were allowed to choose among a variety of tasks (laundry service, dietary service, etc.) for which they were to be rewarded. The reward took the form of tokens, which were convertible into commissary articles (clothing, toiletries, cigarettes, etc.) or into hospital privileges (e.g., privacy, leave from the ward).

During the first 20 days, patients were (as promised) rewarded with tokens upon completion of their chosen tasks. After 20 days, however, it was announced that the same number of tokens as before would be paid to each patient *whether or not the tasks were completed*. During the first 20-day period of "contingent reinforcement" (i.e., positive wages for services) the 44 patients worked in total 45 hours per day, on the average. Upon the shift to "non-contingent reinforcement" (i.e., to free gift of tokens) the total number of hours worked by the 44 patients rapidly dropped to 35 on the first day and to 20 hours on the third. Shortly afterward the bottom dropped out, and close to zero hours were worked thereafter.

Then, at the end of a second period of 20 days, the earlier system of contingent reinforcement was reinstated. The total number of hours worked jumped immediately to 45 hours per day, and remained near this level to the end of the experiment 20 days later.

Conclusion: Psychotics can still, at least in some domains, behave rationally.

[3]Discussion based upon T. Ayllon and N. H. Azrin, "The Measurement and Reinforcement of Behavior of Psychotics," *Journal of the Experimental Analysis of Behavior*, v. 8 (Nov. 1965).

Rationality is an instrumental concept. It requires the prior existence of goals aimed at. The economist, by and large, regards the process whereby individuals somehow become pointed toward particular desired ends as outside his sphere of competence. He is only interested in the net result of this process, the patterns that he calls *tastes* or *wants* or *preferences*. These are, from his point of view, arbitrary. In one society individuals may be protective of children but eat cattle; another society may be protective of cattle but expose unwanted infants. Either way, the scientific economist is prepared to make predictions about the social consequences of the given preferences.

This undoubtedly leaves a great territory, including what are perhaps the most important aspects of social phenomena, for other sciences to study. Goals and preferences are not determined randomly. Psychology brings explanations to bear in terms of primitive instincts, as reinforced or suppressed by socialization processes. The anthropologist analyzes the relevance of culture for goal formation, and the sociologist the relevance of class or other group identification. The economist is content to let the division of intellectual labor operate in this way, and leave the explanation and prediction of changes in tastes or goals as a task for the sister social sciences. (A task on which they have made regrettably small scientific progress!)

The economist's mode of procedure inclines him to suppose that preferences are generally quite *stable*, only rarely constituting the dynamic element in social changes. If a tax on liquor is imposed, his analysis will almost automatically assume that the desire to drink is just as great—only that the tax makes it more expensive to indulge that desire. For the economist this represents a possible blind spot, and scientific caution is indicated. Take liquor: Without any change in taxes the temperance campaign of Father Mathew around 1850 in Ireland reduced that country's consumption of spirits from 12,000,000 to 5,000,000 gallons per annum.[4] And if there is a higher tax on liquor, its imposition may itself reflect a change of tastes in the form of increased revulsion against drinking. Nor is the assumption of unchanging tastes very helpful for analyzing the element of fashion and style in consumption. Far more important, many of the really great social changes in human history have clearly stemmed from shifts in people's goals for living. Indeed, the economist is in danger of trivializing these fundamental values and goals by suggesting that they are merely arbitrary "tastes." From the prophets of ancient Israel to the ministry of Jesus to the recent decline in effective belief in God, the changes in the kinds of rewards that people seek from life have had enormous effect upon the shape of the social system of the West. The ethical messages of Buddha and Confucius have perhaps had similar impacts upon the civilization of the East. The areas the economist leaves out of his cognizance are therefore at least as important as those he feels equipped to examine.

It is sometimes charged that economics also postulates that people's preferences are completely selfish. This is an uninformed criticism. It is true

[4]But alas, only temporarily.

that, observing facts as they really are, the economist normally finds it useful to operate on the premise that individuals seek their own advantage. "It is not from the benevolence of the butcher, the brewer, or the baker, that we expect our dinner, but from their regard to their own interest."[5] That this is a main truth about human activity it would be absurd to deny. Nevertheless, charity is an important feature of economic life; people have, in a sense, a taste for benevolence. Even so, the economist is likely to say, if benevolence were made less costly (for example, if the Internal Revenue Service permitted more ample deductions for charitable giving against income tax), we would see more of it. As another example, the economist can hardly explain the economic relations between parents and children—expenditures for protection and education, and provision for inheritance—with a postulate of complete parental selfishness. But again, if we want to elicit a higher degree of love and care on the part of parents, a financial inducement would help.

Rationality, the sensible selection of means for achieving given ends, does not suffice to delimit the core domain of economics. Something must be said about the ways in which people's rational decisions interact. If consumer A wants bread from baker B, it may seem like rational behavior for A to get a job and earn the price of a loaf. But it may also be rational, in certain circumstances, for A to simply steal the bread from B. Alternatively, A might organize a political party with the object of passing laws dictating that B's must give bread to A's. Or, A might attempt to persuade B that it is the latter's charitable duty to help out hungry A's. Economics concentrates upon the first of these forms of interaction: i.e., the integration of individuals' separate goal-seeking activities *through the market*. For the most part crime has been left to sociology, the uses of state power to political science, and techniques of persuasion to psychology. But the vigor and rigor of economic science are proving increasingly useful in these related areas. Economics has tended, therefore, to overflow these boundaries, as the following example shows.

[5]Adam Smith, *The Wealth of Nations*, Book I, Chap. 2.

Example 1. 4
Rational
Bank Robbers?

Comparing a cross-section of states, T. O. Ozenne related the mean dollar loss per bank robbery (y) in the state to the average months of imprisonment per robbery (F) in the state. If bank robbers were rational, they would engage in robbery in a higher-imprisonment state only if higher-yielding robberies were anticipated (on the average). The equation obtained for 1966–70 was:

$$y = 3238 + 24.5F$$

The interpretation is that, for each month increase in average imprisonment per robbery, there was an average rise of $24.50 yield per robbery.

The direction of effect is right—though the receipt of $24.50 seems only a small recompense for the additional risk![6]

[6]T. O. Ozenne, "The Economics of Theft and Security Choice," UCLA Ph.D. dissertation, 1972, p. 67.

Results in the area of non-market decision-making will be studied further in Part Six of the book.

Market interactions have distinctive characteristics that set them apart from other forms of human relationships. The market relation is *mutual* and *voluntary*. Criminal taking is involuntary on one side, while gifts are voluntary but not a relation of mutuality. Two different objections can immediately be raised on this score. First, if A is hungry and B has bread, can their relation really be voluntary? Must not the A's of this world be "wage slaves" of the B's? Then how does the market differ from coercive dominance? Second, suppose some highwayman declares to his victim, "Your money or your life!" Isn't he offering a voluntary deal? Then how can criminal transfers be distinguished from market exchange?

The explanation of these conundrums turns on the legal concept of *property*. To take up the highwayman first, he is indeed proposing a market deal: to "sell" the victim back his own life, in exchange for his money. But under our legal system each person has property in his own life. The seemingly voluntary transaction proposed by the highwayman is premised upon his seizing power over something he has no right to—his victim's life. As for the "wage slave" contention, it is of course true that those endowed with more valuable property will be better off in the market than those possessing little in the way of resources. But there is a vast difference between the laborer possessing property rights in his own labor power, in a position to bargain with alternative employers for the best available terms, and the slave. The latter has no property; indeed, he is property. He cannot market or trade his labor power, for it is not legally his to dispose of.

1. A. 3 Normative versus Positive Analysis

In its scientific aspect economics is strictly *positive*. It answers the question "What is reality like?" But *normative* issues in public policy, turning upon the question "What *should* be done?", also always require economic analysis. Given the social objective aimed at (with which he might in fact personally disagree), the scientific economist can use his knowledge of reality to analyze the problem and suggest efficient means for attaining the desired end. This book will touch upon many policy issues, but always emphasizing the positive point of view.

Apart from this technical or instrumental use of economic science, however, the economic approach can claim to parallel all straight thinking on normative issues. Any policy proposal involves gains and losses, benefits and costs, favorable and unfavorable features. The enthusiastic advocate will only consider one side, his own side, of the question. The training of the economist, and the set of mind that the subject tends to establish, lead him always to ask: "Yes, but how much will it cost?" That is, what has to be sacrificed to achieve the ends of the enthusiast? Always insisting that attention be paid to both sides of the balance, the economist is likely to be unpopular—but indispensable.

When economists disagree on policy issues, it may be because they are seeking divergent goals; one may be more concerned with achieving social equality, another, with achieving individual freedom. Where the divergence is indeed on such a philosophical plane, even the most complete scientific understanding of economic reality will not resolve the conflict. But it is often the case that variance of opinion among economists is over *means* rather than *goals*. Further scientific progress in positive economics will, over time, tend to eliminate this source of disagreement.

1. B THE INVISIBLE HAND

As astronomy has Newton's principle of universal gravitation, and biology Darwin's principle of evolution through natural selection, economics also has a great unifying scientific conception. Its discovery was, like Newton's and Darwin's, one of the important intellectual achievements of humanity.

Adam Smith's *The Wealth of Nations* appeared in 1776. The key idea is suggested by the following quotation:

But it is only for the sake of profit that any man employs his capital in the support of industry; and he will always, therefore, endeavour to employ it in the support of that industry of which the produce is likely to be of the greatest value, or to exchange for the greatest quantity either of money or of other goods. . . . He is in this, as in many other cases, led by an invisible hand to promote an end which was no part of his intention. Nor is it always the worse for the society that it was no part of it. By pursuing his own interest he frequently promotes that of the society more effectually than when he really intends to promote it.[7]

We can amplify this, in more modern language, as follows. Each person will be motivated by rational self-interest to employ the resources under his control wherever he can get the highest possible price. But high prices reflect scarcity of supply relative to intensity of consumers' demands. Hence the private incentives will work continuously to overcome scarcity and meet consumer demands, i.e., to direct resources to the employments most suited for satisfying consumers' desires.

This seems obvious enough, though it was not so obvious two centuries ago. At that time it was commonly believed that untrammeled selfishness must lead to mutual harm, if not to total chaos. Even today many people hardly understand how, for example, the city of New York can be regularly

[7]Book IV, Chap. 2.

fed by convergence of food shipments from all corners of the earth—without any governing plan to make sure that the Iowa farmer, the New England fisherman, and the Florida orange-grower actually deliver to the hungry city. Yet the city is fed, although none of its suppliers need be motivated by any particular love and concern for New Yorkers. The Iowa farmer simply finds it more profitable to ship to New York than to eat his own wheat, and similarly for the others.

Adam Smith's object in composing *The Wealth of Nations* was largely policy-oriented or *normative*; he argued that national wealth would expand if mercantilism[8] were replaced by a policy of "natual liberty."[9] But it is not his policy recommendations that will mainly concern us. For our purposes, his key conception is that *the economy is an integrated system whose behavior follows scientifically determinable laws.* In early times, the motion of the planets was so incomprehensible that it was thought they were pushed in their courses by angels. The development of astronomy eventually led to the scientific idea of gravitation as the integrating mechanism that explains these motions. Similarly today, all too many people find it utterly incomprehensible why (for example) water is cheap and diamonds expensive, a strange situation that they are all too likely to attribute to the actions of angels or devils. We owe to Smith the conception of the market economy as a self-regulating mechanism, harnessing as motive power the self-interest of participants, yet so integrating their activities that each is led to serve the desires of his fellows. How this leads to water being cheap and diamonds expensive we shall see in the pages to come.

1. C ELEMENTS OF THE ECONOMIC SYSTEM, AND THE CIRCULAR FLOW OF ACTIVITY

That *there is an economic system*—that there are laws of economics—is the first message to learn. We can now survey some of the necessary elements going into the make-up of the economic system.

1. C. 1 Decision-Making Agents in the Economy

Economics concerns the making of rational decisions, as well as the social interactions of the choices so made. What are the active entities to be regarded as engaging in the process of choice? We shall deal in this book with three main categories of decision-making units: individuals, firms, and governments.

Individuals are the ultimate active members of social systems, the only agents said to have goals or *preferences* and to engage in the process of *consumption* (to be discussed in Part Two). Actually, recognizing the mutual support and cohesiveness of the family some economists prefer to consider

---

[8] The mercantilists believed that a nation's well-being could best be furthered by accumulation of gold and silver, to be achieved by systematic government interventions designed to encourage exports and restrain imports.
[9] Smith recommended free trade among nations and *laissez faire* within.

the "household" to be the effective consumptive unit. Except where otherwise specified, the individual here will be understood as making decisions for his or her family or household.

The business firm is an artificial unit; it is ultimately owned by or operated for the benefit of one or more individuals. Surprisingly, this fact is often not appreciated. It is sometimes argued, for example, that "soulless corporations" can be taxed without cost to the people. But while taxing a corporation will benefit *some* people (possibly, the great majority), it will do so only at the expense of some *other* people (possibly, a wealthy few). The economist finds it convenient to think of firms as distinct agents specialized in the process of *production*, the conversion of resource inputs into desired goods as outputs. Firms will be the center of attention in Part Four of the text. In point of fact, however, much production actually takes place within the household; cooking, gardening, and home maintenance are examples.

Individuals and firms are not the only economic decision-making agents. A third category, government, is of great and growing importance. Governments like firms are artificial groupings; they are distinguished by not being owned by individuals, and also by having powers to take property involuntarily, yet legally (as by taxing). From the economic point of view governments are agencies engaging in a number of collective productive and consumptive activities, the scope of which is determined by a political rather than market process. Perhaps even more important, government establishes the legal framework within which the entire economy works. Just as ownership of valuable resources normally leads some individuals to superior outcomes through the market mechanism, similarly possession of influence over government policies can be expected to lead some individuals to superior outcomes through the political mechanism. (The role of government is examined specifically in Part Six.)

In complex modern economies there are still other "collective" decision-making units, aggregations of individuals (or of firms or other collective units) designed to facilitate some form of united action. Trade unions and cartels are of particular interest as representing organizations of buyers or sellers in markets, and will be discussed in the text below. Of lesser economic importance are voluntary associations like clubs, foundations, and religious institutions, which can be regarded as instrumentalities whereby individuals combine for certain collective consumption choices.

1. C. 2 Scarcity, Objects of Choice, and Economic Activities

The all-pervasive economic problem is that of *scarcity*. Not all desired things are available to individuals, the ultimate decision-making agents, when and as desired. Even if all desired physical commodities were present in unlimited quantities, we would not have enough *time* to enjoy them all. It is the fact of scarcity that forces us to make economic decisions, that is, to organize our efforts for production and/or to engage in trade with a view toward obtaining desired objects of consumption.

The physical entities that are the objects of economic decisions are called commodities or goods and services. Commodities or goods as distinguished from services are *physical objects* (wares or merchandise); services are *activities* (like haircuts, concerts, etc.) that are nevertheless the objects of human desires. The distinction between physical wares and intangible services will not be essential for us until the discussion of resources and production in Part Five. For the present, therefore, we will think of commodities or goods as synonymous words covering also desired consumption services.

Consumption of commodities or goods represents one of the main economic activities, engaged in *only* by natural individuals. The consumptive decision of a particular person will range over the various goods available to him, attempting to pick out an assortment within his means that best accords with his given tastes. We shall say that goods are the *objects of choice* for the consumption decision.

Production is another main economic activity. We shall sometimes find it convenient to regard it as engaged in by natural individuals, and sometimes by firms. We usually think of production as the physical conversion of inputs into outputs, i.e., of resources (or the services of resources) into consumable goods. More fundamentally, production is any transformation adding to the social totals of some desired goods at the expense of a reduction in the amount of others. Production might represent a transformation of physical form, as in the conversion of leather and human labor into shoes, but not necessarily so. Transformations would still be regarded as productive if they took place over space (shipment of oranges from Florida to Maine) or over time (storing of potatoes after harvest so as to distribute consumption over the year).

Of course, to be economically rational production should represent a conversion from a less desired to a more desired configuration. To burn an antique Chippendale chair for heat is a kind of production, but ill-advised under ordinary conditions. (On the other hand, an individual on the point of freezing to death might find the conversion from chair to warmth exceedingly advantageous.)

In the process of production, the objects of choice include both output and input elements. The outputs are ultimately consumption goods; the inputs are ultimately the services of resources. (We shall ordinarily disregard intermediate phases that convert resource services into "partially finished" products or "producers' goods.") From the social point of view, the process of production converts services of the given stock of resources into desired consumption goods.

The third main economic activity is *exchange* (to be discussed in Part Three). For the individual, exchange is also a kind of conversion—he trades away some objects for others. But from the social point of view, exchange is distinguished from production in that the totals of commodities are unaffected; goods and services are reshuffled in trade, but wherever one person has less, someone else must have more. Thus, exchange is a kind of transfer. But it is a mutual and voluntary transfer; *all* parties involved are satisfied. The objects of choice in exchange activities may either be consumption goods and services or production goods and services.

1. C. 3   The Circular Flow

In a simplified world with only two types of economic agents, individuals and business firms, the relations between them can be pictured as in Figure 1.1. Individuals and firms have dual aspects, and thus transact with one another in two distinct ways. Individuals are in one aspect consumers of goods, while firms are producers of goods. Thus, the diagram shows a "real" flow of consumption goods (solid upper channel) from firms to individuals. But the goods must be produced. To permit this there must be a "real" flow of productive services, from the individuals in their second aspect as owners of resources, to the firms.

In a command economy these flows of goods and resources would be directly ordered by a dictator. But in a private-enterprise economy the relations are based on exchange and so must be mutual and voluntary. Hence, offsetting the "real" flows are reverse "financial" flows of claims that in a modern economy normally take the form of money payments. The con-

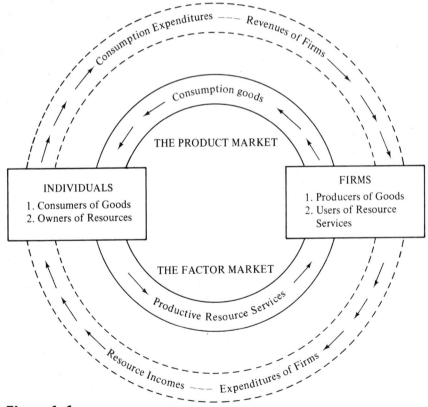

Figure 1. 1
The Circular Flow of Economic Activity

sumers' financial expenditures on goods (dotted upper channel) become the receipts or revenues of the firms. The exchange of consumption goods between individuals and producing firms, and the balancing financial payments, take place in what is abstractly termed "the product market." (Actually, there will of course be a host of separate product markets, one for each distinct class of consumption good.)

The revenues from sales to consumers provide the firms with the wherewithal to compensate resource-owners for the productive services supplied by the latter. This closes the circle, as the firms' payments for productive services become income to the individuals, available once more for consumption expenditures to begin the next cycle. The purchase and sale of productive services take place in what is abstractly called "the factor market," again, really a number of distinct markets for the various types of productive services.

Looking within the box representing the firms as economic agents, what takes place there is the process of *production*, i.e., the physical transformation of resources into products. Within the box representing individuals, *consumption* of the produced goods takes place. Here again, the circle is closed by the fact that consumption is necessary to recreate the main productive resource— labor power—for the next cycle.

1. D MICROECONOMICS AND MACROECONOMICS

A distinguished professor of logic, deploring the division of his subject between deductive reasoning and inductive reasoning, once declared: "In our textbooks on deduction we explain all about logical fallacies; in our textbooks on induction, we then commit them." In economic theory as well, we have an as yet unresolved split of the subject—microeconomics versus macroeconomics. In microeconomics we see how and why the Invisible Hand operates; in macroeconomics we examine the consequences of its failing to do so!

An easy explanation of this unsatisfactory state of affairs is not available. Suffice it to say, for our purposes here, that microeconomics concentrates mainly upon equilibrium states of particular markets, presuming an equilibrium of the market system as a whole. It also examines the shift from one equilibrium state to another in particular markets, in response to changes in the given data of economic systems, i.e., to changes in tastes, technology, resources, and legal provisions. But it seems to be the case, in complex advanced economies at least, that the equilibrium of the market system as a whole is not as robust as might be hoped. The circular flow of economic activity may become disorganized, to greater or lesser degree, without any significant disequilibrium in particular markets. After some types of disturbance there may occur self-reinforcing aggregate movements (e.g., the Keynesian "multiplier") likely, at least for a time, to lead the system of the circular flow away from rather than back to an equilibrium condition. It is these disequilibria of the system as a whole that macroeconomics studies.

For some period of time, starting in the 1930's, macroeconomists attempted to develop modes of reasoning largely independent of any micro-economic foundation; some theorists went so far as to dismiss classical microeconomics as obsolete or irrelevant. It is now generally recognized that this attempt has failed. Significant recent progress in macroeconomics has been made precisely by improving the logical connection of the subject with the microeconomic theories of production, consumption, and exchange. So if we cannot give answers to the key questions of macroeconomics here, we can still with some confidence assure the student that his study of micro-economics will promote even his understanding of the former subject.

1. E ANALYTICAL TECHNIQUES OF ECONOMICS

In any intellectual discipline, the partially-informed individual, i.e., the student, is liable to moments of despair. He will have acquired many bits of knowledge and technique, yet the subject can remain a buzzing, blooming confusion; the parts don't come together into a meaningful whole. In economics, as has already been mentioned, the student can keep hold upon a key unifying concept: the Invisible Hand. He can recall that he is studying the market system as one way of solving the economic problem of society, a way that (at least, when working ideally) harnesses individual self-interest to achieve a kind of mutual cooperation in the face of scarcity. ("Imperfections" of the market system and of alternatives to it are examined in Part Six of the text.)

The student is also helped to set the subject in order by the fact that the great bulk of economic reasoning makes use of only two analytical techniques. These two are the technique of *optimization* and the technique of *determination of equilibrium*. If the student facing any question will ask himself, "Is this an optimization problem, or an equilibrium problem?" he will rarely find himself going astray.

Optimization occurs at the level of the decision-making agent. In his consumption decision the individual wants to determine the best package or combination of goods to purchase out of his income. In his resource-supply decision he wants to find the best employment of his resources—in particular, of his labor power—taking into account the alternatives available. The business firm, engaging in the process of production, is presumed to decide upon the nature and quantities of commodities to be produced and of resources to be employed in order to achieve a best possible outcome for its owners.

Mathematically, the process of optimization can be formulated as finding a maximum (or minimum) of some desired (or undesired) *criterion*. This is the standard problem of the calculus. In this book calculus techniques are not explicitly used (except in specified mathematical footnotes). Economists have devised a variety of methods for optimization, turning upon the idea of "marginal" quantities, which amount to doing calculus without necessarily knowing it! As for the criterion measures, we say that the individual maximizes "utility" while the firm maximizes "profits." The nature and use of these criteria will be explained in Part Two (covering the decisions of the individual) and Part Four (covering the decisions of the firm), respectively.

Equilibrium is a property of the interaction of economic agents in markets. A system is in equilibrium when the forces acting upon it are so balanced that there is no net tendency to change. When the price is such that the quantity supplied equals the quantity demanded, conditions are in balance and there is no tendency for price or for quantity to change—the market is in equilibrium. The process determining an equilibrium can be formulated mathematically as a conditional equation (or system of equations). The student is assumed in this book to have the ability to understand and solve simple equations. Where complications or tricky features arise, however, explanations will be provided.

Questions

1. In what respects can it be said that economics is a science? Give an example of a prediction that modern economic science can confidently make. [Hints: Are vegetables cheaper in season or out of season? How often do you see people throwing away money? Which way would the price of copper change if the copper-exporting nations succeeded in forming an effective cartel?] Are there predictions that economic science has not yet shown itself competent to make?

2. What is rational behavior? Give examples of rational and of irrational behavior. Why may the economist's postulate of rationality be useful even in domains where irrational elements strongly influence behavior?

3. Other things being equal, would you expect the murder rate to be lower in jurisdictions applying capital punishment? If the income-tax exemption granted for each child were increased, would you expect the birth rate to rise?

4. The psychiatrist T. S. Szasz argues that what is called "mental illness" is the result of rewarding people for disability. Not only is the patient motivated to become "ill," but there is a financial advantage to the healing professions in declaring personal problems to be "illnesses." How could mental illness be made less "rewarding"? Would doing so affect its prevalence?

5. Does the economist assume stable preferences? Give an example of a change in preferences that has had important economic effects.

6. Does the economist assume that everyone is selfish? Give an example of an area where unselfish behavior has important economic consequences.

7. Market transactions or exchanges are said to be both *mutual* and *voluntary*. Give an example of a non-market interpersonal transaction that is not voluntary. Of one that is voluntary but not mutual.

8. What are positive issues in economics? Normative issues? Give an example of each.

9. How does the "Invisible Hand" lead individuals in a market economy to cooperate for mutual advantage even without any definite intention on their part to do so? Would self-interested behavior lead to mutual advantage in a monastic economy where all income is equally divided? In a dictatorship where the political authorities confiscate the lion's share? In an economy with no property, so that any person could take what he needs from any other person?

10. What are the most important classes of decision-making units in a modern economy? In what types of activity do they engage? In what sense are firms and governments "artificial" units?

11. In the circular flow of economic activity, distinguish between the "real" and "financial" circuits of flow. What is the relation between the two? Distinguish between the "product market" and the "factor market." How are these connected?

12. In terms of the circular flow of activity, explain what determines the fact that some individuals are wealthy (in a position to consume a great deal in the product market) and others are poor.

13. What are the two main analytical techniques used in economic reasoning? Which concerns the decisions of rational economic agents? Which concerns the interactions of their decisions through the market process?

14. If the Invisible Hand leads individuals to serve their own interests by serving others, why are some people led to a life of crime? Why do some corrupt politicians find it advantageous to serve themselves at the expense of their constituents? Why are dictators motivated to seize power? [Hint: Does the principle of the Invisible Hand apply to all kinds of social interactions, or does it hold only when individuals interact in a particular way?]

Chapter 2
Working Tools

At the end of Chapter 1, it was asserted that the great bulk of economic reasoning makes use of only two analytical techniques: *optimization* (on the level of the decision-making agent) and *determination of equilibrium* (on the market level of analysis). Each of these techniques employs a characteristic working tool. For equilibrium, there is supply-demand analysis. For optimization, there is the relation among total, average, and marginal magnitudes. These will be reviewed, with some applications, in this chapter.

2. A SUPPLY-DEMAND ANALYSIS

2. A. 1 Equilibrium of Supply and Demand

Consider the supply-demand diagram of Figure 2.1. The horizontal axis represents the quantity Q of some good or service. In accordance with the idea of the economy as a circular *flow* of activity, it is sometimes important to think of quantity as a continuing stream of production or consumption over time. Thus, we should speak of quantity per month or per week, etc. That quantities represent flows over time, however, will be taken as understood throughout this book.

The vertical axis of the diagram represents price P. *Price is a ratio of quantities*: the amount of some good Y that must be given up to obtain a unit of some other good X. Thus, one can speak of the price in cigarettes of a hat, or the price in labor-hours of a loaf of bread. However, in modern economies price is normally quoted in terms of *money*,[1] a "medium of exchange." Consequently, the dimensionality of the vertical or price axis in Figure 2.1 is stated in the diagram as the ratio $\$/Q$.

The demand curve DD shows, for each price P, the quantity that purchasers choose to take from the market. Its negative slope is to be accepted for the moment as an empirical fact: Buyers are willing to purchase more, the lower the price. (Verification: We often observe sellers trying to win more customers

[1]The nature and role of the institution of money will be explained in Chapter 8.

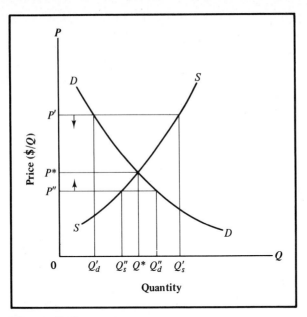

Figure 2. 1
Demand and Supply

by claiming to be offering unusually low prices. Do advertisers ever try to attract customers by asserting that their prices are exceptionally high?) Similarly, the positive slope of the supply curve SS asserts as an empirical fact that sellers will offer more the higher the price. Supply and demand curves will be derived analytically from more fundamental determinants in later chapters, where further light will be cast upon their normal shapes.

In Figure 2.1 market equilibrium is represented by the intersection point of SS and DD, whose coordinates are the quantity Q^* and price P^*.[2] The justification for the assertion that the intersection of the supply and demand curves is an equilibrium position for the market will be familiar from elementary economics. Suppose the market price were momentarily at any price higher than P^*, such as P' in the diagram. At that price the quantity along the demand curve, the number of units Q'_d that consumers are willing to purchase, is less than Q'_s, the number of units that suppliers offer on the market. Not all the suppliers can find customers. What will then happen? It is reasonable to suppose that some suppliers will quote lower prices rather than be left with undesired stocks of goods. Thus, the excess of the supply-quantity Q'_s over the demand-quantity Q'_d generates *downward* pressure on price, indicated in the diagram by the arrow pointing downward from the horizontal line representing the price P'.

What if market price were momentarily at some level lower than P^*, such

[2]In this text we will generally follow the convention of designating solution values (values of the variables associated with equilibrium or optimum positions, as the case may be) by asterisks.

as P'' in Figure 2.1? Then the quantity demanded would be Q''_d, in excess of the supply-quantity Q''_s offered on the market. Not all demanders would be able to find the number of units they desire to purchase, and hence some of them will start to bid up the price. Here there is *upward* pressure on price, indicated in the diagram by the arrow pointing upward from the horizontal line representing the price P''.

Clearly, one or the other process will always be at work so long as price is not at the equilibrium P^*. Only at P^* are the demand-quantity Q_d and the supply-quantity Q_s equal to one another, so as to rule out any upward or downward pressure on price. When Q_d equals Q_s, we have the market equilibrium quantity Q^*.

How realistic is this picture? What we are dealing with here is a *model* of reality, not reality itself. It is a model (as will be explained later) of perfect competition among individuals interacting in a perfect market. The question of scientific interest is not the literal *truth* of the model but rather its usability for understanding reality and predicting the consequences of change. This is the subject of the next section.

Conclusion: The intersection of demand and supply curves determines the equilibrium values of price and quantity exchanged.

2. A. 2 Comparative Statics of Supply and Demand— Shift of Equilibrium

Equilibrium was determined, in the picture of Figure 2.1, by the intersection of *given* supply and demand curves. But the concepts of supply and demand are mainly used to analyze the consequences of *changes* in economic data affecting the relative scarcities of economic goods. Such changes can be interpreted as shifts or displacements of either the supply curve of the good, of its demand curve, or both at once.

Suppose, for example, that buyers suddenly became universally more desirous of consuming the commodity in question. (The underlying change here is in the fundamental data of consumer preferences.) Then more of the good would be purchased at each possible price. This is called an *increase of demand*. As shown in Figure 2.2, the demand curve shifts *to the right* (from a position like $D_1 D_1$ to $D_2 D_2$). Where the old equilibrium price was P_1^* and quantity Q_1^*, the new equilibrium price and quantity are P_2^* and Q_2^*.

How does the revision of the equilibrium position actually come about? We might describe the process somewhat as follows. Suppose the price were originally unchanged at P_1^* after the demand curve shifted to $D_2 D_2$ in Figure 2.2. Then consumers would want to purchase the quantity Q'_d which exceeds Q_1^*. But at price P_1^* suppliers would still be offering only the quantity Q_1^*. There is an excess of quantity demanded over quantity supplied, leading to upward pressure on price. In a free market, price will respond to this pressure and continue to move upward until Q_d equals Q_s at the new equilibrium price P_2^*.

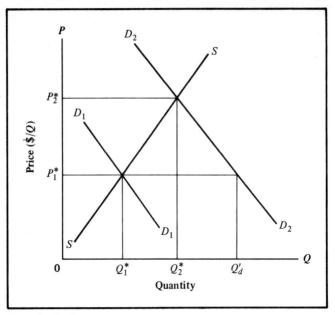

Figure 2. 2
Increase of Demand

While this description of the process of price-quantity adjustment to change is plausible, it is not the only possible scenario of events. Nor is it entirely free of problems. For example, some transactions might actually take place at "wrong" prices (somewhere before P_2^* is reached), which might have effects on the supply or demand curves. That is, the final equilibrium reached might conceivably depend upon the path for getting there. Issues of this kind are studied in the branch of economics called *dynamics*. We will, except where the contrary is indicated, waive consideration of such problems. Thus, we limit ourselves to comparisons of the initial and the final equilibrium situations. This is called *the method of comparative statics*. While some aspects of reality cannot be successfully modeled without use of dynamics, the relatively simple tools of comparative statics can still tell us a great deal about real-world phenomena.

Our basic technique, then, in analyzing the consequences of some change in market circumstances will be to ask: Is the change reflected in a shift of supply, or a shift of demand (or, possibly, of both)? It will be immediately evident from Figure 2.2 that *an increase in demand alone leads to an increase in both equilibrium price and equilibrium quantity*. An increase in *supply* (see Figure 2.3) is to be interpreted as a *rightward* displacement of the supply curve (from S_1S_1 to S_2S_2), since at each price a large quantity is offered. (*Warning:* A common slip is to think of an "increase" of demand or supply as an *upward* shift of the corresponding curve; this is correct for the demand curve but incorrect for the supply curve. The student can avoid error by thinking of an "increase" always as a *rightward* shift of the corresponding curve.) *An*

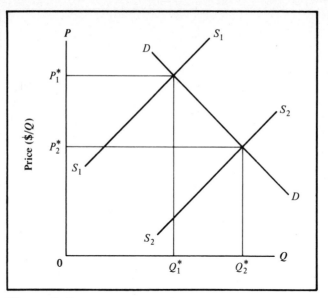

Figure 2. 3
Increase of Supply

increase in supply thus leads to an increase in equilibrium quantity but to a decrease in equilibrium price. (Question for the student: What can be said if both supply and demand increase together?)

Proposition: If demand increases, equilibrium price and quantity *both* rise. If supply increases, equilibrium quantity rises but equilibrium price falls.

Any change in economic data affecting market equilibrium can be expressed as a shift in demand or in supply (or both), upward or downward. But what are the sources of these shifts? It is sometimes useful to distinguish between those sources of change originating "outside" and those originating "inside" the economic system. The outside sources of variation include changes in *tastes, technology, resources,* and the *political-legal system.* A temperance campaign may alter tastes; a new invention modifies technology; a mineral discovery or a gift from a foreign nation can change resources; a new tax or judicial decision may change the political-legal system. These classes of changes are regarded as originating autonomously, rather than in response to economic factors.[3]

Displacement of equilibrium in a particular market may, however, also stem from movements within the economic system as a whole, but outside the

---

[3] There is no hard-and-fast rule as to what elements lie "outside" and what "inside" the economic system. Rates of change of resources like petroleum reserves or even of population (labor supply) do actually respond to economic incentives. The pace of technological change, also, is dependent upon the economic effort applied to the process of invention. Similar statements can be made about the other elements conventionally considered as originating independently of economic factors; the broader the concept of the scope of economics, the fewer the elements determined "outside" the system.

particular market in question. The "inside" or economic variations that may affect the price-quantity equilibrium of a particular good or service include: (1) *Changes in prices (or quantities) of goods related in demand.* For example, an increase in the price of butter (however caused in terms of the ultimate or "outside" sources of variation) will tend to raise the demand for margarine. (2) *Changes in prices (or quantities) of goods related in supply.* For example, a rise in the production of wool will almost necessarily increase the supply of mutton on the market. (3) *Changes in levels of income.* For example, the higher incomes recently received by petroleum-exporting countries would be expected to raise their demands for a variety of consumption goods.

It is of considerable importance for the student to develop his intuition by analyzing a number of situations in which the price-quantity equilibrium of particular markets is observed to vary over space or time.

Example 2. 1
Catholics and
Fish

For over a thousand years, the Roman Catholic church required believers to abstain from consuming meat on Fridays. But a liberalization of the regulations of the Church abolished this requirement for American Catholics as of December 1966 (except for Fridays falling within Lent).

Frederick W. Bell studied the impact of the liberalization upon the price of fish in New England (population approximately 45% Catholic). The study compared a 10-year period before the liberalization with the nine-month period just after (excluding Lenten months). In estimating the shift of the demand curve (price paid for given quantities of fish landed by New England fishermen) it was necessary to adjust for a number of economic factors: imports of fish, prices of closely competitive foods (poultry and meat), cold storage holdings, and personal income among them. Having made these adjustments, the effect of the liberalization on fish prices can be seen in the following Table.

Prices of Fish, Monthly Data, 1957–67

Species	Percent Change Due to Liberalization
Sea scallops	−17%
Yellowtail flounder	−14
Large haddock	−21
Small haddock (scrod)	− 2
Cod	−10
Ocean perch	−10
Whiting	−20

Source: F. W. Bell, "The Pope and the Price of Fish," *American Economic Review*, v. 58 (Dec. 1968), p. 1348.

The results show that, for any given quantity of fish landings (and after adjusting for the other variables mentioned above), the prices received for fish of all seven species were lower after the liberalization than before.

The "Catholics and Fish" example clearly represents a *decrease* in the demand for fish. (The demand curve for fish shifted leftward, rather than rightward as in Figure 2.2.) The source of the variation would seem to lie clearly "outside" the economic system, since the modification in Church regulations was not in any evident way a response to market factors.

Example 2. 2
Potatoes

That vegetables are cheap at harvest time may well have been the first law of economics observed in primitive society. In the case of potatoes, there is some production throughout the year but the major crop is harvested in the Fall. The Table below shows the average U.S. prices and production of potatoes in the various seasons of the year during the period from 1968 to 1970.

Prices and Production of Potatoes, 1968–70

Season	Average Production in cwt.	Average Price Received by Farmers, $/cwt.
Winter	3,765	2.09
Early Spring	5,154	2.48
Late Spring	20,977	2.71
Early Summer	13,483	2.73
Late Summer	29,790	2.07
Fall	237,391	1.90

Source: Data from U.S. Dept. of Agriculture, *Agricultural Prices, 1970 Annual Summary*, p. 22; *Crop Production*, July 9, 1971, p. A2, July 10, 1969, p. 2.

What we see here is obviously an *increase in supply* (rightward shift of the supply curve as in Figure 2.3) in the main Fall harvest season. It is perhaps surprising that the price variation is so small, given the enormous production swings over the year. The main reason is that potatoes are *stored* from harvest on. Therefore, price is still relatively low in the Winter season just after the Fall harvest, even though production is at a minimum in the Winter. As stored holdings are gradually consumed, price rises steadily over the year until the new crop begins to arrive in the Late Summer and Fall seasons.

The original source of agricultural supply variation over the year is the "outside" element of God-given seasonal climate. But note that the "inside" element of economic storage activity greatly modifies the force of the external factors. Other economic activities like improvements in transportation, changes in agricultural practices, development of new seed varieties, etc., may also be at work to minimize the impact of seasonal variation of supply.

Example 2. 3
Markdowns in Men's Furnishings

The supply of men's furnishings in department stores is relatively constant over the year, but demand tends to be concentrated in the month of December for Christmas giving. The first column of the Table below is an index of monthly sales over the year for the period 1928–1933. (An index figure of 100 represents the average sales rate over the entire year.) The second column shows an index of "markdowns" of price—the larger the markdown index, the lower the average price. (Again, a figure of 100 represents the average markdown percentage over the year.) Evidently, markdowns are least in December, most in January.

Sales and Markdowns, Men's Furnishings in North Central and Eastern Department Stores, 1928–33

Month	Index of Monthly Sales	Index of Monthly Markdowns
January	55	264
February	55	120
March	58	77
April	65	73
May	79	82
June	101	85
July	87	115
August	83	113
September	63	85
October	80	68
November	90	63
December	384	55

Source: Edgar H. Gault, *Seasonals in Department Store Merchandising* (University of Michigan Press, 1934), p. 59.

For men's furnishings we clearly see an *increase in demand* (rightward shift of the demand curve) for the month of December, with a correspondingly low markdown index (implying a relatively high price). The source of the variation is the "outside" cultural preference for Christmas giving. Again, the price swings are not as great as might be anticipated, because the possibility of storage permits production to take place over the entire year to meet the sales peak at Christmas.

<table>
<tr><td>

Example 2. 4
Brides

</td><td>

Among the Sebei in Uganda, husbands obtain wives by purchase. The anthropologist Walter Goldschmidt secured data on bride prices paid by husbands in two communities: the cattle-herding district of Kapsirika and the farming district of Sasur.[4]

The Kapsirika herders pay higher prices for brides than the Sasur farmers, although the former are not wealthier on the whole. The immediate explanation appears to be the higher rate of polygyny (plural wives) among the Kapsirika: Their wife/husband ratio is 1.51, whereas among the Sasur farmers it is only 1.17. There is a substantial intermarriage rate, but it takes entirely the form of herder husbands buying farmers' daughters. Thus, the herders' demand curve for brides seems to be higher; they pay more, and so they get more.

[4]Walter Goldschmidt, "The Brideprice of the Sebei," *Scientific American*, v. 229 (July 1973), pp. 74–85.

</td></tr>
</table>

The "Brides" example shows how supply-demand analysis can be used to interpret changes over space or across communities as well as over time within a given community. In the example, the herders' demand curve for brides can be regarded as greater than (lying to the right of) the farmers' demand curve. The *source* of the difference might seem to be just the "outside" factor of differential preferences for brides on the part of the males in the two communities. An alternative explanation is that wives are better "productive assets" for herders than for farmers among the Sebei.

<table>
<tr><td>

Example 2. 5
Computing
Power

</td><td>

An outstanding instance of technological advance in recent decades has been the development of the computer. It is difficult to directly show changes in computer prices (actually, large computers are usually rented, so the "price" is an annual or monthly rental) over time because quality has improved so drastically. Gregory C. Chow developed an index for the quantity of *computing power* represented by the physical stock of computers in existence at any moment of time. Taking account of the improvements in quality variables like multiplication time, memory size, and access time, he expressed this quantity in terms of 1960 rental equivalents. Associating the quantity index with the current prices of computing power for each year led to the results shown in the Table:

</td></tr>
</table>

Quantity and Price of Computing Power

Year	Quantity (thousands of 1960 rentals)	Absolute Price Index
1954	370.26	3.2554
1955	991.67	2.9610
1956	2389.9	2.5336
1957	5087.6	2.3168
1958	8362.0	2.0342
1959	12549.	1.5884
1960	19072.	1.0716
1961	38264.	.9042
1962	64349.	.6873
1963	95815.	.5712
1964	136845.	.4186
1965	194136.	.3416

Source: Gregory C. Chow, "Technological Change and the Demand for Computers," *American Economic Review*, v. 57 (Dec. 1967), p. 1124.

Between 1954 and 1965 the quantity of computing power rose over 50-fold, while the unit price fell to around 10.5% of its original level. Since the rise in the general price level due to inflation between 1954 and 1965 was some 20%, in real terms the fall in the price of computing power was even greater.

In the "Computing Power" example, technological advances brought about an increase in supply, a rightward shift of the supply curve, leading to an increase in quantity but fall in price. Technological improvement is usually regarded as an "outside" source of variation. But in this case advances in computer power emerged for the most part in response to profit incentives—the conflicting efforts of firms to get ahead of the hot quality competition in the computer industry.

2. A. 3　An Application:
Effects of a Tax on Transactions

The familiar "sales tax" is an example of a tax on transactions. Consider what is sometimes called an "excise tax" levied upon *sellers*, in the form of a fixed dollar charge (rather than a percentage) per unit of commodity exchanged, say, $T per unit sold. The situation is portrayed in Figure 2.4. The supply curve SS is shifted *upward* (recall that this is *not* an "increase in supply") by one dollar per unit to the position indicated by the curve S'S'. Why? The original SS curve specifies the number of units suppliers were willing to provide at any price P. They still must be paid the same *net* price if they are to

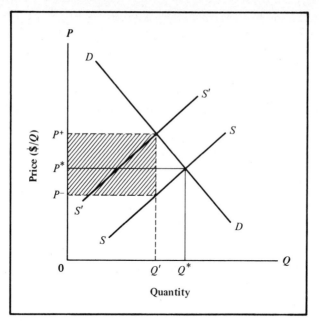

Figure 2. 4
A Tax upon Sales

supply the same number of units. But if the *net* price is P dollars along SS, the *gross* price per unit must be $P + T$ dollars along $S'S'$ if the tax is $\$T$ per unit. Using the symbols P^+ for the gross price and P^- for the net price, we have:

$$P^+ = P^- + T$$

The new equilibrium quantity is determined by the intersection of the shifted supply curve $S'S'$ with the original demand curve DD. Evidently, the equilibrium quantity Q' bought and sold is less as a result of the tax. What about price? Carelessness can cause confusion here, because the new *gross* price P^+ is higher than the previous equilibrium P^*, but the new *net* price P^- is lower than P^*. One must state *which* price, gross or net, in asking whether price has risen or fallen.

Proposition: A tax on transactions lowers the equilibrium quantity exchanged in the market. The new price *gross* of the tax (paid by buyers) is more than before; the new price *net* of the tax (received by sellers) is less than before.

It may seem arbitrary that our analysis here took the form of shifting the supply curve rather than the demand curve. This format seems logical if the tax were, legally, levied upon sellers. What if it were levied on buyers instead? It is left for the student to determine, as an exercise, that a shift of the demand curve from DD downward by $\$T$, to a new position $D'D'$, would lead to exactly the same solution as before for quantity and for gross and net prices.

32

So the supply-demand analysis leads to a possibly surprising conclusion: *It makes no difference whether a tax on transactions is formally levied upon buyers or upon sellers.*

*2. A. 4   Algebra of Supply-Demand Analysis

If we assume that the demand and supply curves are both linear, it is easy to obtain algebraic solutions for the conditions of equilibrium.

Let the equation of the demand curve be $P = A - BQ_d$, where A and B are positive constants. A is the vertical intercept, and $-B$ the slope. Let the supply curve be $P = C + DQ_s$. C is again a vertical intercept (which might be negative here) while D represents the positive slope. The condition of equilibrium is, of course:

(2.1)
$$Q_s = Q_d$$

We thus have a system of two simultaneous equations:

(2.2)
$$\begin{cases} P = A - BQ \\ P = C + DQ \end{cases}$$

The solution values are:

(2.3)
$$Q_1^* = \frac{A - C}{B + D}, \qquad P_1^* = \frac{AD + BC}{B + D}$$

Now consider the comparative-statics problem of shifts in the determinants of equilibrium. From the algebraic point of view, we are dealing with "parametric change," i.e., shifts in the constants A, B, C, or D. An increase (rightward shift) in demand can take the form of an *increase* in the intercept A (this is an upward displacement of the demand curve as in Figure 2.2) or a *decrease* in the absolute magnitude of B (this would be a tilting about the vertical intercept making the curve more horizontal). Consider an increase in A, writing $A' = A + \Delta A$, where ΔA symbolizes a positive increment of A.

Then
$$Q_2^* = \frac{A' - C}{B + D} = \frac{(A + \Delta A) - C}{B + D}.$$

Since B and D and ΔA are all positive, Q_2^* is surely greater than Q_1^* in equation (2.3).

Also,
$$P_2^* = \frac{A'D + BC}{B + D} = \frac{(A + \Delta A)D + BC}{B + D}.$$

Again, since B and D and ΔA are positive, P_2^* is surely greater than P_1^*.

*Starred sections represent optional or advanced material.

An increase (a rightward shift) of supply can take the form of a *decrease* in the intercept C (a downward displacement of the curve) or a *decrease* in D (a tilting that makes the curve more horizontal). Let us consider here only the effect of a decrease in C, writing $C' = C + \Delta C$, where ΔC now represents a *negative* increment.

Then

$$Q_3^* = \frac{A - C'}{B + D} = \frac{A - (C + \Delta C)}{B + D}.$$

Since B and D are positive, but ΔC is negative, Q_3^* is surely greater than Q_1^*.
Also,

$$P_3^* = \frac{AD + BC'}{B + D} = \frac{AD + B(C + \Delta C)}{B + D}.$$

Again, since B and D are both positive but ΔC is negative, P_3^* is surely *smaller* than P_1^*.

These results are consistent with those obtained via the verbal and diagrammatic analysis above. An increase in demand (rightward shift of the demand curve) raises both price and quantity; an increase in supply (rightward shift of the supply curve) raises quantity but lowers price.

2. A. 5 Interferences with Equilibrium

Government policy, as in the case of a tax or a subsidy, may lead to a shift from one equilibrium position to another. The government may also, however, intervene directly in the functioning of markets. Government action may be directed to improving the perfection of the market process. For example, by providing a mechanism for the enforcement of private contracts through the judicial system, the state reduces or eliminates the need for individuals to make costly private enforcement arrangements. This facilitates the process whereby markets attain equilibrium.

We will be concerned here, however, with government interventions designed to *prevent* markets from reaching equilibrium. It is not our purpose to make normative judgments as to the wisdom of such interventions. Rather, we seek only to show how the tool of supply-demand analysis enables the economist to understand and predict the consequences.

In the current inflationary period, we are all familiar with attempts to hold down inflation by "freezes" or other forms of maximum wage-price controls. In the deflationary period of the 1930's there were similar attempts to prevent a feared downward spiral of prices by *minimum* wage-price controls under the NRA (National Recovery Administration). The extent to which such "price ceilings" or "price floors" can actually cure a general inflation or a general deflation, as the case may be, remains a controversial issue in macroeconomics. We shall not be concerned with the macroeconomic problem, but only with the impacts of control policies upon particular markets.

Apart from the macroeconomic motivation, government may interfere with the equilibrium of markets in order to promote the interests of particular economic groups perceived as particularly deserving of aid (or, perhaps, merely as wielding enough political clout).

Figure 2.5 pictures a "meaningful" ceiling price P'. (To be meaningful, the ceiling must be *below* the equilibrium price P^*.) At the ceiling price, the quantity demanded Q'_d exceeds the quantity supplied Q'_s, so there is upward pressure on price, indicated by the upward-pointing arrow. However, the arrow is blocked by the fixed ceiling price P', which remains in effect regardless of the upward pressure. (We do not consider here the possibility of illegal trading at higher prices—black markets.)

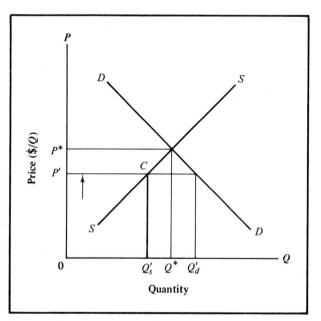

Figure 2. 5
A Price Ceiling

What about the actual quantity traded? There is a fundamental maxim of markets, "It takes two to tango." That is, exchange requires willing buyers *and* sellers. At the fixed ceiling price P' the sellers are willing to offer only Q'_s. The buyers would be delighted to take this much and any larger quantity up to Q'_d, but they can only find trading partners to the extent of the smaller magnitude. Thus, the position denoted C is the actual price-quantity situation. So the effective price is lower than the unregulated equilibrium P^*, but the effective quantity is also lower than the equilibrium Q^*. This sometimes surprises students, as they expect the quantity traded to be some compromise between the larger quantity demanded Q'_d and the smaller quantity offered Q'_s. But the result is no compromise; *it is the smaller of the desired transaction magnitudes that governs*. This is emphasized in the diagram by the bold vertical drawn through the point C.

Example 2. 6
Repressed
Inflation
and Trekking

During and after World War II all the major belligerent powers were troubled by severe inflationary pressures. Wartime and postwar needs led to enormous government deficits, covered largely by increased monetary issues. And yet consumer prices were frozen at low levels. Since the necessities of life were scarce, there was strong upward pressure on price. Indeed, often the absolutely minimal needs of life were not legitimately available. In postwar Germany, for example, the official daily ration at one point was down to the incredibly low figure of 1180 calories.

In these circumstances the curious institution of "trekking" developed in a number of different countries. City-dwellers would leave town for a day and scour the nearby countryside for food, making private black market deals with farmers or, indeed, often simply stealing. The more the governments succeeded in controlling prices in the legitimate means of food distribution, the more the abnormal system of trekking flourished. On one single day, it was reported, over 900,000 persons trekked from Tokyo into the countryside.[5] In Germany, the "Erhard reforms" of 1948 abolished price freezes and thus eliminated trekking. But a curious and unexpected consequence was a financial crisis for the State railroads. Shorthaul railroad passenger traffic dropped immediately to less than 40% of its pre-reform volume, evidencing the massive volume of trekking that had previously been going on.[6]

[5]Jerome B. Cohen, *Japan's Economy in War and Reconstruction* (Minneapolis: University of Minnesota Press, 1949), p. 378.
[6]Lucius D. Clay, *Decision in Germany* (Garden City, N.J.: Doubleday, 1950), p. 191.

A meaningful price floor is pictured in Figure 2.6. At the legal floor P'' the quantity offered by sellers Q_s'' exceeds the quantity desired by buyers Q_d''. There is downward pressure on price. Here the effective price is higher than the unregulated equilibrium P^*, but the effective quantity is again *lower* than the equilibrium Q^*, as indicated by the bold vertical drawn through the point F. Once more, "It takes two to tango." We see, therefore, that although price ceilings and price floors have opposite effects on price they have similar effects upon the real volume of transactions; *in either case, the quantity exchanged is lower than in the unregulated market.* (Again, a kind of black market may come into existence, permitting the trading of somewhat larger quantities at illegally low prices.)

Floors hold up better when they are *supported.* The supply-demand analysis of supported floors shows results drastically different from those of unsupported floors. Support takes the form of a "buyer of last resort"— Uncle Sam in the case of agricultural price supports in the United States. Going back to Figure 2.6, private buyers are only willing to take Q_d'' at the

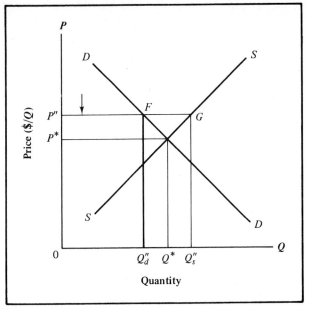

Figure 2. 6
A Price Floor

high floor price P''. But now suppose the government as buyer of last resort is available as trading partner for unrequited suppliers. Then the latter *can* actually dispose of their supply-quantity Q''_s; the actual situation is represented by the position G in the diagram. There is no black market problem with a supported floor, as no supplier would let units of the good go for less than the floor price. Instead there is a "surplus" problem. The buyer of last resort finds himself accumulating larger and larger unwanted stocks of the supported community.

Conclusion: Meaningful ceilings hold down prices; meaningful floors keep them up. In either case, the quantity exchanged is *less* than in unregulated equilibrium. If, however, the floor is *supported*, quantity will be greater than equilibrium but the "buyer of last resort" must accumulate inventories.

Example 2. 7
Agricultural
"Parity" Prices

The U.S. government has attempted since the 1930's to maintain "parity" prices for agricultural products. "Parity" is interpreted to mean the relationship between agricultural and non-agricultural prices that obtained during the years 1910–14, a period of farm prosperity. Throughout the 1950's the primary method employed to achieve parity was price support of farm products: a Federal agency called the Commodity Credit Corporation (CCC) stood always ready to buy any unsold fractions of supported crops at 90% of the parity price.

The "surpluses" purchased by the CCC were for the most part kept in storage, the intention being to release them to the market in years of deficient crops. But as parity corresponded to an unusually favorable price relationship from the farmers' point of view, we might expect that in most years the government would have to purchase sizable shares of the supported crops. As indicated in the Table, the CCC did purchase enormous amounts in the 1950's. By 1960 the CCC held in storage as much wheat as the entire 1960 crop (not to mention amounts that had previously been disposed of).

With the burden of maintaining such huge stores becoming increasingly intolerable, other methods were turned to. Food stamps and school lunch programs were used to subsidize market demand. More important, through acreage limitations farmers were paid *not* to produce. The consequent increase in demand and decrease in supply cooperated to raise the market prices received by farmers. In addition, the price support levels were adjusted downward closer to market. The Table shows the resulting reduction of CCC purchases in the 1960's.

Yearly Acquisitions of Three Supported Crops by
the Commodity Credit Corporation, Selected Years

	Millions of Bushels		
	Grain Sorghum	*Corn*	*Wheat*
1953	40.9	422.3	486.1
54	110.1	250.6	391.6
55	92.6	408.9	276.7
56	32.5	477.4	148.4
57	279.5	268.1	193.5
58	258.0	266.6	511.0
1963	125.1	17.9	85.1
64	66.8	29.1	86.9
65	85.0	11.2	17.4
66	0.3	12.4	12.4
67	9.1	191.0	90.0
68	13.7	34.4	182.9

Source: Commodity Credit Corporation Charts, Nov. 1972, pp. 49, 75, 115.

2. B THE RELATION AMONG TOTAL, AVERAGE, AND MARGINAL MAGNITUDES

As mentioned in Chapter 1, economists have derived a way of thinking about *optimization* problems (problems which always involve maximization of a desired end, or minimization of an undesired one) that does the work of mathematical calculus without requiring formal knowledge of calculus techniques. The key to this process is the relation among total, average, and marginal magnitudes.

It is important to appreciate that the relations among total, average, and marginal magnitudes are ones of fundamental logic. The principles remain the same, regardless of whether we are thinking of Total, Average, and Marginal *Cost* or Total, Average, and Marginal *Revenue* or Total, Average, and Marginal *Utility* (to mention only a few of the variables to which these concepts will be applied in the pages to come). The purpose in this section is to cast light upon the general principles; the application to specific economic variables is only illustrative.

To fix ideas let us start with a curve like that in Figure 2.7, which we may

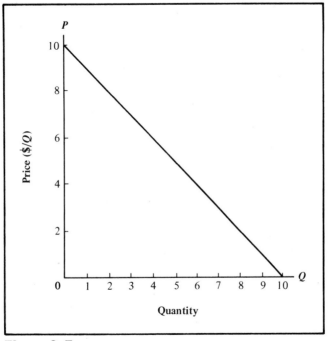

Figure 2. 7
A Demand Curve

suppose represents the familiar market demand curve for some good. Hypothetical data underlying this demand curve are tabulated in the first two columns of Table 2.1, representing Quantity (Q) and Price (P) of the good, respectively.

If we multiply Price times Quantity, we obtain definitionally the magnitude economists call Total Revenue or sometimes simply Revenue (R). Thus:[7]

(2.4) $$R \equiv PQ$$

---

[7]The triple equality sign $\equiv$ represents mathematical identity. This symbol will be used in the text where it is desired to emphasize that both sides of the equality are definitionally equivalent.

Table 2. 1

Total, Average, and Marginal Revenue

Quantity	Price—or Average Revenue (P or AR)	Total Revenue (R)	Marginal Revenue— Better Approximation (MR)	Marginal Revenue— Poorer Approximation
0	10	0		—
			9	
1	9	9		9
			7	
2	8	16		7
			5	
3	7	21		5
			3	
4	6	24		3
			1	
5	5	25		1
			−1	
6	4	24		−1
			−3	
7	3	21		−3
			−5	
8	2	16		−5
			−7	
9	1	9		−7
			−9	
10	0	0		−9

Total Revenue is tabulated in the third column of Table 2.1, and the corresponding data are plotted in Figure 2.8. Both Price and Revenue are regarded as functions of a single variable—Quantity.

Revenue R is a *total* magnitude or function of Quantity. And Price P can be regarded as an *average* magnitude. In Table 2.1, for example, at quantity $Q = 2$ Total Revenue R equals 16. If we ask what is the Average Revenue received per unit of quantity when $Q = 2$, the answer is obviously 8, which is, of course, nothing but the price along the demand curve associated with that quantity. Formally, equation (2.5) defining Average Revenue (AR) follows immediately from equation (2.4):

(2.5) $$AR \equiv P \equiv \frac{R}{Q}$$

Dimensionally, Price is measured in terms of *dollars per unit quantity* ($\$/Q$), whereas Revenue is simply scaled in dollars.

To understand the geometrical relation between total and average magnitudes, it is best to take the *total* measure as the fundamental or primitive concept. In Figure 2.9 we see plotted again the curve of Total Revenue R as a function of quantity. Now, for any level of Q, say $Q = 4$, consider the line from the origin to the curve. The slope of this line is the ratio R/Q—the height R reached along the curve, divided by the horizontal length represented by the level of Q. By equation (2.5), R/Q equals Price (P) or Average Revenue AR. Numerically, at $Q = 4$ we have $AR = 24/4 = 6$.

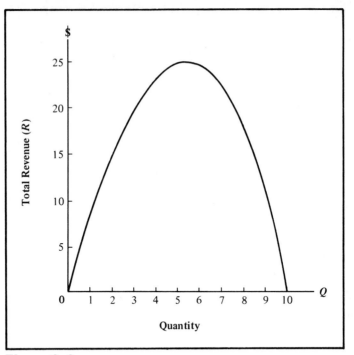

Figure 2. 8
A Total Revenue Curve

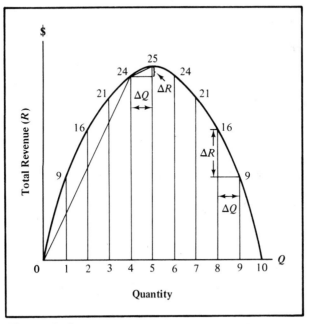

Figure 2. 9
Derivation of Average and Marginal Magnitudes
from Total Function

41

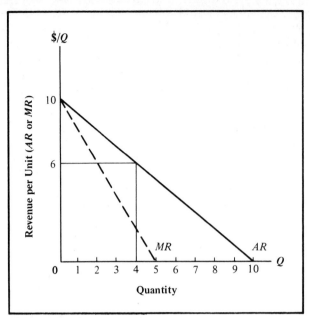

Figure 2. 10
Average Revenue and Marginal Revenue

The Average Revenue AR is plotted separately as a function of Quantity Q in Figure 2.10. Note that at $Q = 4$ we have $AR = 6$. Of course, the Average Revenue function in this diagram is identical with the original demand curve in Figure 2.7. (*Warning:* The vertical axis of the "total" diagram is scaled in terms of R—in dollars. The vertical axis of the "average" diagram is scaled in terms of R/Q—dollars *per unit of quantity*. Total and average magnitudes should never be plotted in the same diagram, since the dimensionality conflicts. Confusion is almost certain to result when this warning is overlooked.)

For the particular data assumed in Table 2.1, the Average Revenue AR is declining throughout (negatively-sloped demand curve). Geometrically, we can see that AR must be falling since, in the "total" diagram of Figure 2.9, the slope of the line connecting the origin to the Total Revenue curve diminishes in moving to the right along the humped shape of the function.

Actually, as can be determined from Figure 2.7, the demand curve or AR function implied by the given data has the specific linear form:

$$P = 10 - Q$$

Since $R = PQ$, we know that the Total Revenue curve satisfies the equation:

$$R = (10 - Q)Q = 10Q - Q^2$$

So much for the connection between average and total magnitudes. The *marginal* function is akin to the average function in that both are measured, geometrically, in terms of slopes derived from a total magnitude. Consequently, marginal and average curves are scaled in the same dimensions (dollars per unit of quantity) and can without danger of confusion be plotted in the same diagram as in Figure 2.10. The difference between average and marginal can be explained as follows. The *average* function AR was defined as the slope of a line connecting the origin to positions on the Total Revenue curve R as already shown in Figure 2.9; the *marginal* function MR, on the other hand, is defined geometrically as the slope *along the curve R* itself. To approximate this slope at a particular point, consider a unit horizontal change or increment in Q (notationally, $\Delta Q = 1$) between $Q = 4$ and $Q = 5$ in Figure 2.9. The corresponding vertical change in R is denoted ΔR. Thus, Marginal Revenue is (approximately) $\Delta R/\Delta Q$, for a unit change in Q. This corresponds to the slope of the hypotenuse of the small right triangle drawn between $Q = 4$ and $Q = 5$ in Figure 2.9; over this interval the slope of the hypotenuse approximates the slope of the curve. Numerically, the Marginal Revenue MR is approximately $(25 - 24)/1 = 1$.

The degree to which the slope of the hypotenuse of the small triangle approximates the exact slope along the Total-Revenue curve itself (the latter being the true Marginal Revenue) can be improved by taking a smaller and smaller variation ΔQ. This leads to the formal definition of Marginal Revenue as:

$$(2.6) \qquad MR \equiv \lim_{(\text{as } \Delta Q \to 0)} \frac{\Delta R}{\Delta Q}$$

Even though the denominator ΔQ approaches zero in the limiting process, it will in general be the case that the ratio of ΔR to ΔQ approaches some definite number, which is the slope *along* the curve. (This ratio is known as the *derivative* in the calculus.[8])

So long as the Total Revenue R is rising as Q increases, it is obvious from Figure 2.9 that the slope along the curve must be positive; hence the Marginal Revenue MR exceeds zero. When R is decreasing in the region past the hump in the diagram, however, MR must be negative. Thus we have:

Proposition 2.1a: *When a total function or magnitude is rising, the corresponding marginal function or magnitude is positive.*

Proposition 2.1b: *When a total magnitude is falling, the corresponding marginal magnitude is negative.*

But when R reaches a maximum it is neither increasing nor decreasing, i.e., it is level. Drawing the obvious inference, we have:

---

[8]*Mathematical Footnote: Marginal Revenue* as a derivative is thus defined as:

$$MR \equiv \frac{dR}{dQ} \equiv \lim_{\Delta Q \to 0} \frac{\Delta R}{\Delta Q}$$

Proposition 2.1c: *When a total magnitude reaches a maximum or a minimum, the corresponding marginal magnitude is zero.*[9]

While the example above applied to a maximum, at a *minimum* along any total function the total curve would again be level, so that the corresponding marginal measure would again be zero.[10]

Table 2.1 shows two alternative representations for MR: a better and a poorer approximation. Consider the first two rows of the Table. For a unit variation ΔQ (from $Q = 0$ to $Q = 1$), the revenue increment is $\Delta R = 9$ (from $R = 0$ to $R = 9$). According to the poorer approximation, MR is said to be 9 *at* $Q = 1$. But the increment of revenue takes place *over the interval* from $Q = 0$ to $Q = 1$. Hence, the better approximation has $MR = 0$ *between* $Q = 0$ and $Q = 1$, or approximately at $Q = \frac{1}{2}$, i.e., halfway between $Q = 0$ and $Q = 1$. As a test, recall Proposition 2.1c, which says that when a total magnitude reaches a maximum, the corresponding marginal magnitude must be zero. It can be verified that, with the equation $R = 10Q - Q^2$, revenue is maximized at 25 when $Q = 5$.[11] But the poorer approximation shows $MR = 1$, not $MR = 0$, at $Q = 5$. The better approximation has $MR = 1$ *between* $Q = 4$ and $Q = 5$ (i.e., at $Q = 4\frac{1}{2}$); between $Q = 5$ and $Q = 6$ (i.e., at $Q = 5\frac{1}{2}$) we have $MR = -1$. By interpolation, the MR at $Q = 5$ is exactly zero, which is correct. The better approximation will in fact be *precisely* correct whenever (as in this case) the underlying demand curve is linear.

There is a geometrical relation between average and marginal functions:

Proposition 2.2a: *When the average magnitude is falling, the marginal magnitude must lie below it.*

This can be intuitively appreciated: If adding one more unit to a previous collection reduces the average of some measure, the additional unit or newcomer must have been below average. In Figure 2.10 the Average Revenue AR is always falling, hence the Marginal Revenue MR lies always below it. Analogously:

Proposition 2.2b: *When the average magnitude is rising, the marginal magnitude must lie above it.*

And, of course, these two propositions imply:

[9]*Mathematical Footnote:* When $dR/dQ > 0$, the Total Revenue function R is increasing; when $dR/dQ < 0$ it is decreasing; and when $dR/dQ = 0$, we have a stationary value of the function, in this case, a maximum.

[10]Some technical qualifications should be made to these assertions. Not all minima or maxima are "flat." Thus, in Figure 2.9 Total Revenue R has an interior maximum at $Q = 5$, for which $MR = 0$. But it also has minima at $Q = 0$ and $Q = 10$ (since revenue R can never be less than zero). But the curve is not flat at those points. In this book we will be dealing almost always with flat minima or maxima, so that Proposition 2.1c holds.

[11]*Mathematical Footnote:* If $R = 10Q - Q^2$, $dR/dQ = 10 - 2Q$. Setting $dR/dQ = 0$ (first-order condition for a maximum), we have $Q = 5$.

Proposition 2.2c: *When an average magnitude is neither rising nor falling* (at a minimum or maximum, or other stationary point), *the marginal magnitude must be equal to it.*[12]

Figure 2.10 illustrates only the relation of Proposition 2.2c, since the average magnitude (Average Revenue AR) is a declining function of Q throughout (negatively sloped demand curve). So another example may be useful. In Figure 2.11 we see a different total function to be employed later

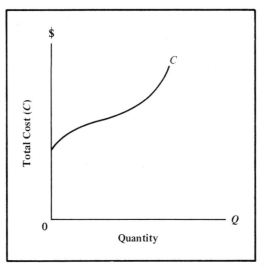

Figure 2. 11
Total Cost

in this book: a firm's Total Cost C as a function of Quantity Q. Unlike the Total Revenue function R of Figure 2.8, Total Cost C is positive even for $Q = 0$, and rises throughout. The initial positive intercept of the C function is called the "fixed cost." This fixed positive quantity dictates that, at $Q = 0$, the average cost $AC = C/Q$ is infinite. But using the technique of determining AC as the slope of a line connecting the origin with a point along the curve, we can see that as Q increases this slope will first fall (become flatter) but then rise (become steeper). Hence in Figure 2.12 the AC curve has at first a declining, and then a rising range—so that it must have a minimum in between. The MC curve is of course below AC in the latter's declining range,

---

[12]*Mathematical Footnote:* Let us verify Proposition 2.2a of the text, and specifically that MR is below AR when the latter is falling (a declining function of Q). For AR to be falling:

$$0 > \frac{d(AR)}{dQ} = \frac{d(R/Q)}{dQ} = \frac{Q\,(dR/dQ) - R}{Q^2}$$

This directly implies $dR/dQ < R/Q$, or $MR < AR$. Similar proofs for Propositions 2.2b and 2.2c can easily be shown.

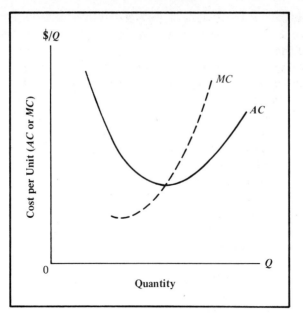

$/Q

Cost per Unit (AC or MC)

MC

AC

0

Q

Quantity

Figure 2. 12
Average and Marginal Cost

always above in the latter's rising range. Therefore, *MC* must cut *AC* at the latter's minimum as asserted in Proposition 2.2c.

Example 2. 8
Taxes

The Table below shows the personal income tax schedule for single taxpayers in the tax year 1973. For any "Taxable Income"[13] bracket on the left-hand side of the Table, the right-hand side shows the Total Tax at the bottom of the bracket and the Marginal Tax for increments of income within the bracket. In the $20,000–$22,000 income bracket, for example, the Tax Due is stated as $5,230 + 38%. $5,230 is the Total Tax for someone earning exactly $20,000, and .38 is the Marginal Tax per dollar of income thereafter (up to the top of the bracket).

Comment: The following fallacy is sometimes encountered. An employee is making an annual income of $19,500 and paying a Total Tax of $5050. His employer offers him a raise of $1000, which the worker refuses on the ground that it would put him in a higher tax bracket! The worker seems to be thinking that, in moving up to a higher *marginal* tax rate (38% instead of 36%) he will be taxed more heavily on his earlier $19,500 in addition to whatever tax he must pay on the $1000 raise. This is incorrect. The worker's additional tax would be at

[13]"Taxable Income" is less than earned income by the amount of exemptions, deductions, etc., as provided in the tax law.

46

the rate of 36% on half the increase (which brings him to the top of the bracket at an income of $20,000), or $180, and would be at the rate of 38% on the second half, or $190. Had he accepted the raise he would be better off by $1000 − $370. His net loss of $630 is one of the costs of being unable to comprehend the marginal concept of economics.

Tax Due for Single Taxpayer
(not qualifying as head of household)

| Taxable Income | | Tax Due | |
Over	but not Over		of Excess Over
$0	$500	$0 + 14%	$0
$500	$1,000	$70 + 15%	$500
$1,000	$1,500	$145 + 16%	$1,000
$1,500	$2,000	$225 + 17%	$1,500
$2,000	$4,000	$310 + 19%	$2,000
$4,000	$6,000	$690 + 21%	$4,000
$6,000	$8,000	$1,110 + 24%	$6,000
$8,000	$10,000	$1,590 + 25%	$8,000
$10,000	$12,000	$2,090 + 27%	$10,000
$12,000	$14,000	$2,630 + 29%	$12,000
$14,000	$16,000	$3,210 + 31%	$14,000
$16,000	$18,000	$3,830 + 34%	$16,000
$18,000	$20,000	$4,510 + 36%	$18,000
$20,000	$22,000	$5,230 + 38%	$20,000
$22,000	$26,000	$5,990 + 40%	$22,000
$26,000	$32,000	$7,590 + 45%	$26,000
$32,000	$38,000	$10,290 + 50%	$32,000
$38,000	$44,000	$13,290 + 55%	$38,000
$44,000	$50,000	$16,590 + 60%	$44,000
$50,000	$60,000	$20,190 + 62%	$50,000
$60,000	$70,000	$26,390 + 64%	$60,000
$70,000	$80,000	$32,790 + 66%	$70,000
$80,000	$90,000	$39,390 + 68%	$80,000
$90,000	$100,000	$46,190 + 69%	$90,000
$100,000		$53,090 + 70%	$100,000

Source: *1973 Instructions for Form 1040*, Department of the Treasury, Internal Revenue Service, Schedule X, p. 27.

Questions

1. Supply-demand analysis is the key tool for which of the two main analytical techniques of economics? For what class of problem is the relation among total, average, and marginal quantities the key tool?
2. In what sense is price a "ratio of quantities"?

3. Explain why market equilibrium is determined by the *intersection* of the supply curve and the demand curve.

4. How does an "increase in demand" shift the demand curve? How does an "increase in supply" shift the supply curve? Do the effects upon equilibrium price and equilibrium quantity go in the same direction in the case of an increase in demand? In the case of an increase in supply?

5. In the analysis of a $T per unit tax described in the text, the supply curve was shifted upward by $T to find the new equilibrium. Would the same result have been achieved if instead the demand curve were shifted downward by $T? Explain.

6. For a particular commodity, suppose that the supply curve is very steep (positively sloped, but almost vertical). In this case would a $T tax tend to have a relatively large or a relatively small effect upon quantity exchanged in the market? Would there tend to be a relatively large or relatively small effect upon the gross price paid by consumers? Upon the net price received by suppliers? In terms of the underlying economic meaning, why would these consequences be anticipated if a tax were imposed upon a commodity with a steeply rising supply curve?

7. Analyze correspondingly the case where the *demand* curve is very steep (negatively sloped, but almost vertical).

8. Suppose that a $S per unit *subsidy* upon sales of a particular commodity is put into effect. What would the implications be for the quantity exchanged? For the gross and the net price?

9. What is a "meaningful" price ceiling or price floor? Why is it that meaningful floors and meaningful ceilings both *decrease* the quantity traded? What happens, however, if a price floor is "supported"?

10. During World War II in Great Britain, a ceiling price was in effect to hold down the market price of bread. Explain why there was upward pressure upon the price of bread. What consequences of the upward pressure would you anticipate, given continuing enforcement of the ceiling? To help reduce this upward pressure, the British government took fresh bread off the market—all bread sold had to be at least one day old. Would you expect this regulation to achieve the desired effect?

11. In the year 302 A.D., the Roman emperor Diocletian "commanded that there should be cheapness." His edict declared:

Unprincipled greed appears wherever our armies, following the commands of the public weal, march, not only in villages and cities but also upon all high-ways, with the result that prices of foodstuffs mount not only fourfold and eightfold, but transcend all measure. Our law shall fix a measure and a limit to this greed.

Why do you think Diocletian found food prices higher wherever he marched with his armies? What result would you anticipate from the command that "there should be cheapness"?

12. Starting from a given Total Revenue function R, show how the Average Revenue function AR is derived. Show how the Marginal Revenue function MR is derived.

13. Starting from a given Total Cost function C, show how the Average Cost function AC and the Marginal Cost function MC are derived.

14. In terms of the general relations among total, average, and marginal quantities, which of the following statements are true:

a. When the total function is rising, the marginal function is rising.

b. When the total function is rising, the marginal function is positive.

c. When the total function is rising, the marginal function lies above it.

d. When the marginal function is rising, the average function is also rising.

e. When the average function is falling, the marginal function lies below it.

f. When the marginal function is neither rising nor falling, the average function is constant.

15. For a Total Revenue function given for integer values of quantity as in Table 2.1, explain the nature of the "better approximation" of Marginal Revenue that provides a greater degree of accuracy.

16. From the tax-schedule data in the text, graph the Total Tax ("tax due") as a function of Taxable Income over the range from $0 to $10,000 of income. Also graph the corresponding Average Tax and Marginal Tax functions. Note that Average Tax and Marginal Tax are percentages. Why?

Two

Preference, Consumption, and Demand

Chapter 3
Utility and Preference

The two basic techniques of analysis over which the student must gain command are *optimization* and *determination of equilibrium*. In this Part Two, covering the topics of Preference, Consumption, and Demand, we shall be concentrating upon the optimization problem of the consumer as decision-making agent.

3. A THE DECISION PROBLEM OF THE INDIVIDUAL

As the circular flow of economic activity pictured in Figure 1.1 shows, the economic problem of the individual (or household) is two-fold. Facing the product market as a demander, he must decide how to spend his income over consumable goods and services. (He can also save, as will be explained more fully in Chapter 16; however, saving is to be regarded as an indirect purchase of *future* consumable goods.) But a consumer's income does not come down from heaven like manna; it must be *earned*, an activity that also involves a decision-making process. Facing the factor market as a supplier, each person in his capacity as resource-owner must decide what employments to accept for the resources (labor power, rental property, etc.) that he owns. The earnings obtained from such employment become the income out of which he can make his consumptive choices.

In this Part Two, however, we limit ourselves to the individual in his aspect as consumer, taking as given the income resulting from whatever decisions he may have made as resource-owner. We need mention here only that in *both* of these aspects, consumer and resource-owner, the rational individual will be optimizing—attempting to make the decision that is best in terms of his existing tastes and preferences within the limit of his knowledge and capacity.

The economist finds it convenient to describe this optimization process as the *maximization of utility*. Utility as a hypothetical magnitude serving as an index for preference will be the central topic of this chapter.

Scientific analysis involves the construction of theories or models, which are always, at best, simplified pictures of reality. They can be regarded as idealizations in which irrelevant or unsystematic peculiarities are stripped away to permit concentration upon the dominant features of the situation for the purpose at hand. Such an idealized picture of the individual's preferences for alternative bundles or baskets of consumptive commodities is presented here.

We postulate that the individual's preferences follow two laws:

1. Axiom of Comparison. *Any two distinct baskets A and B of commodities can be compared in preference by the individual. Each such comparison must lead to one of the three following results: (i) Basket A is preferred to basket B, or (ii) B is preferred to A, or (iii) A and B are indifferent.*

The Axiom of Comparison is an idealization of reality, in that we suppose that the individual never says "I simply can't compare A and B." Nor is he supposed ever to say "Two-thirds of the time I prefer A, but the other one-third of the time B."[1]

2. Axiom of Transitivity. *Consider any three baskets A, B, and C. If A is preferred to B, and B is preferred to C, then A must be preferred to C. Similarly, if A is indifferent to B, and B to C, then A is indifferent to C.*

The Axiom of Transitivity is also an idealization, for violations of it no doubt take place. But suppose an individual were to tell you: "I prefer Apples to Bananas and Bananas to Cherries." If he were then to add, "But I'll always take Cherries over Apples!" you'd surely be inclined to regard him as odd.

---

[1] More advanced studies in economics have attempted to construct models of preference that allow for limited or probabilistic comparisons.

Example 3. 1
Transitivity and Age

Arnold A. Weinstein administered a questionnaire to experimental subjects asking them for preference rankings over ten commodity bundles, offered as pairs in random order. Among the bundles, all having a market value of around $3 at the time, were items such as: (1) $3 in cash; (2) the three latest Beatles 45-rpm phonograph records; (3) three men's clip-on bow ties, all with red polka dots, one brown, one blue, one gray; (4) a brush-stroke print of El Greco's "View of Toledo"; (5) a vanilla malted milk (two glasses) per day for ten days; and so forth.

The intent of the experiment was to detect possible intransitivities of preference over *triads* of offerings, in the course of the subjects' successive *pairwise* comparisons. An intransitivity would occur if, for example, a particular subject were observed to choose cash over malted milk, malted milk over bow ties, but bow ties over cash. The great majority of the triads showed consistent transitive preferences. An interesting result obtained was that transitivity tended to increase with age, as indicated in the Table:

Transitivity Experiment Results

Group	Proportion of Transitive Responses
52 children aged 9–12	79.2%
36 teenagers aged 14–16	83.3
46 high-school seniors aged 17–18	88.0
18 mature adults (mostly teachers)	93.5

Source: Table compiled from data reported in Arnold A. Weinstein, "Transitivity of Preference: A Comparison among Age Groups," *Journal of Political Economy*, v. 76 (March/April 1968), p. 310.

The experimenter's interpretation was that consistency in preference ordering is an acquired skill, hence more difficult for younger people to achieve. More arguably, he concluded that his results lent some support for the legal restrictions and protections placed on youth in our society.

Comment: As an alternative explanation, younger persons are more likely to engage in choices that seem inconsistent only because they are really *exploratory* in nature. "Don't knock it until you've tried it" is a dangerous maxim, but one with some appeal. If *all* possibilities are to be tried at least once, some seeming intransitivities of choice are inevitable. Consider the three possibilities cash, malted milk, and bow ties. If cash is chosen over malted milk and malted milk over bow ties, the only way to try out the bow ties is to choose them when offered next—even over cash. So the Laws of Preference presume an already well-settled pattern of consumer desires.

The Axiom of Comparison and the Axiom of Transitivity taken together lead to the:

Proposition of Rank Ordering of Preferences: *All conceivable baskets of commodities can be consistently ranked in order of preference by the individual.* This ranking is called "the preference function."

Suppose there are only two commodities, X and Y. Amounts x and y consumed by an individual[2] are scaled along the horizontal and vertical axes respectively of Figure 3.1. Four possible combinations of X and Y are

[2]Capital letters X and Y here designate the two commodities; lower-case letters x and y indicate particular quantities thereof.

being considered by the consumer: the baskets represented by the points *A, B, C,* and *D* in the diagram. Notice that basket *A* represents more of both commodities than Basket *D*. Also, basket *A* has as much of commodity *Y* as has basket *B*, and more of commodity *X*; in comparison with basket *C*, basket *A* has as much of *X* and more of commodity *Y*. What do the Laws of Preference tell us about this situation? Only two things: (1) that the individual is capable of ranking all four combinations; (2) that if, for example, *A* is preferred to *B* and *B* to *D*, then (by transitivity) *A* must be preferred to *D*.

It may seem plausible to assert that the combination *A*—containing at least as much of either commodity as any other basket, and exceeding every other basket in quantity of *X* or of *Y* or both—must be preferred to all the others shown in Figure 3.1. This plausibility is sometimes erected into a

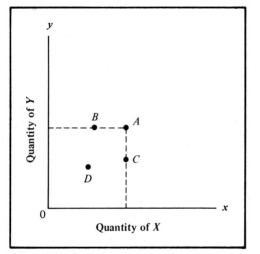

Figure 3. 1
Alternative Consumption Baskets

principle known as: *More is preferred to less*. But "More is preferred to less" is not an inviolable law of preference. Rather, it can be regarded as the defining characteristic of the subclass of commodities called *goods*. Undesired commodities, *bads*, also surely exist; household garbage is a homely example. Some commodities, like tapioca pudding, may be goods for some individuals and bads for others. And even for a great many (all?) undoubted goods, beyond a certain point of satiation they would become bads. (See Example 3.5, "Ball-Point Pens and French Pastries.") If disposal of undesired objects were always free, it would do no harm to assume that all commodities were goods. Any bads would be immediately and costlessly discarded. But as a practical matter, disposal is a seriously costly economic activity; more is *not* always better than less.

Definition: A *good* is a commodity for which more is preferred to less.

The term "utility" was introduced by the British philosopher Jeremy Bentham. Bentham declared:

Nature has placed mankind under the governance of two sovereign masters, *pain* and *pleasure*. . . . The *principle of utility* recognizes this subjection. . . . By the principle of utility is meant that principle which approves or disapproves of every action whatsoever, according to the tendency which it appears to have to augment or diminish the happiness of the party whose interest is in question. . . .[3]

For Bentham, then, the maximization of utility is an assertedly true psychological principle—that men avoid pain and seek pleasure or happiness.

While economists have held to the term "utility," they have felt uneasy about erecting the economic theory of choice upon an arguable psychological premise that pleasure is man's sole goal. The hedonistic connotations of "utility" have therefore been gradually stripped away by successive economic thinkers. The dominant current conception is based upon the observed *fact* of choice rather than any psychological interpretation thereof. There still remains an underlying empirical assertion, to wit: that the Laws of Preference of the previous section, while undoubtedly idealized, are a good approximation of actual behavior observed in the world. Since the Laws of Preference are really rules of rational choice, this reduces to the postulate of rationality discussed in Chapter 1.

What modern economists call "utility" reflects nothing more than rank ordering of preference. The statement "Basket *A* is preferred to basket *B*" and the statement "Basket *A* has higher utility than basket *B*" are equivalent. They both lead to the empirical prediction: "Basket *A* will be chosen over basket *B*."

Conclusion: Utility is the variable whose relative magnitude indicates strength of preference: In finding the most preferred position, the individual maximizes utility.

3. D UTILITY: CARDINAL OR ORDINAL MAGNITUDE?

Early writers had no doubt that utility was a quantitatively measurable entity like length or temperature. They would have regarded it as perfectly reasonable to employ a construction like Figure 3.2 in which any individual's utility (scaled in "utils" according to the vertical column of numbers *U* in the diagram) is shown as a function of the quantity taken of some generalized consumption good *C*. Some even believed it possible to add up these "util" numbers interpersonally: that 5 of John Doe's utils could be added to 7 of Richard Roe's so as to make a total of 12 utils for the pair. This is perhaps

---

[3]J. Bentham, *An Introduction to the Principles of Morals and Legislation* (1823 edition), Chap. 1.

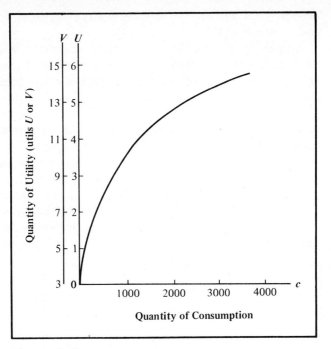

Figure 3. 2
A Cardinal Total-Utility Function

what Bentham meant in recommending public policies designed to achieve "the greatest good of the greatest number," a mystifying though noble-sounding expression. Economists today generally believe that summation of the utilities of different people is meaningless, and cannot be used as a basis for economic policy.[4]

3. D. 1 Cardinal Magnitudes

The common-sense notion of a "quantitatively measurable" variable is known more technically as a *cardinal magnitude*. A cardinal magnitude is a variable whose measurement permits arbitrary choice only of zero-point and unit interval. Along the vertical axis of Figure 3.2, an alternative "util" scale is indicated by the V column of numbers. Note that, in comparison with the original U scale, the zero-point has been shifted (what was formerly 0 utils on the U scale is 3 on the V scale) and the unit interval doubled (a vertical difference of 1 util on the U scale is a difference of 2 on the V scale). Nevertheless the diagram still has the same appearance. And in particular, one crucial property is preserved: the *relative magnitudes of utility differences* as between consumption levels remains the same. For example, in Figure 3.2 we can say that moving from 1000 to 2000 consumption units yields a bigger utility improvement than moving from 2000 to 3000. This assertion

[4]The modern economic approach to interpersonal comparisons will be studied in Part Six.

remains valid whether we measure utility increments according to the U scale or the V scale.[5]

Altitude is an example of a cardinal magnitude. Whether we measure from sea level or from the center of the earth (shift of zero-point) or in units of feet or meters (shift of unit interval), we know that there's a bigger altitude difference between the base and crest of Mount Everest than between the ground floor and the roof of even the tallest man-made building. Temperature provides another familiar instance: the Centigrade and Fahrenheit scales differ, but only in zero-point and unit interval.

Utility in Figure 3.2 is a *total* concept. The corresponding *Marginal Utility* function, defined (as described in Chapter 2) as the slope or rate of change of the Total Utility function, is shown in Figure 3.3. Since the Total Utility rises throughout, by Proposition 2.1a Marginal Utility MU is always positive. But since Total Utility in Figure 3.2 is increasing *at a steadily decreasing rate*, the MU curve in Figure 3.3 is declining. This property, called *diminish-*

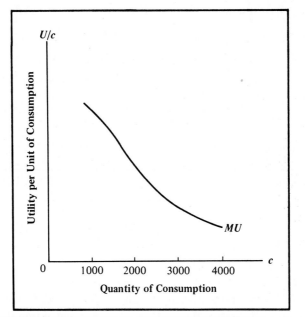

Figure 3. 3
A Marginal Utility Function

[5]*Mathematical Footnote:* The cardinally equivalent U and V scales are related by the equation:

$$V = a + bU \qquad (b > 0)$$

The constant a represents the shift of zero-point and the (positive) constant b the change in unit interval.

Consider three quantities U_1, U_2, and U_3 along the U scale, and suppose that the difference $U_3 - U_2$ exceeds the difference $U_2 - U_1$. The corresponding quantities along the V scale are V_1, V_2, V_3 where $V_i = a + bU_i$ $(i = 1, 2, 3)$. Then $U_3 - U_2 > U_2 - U_1$ obviously implies $V_3 - V_2 > V_2 - V_1$. So the *ranking of differences* is preserved for all cardinally equivalent scales.

ing *Marginal Utility*, also remains valid regardless of whether the U or the V scale is used. Putting it more generally: If the underlying total variable is a cardinal magnitude, it is possible to say when the corresponding marginal variable is an increasing or decreasing function. This is so because marginal quantities are of the nature of differences of total quantities, and the comparison of differences is unaffected by shift of zero-point or unit interval.[6]

The assertion that people are characterized by diminishing Marginal Utility as consumption income rises is an empirical one. This assertion was and is widely believed, despite the absence of a generally accepted measuring rod for utilities. It corresponds to our common-sense notion that more income makes us happier, but that our first million gives us more of a kick than our tenth.

[6]*Mathematical Footnote:* Since $V = a + bU$, $dU/dc > 0$ implies $dV/dc = b(dU/dc) > 0$ (since b is positive).

Diminishing Marginal Utility with respect to the U scale is the property $d^2U/dc^2 < 0$. But $d^2V/dc^2 = b(d^2U/dc^2) < 0$ and so we have diminishing Marginal Utility according to the V scale as well.

Example 3. 2
Does Money
Buy Happiness?

While most economists do not believe that there is a valid "cardinal" scale for utilities, the economist Julian Simon disagrees. He has proposed to measure utility, among other ways, by asking people, "Are you happy?"[7] Psychologists have carried out questionnaire surveys asking people to classify themselves as very happy, pretty happy, or not too happy. The percentage results in the Table were obtained from a survey of residents in four small Illinois towns reported in 1965.

Income and Happiness

Income	Very Happy (%)	Pretty Happy (%)	Not Too Happy (%)	Score[a]
Less than $3000	14	55	31	−.17
$3000–3999	21	63	16	+.05
$4000–4999	27	61	12	+.15
$5000–5999	26	64	10	+.16
$6000–6999	24	65	10	+.14
$7000–7999	30	60	10	+.20
$8000–9999	29	63	7	+.22
$10,000 or more	38	54	8	+.30

Source: N. M. Bradburn and D. Caplovitz, *Reports on Happiness* (Chicago: Aldine, 1965), p. 9.
[a]Column headed "Score" computed as described in text.

In interpreting these data, we still need a numerical utility (happiness) scale. Let us count "very happy" as +1, "pretty happy" as 0, and

[7]One of the "other ways" he proposes is to look at the suicide rate. See Julian L. Simon, "Interpersonal Welfare Comparison Can Be Made—And Used for Redistribution Decisions," *Kyklos*, v. 27 (1974).

"not too happy" as -1. The average for each income group is then shown by the column headed "Score." If plotted, the Score data would show (despite some irregulartities) a picture not too different from Figure 3.2.

Example 3. 3
The
Weber-Fechner
Law

An empirical generalization was developed by the psychologists E. H. Weber (1846) and G. T. Fechner (1860) concerning the relation between degree of stimulus and subjective sensitivity. The assertion is that subjective ability to discriminate is a function of *proportionate* change in the magnitude of stimulus.

Applying this to utility, subjective satisfaction can be regarded as sensitive to *proportionate* changes of income (or material well-being) regarded as stimulus. For example, if an increase in income from $10,000 to $12,000 (i.e., by 20%) is valued as a "one-util" improvement, then a further 20% increase from $12,000 to $14,400 would add a second util and still another 20% increase from $14,400 to $17,280 would provide a third util. If this is the case, utility would be a *logarithmic* function of income. Such a function would accord with the general picture of Figure 3.2, and in particular would imply diminishing Marginal Utility.

The idea of diminishing Marginal Utility has, therefore, some evidential basis. It also provides a way of explaining the fact that, for instance, people *save* more (i.e., buy more *future* consumption) as their wealth increases. If current consumption yields diminishing Marginal Utility, it is reasonable to respond to increments of income by arranging for part of the increment to be spent on *future* consumption. Unfortunately, this argument is not quite iron-clad. For, in general, we would expect the quantity of the one type of consumption to affect the utility of the other. It may be that an extra unit of current consumption *raises* its Marginal Utility (increasing *MU*) but raises the Marginal Utility of future consumption *even more*. So the evidence of saving more as income rises is not conclusive as to diminishing Marginal Utility. What we need is a way of considering utility as depending simultaneously upon the amounts of all the different goods consumed. That is the topic of the next section.

3. D. 2 Utility of Commodity Baskets

Usually in economics we think of utility as a function of several variables, i.e., as depending upon the quantities consumed of a number of different commodities. (It may also depend upon quantities supplied of factor-services like labor effort, but the resource-supply decision is not being considered here.) Suppose we take for simplicity a world of two goods X and Y. In some very special cases the utility function might have an *additive* form like $U(x, y) \equiv U_x(x) + U_y(y)$. That is, there might be two entirely separate utility components, associated with quantities of X and Y, respectively. In such a case we would be able to draw two distinct diagrams, each looking like Figure 3.2, one showing the X-utility component $U_x(x)$ as a function of the consumption of X and the other the Y-utility component $U_y(y)$ as a function of consumption of Y. The total of "utils" would then be simply the sum of these components. But in general this is not possible. The Marginal Utility a consumer derives from another pound of butter normally depends also upon his current rate of consumption of other commodities like margarine (a "substitute") and bread (a "complement").

Figure 3.4 pictures a cardinal utility function $U(x,y)$; the arguments x and y are the quantities of X and Y consumed. Utility is measured in the

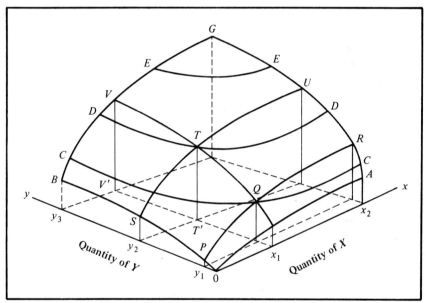

Figure 3. 4
A Cardinal Total-Utility Function of Two Goods

upward direction, as the height of the surface above the base plane. When $x = x_1$ and $y = y_2$, for example, utility is the height $T'T$. If the quantity of Y is held constant at $y = y_1$, we can see how utility varies with x. This is shown by the curve PQR lying on the utility surface; note that Total Utility rises steadily as X increases. If Y is held constant at $y = y_2$ instead, we obtain a similar curve STU; or if Y is held constant at $y = y_3$, we observe the curve BVG. In each case the curves are rising (Total Utility is increasing) as x increases, and so (in accordance with Proposition 2.1a) the Marginal Utility of X is positive. Similar statements can be made about the Marginal

Utility of the other commodity Y. But, in general, the Marginal Utility for *either* commodity depends upon the specific amounts of *both* commodities. For example, the Marginal Utility of X at the point T (i.e., when $x = x_1$ and $y = y_2$), given by the slope at point T in the x-direction along the curve *STU*, is not necessarily the same as the Marginal Utility of X at the point V (where $x = x_1$ but $y = y_3$), given by the slope at V along *BVG*. So we see that Marginal Utility of X may depend upon the quantity of Y, and vice versa. Since we do not have separate utility components attributable to each of the commodities independent of the other, the function of Figure 3.4 is not of the special additive type.[8]

Take particular note of the *contours CC, DD*, and *EE* drawn on the surface in Figure 3.4. These curves connect points of equal altitude on the "utility hill"; in effect, they show slices into the hill at fixed heights parallel to the base plane. These contours therefore are *curves of constant utility*. They were first employed by Edgeworth (1881)[9] who called them *indifference curves*. Along any contour such as *CC* through the point Q on the surface lie all the alternative consumption baskets (combinations of X and Y) that the consumer regards as *indifferent* to the basket $X = x_1$, $Y = y_1$. In Figure 3.5, looking through the transparent utility surface we can see on the base plane the *projections C'C', D'D', E'E'* of the various indifference contours.

Next, suppose we simply deleted the vertical dimension of Figure 3.5, so

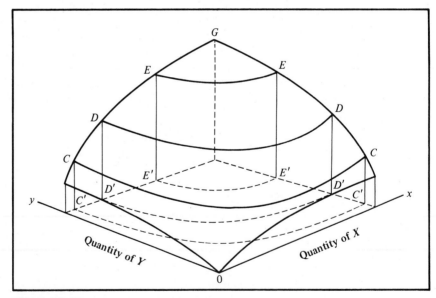

Figure 3. 5
Cardinal Utility and Indifference Curves

[8]*Mathematical Footnote:* In the additive case, where $U(x, y) = U_x(x) + U_y(y)$, the second cross-derivative $\partial^2 U / \partial x\, \partial y = 0$. Where this does not hold, the Marginal Utility of X, $\partial U / \partial x$, and the Marginal Utility of Y, $\partial U / \partial y$, are functions of both x and y.
[9]Francis Y. Edgeworth, British economist, 1845–1926.

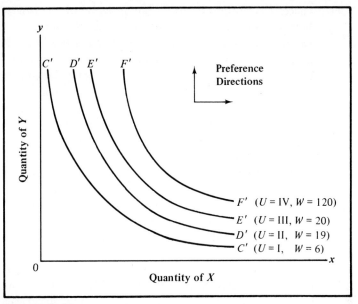

Figure 3. 6
Indifference Curves and Preference Directions

as to leave *only* the base plane. We are left with the pure projection map shown in Figure 3.6. We can now think of the projections of the contours as being themselves the indifference curves; this step was taken by Pareto (1906).[10] Since X and Y are both goods, "More is preferred to less." Hence the preference directions are north and east as indicated by the arrows on the diagram. Thus, as between any two indifference curves, the one that can be reached moving northeast of the other is "higher up" on the invisible utility hill. Apart from the indifference curves, the preference directions are all we need to know for evaluating the *relative* preference status of alternative consumption combinations. So long as we know which of two baskets is on the higher indifference curve, we will choose that one over the other.

But if the contour map of indifference curves (with preference directions) fully describes preference, it is unnecessary to think of the invisible vertical dimension—utility—as having any particular quantification (other than *direction* of increase up or down). To put it another way, if the original util scale U is represented by the magnitudes shown in roman numbers I, II, III, IV in Figure 3.6, we can just as well replace these numerical values by the scale W represented by arabic numbers such as 6, 19, 20, 120, respectively. Note *that this is a more drastic change than permitted by "cardinal" quantification.* More than the zero-point and unit interval has been changed as between U and W. This will be evident if we consider the measurement of utility differences. In terms of the original U (roman number) scale, the indifference curves are all equally spaced: The utility differences between

[10]Vilfredo Pareto, Italian economist and sociologist, 1848–1923.

successive curves are all 1. But in terms of the new W scale the distances between successive curves differ; in particular, the numerical labels on the two middle curves are much closer together than any other pair. To describe this situation we say that the underlying utility concept is an *ordinal* magnitude. For an ordinal magnitude the only meaningful comparisons are equality or else ranking of magnitudes (*direction* of difference).[11] The two radically disparate preference scales U and W are equally satisfactory, since *they give the same answers as to which baskets are equal in utility* (lie along the same indifference curve) *and as to how baskets that are unequal in utility should be ranked* (direction of preference). This is all we need to know.

While Pareto's interpretation says in effect that only the indifference curves are important, Edgeworth, the inventor of the indifference curve, strongly resisted this development. Edgeworth firmly believed in the measurability of utility in the cardinal sense, for which he hoped even to devise a "hedonimeter." And indeed, in recent years it has been found both useful and possible to employ a cardinal scale for income in order to explain individuals' choices over alternatives representing different degrees of *risk*, balancing portfolios between stocks and bonds, for example. We cannot, however, discuss the recent revival of cardinal utility here. In standard price theory, the ordinal concept of utility meets all our needs.

3. E   CHARACTERISTICS OF INDIFFERENCE CURVES FOR GOODS

If we are dealing only with *goods*, indifference curves have four crucial properties: (1) Indifference curves are negatively sloped; (2) indifference curves cannot intersect; (3) one indifference curve passes through each point in commodity space; (4) indifference curves are "convex" with respect to the origin (i.e., they bulge toward the origin).

1. *Slopes of Indifference Curves:*   For simplicity we assume there are only two goods X and Y. We plot their quantities as before in the x,y-plane (the *commodity space*). Then if we consider some initial point like A in Figure 3.7, all points northeast of A (within the upper-right quadrant formed by the vertical and horizontal lines through A) in commodity space represent larger quantities of *both* goods. But for goods, "More is preferred to less." Hence, moving northeast is moving up the invisible utility hill. By a corresponding argument, moving from A southwest is moving down the utility hill to lower levels of satisfaction. It follows that all points *indifferent* to A must lie either to the southeast like points R or Q or to the northwest like points S or T.

[11]*Mathematical Footnote:* If the two utility scales are only ordinally equivalent, all we can say is that $W = F(U)$ and $dW/dU = F'(U)$, where $F'(U) > 0$. The positive derivative dW/dU always preserves rankings of *magnitudes:* If $U_1 > U_2$, the associated $W_1 > W_2$. Since the second derivative $d^2W/dU^2 = F''(U)$ has indeterminate sign, however, the ranking of *differences* according to the W scale need no longer correspond with their ranking on the U scale.

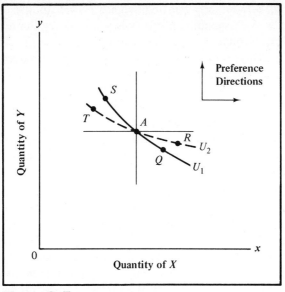

Figure 3. 7
Properties of Indifference Curves

And so the indifference curve must have a negative slope more or less like U_1 or U_2 in the diagram.[12]

2. *Non-intersection of Indifference Curves:* Non-intersection is a logical necessity in a commodity space of goods. Employing Figure 3.7 again, suppose we use the indirect method of proof and tentatively assume that two indifference curves like U_1 and U_2 can actually intersect as in the diagram. According to indifference curve U_1, points A and Q are indifferent. According to indifference curve U_2, points A and R are indifferent. By transitivity, Q and R must be indifferent. But R lies northeast of Q, and "More is preferred to less," so R and Q cannot be indifferent. This logical contradiction disproves the premise that indifference curves can intersect. Hence the intersection in Figure 3.7 is *not* a valid representation of preference.

3. *Density of Indifference Curves:* The proposition that one indifference curve passes through each point in commodity space is expressed in compact language as "Indifference curves are everywhere dense."

[12]*Mathematical Footnote:* In terms of calculus, along any indifference curve utility $U(x,y)$ is constant. So:

$$0 = dU \equiv \frac{\partial U}{\partial x}\,dx + \frac{\partial U}{\partial y}\,dy$$

Then the slope along the indifference curve is:

$$\frac{dy}{dx}\bigg|_U = -\frac{\partial U/\partial x}{\partial U/\partial y}$$

Since $\partial U/\partial x$ and $\partial U/\partial y$ are both positive (X and Y are both *goods* with positive Marginal Utilities), the slope is negative.

That is, between any two indifference curves another can always be drawn. A corresponding property is possessed by the real number system. For example, between any two numbers like 17.4398 and 17.4399 we can always find another number like 17.43986 larger than the first and smaller then the second. The proposition itself follows directly from the first law of preference in Section 3.B above, the Axiom of Comparison. It is assumed *always possible to compare* the preference levels of any baskets of commodities whatsoever. Hence, any describable basket must lie on some indifference curve. Empirically, as already mentioned, this is to be regarded as an idealization rather than a literal description of reality.[13]

4. *Indifference Curves Convex to Origin:* In the two panels of Figure 3.8 we see respectively illustrated the curvatures defined as "convex" and "concave" to the origin. It is the convex curve of Panel (a) that corresponds to the picture of Figure 3.6 and represents the standard assumption applicable to indifference curves between two goods. While a common-sense interpretation can be given to this property of indifference curves, in contrast with the previous three properties (negative slope, non-intersection, and density) *convexity cannot be proved from the postulates of rational choice.* Rather, it is based upon a well-established empirical generalization about the world called "the principle of diversity in consumption" (to be discussed in Chapter 4).

The common-sense explanation may be convincing, however. Suppose an individual is to be held on an indifference curve (constant utility level) between two commodities like food *X* and entertainment *Y*.[14] If his initial position is far to the southeast or lower right on the indifference curve, he is consuming a great deal of food (*x* is great) but is bored for lack of entertainment (*y* is very small). Then it is reasonable to expect him to be willing to give up a relatively large amount of his very ample food for even a small amount of fun. So starting at an extreme position toward the southeast, we would expect to be able to find an indifferent point along the same curve that is well to the left (considerably less *X*) but only a little higher (a bit more *Y*). This implies relatively flat indifference curves in the southeast sector of the preference map. By a corresponding argument, toward the northwest sector of the preference map indifference curves are likely to be steep. Thus the picture of Panel (a) of Figure 3.8, and not of Panel (b), seems to fit our normal patterns of preference.

---

[13]Psychological experiments indicate that there is a minimum "threshold" below which sensations cannot be distinguished from one another. This suggests that indifference curves have some "width" in actuality, which would not fit very conveniently into our picture. But this is no more disturbing than the fact that Euclid's "lines" (straight curves with no breadth) cannot actually be observed in the world, since the best we can do in line-drawing still leaves some crookedness and some breadth. (Nevertheless, some economists in the interests of a more powerfully predictive theory are currently attempting to construct models of choice that incorporate perception thresholds.)

[14]Food and entertainment are aggregations, rather than simple commodities, but this does not affect the point at issue.

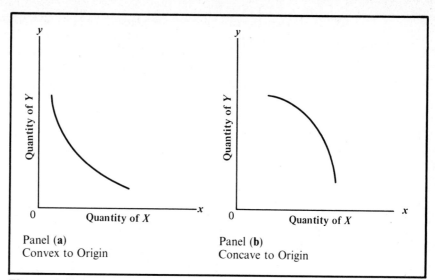

Figure 3. 8
Convexity and Concavity

Example 3. 4
Preferences
for Children—
Number and Sex

The Table here shows the result of a survey of 4,796 families who had two or more children as of 1967. The intention was to determine the proportion of parents who chose to have *more* children, given an initial number of children distributed between boys and girls.

Fraction of Families Who Had Another Child or Expect Another Soon—by Number and Sex of Children

No. of Children	No. of Boys	No. of Families	Fraction Who Had or Expected To Have Another Child
2	0	1159	.67
	1	2385	.61
	2	1252	.67
3	0	337	.58
	1	1025	.55
	2	1023	.51
	3	336	.54
4	0	72	.58
	1	351	.45
	2	520	.48
	3	320	.52
	4	102	.54

Source: Bureau of Census data sampled by James Smith, cited in Y. Ben-Porath and Finis Welch, *Chance, Child Traits, and Choice of Family Size*, Rand Report R-1117-NIH/RF (Santa Monica, Calif., Dec. 1972), p. 14.

Here the two "goods" are taken to be boy children and girl children. (These happen to be produced at home rather than purchased in the market.) The proportion of families having or planning to have *more* children can be interpreted as the proportion for whom children are still a good (for whom the preference directions along the utility map remain north and east as in Figure 3.6). The Table shows that the fraction of parents planning on *more* children is on the whole greatest for those families initially having only two children (regardless of the sex distribution) and least for those families who already have four. But the essential point for our purposes is the somewhat subtler one that, for any given total number of children, the *families with more balanced sex distributions are notably less interested in having more children.*

Going on, or planning to go on, to have more children evidently signifies dissatisfaction with the present situation. For two-child families 67% of those with unbalanced sex distributions (two boys or two girls) were dissatisfied but only 61% of those with one boy and one girl were dissatisfied. While this difference is perhaps not very large, balanced sex distributions remain preferred over unbalanced distributions for three-child and four-child families as well.

Comment: This pattern of choices can be interpreted as showing that indifference curves are *convex* as in Figure 3.6. Recall that a high fraction in the right-hand column of the Table expresses dissatisfaction. For any given number of children, the dissatisfaction tends to be greater at the unbalanced positions (to the southeast or northwest) than toward the middle. With two children, for example, the position (1,1) is preferred to (on a higher indifference curve than) either (0,2) or (2,0). Such a pattern of preferences implies that the indifference curves bulge toward the origin.

3. F GOODS, BADS, AND NEUTERS

As has been suggested above, it is by no means a logical necessity that all commodities of economic significance be *goods*, i.e., desired objects. An obvious example is the problem of pollution. Our society has to choose a combination of industrial production (a *good*) in association with an amount of undesired by-products in the form of contaminants of the environment (a *bad*).

One very important application of utility theory in recent years has been to the problem of *portfolio selection*, the balancing of an individual's wealth over such asset types as stocks, bonds, real estate, etc. In that application it is standard practice to construct utility functions into which M, the *mean* asset return (average percent yield of the portfolio) enters as a desired feature or good, while the *riskiness S* of the return enters as an undesired feature or bad. Figure 3.9 is an illustration of an indifference map of such a utility function. For the good element *M*, more is preferred to less. For the bad element *S*, less is preferred to more. The arrows show that preference directions are north and *west*. Hence the indifference curves here have *positive* slope.

Given the phenomenon of satiation, it is also possible for a commodity to be a good *up to a point*, and then become a bad.

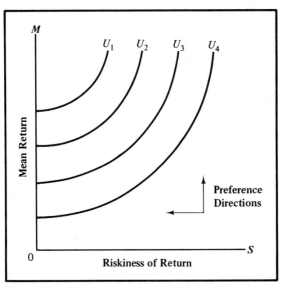

Figure 3. 9
Indifference Curves between a Good and a Bad

Example 3. 5
Ball-Point Pens
and
French Pastries

MacCrimmon and Toda[15] conducted an experimental study of indifference-curve patterns. The subjects were college students. The first choice offered was between money (which we may interpret here as the equivalent of a generalized consumption commodity) and ball-point pens. The subjects' indifference-curve patterns all showed negative slope. The next choice offered was between money and French pastries, with the proviso that the pastries had to be actually eaten on the the spot! Not surprisingly, French pastries became a bad after the first one or two; the subjects would eat more only if paid more money for doing so. Consequently, these indifference curves had normal negative slope only in the region marked as Zone I in Figure 3.10, west of the curve drawn through the lowest points of the successive indifference curves. In Zone I the preference directions are north and east as usual. In Zone II, east

[15]K. R. MacCrimmon and M. Toda, "The Experimental Determination of Indifference Curves," *Review of Economic Studies*, v. 36 (Oct. 1969).

of the dividing curve, French pastries have become a bad so that the preference directions are north and west, and the indifference curves take on a positive slope.

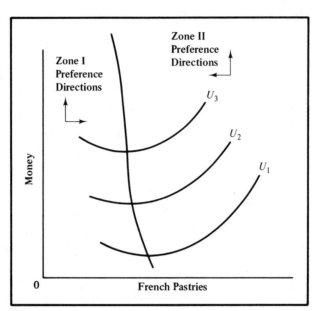

Figure 3. 10
Satiation

So long as commodities are definitely goods or definitely bads, there is no problem with the properties of indifference curves: Making the obvious changes where called for by the reversal of preference direction leads to a correct description, whether we are dealing with two goods, two bads, or a bad and a good. What if there were a commodity that was a *neuter*, neither adding to nor detracting from utility? Then the indifference-curve picture will be as in Figure 3.11. (*Questions for the student*: Which commodity is the neuter in Figure 3.11? Is the other commodity a good or bad?)

3. F. 1 An Application of Utility Theory:
The Economics of Charity.

The following observations, among others, can be made about charity: (1) Not everyone makes charitable contributions. (2) But some people do. (3) Those that give charity almost always give to persons poorer than themselves. The problem is to construct an indifference-curve picture or pictures consistent with these observations.

One approach is as follows. Figure 3.12 has as axes "My Income" (measured horizontally to the right) and "His Income" (measured vertically

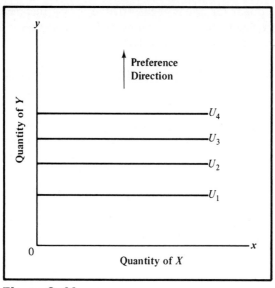

Figure 3. 11
A Neuter Commodity

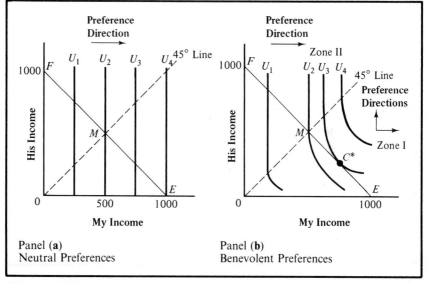

Figure 3. 12
Preference and Charity

upward). The income distribution as initially given is some point along the line *EMF*. At the point *E*, for example, My Income is 1000 and His Income is 0. At the point *F* the situations are reversed. *M* is the mid-point (obtained geometrically by the intersection with the 45° line) where each of us has income of 500. By making charitable contributions, I can increase His

73

Income dollar for dollar at the expense of My Income, that is, I can move along the line *EMF* in the direction of *F*. (Moving in the direction of *E* would amount to his making a charitable contribution to me, but we are looking only at "my" decisions.)

Suppose I am completely uninterested in whether he has any income or not. Then His Income is a neuter commodity on my preference map. Consequently, since My Income is surely a good, the only preference direction for me in Figure 3.12 would be horizontal to the right. Then the indifference curves must be vertical lines as shown in Panel (a). Panel (b) displays a more interesting "benevolent" case. But as indicated in observation (3) above, my benevolence applies only to people poorer than myself. Then His Income is a good for me, *but only when "he" is poorer than I am*. The preference directions are north and east, and my indifference curves take on the negative slope appropriate between two goods, *but only below the 45° line* (in Zone I). For, only below the 45° line is His Income less than My Income.

Questions

1. An individual is offered his choice between a ski trip to Aspen and four cases of Cutty Sark whiskey. Which of the following possible responses violate the laws of preference:

a. "They're so different, I can't choose."
b. "I don't care, you choose for me."
c. "Whichever I choose, I know I'll be sorry."

2. Name a commodity which is a good for many people, but is a bad for you. Name a commodity which is a good for you, but only up to a point; after that it becomes a bad.

3. Draw possible indifference maps between:

a. Two goods.
b. A good and a bad.
c. A good and a neuter.
d. A good and a commodity which is a good up to a point, but then becomes a bad.

4. What do modern economists mean by the term "utility"?

5. Can you give an exact meaning in utility terms to the expression "greatest good of the greatest number"?

6. From a "cardinal" (quantitatively measurable) Total Utility function, show how a corresponding Marginal Utility function is derived. What can be said about the Marginal Utility function if Total Utility is given only in "ordinal" terms?

7. What are the four essential properties of indifference curves between two goods? Explain the justification for each of the four properties.

8. Which of the following requires only *ordinal* utility, which requires cardinal utility, and which requires *interpersonal comparability* of cardinal utilities:

a. Indifference curves can be drawn.

b. A Marginal Utility function can be used to see how Total Utility changes as consumption of a good increases.

c. It can be determined which person in a group is most desirous of receiving a particular prize.

9. An example of an ordinal measure is the military rank system. A sergeant has more authority than a private, a lieutenant more than a sergeant, and so on. Give another example of an ordinal scale of magnitude.

10. *A More Advanced Question:* In the "Economics of Charity" diagram (Figure 3.12), suppose that the initial situation in either Panel is point *E* ("My Income" is 1000, "His Income" is 0). If by charitable transfer of income I can attain any position along the line *EMF*, can you see what my preferred position will be if my tastes are represented by Panel (a)? If my tastes are represented by Panel (b)? How much charity will I give in each of the two cases?

11. *A Still More Advanced Question:* In surveys of income and happiness (see Example 3.2), a puzzling discrepancy has been noted. While there is higher reported happiness with higher income *at a moment of time*, this conclusion does not seem to hold for comparisons *over time*. Even though wealth has risen over the years in the United States all across the scale so that both rich and poor have higher incomes than before, reports on happiness do not average higher than before.[16] The most natural explanation of this paradox is that happiness is more powerfully affected by *relative* income status than by actual consuming power represented by income. The poor are richer than before, but are still on the bottom of the heap in the comparative sense; therefore they may still feel just as unhappy as before. Is this preference pattern consistent with either Panel of Figure 3.12? If not, how would you draw the preference map?

[16]See R. A. Easterlin, "Does Economic Growth Improve the Human Lot? Some Empirical Evidence," in P. David and M. Reder, eds., *Nations and Households in Economic Growth Essays in Honor of M. Abramovitz* (New York: Academic Press, 1974).

Chapter 4
Consumption and Demand

The present chapter connects the *subjective* patterns of individual preferences with the *objective* observable behavior of consumers in markets. The market behavior of the consumer is summarized, from the viewpoint of the economist, by the responsiveness of consumption decisions to *changes in prices* and to *changes in incomes.*

4. A   THE OPTIMUM OF THE CONSUMER

As has already been emphasized, two theoretical techniques—optimization, and determination of equilibrium—account for the great bulk of formal economic analysis. Our first application of the technique of optimization will be to the consumption choices of an individual in the product market.

The class of behavior we call "rational" is characterized by a relation between two sets of data underlying an individual's decisions: his *preferences,* and his *opportunities.* The rational individual will, within the opportunities available to him, so arrange his affairs as to best satisfy his preferences. Or with specific reference to the consumption decision, and employing the utility concept introduced in the previous chapter, we can say: The rational individual will select, from among his opportunities, the one consumption basket or combination that *maximizes* his utility. This selection process is called "consumptive optimization"; the position arrived at (the consumption basket chosen) is the *optimum of the consumer.*[1]

4. A. 1   Optimum of the Consumer—Geometry

Preferences and opportunities are brought together, for a particular individual, in the illustration of Figure 4.1. Here there are just two commodities,

[1]This is sometimes carelessly called the "equilibrium" of the consumer. Such wording blurs the distinction between the two key analytical tools—equilibrium and optimum—that the student must learn to handle, each in its proper place. Logically, an *optimum* is the result of the exercise of willed rational choice on the part of an economic agent. An *equilibrium* is the outcome of a balance of forces, and can be a completely impersonal or even mechanical process involving no human decision or will.

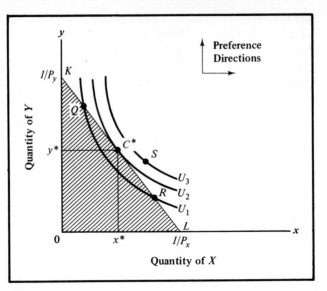

Figure 4. 1
Optimum of the Consumer

X and Y, both assumed to be *goods*. Consequently the indifference curves $U_1, U_2, \ldots$ are negatively-sloped (as in Figure 3.6). This is equivalent to saying that the *preference directions* are north and east. In addition, the indifference curves are shown as *convex* to the origin.

Since preferences are defined for all conceivable combinations (baskets) of X and Y, the indifference curves should be regarded as covering the entire positive quadrant between the X- and Y-axes. But the range of opportunities of the individual, his *opportunity set*, constitutes only a limited portion of the positive quadrant. It is shown as the triangular shaded region in Figure 4.1. More particularly, we are dealing here with the *market* opportunity set for consumption decisions, the alternative consumption bundles available to the individual through transactions in the product market.[2]

The amount of *income*, I, available for spending on consumption is one determinant of an individual's market opportunity set. The *prices* of consumer goods, specifically here the prices P_x and P_y of commodities X and Y respectively, constitute the other determinant. The consumer will ordinarily have obtained income, of course, by selling productive services to business firms.

In a modern economy prices are generally quoted in money terms. And income is also measured as a money flow of earnings from resource services, per unit time. How money functions as a *medium of exchange*, i.e., as a counter whose universal acceptability facilitates the process of trade, will be examined in Chapter 8. For our purposes here we want to "pierce the veil" of

[2]Other types of consumption opportunity sets can also exist. Robinson Crusoe, for example, could be regarded as having an opportunity set as between combinations of commodities like fish and bananas available to him on his island. Crusoe's consumption opportunity set evidently depends entirely upon his own isolated efforts, and in no way upon the possibility of transactions in markets.

money and deal with the underlying *real* magnitudes. Consequently, we will think of prices and income as measured in terms of some standard real good called a "numeraire." Then P_x, the price of X, is the amount of the standard good that must be paid for a unit of X; P_y is the amount that must be paid for a unit of good Y; and income I is the amount earned in units of the standard numeraire good.

Suppose that expenditures on commodities X and Y exactly exhaust income. Then we have the equation:

(4.1) $$P_x x + P_y y = I$$

Alternatively, suppose that we wanted to allow for the possibility of *not* expending all of income on X and Y. Then a more general relation would hold in the form:

(4.1′) $$P_x x + P_y y \leqq I$$

The more general expression (4.1′) describes the entire shaded opportunity region of Figure 4.1. The exact equality (4.1), on the other hand, represents the line in the diagram forming the northeasterly boundary of the opportunity set. More specifically, this boundary is called the *budget line* of the consumer.

Since X and Y are suppose to be the only desired goods,[3] and since the preference directions are north and east, only the budget line itself is of concern to the consumer. (He can get to any position in the interior of the shaded region, starting from a point on the budget line, simply by throwing away some X or some Y or both. But with X and Y both goods, he would never want to do so.)

Let us now consider the shape and position of the budget line more closely. When no X is purchased at all ($x = 0$), there is a maximum possible amount of Y that can be purchased out of income. Equation (4.1) tells us that this maximum number of Y-units equals I/P_y. Geometrically, I/P_y is the ordinate of the intersection of the budget line with the Y-axis, the point K in Figure 4.1. And when no Y at all is purchased, I/P_x units of commodity X can be acquired. So the budget line intersects the X-axis at the abscissa I/P_x, represented by the point L in the diagram. Any mixed basket of X and Y will lie somewhere along the budget line KL between K and L.

In the analysis of optimization, emphasis will very frequently be placed upon the *slope* of curves or lines drawn on x,y-axes. The slope of a curve or line will be symbolized as $\dfrac{\Delta y}{\Delta x}$, the change in y divided by the change in x. In the case of a line, the slope is of course constant throughout its length. The slope of the budget line specifically, symbolized as $\left.\dfrac{\Delta y}{\Delta x}\right|_I$, can be expressed as the ratio of the vertical intercept I/P_y to the horizontal intercept I/P_x.

(4.2) $$\left.\frac{\Delta y}{\Delta x}\right|_I = -\frac{I/P_y}{I/P_x} = -\frac{P_x}{P_y}$$

---

[3]Saving, as representing the purchase of future goods, is therefore excluded.

This slope carries a negative sign since, along the budget line, an *increase* in x is associated with a *decrease* of y.[4]

Algebraically, equation (4.2) tells us that the slope is also equal to the negative of the *price ratio* P_x/P_y. This has a natural economic interpretation. Giving up one unit of X is equivalent to moving up to the left along the budget line. How far up? The unit of X given up makes available the amount P_x for spending on Y, so that the number of units of Y obtainable in exchange is just P_x/P_y. If P_x were 10 and P_y were 2, giving up one unit of X would permit purchase of $\frac{10}{2} = 5$ units of Y, so that -5 would be the slope of the budget line.

We have now seen how the market opportunity set depends upon commodity prices P_x and P_y (whose ratio determines the *slope* of the budget line), and upon income I (whose magnitude determines the distances of the intercepts I/P_x and I/P_y from the origin and therefore the *position* of the budget line). With the data both as to preferences and opportunities in hand, we can proceed to the optimum of the consumer.

From inspection of Figure 4.1, it is evident that the consumer's best attainable position along the budget line KL (and, therefore, the best position attainable within the shaded market opportunity set) is the point C^*—the consumption combination containing x^* of commodity X and y^* of commodity Y. At C^* the indifference curve U_2 is just *tangent* to the budget line. The geometrical relationships are such that the consumptive optimum must be at a tangency, if a tangency position exists (as discussed below). Non-tangency points like Q and R in the diagram, both lying on indifference curve U_1 at the points where U_1 cuts the budget line, must necessarily be inferior in terms of preference to the tangency point C^* on indifference curve U_2. In terms of the invisible "utility hill" of Chapter 3, Q and R lie along a lower contour than C^*; the highest contour attainable is the one that can just barely be reached at the single (tangency) point C^*. It is true that a point like S on indifference curve U_3 would be even superior to C^*—but the combination S is not attainable since indifference curve U_3 never lies within the opportunity set.

Conclusion: The optimum of the consumer is found at the tangency between the budget line and a convex indifference curve (if such a tangency exists).

In Section 3.E the convexity property of indifference curves was asserted to follow not from the logic of the Laws of Preference but rather from observation of behavior in the world. This point can now be demonstrated. Imagine hypothetically that curves of indifference between goods X and Y have negative slope but the opposite concave curvature. Such a situation is

---

[4]*Mathematical Footnote:* With the equation of the budget line as $P_x x + P_y y = I$, the slope is found as the derivative:

$$\left.\frac{dy}{dx}\right|_I = -\frac{P_x}{P_y}$$

Since this derivative is a constant, it equals the ratio of finite increments $\left.\frac{\Delta y}{\Delta x}\right|_I$ in equation (4.2) of the text.

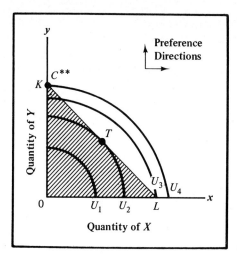

Figure 4. 2
Concave Indifference Curves
and Corner Solution

pictured in Figure 4.2, where the preference directions, shaded opportunity set, and budget line *KL* remain as in the previous diagram. Here there is again a tangency, the point *T*. But *T* is not the consumptive optimum. Indeed, *T* is the *least* preferred point on the budget line, lying as it does on U_2, the *lowest* indifference curve reached along *KL*. With concave indifference curves, the highest level of preference along a budget line will necessarily be found at the intersection of the budget line with one or the other axis. This means that the best use of income would always be to devote expenditure exclusively to the purchase of one commodity—to consume only one of the two goods available. In Figure 4.2 the optimum position is denoted C^{**} on indifference curve U_4, at point *K* on the *Y*-axis. Such an outcome is called a *corner solution*, as opposed to the ordinary *interior solution* as at C^* in Figure 4.1.

Now in the actual world individuals are observed to *diversify* their consumption, to purchase a *mixture* of many different commodities. Only a convex indifference-curve map like Figure 4.1 can lead to interior solutions and thereby explain this observation.

There is one difficulty with the explanation, however. Let us drop the limiting assumption of exactly two commodities and recognize that the typical individual makes consumption choices among many thousands of alternative goods. We are really dealing with a multi-dimensional preference function, with a separate axis for each commodity available. For three commodities there would be three axes. The three-dimensional indifference contours become indifference *shells*, nested like the skins of an onion. Beyond three dimensions we cannot carry the geometrical representation, but can still imagine the generalization to more commodities. Now in point of fact we actually do observe "corner solutions" with respect to many or even most goods; the typical individual buys positive quantities of only a small number of the distinct commodities that he might conceivably purchase. In some cases this may be because a commodity that is a *good* for some people is a *bad* for others (tapioca pudding). But even among the vast numbers of commodities that consumers recognize as goods, many are not actually purchased. The reason is, of course, that the price is regarded as too high relative to the consumer's desires. You may enjoy the flavor of Beluga caviar, be able to afford at least a small quantity of it, and yet not be willing to pay the steep price required. Thus, you are at a corner solution with regard to the "caviar axis" of your multicommodity utility function.

Observation of actual corner solutions for *some* goods does not, however, require us to abandon convexity to the origin as a property of indifference curves. Figure 4.3 shows in two dimensions how a corner solution can be

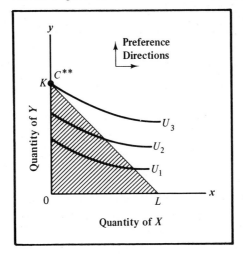

Figure 4. 3
Convex Indifference Curves
and Corner Solution

perfectly consistent with convexity. Here again the most preferred position (highest indifference curve attainable in the market opportunity set) is at C^{**}, reached along the vertical axis at K, where only Y and no X is consumed. We do not have a tangency, but the optimum is the *closest to tangency* (equality of slopes) that the consumer can achieve along the budget line KL. Convex indifference curves are thus capable of explaining *both* the observation of interior solutions in some cases and corner solutions in other cases.

We may summarize this geometrical discussion as follows.

Geometrical Optimum Principle: The optimum of the consumer, the position where he maximizes utility or satisfaction subject to his limited income, is the point on the budget line touching his highest attainable indifference curve, assumed to be convex to the origin. This point may be a tangency of budget line and indifference curve, in which case it will generally be in the interior of the commodity space. This is called an interior solution. But if no tangency exists, then one or the other of the intercepts of the budget line with the axes will be on the highest attainable indifference curve. This is called a corner solution.

4. A. 2 Optimum of the Consumer—Analysis

Setting aside geometry, let us now reconsider the problem of consumer choice in terms of underlying concepts. The consumer is seeking to maximize satisfaction, to distribute his given income I optimally over the different commodities he might conceivably purchase, in our example, over the two goods X and Y.

Suppose that we were allowed to think in terms of a "cardinal" preference function, measured in units of utils. Then it would be meaningful to speak of the magnitude of Marginal Utility. The older economists postulated "diminishing Marginal Utility" with respect to additional units consumed of goods like X or Y. Holding Y constant, let the individual increase his consumption of X. Then, assertedly, the additional satisfaction (marginal utils) per unit of X would be steadily falling as the rate of consumption of X increased. Similarly there would be diminishing Marginal Utility for consumption of commodity Y, holding the quantity of the other good X constant.

Given diminishing Marginal Utility for each of the two goods, the consumer will be at an (interior) optimum when the Consumption Balance Equation (4.3) is satisfied:

$$\text{(4.3)} \qquad \frac{\text{Marginal Utility of } X}{\text{Price of } X} = \frac{\text{Marginal Utility of } Y}{\text{Price of } Y} \qquad \text{Interior Solution}^5$$

The explanation is immediate. For any commodity, Marginal Utility divided by price is *Marginal Utility per dollar* spent on that commodity. For the consumer not to want to change his purchase rate of X relative to Y, the Marginal Utility per dollar of X and Y must be equal. The last dollar must yield equivalent satisfaction, whether spent on X or spent on Y. If this were not the case, the consumer would buy more of the commodity for which Marginal Utility per dollar was high, and less of the one whose Marginal Utility per dollar was low. He would continue to reallocate his spending in this way until Marginal Utilities per dollar became equal over all commodities being purchased.

---

[5]*Mathematical Footnote:* In optimization problems in economics, a very neat technique called "the method of Lagrangian multipliers" is generally used. Specifically, in the present case we seek to maximize a cardinal utility function $U(x,y)$ subject to the constraint $P_x x + P_y y = I$ (where P_x, P_y, and I are constants). The technique involves setting up an artificial maximand in the following form:

$$\underset{(x,\,y,\,\lambda)}{\text{Max }} L = U(x,y) - \lambda(P_x x + P_y y - I)$$

The maximization is with respect to x, y, and λ.

$$\frac{\partial L}{\partial x} = \frac{\partial U}{\partial x} - \lambda P_x = 0$$

$$\frac{\partial L}{\partial y} = \frac{\partial U}{\partial y} - \lambda P_y = 0$$

$$\frac{\partial L}{\partial \lambda} = P_x x + P_y y - I = 0$$

The first two conditions imply:

$$\frac{\partial U/\partial x}{P_x} = \frac{\partial U/\partial y}{P_y}$$

This is, of course, the Consumption Balance Equation (4.3). The technique works because in taking the partial derivative with respect to λ we obtain $P_x x + P_y y - I = 0$. This guarantees that the constraint condition (the budget equation) is always met, and also assures that the maximum of the artificial variable L is the same as the desired maximum of U.

What about the possibility of a corner solution? Suppose that, for some commodity like Beluga caviar, the Marginal Utility per dollar remains lower than that of the other commodity even when zero units of caviar are purchased. Then we would have a corner optimum, which can be expressed (letting X represent caviar) as the inequality:

(4.3′)
$$\frac{MU_x(x=0)}{P_x} < \frac{MU_y(y>0)}{P_y} \qquad \text{Corner Solution[6]}$$

In either case, of course, the budget-line condition (4.1) as well as the Consumption Balance Equation (or Inequality, in the case of a corner solution) holds at the optimum of the consumer.[7]

What if utility is an "ordinal" magnitude only? Then we must think in terms of *substituting* Y for X (or vice versa) in the individual's consumption bundle. The rate at which a consumer *can* substitute Y for X in his market purchases, given his fixed income I, is determined by the price ratio P_x/P_y. For example, if $P_x/P_y = 5$, within a total expenditure I he can substitute in his consumption basket 10 units of Y for 2 units of X. More formally, let us define the *Marginal Rate of Substitution in Exchange*, MRS_E, as this ratio governing possible substitutions between X and Y in market exchanges. Then $MRS_E \equiv P_x/P_y$. Since commodity prices are taken as constant by the consumer, MRS_E is a constant. Indeed, we see immediately from equation (4.2) that MRS_E is equal to the absolute value of the constant slope $\frac{\Delta y}{\Delta x}\Big|_I$ of his budget line.

We thus have a concept explaining the terms according to which the consumer *can* make market substitutions of Y for X in his consumption basket. The next question is, what are the terms on which he would be *willing* to make substitutions of Y for X? More explicitly, what is the ratio $\frac{\Delta y}{\Delta x}\Big|_U$ at which he would be just willing to make exchanges between X and Y, of small amounts, in either direction? This is defined as the *Marginal Rate of Substitution in Consumption*, denoted MRS_C. The expression "*just willing* to make exchanges in either direction" is equivalent to the expression "*indifferent* between substitutions in either direction." This suggests that MRS_C refers to a small movement along an indifference curve. And indeed MRS_C is the

---

[6]If there were many commodities, there might be corner solutions as between some pairs of goods and interior solutions for others. In the case of just three goods, the solution might take the form:
$$\frac{MU_x(x=0)}{P_x} < \frac{MU_y(y>0)}{P_y} = \frac{MU_z(z>0)}{P_z}$$

Here commodities Y and Z, but not commodity X, are being purchased in positive amounts at the consumptive optimum.

[7]*Mathematical Footnote:* The reason for corner solutions is that there are *non-negativity constraints* ($x \geqq 0$ and $y \geqq 0$) on amounts of goods consumed. Where such constraints are dictated by the economics of the problem, calculus techniques must be used with caution.

absolute value of the indifference-curve slope,[8] just as MRS_E is the absolute value of the budget-line slope.

Clearly, the consumer cannot be at an optimum position unless the rate at which he is *willing* to make substitutions in his consumption bundle (MRS_C) equals the rate at which he *can* make substitutions via market trading (MRS_E).

[8] *Mathematical Footnote:* In terms of derivatives,

$$MRS_C \equiv -\frac{dy}{dx}\bigg|_U$$

Example 4. 1
Prisoners
of War—
Tea versus
Coffee

The economist R. A. Radford had the unfortunate opportunity of studying, from the inside, social behavior in prisoner-of-war camps in Germany and Italy during World War II. He found that highly active economies functioned in these camps, particularly under the relatively "favorable" conditions that obtained in the earlier war years.

Cigarettes served generally as the numeraire or standard good in terms of which prices were quoted. Coffee might go for about 2 cigarettes per cup, a shirt might cost 80, washing service 2 cigarettes per garment, etc.

In the camp section holding English prisoners, tea was definitely preferred to coffee—and the reverse in the French section. A regular smuggling trade was conducted between the two, permitting prisoners in each section to adjust their consumption choices to the price ratio reflecting the overall supply-demand balance in the camp as a whole.[9]

Comment: The two panels of Figure 4.4 illustrate the situations of typical English and French prisoners. In both camp sections prices were quoted, in cigarettes, for coffee (P_c) and for tea (P_t). The efficient smuggling trade between sections prevented disparities from developing between the coffee prices or between the tea prices in the two sections. Therefore, the Marginal Rate of Substitution in Exchange, $MRS_E = P_c/P_t$, was the same for both groups of prisoners. But for the English prisoners, the tangency point C^* where $MRS_C = MRS_E$ was well over toward the tea axis while for the French prisoners the consumptive optimum lay in the opposite direction toward the coffee axis.

[9] R. A. Radford, "The Economic Organisation of a P.O.W. Camp," *Economica*, v. 12 (1945). In his enforced period of stay Radford made many other striking observations, some of which will be mentioned below.

We see, therefore, that (in the case of an interior solution) the optimum of the consumer occurs where the following condition, the Substitution Equiva-

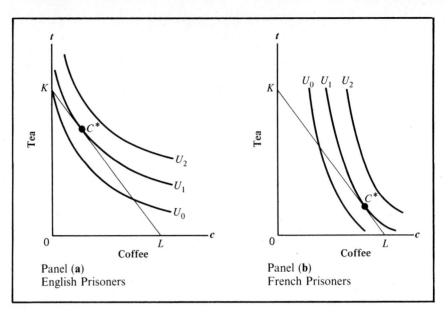

Figure 4. 4
Coffee versus Tea in a POW Camp

lence Equation, holds:

(4.4) $\qquad MRS_C = MRS_E,$ or equivalently $\left.\dfrac{\Delta y}{\Delta x}\right|_U = -\dfrac{P_x}{P_y}$

Analytical Optimum Principle: The optimum of the consumer, the point where he maximizes utility or satisfaction subject to his limited income, is characterized by equality between the Marginal Rate of Substitution in Consumption (MRS_C) and the Marginal Rate of Substitution in Exchange (MRS_E). In addition, the amounts spent must exhaust the consumer's budget. These conditions are the equivalent of the geometrical tangency of indifference curve and budget line, and therefore determine an interior optimum. (If MRS_C and MRS_E cannot be equated, i.e., if no tangency exists, they are to be brought as near to equality as possible by reducing the quantity taken of one of the commodities to zero. This is the equivalent of the geometrical corner optimum.)

The Consumption Balance Equation (4.3) applicable for *cardinal* utility, and the Substitution Equivalence Equation (4.4) that remains valid even if utility is only ordinally quantifiable, must of course be closely related. The former can be rewritten as:

$$\frac{\text{Marginal Utility of } X}{\text{Marginal Utility of } Y} = \frac{\text{Price of } X}{\text{Price of } Y}$$

The price ratio on the right-hand side is the Marginal Rate of Substitution in

Exchange, MRS_E. And, given cardinal utility, the ratio of Marginal Utilities on the left-hand side is equivalent to the Marginal Rate of Substitution in Consumption, MRS_C. Suppose, for example, that $MU_x/MU_y = 2$. Then the individual would be *just willing* to make a small substitution of, say, two units of Y for one unit of X in his consumption basket. But this interpretation is exactly equivalent to saying that his $MRS_C = 2$, and so the ratio of Marginal Utilities can be identified with the Marginal Rate of Substitution in Consumption.[10] But MRS_C *can* be defined independently of cardinal utility, and so the optimum condition (4.4) is more general than equation (4.3).[11]

In justifying the Consumption Balance Equation (4.3) as optimum condition, the traditional argument used the postulate of *diminishing* Marginal Utility. A somewhat analogous specification is needed to justify the Substitution Equivalence Equation. That is, we need some kind of additional restriction, not involving any cardinal utility concept, but still assuring that $MRS_E = MRS_C$ actually represents a best position. Geometrically, the tangency position is an optimum given *convexity* of the indifference-curve map with respect to the origin. The analytical equivalent of the geometrical property of indifference-curve convexity is called the postulate of *decreasing Marginal*

[10]*Mathematical Footnote:* Along an indifference curve,

$$0 = dU = \frac{\partial U}{\partial x}\,dx + \frac{\partial U}{\partial y}\,dy$$

Then

$$-\frac{dy}{dx}\bigg|_U \equiv \frac{\partial U/\partial x}{\partial U/\partial y}$$

i.e., MRS_C equals the ratio of the Marginal Utilities of X and Y.

[11]*Mathematical Footnote:* In ordinal-utility terms, let the consumer maximize $V = F[U(x,y)]$, where $F(U)$ is *any* monotonically increasing function of U. That is, $dF(U)/dU > 0$ for all U. Then the Lagrangian artificial maximand and the optimum conditions become

$$\underset{(x,y,\lambda)}{\text{Max }} L = F[U(x,y)] - \lambda(P_x x + P_y y - I)$$

$$\frac{\partial L}{\partial x} = \frac{dF}{dU}\frac{\partial U}{\partial x} - \lambda P_x = 0$$

$$\frac{\partial L}{\partial y} = \frac{dF}{dU}\frac{\partial U}{\partial y} - \lambda P_y = 0$$

$$\frac{\partial L}{\partial \lambda} = P_x x + P_y y - I = 0$$

Write the first two conditions as:

$$\frac{dF}{dU}\frac{\partial U}{\partial x} = \lambda P_x$$

$$\frac{dF}{dU}\frac{\partial U}{\partial y} = \lambda P_y$$

Dividing the first by the second, we see that dF/dU cancels out:

$$\frac{\partial U/\partial x}{\partial U/\partial y} = -\frac{dy}{dx}\bigg|_U = \frac{P_x}{P_y}$$

So condition (4.4) holds for ordinal as well as cardinal utility.

Rate of Substitution in Consumption. That is, geometrical convexity corresponds to the condition that MRS_C decreases as x increases.[12]

4. B VARIATION OF THE CONSUMER'S OPTIMUM

With the data as to *preferences* assumed unchanging, the optimum of the consumer can vary only in response to changes in *opportunities*. The consumer's market opportunity set, we have seen, depends upon two elements: (1) income, and (2) commodity prices. In this section we shall see how the consumer adjusts his consumption basket in reaction to changes in these two elements governing his market opportunities.

4. B. 1 Income Expansion Path and Engel Curve

Let us suppose, to begin with, that income I increases while all prices remain unchanged. Then, in a simplified world of only two commodities X and Y, we can picture the situation as in Figure 4.5. The original consumptive optimum is at point Q, the tangency of the budget line KL with the indifference curve U_0. (This position corresponds to point C^* in Figure 4.1.) Now let income rise from I to I'. Since the intercept of the original budget line KL on the Y-axis was I/P_y and the intercept on the X-axis was I/P_x, an increase in income from I to I' that leaves prices unchanged will increase both intercepts proportionately. Therefore the new budget line, $K'L'$, must be parallel to the original KL. Put another way, the slope of the budget line depends only upon the price ratio P_x/P_y and so any change in the opportunity set that leaves all prices unaffected must keep the *slope* of the budget line the same as before. (A corollary of this is that a proportionate change of *all* prices simultaneously

[12]*Mathematical Footnote:* We are dealing here with the *second-order* conditions for a maximum. The condition for indifference-curve convexity is $d(MRS_C)/dx < 0$. Or, recalling that MRS_C is defined as the absolute value of the slope, this can also be expressed as

$$\frac{d}{dx}\left(\frac{dy}{dx}\right) \equiv \frac{d^2y}{dx^2} > 0$$

where dy/dx is the indifference-curve slope usually expressed more explicitly as $\frac{dy}{dx}\Big|_U$.

$$\frac{d^2y}{dx^2} \equiv \frac{d}{dx}\left(\frac{dy}{dx}\right) \equiv \frac{\partial}{\partial x}\left(\frac{dy}{dx}\right) + \frac{\partial}{\partial y}\left(\frac{dy}{dx}\right)\frac{dy}{dx}$$

But

$$\frac{dy}{dx} \equiv -\frac{\partial U/\partial x}{\partial U/\partial y} \equiv -\frac{U_x}{U_y} \qquad \text{(in more compact notation)}$$

Then

$$\frac{d^2y}{dx^2} \equiv -\frac{U_y U_{xx} - U_x U_{xy}}{U_y^2} - \frac{U_y U_{xy} - U_x U_{yy}}{U_y^2}\left(-\frac{U_x}{U_y}\right)$$

$$\equiv \frac{-U_y^2 U_{xx} + U_x U_y U_{xy} + U_y U_x U_{xy} - U_x^2 U_{yy}}{U_y^3}$$

The main significance of this result is to show that diminishing Marginal Utility (U_{xx}, $U_{yy} < 0$) does not *necessarily* imply decreasing MRS_C (positive d^2y/dx^2). For the cross-derivative U_{xy} has indeterminate sign. So even with cardinal utility, it is indifference-curve convexity rather than diminishing Marginal Utility that should be relied on as the proper second-order condition for a maximum.

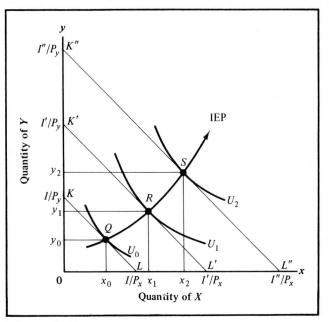

Figure 4. 5
Changes in Income

is equivalent to a corresponding change, in the opposite direction, of income.) The new optimum position is shown as point R, where the budget line $K'L'$ is tangent to the higher indifference curve U_1.

A further increase in income from I' to I'' leads to a further expansion of the market opportunity set, as the budget line shifts outward to $K''L''$. Here the consumptive optimum becomes the tangency position S on indifference curve U_2.

More generally, if we think of I as hypothetically varying while prices and tastes remain unchanged, an entire curve—an Income Expansion Path (IEP) —will be traced out that connects all the different consumptive optimum positions like Q, R, and S in Figure 4.5. The Income Expansion Path indicates the response of the rational consumer to changes in income alone. It should be kept in mind, however, that the Income Expansion Path as a whole depends upon the price ratio; if prices were held constant but at some differing ratio, a different IEP curve would be obtained. More specifically, a price change leading to an increased ratio P_x/P_y (a steepening of the budget lines KL, $K'L'$, etc.) will have the effect of displacing the entire IEP to the northwest. (The student should check this point to verify his understanding of the nature of the IEP curve.)

What shapes are possible for the Income Expansion Path? Consider the three panels of Figure 4.6. In all three cases the original situation is at the point Q, a tangency with indifference curve U_0 along the budget line KL. Now let income increase, so that the budget line shifts out to the position $K'L'$. In

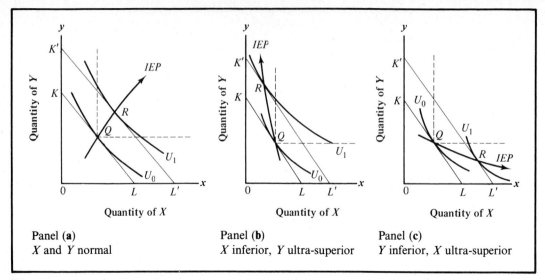

Figure 4. 6 Income-Expansion Paths, Three Cases

Panel (a), the new tangency R along indifference curve U_1 is within the northeasterly quadrant formed by the vertical and horizontal dashed lines through Q. This means that the quantities purchased of X and of Y have both increased with the rise in income; in this case X and Y are called *normal* goods.

In Panel (b), the new tangency R lies to the northwest of Q, outside the normal quadrant; at the higher income, the quantity of Y purchased has increased but the quantity of X decreased. Thus in Panel (b) the IEP has negative slope through the consumptive optimum positions Q and R. A commodity like X here, whose consumption falls when income rises, is called an *inferior* good.

Unfortunately, there is no terminological agreement as to what to call the other commodity Y in this case. The term "superior good" refers to any good that is not inferior, i.e., whose consumption rises with income. Hence Y would be regarded as superior in either the situation of Panel (a) or of Panel (b), leaving us still in need of a way to express the distinction between the two cases. Let us adopt the term *ultra-superior* for the good that is a "partner" of an inferior good. Then Y is ultra-superior in Panel (b). The defining characteristic of an ultra-superior good may be expressed as follows: Since less of an inferior good is purchased when income increases, it follows that *more than 100%* of the increase in income has been devoted to additional purchases of the associated ultra-superior good.

Finally, Panel (c) shows the opposite situation where Y is inferior and X ultra-superior. The IEP is again negatively sloped, but the new consumptive optimum position lies to the southeast (rather than northwest) as income rises.

In all three cases, the IEP curve is drawn with an arrowhead pointing in the direction of rising utility (upward on the invisible utility hill). The arrow is convenient in permitting an immediate distinction, by inspection, between the X-inferior [Panel (b)] and the Y-inferior [Panel (c)] cases.

Conclusion: A positively-sloped Income Expansion Path, between two goods X and Y, means that consumption of each rises as income grows. Then both goods are superior, and the relation between them is normal. Alternatively, if the IEP has negative slope one of the goods must be inferior. The other good must of course be superior, but more specifically may be called ultra-superior as it accounts for more than 100% of the increment of income.

Example 4. 2
Luxuries versus
Necessities in
a POW Camp

Goods that are predominantly purchased by relatively wealthy people are commonly called luxuries. Correspondingly, a good which accounts for a large portion of the consumption budget of poorer people, the proportion in the budget declining as people become richer, is sometimes termed a "necessity." Standard items of food like bread are generally considered necessities. For, while richer people can afford to and generally do buy more loaves of bread per person than poorer people (i.e., bread is not an inferior good), the *proportion* of the budget spent on bread falls as income rises.

In the prisoner-of-war economy already mentioned in Example 4.1 above, R. A. Radford[13] also made interesting observations about necessities and luxuries. Toward the end of the war, prisoners were living in severe privation as a result of the steady deterioration of the German economy under bombing and other wartime strains. In August 1944 a further halving of real income rations, the two main items being food and cigarettes, took place. Unexpectedly, cigarettes proved to be more of a "necessity" than food (by the standard definition above). Despite the presence of many non-smokers, in the market as a whole there was a net attempt after real income fell to trade food for cigarettes. As a result, the price of food (in terms of cigarettes) became actually lower than before.

Comment: The implied shape of indifference curves between cigarettes C and food F at the higher income level (point $Q°$) and the lower income level (point Q'), for a typical prisoner, is indicated in Figure 4.7. The Marginal Rate of Substitution in Consumption, $MRS_c \equiv -\dfrac{\Delta c}{\Delta f}\Big|_U$ is less (indifference curve has flatter slope) at the lower real-income point.

[13]R. A. Radford, "The Economic Organization of a P.O.W. Camp," *Economica*, v. 12 (1945).

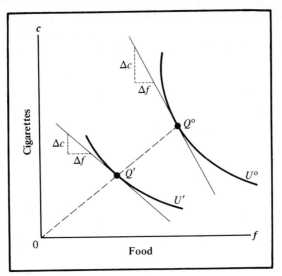

Figure 4. 7
Food versus Cigarettes in a POW Camp

The analysis to this point has showed the reaction of the consumer's optimum basket of commodities to changes in income—prices and preferences being taken as constant. For any single good such as X, the relation between income and consumption can be summarized in a convenient form for statistical determination known as the *Engel Curve*.[14] A portion of a typical Engel Curve is shown in Figure 4.8. In the case illustrated, the quantity of X consumed rises as income rises, i.e., X is a superior good.

In practice, however, we are almost always interested in broader categories or aggregates of consumption like food, clothing, vacation travel, etc., rather

[14]Ernst Engel (1821–1896), German statistician.

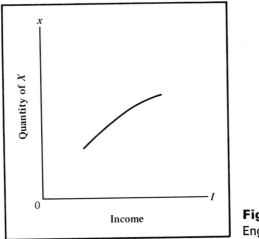

Figure 4. 8
Engel Curve

than in specific single commodities. There is, however, no natural or usable quantity unit for a broad commodity grouping like food or clothing. To handle this, we can replace quantity of X on the vertical axis of the Engel-curve diagram of Figure 4.8 with consumer *expenditures* on X. If X is a single good, expenditures on the good would of course be price times quantity purchased, or $P_x x$. And if X represented an entire grouping of consumption goods $(X_1, \ldots, X_G)$, expenditure is $P_1 x_1 + P_2 x_2 + \cdots + P_G x_G$. Or, in more compact notation, $\sum_{g=1}^{G} P_g x_g$, the sum of the quantities of the separate goods each multiplied by its respective price. The latter version of the income-consumption relation in terms of expenditures may be called the *Engel Expenditure Curve*. Both relations represent a transfer, onto different axes, of the data summarized by the Income Expansion Path.

Definitions: The *Engel Curve* relates consumption quantity x to income I. The *Engel Expenditure Curve* relates expenditure $P_x x$ to income I.

The Engel Expenditure Curve has the additional advantage (over the simple Engel Curve) of directly displaying the difference between a normal superior good and an ultra-superior good. Indeed, the alternative slopes for the Engel Expenditure Curve in the three panels of Figure 4.9 correspond to the three cases of Figure 4.6. To interpret Figure 4.9, first note the dashed 45° line emerging from the origin. If for any commodity (or commodity grouping) the Engel Expenditure Curve lay along this 45° line, the consumer's entire income would be devoted to purchase of that commodity or grouping. Hence the 45° line constitutes an upper limit for the Engel Expenditure Curve.

In the situation pictured in Panel (a), expenditures on X rise as income I increases. But the slope of the rising curve is less than 45°. This means that expenditures on X have risen by *less* than the rise in income, i.e., some of the increment of income must have been spent on a good or goods other than X. Hence, this corresponds to the "normal" case in Panel (a) of Figure 4.6.

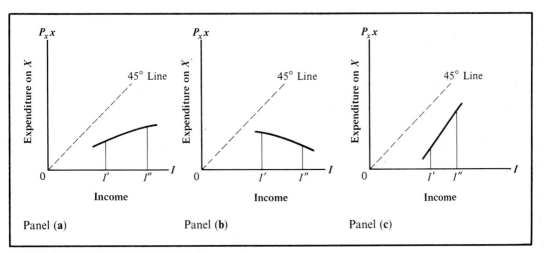

Figure 4. 9 Engel Expenditure Curves

Jumping to Panel (c) of Figure 4.9, we see here that in the range between I' and I'' the Engel Expenditure Curve is rising *more* sharply than the 45° line. Hence more than the total increase in income is being devoted to consumption of X. This means that X is ultra-superior, as in the Panel (c) situation of Figure 4.6. Finally, in the middle Panel (b) of Figure 4.9, expenditures on X actually decline as income rises. Since P_x is constant, the quantity of X taken must have fallen; hence X is inferior, as in the situation pictured in Panel (b) of Figure 4.6.

Recall that the Engel Curve as in Figure 4.8 is a re-plotting of the data summarized by the Income Expansion Path. We know that the IEP will in general shift in response to changes in the price ratio P_x/P_y, and specifically, a rise in P_x (with P_y held constant) will displace the IEP to the northwest. In the Engel Curve, the effect of a rise in P_x will normally be a lowering of the curve, showing that, for any given income I, at a higher P_x less of X will be taken. (See the discussion of the Law of Demand below.) On the other hand, for the Engel Expenditure Curve there are offsetting effects; since P_x rises but the quantity of X falls, the direction of change in $P_x x$ is indeterminate.

Example 4. 3
Engel's Laws
after a Century

The 19th-century statistician Engel did more than merely posit a relation between income and consumer expenditures on specific goods or classes of goods. He went on to assert more specifically that, as income increases: (1) The proportion of the budget spent on food will fall; (2) the proportions spent on lodging and clothing will remain about the same; and (3) the proportion spent on all other goods will increase.

The Table below shows the proportionate expenditures on certain categories of consumer goods, for U.S. urban families in 1960–61 classified by income.

Distribution of Expenditures[a]

	Family Income Level, after Taxes			
Expenditure Category	Under $2000	$2000– 2999	$3000– 3999	$4000 and Over
Food	29.5%	28.4%	25.9%	23.7%
Shelter, fuel, light, refrigeration, water	29.4	24.3	20.6	17.4
Clothing	5.9	8.2	9.0	10.8
Medical care	8.2	8.1	7.3	6.4
Automobile	3.2	6.5	11.3	13.9
All other	23.8	24.5	25.9	27.8
Total	100.0	100.0	100.0	100.0

Source: Bureau of Labor Statistics, "Consumer Expenditures and Income, with Emphasis on Low Income Families," July 1964.
[a]For a more complete survey, see H. Houthakker, "An International Comparison of Household Expenditure Patterns, Commemorating the Centenary of Engel's Law," *Econometrica*, v. 25 (Oct. 1957).

The data confirm Engel in showing a declining proportion spent on food as income rises. But where he predicted constant proportions spent on lodging and clothing, the 20th-century data show a falling proportion in the former and a rising proportion in the latter category. The "All other" category also rises with income, as Engel predicted. One striking feature of the Table is the very sharp increase in the proportion spent on the *automobile* as income rises.

4. B. 2   Price Expansion Path and Demand Curve

Let us now consider the effect of parametric variation in the other determinant of opportunities—market prices. It will be convenient to hold the price of one of the commodities, P_y, constant. Then variation in prices will take the specific form of changes in P_x, the price of commodity X. Here again the change in data affects the shape of the market opportunity set. But whereas a rise in income leads to a *parallel* outward displacement of the budget line representing the northeasterly boundary of the opportunity set, a change in price leads to a *tilting* of this boundary.

In Figure 4.10, as before the initial situation is represented by the consumer optimum at Q where the budget line KL is tangent to the indifference curve U_0. Now let the price of X *fall*. Since the intercept of the budget line with the vertical Y-axis is at I/P_y, nothing has changed there; the point K remains as before. But the intercept of the budget line with the horizontal X-axis is at I/P_x, so the fall in P_x is associated with an expansion of the

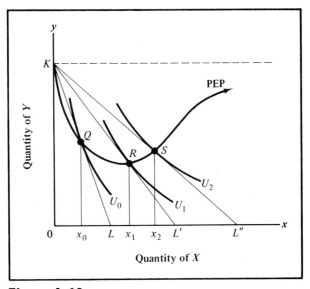

Figure 4. 10
Price Expansion Path

opportunity set taking the form of an outward tilting of the budget line to a new position like KL'. This makes sense, since the enhanced market opportunities are associated entirely with the improved terms for purchasing good X. The new optimum of the consumer is then the point R where the new budget line KL' is tangent to a higher indifference curve U_1. And a still further decline in the price P_x leads to a further outward tilting of the budget line, to the position KL''; here the associated optimum of the consumer is at S on the still higher indifference curve U_2.

A curve can now be passed through all possible consumptive optimum positions like Q, R, and S that are generated by changes in P_x (when income I and the price P_y of the other commodity are held constant). The curve so generated can be called, in analogy with the Income Expansion Path (IEP) of the previous section, the Price Expansion Path (PEP). The PEP curve indicates the response of the rational consumer to changes in P_x alone, income I and the price P_y being held fixed. However, just as the IEP curve in its entirety is shifted when prices change, the entire Price Expansion Path will be displaced to a different position if income I changes. Specifically, if goods X and Y are normal, then a parametric increase in income will tend to shift the Price Expansion Path upward and to the right. (The student should check this point to verify his understanding of the PEP curve, and also work out the implications for the PEP of a parametric shift in the price of the *other* commodity.)

A number of aspects of the Price Expansion Path are of interest.

1. As the price P_x falls, the PEP curve enters regions of higher and higher levels of utility. Again, an arrowhead shows the direction of utility improvement along the PEP in Figure 4.10. The level of satisfaction increases since, with income I in numeraire terms held constant, a fall in P_x is equivalent to a rise in *real* income—in the sense of ability to purchase desired commodities.

2. If the PEP curves downward (southeasterly), as in the range between Q and R along the curve in Figure 4.10, at lower prices P_x the consumer purchases more of X but takes less of Y. If the PEP bends upward into a positive slope, as in the range between R and S in the diagram, the consumer is willing and able at the lower price P_x to obtain more X while consuming more Y as well.

3. If there is some price P_x so high that no X is purchased, at that price the optimum of the consumer is a *corner solution* on the Y-axis. If this condition holds, the Price Expansion Path will have a terminating point on the Y-axis as at K in Figure 4.10. On the other hand, no matter how low the price P_x falls so long as it does not become negative, the budget line (boundary of the market opportunity set) must lie below the dashed horizontal drawn through K in the diagram. Then, the Price Expansion Path must also lie everywhere below this horizontal.

4. Astonishing as it may seem, the PEP curve may actually curl back so

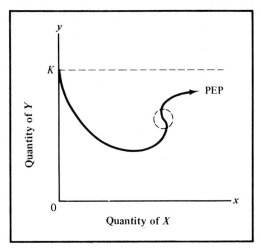

Figure 4. 11
Price Expansion Path—Giffen Case

as to be moving for a time in a northwesterly direction, as in the circled region in Figure 4.11. In this region as price P_x falls, the quantity of X consumed also falls! When this condition applies, the commodity is called a "Giffen good"[15] for this consumer. But the Giffen property can only hold over a limited range; with negatively-sloped indifference curves and positive preference directions, the PEP cannot move northwesterly very long and still be entering regions of higher and higher utility. Giffen goods will be discussed further below.

Finally, we can re-plot the data summarized by the Price Expansion Path as a relation between the quantity consumed of commodity X and the price of X, as in the curve *dd* of Figure 4.12. This is of course the individual's *demand curve for X*. It will be evident from the derivation that so long as the PEP is moving easterly as in Figure 4.10 (whether southeasterly as in the range *KQR*, or northeasterly as in the range *RS*), the demand curve must have a normal negative slope: A lower price P_x is associated with a larger quantity of X entering into the optimum position of the consumer. But if there is a Giffen range in which the PEP curls northwesterly (the circled region in Figure 4.10) then there will be a corresponding range along the demand curve where the demand curve is positively sloped (the circled region in Figure 4.13). In this range the demand curve has the "Giffen property" that at lower prices a smaller quantity is demanded.

That the Giffen demand curve is never (or almost never) observed is a principle called the *Law of Demand*. This principle, like convexity of indifference curves with respect to the origin, does *not* follow from the pure logic of choice. Its justification is empirical observation of the world.

[15]Sir Robert Giffen, British statistician and economist (1837–1910).

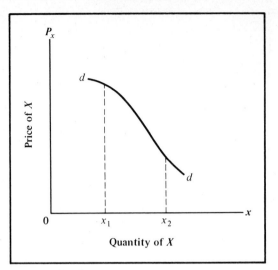

Figure 4. 12
Demand Curve

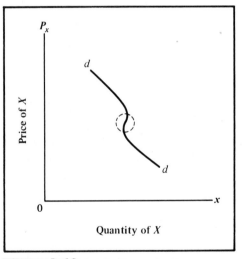

Figure 4. 13
Demand Curve—Giffen Case

Example 4. 4
Alcoholics and
the Law
of Demand

It is often thought that alcoholics lose self-control in the presence of liquor, and so the Law of Demand might not be expected to apply. But in a recent laboratory study, Dr. George Bigelow found that alcoholics' liquor consumption is responsive to price, at least in real terms. In one experiment, alcoholics had to pull a one-pound lever a large number of times to get a drink. The observed result was that the higher the "price" in terms of number of pulls required, the less the alcoholics drank. Other experiments charged "prices" in the form of waiting time between drinks, sacrifice of hospital privileges, and periods of isolation. In every case the higher the price charged, the less the drinking.[16]

[16]Reported in *The Public Interest*, No. 32 (Summer 1973), pp. 119–20.

Since the demand curve is in effect a re-plotting of the data in the Price Expansion Path, and since the latter shifts position as income I changes, we would expect a change in income to affect the position of the demand curve as well. An increase in income, as mentioned above, displaces the PEP curve outward from the origin when X and Y are normal goods. For normal goods, more of *both* commodities X and Y are consumed at any given price ratio when income rises. Along the demand curve for commodity X, we will of course see only the effect upon the consumption of X. Thus, a rise in income tends to move the demand curve *dd* outward from the origin to a position like *d'd'* in Figure 4.14, which shows that an increased quantity would be

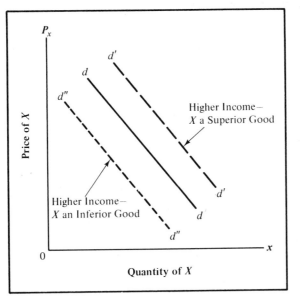

Figure 4. 14
Effect of Income Shifts on Demand Curve

consumed at any give price P_x. But if X is inferior, the shift will be *inward* to the origin as indicated by the position *d"d"* in the diagram; less will be purchased at any given price. (The student should work out the implications of a shift in P_y, the price of good Y, upon the PEP that shows the response of the consumer optimum to variation in P_x.)

4. C INCOME AND SUBSTITUTION EFFECTS OF A PRICE CHANGE

The previous section showed how changes in the two determinants of the opportunity set, *income* and *prices*, affect the optimum of the consumer. However, this classification does not provide a clean separation or "disjunction" of the effects of price changes versus income changes upon individual opportunities. For, if income I in numeraire terms is unchanged while the price P_x falls, with the other price P_y held constant, in a sense *real* income has increased. That real income has increased is also evident from the expansion of the individual's market opportunity set that takes place when P_x falls (the outward tilting of the budget line KL in Figure 4.9). Correspondingly, of course, a *rise* in P_x, with P_y and income I held constant, would represent a contraction of opportunities and in that sense a fall in real income.

For some purposes it is desirable to correct for and thus eliminate the real-income effect of a price change upon the consumer optimum. When this is done we are left with what is called the pure *substitution effect* of the price change. The usual method of adjustment, due to the British economist J. R. Hicks,[17] is illustrated in Figure 4.15. The budget line KL associated with

[17]Another method of adjustment, more convenient for some purposes, will be introduced in Chapter 6.

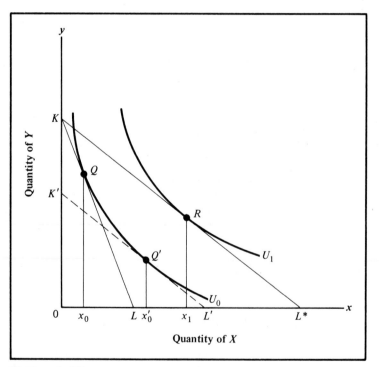

Figure 4. 15
Income and Substitution Effects—Hicks Decomposition

the original price P_x leads to the optimum of the consumer at Q along the indifference curve U_0, where the quantity taken of X is x_0. The budget line KL^* reflects a lower price P'_x leading to the new optimum at R along indifference curve U_1, where $x = x_1$. Now construct an artificial budget line $K'L'$ (dashed in the diagram) *tangent to the original indifference curve U_0 but whose slope reflects the new price ratio P'_x/P_y.* The tangency of $K'L'$ with U_0 is at the point Q', where $x = x'_0$.

Between the original consumer optimum Q and the artificial optimum Q', real income is constant—in the sense that utility is unchanged (the individual remains on the same indifference curve as before). Thus the shift of the optimum from Q to Q' (or, in terms of quantities of X, the difference $x'_0 - x_0$), is the pure "substitution effect" due to the price change. The remainder of the movement of the consumer optimum from Q' to R (or, in terms of X, the difference $x_1 - x'_0$) is the "income effect." Since Q' and R are tangencies along budget lines of parallel slopes, the change in the price ratio plays no role between Q' and R. Thus the income effect isolates the income equivalent of the consumer's gain from the price decrease.

The usefulness of this separation turns upon the qualitatively different elements responsible for the income and the substitution effects. With negatively-sloped and convex indifference curves, the substitution effect is always in the normal direction: A *fall* in P_x necessarily leads to a *rise* in the quantity of X taken. For the fall in P_x flattens the budget line (note that $K'L'$ is less steep than KL in Figure 4.15) and so the Q' tangency along U_0 must be at a point where $x'_0 > x_0$.

Turning to the income effect, we can see by comparison with the three panels of Figure 4.6 that R might lie to the northwest, northeast, or southeast of Q'. In the normal case [Panel (a)], or if X is ultra-superior [Panel (c)], the income effect (due to the enrichment of the consumer after the fall in P_x) *reinforces* the substitution effect so as to lead to a further increase in consumption of X. (Figure 4.15 illustrates a normal relation between X and Y, and so the income effect $x_1 - x'_0$ is positive.) But if X were *inferior* [as in Panel (b) of Figure 4.6], the income effect would tend to offset the substitution effect. And indeed it is at least a logical possibility that an abnormal (negative) income effect might outweigh a normal substitution effect. If this occurs a *fall* in price would lead to a net *fall* in quantity purchased; this is, of course, the aforementioned "Giffen case."

4. D FROM INDIVIDUAL DEMAND TO MARKET DEMAND

The passage from demand of the individual to the aggregate demand in the market as a whole is simplicity itself. The *individual's* demand function, shown in Figure 4.16 as the curve $d_j d_j$, gives the quantities that would be purchased by a particular consumer (designated as j) in response to any specific price for commodity X ruling in the market. The *market* demand function, the curve DD in the diagram, shows the aggregate quantities that would be purchased

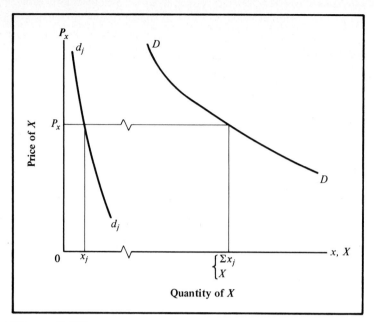

Figure 4. 16
Individual and Aggregate Demand

by all consumers together at that price. If x_j is the quantity taken by the individual j at price P_x, then the aggregate quantity must obviously be the summation over all such individuals. Symbolically, aggregate quantities will generally be designated by upper-case letters.[18] So we can write:

(4.5) $$X = \sum_{j=1}^{J} x_j$$

This says that the aggregate quantity (along the market demand curve DD) is the sum of the individual quantities, where the subscript j is an index running over all of the individuals $1, 2, \ldots, J$ in the market.

Geometrically, the summation is *horizontal* (i.e., over quantities and not over prices). Note that, in Figure 4.16, the market demand has a much flatter *slope* than the individual demand curve. This tells us that if P_x decreases, for example, the quantity increase for the market as a whole will ordinarily be much greater than the increase in quantity consumed by any single individual. If we think, however, in terms of percentage changes instead of numerical changes in the quantity demanded, the *proportionate* increase in X along the aggregate demand curve DD as P_x falls need not be any greater than the proportionate increase along the individual demand curve $d_j d_j$. This point will be considered further when we take up the concept of "Elasticity" in the next chapter.

[18]Symbols like X and Y are used here both as *names* of commodities and to represent aggregate *quantities* of the corresponding commodities. The ambiguity will not be disturbing, as the meaning will always be clear from the context in which the symbol appears.

An implicit assumption of the foregoing analysis, one which will become the subject of attention in Chapter 7, is that the *same* price P_x is being charged to every individual in the market. Where this assumption is not appropriate, a market demand curve in the ordinary sense cannot be constructed.

Conclusion: The market demand curve is the *horizontal* sum of the individual demand curves.

4. E AN APPLICATION: SUBSIDY VERSUS "VOUCHER"

Suppose that the decision-making agencies of government wish to increase consumption of a particular good—education, let us say. There are a number of possible ways to do so. A general *subsidy* to producers or consumers of education is one possibility. (Free public education is of course an extreme kind of subsidy.) But there might be objections on a variety of grounds to a general subsidy. *Voucher* schemes represent a somewhat different technique for achieving the desired end.

In Figure 4.17, E represents education and Z "all other goods." Panel (a) shows the effect of a subsidy to education upon the individual's consumption decision. The original (unsubsidized) tangency optimum is at Q on indifference curve U_0. A subsidy acts like a reduction in price; it rotates the budget line from KL outward to a new position KL'. The new optimum is at R, on indifference curve U_1. Apart from the unlikely possibility that E is a Giffen good in this range, there will be an increase in the consumer's purchases of

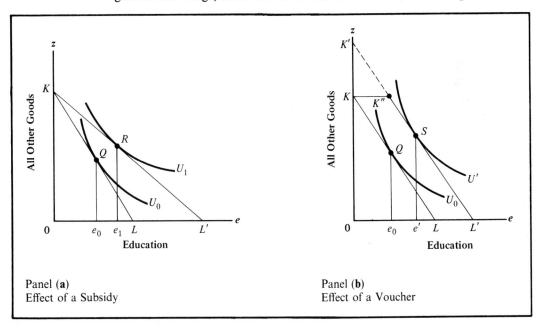

Panel (a)
Effect of a Subsidy

Panel (b)
Effect of a Voucher

Figure 4. 17   Subsidy versus Voucher

education. In the diagram, the increase is the distance $e_1 - e_0$ on the horizontal axis.

Panel (b) of Figure 4.17 shows the effect of a voucher scheme. The initial position Q on indifference curve U_0 is the same as before. The "voucher" is a *gift of income spendable only on the specified commodity E.* The distance KK' on the vertical axis represents the amount of the gift in Z-units, so that the consumer's budget line shifts upward from KL to $K'L'$. But the gift of KK' is only valid to the extent that it is spent on E. Note the dashed portion of the new budget line between K' and K''. This range along the new budget line represents positions for which a lesser amount of income than the voucher gift KK' is devoted to purchases of E and so is not available to the consumer. That is, he is not permitted to move to a consumption position in this range. (If he were permitted to do so he would be converting some of the gift into increased purchases of "other goods" Z, which is what the voucher scheme is intended to prevent.) Therefore, the *effective* new budget line is only the range $K''L'$ along $K'L'$. In Panel (b) of Figure 4.17 the new optimum is at S on indifference curve U'. The quantity purchased of commodity E will rise $(e' > e_0)$ whenever E is a normal or superior good (positive income effect).

So far it might appear that there is no great difference between the subsidy and the voucher. The former works through what is in effect a price change, the latter through what is in effect an income change. But the voucher does have a certain special power in the case of a consumer who would *otherwise take very little or nothing* of the commodity whose consumption it is desired to increase.

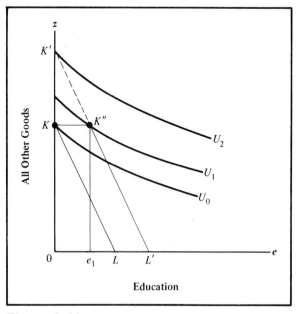

Figure 4. 18
Corner Solution and Voucher

Consider Figure 4.18. Here the individual is initially at a *corner solution*. That is, at the existing prices (slope of market line *KL*) his consumptive optimum is the corner point *K* on indifference curve U_0, where he is consuming a zero quantity of commodity *E*. Even a fairly substantial subsidy, rotating the budget line outward by a considerable angle from *K*, might have little or no effect on his consumption of *E*. But the voucher displaces the entire budget line upward to *K'L'* (of which only the solid range *K''L'* is effective). If he were free to spend his enlarged income, he might still ideally prefer the new corner point *K'* on indifference curve U_2. But the farthest he is permitted to go in this direction along *K'L'* is the point *K''*, on indifference curve U_1. (Note that his achievable optimum *K''* is *not* in general a tangency position.) Here he has spent the entire voucher amount on purchases of *E*, but without spending anything further on *E* out of his own non-voucher income. The voucher will always be effective in increasing consumption for someone previously not consuming *E* at all, or previously consuming an amount less than the voucher equivalent. The only exception would be if *E* is not even a good (i.e., if it is actually a *bad*) from the viewpoint of the consumer.

Questions

1. What is the meaning of the expression "the optimum of the consumer"?

2. How does the amount of income *I* affect the shape of an individual's market opportunity set? How do the prices of the two goods affect the shape?

3. What is the "budget line"? What is its equation? What determines the slope of the budget line?

4. What is the geometrical condition for the optimum of the consumer? Distinguish between a corner solution and an interior solution.

5. What is the Consumption Balance Equation that expresses the optimum of the consumer? Relate this to the Substitution Equivalence Equation. Do the equations hold for an interior solution, a corner solution, or both?

6. Why is diminishing Marginal Utility necessary if the Consumption Balance Equation is to express an optimum? Why is decreasing Marginal Rate of Substitution in Consumption necessary if the Substitution Equivalence Equation is to express an optimum?

7. Characterize a normal good, an inferior good, and an ultra-superior good. Give examples of each. For two goods *X* and *Y*, which of the above must they be if the Income Expansion Path has positive slope? What can you say if the *IEP* has negative slope?

8. A positively sloped Income Expansion Path implies what shape for the Engel Curve? For the Engel Expenditure Curve? If good *X* is inferior, what can you say about its Engel Curve?

9. Show how an individual's demand curve can be derived from his Price Expansion Path. Given the Laws of Preference and the statement that commodities X and Y are both goods, can we infer that his demand curve for X must have negative slope (the Law of Demand)? Explain.

10. How is the market demand curve derived from knowledge of individuals' separate demand curves? Can individual demand curves be determined from knowledge of the market demand curve?

11. "Since 1900 real income has increased tremendously, yet the average number of children per family has decreased." Consider the following possible explanations, and illustrate in terms of market opportunity sets and family indifference curves between number of children (x) and "all other goods" (y).

   a. Children are an inferior good; since we're richer now, we want fewer of them.

   b. Children are *not* an inferior good; however, it has become more expensive to bear and raise children.

   c. Children are not an inferior good, nor have they become relatively more expensive. What has happened is that tastes have changed; couples today want smaller families than couples did in 1900.

12. "As compared with a simple subsidy, the voucher scheme is particularly effective for consumers who would otherwise have chosen little or none of the commodity." Illustrate and explain.

13. In the comparison of subsidy versus voucher in the text, it was assumed that in either case the market base price of the good remained unchanged. Would it be correct to anticipate some change of price? In which direction is this likely to go? Show the effect upon the market opportunity set.

14. Still another consideration is that government expenditures on subsidies or vouchers must ordinarily be financed by taxes. Suppose that the mode of financing works out as a reduction in the typical individual's income I. Show the effect upon his market opportunity set of a tax-financed subsidy. Of a tax-financed voucher.

15. *A More Advanced Question:* The following is sometimes given as an example of a Giffen-good situation. A person must make a 1,000-mile train trip and has only $100 in funds available. If it is at all possible, he prefers first-class travel to third-class travel, but his first priority is to complete his trip. Suppose that first-class travel costs 20¢ per mile and third-class travel 5¢ per mile. Then it can be verified that he will travel 333 1/3 miles in first class and 666 2/3 miles in third class. Now let the price of third-class travel rise to 10¢ per mile. Then the traveler cannot afford any first-class miles at all if he is to complete his trip, so the amount of third-class travel will rise from 666 2/3 to 1000 even though its price has doubled! Question: Is third-class travel an inferior good here? (What would happen if the travel budget were to rise above $100?) Under what circumstances will the traveler choose a corner solution with only third-class travel? With only first-class travel?

Chapter 5
Measures
and Determinants
of Demand

W̶e saw in Chapter 4 that a consumer's demand for any good X depends upon his income I, upon the price P_x, and also upon the prices of other commodities. But an important practical question is: How *sensitive* is demand to changes of prices and to changes of income? If it were government policy to reduce gasoline use, for example, among the relevant considerations might be the effectiveness of a gasoline tax (which raises price to the consumer), and the degree to which gasoline demand is influenced by fluctuations in business conditions (which raise or lower consumer incomes). This chapter concentrates upon *measures* of the responsiveness of quantity demanded to changes in income and prices, and upon the underlying forces that cause strong responses in some cases and weak responses in others.

5. A THE ENGEL CURVE AND THE INCOME ELASTICITY OF DEMAND

The most direct measure of the sensitivity of a consumer's purchases of a good X to changes in his income I would be the ratio $\Delta x/\Delta I$. For small changes Δx and ΔI, this ratio can be interpreted as the slope of the Engel curve.[1] In Figure 5.1 we see alternative Engel curves I, II, III, IV; the very different slopes of the curves indicate differing responses of consumption to changes in income.

There is one serious difficulty in the use of the simple ratio $\Delta x/\Delta I$, however: it is affected by the choice of conventional *units of measurement*. If the commodity X were butter, the numerical value of the ratio would vary by a factor of 16, depending upon whether we measured butter in ounces or pounds. And similarly, the ratio would differ depending upon whether income I were measured in cents or dollars. This type of problem arises in many different branches of economics. To eliminate the difficulty, we make

[1] *Mathematical Footnote:* We can write this as the derivative $\delta x/\delta I$, where the symbol δ indicates a partial effect of varying one of the underlying parameters with all others held constant.

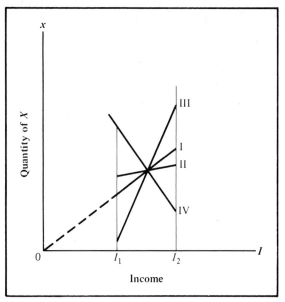

Figure 5. 1
Engel Curves

use of the concept of *elasticity. Elasticity is a measure of relationship in which the changes in both numerator and denominator are expressed in proportionate or percentage terms.*[2] In this case we are interested in proportionate response of quantity purchased to a proportionate change in income. This concept is called "the income elasticity of demand."

Definition: The income elasticity of demand is the proportional change in the quantity purchased divided by the proportional change in income.

We are generally interested, as before, in small changes Δx and ΔI. Then the income elasticity (ϵ_x) is given by the formula:[3]

(5.1)
$$\epsilon_x = \frac{\Delta x/x}{\Delta I/I} = \frac{\Delta x}{\Delta I}\frac{I}{x}$$

To illustrate the geometrical significance of the income elasticity of demand, consider the positively-sloped line-segment ADB in Figure 5.2. This is an Engel Curve characterized by "unitary income elasticity of demand," i.e., $\epsilon_x = 1$. Note that the two points A and B lie on a straight line through the origin. By the elementary properties of similar triangles it is easy to see that, in moving from A to B, the two variables x and I have increased in the same proportion. If we write $I_2 - I_1 = \Delta I$ and $x_2 - x_1 =$

[2]The student should be warned, however, not to fall into the trap of using proportionate elasticity units in cases when it would be more appropriate to employ the natural physical units.

[3]*Mathematical Footnote:* In terms of derivatives, $\epsilon_x = \dfrac{\delta x}{\delta I}\dfrac{I}{x}$.

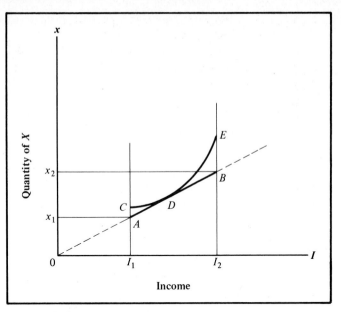

Figure 5. 2
Engel Curve and Unitary Income Elasticity

Δx, then $\Delta x/x_1 = \Delta I/I_1$; the percent change in x equals the percent change in I. Thus, if commodity X accounted for any given proportion of the budget at position A, it accounts for exactly the same proportion at position B.

Now consider the curve CDE lying above the line-segment AB but just tangent to it at the single point D. This is an Engel Curve along which the income elasticity of demand is changing. But at the specific tangency point D, we can think of *very small* changes Δx and ΔI as representing a movement along the line AB. Thus, the Engel Curve CDE has $\epsilon_x = 1$ in the neighborhood of the point D.

Let us return to the four different examples of Engel Curves distinguished by roman numbers in Figure 5.1. Engel Curve I is like ADB in Figure 5.2; it lies on a line through the origin and so represents unitary income elasticity. Engel Curve II has positive slope, but it is flatter than curve I. It is intuitively evident that this means that x increases in a lesser proportion than I as the latter rises, i.e., $\epsilon_x < 1$. By reversing the argument, we see that the steeper Engel Curve III represents an income elasticity $\epsilon_x > 1$. What of Engel Curve IV? This differs from the others in being negatively sloped. Here x *decreases* as I rises, so X must be an inferior good. Its income elasticity is negative, i.e., $\epsilon_x < 0$.

The student should not confuse the geometrical properties of elasticity with slope measures. For *any* positively-sloped straight line through the origin the income elasticity is unity, but such lines can be drawn from very nearly vertical (steep slope) to very nearly horizontal (small slope). It is not the steepness *per se* of an Engel Curve at a particular point that is connected with elasticity, but its steepness at that point *as compared with a line through the origin.*

We have mentioned earlier (in Chapter 2) the distinction between the slope *at a point* along the curve, and the slope over some finite range or *arc* along the curve. Similarly, it is sometimes important to distinguish between elasticity at a point and elasticity over some arc. The definition of income elasticity (5.1), into which the slope enters as the ratio $\Delta x/\Delta I$, is sufficiently general to cover both cases.

Suppose we were interested in the income elasticity ϵ_x over some finite interval along the Engel Curve. Specifically, imagine that 10 units of X are purchased at an income of $5000 and 14 units at an income of $6000. Then the increments, for substitution in formula (5.1), are $\Delta x = 4$ and $\Delta I = 1000. The only question is what particular values for x and I within the arc to use in the formula. The natural answer is to choose the midpoints of the respective intervals. Then:

$$\epsilon_x = \frac{\Delta x}{\Delta I}\frac{I}{x} = \frac{4}{1000}\frac{5500}{12} \doteq 1.833$$

This *arc elasticity*, being greater than unity, shows that consumption of X rises more than proportionately with income I in the interval.

It is evident that arc elasticity is a kind of average of the *point elasticities* along the curve within the range of the arc considered. As the intervals Δx and ΔI shrink down toward zero, their ratio $\Delta x/\Delta I$ approaches a limiting value (the slope of the Engel Curve) that is used in formula (5.1) for determining the point elasticity for a particular x,I combination along the curve.

One simple quantitative statement can be made about income elasticities: *On the average over all goods, income elasticity must be unity.* If there is, say, a 10% increase in income, then consumption of some goods may fall and of others rise, by greater or lesser percentages. But since all of the increase in income must somehow be spent, those goods for which consumption rises by less than 10% must be offset by others for which consumption rises by even more than 10%. On the average, consumption must rise by the same proportion as income. If there are just two commodities X and Y, the following equation must hold:

(5.2) $$k_x\epsilon_x + k_y\epsilon_y = 1$$

Here $k_x = xP_x/I$ is the proportion of the consumer's budget spent on commodity X. Similarly, $k_y = yP_y/I$. These are the weights in the averaging of ϵ_x and ϵ_y that lead to the result of unity.

Example 5. 1
The Declining
Public-Transit
Industry

Table 5.1 illustrates the declining trend of rapid-transit ridership. Generally speaking, ridership declined sharply between 1946 and 1956, and then more slowly between 1956 and 1962. (For some cities, such as Cleveland, the trend is distorted by the opening of new transit lines.)

The declining trend has since continued beyond the period shown in Table 5.1.

Table 5. 1

Rapid Transit System Ridership (1956 = 100.0)

Year	New York	Chicago	Philadel- phia	Boston	Toronto	Cleve- land
1946	151.8	136.8	177.8	185.1		
1950	121.9	95.2	137.3	140.2		
1951	117.5	97.1	126.3	132.3		
1952	114.1	97.0	123.0	127.0		
1953	114.0	96.1	114.8	122.8		
1954	103.9	95.8	109.2	112.1		
1955	101.0	97.2	102.8	103.6	97.0	
1956	100.0	100.0	100.0	100.0	100.0	100.0
1957	99.5	97.2	95.6	96.6	101.0	107.0
1958	96.7	92.8	92.0	94.1	99.1	105.7
1959	97.2	98.1	89.5	92.4	99.1	121.0
1960	98.7	97.6	90.1	91.2	95.7	124.7
1961	100.0	95.2	92.9	—	91.0	120.9
1962	100.5	98.9	89.4	—	91.0	117.5

Source: J. R. Meyer, J. F. Kain, and M. Wohl, *The Urban Transportation Problem* (Cambridge, Mass.: Harvard University Press, 1965), p. 96. (A number of footnotes have been deleted.)

The major factor at work has been the differential income elasticities as between transit and its close substitute—the private automobile. Example 4.3, "Engel's Laws after a Century," indicated the strong positive relationship between income and expenditures on the automobile. In the $2000–2999 income bracket, for example, 6.5% of total expenditure was devoted to the automobile; in the $3000–3999 bracket, 11.3%. Using mid-points of the brackets, the income elasticity of auto expenditures[4] over the arc can be computed as:

$$\epsilon_x = \frac{11.3 - 6.5}{3500 - 2500} \cdot \frac{3000}{8.9} = \frac{4.8}{1000} \cdot \frac{3000}{8.9}$$

$$\doteq 1.6$$

In contrast, the income elasticity of public transit appears to be very low, or even negative. Using degree of housing privacy (multiple, 2-family, and 1-family) as a guide to or proxy for income, Table 5.2 suggests that income elasticity is indeed negative.

[4]We can use auto *expenditures* $P_x x$ in the income elasticity formula since

$$\frac{\Delta(P_x x)}{\Delta I} \cdot \frac{I}{P_x x} \equiv \frac{\Delta x}{\Delta I} \cdot \frac{I}{x}$$

Table 5. 2

Percentage of Detroit White Workers Using Transit

	Structure Type		
Workplace Ring	*Multiple*	*2-Family*	*1-Family*
1	60.7	58.7	50.6
2	28.5	28.6	19.5
3	29.4	26.8	18.9
4	27.3	23.1	14.4
5	17.8	11.1	8.4
6	5.8	4.1	3.5

Source: J. R. Meyer, J. F. Kain, and M. Wohl, *The Urban Transportation Problem* (Cambridge, Mass.: Harvard University Press, 1965), p. 132.

Comment: There have been repeated attempts at encouragement of public transit as against the private automobile—to reduce road congestion, to counter "urban sprawl," to minimize air pollution, to save energy, etc. Despite very substantial public subsidies to transit, these efforts seem inevitably to fail. So far, at least, the higher income elasticity of the auto, given the historical trend of rising levels of income and wealth, has defeated efforts to encourage public transit.

5. B THE DEMAND CURVE AND THE PRICE ELASTICITY OF DEMAND

In the previous section, measures of the responsiveness of consumption to changes in *income* were obtained. Let us now consider the sensitivity of consumption to changes in *price*. Again the most obvious measure would be the ratio of differences $\Delta x/\Delta P_x$.[5] Recall that the demand curve represents the functional relationship between price P_x and the quantity x demanded. For small changes Δx and ΔP_x, therefore, the ratio $\Delta x/\Delta P_x$ corresponds to the *reciprocal* of the slope[6] of the demand curve. The alternative demand curves labelled I, II, III, IV in Figure 5.3 illustrate more and less steep slopes. The steeper the slope, the smaller the numerical or absolute magnitude of $\Delta x/\Delta P_x$. But given the Law of Demand, both the slope and its reciprocal must be negative. (Only in the Giffen case, represented by curve IV in the diagram, would the ratio $\Delta x/\Delta P_x$ be positive.)

As in the case of income, a slope measure like $\Delta x/\Delta P_x$ would be affected by changes in conventional units of measurement for the numerator (e.g., changes from pounds to tons) or of the denominator (e.g., changes from dollars per ton to cents per ton). To avoid this difficulty, we are led once

---

[5]*Mathematical Footnote:* In terms of derivatives, this is $\delta x/\delta P_x$.

[6]It is the reciprocal of the slope, because economists conventionally draw demand curves with price P_x on the vertical axis.

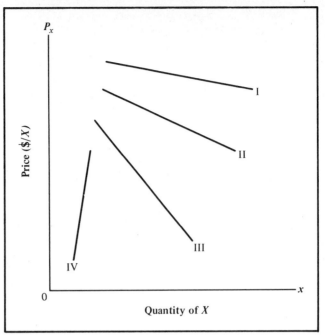

Figure 5. 3
Alternative Demand Curve Slopes

again to an elasticity measure, a ratio of *proportionate* changes. This concept is formally known as "the price elasticity of demand." In common use, the expression "elasticity of demand" standing alone is understood to refer to the price elasticity.

Another very important advantage of the elasticity concept stems from this elimination of dependence upon conventional units of measurement. Comparisons of sensitivity to price changes are often desired between entirely disparate commodities. As the *slope* measure varies with units, it would be meaningless to assert, for example, that the demand curve for wheat is steeper than the demand curve for haircuts, and therefore that the former is less responsive to price changes. The demand curve for wheat could be made to seem as steep or flat as desired, by converting from tons to pounds to ounces as quantity units, or the reverse. But it would be meaningful to say that the demand for wheat is *less elastic* than the demand for haircuts, and in that sense less responsive to price changes.

Definition: The price elasticity of demand is the proportional change in the quantity purchased divided by the proportional change in price.

For small changes Δx and ΔP_x, the price elasticity η_{xx} is given by:[7]

(5.3) $$\eta_{xx} = \frac{\Delta x/x}{\Delta P_x/P_x} = \frac{\Delta x}{\Delta P_x}\frac{P_x}{x}$$

[7]*Mathematical Footnote:* In terms of derivatives,

$$\eta_{xx} = \frac{\delta x}{\delta P_x}\frac{P_x}{x}$$

114

When the demand curve is negatively sloped (the Law of Demand), the changes Δx and ΔP_x have opposite signs. Thus, the price elasticity of demand η_{xx} is normally negative. Nevertheless, when we speak of elasticity being "high" we mean large in absolute value, and "low" elasticity means small in absolute value. More specifically, the term "elastic demand" refers to an absolute value $|\eta_{xx}|$ greater than unity, while "inelastic demand" means $|\eta_{xx}| < 1$.

There is a well-known relation between elasticity of demand and the amount of income spent by the consumer on a good. Suppose the price elasticity is unity (i.e., $\eta_{xx} = -1$, or $|\eta_{xx}| = 1$). What happens if there is a small decrease in price? From the definition (5.3), we know that with unitary elasticity the proportionate *increase* in quantity $\Delta x/x$ is the same as the proportionate *decrease* $\Delta P_x/P_x$ in price. But since the consumer's expenditure on good X equals $P_x x$, the proportionate increase of the one component just offsets the proportionate decrease of the other—total expenditure remains unchanged. If the price elasticity is greater than unity ($|\eta_{xx}| > 1$, or "elastic demand") the proportionate increase in quantity x is larger than the proportionate decrease in price P_x; hence total expenditure $P_x x$ increases when price falls. By a similar argument, if demand is "inelastic," a decrease in P_x leads to a less-than-offsetting rise in x—total expenditure $P_x x$ decreases.[8]

There is a relation between price elasticity of demand for X and the shape of the Price Expansion Path (PEP) showing the response of the consumer's optimum as P_x varies. Considering a PEP like that in Figure 4.10, recall that the *price* of the other commodity, P_y, is held fixed in deriving this curve. Since P_y is fixed, the expenditure on Y moves in parallel with changes in the simple quantity y. But from the budget equation (4.1), $I = P_x x + P_y y$. So $P_x x$, expenditure on X, varies inversely with $P_y y$, expenditure on Y. It follows immediately that when the PEP curve is falling (y is decreasing), expenditure on X must be rising—demand is elastic. Similarly, the range in which the PEP curve is rising corresponds to inelastic demand for X. At the boundary between the two ranges, where the PEP curve reaches a minimum, the demand for X has unitary elasticity.

For price elasticity as well as income elasticity, it is sometimes necessary to distinguish the *arc elasticity* over a finite interval of the demand curve from the *point elasticity* at a single point along the curve. As in the case of the income elasticity definition in equation (5.1), the price elasticity formula of equation (5.3) is sufficiently general to cover both interpretations. For arc elasticity, the finite differences Δx and ΔP_x are employed in the formula, and the specific values used for x and P_x are the mid-points of their respective intervals. For point elasticity, the differences are conceived as shrinking toward zero so that their ratio $\Delta x/\Delta P_x$ approaches a limit—the reciprocal

---

[8] *Mathematical Footnote:*

$$\frac{\delta(P_x x)}{\delta x} = P_x + x\frac{\delta P_x}{\delta x} = P_x + \left(\frac{x}{P_x}\frac{\delta P_x}{\delta x}\right)P_x = P_x\left(1 + \frac{1}{\eta_{xx}}\right)$$

Recall that the sign of η_{xx} is negative. Then the derivative on the left representing the change in expenditure is positive, zero, or negative depending on whether η_{xx} is greater than, equal to, or less than unity in absolute terms.

of the slope of the demand curve. This limit is then used in the formula, together with the specific values for x and P_x at the point for which the point elasticity is being computed. Note how in either case the elasticity depends both upon the *slope* of the curve and the *position along* the curve.

5. C CROSS-ELASTICITY OF DEMAND

The demand for a commodity X will generally depend not only upon its own price P_x but upon prices of other goods such as P_y. Here again it is convenient to use the unit-free elasticity measure, called in this case the *cross-elasticity* of demand. The definition is:[9]

$$\eta_{xy} = \frac{\Delta x/x}{\Delta P_y/P_y} = \frac{\Delta x}{\Delta P_y} \frac{P_y}{x}$$

Cross-elasticity can be either positive or negative. If it is positive the two goods are called *substitutes*; a rise in the price of Y raises the consumption of X. If the cross-elasticity is negative the two goods are called *complements*; here a rise in the price of Y *lowers* the consumption of X. The distinction between substitutes and complements will be discussed in more detail in Section 5.E.

[9] *Mathematical Footnote:* In terms of derivatives,

$$\eta_{xy} = \frac{\delta x}{\delta P_y} \frac{P_y}{x}$$

Example 5. 2
Elasticities
of Electricity
Demand

The Table below shows results from an economic study of electricity demand over the period 1946–72. Among the determining variables examined were: (1) electricity price, (2) income, and (3) the price of a competing commodity—gas. It was found convenient to classify the data according to residential, commercial, and industrial use.[10]

Elasticities of Electricity Use

With Respect to:	Electricity Price	Income	Gas Price
Residential	−1.3	+0.3	+0.15
Commerical	−1.5	+0.9	+0.15
Industrial	−1.7	+1.1	+0.15

Source: D. Chapman, T. Tyrrell, and T. Mount, "Electricity Demand Growth and the Energy Crisis," *Science*, v. 178 (Nov. 17, 1972), p. 705.

[10] The industrial and commercial demands are for electricity as a *factor of production* rather than as a consumer good. We have not yet come to the topic of demand for factors of production, but it is of interest to see the comparative data here.

The price elasticities are negative and in the elastic range ($|\eta_{xx}| > 1$), showing a more than proportionate response of consumption to price change. This was the most important result of the study, running counter to the common but uninformed opinion that electricity use is some kind of absolute "requirement" independent of price. The positive elasticities with respect to income show that electricity is a normal superior good. And the positive elasticity with respect to gas price shows that gas and electricity are *substitutes*.

Comment: The authors of the study emphasize that their results refute the crude techniques for projecting future electricity demands usually employed in "energy crisis" debates. Government planners, industry insiders, and outside critics have often argued as if simple mathematical extrapolations that compound historically observed rates of demand growth into the indefinite future represent valid estimates of what will happen in the absence of some extraordinary government intervention. This is surely mistaken, since the rate of growth of electricity demand is *strongly* responsive to price. And the price of electricity is bound to increase as fuels become more expensive and as requirements for environmental protection add to cost. (Indeed, since the period of the study electricity prices *have* gone up sharply, with the anticipated discouraging effect upon electricity use.)

*5. D FITTING A DEMAND FUNCTION

The technical statistical problems involved in estimating demand functions from empirical data are studied in courses in econometrics, and will not be considered here. Rather, attention will be devoted to certain theoretical questions involved in making statistical inferences about the nature of the relationship between consumption and its determinants: price, income, prices of related goods, etc.

Let us now concentrate upon a single determinant of demand, the price of the commodity itself, in order to focus attention upon the *form* of the relationship. That is, we will suppose that such determinants as income, prices of related commodities, etc., are held constant or statistically allowed for so that we can isolate the price-quantity relationship summarized in the demand curve. What can we say about the shape of the demand curve? In one sense, of course, the statistical data speak for themselves; the curve fitted should be whatever is the best representation of the evidence. Looking at it another way, however, the curve we fit is an artifice. Since it will never *exactly* represent the evidence, there is some choice as to the nature of the approximation to be employed.

*Starred sections represent optional or advanced material.

In the great bulk of statistical studies, we are constrained to use very simple assumptions about the underlying relationships. The ones most commonly employed are the *linear* demand curve, and the *constant-elasticity* demand curve. They are compared in the two panels of Figure 5.4, as fitted to hypo-

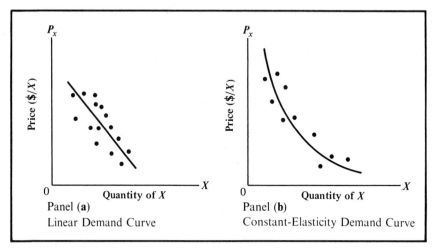

Figure 5. 4
Linear- and Constant-Elasticity Demand Curves

thetical sets of data represented by the clusters of points in the diagrams. The constant-elasticity demand curve is *not* a straight line on X,P_x-axes.[11] Correspondingly, the elasticity must change along a straight-line demand curve.

Let us consider this latter point first, in terms of the linear demand curve DTD' in Figure 5.5. First of all, it is evident from the definition $\eta_{xx} = \frac{\Delta X}{\Delta P_x} \frac{P_x}{X}$ that elasticity is zero at the intersection D' with the horizontal axis, since, at that intersection, P_x is zero. Correspondingly, elasticity is infinite at the intersection D with the vertical axis where X is zero. More generally, it is possible to determine the elasticity at any point such as T along a linear demand curve by the following graphical procedure.

The ratio $\Delta X/\Delta P_x$ entering into the definition of price elasticity is the reciprocal of the absolute slope along the demand curve. Since the demand curve is linear, its constant absolute slope in Figure 5.5 is the ratio of the distances $\overline{OD}/\overline{OD'}$. Then the absolute value of the elasticity anywhere along DTD' is:

$$|\eta_{xx}| = \frac{\overline{OD'}}{\overline{OD}} \cdot \frac{P_x}{X}$$

[11]We use the upper-case symbol X to emphasize that we are now dealing with *aggregate* consumption or demand in the market, rather than with measures derived from choices of an individual.

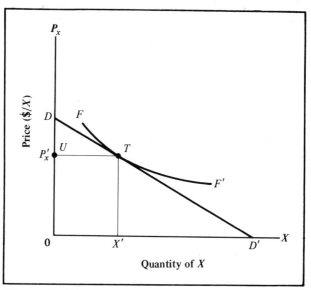

Figure 5. 5
Graphical Measure of Elasticity

Now note that the large triangle DOD' is similar to (has all angles equal to) its smaller component triangle DUT. The base UT of the latter equals $\overline{OX'}$, which is simply the quantity X' associated with the particular point T. By similar triangles, $\overline{OD'}/\overline{OD} = \overline{UT}/\overline{DU} = X'/\overline{DU}$. So at point T:

$$|\eta_{xx}| = \frac{X'}{\overline{DU}} \frac{P'_x}{X'} = \frac{P'_x}{\overline{DU}}$$

That is, the absolute value of the elasticity at a price-quantity point (X',P'_x) equals the ratio of two distances along the vertical axis: the distance from the origin to the price ($\overline{OU}$ or P'_x) divided by the distance remaining from the price to the vertical intercept ($\overline{DU}$). Or, we can equivalently use as geometrical measure the corresponding ratio of distances along the hypotenuse DTD' of the large triangle. As justified again by similar triangles, the ratio $\overline{OU}/\overline{DU}$ along the vertical axis equals the ratio $\overline{TD'}/\overline{TD}$ along this hypotenuse. So at a point T on a linear demand curve, *the absolute elasticity is measured by the distance along the demand curve from T to the horizontal axis divided by the distance from T to the vertical axis.* It can be verified immediately that the elasticity at D' on the horizontal axis is indeed zero, while the elasticity at D on the vertical axis is infinite.

A very simple corollary of this proposition is: Elasticity is unitary at the *mid-point* of a linear demand curve. To the northwest of the mid-point elasticity is greater than unity; to the southeast it is less than unity.

This geometrical measure of elasticity along a linear demand curve can be generalized to any demand curve whatsoever. Consider the point T as lying not on DD' but on a *non-linear* demand curve FF' in Figure 5.5. Then DD'

could be *constructed* as a line tangent to FF' at the point T. Consequently, the constant slope along DD' equals the slope of the non-linear demand curve FF' in the neighborhood of the point T. So the ratio $\overline{TD'}/\overline{TD}$ measures the absolute value of the elasticity at T along the non-linear demand curve FF' as well as along a linear demand curve like DD'.

Let us now consider demand curves along which *elasticity* is constant. Figure 5.6 provides an example, the curve EE', for which the elasticity is in fact *unity* throughout. The point A on the curve is equidistant from the two

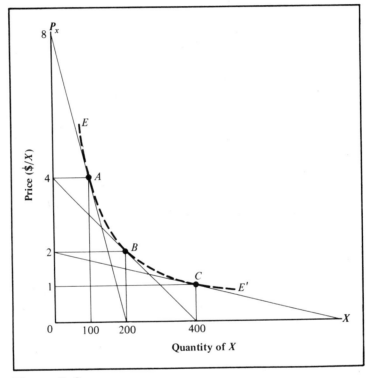

Figure 5. 6
Constant-Elasticity Demand Curve

axes, measuring along the straight line constructed as tangent to EE' at the point A. Similarly for the other points like B and C shown along the curve. The illustrative numerical values along the axes show that, for this curve of unitary elasticity throughout, the *product* of price times quantity is a constant (equal to 400), confirming the argument in the text above about unitary elasticity and constant consumer expenditure. If elasticity were constant but greater than unity, any proportionate decrease in price would lead to a proportionately greater increase in quantity, and the reverse for constant elasticity less than unity.

5. D. 2   Slope and Elasticity: Analysis

A demand curve of constant slope is of course a straight line. It may be expressed in the form of a linear equation:

(5.4) $$X = A + BP_x$$

Here A and B are constants; B is normally *negative* according to the Law of Demand. When we take into account other determining variables, such as income I and the price of a related good Y, we obtain a generalized *demand function in linear form*:

(5.5) $$X = A + BP_x + CI + DP_y$$

Here A, B, C, and D are all constants. B is again normally negative. C is the slope of the Engel Curve, and is only negative when X is inferior. The sign of D would be the same as the sign of the cross-elasticity: positive if X and Y are substitutes, negative if they are complements.

A generalized demand function of this form (or, possibly, extended to take into account additional variables) could be fitted statistically to a body of data. In general, such a fitted function would only be expected to be a reasonable description of the true demand relation within a limited range. Indeed, pushed to extremes it must lead to logical contradictions. For example, equation (5.5) would, for some prices P_x and P_y, indicate a positive quantity X demanded *even when income* I *is zero*. This is of course impossible.[12]

[12]But recall that our model of consumption is timeless. In a multi-period model (to be considered in Chapter 16), the total of consumption expenditures in any single period may diverge from income of that period. The difference is accounted for by borrowing and lending between periods, or repayments of previous loans made or incurred.

Example 5. 3
Demand for
Distilled Spirits

A study by T. J. Wales employed sales data of different states for estimating demand for distilled spirits.[13] It was found convenient to use a simple linear equation. Straightforward statistical regression led to the equation:

$$X_j = .5084 + .0004079I_j - .1771P_j$$

Here X_j represents the number of cases of spirits per adult resident sold in state j; I_j is the disposable income per adult resident of state j; and P_j is the average liquor price, in dollars, within the state. This equation indicates that, for example, a $1000 increase in average income

[13]T. J. Wales, "Distilled Spirits and Interstate Consumption Effects," *American Economic Review*, v. 58 (Sept. 1968), esp. p. 858.

leads to a consumption increase of about 0.4 cases per adult resident per year. (A case consists of 12 fifths, so the increase is about 5 bottles per year.) A one-dollar increase in price leads to a decrease of around .18 case, or around 2 bottles per year.

But Wales was dissatisfied with this result, partly for technical statistical reasons that need not concern us here. He suspected that the data were distorted by failure to allow for liquor sales to *non*-residents crossing state lines to take advantage of lower prices. Correcting for the estimated effect of this factor led to the revised linear equation:

$$X_{jj} = -.4615 + .0004379I_j - .00375P_j$$

Here X_{jj} represents the cases sold in state j to *residents* of that state.

As may be seen, the effect of income differences remains about the same. But the effect of price is much less; demand is now highly price-inelastic. Thus, these data suggest that the impact of price differences between states is almost entirely limited to the effect upon out-of-state purchasers!

Comment: The differences in prices of distilled spirits between states are mainly due to differences in liquor *taxation*. (In some states liquor is a state monopoly, in which case a high monopoly price is substantially equivalent to a high tax.) Very small sensitivity of quantity purchased to price (inelastic demand) is convenient if the purpose of the tax is simply to generate tax revenues. But if the purpose is to discourage consumption, it appears that liquor taxation is not very effective.

A demand curve of constant elasticity also has its own particular algebraic form. This form involves the *logarithms* of quantity and price (and of other determining variables of the demand function). The crucial property of logarithms for our purposes is that equal *arithmetic* steps of the logarithm represent equal *proportionate* steps of the variable. For example, as $\log_{10} X$ (the logarithm of X to the base 10) goes from 1 to 2 to 3, the variable X goes from 10 to 100 to 1000.

For a demand curve of constant elasticity,

$$\eta_{xx} \equiv \frac{\Delta X/X}{\Delta P_x/P_x}$$

is a constant. It follows immediately that the proportionate change in quantity ($\Delta X/X$) is a constant multiple of the proportionate change in price ($\Delta P_x/P_x$) along the demand curve. Using the property that arithmetic changes in the logarithm represent proportionate changes in the variable), we can write:

(5.6) $$\Delta (\log X) = b \, \Delta (\log P_x)$$

Here b is the constant multiple referred to, which (we can see from the definition of elasticity) must be equal to η_{xx}.

Equation (5.6) is equivalent to:

(5.7) $$\log X = \log a + b \log P_x$$

Here $\log a$ is some constant. The linear equation (5.7) in the logarithms implies the previous relation (5.6) between changes ΔP_x and ΔX in P_x and X. It is the linear equation (5.7) that would actually be fitted statistically to the observations reduced to logarithmic form.

Taking anti-logs on both sides of (5.7), where M is the base used for the logarithms, we have:

$$X = M^{\log a + b \log P_x}$$

or

(5.8) $$X = aP_x^b$$

This is the form of the constant-elasticity demand equation after conversion into natural units. The multiplicative constant a and the elasticity $b = \eta_{xx}$ are the parameters estimated from the statistical data.

Generalizing (5.7), the constant-elasticity demand function (of own-price P_x, income I, and price of some other good P_y) would be expressed in logarithmic form as:

(5.9) $$\log X = \log a + b \log P_x + c \log I + d \log P_y$$

Converting to natural units as above, this becomes:

(5.10) $$X = aP_x^b I^c P_y^d$$

Here b is as before the price elasticity η_{xx}, c is the income elasticity ϵ_x, and d is the cross-elasticity η_{xy}.

Example 5. 4
More on Fish

The relaxing of the fish-on-Friday rule for American Catholics led, we saw in Example 2.1 of Chapter 2 ("Catholics and Fish"), to a fall in the price of fish in New England. The same study by F. W. Bell[14] also provided estimates of a number of other parameters of the demand function for fish.

The function fitted in Bell's study was in the logarithmic form of equation (5.9), with two main differences. First, a number of determining variables other than prices and incomes were considered; among them, cold storage holdings, imports, and of course the status of the fish-on-Friday rule. We shall ignore these other variables here. Second, the equation was fitted statistically with the *price* of fish rather than the *quantity demanded* as the dependent variable on the left-hand side.

[14] F. W. Bell, "The Pope and the Price of Fish," *American Economic Review*, v. 58 (Dec. 1968).

Thus, Bell's statistically determined equation took the form:

$$\log P_i = \log \alpha + \beta \log Q_i + \gamma \log I + \delta \log P_m + \ldots$$

Here P_i is the price of fish species i (in cents per pound); Q_i is the quantity landed (in thousands of pounds); I is personal income in New England for 1957–59 (in tenths of millions of dollars); and P_m is the consumer price index for a related consumption item, meat and poultry (index based on taking the average 1957–59 price as 100). The study estimated the constants α, β, γ, and δ for each of seven fish species. A typical set of results, that for "large haddock," is: $\alpha = -.237$, $\beta = -.460$, $\gamma = +.212$, and $\delta = +.878$.[15]

It is possible to reformulate these results in terms of the constants a, b, c, and d of equation (5.9) that relate to the desired elasticities, by rearranging the statistical equation of the study. Solving the latter for $\log Q_i$, we can write:

$$\log Q_i = -\frac{1}{\beta} \log \alpha + \frac{1}{\beta} \log P_i - \frac{\gamma}{\beta} \log I - \frac{\delta}{\beta} \log P_m$$

But equation (5.9) tells us that $\log Q_i = a + b \log P_i + c \log I + d \log P_m$. Then the desired parameters (apart from the constant term which is not needed) are $b = 1/\beta$, $c = -\gamma/\beta$, and $d = -\delta/\beta$. Remembering that the price elasticity is $b = \eta_{ii}$, the income elasticity is $c = \epsilon_i$, and the cross-elasticity is $d = \eta_{im}$, the results imply that for large haddock:[16]

$$\eta_{ii} = \frac{1}{\beta} = -\frac{1}{.460} = -2.174$$

$$\epsilon_i = -\frac{\gamma}{\beta} = \frac{.212}{.460} = .461$$

$$\eta_{im} = -\frac{\delta}{\beta} = \frac{.878}{.460} = 1.909$$

Thus the price elasticity is in the normal negative range. The positive income elasticity indicates that large haddock is a superior good, though not very strongly superior. And the positive cross-elasticity verifies our presumption that meat and chicken on the one hand, as against fish on the other hand, are substitutes in consumption—a rise in the price of the former leads to a rise in the consumption of the latter.

---

[15] *Ibid.*, p. 1348.
[16] For statistical reasons that we need not explore here, these implied estimates are not *exactly* the same as would have been obtained had the equation been initially set up in the form of (5.9), with $\log Q_i$ as the dependent variable.

We will be concerned, in the sections following, with the economic determinants of the measures of demand developed in this chapter. These determinants can be regarded as operating through *income* and *substitution* effects upon individuals' market opportunity sets. The shape of the Engel Curve satisfactorily describes the nature of the income effect, but the substitution effect raises somewhat more complicated questions. While we do have the *cross-elasticity* η_{xy} as one measure of the possibilities of substitution between commodities X and Y, this measure is not fully satisfactory. For one thing, like the ordinary demand relation it confounds a change in real income with a measure of substitution. A fall in the price P_y (with I and P_x held constant) will enrich the consumer; so the responsiveness of the quantity of X demanded to changes in P_y, as measured by η_{xy}, will contain an income-effect element as well. What we seek is a measure of the "closeness" of commodities as substitutes that abstracts from any changes in real income.

Consider two commodities that the consumer regards as *perfect* substitutes throughout. For example, he might be completely indifferent between 2 nickels and 1 dime, or between 200 nickels and 100 dimes, or between 2000 nickels and 1000 dimes, etc. Then his preference map will have the appearance of Panel (a) of Figure 5.7: All the indifference curves will be parallel straight lines. If there were two goods that approached but did not quite attain perfect substitutability, the indifference curves would show a slight degree of normally convex curvature but would be very nearly linear, as in Panel (b) of Figure 5.7. For a particular consumer, bread and rolls might perhaps be so related. The observable market characteristic of strong substitute commodities is: *Small changes in price ratios, with no change in real income, will lead to large shifts in relative quantities purchased.* As can be seen in Panel (b), with the steeper budget line SS' (high ratio of bread price P_b to roll price P_r) the optimum solution S^* is well over toward the northwest of the diagram. But the only slightly flatter budget line FF' (lower ratio P_b/P_r) is associated with a drastically different quantity solution F^* along the same indifference curve U_2 toward the southeast of the diagram.

The opposite of substitutability is called *complementarity*. With perfect complementarity there would be some fixed ratio of quantities (such as one left shoe for each right shoe) of interest to the consumer. If this ratio is departed from, the additional units of whichever commodity is in excess are completely useless. Panel (a) of Figure 5.8 shows the right-angled indifference curves implied by perfect complementarity; the slope of the dashed line through the "elbows" represents the desired ratio of the two commodities. For two goods that approach very nearly to, without quite attaining, perfect complementarity, the indifference map would be as in Panel (b) of Figure 5.8. Possible examples of complementary pairs are bacon and eggs, electricity and appliances, highways and automobiles. The observable market characteristic of strong complementary commodities is: *Large changes in price ratios, with no change in real income, will lead to only small shifts in*

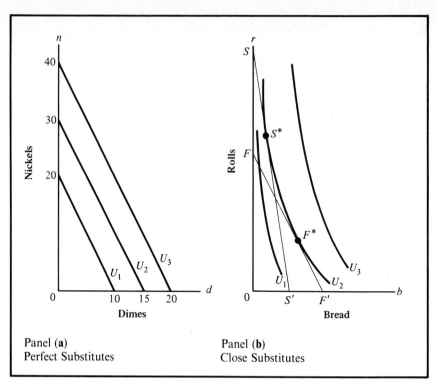

Figure 5. 7
Substitute Commodities

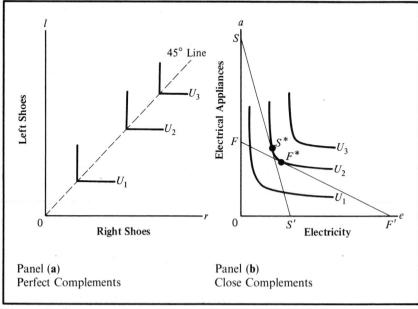

Figure 5. 8
Complementary Commodities

relative quantities purchased. As can be seen in Panel (b) of Figure 5.8, along the steeper budget line SS' (representing a high price ratio P_e/P_a) the tangency solution S^* diverges very little from the optimum F^* along the flatter budget line FF'.

5. F DETERMINANTS OF DEMAND

Why is it that demand for some commodities is great, for others small? Why is it that some commodities are demanded *relatively* more by poor people ("necessities"), others relatively more by rich people ("luxuries")? Economics does not, for the most part, attempt to answer such questions; as indicated in Chapter 1, the study of the formation of goals and preferences is regarded as falling within the province of our sister social sciences.

Of course, the economist working in business or government may be required to come to judgments on such issues. In some cases the forces involved are well understood. It is not hard to predict that cooling drinks will be more popular in Georgia than in Alaska; that diapers are not a big item in retirement communities; that bagels will sell better in Jewish neighborhoods, and soul food in Harlem. Very poor people, we know, must concentrate upon meeting physiological needs; richer people can afford to indulge their tastes for esthetics or social distinction. For novel goods and services, there tends to be an initial penetration phase when the product is still new and demand is affected by the learning process, followed by a replacement phase after saturation is achieved.[17] All of these pose problems of considerable interest, and in fact economics has been recently extending its domain more deeply into issues of consumption and preference theory.[18] But here we must still, for the most part, take as given the consumer tastes and preferences governing demand, without attempting to look into their underlying sources.

5. F. 1 Responsiveness of Demand to Price

A topic that has more traditionally interested economists is not the *magnitude* of demand, but rather its responsiveness to price. Here we are dealing not with preferences *per se*, but rather with sensitivity (in the light of given preferences) to changes in market *opportunities*. As we know, individual responsiveness to price could be measured by the slope $\Delta x/\Delta P_x$, but it is generally more convenient to use the elasticity

$$\eta_{xx} = \frac{\Delta x}{\Delta P_x} \frac{P_x}{x}$$

[17]Texts in marketing or in business economics discuss such topics. See, for example, E. E. Nemmers, *Managerial Economics* (New York: John Wiley & Sons, Inc., 1962), Part II. A somewhat more socio-psychological approach can be found in P. Kotler, *Marketing Management*, 2nd ed. (Englewood Cliffs, N.J.: Prentice-Hall, 1972), Chap. 4.

[18]See the discussion of the "New Theory of Consumption" in Chapter 6.

Thus the question here can be expressed as: What are the determinants of the elasticity of individual demand? Brief discussions of a number of suggested determinants follow below.

1. *Closeness of Substitutes:* The contention is that demand for a commodity will be more elastic, the more numerous and the closer are the substitutes available. This argument is based upon the substitution effect alone. If the preference picture is as in Panel (a) of Figure 5.9 [comparable to the "close substitutes" in Figure 5.7, Panel (b)], a tilt-

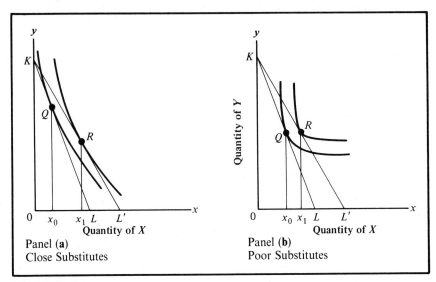

Figure 5. 9
Closeness of Substitutes and Demand Elasticity

ing of the budget line from *KL* to *KL'* would lead to a relatively large change in the quantity of *X* demanded. Here x_1 is considerably greater than x_0. If the picture were as in Panel (b) of Figure 5.9 [comparable to the "close complements" of Figure 5.8, Panel (b)], the corresponding effect on the quantity of *X* demanded would be much smaller. And so, in Panel (b), x_1 is only a little larger than x_0.

2. *Luxuries versus Necessities:* The contention here is that demand for a "luxury" will be more elastic than demand for a "necessity." (As before, a luxury is taken to be a strongly superior good, much more heavily purchased as income rises. A necessity is a good for which almost as much is consumed at low as at high incomes; or even, conceivably, more is consumed at lower incomes.) Thus the argument runs in terms of the *magnitude and direction of the income effect* alone. A fall in the price P_x will tend to enrich the consumer. Then if *X* is a strongly superior good (a luxury) the income effect will powerfully reinforce the substitution effect so as to augment the increased purchases of *X*. If *X* is only weakly superior (a necessity) there will be little reinforcement; if

X is actually inferior, the income effect will tend to offset the substitution effect. So the contention is a valid inference from the income effect.

3. *Importance of the Commodity:* The hypothesis here is that a commodity that is "important," in the sense of accounting for a large fraction $k_x = P_x x/I$ of the consumer's budget, tends to have elastic demand. Again we are dealing with the income effect, assumed to be normal in direction (X a superior good). Then it will be evident that the real *enrichment* due to a fall in P_x will be greater, the larger is the consumer's initial expenditure $P_x x$ on commodity X. Thus, the increased purchases due to superiority will tend to be large simply because of a large real income change as P_x falls. However, this argument is not clear-cut. There is indeed reason to expect a large *absolute* increase in purchases of X due to this enrichment. But elasticity measures *proportionate* increases of consumption. Since the absolute quantity of X consumed may already be large, there is no reason to anticipate that the *proportionate* increase $\Delta x/x$ should be particularly great just because $k_x = P_x x/I$ is large.[19] Thus, a traditional argument given for the *inelasticity* of the demand for salt—that salt accounts for only a tiny fraction of the consumer's budget—is fallacious. The true explanation is that salt is a *necessity*, and has no close substitutes.

4. *High-Priced versus Low-Priced Goods:* The contention here is that high-priced goods tend to have elastic demands, and low-priced goods inelastic demands. A "high" price can be interpreted as one for which the individual's desired quantity approaches zero, i.e., is near the vertical intercept of his demand curve.[20] As shown in Section 5.D.1, if the demand curve actually intercepts the vertical axis the elasticity is indeed infinite at that point. And at an intercept with the horizontal axis where P_x goes to zero, elasticity must be zero. But we also saw, in Figure 5.6, that it is perfectly possible to have a constant-elasticity demand curve, for which elasticity remains constant however closely the axes are approached. (Of course, such a demand curve cannot actually *intersect* either axis.) So the logic of the argument here is less than fully compelling.

5. F. 2 Application to Giffen Good

An interesting application of these concepts is to the Giffen case, for which the Law of Demand is violated—a lower price P_x is associated with a *smaller* quantity demanded. It follows that the elasticity η_{xx} has reversed (positive rather than the normal negative) sign.

---

[19]Consider the special case of an "all-important" commodity, accounting for 100% of the consumer's budget ($k = 1$). For such a commodity the price elasticity of demand is not extraordinarily large. Indeed, the elasticity must be exactly -1.

[20]A demand curve intersecting the vertical axis implies the existence of a "corner solution" at sufficiently high prices.

To have a Giffen good, the income effect must be perverse (negative) and also large enough to overcome the substitution effect, since the latter is *always* in the normal negative direction. Two elements tend to increase the likelihood of Giffen goods:

1. The larger the proportion of the consumer's budget accounted for by an inferior good (e.g., potatoes as the main staple of life in Ireland), the weightier the perverse income effect relative to the (normal) substitution effect. If, on the other hand, a good accounts only for a small fraction of the budget, the income effect due to a change in its price will be trivial in magnitude—even if in the perverse direction.

2. The Giffen good must have a rather close "superior" (and dearer) substitute, such that the two are regarded as *closer equivalents at lower incomes than at higher incomes.* In the potatoes example, if the consumer is so poor that he can just barely meet his minimal calorie needs to stay alive, little importance is attached to the taste superiority of more expensive calorie sources—wheat bread, for example. For minimal survival, it is calorie intake that counts and the cheapest source will be purchased at a corner or near-corner solution. But under more affluent conditions potatoes and bread are not such close substitutes, and an interior solution may be obtained at which less potatoes are consumed.

The interaction of these conditions is illustrated in Figure 5.10. On the horizontal axis is quantity of potatoes; on the vertical axis, quantity of bread.

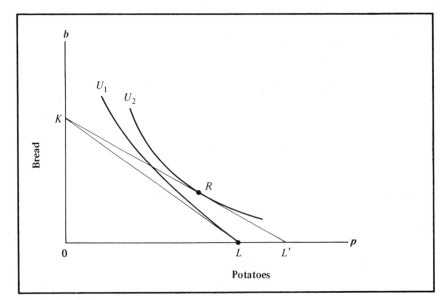

Figure 5. 10
Conditions for Giffen Good

At the original high price of potatoes represented by the steeper budget line *KL*, the consumer's nearly-linear indifference curve U_1 leads him to a corner solution at *L*. (Potatoes are dear, but still a cheaper source of calories than bread.) Since he is consuming only potatoes at *L*, any income effect due to a change in the price of potatoes will be large. Now the price of potatoes falls, the new budget line being *KL'*. The consumer is substantially enriched. However, potatoes are inferior (as can be detected from the fact that U_2 is flatter than U_1 along any vertical line drawn in the neighborhood of the initial solution point *L*). Thus the income effect will be both large and negative in direction. This, and the sharper curvature of U_2 (potatoes and bread are weaker substitutes at higher real incomes), constitute the forces leading to an interior solution at *R* on U_2 *northwest* of *L*: fewer potatoes being consumed when the potato price is low than when it was high!

Questions

1. What is the general definition of all elasticity measures? Why is the income elasticity of demand considered a more useful measure than the simple slope along an Engel Curve? Why is the price elasticity of demand considered a more useful measure than the simple slope along a demand curve? Are elasticity measures always better than the simple measures? (See the question following.)

2. Consider this paradox: "Income elasticity is supposed to measure the responsiveness of consumption to changes in income. But income elasticity is unity along *any* Engel curve which is a straight line through the origin, whether very steep or very flat. Since Engel curves of different steepnesses surely show different responses of consumption to income, how can they all be characterized as having the same income elasticity?"

3. True or false: "Income elasticity is unity at any point along an Engel Curve such that the tangent at that point extends through the origin." Explain.

4. True or false: "Since income elasticities must *average* out to unity, any commodity accounting for a very large fraction of income expenditure cannot have an income elasticity very far from unity." Explain.

5. What is meant by "elastic demand" and "inelastic demand"? How can elasticity at a point along a linear demand curve be determined by inspection? Along a nonlinear demand curve?

6. In 1696 the British statistician Gregory King formulated an alleged "law": The greater the crop, the smaller its money value. What was he implicitly asserting about the price elasticity of demand for crops?

7. What is the analytical form of a demand function that is *linear* in both income and price? What is the analytical form of a demand function that has constant elasticities with respect to both income and price? Explain the economic meaning of each form.

8. The price elasticity of demand for a given commodity is alleged to be greater:

    a. The more numerous and closer the substitutes.

    b. If it is a luxury rather than a necessity.

    c. If it accounts for a large portion of the consumption budget.

    d. At high prices rather than low prices.

Explain the supporting argument in each case and analyze its validity.

9. The American economist Irving Fisher argued in 1891 that a poor community will hardly distinguish quality grades of a commodity like beef, while a rich community would.

In the country districts of "the west" all cuts of beef sell for the same price (about 10 cts. per lb.). In the cities of the west two or three qualities are commonly distinguished, while in New York a grocer will enumerate over a dozen prices in the same beef varying from 10 to 25 cts. per lb.[21]

Construct the implied indifference curves, at low and high levels of income, between "low-quality beef" and "high-quality beef." Why should the different beef qualities be better substitutes at low incomes than at high incomes? What would you anticipate about the price elasticity of demand for low-quality beef? For high-quality beef?

10. Footnote 19 above asserts that, in the special case where there is a single "all-important" commodity accounting for 100% of the consumer's budget, the price elasticity of demand for that commodity is −1. Justify the assertion. What is the income elasticity of demand?

[21]Irving Fisher, *Mathematical Investigations in the Theory of Value and Prices* (New Haven: Yale University Press, 1925), p. 74.

Chapter 6
Applications and Extensions of Demand Theory

In this chapter the topics taken up are intended to give the student some partial idea of the richness and growing power of the modern theory of consumption and demand. The potential applicability of demand theory to realms of behavior not so far considered, for example, the "purchase" of safety or of charity, will be suggested. And a number of theoretical extensions are analyzed, including the index-number problem and the topic of choice under non-income constraints (as in the case of wartime product rationing).

6. A SOME SUBTLER APPLICATIONS OF DEMAND THEORY

In the previous chapter, the effects of variations of prices and incomes upon the optimum of the consumer—and, therefore, through the process of aggregation over all consumers, upon market demand—were analyzed. A variety of illustrative applications were described, among them the division of income among major expenditure categories (food, clothing, shelter, etc.), and certain aspects of the demands for commodities like electricity, fish, liquor, and so forth. All of these are rather conventional applications of the theory of consumer choice—to goods that we ordinarily think of as obtained by consumers through the market.

What is more surprising is that the theory of consumer choice can be applied to a variety of subtler or less obvious decision situations, involving "goods" other than those normally regarded as provided through a market-like process. Two such applications are discussed in this section: the "demand for charity" and the "demand for safety."

6. A. 1 The Demand for Charity

Panel (b) of Figure 3.12 showed a preference function consistent with the observations that the subject individual: (1) may give charity, but (2) only to persons poorer than himself. This situation is repeated here in the diagram of

Figure 6.1. Below the 45° line, "My Income" I is greater than "His Income" H, and so both I and H are goods for me. But above the 45° line, where H exceeds I, His Income is a neuter commodity for me.

We now want to consider charity as the "purchase" of increments to the other person's income H, at the expense of the contributor's income I. Suppose that, to begin with, $I = \$1000$ and $H = 0$, i.e., My Income is $1000, but the potential object of charity is absolutely penniless.[1] Then the initial or *endowment* position is at point E on the horizontal axis of Figure 6.1. In the absence of any special tax considerations, I can transfer income to

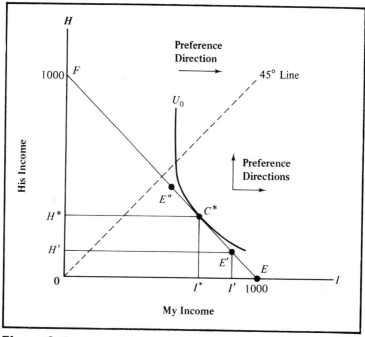

Figure 6. 1

Charity and Relative Income Endowments

the other person dollar for dollar, i.e., the "price" of H is unity in terms of I. Then EF can be regarded as a *budget line* (in complete analogy with the line KL in Figure 4.1) with a slope of -1, at an angle of 135° from the horizontal. The optimum of the "consumer" (i.e., of "me" as donor) along EF is at C^* in Figure 6.1, with associated quantities I^* for my after-contribution income and H^* for his after-charity income. My donation is of course $1000 - I^*$, which numerically equals his receipt OH^*.

Now consider what would happen if our relative income status were initially different. In particular, suppose that the initial endowment position were at E' rather than at E along the line EF. Here My Income is I', and His

[1]For convenience, we speak of income as accruing in monetary units in this discussion, but the reader should still be thinking in terms of *real* incomes.

Income is H'. The tangency position C^* remains the donor's optimum, but it can now be achieved with a substantially smaller charitable contribution. Specifically, the donor gives only $I' - I^*$, which will equal the charitable receipt $H^* - H'$. What if the endowment position were at E'' along EF, lying beyond (to the northwest of) my tangency optimum C^*? Then, my preferences say that he should make some contribution to me! Unfortunately, however, this decision is not within my control.

We have seen that the amount of charitable contribution can be expected to be greater, the higher the initial income status of donor relative to donee. *Tax* considerations are also relevant, in that they affect the "price" of transferring income. In particular, suppose that I must pay a flat 40% tax upon my income *after* deducting charitable donations. Then each dollar of H that I contribute only costs me 60 cents. In effect, then, I can "buy" income H for a donee at the "price" $P_H = 0.6$. In Figure 6.2, we consider once again

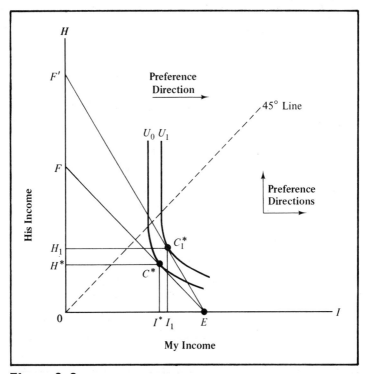

Figure 6. 2
Tax Rates and Charity

an endowment position E along the horizontal axis (the potential object of charity has no income). The previous C^* solution along EF is shown once more for purposes of comparison. But now suppose that the distance OE along the horizontal axis represents my *after-tax* income in the absence of charitable contributions. The fact that $P_H = 0.6 < 1$ means that the new "budget line" EF' is steeper than EF. (The absolute slope of EF' is $1/0.6 = 5/3$, whereas the absolute slope of *EF* is unity.) The new optimum is C_1^*, and the associated contribution OH_1 is now greater than the amount OH^* donated in the no-tax situation.[2] Evidently, in the range where H and I are both goods for the donor, exemption of charitable contributions from tax leads to increased donations.

[2]With a *progressive* income tax, the price P_H would not be a constant. As the contributor gives more and more, his remaining income falls into lower tax brackets. So P_H does not remain quite so favorable as for the first dollar donated. This complication will not be pursued here.

<table>
<tr><td>**Example 6. 1**
Charitable
Giving</td><td>Robert A. Schwartz studied charitable giving, regarded as a good "purchased" by donors, as a function of a number of variables related to those mentioned in the text above: the "price" of giving P_H (equal to 1 minus the donor's marginal tax rate), the donor's income I, and others' income N. (Unfortunately, a measure of *donees'* income H was not available, and so N representing the per-capita income of all non-donors was used as a very imperfect proxy.) The statistical function fitted was in the constant-elasticity form of equation (5.10), leading to the elasticities given in the following Table.</td></tr>
</table>

Elasticities of Charitable Donations

Income Class	"Price" (P_H) Elasticity	Donor Income (I) Elasticity	Others' Income (N) Elasticity
$0–10,000	−.85	+.19	−.53
$10,000–100,000	−.79	+.76	−.43
Over $100,000	−.37	+.40	−.38

Source: R. A. Schwartz, "Personal Philanthropic Contributions," *Journal of Political Economy*, v. 78 (Nov./Dec. 1970), p. 1279.

The results are all in the directions expected. The lower the P_H, the "cheaper" is charitable giving, and so the greater the contributions (negative price elasticity). The higher the absolute donor income, the more giving (positive income elasticity). But the higher the income of others, the less giving; there is a negative effect on donations, the poorer is the *relative* income status of the donor. One point of interest is the big jump in the donor income elasticity between the top and middle lines of the Table. If people are quite poor, a small enrichment will be devoted almost entirely to urgent personal needs. But in the middle income brackets, increments to income are spent in greater degree on behalf of those less well off.

6. A. 2 The Demand for Safety

In Chapter 15 we will see just how the decision as to *employment* can be approached with the tools of demand theory. The worker, for example, can be regarded as "buying" consumption income with his labor power. But in this section we will be considering only an ancillary aspect of the employment decision: the choice of jobs with more or less safety.

In the job market it is reasonable to anticipate that, other things equal, employments with greater injury or death hazard (lower *safety S*) will offer a higher income return *I* than safer jobs. A worker choosing between more and less hazardous jobs can be regarded as facing a curve like *AB* in Figure 6.3; he can choose a low-income high-safety job toward the southeast end, or a high-income low-safety job toward the northwest end along *AB*. The curve *AB* thus plays the role of a "budget line" bounding the job-seeker's oppor-

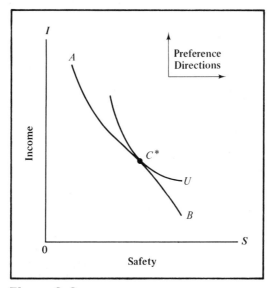

Figure 6. 3
The Demand for Safety

tunity set. However, we do not know whether *AB* is actually linear in form. (Also, as there are neither *perfectly safe* nor totally *sure-death* jobs, *AB* does not extend out to either axis.) Evidently, for people of non-pathological preferences both income *I* and safety *S* are *goods* (preference directions are north and east). Then, normally shaped convex indifference curves can be expected to lead each particular individual to a tangency optimum as at *C** in the diagram. Different workers would, in accordance with their relative preferences for safety and income, distribute themselves at various points along the *AB* opportunity boundary.

Example 6. 2
The Value
of Safety

A study by Richard Thaler and Sherwin Rosen[3] estimated the amount of income necessary to induce workers to accept higher death hazards. Here safety $S = 1 - p$, where p is the *added* annual probability of death due to the job. In current American experience, p does not rise to very high levels for any job category employing substantial numbers of people. Among the relatively high-risk jobs are lumbermen ($p = .00256$) and guards, watchmen, and doorkeepers ($p = .00267$). Police and detectives represent a surprisingly safe category ($p = .00078$), with firemen even safer ($p = .00044$).[4] Thus, the data available all fall toward the extreme southeast end of the *AB* curve of Figure 6.3.

Within this limited interval, the income-safety opportunity boundary did not diverge substantially from linear form. The result obtained was that an extra death probability of one-thousandth (.001) required an income increment of around $200 per year in 1967 dollars.[5]

Comment: An increment to p of .001 means that, for each thousand workers employed, one per year will actually lose his life, on the average. So in a sense $200,000 is the "price of a life"! Needless to say, any such interpretation raises philosophical questions that we cannot take up here.

[3]R. Thaler and S. Rosen, "The Value of Saving a Life: Evidence from the Labor Market," Dept. of Economics, University of Rochester (Dec. 1973).
[4]*Ibid.*, p. 29.
[5]*Ibid.*, p. 38.

6. B INDEX NUMBERS

Suppose we want to know, in comparing two situations, whether consumers are better off in the one or the other. If the commodities involved are *good*s so that "more is preferred to less," this question can be reformulated as: In which situation does the individual get, on the average, a larger quantity of commodities to consume? The average measure designed to answer such a question is called an *index number of quantity*. A closely related question is: In which situation does the consumer, on the average, have to pay a higher price for the goods he consumes? An average measure constructed to answer this question is called an *index number of price*.

Practical applications of index numbers of prices or quantities are almost always associated with problems involving monetary inflation or deflation, i.e., overall swings in the prices of goods measured in money terms. For example, a worker may want to know if his rising money income in an inflationary period has kept up with the rising money prices of the commodities in his consumption basket. Therefore, in this section we diverge from our previous insistence upon dealing in real units only (so as to "pierce the veil" of money). Rather, "income" here is to be understood as accruing to the consumer in the form of a money sum per period (symbolized as I^m). And similarly, prices are to be understood as quoted in money units.[6]

6. B. 1   Index Numbers of Quantity

Consider Panel (a) of Figure 6.4. Here a person's levels of satisfaction or "standards of living" in two different time periods (period 0 and period 1) are to be compared by an observer who does *not* have knowledge of the subject's

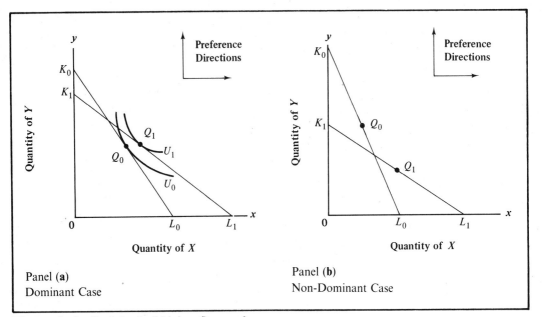

Figure 6. 4   Standard of Living Comparisons

preference map. What the observer knows is that the consumer makes rational choices. He can thus infer that, in the "base year" (period 0), the consumer was at his consumptive optimum combination Q_0 (the corresponding quantities being q_x^0 and q_y^0 of commodities X and Y respectively). This optimum depends, of course, upon base-year income I_0^m and the prices P_x^0 and P_y^0 which enter into the determination of the period-0 market opportunity set and budget line $K_0 L_0$. In the "given year" (period 1) these three determining variables will in general change to new levels I_1^m, P_x^1 and P_y^1, determining a new budget line $K_1 L_1$ and optimum solution Q_1 (with corresponding quantities q_x^1 and q_y^1).

Suppose prices and money income so changed that the individual's new (given-year) budget line has greater intercepts on both the X- and Y-axes

     [6]An explicit rationale for the existence of money will be provided in Chapter 8 below.

than the old (base-year) budget line, i.e., the budget line has shifted outward from the origin. Then the consumer's market opportunity set has increased in both the X- and Y-directions; the observer knows that the consumer must be better off in period 1. Similarly, if the budget line were entirely displaced inward, the consumer would surely be worse off. The difficult case is when income and prices change in such a way that one intercept of the budget line increases while the other decreases. In Figure 6.4, for example, in period 1 the opportunities are greater in the X-direction but poorer in the Y-direction. In other words, the new and the old budget lines intersect.

It is nevertheless possible in some cases to detect immediately an unambiguous improvement or an unambiguous worsening in standard of living. Since X and Y are both goods, the preference directions are north and east. Hence the situation of Panel (a) of Figure 6.4, with the new consumptive optimum at Q_1 lying northeast of the old one at Q_0, represents an unambiguous improvement. We say here that the attained consumption basket Q_1 *dominates* Q_0. Correspondingly, if Q_1 were southwest of Q_0 the new position Q_1 would be *dominated* by the old Q_0, so that an unambiguous reduction in standard of living must have occurred.

In the situation of Panel (b) of Figure 6.4, on the other hand, there is no dominance. With Q_1 lying southeast of Q_0 it would be possible to construct preference maps in which the combination Q_0 is preferred to Q_1, but equally possible to construct maps for which Q_1 is preferred to Q_0. The same would apply if Q_1 were northwest of Q_0. Since the indifference maps are not known to outside observers, no obvious conclusion could be drawn from merely observing Q_0 and Q_1.

However, there is one other consideration that can be brought to bear. Consider now the situation in Panel (a) of Figure 6.5. Here Q_1 lies southeast of Q_0, so this might seem to be a doubtful case. But without knowledge of the preference map the observer can still see that *in period* 0, *the position* Q_1 *was attainable;* Q_1 lies within the shaded market opportunity set bounded by the axes and the budget line $K_0 L_0$ that was effective at time 0. Since the basket Q_1 was attainable in period 0 but was *not* purchased and Q_0 was purchased instead, Q_0 must have been preferred to Q_1. On the assumption that preferences have not changed, the observer can infer that the standard of living must have declined between the base year and the given year as a result of the price and income changes. And he can know this even if the indifference map in the diagram were hidden from him.

Panel (b) of Figure 6.5 shows the opposite case. As Q_1 lies northwest of Q_0, the *dominance* test in terms of preference directions does not lead to a clear conclusion. But in the given year the shaded market opportunity set, bounded by the axes and the budget line $K_1 L_1$, includes the position Q_0. That is, in period 1 the combination Q_0 is attainable but is *not* being purchased. Hence Q_1 is surely preferred to Q_0, and there has been an improvement in the standard of living.

We can now turn to an algebraic measure or index as to when the basket Q_1 (the combination q_x^1 and q_y^1) is—on the average, or in utility terms—

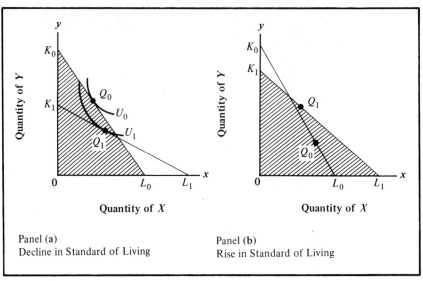

Panel (a)
Decline in Standard of Living

Panel (b)
Rise in Standard of Living

Figure 6. 5
Unambiguous Changes in Standard
of Living

greater than and so preferable to Q_0 (the combination q_x^0 and q_y^0). There are two standard ways of constructing these averages or indexes: the Laspeyres ($\mathcal{L}$) using "base-year weights" and the Paasche ($\mathcal{P}$) using "given-year weights."

The Laspeyres index of quantity is defined, where the "sigma" notation for summation provides a helpful short-hand for extending the 2-good geometrical discussion to any number of commodities, as:

$$(6.1) \qquad \mathcal{L}_Q = \frac{P_x^0 q_x^1 + P_y^0 q_y^1}{P_x^0 q_x^0 + P_y^0 q_y^0} = \frac{\sum P^0 q^1}{\sum P^0 q^0}$$

The Laspeyres index provides an estimate as to whether quantities have increased "on the average" between period 0 and period 1, where, to make the quantity comparison a meaningful one, the same weights (in this case the base-year price weights P_x^0 and P_y^0) are used in calculating the average.

The Paasche index of quantity differs from the Laspeyres only in using given-year weights instead:

$$(6.2) \qquad \mathcal{P}_Q = \frac{P_x^1 q_x^1 + P_y^1 q_y^1}{P_x^1 q_x^0 + P_y^1 q_y^0} = \frac{\sum P^1 q^1}{\sum P^1 q^0}$$

In Figure 6.6, Panel (a) represents the same situation as in Panel (a) of Figure 6.5. The indifference curves and shading have been suppressed; instead, an artificial budget line represented by the dashed line CC' parallel to the base-year budget line $K_0 L_0$ has been passed through the given-year quantity solution Q_1. The total expenditure (the income I_0^m) represented by the original solution Q_0 at the base-year prices can be written as $I_0^m =$

142

$P_x^0 q_x^0 + P_y^0 q_y^0$ or $I_0^m = \sum P^0 q^0$. The new line CC' applies to the *quantities* associated with the given-year solution Q_1, but its slope represents the *base-year* prices. Hence the consumption expenditures associated with CC' can be written in summation notation as $\sum P^0 q^1$. It is evident that, at the P^0 prices, the basket Q_0 represents a higher expenditure level than Q_1. Hence, in Panel (a) of Figure 6.6:

$$\sum P^0 q^0 > \sum P^0 q^1 \quad \text{or} \quad \mathcal{L}_Q = \frac{\sum P^0 q^1}{\sum P^0 q^0} < 1$$

The conclusion is that when the Laspeyres quantity index is *less* than unity, the consumer has surely become worse off in the given year. He had the opportunity to buy Q_1 in place of Q_0 in period 0 but chose *not* to do so; therefore, when he actually was observed to purchase Q_1 in period 1 he must have become worse off than he was at Q_0 in the previous period.

By a corresponding argument, Panel (b) of Figure 6.6 represents the situation where:

$$\sum P^1 q^0 < \sum P^1 q^1 \quad \text{or} \quad \mathcal{P}_Q = \frac{\sum P^1 q^1}{\sum P^1 q^0} > 1$$

The conclusion is that when the Paasche quantity index is *greater* than unity, the consumer has surely become better off in the given year. For, he has in the given year the opportunity of buying Q_0 in place of Q_1, and chooses not to do so.

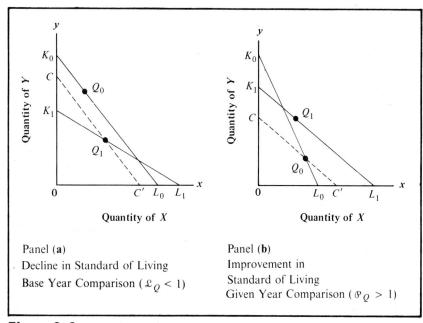

Figure 6. 6
Unambiguous Changes in Standard
of Living—Quantity Indexes

These conclusions are in each case *sufficient* to determine the direction of improvement, but not *necessary*. If the Laspeyres quantity index is less than unity, the observer knows that the consumer must have become worse off in the given year. But he *can* be worse off without this condition holding. In Figure 6.4, Panel (b), it is not the case that $\mathcal{L}_Q < 1$. Nevertheless, it would be possible to construct an indifference map for that diagram for which Q_1 is inferior to Q_0. Similarly, if the Paasche quantity index is greater than unity the consumer must be better off in period 1—but he *can* be better off without this condition holding. Again, it would be possible to show this in terms of Panel (b) of Figure 6.4.

6. B. 2   Index Numbers of Price

We now turn to index numbers of *prices*. Laspeyres and Paasche indexes of prices may be defined algebraically in the same way as for quantities. But here, as it is the prices which are being averaged, the quantities serve as weights. The definitions are:

(6.3)
$$\mathcal{L}_P = \frac{\sum P^1 q^0}{\sum P^0 q^0}$$

(6.4)
$$\mathcal{P}_P = \frac{\sum P^1 q^1}{\sum P^0 q^1}$$

It is also useful to define an index of money-income change as:

(6.5)
$$\mathcal{E} = \frac{\sum P^1 q^1}{\sum P^0 q^0} = \frac{I_1^m}{I_0^m}$$

This is of course simply the ratio of total expenditures in the two periods.

It is intuitively clear that there must be a close connection between the quantity and the price indexes. This connection turns out to involve the index of income change $\mathcal{E}$ as well.

We know from the discussion above that the consumer is surely better off in the given year if $\sum P^1 q^0 < \sum P^1 q^1$ so that the Paasche quantity index is greater than one. Dividing both sides of the inequality by $\sum P^0 q^0$, we have:

$$\frac{\sum P^1 q^1}{\sum P^0 q^0} > \frac{\sum P^1 q^0}{\sum P^0 q^0} \quad or \quad \mathcal{E} > \mathcal{L}_P$$

Thus, if the income index $\mathcal{E}$ exceeds the Laspeyres index of prices, the consumer is in an improved situation in the given year as compared to the base year. This result is implied by a Paasche index of quantity exceeding unity.

Correspondingly, of course, the consumer is worse off in the given year when the index of income $\mathcal{E}$ is less than the Paasche index of prices, or $\mathcal{E} < \mathcal{P}_P$. This is equivalent to a Laspeyres index of quantity $\mathcal{L}_Q$ that is less than unity.

The economic interpretation of the relation between the income and price indexes is quite direct. If, for example, income has risen but more than in proportion to prices, on the average, then the average quantity consumed must have increased. If income has risen but less than in proportion to prices, on the average, the average quantity consumed (real income) must have decreased.

Conclusion: If the Paasche quantity index $\mathcal{P}_Q$ is greater than unity, the consumer is surely better off in the given year. And then the income index $\mathcal{E}$ exceeds the Laspeyres price index $\mathcal{L}_P$. If the Laspeyres quantity index $\mathcal{L}_Q$ is less than unity, the consumer is surely worse off in the given year. And then the income index $\mathcal{E}$ is less than the Paasche price index $\mathcal{P}_P$.

Exploration of the theoretical niceties of Laspeyres versus Paasche indexes is helpful in forcing the student to deepen his understanding of the interrelations among price and income changes. In practice, however, the really important issues do not concern these niceties. The Laspeyres and Paasche indexes will not differ very much, unless indeed an attempt is being made to compare situations so different or so far apart in time or space as to invalidate the assumption of *constant preferences* that underlies the entire analysis. In terms of common sense, the main message to be drawn is that if a person's money-income index has risen, but less than in proportion to the index of money prices (Laspeyres or Paasche makes little difference), then he is *not* really better off. For him, *real* income (index of quantity consumed) has fallen rather than risen.

But a further warning is also very much in order. Money income may have risen more than in proportion to some official price index, and even so the consumers can really be worse off! For, by accident or design, a host of devices may mask losses in real income during an inflationary period. Most, though not all, of these sources of distortion are connected with the imposition of price controls that prevent legally quoted prices from rising to a higher equilibrium level (see Section 2.A.5). As a result there may be disguised price rises, not registered in the official price indexes, in such forms as: (1) Open or hidden degradation of quality (including range of varieties offered); (2) elimination of customary discounts, special sales, etc.; (3) provision of some portion of goods through illegal black-market or unofficial channels at unreported high prices; (4) forcing consumers to less-preferred combinations, at existing money prices, by such devices as coupon rationing, queue rationing, or simple unavailability of desired goods; (5) fiscal subsidies to those particular commodities appearing in the officially quoted index! (This last is akin to lowering the recorded temperature in a room by pressing an ice cube against the thermometer.)

*6. C THE INCOME-COMPENSATED DEMAND CURVE

Suppose that an observer wanted to infer the shape of the demand curve of an individual (or group of individuals) for some commodity X on the basis of historical data, but *without* specific knowledge of preference maps. Imagine

*Starred sections represent optional or advanced material.

that there are just two observations, the first being the consumption basket Q_0 chosen in a base year (period 0) and the second a basket Q_1 chosen in a given year (period 1).

In Figure 6.7 the base-year observed basket Q_0 lies on the budget line K_0L_0 associated with the consumer's base-year income I_0. The slope of K_0L_0 is $-P_x^0/P_y^0$, the ratio of the base-year prices P_x^0 and P_y^0. If in fact income I and the price of the other commodity P_y did not change between the base year and the given year, then the new optimum basket Q_1 would lie along a budget

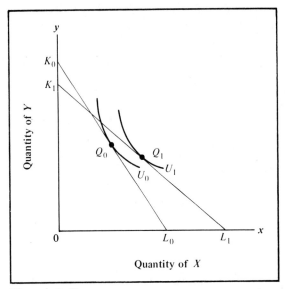

Figure 6. 7
Base Year and Given Year Observed
Solutions

line K_1L_1 representing a simple tilting of the original K_0L_0 about the vertical intercept (as in Figure 4.10). Since this was precisely the process (in the form of a hypothetical experiment) used to derive the demand curve in Section 4.B, the X-quantities and the prices P_x associated with the two positions Q_0 and Q_1 would then correspond to two points on the desired demand curve. But in general, not only P_x but income I and other prices P_y would also change between the base year and given year, and so no such simple inference can be drawn. All we can know (on the basis of the theory of consumer choice of Section 4.A) is that Q_0 and Q_1 are indifference-curve tangencies along K_0L_0 and K_1L_1, respectively.

A proportional change in the prices P_x and P_y together is evidently equivalent to a corresponding change, in the opposite direction, of income I. In either case, there is a parallel inward or outward displacement of the budget line, as in Figure 4.5, which may be interpreted as a change in *real* income, in the sense of an enlargement or contraction of the market opportunity set. A parallel outward shift of the budget line (whether due to a rise in I, or a fall in P_x and P_y together) corresponds to a rise in real income; an inward shift (whether due to a fall in I, or a rise in P_x and P_y together) corresponds to a fall in real income.

It therefore becomes possible to divide the overall observed change, between the consumption combinations attained in the base year and given year, into: (1) a portion due to the change in *real income* (inward or outward displacement of budget line), and (2) a portion due to the change in *relative prices* (shift in the slope $-P_x/P_y$ of the budget line). This of course is similar to the problem addressed in Section 4.C, "Income and Substitution Effects of a Price Change." There it was assumed that income I and other prices P_y remain constant with only P_x varying. The problem was to separate the effect on quantity demanded due to the change in real income ("income effect") from the effect due to the change in relative prices at constant real income ("pure substitution effect"), as two logically distinguishable aspects of the initial shift in P_x. The separation, associated with the British economist J. R. Hicks, made use of the indifference-curve tangency as shown in Figure 4.15. That is, "real income" was held constant in the sense of hypothetically maintaining the consumer along his initial indifference curve while allowing P_x to change.

Here, however, we want to consider a different separation—associated with the Russian economist Slutsky.[7] The division is effected as indicated in Figure 6.8, by passing an artificial budget line CC' parallel to the given-year budget line (i.e., whose slope represents the period-1 price ratio P_x^1/P_y^1) but through the base-year observed position Q_0. In Figure 6.8 the upward shift of the budget line (from CC' through Q_0 to K_1L_1 through Q_1) *is interpreted as the change in real income.*

What is the advantage of the Slutsky over the Hicks decomposition of income versus substitution effects? For one thing, it permits a simple *measure* of the change in real income. For Hicks, the improvement in real income represents only attaining a higher level of utility, a magnitude that is not cardinally measurable. For Slutsky, the real-income change can be measured by the ratio of the expenditures associated with the given-year budget line K_1L_1 (along which the observed Q_1 position falls) to the expenditures associated with the artificial budget line CC' (along which the observed Q_0 position falls). What is this ratio? It is nothing but the *Paasche index of quantity* defined above in equation (6.2) that will be repeated here:

$$(6.6) \qquad \mathcal{P}_Q = \frac{P_x^1 q_x^1 + P_y^1 q_y^1}{P_x^1 q_x^0 + P_y^1 q_y^0}$$

The comparison is of the given-year quantities (consumption combination Q_1) versus the base-year quantities (consumption combination Q_0), averaged in terms of the given-year price weights—represented geometrically by the parallel slopes of K_1L_1 and CC' in Figure 6.8.

While the Paasche quantity index thus provides us with a measure of the

[7]Eugen Slutsky, 1880–1948.

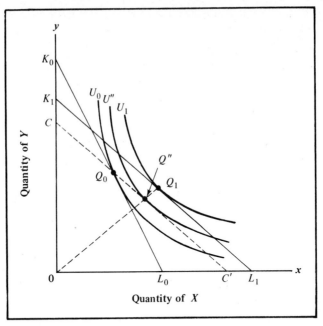

Figure 6. 8
Shift in Real Income versus Change
in Relative Prices—
Slutsky Decomposition

real-income change, we do not yet have a way of separating the *real-income effect* from the *relative price effect* on the basis of the historical observations. Ideally, we would like to know the location of the hypothetical tangency optimum Q'' in Figure 6.8 along the artificial budget line CC'. Combination Q'' would be the Slutsky analog to the artificial tangency optimum Q' for the Hicks decomposition illustrated in Figure 4.15. Since the Slutsky Q'' position is unknowable to an observer (as is the Hicks Q' position), it must be estimated from the observations. This estimation would be based upon the statistical data and the form of the relationship fitted. Suppose, for example, that econometric analysis led to the conclusion that the income elasticity for commodity X (and, therefore, also for Y) is unity. In this case, as explained in Section 5.A, the hypothetical tangency optimum Q'' along CC' in Figure 6.8 would lie on the (dashed) ray drawn from the origin to the point Q_1 along K_1L_1. If the income elasticity for X were greater than unity, Q'' would have to lie along CC' northwest of the intersection with this ray from the origin; if the income elasticity were less than unity, Q'' would lie to the southeast along CC'. But in any case, the statistical evidence would lead to a hypothetical determination of the position of Q''.

As between the points Q_0 and Q'', *real income is constant in the sense of the Paasche quantity index* ($\mathscr{P}_Q = 1$). Then the difference between the X-quantities in these consumption combinations can be attributed solely to the

148

effect of the differing price ratios P_x/P_y (budget-line slopes). Plotting the price ratios against the quantities so obtained leads to what is called the *income-compensated* demand curve d^*d^* shown in Figure 6.9. With this is drawn, for comparison, the "ordinary" demand curve dd previously derived (in Chapter 4, Section B).

The two demand curves in Figure 6.9 are shown as coinciding at the initial observed point A, with quantity q_x^0 and price ratio P_x^0/P_y^0, corresponding to the position Q_0 in the preceding diagram. For the ordinary demand curve

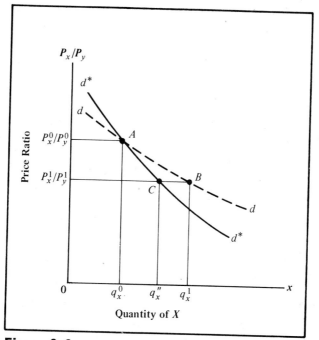

Figure 6. 9
Income-Compensated
versus "Ordinary" Demand Curve

dd, a point like B is obtained at the lower price ratio P_x^1/P_y^1. As indicated in the discussion of Section 4.B.2, the price-quantity point B corresponds to a position on the individual's Price Expansion Path PEP as P_x varies, with income I (in numeraire units) and prices of other goods like P_y held constant. For the income-compensated demand curve d^*d^*, at the lower price ratio the price-quantity point C is obtained. Point C corresponds to the hypothetical consumption combination Q'' in Figure 6.8, estimated from the statistical data while holding real income (Paasche quantity index) constant.

A number of aspects of the income-compensated demand curve are of interest.

1. Since the ordinary demand curve incorporates an "income effect of the price change," which the compensated demand curve excludes, it must be that for a normal or superior good dd is flatter than d^*d^*, as drawn in Figure 6.9. When price falls the income effect is positive for a normal good; the ordinary demand, but not the compensated demand, reflects this (point B lies to the right of point C in the diagram). However, we saw in Chapter 4 that the income effect *may* be negative, indeed conceivably so much so that the Giffen condition obtains (positively-sloped demand curve within some range). Since the compensated demand curve excludes any income effect, the Giffen possibility is also ruled out.

2. In a many-commodity world, it would be arbitrary to pick out some single other commodity Y whose price P_y would serve as the base of the price ratio P_x/P_y in measuring the change in relative prices. Instead, some general average of prices such as the Consumer Price Index would be used in actual statistical work to "deflate" the observed changes in the nominal money price of commodity X.

3. The great importance of the income-compensated demand curve stems from the fact that, as already suggested, this is the relation that is actually obtained from statistical studies of historical price-quantity observations. In such studies it is almost always necessary to allow for *income differences* by fitting a demand function like that of equation (5.5) or equation (5.10) to the observations. For example, it would hardly be possible to simply fit a demand curve to price-quantity data from both California and Mississippi without allowing for the real-income differences between those states. And in time-series analysis, it will similarly be necessary to allow for historical growth of real income over time. But when the statistician makes a separate allowance for differences or changes in real income, he is *eliminating the income effect* from the price-quantity data. This necessarily leaves him with some approximation of the "pure substitution effect"—the income-compensated demand curve.

4. It is sometimes thought that the essential distinction between the ordinary and the compensated demand curves is due to money; some authors regard the ordinary demand curve dd as one that holds *money income constant* while the compensated demand curve d^*d^* holds *real income constant*. This is an understandable confusion, since in modern economies prices are quoted in terms of money. Nevertheless, the existence of money is not the essential here. Suppose money had not been invented so that prices were quoted in terms of some real numeraire commodity. It would still be possible logically to distinguish the "ordinary" demand relation that holds income endowment and other prices constant (see the derivation using the Price Expansion Path of Section 4.B.2) from the "compensated" demand relation that eliminates the income effect of price changes (as derived here and illustrated in Figure 6.8).

5. Nor is it true that the income-compensated demand curve is intrinsically superior to or more valid than the ordinary demand curve (along which consumers' real income rises as price P_x falls). Each has its uses. The ordinary demand curve, for example, is the function that is relevant for the businessman considering alternative prices he must charge, or, as we shall see in Chapter 7, for determining the equilibrium of a market or an economy as a whole.

6. D   MULTIPLE CONSTRAINTS

In Section 4.A, the *budget line* was introduced as the upper (northeast) boundary of an individual's market opportunity set. Or, we may say, the budget line is the binding *constraint* upon the individual's choices. This constraint is due, of course, to his limited income I available for expenditure upon consumption goods.

The familiar equation of the budget line is:

$$(6.7) \qquad\qquad P_x x + P_y y = I$$

The market opportunity set as a whole, the shaded region of Figure 6.10, was previously described as the area bounded on the northeast by the budget

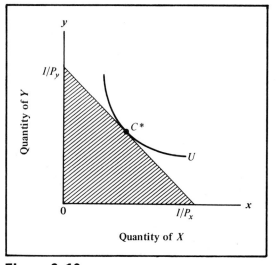

Figure 6. 10
Market Opportunity Set

line. But we must now be more precise. It is the area bounded by the budget line *and the coordinate axes*, the set of points satisfying the inequalities:

$$(6.8) \qquad\qquad \begin{cases} P_x x + P_y y \leqq I \\ x \geqq 0 \\ y \geqq 0 \end{cases}$$

The latter two conditions express the physical reality that goods cannot be purchased or consumed in negative quantities.

6. D. 1 Rationing

It sometimes happens, however, that the consumer faces constraints upon his market decisions apart from his limited income. In wartime, for example, a ration limit R_x might be placed upon consumption of commodity X. Three cases of interest are shown in the three panels of Figure 6.11.

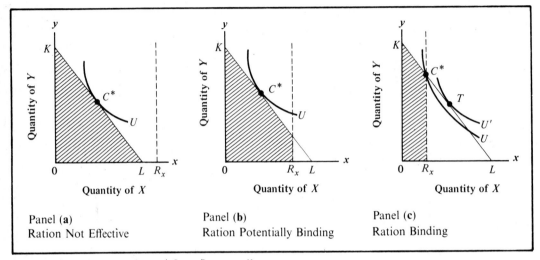

Figure 6. 11 Rationing of One Commodity

In Panel (a) of Figure 6.11, the ration limit is indicated by the vertical dashed line at the quantity $x = R_x$. Here the ration is so large, relative to the consumer's income that establishes the size of his market opportunity set (shaded area), as to be ineffective. In Panel (b) the ration limit R_x is *potentially* binding; it does bite into (truncate) the market opportunity set so as to reduce the size of the shaded area. However, given the individual's preferences the ration limit is not *actually* binding for him; he does not even want to consume as much of X as his ration permits. Only in Panel (c) is the ration limit R_x actually binding; it forces the individual to a *non-tangency* solution C^*, where, without the ration limit, he would have attained the preferred tangency position T.

As an obvious implication, ration limits are less binding for poorer people, for whom income already serves as a severe constraint. Note also that after imposition of a ration limit upon consumption of some commodity X, consumers' demands tend to "spill over" so that more is consumed of those commodities left unrationed.

What if commodities X and Y were *both* rationed? Here there are a considerable variety of cases, not all of which will be diagrammed. In Figure 6.12 we see only the more interesting situations where both of the ration

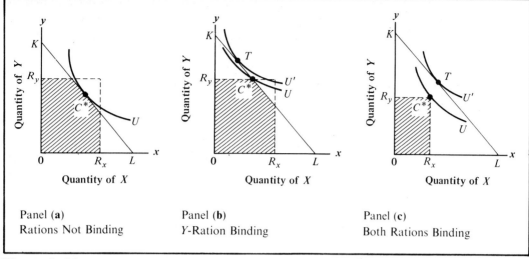

Figure 6. 12
Physical Rationing of Two Commodities—Potentially Binding Cases

limits R_x and R_y are at least *potentially* binding, i.e., the market opportunity set is truncated at both ends. Panel (a) shows that even when both ration limits are potentially binding, neither may *actually* be effective at the consumptive optimum position C^*. In Panel (b), only the ration limit R_y for commodity Y is actually binding; it forces the individual to a position C^* inferior to the tangency optimum T that he would otherwise have chosen. (There would of course be an opposite case, not diagrammed here, in which the ration limit R_x is the only one binding.) In Panel (c), we see the interesting case in which *both* ration limits are actually effective. Here it is the budget constraint that is not binding. This would correspond to the situation of a rich person, well endowed with income, but unable to legally spend it all in a situation where all desired commodities are subject to severe rationing.

Analytically, it is interesting to interpret these possibilities in terms of opportunity sets. The *market* opportunity set, for which income I is the effective constraint, is the familiar triangular area bounded by the budget line and the axes in the diagrams of Figure 6.12. The *ration* opportunity set, where fixed quantitative limits on both commodities are imposed, is in the shape of a rectangle. The lower bounds of the rectangle are the axes, and the upper bounds are the dashed lines $x = R_x$ and $y = R_y$. The *effective* opportunity set, shown as the shaded area in all three situations, is the intersection of the market opportunity set and the ration opportunity set; i.e., it is the collection of all points that satisfy both constraints. Formally, the shaded areas are determined by the inequalities:

(6.9)

$$\begin{cases} P_x x + P_y y \leq I \\ 0 \leq x \leq R_x \\ 0 \leq y \leq R_y \end{cases}$$

153

In the latter years of World War II a number of the belligerent powers, including the United States, introduced relatively sophisticated rationing systems. Instead of absolute quantity limits like R_x and R_y on specific commodities, a consumer was granted a certain amount of "point income" N that could be spent very much like ordinary income. Rationed commodities were then assigned "point prices" p_x and p_y in addition to money prices P_x and P_y. The effective opportunity set, in the case where both income and points are at least potentially binding, is the shaded area in Panel (a) of Figure 6.13.

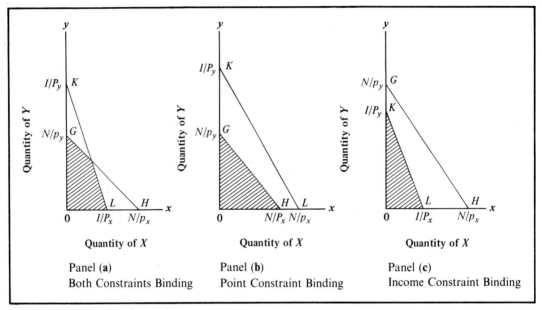

Figure 6. 13   Point Rationing

Formally, the opportunity set under point rationing is determined by the inequalities:

$$\text{(6.10)} \qquad \begin{cases} P_x x + P_y y \leqq I \\ p_x x + p_y y \leqq N \\ x \geqq 0, \qquad y \geqq 0 \end{cases}$$

In the cases illustrated in Figure 6.13, the income budget line KL is steeper than the point budget line GH. That is, $P_x/P_y > p_x/p_y$. Hence, those consumers extremely desirous of purchasing commodity X would tend to find the income constraint binding; those more interested in Y would tend to find the point constraint binding. Nevertheless, an individual sufficiently well endowed with income I might find *only* the point constraint binding for both commodities, as in Panel (b) of Figure 6.13. And a very poor individual in terms of income might correspondingly find *only* the ordinary prices and not the point prices binding, as shown in Panel (c) of the diagram.

The point allowance system of rationing provides some desirable flexibility. Suppose both tea and coffee had been rationed by equal quantity limits. Then consumers whose tastes tolerated both tea or coffee would have an advantage over those disliking one or the other; the latter would find half their beverage rations unusable. (*Sale* of ration coupons is assumed prohibited.) But assigning point prices to tea and coffee permitted consumers to select preferred combinations in accordance with their tastes.

Example 6. 3
Wartime Point
Rationing

Among the commodities rationed by points during World War II in the U.S. were cheese and canned fish. The Table below compares the 1942 (pre-rationing) purchases of different income groups with the quantities purchased during 1944 when rationing was effective.

Average Weekly Purchases (lbs.) by Housekeeping Families in Cities

	Income:	$1000 or Less	$1000– 2000	$2000– 3000	$3000– 4000	Over $4000
1942						
Cheese		.26	.57	.64	.81	1.03
Canned fish		.21	.36	.56	.44	.37
1944						
Cheese		.24	.33	.44	.49	.52
Canned fish		.06	.12	.17	.22	.18

Source: L. A. Epstein, "Wartime Food Purchases," *Monthly Labor Review*, v. 60 (June 1945), pp. 1148, 1150.

One aspect of interest in this Table is the overall binding power of income versus points as constraints. Looking only at the three highest income groups (last three columns), we see that their consumption patterns *in 1944* were almost identical. Hence it appears that consumers in this income range were in the situation pictured in Panel (b) of Figure 6.13—consumption of cheese and canned fish was almost entirely limited by points rather than by income. That the lower income groups and not the upper groups were sensitive to *both* points and income may also be appreciated when it is realized that the dollar price of canned fish relative to cheese approximately doubled between 1942 and 1944. The fish/cheese consumption ratio for the lowest income group consequently fell from .21/.26 to .06/.24, a sharp change indeed. But for the highest income group, the 1942 fish/cheese consumption ratio .37/1.03 remained almost unchanged (at .18/.52) in 1944.

A very important recent development in theoretical and applied work on demand has been the explicit consideration of *time* as well as *income* constraints on consumption. Most consumption activities—playing a round of golf, watching a movie, eating a meal—require significant time inputs as well as cash sacrifices on the part of the consumer.

If time and income were inconvertible, there would be a dual constraint situation like that pictured for point rationing in Figure 6.13. Let t_x and t_y be the time inputs (assumed constant for simplicity) per unit consumed of X and of Y, respectively. The consumer's effective opportunity set would then have to satisfy not only the income constraint $P_x x + P_y y = I$ but also a time constraint $t_x x + t_y y = T$, where T is the total time devoted to consumption activities.

But time and income are not inconvertible for an individual who is employed at income-earning activities outside the home, or in household activities that reduce the need to earn outside income (to pay for repair services, maids, etc.). Consequently, time and income should be regarded as convertible into a single constraint.[8] Suppose the individual devotes T_c hours to consumption. For an hour on the margin, suppose that he could have alternatively been working and receiving an hourly money wage w.[9] Then his consumption time is worth wT_c in money units. If he has non-labor income I_0, the total constraint upon him is given by:

(6.11) $$(P_x + wt_x)x + (P_y + wt_y)y \leqq I_0 + wT_c$$

It is evident from this formulation that the *effective price* π_x for commodity X is not the money price P_x alone but the expression $P_x + wt_x$, the money price plus the income value of the required time input. And similarly, of course, for commodity Y the effective price is $\pi_y = P_x + wt_y$.

For some purposes it is of interest to distinguish elasticity of demand with respect to the cash component of effective price, $\eta_{x \cdot P}$, from the elasticity of demand with respect to the time element, $\eta_{x \cdot wt}$. The definitions are:

(6.12) $$\eta_{x \cdot P} = \frac{\Delta x}{\Delta P_x} \frac{P_x}{x}$$

(6.13) $$\eta_{x \cdot wt} = \frac{\Delta x}{\Delta wt} \frac{wt}{x}$$

---

*Starred sections represent optional or advanced material.

[8] In contrast, the sale of "points" for cash was definitely illegal under wartime rationing systems; for law-abiding persons, there was no convertibility.

[9] This is of course a simplification. Shifting an additional hour from consumption to work might actually yield more than the normal wage w (if, for example, overtime work at time-and-a-half is available). Alternatively, the individual might only be able to earn a lower rate of pay for additional hours because of fatigue, or because he must take a less desirable second "moonlighting" job. The optimum balance between time and income will be considered further when we analyze the labor-supply decision in Part Five.

Since the wage w is assumed constant, (6.13) can be rewritten:

(6.13′)
$$\eta_{x \cdot wt} = \frac{\Delta x}{w \Delta t} \frac{wt}{x} = \frac{\Delta x}{\Delta t} \frac{t}{x} = \eta_{x \cdot t}$$

Thus, the wage w cancels out, and we can speak in terms of the "elasticity with respect to time input."

The following proposition is very easy to prove by calculus: The elasticity with respect to cash price $\eta_{x \cdot P}$ will be greater or less (in absolute value) than the elasticity with respect to time input $\eta_{x \cdot t}$, according as the cash price P_x weighs more or less heavily than the income value of the time input wt_x in the sum representing the overall effective price $\pi_x = P_x + wt_x$. For example, if the cash price P_x accounts for more than half of π_x, then $|\eta_{x \cdot P}| > |\eta_{x \cdot t}|$.[10]

[10]*Mathematical Footnote:* The elasticity of demand with respect to effective price, π_x, is:

$$\eta_{x\pi} = \frac{dx}{d\pi_x} \frac{\pi_x}{x}$$

For *partial* variation of cash price P_x (t_x held constant), $dx/d\pi_x = \partial x/\partial P_x$. Then

$$\eta_{x \cdot P} = \frac{\partial x}{\partial P_x} \frac{P_x}{x} = \frac{dx}{d\pi_x} \frac{P_x}{x} \frac{\pi_x}{\pi_x} = \eta_{x\pi} \frac{P_x}{\pi_x}$$

Similarly, for partial variation of t_x, $dx/d\pi_x = \partial x/\partial wt_x$. Then

$$\eta_{x \cdot t} = \eta_{x \cdot wt} = \frac{\partial x}{\partial wt_x} \frac{wt_x}{x} = \frac{dx}{d\pi_x} \frac{wt_x}{x} \frac{\pi_x}{\pi_x} = \eta_{x\pi} \frac{wt_x}{\pi_x}$$

So $|\eta_{x \cdot P}|$ will be greater than $|\eta_{x \cdot t}|$ if and only if P_x exceeds wt_x.

Example 6. 4
Time-Prices
of Medical Care

Jan Acton studied a number of factors determining the demand for medical care on the part of residents of two neighborhoods in Brooklyn, New York—Red Hook and Bedford-Crown. He explicitly distinguished the time input from money price. For medical services, residents of these neighborhoods made substantial use of both (1) free municipal clinics and out-patient departments, and (2) private physicians for pay. Data were obtained on the number of visits to both sources of medical care. For the private sources, both a cash payment and a time input were involved. For the free sources, *only* the time input could play a role. (The time input involves both travel time and average waiting time for service; the data in the Table below refer to travel time only, however.)

The results for the two neighborhoods are very similar. For both free and paid (private) medical care, the elasticity with respect to the time price (travel time to the source) was negative. For Red Hook the time-elasticity for free sources was −.958; this means that a 1% rise in travel time to free sources was associated with slightly less than a 1% fall in number of visits. The absolute value of this elasticity was

	Red Hook		Bedford-Crown	
	Travel Time to FSMC	*Travel Time to PPO*	*Travel Time to FSMC*	*Travel Time to PPO*
Visits to free sources of medical care (FSMC)	−.958	+.332	−.619	+.137
Visits to private physicians' offices (PPO)	+.640	−.252	+.629	−.337

Source: Jan P. Acton, "Demand for Health Care among the Urban Poor, with Special Emphasis on the Role of Time," The New York City Rand Institute, Report R-1151-OEO-NYC (April 1973), p. 27.

much lower for private care, however; for Red Hook, −.252 as compared with −.958. This is evidently explicable in terms of the proposition in the text above. For free sources, the time input is the sole element of effective price. Hence *all* the elasticity of effective price must show up in the time-elasticity. For private sources of medical care, the elasticity with respect to *effective* price will be divided between time-elasticity and elasticity with respect to cash price.

The positive coefficients in the Table represent cross-elasticities: the effect on usage of one source of medical care associated with increases in travel time to the other source. The positive elasticities show that the two types of medical services are substitutes, as of course would be expected.

6. E   THE "NEW THEORY OF CONSUMPTION"

In recent years a novel and somewhat richer theory of consumption has been developed by economists. The key idea is a distinction between *market goods* and utility-relevant qualities or *attributes*. In this new approach a market commodity like bread is no longer supposed to be desired in and of itself, but only insofar as it is capable of yielding satisfaction through its attributes: tastiness, calories, proteins, etc. Similarly an automobile is desired only insofar as it can be the source of transportation, comfort, prestige, and the like. One interesting aspect of this approach is a recognition that often, if not always, the market commodity does not generate its satisfying attributes unaided. Rather, the consumer generally elicits satisfaction from commodities by combining his own time and effort with the market goods themselves. Utility can thus be regarded as generated by activities subject to *income constraints* (upon the purchase of market goods) and *time constraints* (upon the hours to be allocated for their enjoyment), as discussed in the previous section.

We will not attempt to develop the formal theory here, but will point to two interesting implications:

1. Why some market goods are close substitutes, and others are not, becomes much easier to understand in this approach. Bread and potatoes (substitutes) have generally similar attributes; bread and haircuts do not. Substitutability thus, to a considerable extent, becomes an analyzable rather than a merely arbitrary fact.

2. The process whereby market commodities are combined with consumers' time and efforts can be regarded as *production within the household*, analogous to the ordinary productive process within business firms. Indeed, production within the home often competes directly with outside production, as in home washing versus commercial laundries. It is an interesting empirical question how much of the historical advance in standards of living is due to improved methods of business production, such as interchangeability of parts, more powerful energy sources, newer and better-yielding crops, etc., and how much is due to improvements that operate mainly in the consumption sphere, such as electric light, radio and television, or new fabrics for clothing.

Questions

1. In terms of the example "Charitable Giving," is charitable donation (regarded as a consumption "commodity") a luxury? What is the "price" of charitable giving? Is elasticity with respect to this price greater at high prices or low prices?

2. What is the difference between a Laspeyres index and a Paasche index? Show the geometrical meaning of a Laspeyres quantity index that is less than unity. Show the geometrical measuring of a Paasche quantity index that exceeds unity. What conclusions as to relative well-being can be drawn in these two cases? Why can no conclusion be drawn in the opposed cases?

3. What is an income-compensated demand curve? How does it differ from the ordinary demand curve? For a normal good (positive income elasticity), which of the two curves is the more elastic?

4. Gasoline rationing has been proposed as one possible remedy for the recent "energy crisis." If rations were distributed on an egalitarian basis, show the situations of a wealthy and a poor consumer in terms of opportunity set for gasoline consumption versus "all other goods." Show typical indifference maps if automobile usage is a luxury. Would permitting sale of coupons be a good idea?

5. It is often thought that the wealthy must have a great deal of leisure. On the other hand, members of present-day richer societies tend to be more harried and pressed for time than were their own grandparents who lacked so many modern time-saving devices. Interpret in terms of the time constraint on consumption.

Three

Equilibrium and Exchange

Chapter 7
Equilibrium, Exchange, and the Gains from Trade

Up to now we have analyzed only the private decisions of individuals (or households)—the ultimate economic agents. In this chapter we make the transition from *individual* behavior to *market* phenomena, with a corresponding shift of emphasis from the technique of *optimization* to the technique of *determination of equilibrium*.

7. A THE FUNDAMENTAL THEOREM OF EXCHANGE

Voluntary trade is mutually beneficial (i.e., utility-increasing for both parties). This is the Fundamental Theorem of Exchange. An alternative, mistaken view is the "exploitation theory," that in exchange one party's gain is the other party's loss. The proof of the Fundamental Theorem, and disproof of the exploitation theory, would hardly seem to require any long or difficult reasoning. It follows immediately from the postulate of rational behavior. If exchange were not beneficial for both parties, one or the other would refuse to trade. And yet it is astonishing how many misconceptions of economic problems, for example, the most commonly encountered arguments for protective tariffs, rest upon failure to appreciate the obvious truth that exchange is mutually beneficial.[1]

There are, it is true, debatable aspects of this sweeping theorem. (1) Suppose trickery has taken place: A purchaser pays good money for a beachfront lot that turns out to be a mile out to sea. In this case there was no actual *agreement*, no meeting of minds. Hence the transaction was not really a mutually voluntary exchange. (2) More problematically, it may be that the momentary desires on which an exchange is based do not represent an individual's true considered preferences. Esau sold his birthright to Jacob for a mess of pottage, and regretted the transaction afterward. (3) Still more seriously, the question remains as to whether individuals truly benefit from

[1]This should not be understood as denying the possible validity of more sophisticated arguments for protective tariffs (or for other trade-hindering interventions).

having even their fully-considered preferences satisfied. That a person's desires do not necessarily lead him to where his true benefit lies has been a theme of moralists through the ages.

While these philosophical questions cannot be studied here, we see that there are possible qualifications to the Fundamental Theorem. Nevertheless, accepting the postulate of rationality, it remains the case that each participant in exchange benefits *according to his own lights at the time of decision*, though possibly not in the opinion of an outside observer (or even in his own opinion at some later date).

There are two distinct elements in the mutual gain from trade. The first element is an *improved allocation of consumption goods* over individuals. Suppose there are two persons, let us call them John and Karl, somehow endowed with equal quantities of tea and coffee (perhaps as a result of a wartime rationing system). If John prefers tea and Karl prefers coffee, the potential gain from trade will be obvious. Nor are differences of taste necessary. Suppose that John and Karl, having the same preferences, find themselves in possession of quantities of bread and butter, except that John has all the bread and Karl all the butter. Again, we see that trade can improve consumptive allocations for both.

The second source of improvement, an indirect consequence of the first, is due to *rearrangement of production* rather than of consumption. In the illustration just given, if John were better at baking bread and Karl at churning butter, the possibility of later trading would permit each to concentrate productively upon the activity for which he is better suited. Improved production would make a greater total of goods available to all, apart from the improved consumptive distributions that trade brings about once the goods are produced.

Conclusion: Voluntary trade is mutually beneficial because traders can: (1) reallocate existing stocks of consumption goods so that each achieves a preferred bundle, and (2) specialize in production so as to increase the social totals of goods available.

Sections 7.B and 7.C immediately following concentrate upon the *consumptive* improvement due to trade. Afterward, attention will be turned to the *productive* improvement and to its interaction with the consumptive gains.

7. B THE EDGEWORTH BOX, THE ADVANTAGE OF TRADE, AND COMPETITIVE EQUILIBRIUM

How exchange makes possible mutually advantageous improvements in the allocation of consumption goods can be conveniently illustrated, for two persons John and Karl, by the geometrical device of the "Edgeworth box" in Figure 7.1. For John, the origin O_j is at the lower-left corner as usual; his preference map (consisting of indifference curves U'_j, U''_j, ...) is drawn upon axes representing his consumption quantities x_j and y_j of commodities X and Y, respectively. For Karl, the directions are reversed. Karl's origin O_k is at

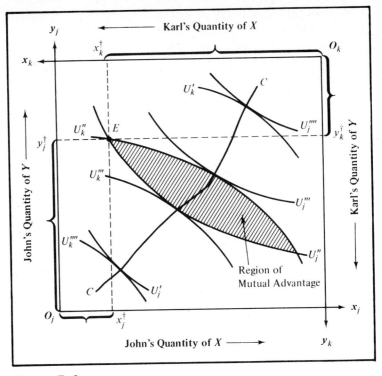

Figure 7. 1
Edgeworth Box

the upper-right corner of the box; his indifference curves are drawn with respect to his consumption quantities x_k and y_k. The arrows attached to the axes indicate that, for commodity X, John's quantity x_j is measured by distance to the *right* of O_j and Karl's quantity x_k by distance to the *left* of O_k; similarly, John's y_j is measured *upward* from O_j and Karl's y_k *downward* from O_k.

The width and height of the Edgeworth box are determined by the pairwise social totals $\bar{X}$ and $\bar{Y}$ of the two commodities, where $\bar{X} = x_j + x_k$ and $\bar{Y} = y_j + y_k$. These social totals are assumed fixed in the present model, in order to isolate the consumptive from the productive aspect of trade. Since the individuals in this two-person economy do not produce (production being a process that changes the social totals of commodities), their opportunity sets reflect *only* the possibilities of reallocating the fixed social totals of commodities through exchange. It follows that if John's consumption x_j increases then Karl's x_k must correspondingly decrease unit for unit, and similarly for the consumed quantities y_j and y_k of commodity Y.

The initial allocation of the two goods between John and Karl is shown by the *endowment* position E in Figure 7.1. John's endowment consists of the quantities $x_j^{\dagger}$ and $y_j^{\dagger}$ measured to the east and to the north, respectively, from his origin O_j. Karl's endowment consists of the quantities $x_k^{\dagger}$ and $y_k^{\dagger}$ measured

166

to the west and to the south from his origin O_k. Trading entails a shift to some other allocation of the social totals, i.e., to some position other than E in the box. If X and Y are *goods* for both parties, then each will insist upon receiving more of the one commodity in exchange for giving up some of the other. The allocations permitted by this condition (i.e., achievable by voluntary exchange) are those lying either toward the southeast *or* toward the northwest of the initial endowment position E.

But a still stronger condition can be placed on the mutually advantageous exchanges that are possible. Consider the traders' respective indifference curves U_j'' and U_k'' that pass through the endowment position E. If trade is voluntary and the individuals are rational, neither will ever move to a point at a lower preference level than he has already attained at E. Each will only move "uphill" from E on his utility surface. Consequently, the possible final allocations are only those lying within the shaded lens-shaped region in the diagram between U_j'' and U_k''. This area is called the *region of mutual advantage*.

Example 7. 1
Economic
Exchange and
the American
Civil War

Before the Civil War, the Northern and Southern states had engaged in a mutually advantageous economic exchange. The South produced a vast surplus of cotton, which was sold in the North (and also abroad), the proceeds being used to purchase manufactured products. Less than 10% of the total pre-war (1860) national value of manufactures had been produced in the seceded states.[2]

With the onset of the war, direct North-South trade was interrupted. The interruption hit the Confederacy much harder than the Union. While cotton prices in the North jumped, the negative impact upon textile availability was an inconvenience rather than a catastrophe. But the Union blockade largely prevented the export of Southern cotton, and then took a heavy toll of the limited amounts of manufactured products that could be purchased with the cotton that did slip through. (The small blockade-running traffic was largely used for the import of luxury goods. "When Captain Hobart Pasha of the *Venus* asked a Southern woman in England what was most needed in the Confederacy, she unhesitatingly replied, 'Corsets'.")[3] Despite valiant effort to redirect production, the South was brought to economic and military collapse by its inability to acquire essential manufactured civilian products and implements of war, while huge stocks of unsalable cotton piled up uselessly in her storehouses.

Confederate trade policy was seriously misguided. Export of the

[2]Albert D. Kirwan, ed., *The Confederacy* (New York: Meridian Books, 1959), p. 63.
[3]Clement Eaton, *A History of the Southern Confederacy* (New York: Macmillan, 1954), p. 144.

huge cotton crops of 1861 and 1862 to earn credits abroad would have been possible, as the Union blockade only really became effective in later years. The Confederate government discouraged this export! They reasoned that, since "Cotton was King," withholding the crop would force Northern (and foreign) industrial interests to support the secession. Relying on their opponents' loss of the advantage of trade, the South's leaders failed to realize how much more vulnerable their own largely one-crop economy was to the interruption of mutually advantageous exchange.

An even more striking error was the policy of the Confederate government that banned trade through the lines with the North, partly on moralistic grounds, partly again to withhold "King Cotton." This was illogical for several reasons, one of which was that most of the cotton run through the blockade to Cuba or Bermuda was transshipped to the North anyway. But more important, a strict ban on trade through the lines was, for the Union, a logical complement to the sea blockade, a component of the "anaconda" policy of strangling the Southern economy. In contrast, it was in the interest of the South to break this overland ban almost as much as it was to evade the sea blockade. It is true the the cotton and tobacco that could have been sent North would, to some degree, have helped the Northern war economy. But the Confederacy, its economy collapsing because of inability to dispose of its surpluses for needed imports of all kinds, was in a position where it had to grasp every opportunity. Actually, a substantial (though unrecorded) amount of illegal trade did pass through the lines; despite the attempts of officials on both sides to stop the practice, the temptations of corruption and the real needs of the Southern economy at times proved to be an overwhelming combination. Curiously, even today historians commonly take a moralistic attitude on this question, and fail to appreciate the fundamental asymmetry in position that made maintenance of the land blockade a wise policy for the Union, but an unwise one for the Confederacy.[4]

[4]This discussion is based on J. Hirshleifer, "Disaster and Recovery: A Historical Survey," The Rand Corporation Memorandum RM-3079-PR (April 1963), Section IV.

The lens-shaped region of mutual advantage is shown again in Figure 7.2. Suppose that market *prices* are now established, by some impersonal process not dependent upon the decisions of our two individuals John and Karl. We say that each is a *competitive* trader or "price-taker." The price ratio P_x/P_y, we know, is the absolute value of the slope of the budget line in an indifference-curve diagram like Figure 4.1. But the Edgeworth box, Figure 7.2, is a double indifference-curve diagram. Suppose hypothetically that prices are such that the dashed line *KL* is the budget line. For John, *KL* passes through

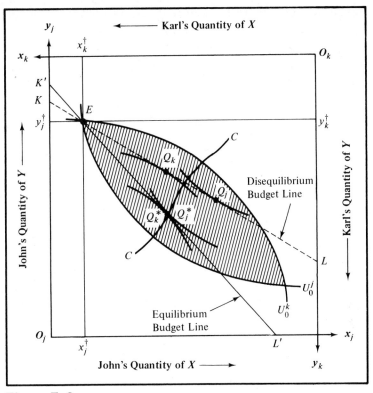

Figure 7. 2
Budget Lines and Competitive Equilibrium

his endowment position $E = (x_j^\dagger y_j^\dagger)$ and represents an upper (northeast) boundary of his market opportunities (just as in Figure 4.1). But in the Edgeworth box KL must also serve as budget line for Karl, passing through his endowment position $E = (x_k^\dagger, y_k^\dagger)$. Since Karl's axes are inverted, KL as upper limit for him bounds the market opportunity set toward the *southwest* rather than northeast.

With KL as budget line in Figure 7.2, John would want to proceed to a consumptive optimum indicated by the position Q_j. Similarly, Karl would want to move to his optimum along KL at Q_k. But the two points Q_j and Q_k do not coincide! This means that the quantity of X that John wishes to purchase, offering Y in exchange in accordance with the price ratio represented by the slope of KL, is *not* equal to the quantity that Karl is prepared to supply at that price ratio. If John and Karl are the only two transactors, the situation is not one of competitive equilibrium. The difficulty is that KL represents a price ratio P_x/P_y such that X is too cheap relative to Y, the buyer (John) seeking to take more X than the seller (Karl) is willing to offer.

An *equilibrium price ratio* for competitive trading is represented by the steeper line $K'L'$ in Figure 7.2, corresponding to a higher price ratio P_x'/P_y'. At this price ratio both parties are led to *coinciding* preferred positions $Q_j^* = Q_k^*$, meaning that the amount of commodity X offered by Karl equals the amount willingly purchased by John. (Correspondingly, of course, the quantity of Y offered by John in payment must also exactly balance the amount required by Karl.) This discussion can be summed up as follows.

Proposition: In the Edgeworth box, the competitive equilibrium allocation of the two commodities (1) lies in the region of mutual advantage, and (2) represents a mutual tangency of both traders' indifference curves with one another and with a common budget line.

Now imagine a number of possible variations of the endowment position E. For each such E, there will be a different region of mutual advantage and equilibrium budget line. But the only *potential* competitive equilibria are the points representing mutual tangencies of indifference curves of John and Karl, since only then do the consumptive optimum positions coincide. The curve connecting these mutual tangencies is known as the *contract curve*, shown as CC in both Figure 7.1 and Figure 7.2.

In Section 4.A, the concept of the Marginal Rate of Substitution in Consumption, MRS_C—the rate at which an individual is just willing to make a small exchange of X for Y—was introduced. It was also shown that MRS_C corresponds to the absolute value of the indifference-curve slope between commodities X and Y. Consumptive *optimality* was attained, as indicated in equation (4.4), where $MRS_C = P_x/P_y$, i.e., where the indifference-curve slope equals the budget-line slope. We see from the above discussion that *a condition of competitive equilibrium is that consumptive optimality holds for both traders:*

$$(7.1) \qquad MRS_C^j = P_x/P_y = MRS_C^k$$

Generalizing, the consumptive optimality condition $MRS_C = P_x/P_y$ (developed in Chapter 4 for *any single* trader) must, in competitive equilibrium, be holding for *every* trader.

The other formal condition of equilibrium can be expressed as:

$$(7.2) \qquad \left\{ \begin{array}{l} x_j + x_k = \bar{X} \\ y_j + y_k = \bar{Y} \end{array} \right.$$

In general terms, we can say: The price ratio must be such that the sum of the individuals' desired consumption quantities must equal the social total available, for every commodity.

7. C SUPPLY AND DEMAND IN PURE EXCHANGE

Competitive equilibrium is only rather artificially pictured in the 2-person Edgeworth box diagram, though this picture was useful in showing how trade contributes to mutually desired consumptive reallocations. More familiarly, we think of competitive equilibrium as determined by an intersection of supply and demand curves (as in Section 2.A). The demand-supply formulation overcomes the limitation of the Edgeworth box to two *persons*, but we will continue for the present to maintain the simplifying assumption of only two *goods*.

The elements underlying the determinants of equilibrium stand out most clearly if we continue to assume a hypothetical world without production—a world of *pure exchange*. In such a world the only purpose of trade is the reallocation of consumption goods. Each individual i comes to market with an endowment $E_i = (x_i^\dagger, y_i^\dagger)$ of consumptive commodities X and Y; trade redistributes the goods among persons, but there is no change in the social totals of commodities. Later on in the chapter, *production* will be introduced as a process that transforms the social totals of commodities, leading to a generalized conception of supply-demand equilibrium.

We have already seen (in Section 4.B.2) how an individual's demand curve for a commodity X is derived—by parametric variation of his consumptive optimum in response to changes of the price ratio P_x/P_y (or simply of P_x, since P_y can be assumed constant). This process led to the Price Expansion Path (PEP) of Figure 4.10 which, upon translation to x, P_x-axes, yielded the individual's demand curve as in Figure 4.12.

Panel (a) of Figure 7.3 here looks very much like Figure 4.10 of the earlier

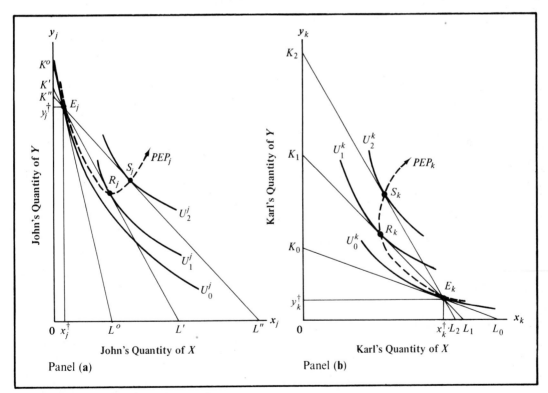

Figure 7. 3 Price Expansion Paths

chapter. We see once again a Price Expansion Path PEP_j, for an individual j (John), drawn through the various possible consumptive optimum positions (tangencies of indifference curves U_0^j, U_1^j, U_2^j, . . . with respective budget lines $K°L°$, $K'L'$, K'', L'', . . .) at points like E^j, R^j, and S^j. The novel feature, carried over from the Edgeworth-box picture of Figures 7.1 and 7.2, is the assignment to John of a specific starting point or *endowment position* E_j. That is, John comes to market already in possession of specific amounts $x_j^\dagger$ and $y_j^\dagger$ of commodities X and Y, respectively. Since he is relatively better endowed with commodity Y, we would normally expect John to be a *net demander* of X (and, therefore, a *net supplier* of Y). For Karl, pictured in Panel (b) of the diagram, the opposite holds. As his endowment $E_k = (x_k^\dagger, y_k^\dagger)$ is heavily weighted in favor of commodity X, we would normally expect him to be a *net supplier* of X (and therefore a *net demander* of commodity Y). For Karl, the Price Expansion Path PEP_k in Panel (b) is also drawn through all his consumptive optimum positions associated with the different possible budget lines such as K_0L_0, K_1L_1, and K_2L_2.

In Panel (a), we see that John's endowment position E_j is itself a point on his Price Expansion Path PEP_j. This means that, although we expect John to be a net demander of X, there is some price ratio P_x/P_y so high that he will prefer to stand pat with his endowment and not make any additional purchases of X. This "sustaining" price ratio corresponds geometrically to the absolute slope of the steep budget line $K°L°$ in the diagram, tangent at position E_j with John's indifference curve U_0^j. Indeed, P_x/P_y might conceivably rise so high (higher even than the sustaining price ratio) as to make John a *net supplier* rather than a net demander of X. That is, a budget line even steeper than $K°L°$ would lead in Panel (a) to a tangency optimum for John somewhere northwest of E_j, as reflected by the extension of the PEP_j curve into that region. Normally, however, John would encounter in the market a somewhat lower price ratio (reflected by the slopes of budget lines like $K'L'$ or $K''L''$) and would accordingly find an optimum consumptive position somewhere to the southeast of E_j. In moving from the endowment position E_j to an optimum position like R_j or S_j to the southeast, John would be giving up units of Y for units of X, i.e., he would be a net demander of X from the market and thus a net supplier of Y.

A corresponding analysis applies for Karl. The low price ratio corresponding to the rather flat absolute slope of the budget line K_0L_0 "sustains" his endowment position E_k; at this price ratio he will stand pat with his endowment at the tangency with indifference curve U_0^k. At still lower price ratios Karl would even be a net demander of X, as represented by the extension of PEP_k to the southeast of E_k. But more normally, at the higher price ratios reflected in the slopes of budget lines like K_1L_1 and K_2L_2, Karl would move northwest from E_k to an optimum position like R_k or S_k. That is, he would give up some of his ample X-endowment for Y; he would be a net supplier of X to the market, and so a net demander of Y.

The next step is the transfer of the data represented by the Price Expansion Paths of the panels of Figure 7.3 into demand and supply curves on x,P_x-axes.

It is very important to appreciate that this can be done in two different meaningful ways: The first way makes use of *net* (or "excess") quantities, and the second of *gross* (or "full") quantities, demanded and supplied.

The relation between net and gross magnitudes, for any individual *i*, is given by:

(7.3)
$$\begin{cases} x_i^n = x_i - x_i^\dagger \\ y_i^n = y_i - y_i^\dagger \end{cases}$$
Net and Gross Demands

The first equation of (7.3) says that the *net* quantity of commodity *X* demanded by individual *i* from the market, x_i^n, is equal to his *gross* quantity demanded for purposes of consumption, x_i, minus the quantity already in his possession before trading, $x_i^\dagger$. The second equation expresses a corresponding relation for commodity *Y*. In Panel (a) of Figure 7.3, the gross quantity of *X* associated with any consumptive optimum position like E_j, R_j, or S_j along the PEP_j curve is simply the *x*-coordinate of that position—the horizontal distance from that point on the PEP_j curve to the vertical axis. The net quantity is this horizontal distance *less* the endowed amount $x_j^\dagger$, the *x*-coordinate of E_j. It follows, of course, that at the price ratio for which E_j is a consumptive optimum position (at the sustaining price ratio), John's *gross* demand for *X* equals $x_j^\dagger$—and his *net* demand for *X* is zero.

The net or excess demands x_i^n and y_i^n in equation (7.3) can be positive or negative. Negative net demand is, of course, positive net supply. But note that the *gross* magnitudes x_i and y_i and the endowed quantities $x_i^\dagger$ and $y_i^\dagger$ are necessarily non-negative; neither consumption nor endowment can ever be less than zero.

The distinction between gross and net magnitudes is important in a number of areas, among them the theory of taxation. A tax on *consumption* of a good *X* is one levied upon the gross demands; a tax on *purchases* of *X* is one that burdens only the net or market demands. Put another way, endowed quantities that are self-consumed escape a "transaction tax" on purchases, but do not escape a tax on consumption. In advanced, highly specialized economies, it is true, we do not ordinarily regard individuals as already endowed with significant quantities of each of the host of goods consumed. But a large group of people—in particular, a nation as a whole—may well be in a position to self-supply desired commodities to some extent, aside from whatever amounts can be obtained from other groups or nations by purchase in the market.

We can now turn to the geometrical relations between gross and net demand and supply.

Any price P_x (corresponding to a price ratio P_x/P_y, since P_y is assumed constant) is associated with a particular consumptive optimum position along an individual *i*'s PEP_i curve. Plotting the *x*-coordinate of that position against the price P_x gives a point on his *gross* demand curve d_i in Figure 7.4. Speaking more generally, the data represented by the PEP_i curve can be replotted on x,P_x-axes to yield the gross demand curve d_i.

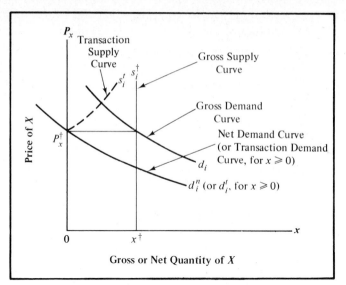

Figure 7. 4
Demand and Supply, Gross
and Net, in Pure Exchange

The *net* demand curve d_i^n is obtained by simply subtracting (horizontally) the endowment quantity x_i^t from the gross demand d_i. It is instructive to think of the vertical line, representing the individual's fixed X-endowment x_i^t, as his (gross) *supply curve of X*—symbolized as s_i^t. Then in correspondence with equations (7.3) relating gross and net magnitudes we have the geometrical relation:

(7.4) $$d_i^n = d_i - s_i^t$$

This says that, at any price P_x, an individual's net demand equals his gross demand less his endowed supply.[5] Note that at the price P_x^t representing the individual's *sustaining price*, his gross demand equals his endowed supply, so that his net demand becomes zero.

At prices *higher* than the sustaining price, the net demand curve d_i^n enters a negative region. Rather than deal with an individual's *negative net demand*, it is usually more convenient to speak of his *positive net supply*. This is represented geometrically, in Figure 7.4, by the dashed curve s_i^t, representing the mirror image of the negative range of d_i^n for prices above P_x^t. The superscript "t" signifies that s_i^t is a *transaction supply* curve, representing the necessarily non-negative magnitudes offered on the market at prices higher than P_x^t. On

---

[5] In Chapter 4 the individual was endowed with a quantity I of *income* in numeraire units, rather than with specific x_i^t and y_i^t amounts of X and Y. But since P_x was allowed to vary with P_y held constant, in effect the person could be regarded as endowed with I/P_y units of commodity Y and none of X, so that position K on the Y-axis of Figure 4.10 served as the equivalent of an initial endowment position. Hence for the individual in Chapter 4 the gross and net demands for X were identical.

the demand side, individual i's *transaction demand* curve d_i^t, the non-negative range of his net demand curve d_i^n, represents the positive net amounts demanded when $P_x < P_x^t$.

We can now return to the two price-taking traders, John and Karl, for whom PEP curves were pictured in Figure 7.3. Karl's *transaction supply* curve s_k^t, and John's *transaction demand* curve d_j^t, are plotted in Panel (a) of Figure 7.5. John's sustaining price $P_x^t(j)$ is at the point where d_j^t contacts the vertical axis. Similarly, Karl's sustaining price $P_x^t(k)$ is where s_j^t contacts the vertical axis.

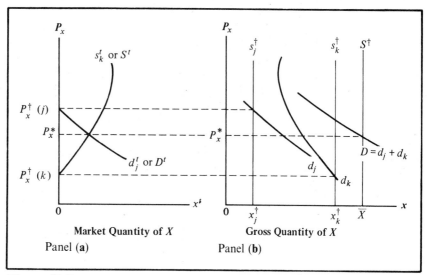

Figure 7. 5
Supply-Demand Equilibrium

If the two traders, John and Karl, can be regarded as constituting the demand and supply sides of a competitive market, the equilibrium price P_x^* is of course at the intersection of d_j^t and s_k^t in Figure 7.5. More generally, of course, *all* the individual demanders' d_j^t curves would be aggregated (summed horizontally) into an aggregate transaction demand curve, or *market* demand curve, D^t, and *all* the suppliers' s_k^t curves into an aggregate transaction supply curve or *market* supply curve S^t. It is the intersection of D^t and S^t that would determine the equilibrium price and quantity. Henceforth in this chapter the aggregation process will be short-circuited by assuming that the two traders John and Karl can serve as a microcosm of the supply and demand sides of the entire market.

Panel (b) of Figure 7.5 shows the other instructive way of looking at the 2-person supply-demand equilibrium. Here, instead of net quantities supplied to or demanded from *the market*, we consider the gross magnitudes demanded (for consumption) from or supplied (via endowment) to *the economy*. The difference between the two concepts is due to the quantities self-supplied for consumption out of a trader's own endowment.

Consider the supply side first. Panel (b) of Figure 7.5 shows John's endowed-supply curve $s_j^\dagger$ (at horizontal distance $x_j^\dagger$ from the origin) and Karl's endowed-supply curve $s_k^\dagger$ (at horizontal distance $x_k^\dagger$ from the origin). The horizontal sum of $s_j^\dagger$ and $s_k^\dagger$ is the two-person aggregate endowed supply $S^\dagger$—the fixed social total $\bar{X}$ available to the economy in this pure-exchange world. On the demand side, of course, the aggregate gross demand D is simply the sum of the individual gross demands d_j and d_k.

The equilibrium price P_x^* in Panel (b), at the intersection of $S^\dagger$ and D, must represent the same price as the intersection of S^t and D^t in Panel (a). At this price John's net demand is positive (his gross demand d_j exceeds his endowed supply $s_j^\dagger$) but this is exactly offset by Karl's positive net supply (the excess of Karl's $s_k^\dagger$ over his gross demand d_k).

The intersection of S^t and D^t in Panel (a) of Figure 7.5, or of $S^\dagger$ and D in Panel (b), determine the equilibrium for commodity X. But it will be evident that the equilibrium for commodity Y is also being implicitly determined. The mathematics of this process, and in particular the demonstration that equilibrium is associated with the level of *relative* prices or price ratio P_x/P_y, are set forth in Section A.1 of the Appendix at the end of the text.

We may note that the demand curves entering into the determination of equilibrium are *not* the "compensated" demands (discussed in Section 6.C above) but rather the "ordinary" demand curves. It is the ordinary demand curves (and associated supply curves) that summarize the market reactions that lead to equilibrium.[6]

We should, of course, be thinking of the equilibriating process as taking place not as between only two commodities X and Y but over all goods simultaneously. The result is a *general* equilibrium of prices and quantities. However, the underlying principles—individual optimization, and the balance of transaction demand and transaction supply in the market—are in no way different from the principles illustrated in the simplified 2-good world.

7. D EXCHANGE AND PRODUCTION

So far in this chapter we have considered trade in a world without production, a world of "pure exchange." Under pure exchange individuals can alter their endowments of commodities *only* through the market process, as illustrated in the Edgeworth box of Figure 7.1. But in the actual world individuals can also modify endowments by *production*, by dealing (so to speak) with Nature rather than or in addition to engaging in transactions with other people. To take the extreme opposite case, Robinson Crusoe (before Friday's arrival) could deal *only* with Nature; he could physically produce and consume, but could not trade. What we really want to consider, of course, is the interaction of the economic processes of production, consumption, *and* exchange in a multi-person economy.

[6]The importance of the "compensated" demand functions, as discussed in the preceding chapter, lies in the analysis of the sources of observed historical *changes* in equilibrium positions.

To begin with, production appears here only in a limited sense that is sometimes called *productive transformation*. This means taking account of production only as offering the physical possibility of alternative "output" baskets of consumptive commodities like X and Y. The role of "factors of production"—commodities not desired in and of themselves, but only as *inputs* for generating consumptive goods—is left in the background. Only in Part Five following will we take up production as an explicit input-output process that converts factors into products.

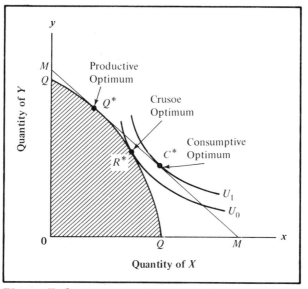

Figure 7. 6
Productive and Consumptive Optimum
Positions

In Figure 7.6, the alternative output baskets of commodities X and Y that an individual might be able to produce are shown as the shaded region, called his *productive opportunity set*. Compare its shape with that of the pure-exchange *market opportunity set OKL* in Figure 4.1. The northeast boundary of the market opportunity set in the earlier diagram was the budget line. The northeast boundary QQ of the productive opportunity set here is called the *transformation locus* or *Production-Possibility Curve* (PPC), whose "concave" shape represents a kind of diminishing returns in productive transformation. Suppose an individual producer (or a nation) tried to "specialize" by concentrating upon the production of commodity X, i.e., tried to produce a combination well toward the X-axis along QQ. As specialization is pushed further and further, each increment of X requires a greater and greater sacrifice of Y. We say that *increasing opportunity costs*, sacrifices of potential output of the other commodity Y, are encountered. Diminishing returns in productive transformation are not derivable from the pure logic of economic theory; rather, they supposedly constitute an observed fact of Nature.

(Concavity of the transformation locus thus rests upon the same observational basis as the convex shape of indifference curves discussed in Section 3.E.)

Returning for the moment to the case of a Robinson Crusoe possessing *only* productive transformation opportunities, his optimum consumption basket in Figure 7.6 is R^*, the tangency of his transformation locus QQ with his highest attainable indifference curve U_0. Since Crusoe cannot engage in trade, R^* represents for him a joint *productive-consumptive optimum*. The tangency condition can be expressed as the equation:

$$ (7.5) \qquad\qquad MRS_C = MRS_T \qquad \text{Robinson Crusoe Optimum} $$

MRS_C, the Marginal Rate of Substitution in Consumption, corresponds as we know to the absolute indifference-curve slope. The new symbol MRS_T stands for the *Marginal Rate of Substitution in Productive Transformation;* more briefly, *Marginal Rate of Transformation*. Note how the opposing curvatures (of the transformation locus QQ versus the indifference curves) guarantee that there will be a unique tangency R^*.[7] We say that there is *decreasing* Marginal Rate of Substitution in Consumption, but *increasing* Marginal Rate of Transformation.

Now let us drop the mythical Robinson Crusoe case and consider the interaction of productive and trading opportunities. We can imagine that Crusoe is discovered by the world and thus is put into contact with a market in which he becomes a competitive trader or "price-taker." His market opportunities are shown in Figure 7.6 by the *market line MM* just tangent to the transformation locus QQ. The absolute slope of the market line represents the ruling price ratio P_x/P_y. The existence of market opportunities permits a trader *to separate his productive and consumptive decisions*. Specifically, the formerly isolated individual can now attain his *consumptive optimum* (most preferred combination of x and y) at C^* on indifference curve U_1 by a two-step procedure. First, he moves along QQ to his *productive optimum* Q^*, the tangency of the Production-Possibility Curve with the market line MM. From Q^*, by exchanging X for Y he can move southeast along MM so as to finally achieve the consumptive optimum at C^*. A comparison of the Crusoe solution R^* with the optimum C^* attainable in a world with exchange reveals the advantage gained from the separation of productive and consumptive optimum positions that is made possible by trade.

The productive optimum position Q^* is associated with the equation:

$$ (7.6) \qquad\qquad MRS_T = MRS_E \equiv \frac{P_x}{P_y} \qquad \text{Productive Optimum Condition} $$

[7]*Mathematical Footnote:* In terms of derivatives, the condition can be expressed as:

$$ \frac{dy}{dx}\Big|_U = \frac{dy}{dx}\Big|_Q $$

In addition, the individual must be on his Production-Possibility Curve, which can be expressed as the equation $Q(x,y) = 0$.

The individual sets his Marginal Rate of Transformation along QQ equal to the Marginal Rate of Substitution *in Exchange*, the absolute price ratio P_x/P_y ruling in the market. This condition in effect moves the individual *onto* the market line MM at point Q^*. The consumptive optimum condition, achieved by movement *along MM* to C^*, is:

$$(7.7) \qquad \frac{P_x}{P_y} \equiv MRS_E = MRS_C \qquad \text{Consumptive Optimum Condition}$$

The latter condition is the same as equation (4.4).

Since (7.6) and (7.7) together imply $MRS_T = MRS_C$, (7.5) holds in a world of exchange as well as for an isolated Robinson Crusoe. But for Crusoe MRS_C and MRS_T are equated *at the same point* R* *along* QQ, whereas for a trader the productive and consumptive solutions are separated. MRS_T is defined along QQ, and MRS_C along an indifference curve lying above QQ, this separation being made possible by trading along the market line MM.

We have not yet discussed the forces that determine the equilibrium price ratio P_x/P_y, and therefore the slope of the market line MM facing particular producer-traders. These forces can be expressed, of course, in terms of supply and demand.

Just as in the case of pure exchange, it will be useful to define gross and net supply and demand concepts in a world of productive transformation. Figure 7.7 is analogous to Figure 7.4. In pure exchange the individual's gross supply of X to the economy was simply his given endowed quantity x_i^t, independent of price, and therefore represented by the vertical line s_i^t in Figure 7.4. But in

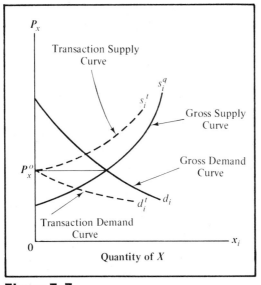

Figure 7. 7
Demand and Supply,
Gross and Net, with Production

a world of production and exchange, an individual's gross supply of X is the result of his productive decision in response to the ruling market price. In Figure 7.7, the person's gross supply curve s^q represents, for any price P_x, the x-coordinate of the *productive optimum* Q^* in the preceding Figure 7.6. As P_x rises (with P_y held constant), the market line MM in Figure 7.6 grows increasingly steep. The tangency of MM with the transformation locus QQ at Q^* therefore shifts around to the southeast. This shift represents an increased quantity of X produced, thus demonstrating that the individual's produced-supply curve s^q for commodity X is a rising function of price P_x. (Of course, the quantity of Y produced will be a correspondingly falling function of P_x.)

The gross demand curve d_i of Figure 7.7 similarly represents, for any price P_x, the x-coordinate of the individual's *consumptive optimum* C^* in Figure 7.6. The shape of the d_i curve reflects the movement of the C^* position in response to price changes that alter the slope of the market line MM tangent to the production possibility curve QQ. Consider first that particular price P_x^o leading to a market line MM for which Q^* and C^* coincide at the Crusoe solution R^* of Figure 7.6. This is called the individual's "autarky price."[8] Since at P_x^o the individual's consumptive demand for X just equals his own produced supply, the gross supply curve s_i^q and the gross demand curve d_i coincide at that price. For prices lower than the autarky price, the market line MM will have flatter slope than the slope of QQ at R^*. Then the productive optimum Q^* will shift around to the northwest along QQ, and the consumptive optimum will move out along MM to the southeast. The reverse holds true as P_x rises above the autarky price.

What about the individual's transaction demand from or transaction supply *to the market*? In analogy with the discussion of the preceding section, the s_i^t curve of Figure 7.7 represents the positive net amounts supplied (for prices higher than P_x^o) and the d_i^t curve the positive net amounts demanded (at prices lower than P_x^o). Of course, at the autarky price itself there is zero net amount demanded and supplied.

Figure 7.7 describes the supply and demand curves for a single person. Equilibrium in the market as a whole is based of course upon balancing the aggregate market or transaction supply and market or transaction demand of all individuals. This is pictured in Figure 7.8, which simultaneously shows the solutions for: (1) X^*, the gross social total of X produced and consumed, and (2) X^{*t}, the aggregate amount of X exchanged in the market.

At the equilibrium price P_x^*, the aggregate quantity *produced* (along the aggregate gross supply curve S^q) must equal the aggregate amount *desired for consumption* (along the aggregate gross demand curve D). Of course, S^q is the horizontal sum of the individuals' s_i^q curves, and D the horizontal sum of their d_i curves. The same price P_x^* obtains at the intersection of the aggregate *market* supply curve S^t and the aggregate *market* demand curve D^t. Note

---

[8] The autarky price is analogous to the "sustaining price" P_x^t of pure exchange; each represents the price at which the individual does not participate in trade.

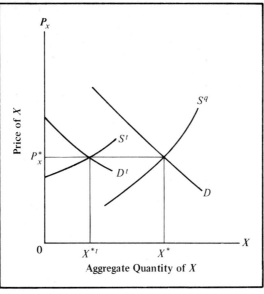

Figure 7. 8
Equilibrium of Supply and Demand
with Production

that for any single individual as in the preceding Figure 7.7, s_i^t and d_i^t intersect only along the vertical axis; no person is ever simultaneously a positive net supplier and a positive net demander. But at the equilibrium price *some* persons will be supplying and others demanding, so that X^{*t}, the volume of transactions, is positive. The difference between the X^* and X^{*t} quantities represents, in equilibrium, the amount of X produced by individuals for personal consumption rather than for trade in markets.

The "net" solution in Figure 7.8 (intersection of S^t and D^t) is the analog for a world of production and exchange of the intersection of the correspondingly labelled curves in Panel (a) of Figure 7.5 for the pure exchange case. And the "gross" solution of Figure 7.8 (intersection of S^q and D) corresponds to the intersection of S^t and D in Panel (b) of Figure 7.5. This permits us to see how the artificial illustrative world of pure exchange in Section 7.C above can be regarded as a "degenerate" instance of a realistic world in which production and exchange interact. The pure-exchange model simply replaces the upward-sloping supply curve S^q here (representing the *productive* response to changes in price) with a fixed vertical supply curve S^t, so as to permit concentration of attention upon the *consumptive* response to changes in price.

The equations of equilibrium in a world of individuals who engage both in production transformations and in exchange are set forth Section A.2 in the Appendix at the end of the text.

We can now see how trade permits a greater total of goods to be made available through *productive specialization*. The two panels of Figure 7.9 show

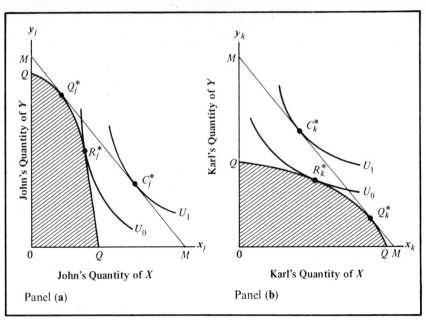

Figure 7. 9
Productive Specialization

the QQ for John and Karl respectively. The Production-Possibility Curves shapes assumed are such that John can more easily or efficiently produce commodity Y, while Karl can advantageously specialize in producing X. Yet, in the absence of trade, their diversified preferences would dictate "Robinson Crusoe solutions" R_j^* and R_k^* that both lie toward the middle of their respective Production-Possibility Curves QQ. To meet his desires for both commodities, each would have to devote a large portion of his efforts to manufacturing the good that is unsuited to his productive talents.

The opening of trade makes available market lines MM (of slope $-P_x/P_y$) to both John and Karl. The former takes advantage of the market by shifting his productive solution northwest along QQ to Q_j^*, i.e., he now *specializes in producing* Y. And this does not in any way require of him a corresponding loss of "diversity in consumption" (see Section 3.E), for he will trade the excess Y to Karl. Correspondingly, of course, Karl is enabled to become a specialist in the production of X, the excess to be traded to John. It is the adjustment of relative prices P_x/P_y (that reflect relative scarcities of goods in society as a whole), determining the slope of the market line MM, that leads each person (as if by an "Invisible Hand") to serve the interests of the other in his production decisions.

That both individuals benefit is evident from the superiority of their C_j^* and C_k^* consumptive optima in a world of exchange, in comparison with their "Crusoe" solutions R_j^* and R_k^*. And inspection reveals that the social totals available of *both* X and Y have increased.

Example 7. 2
International
Specialization
and Trade

We observe that individuals specialize in production but diversify in consumption. Should we expect the same thing of countries? To some extent, surely yes. But we would probably anticipate that the *degree* of productive specialization will be less for larger countries, which tend to have more highly varied resources and productive opportunities, and thus are less dependent upon international trade to secure diversity in consumption.

A study by M. Michaely compared the degree of specialization in the exports and imports of 44 countries, in terms of 1954 (or, in some cases, 1953 or 1952) data. The Table below shows, for a number of countries, indexes of specialization in exports and in imports. The measure of specialization employed was the "Gini coefficient," which in this case had a possible range of from 8.2 to 100.0.[9] The countries in the Table are ranked in decreasing order of export specialization. As can be seen, the group at the top tend to be small countries and the group at the bottom tend to be large. No particular pattern is evident in the specialization index for imports, a result consistent with the principle of diversity in consumption.

Indexes of Specialization of International Trade

	Exports	*Imports*
Egypt	84.2	18.6
Colombia	84.0	23.9
Gold Coast	83.5	21.4
Iceland	80.3	19.1
Finland	38.1	19.2
Mexico	35.0	26.8
Libya	34.1	18.9
Spain	33.9	24.5
Italy	20.5	20.7
U.K.	19.2	16.1
U.S.	18.8	20.5
France	18.0	20.4

Source: Michael Michaely, "Concentration of Exports and Imports: An International Comparison," *Economic Journal*, v. 68 (Dec. 1958), p. 725.

[9] The coefficient for exports is defined as $100 \sqrt{\sum_{i=1}^{n} (x_i/X)^2}$; x_i is a nation's annual value of exports of a particular good i, and X is its total annual value of exports. The goods were classified into 150 categories. If only a single good was exported by a country, the formula would show a specialization index of 100.0. If it exported all 150 goods in equal amounts, the result would be an index of 8.2. The measure of import specialization is similarly defined and has the same range.

According to the Fundamental Theorem of Exchange, trade is mutually beneficial. In practical applications it is very helpful to have a measure of the benefits of trade, scaled in objective units apart from individuals' subjective utilities. *Consumer Surplus* and *Producer Surplus* are such measures. Actually, these terms are misnomers. The benefit in question is due to the act of *trading*, rather than to the mere fact of consumption or production.

The traditional measures of Consumer Surplus (really "buyer surplus") and Producer Surplus (really "seller surplus") are illustrated in Figure 7.10.

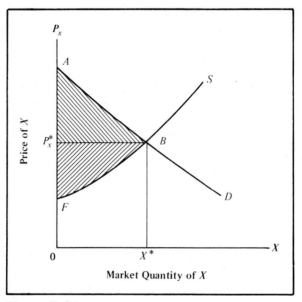

Figure 7. 10
Consumer Surplus and Producer
Surplus—Traditional Measures

In this section all supply and demand quantities are to be interpreted as aggregate transaction or *market* magnitudes; the supply and demand curves are thus the S^t and D^t curves of the previous section. This being understood, however, it is convenient to drop the superscript "t" for the remainder of the chapter. The market supply-demand equilibrium is at price P_x^* and quantity X^*. The Consumer Surplus is represented by the upper shaded area, lying beneath the demand curve D but above the horizontal line $P_x^* B$. The general intention is to show *the net advantage to consumer-buyers of being able to buy all their desired units at the ruling price P_x^**, when they would have been willing to pay higher prices (as shown by the downward-sloping demand curve) for smaller numbers of units. The Producer Surplus is the analogous lower shaded area, lying above the supply curve S but below the horizontal $P_x^* B$. It shows the net gain to producer-sellers of receiving a price as high as

P_x^* when they would have been willing to supply smaller numbers of units at lower prices (as shown by the upward-sloping supply curve).

The concepts of *demand price* (height of demand curve for any X-quantity) and *supply price* (corresponding height of supply curve) are useful here. For the very first unit purchased, the demand price in Figure 7.10 is OA. But the price charged is only OP_x^*—hence a Consumer Surplus of $OA - OP_x^* = AP_x^*$ is gained on the first unit bought. Extending this argument to all successive units suggests that, at $X = X^*$, the sum of successive demand prices (which may be called the consumers' aggregate *willingness to pay* for quantity X^*) is the roughly trapezoidal area $OABX^*$ in Figure 7.10. Since the aggregate amount charged is only the rectangle $OP_x^*BX^*$, the upper shaded roughly triangular area AP_x^*B is the Consumer Surplus.[10] A corresponding argument applies, of course, to Producer Surplus.

7. E. 1 An Application: The Water-Diamond Paradox

Many people have found it difficult to understand why a truly vital commodity like water is very cheap, while diamonds—satisfying relatively insignificant human needs—are so dear. Of course, comparisons like "cheaper" or "dearer" can be made only in terms of some common unit, and it is rather an absurdity to compare the cost of gallons of diamonds with gallons of water, or carats of diamonds with carats of water! Nevertheless, the conclusion is sometimes drawn that there is something wrong with a market system that makes the less vital commodity, diamonds, so much more expensive. This anomaly leads some people to suspect that market prices are merely arbitrary measurements, imposed in a capricious manner on goods and services.

Elementary textbooks explain the supposed "paradox" in terms of downward-sloping demand curves for both water and diamonds, together with the enormously greater supply available of the former. If water as a necessity of life were also very scarce, it would be far more valuable than diamonds. Thus, using some common physical unit (e.g., gallons) as in Figure 7.11, for equivalent quantities the demand curve for water D_w is surely far higher than the demand curve for diamonds D_d. But at the actual tremendously disparate quantities, the market price of water is lower. A fairly typical retail price of municipal water is $100 per acre-foot, or about 3 cents per hundred gallons. At this price municipal water consumption is commonly about 150 gallons (five-eighths of a ton) per capita *per day*. Diamond quantities are measured in terms of the carat (one-fifth of a gram), and gem-quality prices run upward from $1000 per carat. At such prices (on the order of $20,000,000 per *gallon*) the number of gallons of diamonds demanded per day (or even per year or per lifetime) is small!

In terms of the benefits of trade, the Consumer Surplus in water consumption must then be enormously great, not only in comparison with the Consumer Surplus for diamonds (which is only the small hatched area under the

---

[10]This argument is strictly valid only under certain special assumptions that will be discussed in the optional Section 7.E.3 below.

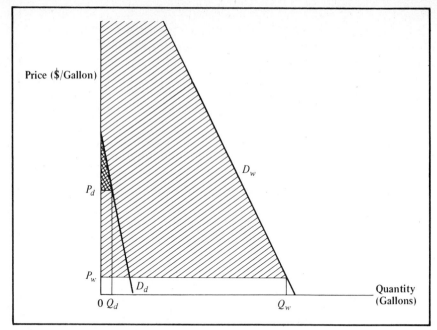

Figure 7. 11
The Water-Diamond Paradox

D_d curve), but in comparison with the actual market value of water bought and sold. The market value, $P_w q_w$, is represented in Figure 7.11 by the very low, flat rectangle lying just above the horizontal axis. The enormously greater area lying above this rectangle but below the demand curve D_w approximates the Consumer Surplus. Using the instructive terminology of Adam Smith, the aggregate *value in use* of water (total worth to consumers, or willingness to pay) is very, very large in comparison with its *value in exchange* —the difference between the two being the Consumer Surplus. For diamonds, on the other hand, there is comparatively little Consumer Surplus; the market value represents the great bulk of the aggregate value in use.

7. E. 2   Hindrances to Trade

In Section 2.A.3, taxes on transactions were analyzed. The conclusion was that, regardless of whether a tax is imposed upon buyers (shifting the demand curve down) or upon sellers (shifting the supply curve up), the effects are identical. As illustrated in Figure 7.12 (essentially equivalent to Figure 2.4), the quantity of X traded falls from a pre-tax amount X^* to a post-tax $X^\sim$. As for price, post-tax, there are *two* prices to consider: a "gross price" P_x^+ inclusive of tax and a "net price" P_x^- exclusive of tax. Buyers would be paying the gross price, whereas sellers would be receiving only the net price; hence, it is P_x^+ that is relevant for transaction demand decisions and P_x^- that is relevant for transaction supply decisions. Figure 7.12 shows that the gross

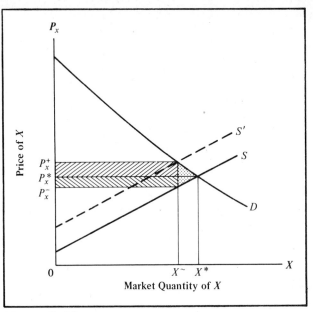

Figure 7. 12
A Tax on Transactions

price is higher than, but the net price lower than, the pre-tax equilibrium price P_x^*.

The effects of the tax upon the *gains from trade* can be analyzed in terms of the shaded and dotted areas of Figure 7.12. The entire shaded rectangle, equal to $(P_x^+ - P_x^-)X^\sim$, represents the aggregate tax collections. The upper shaded portion, lying above the previous equilibrium price P^*, is at the expense of what was formerly Consumer Surplus (since the buyers now must pay the higher price P_x^+); the lower portion, lying below P_x^*, represents a corresponding loss of Producer Surplus. However, these two losses are offset by whatever benefits stem from the uses government makes of the funds collected. And indeed, measuring in dollar units, the uses of funds must exactly balance the losses of surplus. Hence, the rectangular shaded area is a *transfer* from buyers and sellers to the beneficiaries of government expenditures.

The dotted areas in Figure 7.12 represent something quite different. The triangular upper dotted area is a *net loss* of Consumer Surplus, and the corresponding lower area a *net loss* of Producer Surplus. Here there is no gain to any other party offsetting the loss to traders. The tax, by raising the effective price to buyers and lowering the effective price to sellers, *has reduced the volume of transactions* and consequently the benefits derived from trade. The dotted areas therefore represent dead-weight losses. Their aggregate magnitude constitutes the *efficiency loss* due to the tax.

But it cannot therefore be inferred that taxes should be abolished! The transfer (shaded rectangular area) represents an equivalence *in numeraire*

187

terms between losses in Consumer and Producer Surplus on the one hand, and gains to beneficiaries of government expenditures on the other. The deadweight loss (dotted area) represents an additional loss of surplus, but it cannot be said that the "social value" (a term not defined here, and perhaps undefinable) of the government expenditures is necessarily less than the sum of the transfer and deadweight losses to traders taken together. It cannot even be proved that government revenue "should" be acquired in a way that minimizes these deadweight losses, though the analysis here is perhaps suggestive in that direction. What economics can say about such policy issues will be examined in Part Six following.

Proposition: Taxes on transactions involve a transfer from both consumers and producers to government. In addition, there is an efficiency loss due to a reduction in the volume of trade.

Taxes hamper trade through their effect on *prices*, more specifically, by driving a "wedge" between the gross price P_x^+ effective for buyers and the net price P_x^- effective for sellers. *Quantitative* restrictions on trade, to be considered next, operate somewhat differently.

Using Figure 7.13, suppose that a *quota* equal to $X' < X^*$ were imposed on the amount of commodity X that could be supplied to the market—with no restriction upon demand. The reduced quantity X' would then be sold at "whatever price the market will bear," determined along the demand curve D

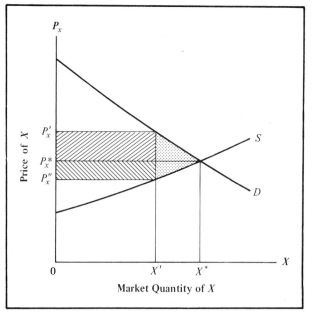

Figure 7. 13
Quota Limit on Supply

at the level P'_x. We want to compare this outcome with the unregulated equilibrium at price P^*_x and quantity X^*. The upper transfer (shaded) rectangle $(P'_x - P^*_x)X'$ is a loss of Consumer Surplus that now goes *to the suppliers* rather than to government. (And, of course, the suppliers retain the lower shaded area.) It follows that suppliers in the aggregate *may* benefit from the quantitative restriction on trading; they will do so if their transfer gain (upper shaded area) is less than their deadweight loss from the reduced volume of transactions (lower dotted area). The buyers, on the other hand, upon the imposition of a supply quota suffer *both* a transfer loss and a deadweight loss.

Now consider a quantitative restriction $X'' < X^*$ on the demand side, as by *rationing*. Then the effective price would be the lower P''_x along the supply curve in Figure 7.14. An exactly corresponding analysis will show that then the buyers *may* gain on balance, though the suppliers *must* lose.

There is one important respect, however, in which this analysis of quantitative restrictions is misleading. Indeed, the cases just discussed are ideal limiting situations; in general, the deadweight losses due to quantitative restrictions upon trade will be *much greater* than has been indicated. Let us reconsider Figure 7.14, showing consumption rationing that limits demand to the quantity X''. At the price P'' that suffices to elicit the desired quantity X'' from suppliers, the shaded area in Figure 7.14 would represent the total remaining Consumer Surplus in the "ideal" case just analyzed. But at a price as low as P''_x the buyers are desirous of purchasing not X'' but the much

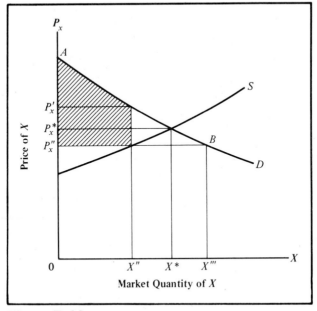

Figure 7. 14
Ration Limit on Demand

larger X'''. Somehow or other the ration tickets must be distributed so as to validate only X'' of the X''' units demanded. Only if the validated demand units correspond exactly to the most intense demands (as measured by willingness-to-pay, or demand price) will the Consumer Surplus actually received remain the shaded area in the diagram.

Consider the single most intensely demanded unit, for which some buyer is willing to pay as much as OA (where the demand curve intersects the vertical axis). It may be that the desirous buyer of this unit *does not obtain even a single ration ticket* and so cannot buy in the rationing situation. In contrast, consider the low-demand-price unit of demand at the point B along the demand curve, where some consumer is only barely willing to offer P''_x. Nonetheless, this last unit may represent demand that is validated by a ration ticket, and thus effective in a rationing situation. Note the curious consequence that rationing of demand, by leading to a low price P''_x, may induce *greater* consumption on the part of those buyers successful at obtaining ration tickets. The upshot, of course, is that the overall efficiency loss is *much greater* than would be indicated by the previous analysis.

Proposition: Production quotas involve a transfer from consumers to producers; rationing of demand involves a transfer from producers to consumers. In addition, both cause an efficiency loss due to the reduced volume of trade. There will generally be a further efficiency loss as a result of non-ideal assignments of rights to sell or rights to buy.

Example 7. 3
Sugar Quotas

Under the Sugar Act of 1948, the availability of sugar in the United States is limited by specific marketing quotas assigned to foreign countries and to domestic production areas. The U.S. market price for sugar is consequently at a substantial premium over the world price: for example, a 35% premium in 1960, 61% in 1968, 40% in 1970.

The effects of the U.S. quota system were studied by Ilse Mintz for the year 1970; the figures here are based upon her "low" estimates.[11] The underlying situation is pictured in Figure 7.15. Panel (a) represents a hypothetical free-market equilibrium that would have occurred in the absence of quotas. The world price is 5.5¢ per pound, and the domestic price must equal this. United States domestic production along the supply curve S_{US} is 2.9 million tons at this price, and imports are 8.7 million, making up a total of 11.6 million tons along the curve S_w showing world supply to the United States. Since this is an equilibrium situation, the U.S. demand curve D intersects S_w at this price. Producer surplus of the *domestic* producers is the small lower shaded area in

[11]Ilse Mintz, *U.S. Import Quotas: Costs and Consequences*, American Enterprise Institute for Public Policy Research, Washington, D.C. (Feb. 1973).

Panel (a), and the U.S. Consumer Surplus is the huge upper shaded area (because of the steepness of the demand curve, the latter is shown only suggestively).

The effects of the quotas are shown in Panel (b). The quota assignments (6.0 million short tons domestic, 5.2 million short tons of imports) aggregate to only a little less than the 11.6 million tons that would have been supplied under free markets. But with a highly inelastic demand (price elasticity of −0.1, according to the "low" estimate), the U.S. domestic price is sharply higher at the observed 8.07¢ per pound.

The deadweight loss of Consumer Surplus [the smaller dotted triangle in Panel (b)] is estimated by assuming that the demand curve D is linear between 11.2 million and 11.6 million tons. The area of the dotted triangle is $1/2(8.07¢ − 5.5¢)(.8$ billion pounds) or $10,280,000.

But the most obvious feature of the situation is the tremendous cost increase to consumers due to the price difference calculated upon the 11.2 million tons consumed in either case. This amounts to (22.4 billion pounds) $(8.07¢ − 5.5¢)$ or $575,680,000.

The increase, all at the expense of U.S. Consumer Surplus, is broken down into four numbered areas in Panel (b). Area 1 is the transfer from domestic consumers to foreign producers, calculated on the basis of the higher price received for the 5.2 million tons they continue to deliver to the U.S. market. This amounts to $267,280,000. Area 2 is the transfer to domestic producers, calculated on the 2.9 million tons they would have delivered in either case. This amounts to $149,060,000. Areas 3 and 4 are equal (assuming for simplicity that the domestic supply curve S_{US} is linear), and amount together to the remaining $159,340,000. However, they are conceptually quite different. The upper area 3, like area 2, is a transfer from Consumer Surplus to domestic Producer Surplus. But the lower area 4 is a deadweight loss. It represents increased cost of production (higher supply price) on units produced domestically that could have been obtained more cheaply from foreigners. Note that this is the type of deadweight loss, described in the text above, that is due to a *non-ideal distribution* of quantitative restrictions upon trading. That is, granting that only 11.2 million tons of sugar are to be sold in the United States, there is an additional loss to the extent that quotas are assigned to high-cost domestic rather than to low-cost foreign producers. This additional deadweight loss, the larger dotted triangle in Panel (b), amounts to one-half of $159,340,000—or $79,670,000.

If we regard the transfers as cancelling out, the aggregate of the deadweight losses (the "efficiency loss" due to the sugar quotas) amounts to $89,950,000.

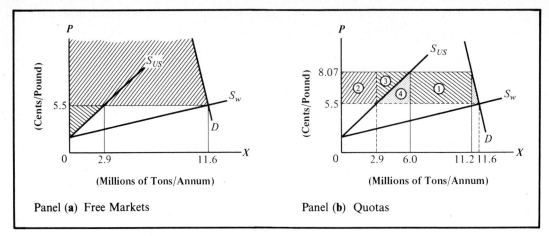

Figure 7. 15 Sugar Supply and Demand

*7. E. 3   Rationale of Consumer and Producer Surplus

In the discussion of Section 7.A, the benefits of trade were divided into two categories: those due to improved consumptive reallocations of given commodity totals, and those due to the increased production of consumable goods stemming from the specialization that exchange makes possible. Consumer Surplus measures the first type of benefit, and Producer Surplus the second. But the traditional geometrical representations of these concepts, the shaded areas of Figure 7.10, are precisely valid only under certain restrictive assumptions.

Consider Producer Surplus first. In Figure 7.16 we see an individual's Production-Possibility Curve QQ, market line MM, and productive optimum Q^* (as in Figure 7.6). We now make the following assumptions: (1) Commodity Y represents "all other goods," and serves as numeraire so that price P_y is unity; "surplus" will be measured in terms of units of Y gained or lost. (2) We consider only the individual's productive aspect, summed up in his attempting to achieve his productive optimum at Q^*. (3) The individual has an initial *endowment* position E on the Y-axis, so that he can generate units of X only by sacrificing Y along the transformation locus QQ.

In moving from his endowment position E to the productive optimum Q^* along QQ, the individual has transformed (sacrificed) EH units of Y to generate his produced-supply x^q. But at the equilibrium price ratio, corresponding to the slope $-P_x/P_y$ of the market line MM with $P_x = P_x^*$ and $P_y = 1$, the x^q units of X produced have a market value of KH in Y-units. Thus, in Figure 7.16, the individual's Producer Surplus or *net gain in terms of Y-equivalents* is the distance $KE = KH - EH$ along the vertical axis. In order to translate into the picture of Figure 7.10, we can assume that this individual is typical of the supply side as a whole. The distance KH, the worth in Y-units of the X-production at the equilibrium price ratio, corre-

*Starred sections represent optional or advanced material.

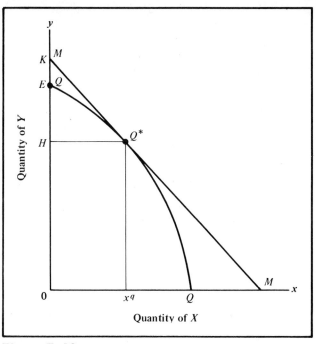

Figure 7. 16
Derivation of Producer Surplus

sponds to the price-times-quantity rectangle $OP_x^*BX^*$ in Figure 7.10. The distance EH, opportunity cost or amount of Y sacrificed in producing X, corresponds to the area $OFBX^*$ lying below the supply curve. The lower shaded area FP_x^*B in Figure 7.10 is thus the analog on the aggregate level of the individual Producer Surplus KE of Figure 7.16.

Now consider Consumer Surplus, illustrated in Figure 7.17. Here we make the following assumptions: (1) The individual is considered only in his consumptive aspect, leading him from an endowment position E to a consumptive optimum C^* along his budget line EC^*L. (2) The endowment position is along the Y-axis, so that the individual can acquire X *only* by paying out "other goods" Y. (3) The preference map is characterized by parallelism in the Y-direction; i.e., for any vertical line in the diagram of Figure 7.17, the indifference-curve slopes encountered along that vertical (whether steep as along $A'B'$ or flat as along $A''B''$) will all be the same. (The significance of this assumption will become clear shortly.)

If the individual in Figure 7.17 could not trade, he would have to remain at his endowment position E on indifference curve U_0, rather than attaining the position C^* on indifference curve U_1. Two possible measures, in Y-units, of the gain from trade are the vertical distances C^*D (along the vertical $x = x^*$) and GE (along the vertical axis $x = 0$).

The distance GE corresponds to what may be called the "compensation" concept of the gain from trade. Consider the question: If the individual at the

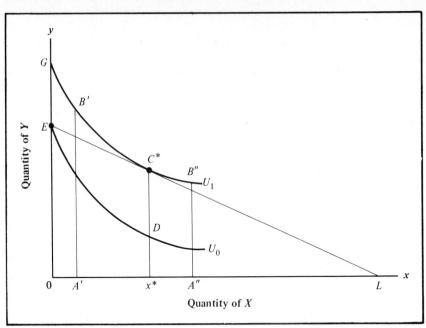

Figure 7. 17
Derivation of Consumer Surplus

endowment position E were forbidden to purchase commodity X along the budget line EL, what amount of "other goods" Y would be required to just compensate him? The answer is GE, since the position G is at the same U_1 utility level that he would have attained by trading from E to his consumptive optimum C^*. The distance C^*D, in contrast, may be called the "deprivation" concept of the benefit of trade. Here the question is: Having attained C^* by trading along the budget line, how many units of Y can the consumer be deprived of and still be no worse off than he was at E? The answer is C^*D, since the position D is at the same U_0 utility level as the endowment E.[12]

Now we can see the point of the special "Y-parallelism" assumption. First of all, if indifference curves are everywhere vertically parallel then they remain the same vertical difference apart (by the fundamental geometrical property of parallelism). Then the distances GE and C^*D are identical; the compensation and deprivation measures coincide.

Even more important is the following consideration: Y-parallelism means that the Marginal Rate of Substitution in Consumption, MRS_C, is a function only of the X-quantity and not of the Y-quantity. With Y-parallelism, when we move along a vertical and thus hold the X-quantity constant, the indifference-curve slope (whose absolute value is MRS_C) is unchanged. *This is equivalent to assuming that* X *is a commodity with zero income elasticity:* As the budget line shifts outward with increased income, the consumptive

---

[12]Other measures of the benefit can be defined; for example, in terms of deprivation or compensation quantities of the commodity X itself.

optimum shifts vertically upward. Put another way, *under this assumption the consumer's demand price for any quantity of* X *is independent of income.* It is this that justifies the simple aggregation of successive demand prices as the traditional measure of the consumer's total "willingness to pay," i.e., as the roughly trapezoidal area $OABX^*$ under the demand curve in Figure 7.10.

What if the demand price for X were *not* independent of income? Specifically, consider the normal case where the consumer's demand price for any X-quantity *rises* with income (positive income elasticity for X). In Figure 7.10, if the individual hypothetically paid OA for the first unit instead of the lower market price P_x^*, this would be an impoverishment. If the income effect is normal, he would no longer be willing to pay as high demand prices for successive units as suggested by heights along the "ordinary" demand curve D in Figure 7.10. Consequently: *For a superior good, the aggregate willingness to pay is less than the area under the demand curve* (less than the area $OABX^*$ in Figure 7.10). Since Consumer Surplus is willingness to pay less actual cost of purchase, it follows immediately that for a good with positive income elasticity, the true Consumer Surplus is less than the traditional roughly triangular area ABP_x^* (upper shaded area in the diagram). For an inferior good, of course, the true Consumer Surplus would be larger than the conventional representation.[13] What makes the conventional representation a usable approximation is the consideration that the *income effect*, the enrichment or impoverishment due to changes in P_x, is ordinarily only a minor factor affecting the demand for X itself.

Questions

1. Explain how the possibility of trade can lead both to *consumptive* benefits (preferred allocations of given social totals of goods over the different individuals) and *productive* benefits (larger social totals of desired goods). How is the consumptive improvement illustrated in the Edgeworth box of Figure 7.1? Which diagram illustrates the productive improvement?

2. If two persons have identical preferences (indifference-curve maps), does it follow that they cannot trade to mutual advantage? What if they have identical preferences *and* identical endowments in a world of pure exchange? In a world of production, what if they have identical preferences and identical productive opportunities?

3. We normally observe a strong tendency toward specialization in production but diversification (non-specialization) in consumption. What shapes of the individuals' Production-Possibility Curves and preference maps lead to this pattern of behavior? Is trade necessary to bring it about?

---

[13]On the other hand, the conventional representation of consumer surplus is correct if the demand curve employed is the *income-compensated* demand curve (of Section 6.C). It is left for the student to justify this assertion. (*Hint:* What can be said about the "income effect" along the income-compensated demand curve?)

4. What is meant by an individual's "sustaining price" for a particular good? What happens at higher prices? At lower prices? How does the "sustaining price" differ from the "autarky price"?

5. What condition must hold for each individual at competitive equilibrium in a world of pure exchange? What additional condition characterizes the market as a whole?

6. What are the productive and consumptive conditions that must hold for each individual in a world of production and exchange? What additional conditions characterize the market as a whole?

7. Justify the assertion that the *productive* improvement due to trade necessarily implies greater social totals of desired goods. [*Hint:* Consider the two individuals' Marginal Rates of Transformation with and without trade.]

8. If market equilibrium takes place at the intersection of the aggregate *transaction* demand and *transaction* supply curves, how can the intersection of the *gross* demand and *gross* supply curves also determine the equilibrium?

9. Consider the following assertion:

If we destroyed half the nation's stock of a certain good X, its price P_x would rise so high that the remaining half would be more valuable in economic terms than was the original total. Then economics would tell us to go ahead and destroy half the stock, which shows how absurd economics is![14]

If half the stock were destroyed, would the value of the remainder *necessarily* exceed the value of the original total? Could it *possibly* do so? If it did, would destroying half the stock be a good idea? Would economics tell us to go ahead and do so? [*Hint:* Distinguish between market value and aggregate "value in use" (market value plus Consumer Surplus).]

---

[14]This assertion is the substance of a passage in *The Report of the President's Water Resources Policy Commission*, v. 1 (Washington, D.C.: Government Printing Office, 1950) pp. 60-61.

Chapter 8
Costs of Exchange and the Role of Money

It is perhaps surprising that, up to quite recently, economists have paid relatively little attention to the *process of exchange* itself. Closely analyzed, this process is found to involve inevitable costs and imperfections. It is as an attempt to cope with these imperfections that the crucial institution of *money* comes into existence (together with banking, credit cards, and other puzzling phenomena of our modern world). The role of money is generally emphasized as a topic in *macro*economics, an application that lies beyond the scope of the present book. However, the foundations of money as an artificial or invented commodity lie in the *micro*economics of the market process.

8. A PERFECT COMPETITION AND PERFECT MARKETS

A competitive trader, we know, is a *price-taker*. The terms of exchange facing him in the market are, in his view, outside his sphere of control; he regards himself as able to buy or sell any desired quantity at the current ruling price.

There is a paradox here. Suppose individual i is a net demander in the market for a good X, where the *overall* supply-demand equilibrium is as pictured in Figure 8.1, Panel (a). The equilibrium price is P_x^* and aggregate transaction quantity is X^*. Note the normally upward-sloping market supply curve S.[1] But if the individual's own purchases do not affect price, the supply curve S *as viewed by him* in Panel (b) is horizontal (at the supply price P_x^*). At this price his individual market demand curve d_i indicates that he will purchase the quantity x_i^*. But how can a supply curve that is upward-sloping in Panel (a) be horizontal in Panel (b)?

The explanation is simple: The supply curve is not *really* horizontal in Panel (b). However, if an individual i is a negligible element in the overall supply-demand picture, variations in his x_i will not sensibly affect the price

[1]In this chapter, and henceforth in the text, supply and demand curves will be understood to be the *transaction* supply and demend curves that were symbolized as S^t and D^t (on the aggregate level) and s^t and d^t (on the individual level) in the previous chapter.

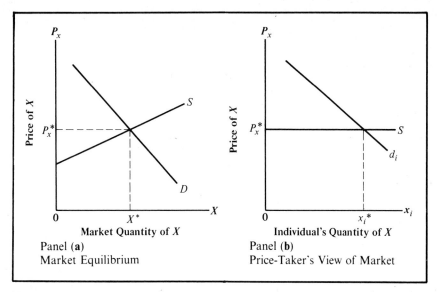

Figure 8. 1
A Price-Taker in the Market

in equilibrium. In effect, the supply curve viewed by the individual demander in Panel (b) is a very tiny segment of the total supply curve S, lying in the immediate neighborhood of the quantity X^* in Panel (a). In shifting from the aggregate X-scale in Panel (a) to the individual x_i-scale in Panel (b), this segment is stretched out horizontally so that in appearance it becomes practically flat. Thus, we see that a competitive demander cannot literally be a "price-taker" in the sense of being able to buy *any* quantity at a given price P_x. Rather, the supply price is effectively constant with respect to the relatively negligible quantities he might be *able and willing* to purchase.

Numerical Illustration

Suppose that the market supply equation is $X_s = 10,000P_x$ and the market demand equation is $X_d = 75,000 - 5000P_x$. By letting $X_s = X_d = X^*$, the equilibrium price is seen to be $P_x^* = 5$ and equilibrium quantity $X^* = 50,000$ units. If we imagine that the demand side of the market actually consists of 1000 identical individuals, each has an individual demand function $x_d = 75 - 5P_x$. At the equilibrium price $P_x^* = 5$, each is of course purchasing 50 units.

Now suppose that one single demander were to reduce his purchases to zero. Then the market demand equation becomes $X_d = 999(75 - 5P_x)$, and the equilibrium price falls from $P_x^* = 5$ to $P_x^* = 4.997$. If, on the other hand, any single demander were to double his purchases from 50 to 100 units, the equation becomes $X_d = 100 + 999(75 - 5P_x)$, and the market price rises from $P_x^* = 5$ to $P_x^* = 5.003$.

The price shift in either case is negligible, though not literally zero.

The ideal concept of *perfect competition* goes beyond mere price-taking behavior on the part of individual traders, however. It involves *perfect markets* as well. There are three main characteristics of perfect markets:

1. *Perfect Communication:* The market must be an integrated whole, not segmented by limitations of information. In actuality there are cases in which an individual i is in communication with j, and j with k, but where i and k are not themselves able to make direct contact. A number of observed phenomena in the world are explicable as attempts to overcome informational imperfections of markets: the use of classified newspaper advertising to communicate supply-demand offers, specialized "middlemen" (such as real-estate brokers) through whom buyers and sellers can reach one another, and organized exchanges (such as the New York Stock Exchange) which aim to bring all relevant offers into a single combined marketplace.

2. *Instantaneous Equilibrium:* A market can be viewed as a mechanism, taking as input all potential traders' supply and demand functions, and yielding as output the equilibrium or "market-clearing" price at which purchases and sales are all to be executed. A perfect market would instantaneously digest the inputs and proclaim the correct market-clearing price. But in the real world a farmer bringing his vegetables to a city produce market, for example, may by cleverness or chance realize a sale at a price higher than the (unknown) true equilibrium. Or, unluckily, he may accept a price lower than the one he should have held out for. Thus, in real-world markets there is some "trading at false prices." (One of the functions of *speculation* is to minimize such accidental fluctuations of price that lead to false trading, since speculators enter the market so as to buy when they perceive that the price is accidentally too low and to sell when price is accidentally too high.)

3. *Costless Transactions:* Markets that are perfect would also be costless. In the real world, market "middlemen" such as wholesalers and retailers, brokers, jobbers, etc., exist and obviously must be paid for their services. While these middlemen may improve the perfection of the market in other respects, the fees and payments they receive constitute a burden on the process of exchange. Transaction taxes, in which *government* collects "middleman" payments (possibly reflecting actual services to taxpayers, but possibly not), are another important factor. (One famous transaction tax that played an important role in American history was the Stamp Act of 1765.)

Example 8.1
Experiments in
Perfect and
Imperfect
Markets

An interesting series of economic experiments on the functioning of markets has been conducted by Vernon L. Smith.[2] One question studied

[2]V. L. Smith, "An Experimental Study of Competitive Market Behavior," *Journal of Political Economy*, v. 70 (April 1962); "Effects of Market Organization of Competitive Equilibrium," *Quarterly Journal of Economics*, v. 78 (May 1964); "Experimental Auction Markets and the Walrasian Hypothesis," *Journal of Political Economy*, v. 73 (Aug. 1965).

was the following: Given that real-world market situations, whether arising naturally or in artificially constructed experiments, can never fully meet the theoretical conditions of "perfect markets," how far can the conditions diverge from "perfection" and still achieve the same essential *results*? For example, if traders are not in perfect communication, or if "trading at false prices" may occur, to what extent is it the case that equilibrium is nevertheless attained quite quickly and at a price-quantity outcome close to the theoretical ideal?

In a typical experiment, Smith provided each subject with information as to demand price (the maximum unit price he should be willing to bid), if a buyer, or as to supply price (the minimum he should be willing to accept), if a seller. With different subjects having different demand prices and supply prices, demand and supply curves were brought into implicit existence (though not visible as such to any single participant). Under the experimental conditions, any buyer (or seller) could at any time make a bid (or offer) which, if accepted by a seller (or buyer), became a binding contract. The process was public, so that the terms of contracts become known to as-yet-uncommitted traders.

In the experimental situations almost all contracts took place near the "true" (but unknown) equilibrium price, except possibly for the first few transactions in any series. When an initial divergence occurred, convergence toward the "true" price was very rapid. While it was not the case that literally all transactions took place at the equilibrium price, even toward the end of a market sequence, the model of perfect markets nevertheless provided a high degree of approximation of actual transaction prices. Furthermore, the *quantities* exchanged were also very close to the theoretical ideal. In short, substantially all the potential advantages of trade (in the form of Consumer Surplus and Producer Surplus) were in fact achieved despite the experimental departure from ideal conditions.

Results such as these suggest that the economist's perfect-market model is "robust," in the sense of having a high degree of predictive reliability even though the exact conditions for its validity are not fully met. A very similar situation in physics is the model of a "perfect gas" that leads to the prediction known as Boyle's Law. No actual gas can meet the requirements of a "perfect gas," and yet Boyle's Law is a very reliable predictive equation in physics.

8. B TRANSACTION COSTS AND MARKET EQUILIBRIUM

In the discussion that follows, markets will be assumed perfect *except* for the existence of transaction or exchange costs. This amounts to assuming that middlemen function so effectively as to totally eliminate the other two types of market imperfection—informational segmentation, and false trading at non-equilibrium prices. But of course these efficient middleman services must be compensated by fees or charges upon transactions. Costs of exchange have, we shall see, important consequences for the scope of trading and for the degree of specialization in production and consumption.

Example 8. 2
Costs of Trading on the New York Stock Exchange

An organized exchange like the New York Stock Exchange goes a considerably way toward the ideal of a perfect market. The key feature of an organized exchange is the guarantee of the transaction, i.e., of the quality of merchandise delivered, of payment arrangements, etc., by the exchange authorities themselves. As a result the buyer can forego personal inspection of the merchandise, and the seller need not be concerned with the credit standing or the character of the buyer. In the case of the New York Stock Exchange, the buyer does not have to worry about whether the stock certificates he acquires are counterfeit, nor need the seller fear that the buyer may be making payment with a bad check.

However, there are costs of dealing on the New York Stock Exchange. These fall into two main categories: (1) commission charges, and (2) bid-ask price spread. The *commission charges* are the explicit fees paid to brokers by buyers and sellers. These charges are quoted separately from the amounts paid or received for the securities themselves. The *bid-ask spread* is a less obvious portion of the cost of transacting. At any instant of time the market price of a stock like General Motors to a seller, the "bid price," is less than the "ask price" that a buyer of GM stock would have to pay. The difference goes mainly to the Exchange's "specialist" in General Motors stock who serves the role of making a continuous market in (standing ready always to buy or sell) that security. The specialist, like a retail or wholesale merchant, must on the average buy for less (the bid price) than he sells for (the ask price) if he is to remain in business. (The customer's *broker*, in contrast with the specialist, is normally a pure intermediary who does not buy or sell on his own account.)

A study by Harold Demsetz[3] indicated that in 1965 the bid-ask spread on the New York Stock Exchange comprised about 40% and explicit commission charges about 60% of total transaction cost, on the average. The two together amounted to about 1.3% of the value of the securities exchanged. One point of interest, understandable in terms of the analogy of the specialist with a retail or wholesale merchant, is that the bid-ask spread is normally much lower for high-volume (frequently-traded) securities than for low-volume (infrequently-traded) securities. The commission charges are also relatively lower for large than for small transactions.

[3]H. Demsetz, "The Cost of Transacting," *Quarterly Journal of Economics*, v. 82 (Feb. 1968).

Costs of exchange are generally a function of: (1) the volume of goods traded; (2) the number of distinct transactions per unit of time; (3) the number of parties involved in a transaction; and (4) the number of distinct commodities per transaction. In the next sections we will be dealing only with two-party, two-commodity trades, ruling out the third and fourth elements above as determining factors of transaction costs. (Some comments upon costs of multi-party and multi-commodity trading will be made in later sections.) For simplicity, we will deal below with special cases that isolate each of the two sources of exchange cost to be considered here. Specifically, the implications of *transaction costs strictly proportional to volume* will be studied first; afterward, *costs dependent solely on the number of separate transactions* will be taken up.

8. B. 1   Proportional Transaction Costs

We have already noted in Chapter 2 (see Figure 2.4) certain consequences of a particular type of proportional transaction cost—a uniform tax on sales. If an impost of \$1 per unit were levied upon purchases of a commodity X, then the *gross price* P_x^+ paid by buyers would necessarily be \$1 greater than the *net price* P_x^- received by sellers. Figure 8.2 here is equivalent to the earlier diagram. It indicates that, as compared with a no-tax situation with price P_x^* and quantity X^*, after imposition of the tax the quantity exchanged would be only X'. As for price, the gross price P_x^+ paid by buyers will always be higher than, but the net price P_x^- received by sellers will be lower than, the no-tax equilibrium price P_x^*. The shaded area in the diagram, equal to $X'(P_x^+ - P_x^-)$, represents the tax collections.

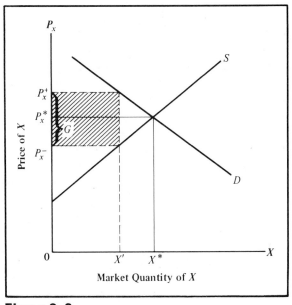

Figure 8. 2
Proportional Transaction Costs

But a more generalized interpretation of the diagram is possible. We can think of it as representing the effects of *any* proportional transaction cost, not just a tax. The *price gap* $G = P_x^+ - P_x^-$ is the rate charged by middlemen (e.g., the "bid-ask spread" of Example 8.2 above) to effectuate the exchange of a unit of X. The shaded area is then the aggregate amount received by middlemen for their services in this market.

Let us now consider the situation from the viewpoint of an individual trader. In Figure 8.3 a price-taking trader in a world of *costless* exchange

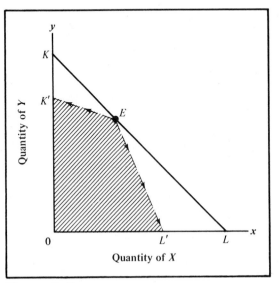

Figure 8. 3
Individual Trading Opportunity

could, starting from an endowment combination E, attain any position along the solid market line KL. The slope of the market line is $-P_x/P_y$, or simply $-P_x$ since, as usual, we interpret Y as a numeraire (representing "all other goods") with price $P_y \equiv 1$. The dashed line-segments show the impact of a proportional trading charge. Here, if the individual tries to buy X by moving southeast from E (note direction of the arrows) he faces a higher price P_x^+ reflected in the steep slope of the line-segment EL'. If he tries to sell X by moving northwest along EK', he receives only the lower price P_x^- reflected in the flat slope of EK'. The existence of transaction costs narrows the individual's opportunity set, from the triangle OKL that would be relevant under costless exchange to the quadrilateral $OK'EL'$ bounded by the dashed line-segments (shaded area in the diagram).

Next, it will be interesting to trace out the implications of transaction charges for *autarky*—self-sufficiency—in a world where individuals have productive transformation opportunities as well as market opportunities. Figure 8.4 shows how autarky may come about even in costless exchange. The individual's autarky optimum is his "Robinson Crusoe solution" R^*,

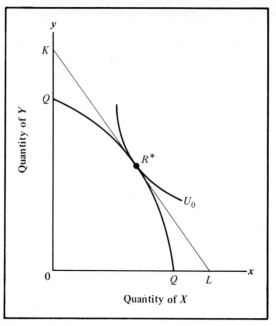

Figure 8. 4
Autarky in Costless Exchange

where his Production-Possibility Curve QQ is just tangent to indifference curve U_0. At this point, as we know from equation (7.5), $MRS_C = MRS_T$, the Marginal Rate of Substitution in Consumption (the slope of his indifference curve) is just equal to his Marginal Rate of Transformation (slope of QQ). Only in the very special case shown in the diagram, where the market price ratio P_x/P_y is just equal to this common value of MRS_C and MRS_T, will there be no way for the individual to gain from exchange. If the market price ratio (absolute slope of the market line) tilts away in either direction from this common value, as it almost always will, the productive optimum and consumptive optimum for the individual diverge (as in Figure 7.6). Such a divergence means that the individual can participate in and benefit from market exchange.

Under costly exchange, autarky becomes a much more likely possibility. In Figure 8.5 the Crusoe solution is R^* as before. R^* on QQ is obviously preferable to any other point in the shaded quadrilateral $OK'R^*L'$ that shows the market opportunities. Autarky now may be best for the individual in a much wider class of cases. For, considerable tilting of the slopes of R^*K' and R^*L' (upward or downward shifts of buying and selling prices) could take place and still leave the R^* position best for the individual in Figure 8.5.

The *limits* of the price range leading to autarky solutions, in a world of production and exchange, are indicated in Figure 8.6. The two dotted areas represent the increments to the overall opportunity set due to the possibilities

205

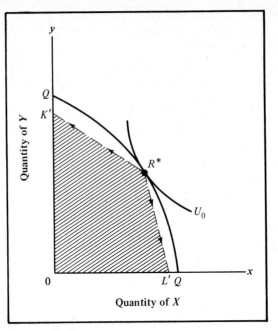

Figure 8. 5
Autarky with Proportional Trading Cost

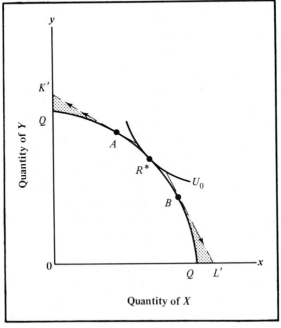

Figure 8. 6
Limits of Autarky Solutions

of costly trading. Consider the dotted area at the upper left. Here A is the point where the Production-Possibility Curve QQ has the same slope as (is tangent to) the dashed market line-segment whose flatter slope represents the lower selling price P_x^-. Hence, in attempting to move northwest (acquire Y by giving up X) beyond A the individual does better along AK' (selling X for Y in the market) than along QQ (converting X into Y via productive transformation). A corresponding argument applies, of course, for the dotted area at the lower right bounded by the steeper line-segment BL' whose slope represents the higher buying price P_x^+.

Now if the preference map is, as shown in Figure 8.6, such that the Crusoe tangency R^* *falls anywhere between* A *and* B, then autarky is preferred. The high buying price P_x^+ and the low selling price P_x^- then *straddle* the common value of $MRS_C = MRS_T$ at the autarky point. On the other hand, if the shape of the preference map and/or transformation locus QQ are such that R^* falls outside the range AB along QQ, the individual will engage in market trade as a net buyer or seller. Specifically, suppose that the R^* tangency falls northwest of A along QQ as in Figure 8.7. But in this range the indi-

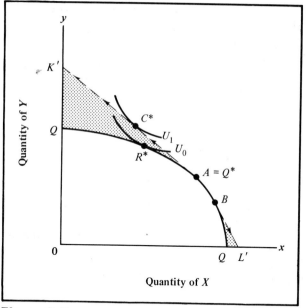

Figure 8. 7
Productive Specialization with Transaction Costs

vidual can do better (can attain a higher indifference curve) along the market line-segment AK' than along AQ. His *productive* optimum Q^* would then be at the point A and he would sell X for Y to attain a *consumptive* optimum C^* along AK'.

Thus, the condition for the individual to become a net seller of X (specializing in production of X), despite the existence of a price gap G due to proportional transaction costs, is that *the low net price* P_x^- *must exceed* the common value of $MRS_C = MRS_T$ at his autarky point. Again, a corresponding argument will apply to the opposite case of specialization in production of Y: This will occur only if the *high gross price* P_x^+ *is less than* the common value of $MRS_C = MRS_T$ at R^*.

Let us now make the connection between the individual's optimizing decision and market equilibrium. We saw in Section 7.D that in costless exchange there is a unique autarky price P_x^o at which the individual's net transaction demand x^t, i.e., the difference between his gross (consumptive) demand x and his total (productive) supply x^q, will be zero. Below this price the individual will be a positive net demander; above, a positive net supplier. Panel (a) of Figure 8.8 represents this situation. The underlying picture is

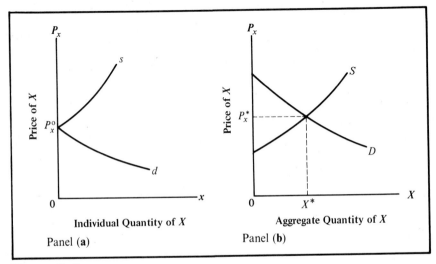

Figure 8. 8
Supply and Demand, Costless Exchange

exactly that portrayed in Figure 7.7, except that we show here only the positive ranges of transaction supply and transaction demand. Furthermore, under conditions of costless exchange we see in Panel (b) that the aggregate market supply and market demand curves—the horizontal summations of the individual transaction supply and transaction demand curves—must intersect at an equilibrium representing a positive volume of transactions ($X^* > 0$). The only exception would be if, by some unbelievable coincidence, every individual in the market had exactly the same autarky price P_x^o!

With proportional costs of transacting, the individual and overall market situations are represented in Figure 8.9. In Panel (a) the autarky price P_x^o for any individual is the common value of $MRS_C = MRS_T$ at his Crusoe solution R^*. If the low *net* price P_x^- exceeds P_x^o, the individual will be a supplier to the market as shown by the dashed curve labelled $s(P_x^-)$. Similarly, he will be a net demander only if the high *gross* price P_x^+ is lower than P_x^o, as

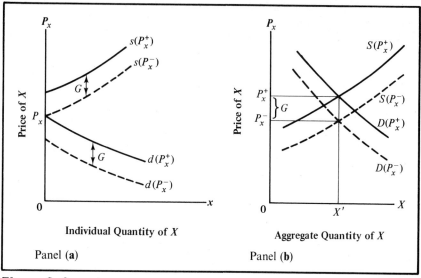

Figure 8. 9
Supply and Demand, Proportional
Exchange Cost

shown by the solid curve labelled $d(P_x^+)$. Thus, it is the *inner pair* of curves that directly show the individual's market behavior. It is convenient, however, also to show the (solid) supply curve in terms of the gross price, $s(P_x^+)$ and the (dashed) demand curve in terms of the net price, $d(P_x^-)$. Each of these differs from its partner by the constant vertical distance G—the price gap.

Summing over all the individuals, we have the corresponding pairs of aggregate market supply and demand curves shown in Panel (b). Now we can see why it was convenient to draw the curves in terms of both gross and net prices. For, the solution that determines the gross or buying price P_x^+ will be at the intersection of $S(P_x^+)$ and $D(P_x^+)$, the two solid curves. This intersection will be at the same market quantity X' as the intersection of the two dashed curves $S(P_x^-)$ and $D(P_x^-)$ that determines the net or selling price P_x^-. The two prices are related by the fixed gap G that was assumed to represent the fee charged in equilibrium by middlemen.

What would happen if the bid-ask spread, the size of the gap G, were to increase? In Panel (a) of Figure 8.9 the *inner pair* of curves would remain unchanged, as they directly represent individual behavior in terms of the relevant (gross or net) prices. But the outer pair of curves would be pushed further outward as G rises. Since the equilibrium solution determined in Panel (b) necessarily involves an intersection with one or the other of the outer curves, the *consequence of higher transaction costs is a fall in the volume of transactions.*

Conclusion: Proportional transaction costs create a gap between buying price and selling price. The higher the transaction charges, the more likely that individuals will choose autarky solutions, and the smaller the aggregate volume of market trading.

Example 8. 3
Urban–Farm
Food Cost
Differentials

In the absence of transaction costs, there would be no reason for a specialist in the *production* of commodity X to be a particularly heavy consumer of X. The tailor would not have an unusually ample wardrobe, the candlestick-maker would not substitute his product for electric lights in his home, and the Detroit assembly-line worker would have no special inducement to drive a car rather than use public transit. It follows that where we *do* observe a producer heavily consuming his own product, transaction costs are likely to be an important factor.

Urban and farm consumption expenditures for 1960–61 were studied by F. Y. Lee and K. E. Phillips. As can be seen in the Table below, farmers spend relatively more on "Food prepared at home," urban-dwellers relatively more on "Food prepared away from home." There seems little reason to doubt that transaction costs impose a greater degree of autarky upon farmers, making it more advantageous for them to consume home-prepared food. Farmers must, on the average, travel a longer distance to non-home sources of food such as restaurants. And upon getting there, they will to some degree be consuming at relatively high prices (after adding on middleman charges of all descriptions) products very similar to those available back home on the farm without payment of transaction charges.

Of course, transaction costs may not be the *sole* explanation of the divergence visible in the Table. It may be that farmers simply have a greater comparative preference for home-prepared food (if not, they might not have chosen farming as an occupation). Perhaps more important, in the period studied farm families on the average were poorer than urban families. Since "Food prepared away from home" is a relatively superior good (income elasticity greater than unity), the income difference may also provide a partial explanation.

Percent of Total Consumption Expenditures

	Northeast		West	
	Urban	Farm	Urban	Farm
Food prepared at home	21.0%	31.0%	18.9%	27.5%
Food prepared away from home	4.8	3.0	4.9	2.9

Source: F. Y. Lee and K. E. Phillips, "Differences in Consumption Patterns of Farm and Non-Farm Households in the United States," *American Journal of Agricultural Economics*, v. 53 (Nov. 1971), p. 575.

For sufficiently large transaction cost G, in fact, there will be no exchange whatsoever in the entire market! With costless trading, total absence of market transactions could occur only with a fantastic coincidence of all the individuals' autarky prices P_x^o. But given that trading costs exist, markets can easily disappear or become non-viable. In poorer economies active trading occurs in products like used containers and cigarettes by the unit (rather than by the pack)—markets not seen in wealthier countries. The market for used clothes is one that has substantially disappeared in recent years in the United States; it has become cheaper to throw used clothes away than to pay for a middleman to resell them.

A per-unit tax on transactions, we have seen, is a special case of proportional trading costs. The analysis here therefore corresponds with the well-known result that a tax can become so large as to be *prohibitive*. "The power to tax is the power to destroy."

*8. B. 2   Lump-sum Transaction Costs

The model of proportional exchange costs discussed above is a simplification. But it does explain a number of important aspects of the process of exchange observed in the world: among them, the normal gap between buying and selling prices, and the viability or non-viability of markets as transaction costs rise or fall. But there is one crucial aspect of exchange not so far explained: the holding of *inventories* (stocks of goods) for purposes of trading. All the models so far studied in the book have taken the form of continuous *flows*—of production, consumption, and exchange—over time. In such models, at least in the simple versions dealt with to this point, there was no need for *stocks* of commodities to be held by anyone. But in point of fact people do not transact continuously; we go to market at discrete separated moments of time. Over the intervals between transactions, traders must accumulate and decumulate inventories of goods purchased or to be sold.

In this section, the role of the elements of cost associated with the discreteness of transactions will be highlighted. Let us make the extreme assumption that costs of exchange take only the form of a fixed lump-sum *charge per transaction*. This obviously provides a strong incentive for the trader to minimize the number of transactions engaged in per unit of time. On the other hand, the less frequent the transactions the larger the inventories needed to bridge over the intervals between successive trips to market. The cost of holding inventories must be balanced against the cost of frequent trading.

Suppose the lump-sum charge is a fixed amount F, incurred for each transaction. The individual trader's decision problem may be interpreted as the choice of an *optimal trading interval* θ. Figure 8.10 shows a possible inventory history for an individual with level production and consumption

*Starred sections represent optional or advanced material.

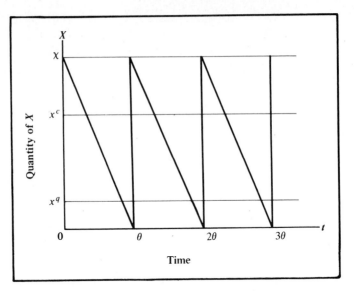

Figure 8. 10
Inventory History for an Individual

flows of a commodity X, making discrete trades at a time-interval of θ. First, he retains a self-supplied productive flow at the rate x^q. At discrete intervals θ, 2θ, 3θ, etc., he purchases a quantity χ (not a flow, but a stock magnitude) of commodity X. This permits him to maintain a level consumption flow of $x^c = x^q + (\chi/\theta)$ continuously. For example, if $x^q = 10$ units per day, χ is 140 units, and $\theta = 7$ days, he can maintain a consumption rate of $10 + \frac{140}{7} = 30$ units per day.

Since this person is a net purchaser of X, he would have to be a net seller of the "other" commodity Y; a similar diagram, showing regular accumulation rather than decumulation of inventory between trades, could be constructed to portray his inventory history for commodity Y.

Now let us consider the individual's decision as to *autarky*, i.e., as to the desirability of engaging in trade at all. Figure 8.11 shows a situation where autarky is preferred; the "Robinson Crusoe solution" R^*, at the tangency of the transformation locus QQ and the indifference curve U_1, is the best position attainable. In the lump-sum transaction cost model, it is important to appreciate that there are two distinguishable disadvantages of trading. The first is *inventory holding costs*. In the diagram these have the effect of contracting the production possibilities of X and Y from the solid QQ curve to the dashed $\hat{Q}\hat{Q}$ curve; resources devoted to maintaining inventories cannot be applied to production. The second disadvantage is, of course, the *lump-sum trading charges* themselves—the explicit fees F paid at each transaction. In the diagram, the average fee incurred per unit of time is represented by the vertical distance $\hat{Q}^* - N^*$. This distance is equal to F/θ, paid out in units of Y. The key point to appreciate is that the individual in this model must, if he does not choose the autarky solution, trade along the market line NN,

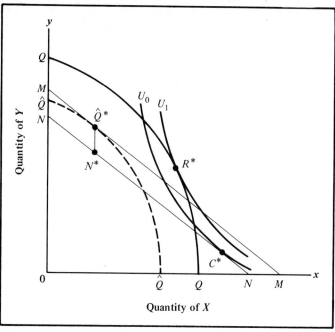

Figure 8. 11
Autarky and Lump-Sum Transaction Costs

parallel to but below the market line MM that is tangent to his $\hat{Q}\hat{Q}$. The line NN represents his *effective* trading opportunities, the combinations of X and Y achievable in the market after payout of the average lump-sum charges F/θ per unit of time.

Autarky is of course not inevitable. Lowered costs of holding inventories would decrease the gap between QQ and $\hat{Q}\hat{Q}$; lowered transaction charges would decrease the gap between MM and NN. Either of these forces would tend to make the trading solution (the tangency C^* with the highest indifference curve attained along the market line NN) relatively more attractive in comparison with the autarky solution R^*. For the trading solution to be superior, C^* would of course have to lie on a higher indifference curve than R^*.

Even with trading costs held constant, the outcome as to autarky or trading will depend upon the market price P_x. Returning to Figure 8.11, as P_x falls the absolute slope of MM and NN will decrease. The tangency of MM with $\hat{Q}\hat{Q}$ (the point $\hat{Q}^*$) will rotate along $\hat{Q}\hat{Q}$ to the northwest, enlarging the trading opportunity set toward the southeast of the diagram. Eventually, a price may be reached at which the trading optimum C^* along NN will be preferred to R^*—the individual will enter the market as a net demander of X. Similarly, at a sufficiently high price P_x he may enter the market as a net supplier of X.

Translating this information into a supply-demand representation, Figure 8.12 is the analog (for lump-sum transaction charges) of Panel (a) of Figure

213

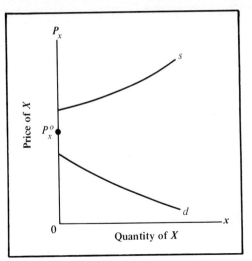

Figure 8. 12
Individual Net Supply and Demand,
Lump-Sum Transaction Cost

8.9 that applied to proportional transaction costs. But here there is no divergence between the buying price and selling price; in this case, middlemen are reimbursed by lump-sum transaction payments F, not by a price gap G. As before, for each individual there is an autarky price P_x^o represented by the common slope $MRS_C = MRS_T$ at his Crusoe solution R^*. There will now be a *range* of prices around the autarky price for which it will not pay the individual to undergo both the inventory holding costs and the lump-sum transaction charges of entering a market. But as the market price P_x increasingly diverges from P_x^o, consumptive combinations attainable only by trading become increasingly attractive. For a sufficiently wide divergence, it will pay to incur the average trading fee F/θ and the inventory costs associated with market exchanges.

The individual net supply and demand curves can again be aggregated, in analogy with Panel (b) of Figure 8.9, into market-wide net supply and demand curves. The market curves *can* intersect in the interior of the positive quadrant, even though for each person separately the s and d curves do not intersect even along the vertical axis. But they may not intersect. If so, that means that the market disappears; there is no price at which traders are willing to incur the transaction charges and associated inventory costs of market dealings in preference to autarky solutions.

Conclusion: Lump-sum transaction costs do not create a price gap. But they dictate that exchanges take place at discrete intervals, so that inventories must be held. Transaction charges and inventory costs due to trading make individual autarky solutions more likely, and reduce the aggregate volume of market trade.

At first sight, very large proportions of our resources appear to be devoted to the process of exchange. In 1971 around 19% of the total U.S. employed civilian labor force was reported as engaged in the occupational category Wholesale and Retail Trade. And many workers classified under other headings—e.g., Transportation and Communication; Finance, Insurance and Real Estate; and Services—might also be regarded as associated with the exchange process. This suggests that "middleman" (transaction-facilitating) activities are a truly enormous drain upon the nation's resources. It might seem astonishing that such heavy burdens remain even after the invention of money, banking, and other sophisticated devices designed to economize upon the costs of market exchange.

This initial impression is misleading. From the social point of view, a crucial distinction must be made between two logically distinct classes of interpersonal "transactions." The *trading* of goods and services between self-interested individuals, i.e., the social process of market exchange, is one thing. The sheer physical transfer or *turnover* of possession or control of commodities is quite another. Any economy that integrates the activities of a multiplicity of individuals so as to take advantage of productive specialization and the division of labor, whether it be an economy of saints, of monks, of slaves, of ants, or of utility-maximizers under *laissez faire*, would still involve physical turnover of commodities. *Activities and costs that are intrinsically due to the mere physical fact of turnover must not be attributed to the particular process that achieves interpersonal integration via market trading.*

For concreteness, consider an extreme "command economy" in which all economic decisions are made by a central authority. The economy might be a slave society in which everyone works as directed for the benefit of a single master. Or it might be a total socialist dictatorship, centrally planned (let us say) to achieve popular well-being. (Egypt, after Pharoah assigned authority to Joseph to meet the threat of the seven lean years, might be an example.) In such a command economy specialization in production still would be desirable. But it would be achieved by visible direction rather than by an "Invisible Hand."[4] Farmers would be ordered to grow crops and turn them over to railroads; railroads ordered to ship them to cities, and turn them over to warehouses; warehouses ordered to store them, and turn them over to the next recipients in the chain, and so forth.

The costs associated with mere physical turnovers that would persist even in a totally dictated economy fall logically under the economic category of *production* costs rather than exchange costs. This accounts for essentially all transportation services, for one thing. "Adding" transportation to a good so as to physically bring it to a consumer is in principle the same as "adding"

---

[4]We leave aside here the question of "comparative economic systems"—the relative effectiveness of *inducing* interpersonal cooperation through self-interest (the "Invisible Hand") on the one hand, or *commanding* it by central direction (with suitable provision for enforcement) on the other.

baking services to dough so as to make bread that the consumer can eat. The consequence is that *the costs of market exchange as a process are not nearly so great as might have first been thought*. Even wholesaling and retailing expenses, as usually classified, are in large part due to the physical warehousing of goods that would still be needed in a total command economy with no market process at all.

What then are the *costs of exchange* proper? These are the costs, in a non-command or "free" economy, that stem specifically from the contending wills and property interests of the parties. In such an economy physical turnovers of commodities take place only if and as consistent with perceived mutual advantage of traders. To arrange transactions, offers must be communicated and alternatives compared. Contracts must be negotiated, and their execution thereafter must be verified. Fraud or other non-performance must be guarded against. All these activities involve costs.[5] All of the expenses of an institution like the New York Stock Exchange, for example, fall under one or more of these headings. (Without private ownership there would be no need for a Stock Exchange, since there would be no corporate shares.) In addition, we shall see that certain "trading inventories" will be held, over and above the necessary stocks of goods that would be carried by an ideal command economy.

---

[5]Of course there would also be great communication and enforcement problems in any actual attempt to construct a functioning *command* economy. Again, it is not our purpose here to engage in an analysis of comparative economic systems.

Example 8. 4
Farmer,
Consumer, and
Middleman

"Consumerists" contend that food prices are too high, while farmers can be counted on to complain that the prices they receive are too low. It is natural for both groups to fasten upon the "middleman" as the culprit. And, in fact, payments to middlemen have over the years been accounting for an increasing share of consumer expenditure on food.

But of course middlemen are providing services for the income they receive: processing, transporting, packaging, distributing, and so forth. Over time the middleman services incorporated into food products have been increasing; we have been choosing to consume food that has traveled further, been processed more elaborately, and distributed in more complex ways than in earlier times.

One explanation of this phenomenon is that middleman services are a relatively superior or "luxury" commodity compared to raw farm products themselves. That is, the *income elasticity of demand* (see Section 5.A) for off-farm food services is greater than for farm products alone. Confirming this, one recent study indicates an overall income elasticity of demand of .705 for food products—but when this figure is divided between the farm and off-farm components, the income elasticity of demand is only .279 for the farm but 1.322 for the off-farm element.[6] So the rising share of the middleman in food sales in the United States is largely a result of rising consumer income, which has permitted an increase in the purchases of middleman services that constitute a relatively superior component of food consumption.

[6]E. W. Bunkers and W. W. Cochrane, "On the Income Elasticity of Food Services," *Review of Economics and Statistics,* v. 30 (May 1957), p. 217.

8. D THE ROLE OF MONEY

Money is a device that reduces the cost of market trading. But it does not, and in the nature of the case *cannot reduce the cost of physical turnovers* that are, as just discussed, essentially an aspect of production. As regards transportation, for example, geographical dispersion of producers and consumers will dictate shipping costs that would have to be incurred even in a perfectly functioning command economy. Money can do nothing to reduce this shipping cost. And similarly, imperfect synchronization of production and consumption will dictate the presence of commodity inventories at various places along the production-turnover-consumption chain. Again, money cannot eliminate this category of expense.

What money does is to reduce trading costs proper, the cost of integrating individual activities through the process of voluntary exchange. Money thus tends to counter the tendency toward autarky so as to promote a more efficient division of labor. It does so by serving the two key functions of *medium of exchange* and *temporary store of value*. These functions can be best visualized if we consider a triad of social regimes in logical succession: (1) pure command economy, with only physical turnover and no trading whatsoever; (2) barter economy, with trading but without any monetary commodity; and (3) money economy.

Money as medium of exchange:

To fix ideas, suppose that there are N commodities, each produced by a single individual. In the absence of any turnover or trading costs, imagine that all N persons would be willing to consume positive quantities of all N goods. Thus, there is specialization in production but diversity in consumption—the normal situation.

Under a pure command regime, suppose the dictator is perfectly efficient and benevolent. In this economy there is no resource "wastage" due to costs of *trading*, i.e., no bidding, negotiating, contracting, etc. Even so, pure costs of *turnover* such as transportation expense may rule out some of the $N(N-1)$ possible commodity movements as uneconomic. Suppose that oranges are produced in California, and lobsters in Maine. Lobsters might be so expensive to ship that, from the viewpoint of overall economic efficiency, the dictator correctly decides that Californians would have to do without them.

But if oranges are not very costly to ship, the dictator might still find it feasible and efficient to command that California oranges be sent to Maine.

Now suppose that a revolution displaces the dictator, substituting a regime of barter trade. In this regime, we will suppose, *only two-party trade is feasible.* (In actuality, multi-party transactions can and do take place, but they seem to be exceedingly costly to negotiate and enforce and are therefore relatively rare.) Then, and this is the crucial point, instead of the $N(N-1)$ possible *one-directional commodity movements* that were available to the dictator in a command economy, under bilateral barter only $N(N-1)/2$ possible *two-way channels of exchange* are possible. If shipment of Maine lobsters to California is barred by the high costs of physical turnover (transportation cost), then the two-way channel is blocked. The California oranges cannot go to Maine either, since the lobstermen cannot provide appropriate compensation. As compared with an ideal command economy (perfectly efficient and benevolent dictator), not only is there wastage of resources due to the necessity of negotiating trades but also an inferior allocation of production and consumption due to a higher degree of autarky.

We can now see how the invention of a universal *medium of exchange* improves matters. The medium of exchange can be one of the original N goods or it can be an artificial $(N+1)$th commodity like paper money. In either case, the effect is *to make multilateral trading indirectly possible through a bilateral accounting device.*

Suppose, to begin with, that one of the N initial commodities is chosen as medium of exchange. In the prisoner-of-war situation of Example 4.1, *cigarettes* served this function. But in keeping with modern economic history, we will speak of *gold* as medium of exchange. Then all the other commodities are no longer traded for one another, but only for gold. This involves a saving, in that there is a drastic reduction in the number of markets that must be provided.

For the moment, let us assume there are no markets blocked under barter by the high real turnover costs in one direction (e.g., by the cost of shipping Maine lobsters to California). In general, the number of two-way trading channels required is $N(N-1)/2$. Then if there are five goods (four ordinary consumption goods A, B, C, D plus gold G), Figure 8.13 pictures the $5(4)/2$ or *ten* trading channels. But if all other commodities are traded only for gold, *four* channels or markets will suffice. In general, the market system of a money (gold) economy would be required to generate prices and to execute exchanges for only $N-1$ types of transactions. As compared with barter, there will be a considerable reduction of the costs associated with disseminating information; buyers locating sellers and vice versa; and negotiating, recording, and enforcing trades.

But this direct saving has less overall import than the *indirect* gain due to the greater degree of productive specialization made possible. Consider the lobster–orange example once again. With gold as medium of exchange, the Maine lobsters will still not go to California; the physical turnover costs

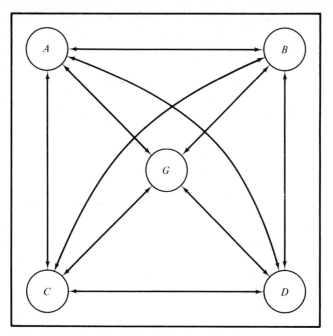

Figure 8. 13
Trading Channels—Five Goods

remain excessive. But the California oranges can now go to Maine! For, the Maine lobstermen can pay for oranges in gold that they obtain by selling lobsters to other, non-Californian customers. Thus, gold makes possible triangular or still more complex turnovers, without requiring anything beyond bilateralism in trading.

There is, however, one element of cost likely to be greater in a gold economy than in a barter economy: There will be greatly increased handling and shipping back and forth of *gold*, the monetary commodity itself. Clearing arrangements, one aspect of banking, will arise to reduce these costs. Also, gold as medium of exchange can be replaced by an artificial commodity (e.g., paper money) for which the shipping and handling costs are less. Ultimately the money economy tends to move toward a non-physical, purely abstract medium of exchange, *banking deposits*, to minimize handling costs of money.

Money as temporary store of value:

So far we have considered money only as medium of exchange, an intermediating commodity in transactions. A mere intermediating commodity could exist as a pure flow—a good produced and consumed at a constant rate over time. The only difference between it and other flow goods would be that it works somewhat harder, entering into multiple transactions on the way from production to consumption. Thus, a single cigarette in the POW

219

camp example might pass through many hands, helping to mediate many transactions, before eventually being smoked as a consumer good. But we generally think of money not as a flow good but as a stock. The butcher and baker, in exchanging, produce and consume flows of meat and bread. But over any time period, each will begin and end with a *stock* holding of money. As temporary store of value ("abode of purchasing power"), inventories of money bridge time gaps between receipts and payments. The baker can obtain meat today, even though he is out of bread for sale until tomorrow, by dipping into his money reserve.

We saw above that, even in a pure command regime where no voluntary exchange occurs, imperfect synchronization of the processes of production, transportation, and consumption will lead to the existence of inventories of all types of goods as they are passed along the interpersonal turnover chain. The unique feature of a *monetary inventory* is that it is held to facilitate the process whereby goods are transferred by the specific mode of market exchange.

Consider once again the revolution that overthrows the dictator of a pure command economy, substituting a regime of barter exchange. Now *trading inventories* come into existence. Let three individuals a, b, c be sole specialized producers of commodities A, B, and C, respectively. Imagine that to meet consumption preferences the desired pattern of trade is triangular: Commodity A is to flow from a to b, commodity B from b to c, and commodity C from c to a. If multilateral trading is ruled out, we have here the famous "double coincidence" problem of barter. Consider individual b. He wants commodity A from individual a, but produces nothing that the latter wants from him; he can provide commodity B to individual c, but the latter produces nothing that b desires.

Under triangular barter, this dilemma is resolved by having some or all individuals hold inventories of the third commodity, i.e., the one they neither produce nor consume. With a great many individuals and a great number of commodities, barter exchange requires an enormous extent and variety of such holdings. Essentially everyone would have to carry trading inventories of numerous commodities he neither produces nor wishes to consume. He must accept goods in exchange for a commodity he does produce, to have something available for exchange when opportunity permits for a commodity he wishes to consume.

Rather than hold a multiplicity of different trading inventories, it is obviously efficient for all traders to agree to accept in exchange some single "store of value" commodity. It should be a commodity both cheap to produce and cheap to store, and preferably one that is not eroded (as were cigarettes in the POW example) by consumption. These criteria will enter into the selection of gold (or some alternative commodity) as the monetary medium. Again, there will be a natural tendency to move toward a money having the form of a purely abstract artificial commodity like banking deposits, almost costless to produce and to store, and not needed for consumption.

Example 8. 5
Barter in
the East Indies

An interesting network of exchanges among primitive peoples in the East Indies was analyzed by the anthropologist M. Sahlins.[7] A puzzling problem encountered was that the Busama as middlemen acquired bowls worth 10 to 12 shillings from the Tami Islanders, which they then used to exchange with southern villagers for pots worth only 8 shillings.

The network can be pictured somewhat as follows. The Busama, producers of taro, want pots from villages in the south and bowls from Tami Island to the north. Pots and bowls are desired throughout the region, but the problem for the Busama is that only the southern villagers want their taro. Hence, the Busama must accept pots in exchange, to trade at Tami Island (even on seemingly adverse terms) for bowls. The upshot is that the Busama carry pots and bowls back and forth, in excess of their needs, in a pattern of trade that permits them to export their taro.

Comment: But it is still not rational for the Busama to carry bowls from Tami where they are, according to the report, *more* highly valued than pots (10 to 12 shillings against 8) to the southern villages where bowls are relatively *less* highly valued (one against one). Indeed, the logic of the situation strongly suggests that the relative values have been misreported: Surely the pots are relatively less highly valued where they are plentiful, at their origin in the south, and the bowls relatively less highly valued at their origin on Tami Island. Only if this is the case does the two-way shipping traffic of the Busama become understandable. The Busama must accept pots from the southern villagers, their only customers for taro, but nothing forces the Busama to carry bowls from north to south at a loss.

The explanation may be that, in this partially monetized circle of exchange, nominal shilling values may be meaningless. Since shillings are not actually employed everywhere in the region as medium of exchange, price quotations may be reported that do not reflect the actual terms in which trades are taking place. Thus, a pot may be "worth" 8 shillings somewhere, but not necessarily on Tami Island, if shillings are not actually exchanged for pots there.

[7] Marshall Sahlins, *Stone Age Economics* (Chicago: Aldine-Atherton, Inc., 1972), Chap. 6.

Questions

1. How can there be "price-taking" behavior if *market* supply curves and demand curves are not horizontal?

2. What are perfect markets? What is perfect competition?

3. Can autarky occur in costless exchange? Why is autarky more likely, the higher the transaction costs? Do you think the increasing weight of payroll taxes (income tax, social security tax) in recent decades has anything to do with the "do-it-yourself" trend observed in such areas of activity as furniture construction and repair, car maintenance, dressmaking, etc.? What about sales taxes?

4. Give examples of markets that have existed historically, but do not now.

5. Some markets are illegal (markets for babies, for narcotic drugs, for government favors, and so on). Law enforcement that is short of being *totally* effective can be regarded as imposing a transaction cost upon participants. In terms of this chapter's analysis, what effects would you anticipate from increased law-enforcement effort against the narcotics traffic? Would the volume of transactions be affected? What about the gross price paid by buyers in comparison with the net price received by sellers?

6. According to the economist K. E. Boulding, a tariff can be regarded as a "negative railroad"—whereas a railroad *connects* trading communities, a tariff *separates* them. Is the analogy valid?

7. How can integration of individuals' productive and consumptive choices be achieved *without* the use of markets? Can it be achieved with markets, but without the use of money?

8. Since the existence of markets necessarily involves some burden of transaction costs, wouldn't a command economy dispensing with markets always be more efficient? Explain.

9. Distinguish between transaction costs and turnover costs. How would you class transportation of goods between producer and consumer? What about the costs of negotiating a contract? Enforcing a contract?

10. Give examples of exchange costs that are reduced by the existence of money as a *medium of exchange*. Of money as a *store of value*.

11. If rationing is introduced (see Section 7.E.2), money is no longer fully effective as a medium of exchange. What types of additional exchange costs emerge in a world where ration coupons and cash are *both* required in order to effectuate a transaction?

12. According to elementary textbooks, a commodity selected to serve as money should be portable, divisible, generally recognizable, and homogeneous. In terms of the discussion in this chapter, why are these desirable qualities? Can you think of other desirable qualities? [*Hint:* Think of cigarettes serving as money in a prisoner-of-war camp.]

Four

The Firm and the Industry

Chapter 9
The Business Firm

In Part Two of this book, the consuming *individual* or *household* held the center of attention. In Part Three, attention shifted to the interaction of individuals through the *market*. We will be concentrating in Part Four upon the *business firm*, and upon the aggregate of firms in a given market that we call the *industry*. This chapter is devoted specifically to the firm. Chapter 10 following will develop the relationships between the competitive (price-taking) firm and the industry; later chapters will be devoted to firms and industries under conditions other than perfect competition.

9. A FIRMS AND THE CIRCULAR FLOW
OF ECONOMIC ACTIVITY

Referring back to Figure 1.1, one of the two poles of the circular flow of economic activity is the class of economic agents we call individuals—natural persons, or groupings of such persons into households. While the existence of natural persons is simply a fact for economics, it has been recognized since the time of Malthus[1] that the *size* of population over time does respond to economic incentives. Until quite recently economists had little to say about the clustering of individuals into families and households, although it is known that phenomena like polygamy (see Example 2.4) are influenced by economic conditions.[2] Individuals or households represent the *demand side* of the "product market," the market for consumption goods and services discussed in previous chapters. And they also constitute the *supply side* of the "factor

[1] T. R. Malthus (1766–1834), English clergyman and economist. Malthus maintained that population would always tend to expand to the limits of subsistence. His views had an important influence upon Charles Darwin's thinking that culminated in the theory of biological evolution.

[2] Following the tendency of economics to overflow conventional boundaries in finding applications for our analytical tools (see Section 1.A.2), there has been a recent flowering of exciting economic investigations into what is now known as the "human capital" area, in which such topics as population size, family formation, and education of children are integrated into an economically understandable system of behavior.

market," the market for resources employed in production. (The factor market will be the object of attention in Part Five of the text.)

The other pole of economic activity is the business firm. The firm, as an artificial entity created in response to economic incentives, is clearly a subject for economic attention. For our purposes, the emphasis will be upon firms as the crucial *productive* agents of society,[3] engaged in the conversion of resources into final goods.[4] Thus, firms constitute the supply side of the product market and the demand side of the factor market.

The invention of *money*, as discussed in the chapter preceding, facilitates the process of exchange and the consequent specialization in production. The diagram of the circular flow of economic activity, Figure 1.1, shows two opposed circuits: a "real" flow of productive services from individuals to firms and then of consumptive goods from firms to individuals, balanced by a "financial" flow of expenditures from individuals to firms (purchase of goods) and then from firms back to individuals (payment for resource services). Even in the absence of a money commodity, resource-supplying individuals could hardly be compensated *directly* out of the physical output of firms, e.g., workers in a candy shop take their wages in bonbons. So firms would have to suffer the inconvenience of barter in converting their products into the various consumption goods desired by resource-suppliers in payment for their services. Under barter conditions firms would therefore tend to be much less specialized, themselves producing a diversity of commodities of interest to their resource-suppliers. Money as a medium of exchange promotes specialization in production. Firms need only provide *indirect* (monetary or financial) compensation to resource-suppliers, which can be done regardless of the physical nature of the firm's own output. Conversely, of course, existence of a medium of exchange permits any individual to supply his productive resources to whatever firm can use them most effectively, even though the person himself may be utterly uninterested in the good produced by that firm.

9. B WHY FIRMS? THE ROLE OF THE ENTREPRENEUR

But we could have productive specialization without firms. Why does a special kind of economic agent, apart from natural individuals, emerge for this purpose? The key to the answer is two-fold: (1) Production opportunities are commonly *multi-personal*, and (2) exchange through the market is, as discussed in the chapter preceding, not a costless process—despite the existence of money.

The productive transformation opportunities examined to this point have

---

[3]Of course, households also engage in production. Indeed, in primitive economies there is *only* household production; the institution we call the firm is absent. The firm is the characteristic unit for organizing production in modern economies.

[4]As was indicated above, our analysis of the productive process will be simplified by excluding complications connected with the existence of partially finished or "intermediate" goods.

pertained only to single individuals. In Figure 7.6, for example, a typical individual has a productive opportunity set bounded by the curve QQ that shows the alternative combinations of commodities X and Y he can produce as a "Robinson Crusoe" apart from the existence of a market. The consequences of opening up a market in which the individual can trade X for Y, or vice versa, were analyzed in Chapters 7 and 8. It was implicitly assumed there that the emergence of the individual from isolation *did not affect the productive opportunity set itself.* But it is a fact of the greatest practical importance that the possibilities of multi-person or "team" production enormously expand output potentialities. The advantages of the division of labor lie not only in specialization in terms of *products* (shoemaker, butcher, baker) but also in the specialization of *tasks* in the joint production of a given end-product (clerk, assembly-line worker, inspector, foreman, etc.) Indeed, our modern economy would be utterly impossible without such specialization of tasks.

But the mere fact that attractive productive opportunities are multi-personal, requiring integration of the skills and resources of a number of distinct individuals, does not suffice to explain the institution of the business firm. For, even without forming a firm, it would in principle be possible to combine resources owned by many different persons via a *multilateral contract* among all the individuals involved. Such a contract would specify for each party what types and quantities of resources he would contribute, at stated times, to the productive process. The contract would also specify, of course, each party's financial reward in the form of the division of output achieved. Such contractual arrangements are relatively rare because of the high costs of negotiating and enforcing multilateral contracts. The business firm provides a way of reaping the advantages of team production without going beyond *bilateral* contracting. Each resource-owner need not deal separately with every other participant in the productive process but instead only with a single artificial entity—the firm itself.

In actuality, of course, the "firm" is an abstraction. People can really deal only with other persons. Therefore some person or group, called the "management," must be authorized to deal in the name of the abstract firm. The management may simply be the *owner or owners* of the firm, the residual claimants to the firm's profits or losses after meeting contractual obligations. But here again, especially where relatively large-scale productive operations are involved, a division of labor tends to come into existence in which management itself becomes a specialized kind of employed resource. The function of the manager is to make contractual agreements with other resource-suppliers and to enforce or monitor performance of these contracts. He does this as a hired agent of the owners.

The manager himself must then be employed and monitored by someone —ultimately, by the owner or owners themselves. Hence, an inescapable decision-making aspect attaches to firm ownership; this combined function is traditionally called *entrepreneurship.* While the institution of the firm emerges in order to achieve certain economies in transacting among resource-suppliers, the execution and enforcement of the contract *among the owners* (if more than one) that constitutes the firm and of the contract *between the owners and the manager* (if those two functions are not combined) both pose considerable difficulties.

A variety of devices have arisen to overcome these problems. With regard to the contract among owners that constitutes the firm, the legal invention of the *corporate form* has opened up the possibility of exploiting even very large and hazardous multi-person productive opportunities. The key features of the corporation are *limited liability* and *transferable shares*. Legal and contractual obligations of the corporation, as a fictional person, cannot be brought home to the individual owner's personal account. His ownership shares may become valueless (at worst), but his individual finances are otherwise safe. And should he be dissatisfied with the policies and procedures adopted by the other owners, or by the manager on behalf of the owners, he has the option of selling out his shares. In consequence, the corporation is enabled to commit large amounts of resources to exploit productive opportunities, far beyond what would be achievable by a partnership without the advantages of limited liability and transferability of ownership interests. With regard to the contract between owners and management, devices like profit-sharing and stock options have emerged with the aim of linking managers' interests more closely with those of the shareholders, thus minimizing the need for detailed owner monitoring of managerial performance.

One interesting question is: Which classes of resource-suppliers tend to become the *owners* of the firm, thereby relying upon compensation out of residual profit and loss rather than receiving fixed payment terms under contract of hire with the firm? For small firms, of course, *management* tends to be combined with ownership (so as to eliminate the difficult problem of contracting and monitoring between the two). But for large firms, management is typically hired. The convenience of the corporate form for large-scale enterprise almost always dictates that "capitalists"—providers of generalized purchasing power for the exploitation of productive opportunities—become the owners (shareholders). Some capital, however, is normally acquired even by corporations on contractually fixed terms through debt instruments like bonds or notes.

9. C   THE GOAL OF THE FIRM AS OPTIMIZING AGENT

Individuals maximize utility, but what do firms maximize? In the traditional formulation, the firm is said to maximize *profit*, which is the difference between *revenue* and *cost*.

Revenue consists of the receipts of the firm from sales, i.e., price times quantity sold. *Cost* is a somewhat more elusive concept. The ultimate economic cost of any activity is to be interpreted as the alternative *opportunities foregone*. The firm, in order to attract the resources or "factors" necessary to engage in production, must pay resource-owners amounts sufficient to induce them to sacrifice their best alternatives, whether these alternatives be employment elsewhere, or leisure. The payments required are, of course, the going market prices for the services of the factors of production. Thus, as will be explained further in Part Five, *cost can be regarded as the sum, taken over all resources employed, of the factor prices times factor quantities.*

There is one tricky feature here. The owner is, as defined above, the *residual* claimant to the firm's earnings. Payment for any factor services supplied by the owner himself will not ordinarily be made by explicit contract but will be mixed with his residual claim. "Profit" in the legal or accounting sense fails to distinguish these two economically distinct categories. If a small merchant works long hours in his own store, his accountant will calculate a "profit" that is likely to amount to little more than a normal wage payment for the merchant's labor services. In the case of a large corporation, "profit" as reported to the Internal Revenue Service will be confounded with a normal interest return upon the funds committed by share-owners to the firm. *Economic* or "pure" profit is arrived at by deducting the normal factor return on owner inputs, sometimes called the "normal" profit, from accounting profit. The *value in alternative uses* of the resources employed in production, whether explicitly hired and paid for, or only implicitly hired and not separately paid for because they are provided by the owner himself, constitute "economic" cost. *Economic profit is thus the difference between revenue and economic cost.* In this book, unless otherwise indicated, the word "profit" will always be used in the sense of *economic* profit.

According to the classical formulation, the aim of the firm as a decision-making agent is to maximize (economic) profit. This view has not gone unchallenged, however. Some observers maintain that the behavior of large modern corporations cannot be explained in terms of the profit-maximizing hypothesis. In such corporations the *separation of ownership and control* may be carried to an extreme degree. Where no single shareowner accounts for more than a minuscule fraction of the shares outstanding, management may (it is contended) be in a position to run things without significant monitoring by nominal owners.

Of course, there are limits. If the shareholders were literally powerless, management could do whatever it wished, even dissipate the value of the firm in the form of enormous executive salaries and expense accounts. But no management ever has such a license to steal. Shareholders as owners have judicial recourse; they can sue for damages if they believe that management has violated the contract with the owners. Such lawsuits frequently do take place, indicating that at least some owners are actually monitoring performance of management. Perhaps a more important check is the presence of competing groups anxious to take over the managerial function. Suppose a self-serving or inefficient management is in control of a corporation. Then the reduced earnings now and in prospect make the value of the corporate shares lower than they would otherwise be. An alternative management group can then try to purchase shares, at their current cheap prices, with the hope of obtaining enough for control. Or they may instead try to win the proxy votes of existing shareholders and thus overturn the current management.

The challenge to the profit-maximizing hypothesis need not, however, postulate a literally all-powerful management. The critics might admit that management aims to achieve at least a certain minimal level of (accounting) profit, enough to placate the shareholders and avoid legal sanctions. But beyond this level, the contention is, management pursues its own goals rather than those of owners. Because of the takeover threat in the background, management's goals may take a somewhat more subtle form than crude monetary emoluments: They may involve power and growth ("empire-building"), advertising or charitable outlays to enhance a favorable "corporate image" (really a management image), amenities like luxurious offices and attractive secretaries, and the pursuit of stability so as to achieve a world without risk of unpleasant surprises.

That forces like those just described are actually operative can hardly be doubted. But are they significant enough, reined as they are by the ever-present takeover threat from outside contenders for managerial positions, to make the profit-maximization hypothesis unworkable? That is a question for empirical investigation. So far at least, there is no convincing evidence for a general formulation of the goal of the business firm that competes successfully with the classical conception of the profit-maximizing firm.

Example 9. 1
Non-Profit
Goals and
"Techno-
structure
Orientation"

J. K. Galbraith has given wide dissemination to the idea that the management-dominated modern American corporation does not aim to maximize profit. Among the possible competing goals satisfying management desires rather than stockholder interests, he lays particular stress upon (1) *growth of sales* and (2) *stability*.[5] In Galbraith's view, those firms he calls "technostructure-oriented" are best able to achieve these goals, through devices like advertising and defense contracts.

Harold Demsetz[6] attempted to test these hypotheses. In order to do so, it was first necessary to convert them into quantifiable form. Demsetz used a variety of statistical criteria to interpret Galbraith's concept of "technostructure orientation," so as to be able to distinguish those firms that could be expected to adhere (on Galbraith's theory) to non-profit goals more than others. The measures of "technostucture orientation" employed by Demsetz included advertising intensity, capital intensity, and proportion of defense contracts.

With regard to sales growth as an alternative to profit-maximization,

[5]J. K. Galbraith, *The New Industrial State* (Boston: Houghton Mifflin, 1967), pp. 171, 199, 210, 309–10.
[6]H. Demsetz, "Where is the New Industrial State?" *Economic Inquiry*, v. 12 (March 1974).

the statistical evidence was examined to see whether firms with high indexes of "technostructure orientation" tended to have high sales growth *relative to* profit rates. Had this in fact occurred, it would suggest that profit had been sacrificed for sales growth (i.e., the interests of owners for the benefit of managers) by these "technostructure-oriented" firms. But no visible effect was found in the data, except that (in contradiction with the tested hypothesis) high advertising intensity was found to be associated with relatively *low* sales growth relative to profit rate.

With regard to Galbraith's second stated goal, a number of alternative measures of *stability* were considered by Demsetz. But in no case was there any indication that firms with high "technostructure orientation" sacrificed profits for stability in such a way as to be distinguishable from firms of low "technostructure orientation."

The book is not yet closed on the issue of conflict between manager and owner. It may well be that, with more precise specification, classes of firms will be detected that can successfully be analyzed in terms of pursuit of non-profit goals. Among the possibilities that come to mind are *monopoly* firms and *regulated* firms, both to be discussed in Chapter 11. And the example following may be suggestive.

Example 9. 2
Savings
and Loan
Associations—
Stock versus
Mutual

Alfred Nicols compared the performance of savings and loan associations organized as *corporations* owned by stockholders ("stock" associations) with those organized as *cooperatives* owned by depositors ("mutual" associations).While J. K. Galbraith (see previous example) had emphasized the separation of ownership and control in the modern corporation, this separation is carried to a far more extreme degree in the savings and loan "mutuals." It may be difficult to overturn management by takeover or proxy fight in a corporation, but it has been made essentially impossible to do so in a "mutual" savings and loan association.

Nicols argued that managers of mutuals, practically free of owner-depositor control, would find ways of diverting association income to their own advantage. While Galbraith had maintained that a main management goal would be *growth* as an alternative to profit, Nicols' position is in sharp contrast. The diversion of association income to managers must mean that mutuals have less to offer their depositors; hence income diversion to management, he argues, is necessarily in *conflict* with rapid growth. The legislation of most states effectively bars stock associations, thus providing a shield for the mutuals. But in

California, where legislation has permitted competition between mutual and stock associations, the latter have indeed grown so as to sharply increase their percentage of the market at the expense of the mutuals.

The Table below provides comparative performance indicators for three classes of institutions: California stock associations, California mutuals under federal charter, and non-California institutions (overwhelmingly mutuals). Note that the indicators for California mutuals generally fall between those of the California stock associations and the non-California institutions; Nicols attributes this to the competitive pressure of California stock associations upon the California mutuals.

1963 Performance Indicators—Mutual and Stock Associations

Indicator	U.S. Non-California	California Federal Mutuals	California Stock
$\dfrac{\text{Gross operating income} - \text{expenses}}{\text{Average assets}}$ (%)	4.31	4.95	5.18
$\dfrac{\text{"Dividends"}}{\text{Average saving capital}}$ (%)	4.04	4.72	4.78
$\dfrac{\text{New Loans}}{\text{Average Assets}}$ (%)	21.2	34.9	45.1

Source: Alfred Nicols, "Stock versus Mutual Savings and Loan Associations: Some Evidence of Differences in Behavior," *American Economic Review*, v. 57 (May 1967), p. 342.

These data suggest better performance by the stock associations, whether measured in terms of association net income (gross operating income minus expenses), or in terms of interest paid out to depositors (called "dividends" in savings and loan jargon), or in terms of growth (new loans divided by average assets). The "mutual" form thus does appear to permit managers to pursue goals in conflict with those of the owner-depositors.

9. D THE OPTIMUM OF THE COMPETITIVE FIRM

According to the classical goal, the firm aims to maximize profit. Such maximization, like all behavior, is subject to constraints; in this case, the constraint is the relation between *revenue* received and *costs* incurred as larger or smaller outputs are contemplated.

More specifically, we are dealing here with the *competitive* or "price-taking" firm: The market price P is assumed, for all practical purposes, to be independent of the firm's level of output. (As we saw in the preceding chapter, while never literally true this may be a usable approximation of reality.) Then

Total Revenue $R = Pq$, plotted as a function of output q in Panel (a) of Figure 9.1, is a ray of slope P out of the origin. If the price P is constant, when output q is increased by any proportion then Revenue R rises by the same percent. Note that the vertical axis of Panel (a) is scaled in dollars.[7]

Total Cost is traditionally represented as a curve like C in Panel (a): starting from a level F of fixed costs incurred independently of any output, Total Cost as a function of output rises throughout, first at a decreasing and then at an increasing rate.

Profit is Revenue minus Cost. In symbols, $\Pi = R - C$. In the diagram, the profit-maximizing output q^* is the level of q such that the positive vertical difference between the R and the C curves is greatest. The maximum level of profit, Π^*, is shown as the bold line-segment in the diagram. It is geometrically evident that this maximum difference occurs where the Total Cost curve C is parallel to (has the same slope as) the Total Revenue curve R. (The parallelism is suggested by the dashed tangent drawn along the C curve at $q = q^*$.) This provides the key to the connection between the solution in "total" units as shown in Panel (a) and the solution in "average-marginal" units portrayed in Panel (b) of Figure 9.1.

The relations that logically must hold among total, average, and marginal magnitudes were expounded in Section 2.B: (1) A *marginal* function corre-

---

[7]Since a rationale for the use of *money* has been provided in the preceding chapter, henceforth in the text it will be assumed that goods and services are valued in terms of money as "numeraire."

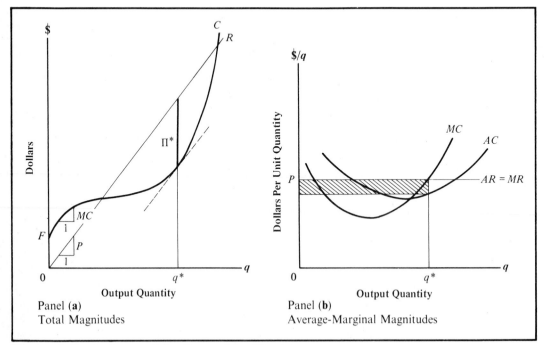

Figure 9. 1 Optimum of the Competitive Firm

sponds to the rate of increase along a total function; and (2) an *average* function is simply the total function divided by the argument or choice variable; in this case, the average functions to be dealt with are R/q and C/q.

First with regard to revenue. Marginal Revenue MR was formally defined in equation (2.6) as[8]:

(9.1)
$$MR \equiv \underset{(\text{as } \Delta q \to 0)}{\text{limit}} \frac{\Delta R}{\Delta q}$$

We will use the notation $\Delta R/\Delta q$, on the understanding that we are dealing with small increments Δ. Geometrically, MR corresponds to the *slope* along the Total Revenue curve in Panel (a) of Figure 9.1; this slope is a constant equal to the market price P. That is, any unit increase of q will yield an increment of revenue equal to the price P received for that unit. Thus, the Marginal Revenue curve MR is plotted in Panel (b) as a horizontal line at the level of P. In terms of dimensionality, note that the vertical axis of Panel (b) is scaled in units of $\$/q$, the dimensions of price.

Average Revenue AR is defined as R/q. But since $R = Pq$ necessarily, it is always definitionally true that $AR \equiv P \equiv R/q$. In this case, price P being taken as constant, the Average Revenue curve AR in Panel (b) must also be a horizontal line at the level of P. Thus, for a price-taking firm the AR and MR curves coincide in the form of a horizontal line at the level P.

For Marginal Cost MC, the formal definition is analogous:[9]

(9.2)
$$MC \equiv \underset{(\text{as } \Delta q \to 0)}{\text{limit}} \frac{\Delta C}{\Delta q}$$

Again, the notation $\Delta C/\Delta q$ will be used on the understanding that we are dealing with small increments Δ. MC corresponds geometrically to the (changing) slope along the Total Cost curve of Panel (a). MC in Panel (b) is shown as first positive but decreasing (corresponding to the region where Total Cost is rising at a decreasing rate) and then positive and increasing (corresponding to the region where Total Cost rises at an increasing rate).

Average Cost AC is C/q. For any output q, Average Cost C/q in Panel (b) corresponds to the slope of the line that could be drawn in Panel (a) from the origin to the point on the Total Cost curve at that q. At $q = 0$, Average Cost must be infinite, as can be seen directly from the definition C/q, or geometrically from the ever-steepening slope of the line from the origin to the C curve as q approaches zero. The AC curve has a falling region so long as MC lies below it (Proposition 2.2a) and later a rising region where MC lies above it (Proposition 2.2b). It then follows that AC reaches a minimum (is neither rising nor falling) at the point where MC equals AC (Proposition 2.2c). Or, we may say, the MC curve cuts through the low point of the AC curve (from below).

---

[8]*Mathematical Footnote:* This definition is equivalent, of course, to the derivative: $MR \equiv dR/dq$.
[9]*Mathematical Footnote:* In derivative notation: $MC \equiv dC/dq$.

The maximum-profit output q^*, as has already been seen, corresponds to the point in Panel (a) where the Total Revenue curve R and the Total Cost curve C have the same slope. Then at q^* in Panel (b), Marginal Revenue and Marginal Cost are equal, i.e., the MR and MC curves intersect.

In terms of economic logic, if a unit increment of output will increase revenue more than it does cost ($MR > MC$) then the increment should be produced; we are not yet at the profit-maximizing output. If $MR < MC$, on the other hand, the last unit caused a decrease in profit so that output has been pushed beyond the optimum. For profit to be a maximum, then, the condition $MC = MR$ must hold. And since we are dealing with competitive (price-taking) firms for which $MR \equiv P \equiv AR$, this condition takes on the specific form:

(9.3) $\quad MC = MR \equiv P \quad$ Maximum-Profit Condition, Competitive Firm

The economic logic also tells us something further. For, we have just seen, if $MR > MC$ the firm should expand output, and if $MR < MC$ it should contract. This suggests that $MC = MR$ is an optimum *only if the* MC *curve cuts the* MR *curve from below*. Note that in Panel (b) of Figure 9.1 there are *two* intersections of the MC curve with the horizontal MR curve. But at the left-hand intersection, MC cuts MR *from above*. By the economic logic we see that it pays to go beyond the left-hand intersection into the range of output where $MR > MC$, until the right-hand intersection is reached[10] where MC cuts MR *from below*.[11]

Proposition: The profit-maximizing output for the firm is that for which Marginal Cost equals Marginal Revenue, provided that the MC curve cuts the MR curve from below.

The *size* of the economic profit, at the profit-maximizing output q^*, was represented in Panel (a) of Figure 9.1 as the bold vertical line-segment Π^* between the Total Revenue and the Total Cost curves. In terms of average-marginal units of measurement, we can think of profit as equal to $(AR - AC)q$. That is, profit equals the difference between *Average* Revenue and *Average* Cost, multiplied by the number of units of output. So in Panel (b), maximum profit is shown as the shaded rectangle whose area is $(P - AC)q^*$.

Table 9.1 illustrates a hypothetical set of revenue and cost data for a competitive profit-maximizing firm. Price is constant at $P = 60$, so that the Total Revenue column (R) is given simply by $R = 60q$. The specific cost function assumed is $C = 128 + 69q - 14q^2 + q^3$. This formula was used to

---

[10]The left-hand intersection of MC and MR in Panel (b) corresponds to the output in Panel (a) where the vertical difference is greatest between a *higher* Total Cost curve C and a *lower* Total Revenue curve R. This is a *minimum*-profit (or maximum-loss) output.

[11]*Mathematical Footnote:* We are maximizing $\Pi = R - C$ with respect to q. Differentiating and setting equal to zero, we have as the *first-order* condition for a maximum: $dR/dq = dC/dq$, or $MR = MC$. The *second-order* condition for a maximum is that $d^2\Pi/dq^2 < 0$, or $d^2R/dq^2 < d^2C/dq^2$. This says that MR must be falling relative to MC, i.e., that MC must be cutting MR from below to have a maximum of Π.

Table 9. 1

Hypothetical Revenue and Cost Functions—Competitive Firm

$$P = 60, \; or \; R = 60q$$
$$C = q^3 - 14q^2 + 69q + 128$$

q	P	R	C	MC_1	MC_2	MC	AC	VC	AVC
0	60	0	128	—		69	∞	0	—
					56				
1	60	60	184	56	(45)	44	184	56	56
					34				
2	60	120	218	34	(26)	25	109	90	45
					18				
3	60	180	236	18	(13)	12	78.7	108	36
					8				
4	60	240	244	8	(6)	5	61	116	29
					4				
5	60	300	248	4	(5)	4	49.6	120	24
					6				
6	60	360	254	6	(10)	9	42.3	126	21
					14				
7	60	420	268	14	(21)	20	38.3	140	20
					28				
8	60	480	296	28	(38)	37	37	168	21
					48				
9	60	540	344	48	(61)	60	38.2	216	24
					74				
10	60	600	418	74		89	41.8	290	29

compute the Total Cost column C. If plotted, the Total Revenue and Total Cost functions would have the general shapes pictured in Panel (a) of Figure 9.1, and the average and marginal functions would resemble those in Panel (b).

Three different Marginal Cost columns are shown in the Table. The first, MC_1, is the "poorer approximation" discussed in Section 2.B. Let $C(q)$ be the Total Cost at a particular level of output q, and $C(q + 1)$ that at a unit greater level of output. Then, according to MC_1, the difference $C(q + 1) - C(q)$ is the Marginal Cost *at* $q + 1$. The "better approximation" discussed in Chapter 2, tabulated as MC_2 here, calls this same cost difference the Marginal Cost *at* $q + \frac{1}{2}$. To find MC_2 for integer values of q, simple interpolation is used; these interpolated numbers are shown in parentheses in the MC_2 column of the table. The precise Marginal Cost, finally, is tabulated as MC; this was determined by calculus techniques which yielded the equation $MC = 69 - 28q + 3q^2$.[12] As can be seen, MC_2 is indeed a much better approximation than MC_1 to the true Marginal Cost MC.

Since $P = 60$, the condition $MC = P$ leads to the profit-maximizing solution $q^* = 9$. (Using MC_2 and interpolating would yield a close approxi-

[12]*Mathematical Footnote:* $C = 128 + 69q - 14q^2 + q^3$. Then $MC \equiv dC/dq = 69 - 28q + 3q^2$.

mation; note that use of MC_1 and interpolating would lead to a substantial error.) At $q^* = 9$, Total Revenue $R = 540$ and Total Cost $C = 344$; hence profit $\Pi^* = 196.$[13]

The last two columns of Table 9.1 show *Total Variable Cost VC* and *Average Variable Cost AVC*. Total Variable Cost is simply Total Cost less Fixed Cost: $VC = C - F$. Average Variable Cost is, correspondingly, $VC/q = (C - F)/q$. The relations between Total Cost and Total Variable Cost are shown geometrically in Panel (a) of Figure 9.2. Evidently, the latter

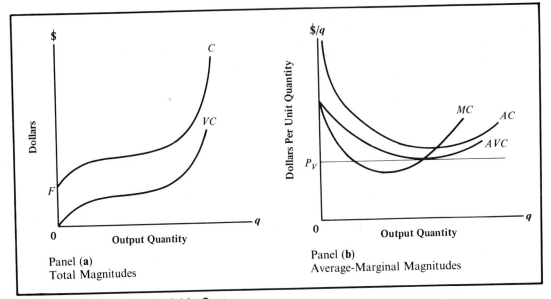

Figure 9. 2   Total and Variable Costs

is everywhere lower than the former, by a constant vertical difference equal to the amount of the Fixed Cost F.

In terms of average-marginal magnitudes, the relations are as shown in Panel (b). The Average Cost AC and Average Variable Cost AVC are vertically farthest apart at the left; indeed, at $q = 0$, AC is infinite.[14] For larger q, the Average Cost $AC = C/q = (F + VC)/q$ approaches nearer and nearer to $AVC = VC/q$, since the term F/q gets smaller and smaller as q increases. As for the Marginal Cost curve MC, this is defined solely in terms of cost *differences*, and hence is in no way affected by the presence or absence of fixed costs. So there is only a single MC curve, reflecting the (parallel) slopes of either Total Cost C or Total Variable Cost VC at any given level of q. By

[13]There is also a false solution (where MC cuts MR *from above*) at $q = \frac{1}{3}$. At this output, Revenue $= P(\frac{1}{3}) = 20$, and Cost can be computed as equalling (approximately) 149.48. Here a loss is being incurred.

[14]*Mathematical Footnote:* What about Average Variable Cost? At $q = 0$, $AVC = 0/0$ is indeterminate. But applying L'Hôpital's Rule, it can be seen that AVC approaches a finite limit as q approaches zero. This limit is the Marginal Cost MC at $q = 0$. So MC and AVC coincide at $q = 0$.

corresponding reasoning, we see that MC is related qualitatively to AVC in the same way as it is to AC (Propositions 2.2a, 2.2b, and 2.2c). Specifically, MC cuts through the minimum point of AVC as well as the minimum point of AC, as shown in the diagram.

In the Table, the true $MC = AVC = 20$ when $q = 7$; hence this is the minimum of AVC. The Table indicates that $MC = AC = 37$ at $q = 8$; this is the minimum of the Average Cost AC.[15]

The maximum-profit condition for the competitive firm is, according to equation (9.3), $MC = MR \equiv P$ (assuming MC cuts MR from below). There is a supplementary condition, however, that runs in terms of the concept of Variable Cost. If the Total Revenue R does not even cover the Total Variable Cost VC, then the firm is losing by producing any output at all. Even though the fixed cost F runs on, the firm would do better incurring that fixed expense rather than generating output whose sales value falls short of the variable cost incurred. Hence we have:

(9.4) $$R > VC \quad \text{or equivalently} \quad P > AVC$$

Condition for Non-Zero Output

In geometrical terms, the optimal output q^* is given by the intersection of MC with the horizontal $MR = P$, as in Panel (b) of Figure 9.1, but only if P is greater than a certain minimum "shut-down" price P_V. This minimum is shown in Panel (b) of Figure 9.2. It is at the level defined by the intersection of the MC and AVC curves, i.e., the shut-down price P_V is the low point or minimum of the Average Variable Cost function. If the actual price P is less than P_V, the optimal output for the firm is simply zero.

Proposition: If market price P is less than the minimum attainable Average Variable Cost AVC, a competitive firm will not produce at all.

But at zero output, and consequently zero revenue, if the fixed cost F runs on then the firm must be incurring a loss. And if $AVC < P < AC$, even though it pays the firm to produce where $MC = P$, still a loss is being suffered. How can a firm stay in business at a loss? The explanation of this possibility runs in terms of the economist's distinction between *short-run* and *long-run* solutions for the firm to be taken up in Section 9.E.

*9. D. 1 An Application: Division of Output among Plants

Sometimes a firm is faced with the problem of allocating a given total of output between two or more plants that it owns. Suppose there are just two

---

[15]*Mathematical Footnote:* To find the minimum of AVC, differentiate $AVC = q^2 - 14q + 69$ and set equal to zero. The solution is $q = 7$. To find the minimum of AC, differentiate $AC = q^2 - 14q + 69 + (128/q)$. A cubic equation is obtained, but the only root in the relevant range is $q = 8$.
*Starred sections represent optional or advanced material.

plants *a* and *b*. Then, by an obvious extension of equation (9.3), the firm's optimizing rule becomes:

(9.5)
$$MC_a = MC_b = MR \equiv P$$

That is, the firm should so divide its production as to make the Marginal Costs of output the same in both plants; the total output, furthermore, should be such that this level of Marginal Cost equals Marginal Revenue *MR*. (In competition, of course, *MR* is identical with price *P*.)

Figure 9.3 is a geometrical representation of the division of output between two plants. The given total of output, $q_a + q_b = q$, is indicated by the

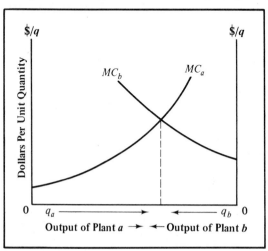

Figure 9. 3
Division of Output between Plants

horizontal distance between the two vertical axes. The output q_a of plant *a* is measured in the usual way, as the distance to the right of the left-hand axis. But q_b is, as indicated by the arrow, measured in the reversed direction as the distance to the left of the right-hand axis. This construction is convenient since the optimal division of output, where $MC_a = MC_b$, is then at the intersection of the two Marginal Cost curves (both assumed rising through-out).[16] The *total* output of the firm will be correct if the $MC_a = MC_b$ so determined is just equal to Marginal Revenue.

The inequality condition of equation (9.4) must, however, also be remem-bered. The revenue R_a or R_b received by *each* plant must exceed the Total Variable Cost VC_a or VC_b incurred by that plant. If this does not hold for any single plant, that plant should be shut down (assigned zero output).

What if the MC_a and MC_b curves, each an increasing function of its own plant output, do not intersect? This means that for the specified total output *q*, one plant *always* produces less cheaply than the other. Then regardless of fixed costs, the higher *MC* plant should not be operated at all.

[16]There are interesting complications if one or both of the plant *MC* curves are falling rather than rising functions of output. These topics cannot be pursued here, however.

Example 9. 3
Load
Dispatching:
Electrical
Engineers as
Economists

Electricity is typically generated by companies that operate a number of separate producing plants, with a transmission network providing connections to consumers as well as ties among the generating plants. Since electricity companies are (with some exceptions) required to meet instantaneously the demands placed upon them by consumers, the operating problem at any moment of time is to assign output most economically among the generating plants. As required total output varies widely within the day, and even from moment to moment, the problem is both practically important and ever-present.

Fred M. Westfield[17] investigated the operating practices of a leading American electric utility. He discovered that this company employs a dispatcher to actually "assign the load" from moment to moment among the different plants. The dispatcher is guided by a Station-Loading Sliderule that shows what the economist would regard as the Marginal Cost function of each plant. By mechanically manipulating his Sliderule, the dispatcher automatically equates Marginal Cost for all plants in operation, satisfying equation (9.5) in such a way as to meet the total generation requirement. For some older plants, Marginal Cost is high throughout. These plants are operated at non-zero levels only in peak-demand periods.

The company's method of division of output, and the Sliderule itself, were developed by engineers lacking the slightest acquaintance with economic theory! The company's engineers thus independently "discovered" Marginal Cost analysis—a striking intellectual achievement, though one that knowledge of intermediate economic theory would have made unnecessary.

[17] F. M. Westfield, "Marginal Analysis, Multi-Plant Firms, and Business Practice: An Example," *Quarterly Journal of Economics*, v. 69 (May 1955).

9. E SHORT RUN VERSUS LONG RUN

"In the short run some costs are fixed; in the long run they become variable." This is the fundamental difference between long run and short run. The distinction between "long run" and "short run" is not a simple dichotomy, however. The longer the run contemplated, the greater the range of costs considered as variable rather than fixed.

Consider a manufacturing firm. Toward the variable end of the fixed/variable cost continuum are the expenses of input elements like electric power, supplies of materials, and common labor services; toward the relatively fixed end are costs associated with ownership or leasing of real estate and machinery. Suppose circumstances (e.g., an interruption of supplies, or breakdown of machinery) call for a very short, say an hour's, reduction of output. Some electric power would be saved in the slowdown, and there would be lesser usage of materials, but little else could or would be changed in the way of cost. If output were cut back over a period as long as a day, some labor might also be laid off. Over a period like a month a large fraction of the labor force might be furloughed (their wages would become a variable cost), and perhaps some leased equipment (e.g., trucks) would be dispensed with. Finally, for a permanent reduction in output the firm will sell off machinery and scale down real-estate commitments.

For simplicity, in the discussion that follows we shall treat the long-short distinction as if it were a dichotomy. The "long run" will mean that *all* costs are variable; the "short run," that some costs are fixed. The relations between *total* short-run and long-run costs, under this assumption, are shown in Panel (a) of Figure 9.4. The single Long-Run Total Cost curve *LRTC* goes

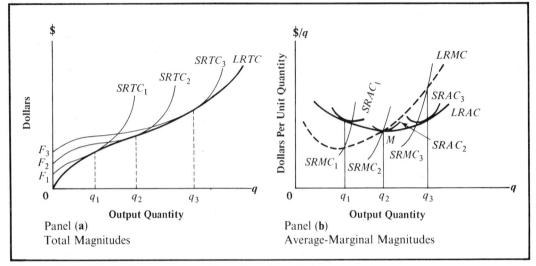

Figure 9. 4 Short-Run and Long-Run Cost Functions

through the origin; since there are no fixed costs, if $q = 0$ then $LRTC = 0$. The *LRTC* function shows the *lowest cost* of producing any given level of output. Why the lowest cost? Because, with all costs variable, for any output q the firm is free to choose the best (most economical) mix and proportion of all resources employed.

Three different Short-Run Total Cost functions are shown in Panel (a). First, $SRTC_1$ represents a low level of fixed cost F_1, adapted for a relatively small rate of output. The adaptation is optimal for the rate of output q_1 at which $SRTC_1$ is tangent to *LRTC*; this is optimal because at q_1, $SRTC_1 = LRTC$, and the latter is the *lowest* cost possible of producing output q_1. Along $SRTC_1$ the fixed costs are small, which is fine if output is to be at a low rate. On the other hand, if the actual production should become greater than initially contemplated, $SRTC_1$ rises steeply—increments of output beyond q_1

rapidly become very costly. $SRTC_2$ is an adaptation that is optimal for a middling rate of output, q_2 in the diagram. The fixed cost F_2 is at a sufficiently high level to make larger output rates cheaper along $SRTC_2$ than along $SRTC_1$; on the other hand, should it turn out that only small output is desired, then it would have been better to be operating along $SRTC_1$. Finally, $SRTC_3$ represents a level of fixed cost F_3 that is optimal for the relatively large output rate q_3. It represents the best of the three situations for high output, but the worst if it should turn out that only a small output is wanted.

A common confusion runs somewhat as follows: "The short run is distinguished from the long run in that certain factors are fixed in the former but variable in the latter. Since short-run costs of expanding output involve increases in only *some* of the resources or factors, while long-run costs may involve increases in *all*, short-run costs must be less than long-run costs. Isn't it cheaper to increase output by expanding only variable cost than by expanding both variable and fixed cost?" Expressed this way, the fallacy is evident. The firm would rationally accept an increase in its fixed cost, in its long-run decision, precisely because doing so is *less costly* (involves a more economical mix or proportion of the various factors) than trying to expand output by increasing variable cost alone.

Let us now translate from the total units in Panel (a) of Figure 9.4 to average-marginal units in Panel (b). Since $SRTC_1$ lies always above $LRTC$ except at the tangency point q_1 it follows that the corresponding Short-Run Average Cost curve $SRAC_1$ will lie always above the Long-Run Average Cost curve $LRAC$ except at q_1.[18] A similar argument applies for the relation between $SRTC_2$ and $SRAC_2$, $SRTC_3$ and $SRAC_3$, etc. The upshot is that the Long-Run Average Cost curve $LRAC$ has the same "lower envelope" property relative to the Short-Run Average Cost curves that $LRTC$ has relative to the Short-Run Total Cost curves.

There is a famous conundrum reflected in the shapes of the various $SRAC$ curves relative to the $LRAC$ curve in Panel (b). Note that while the point of contact of the middle curve $SRAC_2$ with $LRAC$ is at the minimum of the $SRAC_2$ curve itself, this is *not* true for the other two $SRAC$ curves. For $SRAC_1$, the point of contact with $LRAC$ is along the downward slope, and so the minimum of the $SRAC_1$ curve lies to the right of (at a greater output than) the tangency point q_1. For $SRAC_3$ the situation is reversed, and the minimum of $SRAC_3$ is to the left of q_3. This seems puzzling, as suggested by the question: "The point of tangency is a low-cost point. Hence shouldn't the points of tangency coincide with the low-cost points (minima) along the various $SRAC$ curves?"

Exploratory curve-bending will show that it is geometrically impossible to draw an $LRAC$ curve through the *minima* of the $SRAC$ curves, and still have

---

[18] $SRTC_1 > LRTC$ implies $SRTC_1/q > LRTC/q$. But $SRTC_1/q$ is simply $SRAC_1$ and $LRTC/q$ is simply $LRAC$, so $SRTC_1 > LRTC$ evidently implies $SRAC_1 > LRAC$. At the point of contact itself, at output q_1, the equality $SRTC_1 = LRTC$ implies the equality $SRAC_1 = LRAC$.

it lie everywhere *below* these curves. For *LRAC*, what we really want to know is the lowest unit cost of producing any given level of output, i.e., the "lower envelope" of the *SRAC* curves. A point on this envelope is *not generally the lowest-cost output for any given level of fixed cost*, i.e., a minimum along any specific *SRAC* curve.

Consider now the short-run and long-run *Marginal* Costs. At the tangencies of the *SRTC* and *LRTC* curves in Panel (a) of Figure 9.4 not only the *levels* but also the *slopes* of the curves in contact are equal. But the marginal function is always the slope of the corresponding total function. It follows that at output q_1, the short run $SRMC_1$ equals the long run $LRMC$; at q_2, $SRMC_2 = LRMC$; and at q_3, $SRMC_3 = LRMC$. This leads to the relation among the various short-run and the long-run marginal curves shown in Panel (b). Note that *LRMC* has a generally less steep slope than the Short-Run Marginal Cost curves. This feature will play a role in the distinction between the short-run versus long-run *supply function of the firm*, to be discussed in the chapter following.

There is one difficulty with the concept of "fixed" costs that has been pushed into the background, but now ought to be faced. Common sense tells us that, for an hour's shutdown of output, a firm will not sell off its buildings and machinery with the intention of buying them back when output picks up again. But is this consistent with our analytical models? Why should a firm continue to incur any needless "fixed" costs not dictated by immediate production requirements? Why not sell off the buildings if not needed today? It is sometimes said that "fixity" is the result of previous contractual arrangements, for example, a mortgage on an owned building or a long term lease on a rented one. But mortgages and leases on an excessive scale can always be renegotiated; any losses incurred in the process are attributable to past errors of judgment, and are in no way costs of current production.

The explanation of "fixity" is connected in part with the feature of the real world discussed at length in the previous chapter—the fact that exchange transactions are not costless. The costs of negotiating and executing complex contracts are what make absurd the idea of sale and repurchase of factory buildings for an hour's production shut-down. But there is an additional element also involved: the *specialization of resources to the firm*.

Many different types of resources may have a degree of specialization to the firm. Machinery can be made to order, buildings partitioned or remodeled, and labor can incur specific training of little or no use to other employers. The presence of such specialized resources imports a degree of irreversibility into the firm's employment decision. With only unspecialized factors, the firm can indeed, subject to the limitations of transaction costs, purchase or sell off resources as required (or enter into or cancel leases) so as to preclude any significant "fixity" as output expands or contracts. Thus temporary increases or decreases in output can, to the extent permitted by transaction costs, be responded to with "appropriate" resource combinations, i.e., along the long-run cost curves. But highly specialized assets owned by the firm will be of little use to other firms and thus have little or no resale value. Hence, the firm will not be inclined to dispose of such assets to meet a reduction of output evaluated as temporary in nature. Nor will the firm very readily acquire more of such a resource merely to achieve a temporary increase in production. Even if such specialized resources are *leased* rather than *owned* (specialized labor may be placed in this category), the cost of cancellation of the lease will tend to be high. For the owner of such a resource will, before tailoring it to the needs of the firm and thereby reducing its marketability elsewhere, surely protect himself by insisting upon steep penalties in the event of cancellation.

In the absence of transaction costs, and if only unspecialized resources were employed in production, *there would then be only a single cost function*—the distinction between "long run" and "short run" would be meaningless. Continuing to neglect transaction costs, but admitting that specialized resources permit firms to produce more cheaply, there are two modes of response to a decline in demand (for a competitive firm, this would be observed as a fall in product price P). (1) The "short-run" response, appropriate for a *temporary* decline in price and so in output, holds the firm's specialized resources fixed and continues to count their cost as a cost of doing business. Thus, "a loss may be incurred in the short run" (AC may exceed P), meaning that it is rational for the firm to accept a temporary loss rather than dispose of a specialized factor that would shortly have to be reacquired. (2) The "long-run" response, appropriate for a *permanent* decline in output, is to dispose of the specialized resources no longer needed for projected future production. Hence their cost is no longer "fixed," though in general not all the expenses incurred can be recovered in disposing of them. Whatever accounting loss is incurred in the disposition of specialized factors is a "sunk" cost, a record of a past error of judgment, but not a relevant cost for any current decision.

Corresponding considerations apply to an *increase* in demand (for a competitive firm, a *rise* in market price P). If regarded as temporary, it will not pay the firm to incur the cost of specializing additional resources, since the expense of doing so will not be fully recovered when the time comes to dispose of them. To the extent that the demand change is regarded as permanent, however, it will become increasingly attractive for the firm to incur additional "fixed" (specializing) costs that make it possible to produce large rates of output cheaply.

Conclusion: Factors may be held fixed in the face of a temporary demand fluctuation, in order to avoid round-trip transaction costs associated with purchase and re-sale (or sale and re-purchase), and also to save the costs of specializing factors to the firm. When this occurs, the firm is making a *short-run* response to the fluctuation in demand. A *long-run* response, in which all factors are varied in amount, will be made if the demand change is regarded as permanent.

Example 9. 4
Electricity:
Short-Run and
Long-Run Costs

There have been a good many studies by econometricians and by engineers of the *long-run* costs of electricity production. The general conclusion has been that economies of scale exist, i.e., that in the region of historical experience the Long-Run Average Cost curve *LRAC* has been a declining function of output.[19] Thus, electric power firms appear to characteristically choose levels of capacity (i.e., of "fixed" plant) so as to operate to the left of the minimum of the *LRAC* curve in the diagram of Figure 9.4, Panel (b). This means, in particular, that Long-Run Marginal Cost *LRMC* is less than *LRAC*.

The main technological source of economies of scale is in power *generation*; almost without exception, the larger the generating plant capacity, the cheaper the power output. The main counterbalancing force is the cost of power *transmission*. The more that power generation is concentrated in a single plant of huge capacity, the higher are the transmission losses in carrying power to geographically dispersed customers.

With regard to *short-run* costs, the picture is quite different. A power system must provide for enormous variation in usage even within short periods like a single day; since electricity is non-storable, in peak hours far more power must be produced and delivered than in off-peak quiet hours. Of course, it would be absurd to expect the firm to respond by adjusting "fixed" capacity up and down within the day. And in any case, since these demand fluctuations are obviously temporary, the firm would not want to do so. Hence we would expect to find contractions and expansions of short-run output associated with *SRMC* and *SRAC* curves like $SRAC_1$ and $SRMC_1$ in Panel (b) of Figure 9.4. In particular, with capacity held fixed, *rising* average and marginal costs should be encountered, at least at the high outputs required for meeting peak demands.

Technologically, there are two main reasons for rising short-run costs in the range of larger outputs. (1) Pieces of electrical equipment generally have a rated "capacity." This is not an absolute limit; capacity can be temporarily exceeded. But as this is done there are losses from overheating, risk of breakdown, etc. (2) Any power system has plants, and generating units within plants, of greater or lesser "efficiency" (ratio of output to input, particularly with regard to fuel required). Rationality dictates that the most efficient equipment will typically be run continuously to carry the "base load." Only as required by demand will increasingly less efficient units be started up, so that average costs rise. (Less "efficient" units may simply be obsolescent equipment not yet replaced, but not necessarily so. It pays an electrical system to keep

[19]A review of recent studies is contained in D. Huettner, *Plant Size, Technological Change, and Investment Requirements* (New York: Praeger Publishers, 1974), especially pp. 29–39.

some units with relatively poor fuel efficiency, provided that they possess otherwise desirable properties such as low capital costs, rapid start-up, etc.)

Example 9.3 showed that integrated power systems do take account of the rising *SRMC* curves of generating plants. If plant *SRMC* curves were not rising, there would be no need for dispatching; all the load would always be assigned to the single most efficient plant!

Questions

1. Why is most productive activity carried out by firms, rather than simply by individuals who contract mutually with one another?

2. Partnership firms are generally small and are generally managed directly by their owners. Why? How does the corporate form facilitate the organization of larger enterprises?

3. What is meant by economic profit? Is profit maximization an appropriate goal for owners? For managers? What tends to happen if owners are not themselves managers?

4. What would be the effect upon the firm's decisions of a 50 percent tax upon *economic* profit?

5. Explain the nature of the "better approximation" of Marginal Cost in Table 9.1. Why isn't the "better approximation" a perfect one?

6. What are the two conditions necessary for a competitive firm to be producing at a profit-maximizing rate of output? Explain.

7. When will a firm respond to changes in economic conditions by a "short-run" adjustment? When by a "long-run" adjustment?

8. Why will a firm ever keep *any* factors fixed in the face of changing economic conditions? What determines which classes of factors are held fixed, and which varied?

9. Compare the effect upon the firm's decisions of (a) a per-unit tax of $1 upon output versus (b) a license fee of $200 payable each year regardless of output.

10. Is the firm's Total Cost curve necessarily rising, or can it have a falling range? Is the firm's Average Cost curve necessarily U-shaped, or can it be rising throughout (or falling throughout)? What of the Average Variable Cost curve? For each allowable shape of the *AC* and *AVC* curves, show the implied shape of the Marginal Cost curve *MC*.

11. Why is it that a Long-Run Average Cost curve *LRAC* cannot be drawn with the following two properties: (a) It shows the lowest cost at which any given output can be produced (i.e., it is a "lower envelope" of the Short-Run Average Cost curves); and (b) it shows the lowest-cost output at any given level of the fixed factor (i.e., it goes through the minimum points of all the *SRAC* curves)? Which of the two conditions is the correct one?

12. In the problem of division of output between two plants, suppose that the Marginal Cost curves MC_a and MC_b are rising but do *not* intersect. The text asserts that in such a case only one of the plants should be operated. Is this correct? Explain.

13. What is wrong with the following reasoning on the part of a factory manager:

> My plant is working steadily at its most efficient output. Nevertheless, I could always meet a short-run surge in demand simply by running the machines a little faster and deferring maintenance. So in the short run my Marginal Cost is practically zero.

14. Electric utilities commonly keep their most modern and efficient generating equipment, characterized by low ratio of fuel input to power output, working around the clock. Older equipment still on hand is used only to meet periods of higher load. What does this imply about the shape of the Short-Run Marginal Cost curve for generation of electricity? Why doesn't the firm always use only the most modern equipment?

15. An urban rapid-transit line runs crowded trains (200 passengers per car) at rush hours, but very empty trains (ten passengers per car) at off hours. A management consultant makes the following argument:

> The cost of running a car for one trip on this line is about $50 regardless of the number of passengers. So the per-passenger cost is about 25 cents at rush hour but rises to $5 per passenger in off hours. Consequently, we had better discourage off-hour business.

Explain the fallacy. "Commutation tickets" sold by some transit systems (reduced-price, multiple-ride tickets) are predominantly used in rush hours. Are such tickets a good idea?

Chapter 10
Competitive Supply, and Equilibrium in the Product Market

This chapter moves on from the behavior of the single firm as a decision-making agent (an optimization problem) to the supply side of the product market as a whole. Competitive (price-taking) behavior on the part of firms leads to a *supply function* in which the outputs of the firms, and therefore of the industry, respond to changes in the market price of the product. Putting this supply function together with the consumers' *demand function* developed in Part Two, we will have studied the equilibrium-determining elements on both sides of the product market.

10. A FROM FIRM SUPPLY TO MARKET SUPPLY

The competitive firm's maximum-profit condition, equation (9.3), is $MC = P$, product price P being taken as constant by the firm. Since Marginal Cost MC varies with firm output q, as shown in Panel (b) of Figure 9.1, a *supply function* of the firm can be derived. This function shows how firm output q responds to changes in price P. The firm's reaction is also subject to the qualification expressed in inequality (9.4): When market price is less than P_V, the minimum level of the Average Variable Cost AVC, the (short-run) optimal output for the firm is simply zero. Thus, the competitive firm's short-run supply function s_f may have a discontinuity as illustrated by the bold curve of Figure 10.1: After an initial horizontal range $P_V K$, it follows the rising branch of MC above the point K. The discontinuity is associated with a minimum positive output q_V; as P rises from zero, at the level P_V the firm's output response jumps suddenly from $q = 0$ to $q = q_V$.[1]

Aggregating over all firms producing a particular good, the economy-wide supply curve for that good is obtained. This aggregation is analogous to that of Section 4.D. There, the quantities *demanded* by the separate *individuals* at any given price were summed to obtain the economy-wide or market demand

---

[1] *Question for the Student:* Why do we say that the supply function "may" have such a discontinuity? (*Hint:* Is it logically necessary for the curve of Average Variable Cost, AVC, to have an initial falling range?)

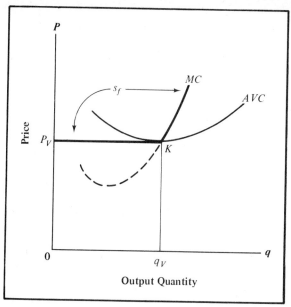

Figure 10. 1
Competitive Firm's Supply Function—Short Run

at that price; doing this for all prices led to the overall market demand curve. Here, the quantities *supplied* by the separate *firms* at any given price are summed to obtain the market supply at that price; doing this for all possible prices, we have the overall market supply function. As a result of *specialization in production*, however, a given good is produced only by a limited subset of firms in the economy—a subset that is called the *industry* associated with that good. So the aggregate of the firm supply curves for a particular product becomes the *industry supply curve*.

There is one complication to consider. The cost of production of the firm is equal to the sum of payments to the various factors, i.e., to the sum of resource prices times resource quantities employed. The individual firm is a price-taker not only with regard to product price but also with regard to factor prices. But when the *industry as a whole* expands or contracts output in response to changes in product price P, there may well be an impact upon the prices of some or all of the resources used in production.

The effect of this consideration is shown in Figure 10.2. Let us suppose that an initial level of product price P' is associated with an industry aggregate output Q'; this price and quantity therefore determine one point on the industry supply curve S. At this initial price each firm has a Marginal Cost curve, like MC in Figure 10.1, which (for prices $P > P_V$) shows the supply reaction of the firm to changes in price. It might then be thought that the effect of a product price increase from P' to P'' can simply be found by moving along the curve denoted $\sum s'_f$ in Figure 10.2, the simple horizontal summation of the firms' supply curves, to the output level $\hat{Q}$. But, if the collective

251

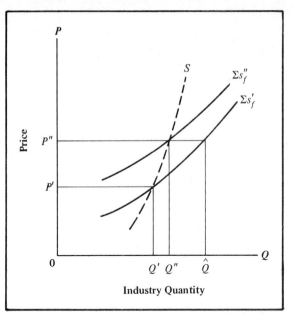

Figure 10. 2
Industry Supply Function (External Diseconomy)

expansion of industry output affects factor prices, the industry *as a whole* cannot expand output along $\sum s'_f$. Normally, the consequence of such an expansion would be a *rise* in the prices of factors used by the industry; this would entail an *upward shift* of all the firms' Marginal Cost curves and, therefore, of their supply functions. The upshot is that with a product price rise from P' to P'', the new quantity supplied by the industry will not be $\hat{Q}$ along $\sum s'_f$ in Figure 10.2. The correct quantity Q'' lies along a somewhat higher summation curve $\sum s''_f$, which reflects the firms' upward-shifted MC curves at the higher level of industry output. The true supply curve, the dashed curve S in Figure 10.2, will therefore tend to be steeper than would be inferred from looking at the separate firms' MC curves. Put another way, an observer who failed to take this factor-price effect into account would be led to predict too big a supply response of the industry to variations in product price P.

Conclusion: The supply curve of a competitive firm is identical to its MC curve (above the minimum of its AVC curve). The supply curve of a competitive industry is the horizontal sum of the firms' supply curves, adjusted for the factor-price effect upon firms' MC curves as the industry output expands or contracts. The factor-price effect normally operates to reduce the magnitude of the supply response to changes in demand, that is, it steepens the industry supply curve.

It is desirable to have a measure of responsiveness of quantity supplied to price, analogous to the corresponding demand measures discussed in Chapter

252

5. The most obvious measure of supply responsiveness would be $\Delta Q/\Delta P$, the ratio of the change in quantity per unit change in price along the supply function. But, as explained in Chapter 5, such a ratio has the disadvantage of being affected by changes of conventional units of measurement. Different values for the measure of responsiveness would be obtained if the unit of quantity were pounds instead of tons, or if price were quoted in dollars instead of in cents.

The *elasticity* concept eliminates this difficulty by expressing changes of quantity and price in terms of proportionate rather than arithmetic variation. In this case, we are interested in proportionate response of quantity supplied to proportionate change in price. This concept is called the "elasticity of supply."

Definition: The elasticity of supply κ is the proportional change in the quantity supplied, $\Delta Q/Q$, divided by the proportional change in price, $\Delta P/P$.

For consistency with the treatment of elasticity of demand in Chapter 5, Sections B and C, a symbol like κ_{xx} should have been used for the elasticity of supply of commodity X in response to changes in P_x. *Cross*-elasticity of supply (response of supply of commodity X to changes in the price of any other commodity Y) could be symbolized as κ_{xy}'. *Income* elasticity of supply could be defined as well.[2] But attention will be limited here to the direct price elasticity symbolized simply as κ:[3]

$$(10.1) \qquad \kappa = \frac{\Delta Q/Q}{\Delta P/P} = \frac{\Delta Q}{\Delta P} \cdot \frac{P}{Q}$$

To distinguish different commodities, appropriate subscripts would of course be used.

Aside from eliminating undesired effects due to shifts in conventional units of measurement, the elasticity concept permits *inter-commodity* comparisons of the degree of supply responsiveness to price: We can meaningfully say that the supply of some commodity X is more sensitive to price (X has greater elasticity of supply) than some other commodity Y. The elasticity concept also allows price-responsiveness comparisons despite wide variations in *scale*, for example, between a firm's supply function and an industry supply function. The relation between the firm supply curves and the industry supply curve derived in the previous section, i.e., the relation between the shapes of the $\sum s_f$ curves and the S curve in Figure 10.2, can be expressed as follows:

[2]The *cross-elasticity* of supply would be relevant for two goods related in production, e.g., wool and mutton. The *income elasticity* of supply might be significant if, for example, higher income led to a withdrawal of labor from the industry. (In this case, the income elasticity would be *negative*.)

[3]*Mathematical Footnote:* In terms of derivatives,

$$\kappa = \frac{dQ}{dP} \cdot \frac{P}{Q}$$

Proposition: The elasticity of supply of the industry is normally *less* than the separate elasticities of supply of its component firms (because of the factor-price shifts that take place with industry-wide changes of output).

10. B   LONG-RUN AND SHORT-RUN SUPPLY

The supply curve of the firm discussed in Section 10.A (in Figure 10.1, the horizontal $P_V K$ followed by that portion of the MC curve lying above the minimum of the Average Variable Cost curve AVC) is a *short-run* supply function. The MC curve involved is a particular *Short-Run* Marginal Cost curve $SRMC$ [like the ones pictured in Figure 9.4, Panel (b)] associated with a given quantity of a "fixed" factor. As explained in Section 9.E, a factor may be held "fixed" in quantity when the firm is responding to price changes regarded as temporary. The short-run supply curve S of the industry is derived by aggregating these short-run supply curves of the separate firms (with due allowance, of course, for the factor-price effect discussed above).

What if a fall in price were regarded as *permanent*? Then the firm has clearly made a mistake in past over-expansion of the "fixed" factor. That is, its past "planning" decision that equated *Long-Run* Marginal Cost $LRMC$ to anticipated price P was based upon an over-optimistic evaluation of the price prospects. It now wishes to contract the scale of the "fixed" factor back to the level associated with the condition $LRMC = P$, using the more realistic value of P.[4] In the opposite case, of course, an *increase* in price regarded as permanent would be reacted to by an output adjustment setting $LRMC = P$ via an increase in the scale of the fixed factor.

Thus, a firm's long-run supply function Ls_f will be the broken bold curve shown in Figure 10.3. It has a horizontal branch at the level of P_C, the low point of the $LRAC$ curve, but above that is represented by the firm's $LRMC$ function. Suppose that a firm is initially in optimal short-run and long-run adjustment to a given level of price P°. In Figure 10.3, we see that at output q° both $SRMC$ and $LRMC$ are equal to P°. Now imagine that price suddenly jumps to P'. If the price change is regarded as *temporary* by the firm, the correct reaction will be to set $SRMC = P'$ at output level q'_S; if regarded as *permanent*, the correct reaction is to set $LRMC = P'$ at output level q'_L. Of course, there will be various degrees rather than a strict dichotomy between "temporary" and "permanent" price changes. In addition, firms may differ in their estimates of the permanence of price fluctuations currently encountered. In consequence, over any period of time we would expect to observe some *mixture* of "short-run" and "long-run" responses to price changes.

---

[4]How *rapidly* it pays to move from the over-expanded to the correct level of the fixed factor depends upon a number of features, including the durability and the resale value of the "excessive" fixed equipment specialized to the firm. If resale value is relatively high, the firm may sell off the excess equipment and move to the correct scale almost immediately. But if resale value is very low, it may pay the firm to retain the equipment until it wears out, rather than dispose of an asset of positive productivity for almost nothing. Note that it may or may not take a long period of *calendar* time to make a "long-run" scale adjustment.

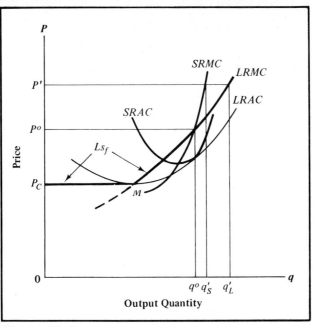

Figure 10. 3
Firm's Long-Run Supply Function

Example 10. 1
Cotton
Spindles[5]

Cotton spinning in the United States is generally regarded as a good approximation of a competitive industry. There are two main geographical concentrations of the industry, in New England and in the South. The Table below shows, for each region, the average variation (by calendar quarters over the period 1945–59) in "spindle hours." Spindles as fixed equipment are of course an essential element of spinning, so that spindle hours can be regarded as measuring output. "Changes in Hours per Spindle" may be interpreted as an index of the firms' "short-run" adjustment to the price changes taking place quarter by quarter. "Changes in Active Spindles" represents a "long-run" adjustment—variation in the amount of fixed equipment.

1945–1959 Quarterly
Changes in Spindle Hours Due to:

	Change in Hours per Spindle (%)	Change in Number of Active Spindles (%)
Southern States	90.5	9.2
New England	76.5	21.8

Source: U.S. Census data cited in G. J. Stigler, *The Theory of Price*, 3rd ed. (New York: Macmillan, 1966), p. 144.

[5]Discussion based upon G. J. Stigler, *The Theory of Price*, 3rd ed. (New York: Macmillan, 1966), pp. 143–44.

Evidently, the quarterly price changes in this period were predominantly interpreted by firms as temporary, since they led only to a small extent to changes in the quantities of "fixed" equipment.

The difference between the two regions appears to be due to the fact that the industry, while relatively static in the South, was definitely declining in New England. In periods of low prices, some of the higher-cost New England firms made long-run adjustments by gradually disposing of their fixed spindle equipment.

The *industry* long-run supply curve, like the industry short-run supply curve, is based upon the horizontal summation of the firm supply curves. As before, allowance must be made for the impact of industry-wide expansions or contractions upon factor prices, the effect of which will be as already pictured in Figure 10.2. As in the case of short-run supply, this factor-price variation makes the industry long-run supply curve LS less elastic than the separate firms' Ls_f curves.

There is one new element that operates in the long run: *entry and exit of firms*. In long-run equilibrium, for every firm that remains in the industry price must cover Average Cost: $P > LRAC$. Or, we may say, *profit* must be non-negative. Profits are the excess of revenue (market value of output) over costs (market value of input). If this excess is negative, in the long run the resources will be freed to move to higher-valued uses elsewhere. As this applies to entrepreneurial resources as well, those firms that can achieve only negative profit at all achievable levels of output will eventually exit or cease to exist (the entrepreneur will move to a new industry or will shift to non-entrepreneurial employments). And if a new firm (whether newly organized, or already in existence but outside the industry) can earn a profit within the industry, it will eventually enter.

The crucial relation between long-run and short-run supply is:

Proposition: *Supply response to price changes will be greater in the long run than in the short run.* Or, we may say, *long-run supply elasticity is greater than short-run.*

A given price change leads to a larger supply reaction when firms in the industry adjust along $LRMC$ (i.e., when they interpret the price change as permanent) than when they adjust only along $SRMC$ (i.e., when they interpret the price change as temporary). And the entry of firms into, or exit from, the industry works in the same direction. A high price leads in the long run not only to a larger quantity response along existing firms' $LRMC$ curves, but also to an increase in the *number* of firms; a low price leads in the long run not only to output reductions along $LRMC$ curves, but to a contraction in the *number* of firms.

The difference this makes for industry-wide supply-demand equilibrium

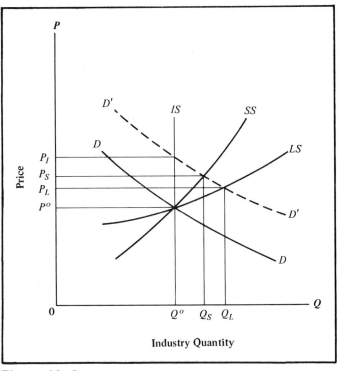

Figure 10. 4
Industry Responses to Demand Shifts

is pictured in Figure 10.4. The initial equilibrium situation is represented by price P^o and quantity Q^o along demand curve DD. Now suppose that demand shifts upward to $D'D'$. The vertical curve labelled IS is what is sometimes called the "immediate run" or "very short run" supply function. It is supposed to represent a period so momentary that production has no time to respond at all. In these circumstances the full brunt of the equilibrating adjustment must fall upon price, which is determined, then, by the intersection of supply curve IS with the demand curve $D'D'$ at the level P_I. In the short run proper, firms will react by varying output along their $SRMC$ curves. These responses, properly aggregated, are represented by the industry's short-run supply curve SS. In the new short-run equilibrium, price P_S is higher than the initial P^o but lower than the immediate-run price P_I. Finally, in the long run a still further supply reaction is elicited, so that price declines still further to the level P_L—still higher, however, than P^o if the industry long-run supply curve LS has any positive slope.

In competitive equilibrium, the movement from short-run to long-run supply reflects itself in a moderating of the price impact of increased demand. Conversely, if price were for some reason maintained at the higher level, the passage from short-run to long-run would reflect itself in steadily increasing quantity supplied.

Example 10. 2
Preclusive
Buying of
Wolfram[6]

A striking example of the responsiveness of supply to price resulted from the Allied powers' "preclusive buying" program in World War II. In this program the U.S. and Great Britain attempted to cut off the flow of strategic materials from neutral countries to the Axis powers, by prior purchase in the open market.

Wolfram is an ore of tungsten, a vital alloying metal for steel. It is produced in Spain and Portugal, countries that were both neutral in the War and potential suppliers to the Axis. In August of 1940, before the commencement of preclusive buying, the market price of wolfram in Portugal and Spain was $1,144 per ton. Since the Allies were trying to buy up literally *all* the wolfram that would otherwise have gone to Germany and Italy, the price was rapidly driven to unprecedentedly high levels; by October of 1941 it had reached $20,000 per ton. Portugal reacted by controlling the price and allotting the wolfram supply (in a presumably "equitable" manner) between the Axis and the Allies. Spain, however, chose to let the market process operate unhindered (to the advantage of the Spanish wolfram miners!).

The program "succeeded" in the sense that Germany eventually (in July of 1943) quit bidding for Spanish wolfram, making do with substitutes for tungsten alloy. But before this occurred, wolfram production in Spain had increased to ten times its pre-war level. It seemed at times to Allied purchasing agents that every man, woman, and child in the country must be back in the hills digging wolfram. In undertaking the program, the long-run supply elasticity of wolfram production had been seriously underestimated.

[6]Discussion based upon D. I. Gordon and R. Dangerfield, *The Hidden Weapon* (New York: Harper & Brothers, 1947), pp. 105–16.

10. C ECONOMIES AND DISECONOMIES OF SCALE, INTERNAL AND EXTERNAL

It is useful to classify the determinants of the industry supply function into: (1) those elements that are *internal* to the separate firms of the industry, and (2) those that are *external* to the separate firms (but still "internal" to the industry as a whole).

The determinant of supply that is *internal* to each firm is its own cost function. The firm's short-run supply function s_f depends upon the minimum level of its Average Variable Cost AVC, and beyond this upon the shape of the Short-Run Marginal Cost curve $SRMC$. The firm's long-run supply function Ls_f depends upon the minimum level of its Long-Run Average Cost $LRAC$, and beyond this upon the shape of the Long-Run Marginal Cost curve $LRMC$.

An "economy of scale" is said to exist when larger output is associated with lower Average Cost; a "diseconomy of scale," when larger output entails higher Average Cost. The shape of the firm's supply function s_f in Figure 10.1 shows that, in the short run, diseconomies of scale are dominant—everywhere beyond the minimum output level q_V. This is due fundamentally to the principle of technology studied in elementary economics, the *Law of Diminishing Returns*. According to this law, if one or more factors are held constant in amount, then beyond a certain point increasing inputs of the other factors will be required per unit of added output. The Law of Diminishing Returns is applicable in the short run, since one or more of the factors is being held "fixed." Hence the internal diseconomies of scale dictate rising short-run supply functions for the firms in an industry.

Matters are not so clear in the long run. Figure 10.3 shows that the *LRMC* curve is *less steep* than the *SRMC* curve; i.e., the individual firm's long-run supply function Ls_f is *more elastic* than its short-run supply function s_f. Indeed, if it were literally the case that in the long run *all* factors were variable, the Law of Diminishing Returns would not be operative at all. It would be possible to choose the best set of factor proportions, and then increase or decrease all factors together as required to produce more output or less. One would then expect to find a *horizontal* Long-Run Average Cost curve *LRAC*, in which case the Long-Run Marginal Cost curve *LRMC* would coincide with *LRAC* (Proposition 2.2c). But it is really not possible to vary literally all factors in proportion together. One or more factors, and most particularly *entrepreneurship*, may not be readily expandable by the firm. This consideration dictates, then, that even in the long run the Law of Diminishing Returns will apply and a range of internal diseconomies will eventually be reached. So the competitive firm's Ls_f curve, while more elastic than its short-run supply curve s_f, will still be a rising function of output.

Even granting that a region of internal diseconomies will *eventually* be reached, for sufficiently great output, it still remains possible that this "eventual" condition will not be encountered until the firm's output is too large to be consistent with the survival of competition. If economies of scale dominate throughout the relevant range, one firm with very large output can always produce more cheaply than its smaller competitors, and will drive them out of business. This is the condition called "natural monopoly," to be discussed in Chapter 11.

Conclusion: In a competitive industry, internal *diseconomies* of scale lead to rising supply curves, though less sharply rising in the long run than in the short run.

We now want to consider the elements *external* to the separate firms, but nevertheless "internal to the industry." We have already encountered one such element, illustrated in Figure 10.2—the effect of industry output upon prices of resources used by the industry. No single firm's output decision, in a competitive industry, has other than a negligible effect upon factor prices. But when the industry *as a whole* expands, the prices of factors heavily employed in that industry tend to be driven up. The factor-price effect is thus normally an external *diseconomy* of scale. As shown in Figure 10.2, it makes the supply curve of the industry less elastic than the simple horizontal sum of the separate firms' supply functions. (This is the normal situation. But we will see in Chapter 15 that the supply curve of a factor may be *negatively* sloped, in which case an increase in demand will tend to lower its equilibrium price. This would be an external *economy* of scale.)

External economies and diseconomies can be divided into two categories: "pecuniary" and "technological." In both cases, the externality exists because changes in the *output of the industry* affect the *cost functions of its component firms*. For a "pecuniary" economy or diseconomy, the interaction between industry output and firm cost function is solely through changes in the market prices of inputs. For a "technological" economy or diseconomy, on the other hand, the interaction is directly upon the physical possibilities of production—the production function. The factor-price effect just discussed is an external *pecuniary diseconomy*. As we have seen, pecuniary external effects are normally (though not necessarily always) diseconomies. Technological external effects, on the other hand, can equally well be economies or diseconomies.

As an example of a *technological external economy*, consider firms in the business of farming on marshy soil. In order for farmer A to produce, he must drain his land. But pumping water out of his marshy soil will necessarily help to drain the lands of his neighboring competitors $B, C, D, \ldots$. These latter find that their lands, being less marshy than before, now produce better (Average Cost and Marginal Cost are lower). Similarly, any drainage efforts of his neighbors $B, C, D, \ldots$ will help to shift AC and MC downward for farmer A. If all try to expand output together, all engaging in more drainage, the situation is as pictured in Figure 10.5. The original industry price-quantity equilibrium is at P', Q'. With a rise in price to P'', the $\sum s_f'$ curve (the simple aggregation of the firms' s_f' curves) would indicate industry output $\hat{Q}$. But with the externality shifting the firms' MC curves downward, the curve $\sum s_f''$ becomes relevant so that the new equilibrium will be at $Q'' > \hat{Q}$. The industry supply curve S is thus more elastic than the separate supply curves of its component firms. It will be apparent that the effect is the reverse of that pictured in Figure 10.2 earlier.

Now consider a *technological external diseconomy*. We can still use an example of neighboring farming firms. But suppose now that the farm lands are too dry rather than too wet. Each farmer must irrigate, pumping water up from underground wells. In doing so, he drains water away from his neighbors' wells, thus *increasing* their Average Cost and Marginal Cost. Here the picture corresponds to Figure 10.2. Note that the diagrams do not of themselves indicate whether the *source* of the externality is pecuniary or technological.[7]

---

[7]The importance of the distinction between pecuniary and technological externalities arises in the context of "Welfare Economics," taken up in Chapter 17.

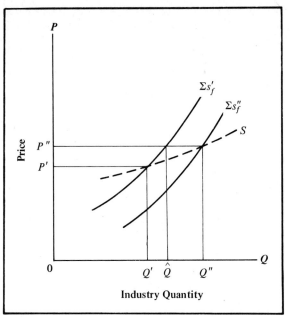

Figure 10. 5
Industry Supply Function (External Economy)

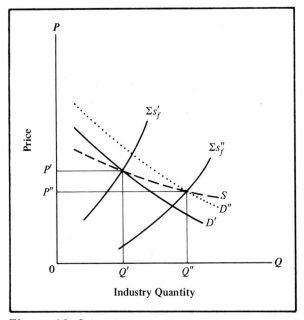

Figure 10. 6
Effect of Demand Shift—
Negatively Sloped Supply Function

261

Is it possible for a favorable externality, an external economy reducing costs of the separate firms as industry output expands, to be so powerful as to make the industry supply curve downward-sloping? That is, can the *external economies* be so great as to over-ride the inevitable *internal diseconomies* of scale? The answer is yes! An industry supply curve that is negatively sloped, despite rising $\sum s'_f$ and $\sum s''_f$ curves, is illustrated in Figure 10.6. Here as the demand curve shifts upward from D' to D'', price actually declines from P' to P''. Note that the *quantity* response to a change in demand is relatively greater for industry supply curves of flatter positive slope (compare Figures 10.2 and 10.5), and becomes still greater for negatively-sloped supply curves.

Conclusion: *External diseconomies* (external to the firm, but internal to the industry) make the industry supply curve rise more steeply; external *economies* make for a less steep supply curve. It is possible for the external economies to over-ride the internal diseconomies of scale, so as to generate a negatively sloped industry supply curve.

10. D FIRM SURVIVAL AND THE "ZERO-PROFIT THEOREM"

Under competitive conditions, there is always pressure on economic profit. This pressure comes both from above and below. Wherever profit exists, product prices tend to move downward and resource prices move upward.

Returning to Figure 10.4, suppose that starting from a position of supply-demand equilibrium at price P^o and industry output Q^o, an unanticipated increase in demand from DD to $D'D'$ takes place. As we saw in Section 10.B, in the *immediate run* the full impact is on product price, which shifts upward to P_I; every firm in the industry will then (momentarily) be receiving increased profit. Moving from the immediate period to the *short run*, the firms in the industry will increase output. The consequence will not only be a fall of product price to P_S, a partial return toward the previous equilibrium price P^o, but also a tendency for *factor prices* to rise in response to the industry's expansion of output. Firms will still be predominantly better off at price P_S than at the previous equilibrium P^o (though it is conceivable that a few who are especially vulnerable to factor-price increases might actually end up worse off). The opportunity of earning an economic profit—revenues greater than economic costs—leads in the *long run* to still further expansion of firm output and also to the entry of new firms. Product price therefore moves still further back downward to P_L, and the additional industry output expansion tends to force factor-input prices upward still more.

Where does this process end? Entry stops (long-run equilibrium is attained) when no firm still outside the industry can see its way to earning a profit within. It follows that the "marginal firm," the one just on the borderline of entering or leaving the industry, can earn only negligibly more within the industry than outside. Thus, its *economic* profit (excess of revenues over the best alternative foregone) in the industry is essentially zero.

Does it follow that the "infra-marginal" firms, i.e., firms whose lower costs in the industry (or poorer alternatives elsewhere) permit them to remain in the industry even at lower prices than P_L, are earning positive economic profits in long-run equilibrium? No, because if they were there would still be upward pressure on *factor* prices. The reasoning goes as follows. If an "infra-marginal" firm is earning positive economic profit, it must be that its Average Costs are lower than those of the marginal firm. Some special resource employed by the infra-marginal firm must be responsible for its unusually low cost of production. *All firms in the industry will be bidding for the right to employ that special resource*, and in the long run its factor price must be driven upward accordingly.

A clear case occurs in mining. Suppose the demand for copper rises, and the long-run equilibrium price for copper is higher than before. New firms will have entered to develop copper ore bodies previously too lean to work. If the marginal firm working a very thin ore just breaks even, it might be thought that an infra-marginal firm exploiting a richer ore body should be making a handsome profit. And indeed it may, in the short run. But in the long run all firms in the industry will be bidding for the right to work the richer ore. Consequently, the owner of the resource, i.e., the owner of the richer body of ore, will be able to renegotiate his contract with the user firm so as to recapture any extra profit earned.

What if the firm is itself the legal owner of the richer ore body? Here is where the distinction between *economic profit* and *accounting profit* (see Section 9.C) becomes essential. The accounting profit attributed to the firm controlling a rich ore body may indeed be high. But in principle, that firm could cease its operations and lease or sell the ore body to another. It should therefore charge itself, as an *economic cost* of its mining operations, the highest bid an outsider would make for the right to exploit its ore. In this way, its *economic profit* as a mining firm becomes zero in long-run equilibrium.

Proposition: In the long run, economic profit for any firm in a competitive industry is zero.

Of course, in an ever-changing world the "long run" may never actually arrive! Something almost always happens to change the conditions of long-run equilibrium before that state is achieved. But the *tendency* toward zero economic profit, due to downward pressure on product price and upward pressure on factor prices, is an important aspect of competitive industries.

Example 10. 3
Economies
of Scale and
the Survivor
Principle—
Medical Practice

The competitive pressure upon firm survival provides a source of information about *efficient scale* of production for firms in a competitive industry. Those firms having chosen inappropriately small or inappropriately large levels of "fixed" factors will have high Average Costs of production. In the long run, if they are to survive in the industry, such firms must shift to a more appropriate scale. "The survivor principle"[8] takes observed changes in the proportions of industry output accounted for by firms of different sizes as evidence concerning typical cost functions in the industry.

The survivor principle was applied to medical practice by H. E. Frech III and P. Ginsberg. They compared the market shares of physicians engaged in solo versus joint practice for the years 1965 and 1969. As can be seen from the Table, the share accounted for by solo- and two-physician practices declined, whereas all larger-sized groups gained in market share between 1965 and 1969. There is a suggestion in the data that moderately-sized groups (3–6 physicians) as well as rather large groups (26 or more physicians) may both have constituted efficient sizes in this period.

Market Share by Group Size, Medical Practice

Group Size	1965	1969	Ratio 1969/1965
1–2	84.69%	78.25%	0.92
3	3.12	4.39	1.41
4	2.33	3.13	1.34
5	1.33	1.87	1.41
6	0.87	1.38	1.59
7	0.73	0.77	1.06
8–15	2.76	3.43	1.24
16–25	1.54	1.66	1.08
26–49	0.75	1.78	2.37
50–99	0.58	1.22	2.10
100+	1.31	2.12	1.62
TOTAL	100.0	100.0	

Source: H. E. French III and P. Ginsberg, "Optimal Scale in Medical Practice: A Survivor Analysis," *Journal of Business*, v. 47 (Jan. 1974), p. 30.

The data in the Table can be interpreted quite differently, however, depending upon whether a static or dynamic viewpoint is adopted. From the former point of view, even in 1969 the great bulk of the market was accounted for by surviving single- or two-physician groups. This strongly suggests that small size must indeed be the most efficient in medical practice. On the other hand, it is precisely this size that is declining, relative to all others. So it appears that, *on the margin*, it is firms of moderate and large size that are the most profitable. New entrants find it advantageous to form groups of moderate or large size, while exiting firms come disproportionately from the small 1–2 physician class.

A reasonable interpretation of the data is that, at any point of time,

[8]See G. J. Stigler, "The Economies of Scale," *Journal of Law & Economics*, v. 1 (Oct. 1958).

there is an efficient *mixture* in an industry of firms varying over a spectrum of sizes. Even though the small 1–2 physician class may on the whole be most efficient in medical practice, there may still at the present moment be relatively *too many* in this size class. So we observe proportions shifting in favor of the larger groups.

10. E AN APPLICATION OF SUPPLY AND DEMAND: MANAGING A "SHORTAGE"

In a world of change, the conditions determining supply and demand—preferences, productivity, and resources—are continually varying. In consequence, equilibrium or "market-clearing" prices are also ever-changing. Some of this variation does not seem to generate serious complaint. People are not disturbed that department-store sales take place after Christmas (i.e., that consumers must pay higher prices in their pre-Christmas shopping). Nor does the fact that vegetables are cheaper after harvest, or cheaper at farm roadstands than in big-city markets, seem to raise controversy. But shifts in supply or demand are sometimes both unexpected and dramatic, drastically affecting the established relations among groups in the community. In such circumstances political pressures may arise for government interventions designed to prevent or to cancel out some or all of the price effects of the shift to a new market-clearing solution.

Interferences with market equilibrium were studied in Section 2.A as an illustration of the use of supply-demand analysis; in Section 7.E their consequences were evaluated employing the concepts of Consumer Surplus and Producer Surplus. Our purpose here is to analyze the repercussions of market interventions by government from the viewpoint of short-run and long-run supply-demand responses.

Interventions designed to prevent price from adjusting to an increase in demand, or to a decrease in supply, tend to create a "shortage."[9] The standard use of the word "shortage" in economics refers not to physical scarcity, but to a supply-demand imbalance at the existing price. This does indeed seem to correspond with popular terminology. People speak of "shortages" when goods become not just expensive but *unavailable*, partially or completely, in the market. Thus, faced with a supply or demand shift dictating a higher equilibrium price, consumers are bound to lose out one way or the other—either from the higher price if the market adjustment proceeds unimpeded, or from the "shortages" consequent upon interventions that succeed in maintaining a lower price.

[9]In the opposite case, where interventions prevent adaptation to decreased demand or to increased supply, commodity "surpluses" are generated.

Example 10. 4
Two San
Francisco
Housing
Crises[10]

In the 1906 earthquake and fire, the city of San Francisco lost more than half its housing facilities in three short days. Nevertheless, the first post-disaster issue of the *San Francisco Chronicle* had no report of a "housing shortage"! Indeed, the newspaper's classified advertisements carried 64 offers of houses or apartments for rent and only 5 ads for apartments or houses wanted. Of course, prices of accommodations rose sharply.

In contrast, in 1946 San Francisco was gripped by the national postwar "housing shortage." In the first five days of 1946 newspapers carried only 4 ads offering houses or apartments for rent, but around 150 ads by persons wanting to rent houses or apartments. The explanation, of course, is that in 1906 the catastrophic reduction in the housing stock led to a sharp rise in rents to a new equilibrium level, whereas in 1946, rents "frozen" below the market-clearing price left an excess of quantity demanded over quantity supplied.

Comment: In the physical sense, housing supply relative to population was clearly much more scarce after the 1906 earthquake and fire than in 1946. The 1946 "shortage" was an outgrowth of the general price freeze aimed at controlling inflation during and after World War II. Actually, housing supply had not decreased at all in the wartime period. But rising money incomes, the return of war veterans, and a high rate of family formation led to an upward shift in demand for housing. With rents frozen, a "shortage" ensued.

[10]Discussion based on M. Friedman and G. J. Stigler, "Roofs or Ceilings?", The Foundation for Economic Education, Inc. (Irvington-on-Hudson, New York, Sept. 1946).

We shall not be concerned here with the normative question of how a shortage "should" be managed but only with the consequences of alternative ways of coping with it. It is important to distinguish between short-run and long-run consequences. Figure 10.7 illustrates a "ceiling," holding price at its previous equilibrium P^o after demand has shifted upward from D to D'. The *perceived* shortage is the magnitude H in the diagram—the demand-supply gap at price P^o. In the unimpeded market process, price would jump in the first instance to the immediate-run level P_I, as previously discussed, but would eventually come down to the long-run equilibrium at P_L. The market would eliminate the shortage, in the short run primarily by a high price choking off demand, but in the long run increasingly via an augmentation of supply. At the price P_L in Figure 10.7, the interval ΔD is the *long-run* reduction in demand quantity and ΔS the long-run augmentation of supply.

With a price ceiling, in the immediate run the effect is often said to be "purely distributive." The same supply remains on the market; holding the

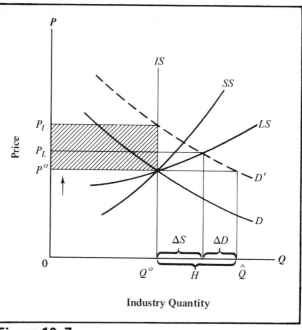

Figure 10. 7
Effect of a Shortage

price at P^o means only that producers fail to make a "windfall" gain (the shaded area in the diagram) at the expense of consumers. But a price ceiling that remains effective for a longer period increasingly forecloses the operation of forces that would have provided additional supply.

The assertion that the immediate-run effect of a price ceiling is purely distributive between consumers and producers is, however, somewhat of an oversimplification. In the absence of a ceiling, price would rise in the immediate run to P_I, and the supply on hand Q^o would go to those consumers willing to pay at least as much as P_I. But at the low ceiling price P^o there will be an *enlarged potential demand*—the amount $\hat{Q}$. It may be, in consequence of whatever commodity allocation scheme is adopted, that some relatively low-valued demands (for which consumers are willing to pay little above P^o) are actually satisfied while some high-valued demands (for which consumers would be willing to pay more than P_I) are not. Thus some consumers may benefit at the expense of others.

Some consequences of blocking the price rise that would adapt supply to demand are not visible in the supply and demand functions themselves. Unable to raise price openly, firms may divert energies and resources to subterfuges. They may eliminate discounts or seasonal sales, reduce quality or variety or convenience of their offerings, or concentrate production in product lines that happen to have received a better break from the price-control authorities. Supplies may be attracted into uncontrolled foreign markets that were previously unremunerative, leaving even less available for domestic consumers. And of course black markets may arise, providing a wider scope for elements of the population specializing in illegal activity. In extreme cases, the cumulative effect may be a breakdown of legitimate trade.

General price inflation, such as has been experienced in much of the world during the decade of the 1970s, is a topic in *macro*economics. But in an attempt to remedy or perhaps only to mask the inflationary process, governments may be led to impose price ceilings or "freezes" in some or all markets. Then, prices over greater or lesser reaches of the economy will no longer be free to reconcile supply and demand. While the initiating source of the disequilibrium lies in the realm of macroeconomics, the imbalances in particular markets are analyzable using the tools of *micro*economics. In this connection, we can learn much that is useful from a previous great inflationary episode—that associated with World War II and its aftermath.

Example 10. 5
Repressed
Inflation in
Postwar
Germany[11]

Germany, like most of the belligerent countries in World War II, had financed her war effort by inflationary expansion of money and credit. Simultaneously, price freezes were employed to prevent this expansion from being reflected in market prices. By 1945, wartime finance had increased liquid funds in the hands of the public around tenfold, while prices were still largely at the levels frozen by the Nazi government back in 1936. And, of course, Germany faced not only the "normal" aftermath of a war that saw her cities and industry smashed by bombing, but also the special problems of a defeated nation—divided, occupied, and subjected to punitive reparations.

The frozen levels of German prices were so drastically out of line with supply-demand reality that over most of the economy production for legal sale could take place only at a financial loss. Industrial production in the first half of 1948 was only 45% of 1938, despite a larger population. The black market was, surprisingly, estimated to account only for 10% of transactions. That this figure is so low is accounted for by the fact that in Germany the term "black market" was given a very narrow definition: to wit, outright trading of goods for cash at illegal prices (a practice professionally engaged in by a specialized class of disreputable individuals). In contrast, *everybody* engaged without moral taint in a form of transaction known as "bilateral exchange" or "compensation trade." This trade took place at entirely legal prices in money, with one catch: No one could acquire goods or services for money alone! In addition to the money price, the purchaser had to provide "compensa-

[11]Discussion based on J. Hirshleifer, *Disaster and Recovery: A Historical Survey*, The Rand Corporation, RM-3079-PR (April 1963), pp. 83–112.

tion" in real goods and services. Estimates are that one-third to one-half of transactions took this form. Even the Occupation authorities engaged in it; the noon meal provided to all German employees of the Occupation administration (at legal prices, of course) was often the chief attraction of such employment. Thus, the "legal" monetary transaction was a fig-leaf. What was actually taking place was the *de facto* elimination of money as medium of exchange—regression to the inefficiencies of barter (as discussed in Section 8.D).

There were two aspects of the German problem: Relative prices were more or less seriously out of line, but the overwhelming feature was that almost *all* money prices were too low. The Erhard policy of June 1948 was correspondingly double-barreled: (1) a drastic "currency reform," exchanging new marks for old, cut down the money supply by a factor of about ten; and (2) price controls were removed. The effect was dramatic. According to one observer: "It was as if money and markets had been invented afresh as reliable media of the division of labor."[12] The German postwar "economic miracle" was under way.

[12]H. Mendershausen, "Prices, Money and the Distribution of Goods in Postwar Germany," *American Economic Review*, v. 39 (June 1949), p. 646.

The German example suggests that a *general* shortage of goods relative to money, i.e., an inflationary situation repressed by price controls, can to some degree be coped with by reduction of liquid funds in the hands of the public. In the extreme situation of Germany, this took the form of actually calling in the old currency and replacing it with smaller amounts of the new. More normally, funds in the hands of the public could be reduced by fiscal and monetary policies—raising taxes, increasing bank reserve requirements, selling bonds to the public, etc.—as discussed in courses in macroeconomics.

Even for specific shortages in narrower sectors of the economy, it remains true that a general reduction of purchasing power will tend to mitigate the upward pressure on price. But more sharply focused measures would have a more concentrated effect. One possibility is a specific *tax* upon consumption of the commodity subject to shortage. As discussed in Section 2.A.3, a tax introduces a gap between the *gross* price P^+ paid by buyers and the *net* price P^- received by sellers. In Figure 10.8, a tax has been imposed that brings the *net* demand back from D' to the same D that it was initially. The consequence, as indicated, is that the price P_I along the immediate-run supply curve is the same as the gross price P^+ paid by buyers; similarly, the price P^- received by sellers is the initial price P°. The consequences of such a tax are: (1) The shortage is eliminated; supply and demand are in balance at the specified gross and net prices. (2) There is no "windfall" benefit to sellers. Buyers

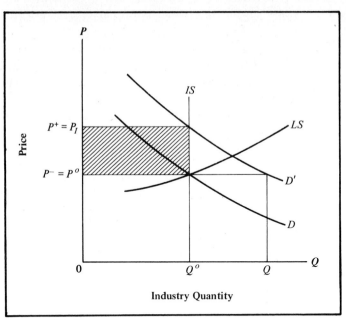

Figure 10. 8
Tax versus Shortage, I

will lose, but the windfall amount (the shaded area in the diagram) goes to the government instead. (3) The limited supply available in the immediate run is allocated only to those with the highest demand prices—those willing to pay at least P_I. (4) But there is no tendency for supply to increase, in the short run or long run. Thus, the supply side of the normal economic response to the upward shift of demand from D to D' has been cancelled out. This last is the great weakness of "managing" a shortage through a tax.

It would be possible, by a tax somewhat smaller than that just described, to achieve an intermediate result. Suppose as before that demand shifts upward from an initial D to D'. Now let a tax be imposed that brings the *net* demand down only to the dashed curve labelled D^- in Figure 10.9. The long-run equilibrium is at output Q', some expansion from Q^o having taken place. The gross price to buyers is P^+, and the net price to sellers P^-. Had such a tax been combined with imposition of a price ceiling at the level of P^+, the net price would have been high enough to elicit the long-run supply increment $Q' - Q^o$—while still lopping off the "immediate-run" tendency of price to go still higher. (Of course, the market would be in disequilibrium during the immediate-run period, since only a price as high as P_I can reconcile supply and demand in the very short run.)

Another line of attack upon a shortage would be through *rationing*. Effective demand for a particular good could be controlled by the requirement that the consumer possess a valid ration ticket for each unit consumed. Rationing was discussed in Section 6.D above. We saw there that ration

270

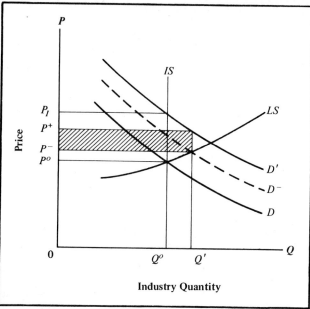

Figure 10. 9
Tax versus Shortage, II

allotments can be regarded as a secondary type of "income" constraining the consumption of individuals, thereby pulling downward their market demands for the rationed good.

Rationing can reduce pressure upon a price ceiling, or rationing may be imposed *instead* of a price ceiling. Under rationing, only the portion of demand validated by coupons can legally enter the market. In Figure 10.7, therefore, imposition of rationing may bring the effective demand curve back down from D' to the original D once more, so that the market can clear at the original price P^o. Sufficiently severe rationing can entirely eliminate the shortage—the difference between quantity demanded and quantity supplied at a price ceiling. But without an increase of price to suppliers, *there will still be no supply response* to the original rise in demand. And, in contrast with a tax, rationing will involve an additional loss of Consumer Surplus unless the coupons are "ideally" assigned to those with highest demand prices for the good (see Section 7.E.2).

This last objection would be eliminated if the ration coupons were legally *salable*. In that case, apart from transaction costs, the coupons would be purchased by those most willing to buy the good. The initial assignment of ration tickets is then irrelevant, except insofar as it involves a redistribution of income. In effect, part of Consumer Surplus is transferred from buyers of the good to those coupon-holders who choose to sell their ration entitlements. As a practical matter, it should be noted that ration tickets may be surreptitiously transferred even where sale is not legal. Also, a black market may come into existence whether or not coupons are salable; either way, there remains a motive to engage in unrationed transactions.

Conclusion: Attempts to protect consumers from the effects of a *price* increase tend to deflect the *quantity* response that suppliers would otherwise be induced to provide. And since supply is increasingly elastic in the long run, this disadvantage increases over time.

Questions

1. Define elasticity of supply. Does elasticity of supply for an industry tend to be great or small if the firms' Marginal Cost curves are sharply upward-sloping? What is the effect on elasticity of supply if higher industry output markedly drives up the prices of factors employed in the industry?

2. At any rate of output, the industry long-run supply curve tends to be less steep than the short-run supply curve. Is it also less elastic? Explain.

3. If there are N identical firms and no "external" effects on factor prices, is the industry supply curve more or less steep than the firm supply curve? More or less elastic?

4. "In a competitive industry, for any firm the internal economies of scale may be effective for a while. But each firm must be operating in the region where internal *diseconomies* of scale dominate over the economies of scale." True or false? Explain.

5. Which of the following is a "pecuniary" effect, which a "technological" effect? Which is "internal" to the firm, which "external" to the firm (but internal to the industry)?

    a. As the number of films produced rises, stars' salaries go up.

    b. As fishing intensifies, each fisherman finds fish scarcer.

    c. As new shops open, existing shops find customers scarcer.

    d. Steel mills along a river use the water for cooling—but the greater the use, the warmer the water gets.

6. In long-run equilibrium why does the marginal firm (the highest-cost firm in the industry) earn zero economic profit? Why do infra-marginal firms earn zero economic profit?

7. If at a certain equilibrium price every firm in the industry is earning zero economic profit, doesn't that imply that a fall in market price would mean that no firms at all could continue to survive? Explain.

8. A number of techniques are available to cope with increased scarcity and higher world prices of petroleum. Analyze the following in terms of supply-demand responses in the short run and long run:

    a. Price freeze and "rationing by queue" (waiting lines for gasoline).

    b. Price freeze and rationing by coupon (non-salable).

c. Rationing by coupon (non-salable) without a price freeze.

d. A tax on all petroleum used.

e. A tariff on *imports* of petroleum.

9. In policy (c) above (rationing by coupon without a price freeze), suppose consumers were permitted to sell ration coupons to one another. Would this tend to elicit more supply? Would the limited supplies be reallocated to those with higher demand prices? Explain the consequences in terms of the concept of Consumer Surplus.

10. Suppose that, after a decline in demand for a product, a *floor* is placed under its market price. Then the problem arises of managing a "surplus" rather than a shortage. What disadvantages would arise? Would the disadvantages tend to increase over time, as in the case of managing a shortage, or would the disadvantages tend to evaporate over time in the "surplus" case? Would "black markets" tend to develop?

Chapter 11
Monopoly and the Question of Economic Efficiency

Perfect competition is one model of *market structure*. Monopoly is another model. Traditionally, market stucture has been associated with the number of firms viable in an industry, a number determined by the economies of scale relative to the magnitude of demand. If the efficient (minimum-cost) scale in an industry is small in relation to demand, the number of firms will tend to be large. Then each single firm has so negligible an effect on price that the assumption of price-taking or competitive behavior will be appropriate. At the other extreme is "natural monopoly," where economies of scale are so overwhelming that one firm can always produce more cheaply than (and thus drive out) any larger number. Not all monopolies need be "natural"; competition may fail to develop, perhaps only temporarily, for a host of reasons. One important source of monopoly is exclusive governmental franchise, as in the case of a "public utility" or a patent grant.

Where more than one but still only a very few firms survive in an industry, the market structure is called "oligopoly"—competition among the few. The essence of oligopoly is that each single firm's output decision noticeably affects the demand conditions faced by *other* firms. As a result there is *conscious interaction* among firms, a condition that leads to "strategic" rather than price-taking behavior, as will be explored in Chapter 13. Another important market structure is called "monopolistic competition"; in monopolistic competition each firm in an industrial grouping produces a unique product and thus has some degree of monopoly power—over a subset of customers that constitute a clientele for its particular output. Chapter 12 treats monopolistic competition as a special topic under the more general heading of "Product as a Variable."

11. A MONOPOLY AND NON-PROFIT GOALS

Non-profit goals of the business firm were discussed in a general context in Section 9.C. There is some reason to believe that a monopoly firm, largely sheltered from competition, would be inclined to give more weight to non-profit goals. In perfect competition (as explained in Section 10.D) there is always a problem of *survival*. Since competitive downward pressure on product prices and upward pressure on input prices are continually forcing profits toward zero, in pure competition no firm can have much leeway for indulging non-profit goals. Monopolistic firms, in contrast, may have some margin for freedom of choice among goals.

<table>
<tr>
<td>

Example 11. 1
Jews and
Monopoly[1]

</td>
<td>

One non-profit goal that owners or managers of a firm might be inclined to indulge in is group prejudice. Under severe profit pressure, the need to survive dictates hiring the best person for the job regardless of sex, race, color, etc. But if a monopoly position provides a degree of security, owners or managers may prefer to deal or associate with "their own kind," avoiding the discomfort of making adjustments to overcome long-held animosities or stereotypes.

A. A. Alchian and R. A. Kessel examined the employment patterns of a sample of Jewish and non-Jewish Harvard Business School graduates. Employments were classified under a number of industry categories. Two industry categories—(1) transportation, communication, and other public utilities and (2) finance, insurance, and real estate—were considered relatively monopolized. Public utilities are almost always protected from competition by exclusive franchises. And the field of finance, in particular banking, has been subject for many years to severe government constraints upon competitive entry.

Jews comprised some 36% of the overall statistical sample used (not a representative sample of the entire population, of course). The ratio of Jews to non-Jews of those in the sample found to be employed in the two relatively monopolized categories was under 18%; in the remaining, relatively competitive categories, over 41%. While more than one explanation is possible, it seems reasonable to infer that monopoly situations do facilitate the exercise of prejudice against Jews—at least for employment in the types of executive positions likely to be filled by Harvard Business School graduates.

[1]Discussion based on A. A. Alchian and R. A. Kessel, "Competition, Monopoly, and the Pursuit of Money," in H. G. Lewis *et al.*, *Aspects of Labor Economics* (Princeton, N.J.: Princeton University Press, 1962).

</td>
</tr>
</table>

11. B MONOPOLY OPTIMUM

11. B. 1 Price-Quantity Solution

Figure 11.1 displays the basic price-quantity solution for the monopolistic firm. As in Figure 9.1 for the competitive firm, Panel (a) here shows the solution in terms of the Total Cost function C and Total Revenue function

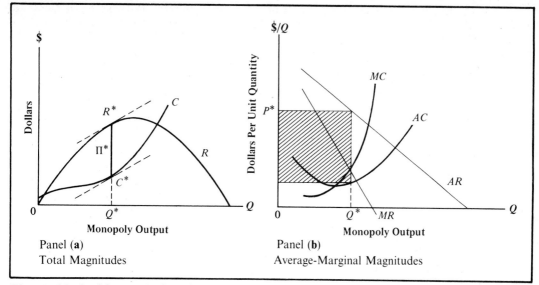

Figure 11. 1   Monopoly Solution

R. And Panel (b) runs in terms of AC, AR, MC, and MR, the corresponding average and marginal functions of output Q.[2] The bold line-segment labelled Π^* in Panel (a) is the maximized profit—the excess of Revenue over Cost at the optimal output Q^*. At this optimal output the R and C curves are farthest apart, so that their slopes must be parallel as suggested by the dashed tangent lines drawn at the points R^* and C^*. Consequently, in Panel (b) the Marginal Revenue MR (representing the slope of the Total Revenue function) and the Marginal Cost MC (representing the slope of the Total Cost function) intersect at this same output Q^*. The maximized profit Π^* is represented in Panel (b) by the shaded rectangle, whose base is the optimum quantity Q^* and whose height is $P^* - AC \equiv AR - AC$. Since Average Revenue AR is R^*/Q^* and Average Cost AC is C^*/Q^*, the shaded area can be written as $Q^*[(R^* - C^*)/Q^*] = R^* - C^*$, demonstrating the equivalence of the representations of profit in the two panels.

The difference between the competitive and monopoly solutions lies on the revenue side. For the competitive firm of Figure 9.1, the constancy of price P led to a Total Revenue curve R taking the form of a ray out of the origin. But for the monopolistic firm, price P is a falling function of output. The consequence is that the Total Revenue curve R in Panel (a) of Figure 11.1 is concave downward, like the cross-section of a mountain.

Geometrically, we know that Marginal Revenue MR is the slope along the Total Revenue curve R. Along the concave-downward R function, slope decreases algebraically throughout (from a high positive magnitude at small Q, to zero slope at the point where R reaches a maximum, and then to increasingly negative slope as the R curve turns downward). The MR curve in

---

[2]The capital letter Q has previously been used to signify *industry* output. Since the monopolist is a single-firm industry, Q can be used to denote the output of a monopolist firm.

Panel (b) is correspondingly first positive, then zero, then negative; it decreases along its entire length. The demand curve, we know, is the Average Revenue curve AR, since price P *is* Average Revenue R/Q. As the monopolist by definition faces a downward-sloping demand curve, AR also declines throughout.

In Panel (b) MR always lies below AR, i.e., Marginal Revenue is less than Average Revenue. This follows from the logical relations between average and marginal magnitudes discussed in Section 2.B. Proposition 2.2a there states: *When the average magnitude is falling, the marginal magnitude must lie below it.*

Warning: It is important not to be confused between the *price* charged for the last unit sold and the *Marginal Revenue MR*. Note the two shaded areas in Figure 11.2. As sales increase from Q to $Q + 1$ units, the demand curve D

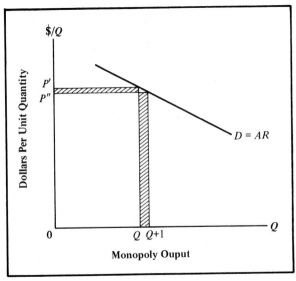

Figure 11. 2
Marginal Price versus Marginal Revenue

shows that price must fall slightly from P' to P''. We can think of P'' as the price received for the last unit, represented by the thin tall rectangle of width unity and height P''. But to see the full effect on Revenue of a unit increase in quantity, it is necessary to remember that price has fallen from P' to P'' on all the other units sold. The effect of this price reduction is represented by the flat thin rectangle of width Q and height $P' - P''$.

There are, therefore, two elements entering into Marginal Revenue. First is the positive price P along the demand curve. Second is the price reduction on all units that could have been sold at higher prices. Since Marginal Revenue is always the *difference* between these two areas, we see again that $MR \equiv P + Q(\Delta P/\Delta Q)$ must always be less than $P \equiv AR$.

The cost function for the monopolistic firm, as shown in terms of total magnitudes in Panel (a) of Figure 11.1 and in terms of average and marginal magnitudes in Panel (b), has essentially the same appearance as for the competitive firm. Of course, the monopolistic firm may be of relatively large size, so that the horizontal scale would then be correspondingly large. Connected with this, there is one difference of substance. The competitive firm was assumed to be a price-taker not only with respect to the product market but also with respect to *factor prices*. In consequence, the competitive firm's cost function does not allow for any effects on factor prices; only after turning to the supply function of the competitive industry (in the discussion of Section 10.A) was the factor-price effect encountered. But the single monopolistic supplier is itself an entire industry. Hence, any factor-price effect would be displayed *within* the cost function of the monopolist firm. As will be recalled from Chapter 10, an increase in industry output will normally tend to push factor prices upward. Hence the factor-price effect makes the monopolist firm's cost functions—total, average, and marginal—all tend to rise more sharply as output increases.

Formally, the monopolist's optimizing problem can be expressed as:

(11.1) $\text{Max } \Pi = R(Q) - C(Q) = P(Q)Q - C(Q)$

Here the parenthesis notation (Q) is to call attention to the fact that the R, C, and P variables are all functions of output Q. (In the solution for the competitive firm, price P was *not* a function of firm output.) As usual, the condition of optimality (maximum of profit or minimum of loss) is the equality of Marginal Cost and Marginal Revenue:[3]

(11.2) $$MC = MR \equiv P + Q\frac{\Delta P}{\Delta Q}$$

Maximum-Profit Condition, Monopolist Firm

As in Section 9.D, there is again the technical qualification that the MC curve must cut the MR curve *from below* to have a profit maximum. If MC cuts MR *from above*, profit is a *minimum* (or loss a maximum) at that output.[4]

On the right-hand side of equation (11.2), Marginal Revenue MR is broken up into the two elements illustrated geometrically in Figure 11.2. The first term is the price P received for the last unit sold; the second term is the revenue change on the units that could have been sold at higher prices.

---

[3]*Mathematical Footnote:* Taking derivatives of profit Π as defined in (11.1), and setting equal to zero:

$$\frac{d\Pi}{dQ} = \frac{dR}{dQ} - \frac{dC}{dQ} = P + Q\frac{dP}{dQ} - \frac{dC}{dQ} = 0$$

Marginal Revenue dR/dQ is $P + Q(dP/dQ)$, and Marginal Cost is of course dC/dQ. The equality of MC and MR is the first-order condition for a maximum of Π.

[4]*Mathematical Footnote:* The second-order condition for a maximum of Π is $d^2R/dQ^2 < d^2C/dQ^2$. That is, MR must be falling relative to MC, i.e., MC must cut MR from below.

Since $\Delta P/\Delta Q$ is the negative slope along the demand curve, this second element is a *negative* magnitude. With a unit quantity increment $\Delta Q = 1$, the second term corresponds to the horizontal shaded area $Q(\Delta P)$ of Figure 11.2. In the competitive case, by comparison, the firm is not aware of any effect of its own output on product price P. Thus the competitive profit-maximizing condition (9.3) was simply $MC = MR \equiv P$. This can be regarded as the special case of (11.2) for which $\Delta P/\Delta Q$ is zero, so that the second term disappears.

The (price) elasticity of demand was defined in equation (5.3). In terms of the notation of this chapter:

(11.3)
$$\eta \equiv \frac{\Delta Q/Q}{\Delta P/P} = \frac{\Delta Q}{\Delta P} \cdot \frac{P}{Q}$$

We can use (11.2) and (11.3) to obtain an important expression connecting Marginal Revenue MR and price elasticity η. First, equation (11.3) can be rewritten:

$$\frac{\Delta Q}{\Delta P} = \eta \frac{Q}{P} \quad \text{or} \quad \frac{\Delta P}{\Delta Q} = \frac{1}{\eta} \frac{P}{Q}$$

Substituting for $\Delta P/\Delta Q$ on the right-hand-side of (11.2), we have

$$MR \equiv P + Q\left(\frac{1}{\eta} \frac{P}{Q}\right) \equiv P + \frac{P}{\eta}$$

This is usually written in the form:

(11.4)
$$MR \equiv P\left(1 + \frac{1}{\eta}\right)$$

Again, since elasticity η is ordinarily negative, $MR < P \equiv AR$.

We saw also in Section 5.B that elastic demand (η greater than unity in absolute value) corresponded to increasing consumer expenditure on a good as its price P falls and quantity purchased Q rises. Consumer expenditure is, of course, the opposite side of the same coin as *Revenue* to the firm. So elastic demand corresponds to the region where Total Revenue R is an increasing function of output Q in Figure 11.1, Panel (a), or equivalently to the region of positive Marginal Revenue MR in Panel (b). Inelastic demand corresponds to the region of falling Total Revenue in Panel (a) or negative Marginal Revenue in Panel (b). Since Marginal Cost MC is surely positive, the condition $MC = MR$ dictates that the monopolist optimum must be in the region where the Total Revenue curve is rising and $MR > 0$, i.e., in the range of *elastic* demand.

11. B. 2   Monopolist versus Competitive Solution

Table 11.1 illustrates a hypothetical set of revenue and cost data for a monopolist firm. The cost data are exactly the same as those employed for a hypothetical competitive firm in Table 9.1. But on the revenue side, the monopolist's demand function is assumed here to be $P = 132 - 8Q$; price is a declining function of output. The equation has been so chosen that if the monopolist *were* following the competitive optimality rule $MC = P$ [equation (9.3)] he would be led to the same numerical output ($Q = 9$) as in the case of Table 9.1. For although the demand curve here is a declining function of Q, the numbers have been so contrived that, at $Q = 9$, Marginal Cost MC and price P are both equal to 60.

The monopolist, therefore, has it in his power to behave like a competitive firm. But, in the interests of profit-maximization he will set $MC = MR < P$ [equation (11.2)]. In the Table here, three approximations for Marginal Revenue are shown. The first, MR_1, is the "poorer approximation" as discussed in Section 2.B. Here the revenue difference $R_{Q+1} - R_Q$ is considered the Marginal Revenue at $Q + 1$. MR_2 is the "better approximation" of Chapter 2, where this same difference is taken as the Marginal Revenue at $Q + \frac{1}{2}$. The numerals in parentheses are interpolated to show MR_2 at integer values of Q. The *true* Marginal Revenue MR (the perfect approximation) is given in the third column. This can be attained by calculus techniques, which show that if the demand function is $P = 132 - 8Q$ then Marginal Revenue is $MR = 132 - 16Q$.[5] As can be seen from the Table, the "better approximation" MR_2 is in this case precisely correct. (This will always be true for a quadratic revenue function.)

It is easy to prove the following, without using calculus:

Proposition: Given any *linear* demand curve $P = A - BQ$, the true corresponding Marginal Revenue function is $MR = A - 2BQ$. Geometrically, starting at the same vertical intercept on the P-axis, the MR curve falls twice as fast as the AR curve. From equation (11.2), $MR = P + Q(\Delta P/\Delta Q)$. Now $\Delta P/\Delta Q$ is by definition the slope of the demand curve, a constant for a linear demand curve. Given the demand equation $P = A - BQ$, this slope is equal to $-B$. Substituting on the right hand side: $MR = (A - BQ) + Q(-B)$ or $MR = A - 2BQ$.

Corollary: The MR curve bisects the horizontal distance between the vertical axis and the AR curve (if the latter is linear).

As for the Marginal Cost MC, only the "true" figures are taken over from Table 9.1. The condition $MC = MR$ is met at $Q = 7$, which is the monopolist's profit-maximizing output. The corresponding profit-maximizing price (or Average Revenue) is $P = 76$. Total Revenue is $R = 532$ and Total Cost $C = 268$, so that maximum profit is $\Pi^* = 264$.

It was argued above that the monopolist's solution must lie in the elastic range of demand, i.e., where $|\eta| > 1$. The last column of Table 11.1 shows the elasticity at the various levels of output. The computation was based on the

---

[5]*Mathematical Footnote:* If $P = 132 - 8Q$, then $R \equiv PQ = 132Q - 8Q^2$. Differentiating: $MR \equiv dR/dQ = 132 - 16Q$.

Table 11. 1

Revenue and Cost Functions—Monopolist Firm

$$P = 132 - 8Q, \text{ or } R = 132Q - 8Q^2$$
$$C = Q^3 - 14Q^2 + 69Q + 128$$

Q	P	R	MR_1	MR_2	MR	C	MC	η
0	132	0	—		132	128	69	∞
				124				
1	124	124	124	(116)	116	184	44	−15.5
				108				
2	116	232	108	(100)	100	218	25	− 7.25
				92				
3	108	324	92	(84)	84	236	12	− 4.5
				76				
4	100	400	76	(68)	68	244	5	− 3.125
				60				
5	92	460	60	(52)	52	248	4	− 2.3
				44				
6	84	504	44	(36)	36	254	9	− 1.75
				28				
7	76	532	28	(20)	20	268	20	− 1.36
				12				
8	68	544	12	(4)	4	296	37	− 1.06
				−4				
9	60	540	−4	(−12)	−12	344	60	− .83
				−20				
10	52	520	−20		−28	418	89	− .65

relation $\eta \equiv P/(MR - P)$, derived by solving equation (11.4) above for η. Note that had the monopolist been following the competitive rule so as to choose $Q = 9$, the solution would have been in the inelastic range from the viewpoint of industry demand.

We thus see that it is quite possible for a *competitive* price-quantity equilibrium, but not a monopolist's price-quantity optimum, to be in the inelastic range of demand. More specifically, suppose that the demand curve here, $P = 132 - 8Q$, were the true industry demand curve for a competitive industry with 1000 identical firms. For simplicity, assume that Q is measured in thousands whereas the competitive-firm cost data shown in Table 9.1 are a function of q measured in units. Then at the price $P = 60$, the aggregate demand quantity would be $Q = 9$ thousands, whereas at the firm output $q = 9$ we know that Marginal Cost $MC = 60$. So the 1000 firms will supply 9000 units in the aggregate, clearing the market at $P = 60$. But this is in the inelastic range of demand! The competitive industry as a whole is actually receiving less revenue by producing more output—in addition, of course, to incurring positive costs of production on the additional output.

Example 11. 2
Competition
and Costs
of Trading

In Example 8.2 ("Costs of Trading on the New York Stock Exchange") it was reported that 40% of the costs of effecting a trade in securities listed on the New York Stock Exchange (NYSE) were due to the "bid-ask spread." This spread, the difference between the buying price and the selling price at any moment of time, reimburses the Exchange's specialist. The function of the specialist is to "make a market" in the stock by always standing ready to buy or sell.

Only one specialist is assigned to a security listed on the New York Stock Exchange and so each such specialist has a monopoly position for dealings on the Exchange. But the Exchange may not have a monopoly on the trading process for a given security; some stocks are listed on other organized exchanges as well as on the NYSE. A study by S. M. Tinic showed that competition worked in the expected direction: The bid-ask spread on the New York Stock Exchange was lower, other things equal, *for those securities that were traded on other exchanges as well as on the NYSE.*[6]

[6]S. M. Tinic, "The Economics of Liquidity Services," *Quarterly Journal of Economics*, v. 86 (Feb. 1972).

Proposition: The monopoly output solution occurs where $MC = MR < P$. Since competitive firms produce to where $MC = P$, a monopolized industry achieves higher price and lower output than would obtain under competitive conditions.

11. B. 3 An Application: Author versus Publisher

In the publishing industry, it is common practice for authors' royalties to take the form of a simple percentage of sales receipts. The question arises: Is there any difference between the incentives of author and publisher as to how high a price should be set on his book?

Since there is only one seller of any single text, monopoly theory is applicable. Suppose that the author receives as royalty just 10% of Total Revenue R. Denote his royalty as $R_a = .1R$. Writing the net revenue to the publisher as R_p, it must be that $R_p = .9R$. This problem is most simply analyzed in "total" units, by an extension of the geometry in Panel (a) of Figure 11.1. In Figure 11.3 the Total Revenue R received from customers is divided between the dashed R_p (nine-tenths the height of R) and the dotted R_a (one-tenth the height of R). The publisher would prefer the output Q_p^* such that the *slopes* along R_p and along the Total Cost curve C are equal; his

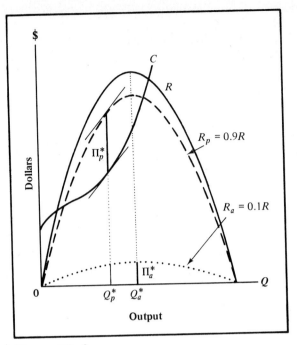

Figure 11. 3
Author versus Publisher

profit Π_p^* at that output is indicated by the height of the upper bold line-segment. The lower solid line-segment drawn along the same vertical, between R_a and the horizontal axis, indicates the corresponding royalty to the author.

It will be evident from the geometry that this is *not* the preferred output from the point of view of the author. *Since the latter incurs no cost of production,* from his point of view the optimum output Q_a^* is simply that which maximizes R_a. (We can think of this as the output where the horizontal slope of R_a equals the horizontal slope of a Total Cost curve that is, from the author's viewpoint, zero everywhere). Since $R_a = .1R$, the author wants to set a price that will simply maximize sales Revenue R, without regard to cost. The author's "ideal" royalty in the diagram is shown by the bold line-segment Π_a^*; it will be evident that the corresponding profit to the publisher will be less than ideal from the latter's point of view. The upshot of the analysis is that *it is in the interests of the publisher to set a higher price (implying a smaller number of books sold) than the author would choose.*

In the publishing industry authors do not normally have the power to fix price, which is in the sole discretion of the publisher. However, it might be advantageous for an author to make a deal accepting a smaller royalty percentage in return for the publisher setting a lower price for his book.

Example 11. 3
Economists
as Authors

P. M. Horvitz[7] surveyed 98 authors of recent textbooks in economics, receiving 71 usable replies to questionnaires. He was interested in determining the degree of participation of authors in the pricing process, and in particular their awareness of the conflict of interest between author and publisher.

The results seemed rather disappointing as clues to the acumen of economist-authors. Only 7 reported participating in the pricing process, and nearly all were satisfied with the publisher's pricing decision. However, the direction of dissatisfaction is of some interest. Of the 5 who reported dissatisfaction, all would have preferred a lower price. And 3 others among the satisfied group also indicated that a lower price would have been preferred. No author would rather have had a higher price set on his book.

[7]P. M. Horvitz, "The Pricing of Textbooks and the Remuneration of Authors," *American Economic Review*, v. 56 (May 1966).

11. C MONOPOLY AND ECONOMIC EFFICIENCY

Monopoly, we have just seen, leads to higher price and lower output as compared with competitive supply. Is this a good or a bad thing? Obviously, while high price is bad for the customers it is good for the monopolist. The possibility of making valid statements concerning the impartial or *social* desirability of alternative economic states of affairs will be discussed under the heading of "Welfare Economics" in Part Six below. However, recall the Fundamental Theorem of Exchange—*trade is mutually beneficial.* We can use the concepts of Consumer Surplus and Producer Surplus developed in Chapter 7 to show that monopoly can be regarded as a *hindrance to trade.* As such, it leads to an "efficiency loss," apart from the transfers associated with high monopoly price.[8]

Figure 11.4 illustrates the interpretation of monopoly as a hindrance to trade. Assume that there are no economies or diseconomies of scale tending to shift the cost function downward or upward for a single producer in comparison with an aggregate of small competitive suppliers. Then the Marginal Cost curve MC of the monopolist is essentially the same as the competitive supply function S of Figure 10.2. (The factor-price effect, if any, due to expanding industry supply is already incorporated in the shape of the monopolist's MC curve.) The monopoly solution is at quantity Q_m (the

[8]However, we cannot therefore conclude that monopoly "should" be abolished. (Any more than we could conclude in Section 7.E that taxes, as the cause of losses in Consumer Surplus and Producer Surplus, "should" therefore be abolished!) There may be other considerations to be balanced against the efficiency loss.

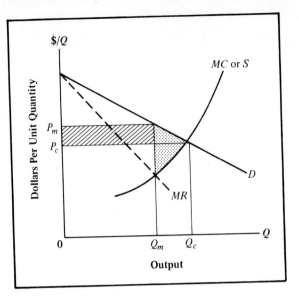

Figure 11. 4
Monopoly and Efficiency Loss

quantity level at which $MC = MR$) and price P_m (the height of the demand curve at quantity Q_m). The hypothetical competitive solution would be at quantity Q_c and price P_c (the intersection of the demand curve D and supply curve S).

The hindrance to trade can be analyzed on the analog of Figure 7.12 that showed the effect of a tax on transactions. The shaded area $(P_m - P_c)Q_m$ is the buyers' loss of Consumer Surplus due to the higher monopoly price on the quantity Q_m. As the monopolist seller derives an exactly equal benefit, this is a "transfer" that does not enter into efficiency calculations. The upper roughly triangular (dotted) area is the deadweight loss in Consumer Surplus for units that *would have been* produced and purchased at the price P_c but are not purchased at the higher price P_m. The lower dotted area is the corresponding deadweight loss in Producer Surplus. The monopolist could have produced these additional units at the successive marginal costs indicated along the MC curve, less than the price P_c he could have received for each unit had he chosen to supply the quantity Q_c. Of course, he chose not to provide so large a quantity because by cutting output he obtained a higher price.

Thus, for the monopolist the net advantage of the monopoly over the competitive solution is the shaded area (a transfer) less the lower dotted area (a deadweight loss). As for the consumers, the upper dotted area represents their deadweight loss, and, in addition, they are on the losing side of the transfer. The transfer cancels out; the *efficiency loss* is measured by the two dotted areas alone.

Conclusion: In comparison with the competitive outcome, monopoly involves a transfer from consumers to suppliers. But the efficiency loss consists solely of the reductions in Consumer Surplus and Producer Surplus that are due to the lessened volume of trade.

<table>
<tr>
<td>

Example 11. 4
Monopoly
Efficiency Loss

</td>
<td>

A. C. Harberger[9] estimated the aggregate magnitude of the efficiency loss due to monopoly in the United States, for the period 1924–28. He was able to do so only by making a number of heroic assumptions, in particular, that Marginal Cost *MC* was constant for all industries, and that the price elasticity of demand was *unity* everywhere. Identifying monopolized industries on the basis of high average profit rate on assets, he obtained a surprisingly low estimate of the loss: only around 0.1% of national income.

Harberger's results were criticized by G. J. Stigler[10] on several grounds, among them: (1) A rational monopolist will always produce in the range where elasticity is *greater* than unity (as we have just seen in Section 11.B); (2) reported profit rates for monopolists may omit monopoly returns in the form of disguised "cost" items such as patent royalties and executive salaries; and (3) for monopoly firms, "intangible" items may become counted among assets, so as to reduce the reported profit as a precent of assets.

A number of later studies examined different sets of data, allowing in various ways for Stigler's objections. D. R. Kamerschen[11] studied the period 1956–61, making rather strong assumptions toward the opposite extreme from Harberger. For example, he included royalties, intangibles, and advertising expenditures with the monopoly returns. He obtained demand-elasticity estimates by industry, averaging around (minus) 2 or 3. On this basis Kamerschen concluded that the annual welfare loss due to monopoly is around 6% of national income. Still later, D. A. Worcester, Jr.,[12] studied the period 1956–69, using *firm* rather than *industry* data for added precision. Taking account of the Stigler objections in a variety of ways, and using an overall elasticity figure of (minus) 2, he still obtained low "maximum defensible" estimates of the welfare loss due to monopoly, in the range of 0.5% of national income.

[9]A. C. Harberger, "Monopoly and Resource Allocation," *American Economic Review*, v. 54 (May 1954).
[10]G. J. Stigler, "The Statistics of Monopoly and Merger," *Journal of Political Economy*, v. 64 (Feb. 1956).
[11]D. R. Kamerschen, "An Estimation of the 'Welfare Losses' from Monopoly in the American Economy," *Western Economic Journal*, v. 4 (Summer 1966).
[12]D. A. Worcester, Jr., "New Estimates of the Welfare Loss to Monopoly, United States: 1956–1969," *Southern Economic Journal*, v. 40 (Oct. 1973).

</td>
</tr>
</table>

Comment: As this very condensed report suggests, we have here an as-yet-unresolved economic controversy, involving issues both of theory and of statistical data. Even if the low estimates prove correct, it would be wrong to infer automatically that anti-monopoly activities of government should be suspended. Perhaps the low monopoly losses are to be attributed to the success of those very activities.

11. D REGULATION OF MONOPOLY

Between the two extremes of *laissez-faire* toleration of monopoly on the one hand, and "trust-busting" on the other, lies a third possibility—regulation of monopoly. Regulation is almost universal for privately-owned public utilities, i.e., power, water, gas, telephone, etc., generally considered to be "natural monopolies." But not all regulation is of monopolized industries, and not all monopolized industries are regulated. The positive factors leading governments to select among policies available will be studied in Part Six. Here our purpose is only to illustrate some aspects of the typical outcome under regulation.

The usual regulatory policy is that monopoly revenue should be allowed to cover only costs plus a *normal profit*, i.e., an amount necessary to attract and retain the resources employed in the industry. But the "normal" profit to the owners of a firm is (as explained in Section 9.C) the economic or opportunity cost of the resources provided by them. Hence regulatory policy can be interpreted as aiming at zero *economic profit* for the firm.

Figure 11.5 repeats the comparison of the monopoly solution (Q_m and P_m) and the competitive solution (Q_c and P_c) of Figure 11.4, and adds the regulatory solution (Q_r and P_r) as interpreted above. As can be seen, the regulatory zero-economic-profit condition is equivalent to setting a price and output such that $AC = AR$. Note that whereas the laissez-faire monopoly solution had "too small" output and "too high" price in comparison with the competitive outcome ($Q_m < Q_c$ and $P_m > P_c$), the regulatory correction "overshoots" the competitive outcome ($Q_r > Q_c$ and $P_r < P_c$).

A striking feature of Figure 11.5 is that, in the range of output greater than Q_c, Marginal Cost MC exceeds demand price (marginal "willingness to pay"). Thus there is an efficiency loss from "too great" a regulated output, as represented by the dotted area in Figure 11.5. This, plus the small cross-hatched triangle, represents *negative* Producer Surplus due to the excessive output. On the other hand, the cross-hatched area is also a region of *positive* Consumer Surplus. So the triangle cancels out, leaving the dotted area as the *net* efficiency loss. Consumers receive also a transfer gain (the shaded area) on the output Q_c.

Regulation is, however, a solution often adopted in the case of a "natural" monopoly—where Average Cost AC is falling throughout the relevant range.

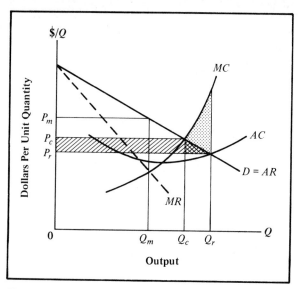

Figure 11. 5
Regulation of Monopoly (Increasing Cost)

This situation is pictured in Figure 11.6. Since AC is falling in the diagram, Marginal Cost MC lies always below it (Proposition 2.2a). Note that in Figure 11.6 the regulatory solution (Q_r and P_r) lies *between* the monopoly solution (Q_m and P_m) and the competitive solution (Q_c and P_c). It follows that, in regulated natural monopoly, there is still "too small" output and "too high" a price. The dotted region shows the efficiency loss due to "too small" a regulated output.[13]

An implication of this analysis is that regulated firms should be rather less interested than unregulated firms in technological advances reducing Average Cost, or in preventing cost increases due to inflation or scarcities. Indeed, if regulation were perfectly effective in maintaining the condition $AC = P_r$, the firm would have no incentive at all to hold costs down. Any cost increase would be immediately reflected in higher prices, maintaining normal profit for the firm. However, there is always a "regulatory lag": If costs rise or fall, it will be some time before the regulatory commission gets around to adjusting prices. Consequently, the cost-reducing incentive, while somewhat attenuated, is not completely eliminated for regulated monopolies.

[13]There is a paradox here. At the competitive solution, since $MC = P$ and $MC < AC$, then $AC > P$. So at the competitive outcome Average Cost exceeds price; the firm suffers a loss! It might therefore seem that the competitive solution could hardly serve as standard of efficiency. Nevertheless, the competitive solution remains the efficient one in the situation of Figure 11.6, as may be seen from the following argument. At the regulatory solution, $AC = P$, and there would be no loss. Now, given that output is at the regulatory level Q_r, is it or is it not efficient to expand production further to Q_c? Clearly it is, since in the region between Q_r and Q_c the demand price is always greater than the Marginal Cost. The resulting price drop, leading to the result $AC > P$, is a pure "transfer" that is not relevant for calculations of efficiency.

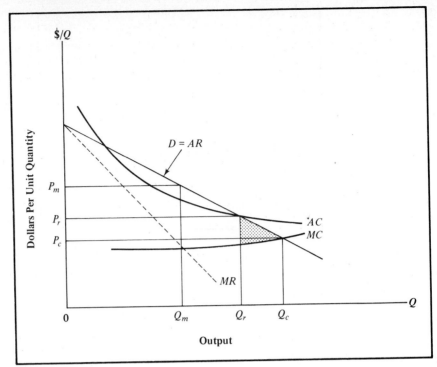

Figure 11. 6
Regulation of Monopoly (Decreasing Cost)

11. E   MONOPOLISTIC PRICE DISCRIMINATION

A monopoly firm is a "price-maker" rather than "price-taker." But up to now it has been assumed that the monopolist offers all customers a single simple price at which they are free to choose desired quantities. In certain circumstances, however, a monopolist might have a greater degree of market power. He might be able to offer different terms to different purchasers, so as to divide the market (*market segmentation*). Or, for any given purchaser, he might be able to impose a price schedule of greater or lesser complexity (*multi-part pricing*). In the limiting case he can charge a different price to each consumer for each successive infinitesimal unit purchased; this is called *perfect discrimination*.

11. E. 1   Market Segmentation

The minimal segmentation scheme involves the monopolist's presenting customers with two different simple prices, one price to each of two portions of the market. Apart from questions of legality, this can only be achieved by the monopolist when the two segments are effectively *insulated* one from another. If they are not insulated, customers in the low-price sector of the market would be able to turn an immediate profit by resale to the high-price sector—and the whole scheme would necessarily break down.[14]

The underlying logic of the market-segmentation solution is perhaps easier to grasp than the geometrical representation. Denote the separate demand or Average Revenue functions of the two segments as $ar_1(q_1)$ and $ar_2(q_2)$. (The parentheses indicate that ar_1 is a function of q_1 and ar_2 of q_2.) There are, of course, corresponding Marginal Revenue functions $mr_1(q_1)$ and $mr_2(q_2)$. The monopolist's Marginal Cost function can be expressed as $MC(Q)$, where $Q = q_1 + q_2$.

Now, at any level of output Q, whenever $mr_1 \neq mr_2$ the monopolist would want to reallocate units from the sector with lower to the sector with higher Marginal Revenue. Consequently, one optimality condition is $mr_1 = mr_2$. Also, he would want to produce more units of output so long as, and only so long as, $MC < mr_1 = mr_2$. Putting these conditions together, we have:

(11.5) $$MC(Q) = mr_1(q_1) = mr_2(q_2) \quad (\text{where } Q = q_1 + q_2)$$

Market-Segmentation Optimality Condition[15]

The geometrical construction appears in Figure 11.7. The key device is the curve labelled $\sum mr$, the *horizontal* sum of mr_1 and mr_2. The intersection of the firm Marginal Cost curve MC with $\sum mr$ at the point W establishes optimal output $Q = q_1 + q_2$. The separation into q_1 and q_2 is determined by picking off the lengths $ST (= q_1)$ and $TW (= SU = q_2)$ along the horizontal $STUW$. The final step is the determination of the segment prices P_1 and P_2; these are simply those associated with the respective quantities q_1 and q_2 along the segment demand curves ar_1 and ar_2.

From equation (11.4), and knowing that $mr_1 = mr_2$, we see that:

(11.6) $$P_1\left(1 + \frac{1}{\eta_1}\right) = P_2\left(1 + \frac{1}{\eta_2}\right)$$

It follows that if, for example, $|\eta_1| > |\eta_2|$ (demand in segment 1 is the more elastic), then $[1 + (1/\eta_1)] > [1 + (1/\eta_2)]$, so that $P_1 < P_2$. Thus, *the segment with more elastic demand receives the lower price.*

This feature explains the phenomenon called "dumping abroad," i.e., selling to foreigners at a price lower than the price a monopolist charges in his domestic market. Suppose a firm has a considerable degree of monopoly power in its own national market. But in the international market, where the suppliers of all nations compete, demand tends to be much more elastic. (More precisely, since any single national supplier may be a relatively small element in the international market, the elasticity of demand there as *perceived* by such a single seller tends to be relatively great.) If the monopolist is able to insulate

---

[14]However, the insulation of the two segments need not be *total*. The monopolist could accept some "leakage" and still remain ahead.

[15]The technical qualification earlier, that MC must cut MR from *below*, here takes the form: MC must cut the horizontal sum of the mr curves (see Figure 11.7) from below.

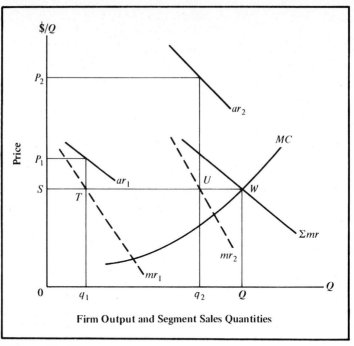

Figure 11. 7
Market Segmentation

his foreign and domestic markets (e.g., by inducing his government to set a tariff or ban upon imports), he generally finds it profitable to charge a lower price abroad than at home.

11. E. 2 Multi-Part Pricing

The minimal multi-part pricing scheme is illustrated in Figure 11.8. It involves the monopolist's presenting a single price *schedule* to each separate consumer, such that a relatively high price P_1 is charged for initial units up to some given limit B, and a lower price P_2 for additional units taken thereafter. The basic intent of such a scheme is to capture for the seller a portion of the Consumer Surplus (see Section 7.E) that would otherwise have gone to buyers.

In Figure 11.8, the monopolist is facing the individual demand curve d of one typical consumer. The cost function cannot be shown in this diagram, but we may assume that the intersection of MC and MR in a diagram like Figure 11.1, Panel (b), leads to the determination of an optimal *simple* monopoly price P^*. At this price the consumer would choose the quantity q^*. Simple pricing would leave the shaded area under the demand curve as Consumer Surplus.[16] A two-part pricing scheme might specify an initial higher P_1 up to

[16]This area is normally a slight exaggeration of the true Consumer Surplus, as explained in Section 7.E.3. See also footnote 17.

the limit B, and the lower $P_2 = P^*$ thereafter as indicated in the diagram. Suppose we can assume that the same total quantity $q_1 + q_2 = q^*$ will still be purchased by the individual as under simple monopoly. The consumer would buy $q_1 = B$ units at the price P_1, and $q_2 = q^* - B$ units at the price P_2. Then the revenue received by the seller would obviously be greater than under simple pricing, by the area $(P_1 - P^*)q_1$ of the rectangle shown as cutting into the Consumer Surplus.

This is, however, somewhat of an idealized situation. The monopolist would ordinarily not be able to do quite so well as pictured. First of all, the "income effect" (Section 4.C) of paying the higher price P_1 for the first B units would *tend to reduce the consumer's demand for additional units.* The ordinary demand curve d is constructed on the hypothesis of simple uniform pricing; only in the case of goods for which the income effect is zero (the income elasticity of demand is zero) will the curve remain the same when multi-part pricing is employed to extract more revenue from the consumer.[17] Consequently, the monopolist must consider, as a partial offset to the advantage gained from selling the first B units at the high price P_1, that there will be a reduction in the overall number of units that can be sold.

Another, generally more important, qualification stems from *differences among consumers.* The monopolist would ideally like to offer differing price schedules to each of his different customers. But legal restrictions, or perhaps the cost of making such distinctions among customers, may dictate a common price schedule in which P_1, P_2, and B are the same for all purchasers. Then

---

[17]The "income effect" is the reason why the true Consumer Surplus is normally less than the shaded area in Figure 11.8. Only when the income effect is zero will the shaded area be the precise measure of Consumer Surplus.

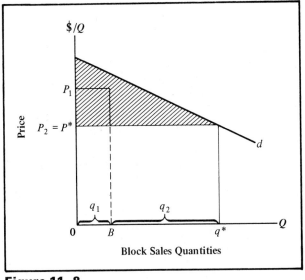

Figure 11. 8
Two-Part Pricing

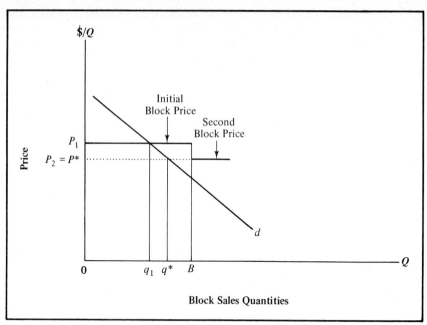

Figure 11. 9
Unsuccessful Two-Part Pricing

there are likely to be a number of customers in the situation of Figure 11.9. For these customers B is so large that the initial price P_1 becomes a simple price for them: they will not purchase any additional units at all at the lower price P_2 quoted for units beyond B. Since $P_2 = P^*$ was by hypothesis the profit-maximizing simple price for the monopolist, inability to offer different multi-part price schedules to different consumers may cut substantially into his profit.

The two qualifications here considered are reinforcing, tending to reduce the advantage of multi-part pricing to the monopolist. In addition, of course, the *transaction cost* of more complex pricing schemes will be greater. Not only will more detailed metering and recording of sales be required, but as in the segmentation case it will again be necessary to control "leakage" of units from low-price to high-price buyers. Thus, it is not always evident that the monopolist will find such discrimination advantageous.

At first sight, it may appear that discrimination via multi-part pricing is very common. Electric and water utilities, for example, normally charge on a "declining-block" basis. There is an initial high price for the first block consumed in any period, and a lower price thereafter. Utility price schedules, indeed, may have four or five parts (blocks), and also, possibly, some segmentation of different classes of customers. Printers and furniture-movers also commonly have declining-block pricing arrangements. Indeed, wherever "quantity discounts" are encountered multi-part discrimination may be suspected.

294

However, the suspicion is not conclusive; the pricing scheme may be due not to discrimination but to the costs incurred in serving different classes of customers. In the case of electric utilities, for example, there may be a recurrent "fixed" cost of providing the consumer's connection to the main cable, a cost that is essentially independent of the number of kilowatt-hours consumed. Ideally, then, periodic bills should have a fixed and a variable component. For a variety of reasons, it may be more convenient for the utility to express the recurring fixed component as a premium price on the first few units taken. For printing similarly, there is normally a "fixed" cost per job or transaction (e.g., the cost of setting up the type for a printing order) and a variable cost representing the actual run of the press. Thus, the question of the actual prevalence of discriminatory multi-part pricing versus "cost-justified" quantity discounts remains subject to some controversy.

11. E. 3   Perfect Discrimination

Finally, we can now go to the logical extreme of *perfect* discrimination. This of course is not a practical possibility, but is illuminating to analyze. It combines the *interpersonal* discrimination of market segmentation and the *intrapersonal* discrimination of multi-part pricing. In addition, these processes are imagined as carried to their limits: Each separate consumer is charged according to an individually tailored price schedule, which specifies a different amount to be paid for each successive infinitesimal unit he purchases.

In Figure 11.10 we see a four-part pricing schedule, a small extension of the two-part schedule pictured in Figure 11.8. As in the previous analysis, we make the simplifying assumption of zero income effect (zero income elasticity of demand) for the commodity. Then the quantities taken at the lower prices are unaffected by the higher amounts paid out (in accordance with the specifics of the price schedule being enforced) for earlier units. As can be seen, the effect of the multi-part schedule is to transfer great portions of the Consumer Surplus to the seller; in Figure 11.10, only the small shaded areas remain as Consumer Surplus to the buyer.

When this process is carried to the limit, with different prices for each successive infinitesimal unit, *all* the Consumer Surplus will have been transferred from the buyer to the seller. Consequently, the buyer receives essentially zero advantage from trade. (Presumably, he can be allowed to retain some negligible benefit, to induce him to engage in trade at all rather than choose an autarky solution.) And, since the seller is not constrained to offer the same price schedule to *all* buyers, he can do this with every separate consumer. So the perfectly discriminating monopolist absorbs essentially all the achievable mutual advantage of trade.

Despite the seeming "inequity" of this totally unbalanced distribution of the benefits from trade, the remarkable thing about the perfect-discrimination solution is that it is *efficient*—there are no deadweight losses! For the last infinitesimal unit purchased by each consumer, the monopolist will charge an amount equal to his Marginal Cost. Since each buyer's marginal willingness

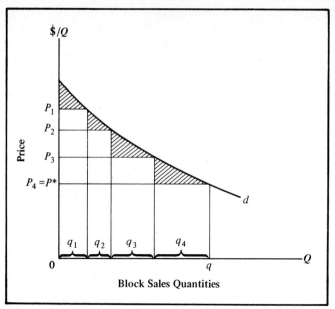

Figure 11. 10
Four-Part Pricing

to pay (demand price) is thus equal to the seller's Marginal Cost of production, there is no social gain available from increasing or decreasing output. So the perfectly discriminating monopolist cannot be said to produce "too little" or "too much" from the point of view of economic efficiency.

11. F CARTELS

A cartel may be defined as a group of independent firms attempting, via collusive agreement, to behave as a collective monopoly. Each firm in a cartel agrees to produce less than it would under unrestrained competition, the overall effect being to drive the price up so that all in the group will benefit.

Cartels have an Achilles heel. However desirable the arrangement is to the firms as a group, for any single firm it pays to "chisel" on the agreement. In the extreme case, consider a firm in a cartelized industry that would otherwise be perfectly competitive.[18] Figure 11.11 illustrates such a situation. At the price P^o that would rule in perfect competition, d^o is the familiar horizontal demand curve as viewed by the competitive firm. Assuming that Average Variable Cost is covered, the firm would produce output q^o where Marginal Cost $MC = P^o$. If a cartel is organized with the objective of raising prices, industry output Q must somehow be cut back—for example, by fixing production quotas for each firm. Suppose that this firm is assigned an output quota q', and furthermore that the cartel is successful in pushing prices up to P'. The

[18]Collusive behavior in market structures that would otherwise be less than perfectly competitive (e.g., oligopoly) will be studied in the chapters following.

incentive to chisel is evident. The new demand curve *as viewed by the firm* (a tiny slice of the industry demand curve) is d'—effectively horizontal, just like the d^o curve before cartelization. By charging an infinitesimally lower price, any single firm can get as much business as desired, taking away sales from others. Even at the old competitive price P^o, the firm was motivated to produce q^o, more than the quota amount q'. (Cartel production quotas must of course be less than competitive firm outputs, or the price could not rise from P^o to P'.) But once the cartel has raised price, the incentive to secretly "chisel" so as to achieve greater sales is that much greater. At the price P' the firm would want to set output q'' in the diagram. The potential profit increment available to a chiseller, assuming all other firms are faithfully abiding by the cartel agreement so that price does not fall, is indicated by the shaded area in the diagram.

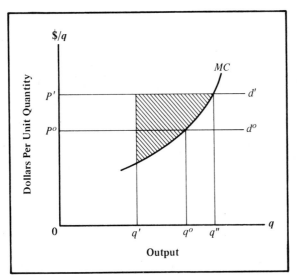

Figure 11. 11
Incentive to Chisel

Conclusion: Cartels can only raise prices by cutting firm outputs. But at the higher prices, member firms are motivated to produce even more than at competitive equilibrium. So the more successful the cartel, the greater the incentive to chisel.

Cartels, therefore, require enforcement devices. The power of the state may do the trick; the law may treat the cartel agreement as a legally enforceable contract. This has indeed been the situation in a number of European countries. Some jurisdictions take a neutral position: the cartel agreement is not unlawful, but the power of the state will not enforce it. Finally, as typically has been the case in the United States, the law may be actively hostile to cartels as "conspiracies in restraint of trade." In such a situation, for the cartel to control chiselling would require enforcement devices that are *both effective and secret*—an unlikely combination when any detected chiseller can threaten to complain to the authorities.

Collusive agreements alleged to be in restraint of trade are prosecuted in the United States mainly by the Anti-Trust Division of the Department of Justice and by the Federal Trade Commission. (In addition, it is possible for individuals or firms to sue for damages suffered as victims of such agreements.) But it is a curious paradox that, in parallel with this activity, other branches of the United States government are themselves active in the organization and enforcement of cartel agreements. A number of agricultural products, for example, are sold subject to governmentally-sponsored "marketing orders" designed to limit production and sales.

Example 11. 5
Agircultural
Marketing
Orders

On the basis of legislation of the Federal government, and some states as well, the growers of certain agricultural products may draw up an agreement to limit supply and assign marketing quotas. If two-thirds of the growers (by number or by volume) vote for such an agreement the Secretary of Agriculture is authorized to make it binding upon *all* growers.

Quantities produced beyond the marketing quotas are "dumped" abroad, used in special government programs outside normal trade channels (e.g., school lunches), or simply destroyed. In effect, the cartel (representing the growers as an aggregate) buys up excess production in order to limit supplies and drive up price in the "primary" market. However, this means that each individual producer has an incentive to produce more and more. In addition, the higher the cartelized price, the more growers of *other* commodities tend to shift over to the cartelized product. Consequently, we would expect to see over time an increasing percentage of the cartelized crops having to be diverted away from "primary" markets. This is illustrated in the following Table.

Percentage of Annual Supply Diverted from Primary
Markets under Federal Marketing Orders

Crop	1960–64 Avg.	1965–68 Avg.
California Raisins	28.2	39.6
California-Arizona Lemons	55.2	62.5
California Almonds	15.0	21.2
California-Oregon-Washington Walnuts	0.8	7.5
Oregon-Washington Filberts	21.8	27.5
California Dates (Deglet Noor)	21.4	28.2

Source: John A. Jamison, "Marketing Orders and Public Policy for the Fruit and Vegetable Industries," *Food Research Studies in Agricultural Economics, Trade, and Development*, v. 10, no. 3 (1971), p. 347.

Of course, there can be hardly anyone in the world unfamiliar with the most successful cartel in history—the Organization of Petroleum Exporting Countries (OPEC).

Example 11. 6
The OPEC

Before 1960 the international oil companies (especially seven or eight "majors" such as Royal Dutch Shell and Standard Oil of New Jersey) dominated the world petroleum market. These companies, while often accused of acting as a cartel, cannot have diverged far from competitive behavior—judging (in retrospect) from the low prices formerly ruling. Indeed, it was the attempt of the majors to cut oil prices further that led the exporting governments to form the OPEC in 1960. With increasing effectiveness over the years, the exporting governments have gained control over production and prices even where they have refrained from total expropriation of the private companies.

While the OPEC kept oil prices from falling in 1960, lack of unity among the exporting nations allowed prices to remain stable for some time thereafter. But in solidarity with the attack of Egypt and Syria upon Israel in late 1973, the Arab countries dominating OPEC decided to use oil as an economic weapon. The effect upon prices was dramatic. On January 1, 1973, the F.O.B. sale price of Saudi Arabian crude oil had been $2.12 per barrel. Most of this amount, in fact $1.52, was already being taken by the Saudi Arabian government, leaving only some $.60 per barrel to cover the private companies' cost of operation and return on investment. But by a year later, price had been raised to $7.61 per barrel. Practically all of the increase went into government take, which now amounted to $7.01 per barrel.[19] By January 1, 1975, the Saudi Arabian government take had risen to $10.12 per barrel, and the price to around $10.50. Other OPEC nations conformed to this price schedule, though government take varied from country to country in accordance with local circumstances. Still, it is evident that the price increase went in its entirety into the coffers of the exporting governments. (It is a tribute to economic gullibility that the Shah of Iran, the King of Saudi Arabia, and other oil potentates succeeded in convincing a large part of Western public opinion that it was the wicked oil companies rather than the exporting governments who were responsible for the higher prices!)

Not surprisingly, the drastic price increases had an impact upon consumption. In 1974 consumption was down from 1973 by 14% in Holland and Belgium, by 10% in West Germany and Spain, by 3.5% in the U.S., and by 2% in Japan and Italy.[20] These percentages are more

[19]Data on prices from *International Economic Report of the President*, Feb. 1974 (Washington: U.S. Government Printing Office), pp. 110–11.
[20]Data on consumption and production from "OPEC Tries To Tackle a World Oil Surplus," *Business Week* (March 17, 1975), p. 20.

impressive when it is appreciated that demand had previously been on a sharp upward trend—growing at the rate of 4% per year in the United States, for example.

The problem for the OPEC, of course, is to hold production down despite the separate countries' incentives to chisel at the high prices achieved. The cartel's task is facilitated by the fact that some of the leading producers—in particular, Saudi Arabia and Kuwait—seem able to cut back enough to make up for others who do not. Thus, while overall crude production of OPEC members declined by 1.3% in 1974 as compared with 1973, in January 1975 Saudi Arabian production was down 8.4% and Kuwait production 35.7% from the year before. Whether this will suffice to hold the line, as the temptation to produce and to sell more oil grows, is a question for history.

11. G SOURCE OF MONOPOLY POWER: NUMBERS VERSUS BEHAVIOR

A monopolist is usually defined as a "single seller in an industry." But the cartel example above shows that small numbers is not the essential. *Any number of sellers*, however large, *are motivated to behave as a collective monopolist*. And, in certain circumstances, they may succeed in doing so.

Alternatively, *there may be essentially competitive behavior even with only a single seller* (i.e., output such that Marginal Cost $MC = P$ rather than the $MC = MR < P$ condition characteristic of monopoly). Consider the case of a "natural monopoly," where economies of scale are so great that only a single producer is viable in the industry. There might nevertheless be a number of alternative claimants willing and ready to enter the industry and be that sole producer. These rivalrous outsiders may, in certain circumstances, impose essentially competitive behavior upon the incumbent producer. "Competition *for* the field" may substitute for the numbers needed to have "competition *in* the field."[21]

A clear example exists today in cable television. This is a natural monopoly in any single geographical area. A firm already providing cable service can supply an increment of output (i.e., increase its coverage) far more cheaply than a new firm, which would have to duplicate facilities that the existing firm already has in place. But communities typically franchise the right to lay cable to the single company making the most attractive bid. The active competition among bidders precludes any significant monopoly profits. Even in the absence of formal bidding and franchise arrangements, the *potential* market presence of alternative suppliers may check the ability of a sole producer to achieve the theoretical monopoly outcome.

[21]See H. Demsetz, "Why Regulate Utilities?", *Journal of Law and Economics* v. 11 (April 1968).

1. Why will a monopolist's profit-maximizing rate of output always be in the region of elastic demand?

2. "Monopoly is a bad thing for consumers, but a good thing for producers. So, on balance, we can't be sure that monopoly is responsible for any loss in economic efficiency." Analyze.

3. Monopoly firms are accused of pursuing "non-profit goals" to a greater degree than would be possible for competitive firms. Why should a monopolist be any less interested in profit than a competitor? What non-profit goals might a monopolist pursue?

4. Compare the profit-maximizing conditions for simple monopoly, for market-segmentation monopoly, and for perfect-discrimination monopoly. Why is only the last of these said to be *efficient*?

5. In comparison with a simple monopolist, does a perfectly discriminating monopolist *possibly* or *necessarily* produce more output? Does a market-segmentation monopolist? A multi-part pricing monopolist?

6. Price discrimination tends to be more common in the sale of services (e.g., discrimination by income for medical services, by age for air transportation services) than for manufactured goods. Explain.

7. Show how behavior of its own members may threaten the survival of a cartel. Show how behavior of outsiders may threaten it.

8. It has been alleged that sellers' cartels are more effective in dealing with *government* as a buyer because of the existence of public records of all transactions in which government engages. Explain. How might the contention be tested?

9. Analyze the equilibrium of an industry characterized by a single very large (price-making) seller surrounded by a "fringe" of many very small (price-taking) sellers. How can the large seller in his profit-maximizing decision take the behavior of the fringe into account?

Chapter 12
Product as a Variable

Up to this point, firms and industries have been assumed to generate products that are defined in some self-evident or natural way not itself the object of economic decision-making. But the "new theory of consumption" (discussed in Section 6.E) indicates that consumers do not really desire brute physical commodities as such. Rather, consumer preferences should be thought of as attaching to the utility-relevant qualities or *attributes* represented by or contained in the commodities. Market goods are desired only because and insofar as they constitute convenient packages of attributes. Firms therefore have another dimension of choice available for their profit-maximizing decisions: Aside from the possibility of quoting alternative prices for any given product, or varying the quantity of product offered, firms can alter the nature or attribute content of the commodities they produce.

In the discussion following, two main types of situations will be investigated. In the first, consumers' tastes and desires for a particular product are assumed to be distributed over a range of some quantifiable attribute such as size, color, or weight. Men with big feet want large shoe sizes; men with little feet, small shoe sizes. Here the market response will typically be to offer an assortment of varieties to consumers. The analytical problem is to determine the *equilibrium nature and extent of the assortment* offered and sold.[1] This situation is associated with the emergence of the market structure known as *monopolistic competition*—where each firm offers consumers its own unique product, but there are many such closely competing firms. In the second type of situation to be considered, the product may be a variable even though differences of tastes among consumers is not involved. Instead, all consumers agree on the desirability of some objective *quality* attribute (e.g., strength or durability) contained, to greater or lesser degree, in the products offered for sale. But higher quality will, in general, involve higher

---

[1] For some commodities, one or more of the preference-determining attributes may not be objectively quantifiable. Toothpaste may have a sweet or spicy taste, clothing may be in mod or in conservative style, an automobile may or may not have a sporty design. We deal here only with attributes that *can* be objectively scaled.

cost of production. The problem is the determination of the *equilibrium level of quality* of the product in the market.

12. A OPTIMAL PRODUCT ASSORTMENT—MONOPOLY

Before bringing in the element of competition, let us consider how a monopolist would solve the problem of determining the profit-maximizing assortment of varieties to be offered on the market. Products may of course vary in an indefinitely large number of ways, but for simplicity we consider a single dimension of variation. In the case of an item of clothing, we might think in terms of the assortment of *sizes* to be offered. Alternatively, the assortment of *colors* might be a relevant consideration.

A *locational metaphor* or analogy will help to visualize the problem. With clothing *size* as the attribute, we can think metaphorically of consumption preferences as distributed over a line-segment as in Figure 12.1 (linear attribute preference). We would expect to find greater density toward the middle of the distribution; as suggested in the diagram, desires for extreme sizes

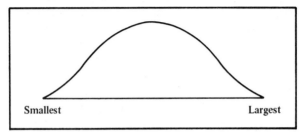

Figure 12. 1
Distribution of Linear Attribute Preferences
(e.g., sizes)

are much less common than desires for middling sizes. It turns out, however, that a somewhat different metaphor employing a *uniform* distribution of preferences is more convenient to deal with. Let us think of clothing color as the attribute instead. Then consumer preferences might reasonably be assumed to be distributed uniformly around a ring, as in Figure 12.2.

In this locational metaphor, the attribute variety (color) preferred by a particular consumer can be regarded as his *consumption locale*, i.e., the geographical location of his residence on the ring. Similarly, any given variety actually produced and offered in the market can be regarded as a *production locale*. In the metaphor, *transport costs* will be incurred due to the distance between a consumer's consumption locale and the production locale nearest to him. This is the locational analog of the *satisfaction loss* involved in the imperfect matching of consumer preferences with the available products on the market.

Using the ring metaphor, the first problem for the monopolist is to determine *how many* varieties to produce, i.e., the number of distinct productive

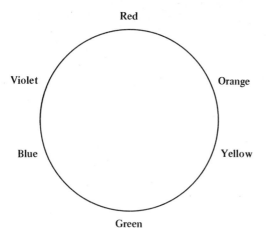

Figure 12. 2
Ring of Circular Attribute Preferences
(e.g., colors)

locales to establish around the ring. (Having done so, he must still face the familiar price-quantity optimization problem, of course.) By increasing the number of productive locales (of "plants"), he can reduce transport costs. What prevents his carrying this process to the limit (a separate plant for each consumer) is the existence of *economies of scale*. Over some range, at least, Average Cost per plant will ordinarily be a decreasing function of plant output. So the monopolist must balance savings in production costs against savings in transport costs, i.e., against the gains achievable by closer matching of product assortment to consumer desires.

For simplicity again, assume that the cost of production is *identical* at all possible locations around the ring. Then, given a uniform distribution of consumers, the producing plants (whatever their number may be) should be spaced evenly around the ring to minimize the transport costs of delivery to consumption locales. And, it also follows from the symmetry of the situation that the price at the factory (the "F.O.B. price") will be identical at each producing plant. Each consumer, of course, must pay this F.O.B. price *plus* the unit transport cost from the nearest plant to his consumption locale.

Looking first at the demand side, note in Figure 12.3 the limiting highest aggregate consumer demand function D_∞. This represents the ideal case in which there are an infinite number of production locales. As consumers then incur no transport costs, their desires for product become wholly reflected in the effective demand curve faced by the monopolist. At the opposite extreme is the curve labelled D_1, which shows effective demand with just a single productive plant (placed at any arbitrary point on the ring). Here the worst-off consumer must pay for shipment halfway around the ring; the *average* transport cost is equivalent to a quarter-circle of circumference about the ring. The curve D_2 represents the effective demand with two plants, where the average consumer is separated by an eighth-circle from the nearest production locale. The D_{10} curve in the diagram shows the effective demand with 10 plants. Note that the curve of effective demand shifts upward, *but at a decreasing rate,* as the number of plants is increased, i.e., as the assortment offered more closely approximates the distribution of consumer preferences.

To arrive at the monopolist's solution, we also need his cost function. This can be conveniently illustrated by making the special assumption that plant production costs are linear so that for the nth plant, $C_n = A + Bq_n$. Here A is the fixed cost of each plant, and B the marginal cost. Then if there are N identical plants, the overall Total Cost will be symbolized here as $TC_N = \sum_{n=1}^{N} C_n = \sum_{n=1}^{N} (A + Bq_n) = NA + BQ$, where $Q = \sum_{n=1}^{N} q_n$ is the monopolist's overall output of product. For a range of possible numbers of plants N, the overall Total Cost functions TC_N are shown by the dashed lines $TC_1, TC_2, \ldots$ in Figure 12.4. Because of the existence of the fixed cost A *per plant,* Total Costs of producing any aggregate output Q rise with *number* of plants N.

The Total Revenue functions corresponding to different numbers of plants are also shown in Figure 12.4. TR_1 is the Total Revenue curve corresponding to the effective demand (Average Revenue) curve D_1 of the previous diagram, TR_2 similarly corresponds to D_2, etc.

For any given number of plants N, the monopolist chooses the F.O.B. price P_m and the associated quantity Q by using the familiar condition $MC = MR$ so as to maximize profit—the vertical distance between the appropriate pair of TR_N and TC_N curves. For different numbers of plants N, the various possible profits are indicated by the vertical bold line-segments in Figure 12.4. As may be seen, there will normally be a range in which profit increases

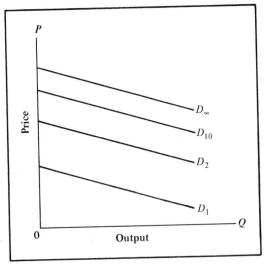

Figure 12. 3
Aggregate Demand as Related to Number
of Producing Plants

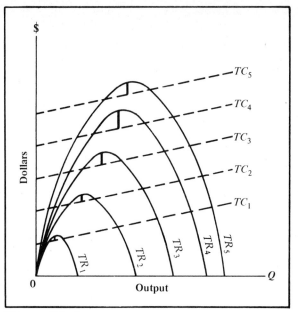

Figure 12. 4
Monopoly Total Revenue and Total Costs
as Related to Number of Plants

as N rises. In this range the gain from better matching of product to consumer desires (i.e., from the fact that consumers are willing to pay more when they avoid the metaphorical "transport costs"), evidencing itself by upward shifts of the TR curve, is greater than the increased cost due to the larger number of production locales. But the gains from increasing N tend to taper off, as indicated in Figure 12.3. Meanwhile the costs tend to rise steadily as N grows, because of the necessity of incurring another fixed-cost element A each time a new plant is added. There will, consequently, be an optimum number of plants, specifically $N = 4$ in the situation pictured in Figure 12.4.

12. B   MONOPOLISTIC COMPETITION

The monopoly solution of the previous section provides the needed background for analyzing the market structure known as *monopolistic competition*. This market structure combines the following characteristics: (1) competition among plants, now treated as independent firms; (2) free entry; and (3) heterogeneous products among firms. The first two characteristics represent the competitive aspects of monopolistic competition. The monopolistic aspect is represented by the third element, the uniqueness of the firm's product offered to the market. This uniqueness corresponds metaphorically to a degree of *geographical* monopoly. Each firm will have a "clientele" consisting of those consumers located closer to it than to any other firm around the ring of preference.

It will be convenient first to provide a reinterpretation of the monopoly solution in terms of an average-marginal diagram as in Figure 12.5. In a monopoly with N identical plants, the effective aggregate demand (Average Revenue) is D_N, a curve some distance below the "ideal" D_∞. Marginal Revenue is MR_N. Now consider the pro-rata shares of D_N attributable to any single plant, $D_n = D_N/N$ and $MR_n = MR_N/N$. Geometrically, these are found simply by dividing the respective aggregate curves horizontally by N. The optimal monopoly *plant* output q_n^* and *firm* output Q_n^* are easy to

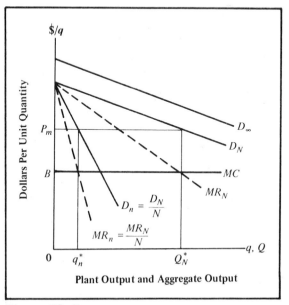

Figure 12. 5
Monopoly Solutions, Aggregate and Plant

see by inspection of Figure 12.5. The *plant* output q_n^* is determined by the intersection of MR_n with MC. (Under the linear cost assumption $C_n = A + Bq_n$, the Marginal Cost curve MC is horizontal at the level B.) The aggregate firm output Q_N^* is found at the intersection of MC with MR_N. The monopoly price, P_m, may be found equally well along the aggregate demand curve D_N (at quantity Q_N^*), or along the plant pro-rata demand curve D_n (at quantity q_n^*). Of course, $Q_N^* = Nq_n^*$.

Figure 12.6 now introduces the element of competition, assuming a fixed number N of *firms*. Furthermore, the competing firms are assumed to possess identical cost functions and to distribute themselves evenly around the ring of preference. Thus, each *firm* here is (aside from its profit motivation) in the same situation as any single *plant* of the monopolist. For purposes of comparison, we see once again the monopoly solution for a typical plant, at output q_n^* determined by the condition that $MR_n = MC$. The key point is that, *for a plant that is an autonomous firm, the demand function* d_n *becomes more elastic (flatter) than the* D_n *curve that represents the monopoly plant's*

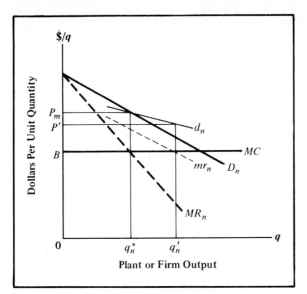

Figure 12. 6
Monopoly Plant versus Monopolistic-
Competition Firm, at Monopoly Solution

pro-rata share of the overall demand curve. The curve d_n is more elastic than D_n because, by lowering price relative to its neighbors, each firm figures that it can win customers away from them—whereas the monopoly plant's demand curve D_n was based on the premise that the *same* (F.O.B.) price P_m will be charged by all N plants. (It is not in the interest of the monopolist, of course, to have his plants cutting price at one another's expense.) Corresponding to the *more elastic* firm demand curve d_n in Figure 12.6 is a *higher* firm Marginal Revenue curve mr_n.[2] The firm in Figure 12.6 will therefore be competitively motivated to attain the larger output q'_n where $mr_n = MC$, setting a lower price $P' < P_m$ for its particular variety of product.

But this solution on the level of the single firm is not consistent with an *overall equilibrium* of the industry. With a fixed number N of producing locations (whether plants of a monopolist, or competing firms), the per-location sales achievable at any given price can be no greater than those represented by the pro-rata demand curve $D_n = D_N/N$. Each firm's flatter demand curve d_n is an illusion (akin to the seemingly horizontal demand curve faced by the firm in pure competition). Any single firm can hope to cut price so as to expand output along d_n. But the symmetry of the situation, with N identical firms, dictates that in equilibrium they must all end up

[2]This will be evident from the geometry, recalling (from the "Corollary" of Section 11.B.2) that the Marginal Revenue curve bisects the horizontal distance from the axis to a linear demand curve. Or, consider the definition $MR = P + Q(\Delta P/\Delta Q)$, where the ratio $\Delta P/\Delta Q$ represents the slope of the demand curve. For a given (P, Q) combination, the smaller the slope in absolute value (the flatter the demand curve), the smaller in absolute magnitude is the second term in the definition of MR. But this second term is of negative sign. So the flatter the slope of the demand curve, the greater is Marginal Revenue.

choosing the same price. They each cut price, hoping to sell output q'_n at price P'. But the result of their collective action is that output expands less than expected, along the steeper pro-rata demand curve D_n in the diagram.

The consequent equilibrium, still holding the number of firms constant, is shown in Figure 12.7. At the quantity q''_n, associated with price P'', the flatter demand curve d_n as perceived by the firm is associated with a Marginal Revenue curve such that $mr_n = MC$ at output q''_n. As the firm's desired price-quantity combination (P'', q''_n) here lies along the true pro-rata demand

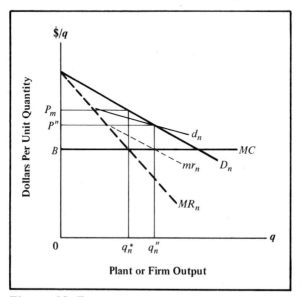

Figure 12. 7
Monopoly Plant versus
Monopolistic-Competition Firm,
at Monopolistic-Competition Equilibrium

curve D_n, this situation is an achievable one. At this solution, firm output is clearly greater (and price to consumers lower) in comparison with the monopoly solution (P_m, q^*_n).

We are not yet at the full or *long-run* equilibrium for monopolistic competition, however. Possible changes in the *number* of firms in the market (associated with the condition of free entry) must also be taken into account. Depending upon the level of the fixed cost per firm, the short-run equilibrium shown in Figure 12.7 might either be a profitable one for firms in the industry (inducing entry) or an unprofitable one (dictating exit). Let us assume that the short-run equilibrium is profitable, with price P'' greater than the representative firm's level of Average Cost AC_n at the production rate q''_n. As entry of new firms occurs, both the true pro-rata demand curve $D_n = D_N/N$ and the illusory d_n as viewed by an existing firm will *shift inward* toward the

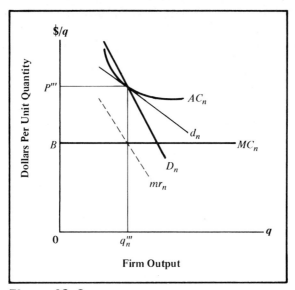

Figure 12. 8
Long-Run Equilibrium,
Representative Firm in Monopolistic Competition

vertical axis.[3] The ultimate consequence is as shown in Figure 12.8 for the representative firm. Here, in addition to the conditions satisfied in the previous diagram, that $MC = mr_n$ and that the firm's price-output combination be consistent with the pro-rata demand curve D_n, we have a zero-profit solution. This is represented in the diagram by the *tangency* of the firm's demand curve d_n with its Average Cost curve AC_n at output q_n''' and price P'''.

Conclusion: Monopolistic competition has lower price—hence greater output in the aggregate—than multi-plant monopoly. It also has greater output per producing locale, as may be seen in Figure 12.6. But there may or may not be a larger *number* of producing locations. Thus, while consumers benefit from a lower price, they may or may not find a better assortment of varieties of product available under monopolistic competition as compared with monopoly.

12. C EQUILIBRIUM QUALITY LEVEL—COMPETITIVE INDUSTRY

In the remainder of the chapter we will be considering quite a different product-variation situation. In this section it is assumed possible to identify and measure some single attribute that *all* consumers desire to obtain from

[3]This shift is due to dividing the aggregate demand curve D_N horizontally by a larger N. There is a countervailing factor, however, since a larger N is associated with a more perfect matching of consumer desires, so that the aggregate curve D_N itself shifts upward as N rises (as shown in Figure 12.3). This latter effect is likely to be minor, except when N is very small.

the product purchased in the market. It is no longer a matter of some customers preferring yellow clothing and others red, or big men wanting big sizes and small men small sizes. Instead we here assume that in the purchase of light bulbs, for example, all buyers agree that light output in lumens is the sole desired feature. In the purchase of gasoline, transportation mileage may be the desired feature. In such cases the amount of the desired attribute obtainable per unit of the physical commodity may be considered the *quality* of the product. Of course, quality will generally be multi-dimensional. Gasoline may be valued for attributes like rapid acceleration and easy starting as well as for cruising mileage. The color or shape or size of light bulbs may be important to consumers in addition to sheer light output. In the interests of simplicity, however, we will deal here only with a one-dimensional quality index.

In this section we will consider whether a *quality assortment* is likely to emerge, analogous to the assortment due to varying consumer preferences that arose in the previous analysis. In the next section, we ask whether a monopolist would tend to produce a quality of product that differs from what a competitive industry will offer.

There is one key idea to be kept in mind: Only superficially are consumers and producers dealing in quantities of *product Q* (e.g., gasoline); more fundamentally, consumers are demanding and firms are supplying quantities of *attribute K* (e.g., mileage). Thus, we are really concerned here with conditions of equilibrium in the *market for the quality attribute* (mileage).

Assume to begin with a fixed number N of competitive firms. Each separate firm will, it is assumed, choose a quality level z_n as well as an output rate q_n for its physical product. Then, the firm's output of attribute k_n will simply be:

(12.1)
$$k_n = z_n q_n$$

For example, a firm producing $q_n = 1,000,000$ gallons of gasoline per day, with quality level $z_n = 20$ miles per gallon, is effectively producing $k_n = 20,000,000$ units per day of "mileage" for sale to consumers.

Consumers have, it is assumed, an implicit demand function for attribute K, e.g., for mileage, relating the aggregate demand quantity K_d to the "price of attribute" P_k that is implicit in the prices charged by the various firms for their physical products. On the assumption that consumers are always fully informed as to quality, the price P_n of the nth firm's physical product depends strictly upon its attribute content:

(12.2)
$$P_n = z_n P_k$$

If one gasoline yields 20% greater mileage per gallon than another, its price must be just 20% higher. The *price of attribute* P_k is determined by the overall supply and demand of attribute. The supply quantity K_s, to be balanced against the demand quantity K_d as a function of price P_k, is simply the sum of the separate firms' outputs of attribute:

(12.3) $$K_s = \sum_{n=1}^{N} k_n$$

The firm's decision problem, as a competitive price-taker in the market for attribute, is to choose the profit-maximizing combination of z_n and q_n. A possible situation is illustrated in Figure 12.9. Suppose an initial quality level $z_n = z^o$ were set by the firm. The associated Average Cost and Marginal

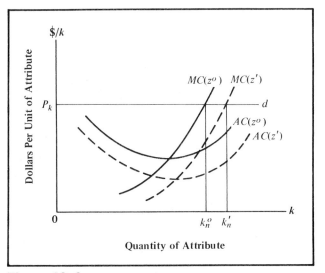

Figure 12. 9
Uniform Best Quality Level

Cost functions for generating output, indicated by the curves $AC(z^o)$ and $MC(z^o)$, lead to the optimal attribute output k_n^o. Knowing k_n and z_n, the required physical output of commodity is then given, from equation (12.1), as $q_n = k_n/z_n$.

But k_n^o is optimal only given the initial choice of quality level as $z_n = z^o$. What would happen if other quality levels were considered? It might be that a 20% increase in quality level z_n (miles per gallon) would only raise cost by 10% per unit of physical commodity (gallons of gasoline). This would imply that the cost *per unit of attribute* (mileage) has fallen. Geometrically, this would be reflected in Figure 12.9 by a downward displacement of *MC* and *AC*, as suggested by the dashed curves $AC(z')$ and $MC(z')$ in the diagram. With $z_n = z'$, the optimal output of attribute is k_n'.

What is the *best* level of z_n to choose? If for some choice of z_n such as z' in Figure 12.9, $AC(z')$ were *uniformly lower* than the Average Cost curve

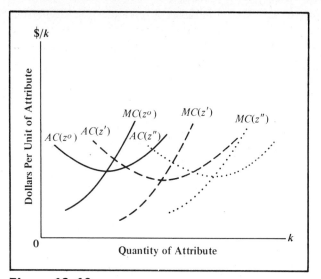

Figure 12. 10
Best Quality Level, Varying with Output

associated with any other quality level z_n, then clearly z' is the profit-maximizing quality level.

In general, however, things may not be quite so simple. It might be the case that, as illustrated in Figure 12.10, some quality levels are better at low production levels ($z_n = z^o$ in the diagram), some at middling output levels ($z_n = z'$), and still others at high production levels ($z_n = z''$). Then the optimal choice of quality level will vary with optimal firm output, which will itself be a function of the market price P^k. At a very high price, for example, the firm will want to produce large amounts of attribute for the market, which can best be done by choosing quality level $z_n = z''$ in the diagram. But at lower prices, a different level of production and consequently a different choice of z_n may be dictated.

Conclusion: The quality level chosen by a firm will be that associated with the lowest Average Cost of producing attribute (at the attribute output supplied by the firm).

When we take into account the possible variation of cost functions as among non-identical firms, we see that there is no presumption that competitive firms will all choose the same quality level. In the case of a mining industry producing ore for sale, for example, some firms will be exploiting richer and others leaner deposits. Each firm will market an ore whose richness (mineral content per ton) represents its quality level z_n. But, assuming informed purchasers, the prices offered for ores of different mineral content will be such as to reflect (after due allowance for any special chemical or physical features affecting extraction cost) a single underlying price P^k for the mineral contained.

Example 12.1
Price and
Quality—Movie
Theaters

R. D. Lamson studied the effect of a number of objective quality attributes upon the prices charged for movie admissions, in a large metropolitan area over the period 1961–64.[4] As suggested by the preceding analysis, there was considerable variation in quality attributes of different theaters.

For 1961, the adult evening admission price P (in cents) was estimated from the data by the equation:

$$P = 4.13 + 31.46 \log_{10} U + 5.77L + 8.21T - 7.68D$$
$$- 1.13F + 27.09S + .81R$$

The symbols used on the right-hand side represent the explanatory (quality) variables:

U: average percentage of unused seating capacity per showing
L: theater location (1 if suburban, 0 if city center)
T: theater age (1 if less than 10 years since construction or major renovation, 0 otherwise)
D: type of theater (1 if outdoor, 0 if indoor)
F: parking (1 if provided, 0 otherwise)
S: screening policy (1 if first-run, 0 otherwise)
R: average film rental (cents per ticket charged by distributor)

The results are generally in the directions anticipated. For example, newer (or renovated) theaters charged on the average 8.21¢ more per admission; first-run houses charged 27.09¢ more; each penny per ticket paid for film rental (a measure of *film* quality or, at least, film popularity) was associated with a 0.81¢ increment to admission price; etc. The one paradoxical component of the equation is parking provision, associated with a 1.13¢ *reduction* in price. This might possibly be due to an inter-correlation of parking availability (a positive quality element) with remote or low-rental location (an unfavorable element) not captured in the crude index L. In any case, the effect is small, and was not found to be statistically significant.

One rather important element is the role of U, unused capacity. This can be regarded as a measure of quality of movie seating—*uncrowdedness*. The equation shows that a 10% increase in unused seating capacity (e.g., from 20% to 22%) is associated with a 1.3¢ increase in admission price. It is of interest to note that since *quality* in the form of U automatically rises when *quantity* of sales fall off in response to a rise in admission price, the true (quality-constant) elasticity of demand for movie admissions must be greater than that implicit in these data.

[4] R. D. Lamson, "Measured Productivity and Price Change: Some Empirical Evidence on Service Industry Bias, Motion Picture Theaters," *Journal of Political Economy*, v. 78 (March/April 1970).

12. D EQUILIBRIUM QUALITY LEVEL— MONOPOLY VERSUS COMPETITION

The question to be considered here is: Will a monopolist producer tend to offer a lower quality level to consumers than would a competitive industry? Since a monopolist produces a lesser *quantity* of product than a competitive industry (see Section 11.B), by analogy one might anticipate a lower *quality* of product as well. But, as it turns out, this superficial analogy is mistaken.

The essential feature at work can be seen in terms of the simplest case of a uniformly best quality level, as illustrated for a competitive firm in Figure 12.9 above. Clearly, if Average Cost is lowest with quality level $z = z'$ for *all* outputs of attribute k, then *that same quality level would be selected by a monopolist as well as by a competitive firm.*

A somewhat more complicated situation is shown by the cost picture of Figure 12.10, where the quality level representing lowest Average Cost of producing attribute k varies at different outputs. Since we would expect the attribute output of a monopolist to be large (in comparison with the output of a *single* firm if the industry in question had a competitive market structure), the monopolist would tend to choose quality levels for which Average Cost is low at high output levels. But there is no reason to presume that a quality level z that is cost-effective at high outputs is necessarily higher or lower than the most economical quality level for small outputs.[5]

[5]Conceivably, at small outputs it might be most economical to use hand labor, and at large outputs machinery. Hand labor may often produce work of higher quality than machinery, but this is by no means a universal phenomenon.

Example 12. 2
Monopoly and Quality: Baseball

H. G. Demmert, in a study of the economics of professional team sports,[6] examined as one topic the determinants of the "quality" choices made by the owners of the various major league baseball clubs. An owner can most obviously upgrade quality by hiring more skilled players, coaches, and so forth. In this case, "output" is produced by two teams meeting in a contest. Hence a natural quality measure is how well a particular team fares in its games relative to other league members.

Using sample of 282 observations on 16 major league baseball teams over the period 1951–1969, two determinants were found to be important. First, teams in more populous areas were, on the average, of higher quality. This seems reasonable, since fans generally prefer winning teams and a greater population base can more afford to "buy" this objective. Specifically, a population difference of 5,000,000 was found to be associated with a difference of .018 in the team's win ratio.

More closely relevant to the discussion of this section, it was found

[6]H. G. Demmert, *The Economics of Professional Team Sports* (Lexington, Mass.: C. D. Heath & Co., 1973), especially p. 71.

that teams facing major league baseball competitors (where more than one team was franchised in a given population area) were of poorer quality than teams with monopoly positions in their area. Specifically, it was found (other things held equal) that the existence of a competitor was associated with a *decrease* of .034 in the win ratio.

At least for this peculiar good, then, a monopolist tended to produce a product of higher quality than a firm facing a competitor or competitors in its market area.

12. E AN APPLICATION: SUPPRESSION OF INVENTIONS

Monopolists are sometimes accused of suppressing inventions. Let us interpret the term "invention" as a discovery permitting production of a higher-quality product at given cost, or a given-quality product at lower cost.[7] Then it can be shown, under the key assumption that buyers are fully informed as to the quality improvement, that suppression is *never* rational!

Take the instance of a monopolist of gasoline, where consumers are interested only in the quality attribute yield (mileage). The monopolist discovers a way, let us say, of doubling the mileage per gallon of his product, without any additional cost of production. We can see immediately that, in terms of a cost function like that in Figure 12.9, the Average Cost of producing mileage will be halved at all output levels if the new invention is adopted. Then, regardless of whether the monopolist decides to produce more output or less, it would surely be absurd for him to suppress such an invention.

The assumption of *full knowledge* on the part of consumers is, however, a strong one. If the invention really improves product quality but the consumers do not believe it, they would not (at least not initially) be willing to pay any more for the higher-mileage gasoline. Under the reasonable assumption that it costs somewhat more per gallon to produce gasoline of doubled mileage yield, the monopolist's incentive to introduce the innovation would be impaired. In this case, however, we should really consider the *cost of informing consumers* as part of the economic cost of the invention. It is not really "suppression" if an invention, even though a genuine improvement of quality, cannot be put on the market except at a cost too great (including the cost of spreading the information) in comparison with the benefit received.

Another possible motivation for suppression emerges in a case where the invention *would destroy the monopoly*. Consider a monopolist of the only currently exploitable aluminum ore—bauxite. Conceivably, this monopolist might come into possession of a cheap process for extracting aluminum from alumina. The latter, one of the most plentiful components of the earth's

---

[7]Obviously, there is no problem in explaining the "suppression" of discoveries that permit production of a *lower*-quality product at the same cost, or a constant-quality product at *higher* cost!

crust, could not effectively be monopolized. Even here, the monopolist can in principle do better using than suppressing the invention. His monopoly *of the information* as to how to reduce alumina is more valuable than his previous monopoly of bauxite. He could patent and license the new process, or alternatively use it while keeping the key steps a secret.[8]

It is of some interest to work through the monopolist's solution for a cost-reducing invention, to see the implications for *output of attribute K* (mileage) versus *output of product Q* (gasoline).

Let us return to the simple assumption that the invention doubles the quality level (mileage per gallon) of the product without any added cost of production. Then the situation may be pictured as in Figure 12.11, a diagram

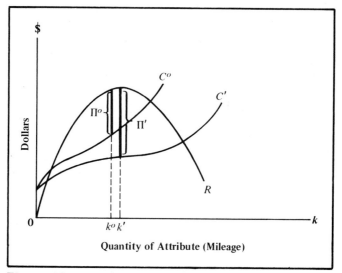

Figure 12. 11
A-Quality Improving (Cost-Reducing) Invention,
Attribute Units

in "Total" units with attribute quantity k (mileage) on the horizontal axis. The original Total Cost curve is C^o. At any given cost of producing the commodity (gasoline), the invention doubles the mileage output k. This shifts the Total Cost curve in mileage units to the position C'—a horizontal doubling (stretching) to the right. The key assumption, that consumers are fully informed, means that the *Total Revenue curve in terms of attribute* k *remains unchanged.* Consumers have no interest in gasoline as such; whether quality is high or low, they can determine and pay for only what concerns them—the mileage content.

In Figure 12.11 the profit-maximizing levels of attribute output are k^o for

[8]In practice, however, there might be difficulties either with patenting or with maintaining secrecy. Thus, a rational motivation for suppression might persist in the case of an invention tending to destroy one's own monopoly.

the pre-invention situation and k' for the post-invention situation. The pre-invention profit Π^o is the bold line-segment indicating the greatest vertical difference between the Total Revenue curve R and the original Total Cost curve C^o. The necessarily larger post-invention profit Π' similarly represents the greatest vertical difference $R - C'$. The diagram illustrates a "normal" case in which output of attribute increases ($k' > k^o$) but by less than a doubling ($k' < 2k^o$). This means that consumers benefit from having more attribute k (mileage), while the firm saves some cost by producing less physical output q (gallons of gasoline).

If the Total Revenue curve were rising almost linearly, however (i.e., if Marginal Revenue MR were almost constant), it might conceivably happen that output of attribute k *more* than doubles. The stretching of the Total Cost curve from C^o to C' may have the effect of lowering Marginal Cost MC in the relevant range. If throughout the doubling interval MC remains lower while MR is nearly unchanged, the profit-maximizing output of attribute k will be more than twice the pre-invention amount.

Paradoxically, it is logically possible for the output of attribute at the post-invention solution to fall ($k' < k^o$). In this case, while the invention will not have been suppressed, the consumers are nevertheless worse off! How this might happen is more clearly visible in the diagram of Figure 12.12, which is constructed in terms of *physical output q* (gallons) on the horizontal axis. In terms of gallons, the Total Cost curve C remains unchanged. It is now the Total Revenue curve that shifts, from R^o to R' (a horizontal halving), since consumers are now willing to pay as much Revenue for half the gallons (i.e., for the same mileage) as before. If the Total Cost curve is shaped like

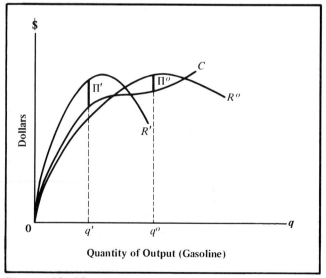

Figure 12. 12

A Quality-Improving Invention Adverse to Consumers, Quantity Units

C in Figure 12.12, with a very steep range in the early portion (high Marginal Cost MC) and then a considerably flatter range (low MC) in the neighborhood of the initial output solution $q°$, it may well be the case that the post-invention physical output has $q' < q°/2$, so that $k' < k°$. Nevertheless, *profit* will still have increased ($\Pi' > \Pi°$).

The upshot, then, is that monopoly cannot validly be accused (granted the assumption of fully informed buyers) of *suppressing* inventions. But it remains open to the accusation of possibly using inventions in such a way that consumers may derive no benefit therefrom, or may even be made worse off.

Questions

1. In Section 12.A, it is argued on the basis of a locational "metaphor" that the aggregate demand for a monopolist's product will be greater, the larger the number of *producing plants*. Translate this metaphor into a statement about the effect on demand of the number of *varieties* offered. How valid is the argument?

2. What stops the monopolist from offering an infinite number of varieties? Under what circumstances will only a single variety be produced?

3. How does monopolistic competition differ from pure competition? From pure monopoly?

4. Is there reason to expect monopolistic competition (rather than pure competition) to emerge when the desired commodity is really a single "quality" attribute contained in the marketed good? Explain.

5. Why is the firm's "illusory" demand curve in monopolistic competition analogous to the horizontal demand curve faced by the firm in pure competition?

6. If a monopolist normally produces less *quantity* of product than a competitive industry would, why is it not correct to presume that the monopolist would normally also offer a product of lower *quality*?

7. Would a monopolist ever suppress an invention reducing the cost of producing its given product? Would it ever suppress an invention raising the quality of product at its given cost? Will consumers in either case be necessarily better off if the invention is adopted?

8. Would imposition of a fixed per-unit tax (e.g., one cent per gallon of gasoline) tend to lead to any change in the equilibrium *quality* of gasoline (miles per gallon) offered on the market? Explain. Would it make any difference if the tax were *ad valorem* (e.g., 5% of the sales price) instead of being a fixed amount per gallon? [*Hint:* Analyze in terms of changes in the Average Cost of providing the underlying attribute with different qualities of product.]

9. It is sometimes argued that only relatively high-quality products can "bear the cost" of shipment to distant locations. Thus, the California oranges shipped to New York are on the average of better quality than those consumed by Californians at home. Does this follow from the analysis in this chapter? [*Hint:* Does it cost much more to ship a high-quality than a low-quality orange?]

Chapter 13
Oligopoly

Oligopoly is competition among the few. But, as explained in Chapter 11, the number of firms in an industry does not conclusively determine how the market functions. While large numbers of firms normally lead to competitive (price-taking) behavior, under certain circumstances the firms may act as a collective monopolist (cartel). Conversely, a single firm in an industry normally behaves as a monopolist (price-maker), but in certain circumstances may be unable to achieve anything but the competitive outcome. In the case of oligopoly, a variety of outcomes are possible *depending upon the degree to which the firms act either as rivals or as cooperators*.

13. A   OLIGOPOLY AND STRATEGIC BEHAVIOR

A "strategic" situation arises when a number of economic agents, with at least partially conflicting interests, are mutually conscious of the interactions of their decisions. In a strategic situation the concept of *optimizing*, choice of a definite "best" outcome, fades into a mist of interacting uncertainties. What is best for one decision-making agent A to do depends significantly upon B's choice, and B in turn must make his decision in the light of the options open to A. Thus, there is conscious conflict of *wills*. Strategic behavior may involve promises, threats, or other communications among the parties apart from price-quantity offers. The time-sequence of moves (i.e., of decisions or communications), the state of information concerning them, and the enforceability of agreements reached may all enter importantly into the outcome. These topics are studied in the *theory of games*, a relatively new field of mathematics stimulated in large part by the economic problem of oligopoly.

In all market situations there are elements of conflict and elements of parallelism or mutuality of interests—among sellers as a group, among buyers as a group, and between buyers and sellers. The sellers always have a common group interest in keeping prices high, but within the group there is a conflict of interest as to which suppliers are to obtain larger fractions of profitable sales. The buyers have a common interest in keeping prices low, but there is a conflict of interest as to which ones will be able to make purchases at a desirably low price. Between sellers as a group and buyers as a group there is of course conflict of interest over the price to be set, but the two still have a strong shared interest in having exchange take place (the mutual advantage of trade).

To some small degree, even in pure competition there will be some interaction among the individual decision-making agents. The decisions of any single buyer or seller contribute to the overall equilibrium involving all other agents in the market. An aggressive buyer or seller might therefore threaten, unless compensated by those who would be adversely affected, to drive price up or down by buying or selling more or less than he otherwise would. But with large numbers of traders any single transactor's leverage on price will be tiny. The costs of communicating threats, negotiating agreements, and enforcing compensation payments are almost certain to exceed the harm that the aggressor could impose on any other single trader. Hence his threat power over others will be essentially zero. Consequently, he will have to treat the decisions of other economic agents as effectively beyond his influence. The choices of others simply become part of his given environment, communicated to him in the ruling market price that integrates the decisions of all transactors. In turn, of course, his own decisions enter into this integration so as to become part of the given environment faced by all other competitive buyers and sellers. So while there is interaction in pure competition, there is no *strategic* situation because no party has effective threat power to harm others. The best any agent can do is to adapt optimally to the price as part of his environment.

In a monopolistic market structure there are numerous buyers, none of whom can have effective threat power so as to affect the choices of other buyers or of the monopolist seller. The seller, on the other hand, can influence the choices of buyers. In simple monopoly he quotes a profit-maximizing price subject to which the purchasers choose their optimal quantities. In discriminating monopoly the seller's range of influence is greater, so that he can quote a more or less complex schedule or pattern of prices to buyers. But there is still no *strategic* situation because the interaction is not a reciprocal one. The buyers, being tiny individually, have no leverage on the seller. Since no single buyer has any threat power, the monopolist seller can consider the decisions of buyers as part of his given environment, communicated to him in the form of their demand function in the market. The monopolist's decision thus takes the form of optimizing adaptation rather than strategic interaction.[1]

In oligopoly we continue to assume that there are a large number of buyers, none of whom has any effective leverage on price or threat power. But here the small number of suppliers do have threat power *upon one another*.

---

[1] An interesting market structure, not studied here, has small numbers on *both* sides of the market. The limiting case is called "bilateral monopoly": a single seller facing a single buyer. This is also a strategic situation.

A number of simplifications will be adopted for the following discussion: (1) There are exactly *two* selling firms, so that oligopoly becomes the special case called "duopoly"; (2) the firms are identical, except possibly in degree of strategic skill or aggressiveness; (3) production is carried on at zero cost (i.e., the Total Cost, Average Cost, and Marginal Cost functions are all zero throughout).

The analysis differs depending upon whether the product is considered *homogeneous* or *heterogeneous*. In the homogeneous case the duopolists produce exactly the same product; hence, even a slightly lower price on the part of one can deprive the other of *all* of his sales. Consequently, no price differential between the two firms can exist in homogeneous oligopoly equilibrium. In the heterogeneous case the products differ to some degree, with the result that a firm raising its price will still generally retain *some* of its customers. Hence, in heterogeneous oligopoly a price differential may persist.

13. B HOMOGENEOUS PRODUCTS

A pure competitor is always a price-taker; his choice variable is *quantity* of output. A monopolist is usually regarded as deciding upon *price*, letting quantity be determined in the market. Sometimes, however, it is convenient to think of the monopolist as choosing quantity and letting the market process determine the price at which that quantity can be sold. Since the result is the same point on the industry demand curve in either case, it makes no difference whether we think of a monopolist as choosing the most profitable price or the most profitable quantity. But in the oligopoly case, whether price or quantity is the decision variable turns out to be important for the *interaction* of the parties. Consequently, the final result may be affected.

Let us first take *quantity* as the decision variable. Table 13.1 categorizes a number of different oligopoly (duopoly) "solutions."[2] The Table was constructed on the hypothesis that the overall *industry* demand curve is expressed by the equation $P = 100 - Q$, where the industry output Q is the sum of the two firm outputs: $Q = q_1 + q_2$. (Zero production cost is assumed.)

Table 13. 1
Duopoly Solutions, with $P = 100 - (q_1 + q_2)$

	q_1	q_2	Q	P	Π_1	Π_2
Symmetrical						
Collusive	25	25	50	50	1250	1250
Cournot	$33\frac{1}{3}$	$33\frac{1}{3}$	$66\frac{2}{3}$	$33\frac{1}{3}$	$1111\frac{1}{9}$	$1111\frac{1}{9}$
Competitive	50	50	100	0	0	0
Asymmetrical						
Pre-emptive	50	25	75	25	1250	625
Threat	50	0	50	50	2500	0

[2]A somewhat similar table appears in M. Shubik, "Information, Duopoly and Competitive Markets: A Sensitivity Analysis," *Kyklos*, v. 26 (1973), p. 748.

The first solution shown in the Table is the Collusive outcome. Here the two firms act as a collective monopolist or cartel, sharing the gain equally. The formal conditions are that Marginal Revenue for the industry, MR (a function of $Q = q_1 + q_2$), must equal the Marginal Cost for each firm: $MR = MC_1 = MC_2$. In the Table, the optimal Collusive output is $Q = 50$, leading to the price $P = 50$. This may be easily verified by using the Proposition (obtained in Section 11.B.2) describing Marginal Revenue when the demand curve is *linear*: If $P = A - BQ$, $MR = A - 2BQ$. In this case the industry demand equation has the linear form $P = 100 - Q$, so that industry Marginal Revenue is $MR = 100 - 2Q$. Since Marginal Cost MC is zero throughout, the monopoly-optimum condition $MR = MC$ becomes $100 - 2Q = 0$, so that $Q = 50$ is the profit-maximizing industry output. Total Revenue R is 2500, equal to combined profit Π (in the absence of any costs). With equal division, the firm profits are $\Pi_1 = \Pi_2 = 1250$.

Skipping to the third outcome in the Table, this is also familiar. It is what would be obtained with *competitive* (price-taking) behavior, as might ensue from utterly shameless "chiselling" on a cartel agreement (see Section 11.F). Suppose each firm produced so as to meet the competitive condition $MC = P$. Then, since costs are everywhere zero, firms would produce indefinitely large amounts whenever price P exceeded zero. The consequence, of course, is that the competitive equilibrium price can only be $P = 0$. Combined output is then 100, as dictated by the demand equation, but revenue and profits are zero. (This self-defeating outcome is known in game theory as the "Prisoner's Dilemma.")

Intermediate between these is the "Cournot solution,"[3] based upon the following considerations. For any output level q_1 that may be chosen (for whatever reason) by the first firm, there will be some unique optimal output choice q_2 for the second firm. In effect, firm 2 becomes a monopolist over the demand not satisfied by the first firm's output q_1 already on the market. Specifically, the demand equation for firm 2 becomes $P = (100 - q_1) - q_2$ with q_1 regarded as constant. This is still a linear demand equation, so for firm 2 the Marginal Revenue is $MR_1 = (100 - q_1) - 2q_2$. For example, if $q_1 = 10$ the condition $MR = MC$ for firm 2 leads to the equation $90 - 2q_2 = 0$, so that firm 2's output would be $q_2 = 45$. Plotting the q_2 chosen by firm 2 as a function of the given output of firm 1 leads to a "Reaction Curve" RC_2 like that shown in Figure 13.1. Since the firms are symmetrically situated, by a corresponding process a Reaction Curve RC_1 can be developed for firm 1. The curves are *mutually consistent only at the point of intersection*, which is therefore declared to be the equilibrium. At the solution point the outputs are $q_1 = q_2 = 33\frac{1}{3}$, intermediate between the Collusive and the Competitive solutions.[4] Thus the Cournot solution may be regarded as representing a kind of imperfect collusion technique.

[3] Antoine Augustin Cournot (1801–77), French mathematician and economist.
[4] To verify that $33\frac{1}{3}$ is indeed the equilibrium, we can proceed as follows: If firm 1 sets $q_1 = 33\frac{1}{3}$, the demand equation for firm 2 is $P = 66\frac{2}{3} - q_2$. The associated Marginal Revenue is $MR_2 = 66\frac{2}{3} - 2q_2$. Setting $MR = MC = 0$, we obtain $q_2 = 33\frac{1}{3}$. Reversing the process, we see that under the assumed reaction conditions both firms are satisfied to set output at $33\frac{1}{3}$.

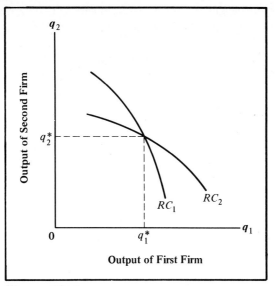

Figure 13. 1
Duopoly Reaction Curves

By postulating different types of reaction functions, a range of alternative solutions can be arrived at as a generalization of the basic Cournot solution for oligopoly. We will not pursue the numerous possibilities thus opened up.

The *asymmetrical* outcomes, in the lower portion of the Table, show certain new solution concepts that emerge with differences in aggressiveness. (The Table pictures a situation where the first firm is the more aggressive.) The *Pre-emptive* solution occurs when firm 1 picks an output level and proclaims that it will not modify that decision regardless of the other firm's behavior. If the proclamation is believed, the best that the second firm can do is to behave as a Cournot reactor. The first firm can then optimize by setting $q_1 = 50$, in which case it achieves as much profit for itself as under the symmetrical Collusive solution. Firm 2 then monopolizes the remainder of the market, setting $q_2 = 25$, and reaping half the profit of the other firm.[5]

The *Threat* solution is a still stronger asymmetrical outcome. Here firm 1 proclaims that if the other firm enters the market at all, it (the first firm) will produce enough to drive price P down to zero! If this proclamation is believed, the second firm will see no way to make a profit in the market. Hence it might as well stay out. (A very small side-payment from the first

[5]This solution may be verified as follows. Firm 1, the aggressor, knows that firm 2 will behave as a Cournot reactor, i.e., that firm 2 will choose output q_2 to satisfy the equation $MR_2 = (100 - q_1) - 2q_2 = 0$. So $q_2 = (100 - q_1)/2$, and this is known to firm 1. Substituting in the industry demand curve:

$$P = 100 - Q = 100 - q_2 - q_1 = 100 - \frac{100 - q_1}{2} - q_1 = 50 - \frac{q_1}{2}$$

This becomes the overall demand curve facing firm 1, and is again linear. Then $MR_1 = 50 - q_1$, and $MR_1 = MC_1 = 0$ leads to $q_1 = 50$. For firm 2, the condition $MR_2 = MC_2 = 0$ becomes $MR_2 = 50 - 2q_2 = 0$, so that $q_2 = 25$. The total industry output is $Q = 50 + 25 = 75$, and market price is $P = 25$.

firm may be postulated to provide a positive inducement for the second to stay out.) In the Threat solution, the first firm does as well as if it itself had the *sole* monopoly of the industry.

What would happen if *both* firms attempted to act as aggressors? Each would make his threat, only to be defied by the other. Actual execution of the threats would then force the situation into the symmetrical Competitive outcome of the upper part of the Table.

Now suppose that *price* rather than output is the decision variable of the firms. The key point here is that, given homogeneity of product, the firm quoting a lower price will (however small the differential) attract *all* the customers. Then the Cournot solution becomes impossible, or, rather, it coalesces with the Competitive solution. Whatever the *price* chosen by firm 1, firm 2 will optimally react by setting a price just infinitesimally lower. There is then no stable outcome short of $P = 0$, the Competitive solution. The asymmetrical Pre-emptive solution also disappears. If firm 1 sets a price of 25, intending to produce an output of 50 while leaving the remaining output of 25 for firm 2, the latter is not effectively pre-empted. By shading price just below 25, firm 2 can obtain all 75 sales rather than only the 25. The other solutions remain as in the Table.

Example 13.1
Predatory
Price-Cutting

The Threat solution of Table 13.1, but with price rather than output as the decision variable, corresponds to what is known as "predatory" price-cutting. A single firm sufficiently well-equipped with resources and ruthlessness might always stand ready to undertake a "price war" to drive out any competitors. Having achieved this reputation, the predator firm need not often have to execute its threat. Occasional punishment meted out to foolish interlopers would suffice to deter all others from entering.

The leading instance one finds cited of a predatory price-cutter firm is John D. Rockefeller's old Standard Oil Company—dissolved in 1911 as a result of a landmark anit-trust decision. Standard Oil had achieved, before this date, a substantial degree of monopoly in oil refining through merger and acquisitions. Common opinion, as illustrated in historical writing about the period, is that these mergers and acquisitions were mainly secured under threat of predatory price-cutting.

A study by John S. McGee demonstrated, however, that the tale is a myth.[6] Standard Oil rarely if ever started costly price wars to achieve its monopoly. Rather, its practice was to buy out competitors on relatively handsome terms, made possible by the prospect of higher monopoly profits achievable by the withdrawal of competition.

[6]J. S. McGee, "Predatory Price Cutting: The Standard Oil (N.J.) Case," *Journal of Law and Economics*, v. 1 (Oct. 1958).

13. C   HETEROGENEOUS PRODUCTS

For oligopolists producing a *homogeneous* product, we have just seen, there are multiple solution concepts depending upon the degree and effectiveness of rivalry among the sellers. These different solutions are all constrained by the condition that the firms' identical products sell in the market at the same price. With *heterogeneous* products, the same forces are still operative: The inducement to cooperate so as to achieve a joint monopoly benefit at the expense of buyers, versus the temptation to benefit at the expense of other sellers by aggressive or rivalrous behavior. But here the fact that the products are not identical (though still similar enough to generate the interaction necessary for a strategic situation to obtain) rules out any necessary identity of prices. One further consequence of eliminating the requirement of identical prices is that the solutions achieved do not depend in any essential way upon whether price or quantity is the decision variable of the interacting firms.

*13. C. 1   Comparison of Solutions

In the discussion following, a number of the different duopoly solution concepts will be described in such a way as to bring out the analogies and differences of the homogeneous and heterogeneous cases. Only the *symmetrical* outcomes will be considered here.

1.   Collusive (monopoly) solution:[7]

HOMOGENEOUS PRODUCT

$$MC_1(q_1) = MC_2(q_2) = MR(q_1 + q_2)$$

HETEROGENEOUS PRODUCTS

$$\begin{cases} MC_1(q_1) = MR_1(q_1, q_2) \equiv \dfrac{\Delta R_1}{\Delta q_1} + \dfrac{\Delta R_2}{\Delta q_1} \\[2mm] MC_2(q_2) = MR_2(q_1, q_2) \equiv \dfrac{\Delta R_1}{\Delta q_2} + \dfrac{\Delta R_2}{\Delta q_2} \end{cases}$$

Here the parentheses indicate the arguments of the respective Marginal Revenue or Marginal Cost functions. In the homogeneous case, the ideal

---

*Starred sections represent optional or advanced material.

[7]*Mathematical Footnote:* In the homogeneous case, the Collusive solution maximizes $\Pi = \Pi_1 + \Pi_2 = PQ - C_1 - C_2$. The first-order conditions are:

$$\frac{\partial \Pi}{\partial q_1} = P + Q\frac{\partial P}{\partial q_1} - \frac{dC_1}{dq_1} = 0$$

$$\frac{\partial \Pi}{\partial q_2} = P + Q\frac{\partial P}{\partial q_2} - \frac{dC_2}{dq_2} = 0$$

But $\partial P/\partial q_1 \equiv \partial P/\partial q_2$, so $P' + Q(\partial P/\partial q_1) = P + Q(\partial P/\partial q_2) \equiv MR$. So the conditions reduce to $MC_1 = MC_2 = MR$ as stated in the text.

In the heterogeneous case, the problem is to maximize $\Pi = P_1 q_1 + P_2 q_2 - C_1 - C_2$. The first-order conditions are:

$$\frac{\partial \Pi}{\partial q_1} = P_1 + q_1 \frac{\partial P_1}{\partial q_1} + q_2 \frac{\partial P_2}{\partial q_1} - \frac{dC_1}{dq_1} = 0$$

$$\frac{\partial \Pi}{\partial q_2} = P_2 + q_1 \frac{\partial P_1}{\partial q_2} + q_2 \frac{\partial P_2}{\partial q_2} - \frac{dC_2}{dq_2} = 0$$

These are the conditions stated, in somewhat different notation, in the text.

Collusive outcome is achieved where the Marginal Cost of each firm equals the industry Marginal Revenue, the latter being a function of the industry total output $Q = q_1 + q_2$. In the heterogeneous case, the profit-maximizing Collusive decision would set the Marginal Cost equal to the Marginal Revenue for each product separately, but *with* recognition of the demand interaction whereby MR_1 and MR_2 are each functions of both of the outputs q_1 and q_2. Specifically, $MR_1(q_1, q_2)$ is the sum of two elements: $\Delta R_1/\Delta q_1 \equiv \Delta P_1 q_1/\Delta q_1$ is the marginal addition to revenue from sales of product 1, while $\Delta R_2/\Delta q_1 \equiv \Delta P_2 q_2/\Delta q_1$ is the marginal cross-effect of increased output q_1 upon Revenue from product 2. (Since q_1 and q_2 are highly similar products of firms in the "same" industry, the cross-effect is certainly *negative*. That is, the two outputs are close substitutes.) A corresponding argument holds, of course, for the effect of output q_2 upon price P_1.

2. Competitive solution:[8]

HOMOGENEOUS PRODUCT   HETEROGENEOUS PRODUCTS

$$\begin{cases} MC_1(q_1) = MR_1(q_1 + \hat{q}_2) \\ MC_2(q_2) = MR_2(\hat{q}_1 + q_2) \end{cases} \qquad \begin{cases} MC_1(q_1) = MR_1(q_1, \hat{q}_2) \equiv \dfrac{\Delta R_1}{\Delta q_1} \\ MC_2(q_2) = MR_2(\hat{q}_1, q_2) \equiv \dfrac{\Delta R_2}{\Delta q_2} \end{cases}$$

In the homogeneous case, each firm sets its own Marginal Cost equal to its own Marginal Revenue, the latter calculated as a function of the industry demand on the (erroneous) supposition of a fixed output of the *other* firm (indicated by the superposed caret as in $\hat{q}_1$ and $\hat{q}_2$). In the heterogeneous case the same type of interaction exists, except that Marginal Revenue for either firm is a function of the two outputs as separate arguments and not simply of their *sum*.

3. Competitive solution:

HOMOGENEOUS PRODUCT   HETEROGENEOUS PRODUCTS

$$\begin{cases} MC(q_1) = P(q_1 + \bar{q}_2) \\ MC(q_2) = P(\bar{q}_1 + q_2) \end{cases} \qquad \begin{cases} MC(q_1) = P_1(q_1, \bar{q}_2) \\ MC(q_2) = P_2(\bar{q}_1, q_2) \end{cases}$$

[8] *Mathematical Footnote:* In contrast with the Collusive solution, here the firms maximize separately *without* attention to any interaction. In the homogeneous case, this leads to the conditions:

$$\frac{d\Pi_1}{dq_1} = P + q_1 \frac{\partial P}{\partial q_1} - \frac{dC_1}{dq_1} = 0$$

$$\frac{d\Pi_2}{dq_2} = P + q_2 \frac{\partial P}{\partial q_2} - \frac{dC_2}{dq_2} = 0$$

And in the heterogeneous case, the conditions are:

$$\frac{d\Pi_1}{dq_1} = P_1 + q_1 \frac{\partial P_1}{\partial q_1} - \frac{dC_1}{dq_1} = 0$$

$$\frac{d\Pi_2}{dq_2} = P_2 + q_2 \frac{\partial P_2}{\partial q_2} - \frac{dC_2}{dq_2} = 0$$

This corresponds to the conditions stated in the text.

The Competitive solution is like the Cournot solution, in that the other firm's output is (erroneously) supposed fixed (indicated by the superposed bar as in $\bar{q}_1$ and $\bar{q}_2$). The difference, of course, lies in the price-taking behavior: In the Competitive solution, each firm sets Marginal Cost MC_1 or MC_2 equal to price P along the demand curve, rather than equal to Marginal Revenue MR_1 or MR_2, respectively. The heterogeneous case again differs only in that price along the demand curve for either product is not a function simply of the *sum* of the two outputs, but of the two quantities as separate arguments.

13. C. 2   The Kinked Demand Curve

The demand curve for any single oligopolist, it has been alleged, has a "kink" at the point of equilibrium (price $P_1 = P^*$ in Figure 13.2).[9] The argument goes as follows. Suppose one oligopolist, firm 1, attempts to sell more by cutting its price P_1. Then all other firms will respond by *meeting* the price cut, so that firm 1 will reap only a relatively small increase in sales. In other words, in the region below the initial equilibrium price P^* the demand curve D_1 as seen by firm 1 will be steep. What if firm 1 attempted to raise price? Then, assertedly, competing oligopolists would *not* meet the price increase, so that firm 1 suffers a relatively large decline in sales. In other words, in the region above the initial equilibrium price P^* the demand curve as seen by

[9]The hypothesis was advanced almost simultaneously in two independent articles: R. L. Hall and C. J. Hitch, "Price Theory and Business Behavior," *Oxford Economic Papers*, v. 2 (May 1939) and P. M. Sweezy, "Demand under Conditions of Oligopoly," *Journal of Political Economy*, v. 47 (Aug. 1939).

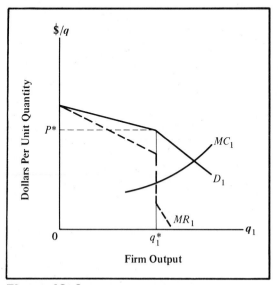

Figure 13. 2
Kinked Oligopoly Demand Curve

firm 1 is relatively flat. Note that this argument makes sense only in the heterogeneous case, since only then can a price difference exist at all.[10]

This hypothesis is not a complete theory. It says nothing about how the original ruling price P^* was arrived at. But there is nevertheless an interesting implication: *That the equilibrium prices arrived at by oligopolistic sellers should be relatively stable over time.*

This hypothesis is based upon the relation between the *marginal* curves in Figure 13.2. Note that the kink in the demand or Average Revenue curve D_1 for firm 1 becomes a *vertical displacement* in the Marginal Revenue curve MR_1. It is simple to verify this geometrically in the special case where the two branches of the demand curve are linear. We know (from the "Corollary" in Section 11.B.2) that for any linear demand curve the Marginal Revenue curve must bisect the horizontal distance to the vertical axis. With two separate linear branches of the demand curve, there must then be a vertical break or jump in the MR_1 curve as shown.

For the price-quantity situation (P^*, q_1^*) to be an equilibrium, it must be the case that Marginal Cost equals Marginal Revenue for firm 1 at q_1^*. Of course, a similar condition must hold for the other oligopolists. Then, as illustrated for firm 1 in the diagram, the MC_1 curve must *cut through* the vertical jump of MR_1. The tendency toward price stability stems from this feature. Suppose some disturbance brought about a moderate change in the cost function of oligopolist 1. Its MC_1 curve would accordingly move up or down. But this could occur, to some extent, *without* affecting the fact that the intersection of MC_1 with MR_1 occurs in the vertical break of the latter, in which case optimal price and output remain unchanged for this firm. Even if the disturbance affected other firms as well, their behavior also might not be affected, leaving the equilibrium unchanged. Alternatively, suppose that a force operated to increase or decrease *demand* for firm 1's output. But so long as other firms continued to respond to firm 1's price changes in the way specified (meeting and following price decreases, but not following price increases), a demand-curve kink would remain at the initial price $P_1 = P^*$. The entire D_1 curve could shift, to the right or the left, but retaining the kink at the same height P^*. The vertical break of the MR_1 curve would then move correspondingly to the right or left, in association with the kink-point of the D_1 curve. Again, it will be evident geometrically that moderate shifts of MR_1 to the right or left are likely to preserve the property that the Marginal Cost curve MC_1 cuts through the vertical jump of MR_1. Where this holds, price $P_1 = P^*$ quoted by firm 1 will remain unchanged, but output q_1^* will increase or decrease in accordance with the direction of shift of the Marginal Revenue function.

The competing oligopolists' behavior, on this hypothesis, is *strongly rivalrous.* We would expect under rivalrous behavior a tendency to approach the Competitive solution of Table 13.1 (following the rule $MC = P$) rather than the

---

[10]Or putting it another way, in the homogeneous case the upper leg of the kinked demand curve would be effectively horizontal—firm 1 would lose *all* its sales if the other oligopolists failed to follow its price increase.

Collusive solution ($MC = MR$) postulated for the initial equilibrium under the kinked-demand hypothesis. However, the hypothesis is not internally inconsistent. It could be imagined that the firms agree on a collusive initial solution, which is then *enforced* by strongly rivalrous behavior as against any single firm that departs from the agreement.

Example 13. 2
Oligopoly and
Price Rigidity

Under the hypothesis of the kinked oligopolist-firm demand curve, demand and cost conditions can vary (to some extent) without affecting the equilibrium prices charged by firms. For a simple monopolist, on the other hand, any shift of the Marginal Cost or the Marginal Revenue curves should lead to a new optimizing price. Consequently, an implication of the kinked-demand hypothesis is that oligopoly prices should be relatively rigid.

This implication was tested by G. J. Stigler. The data in the following Table are typical of his findings. As can be seen, there is a strong indication that oligopoly prices are *less* rigid than monopoly prices. This is certainly true in terms of the *number* of monthly price changes, and tends to be confirmed by the *quantitative* measure of price change represented by the "coefficient of variation" (the standard deviation of monthly prices divided by the mean).

Price Flexibility (June 1929–May 1937)

	No. of Firms in Industry	No. of Monthly Price Changes	Coefficient of Variation of Prices
Oligopolies			
Bananas	2	46	16
Grain-Binder	2	5	3
Plows	6	25	6
Tires	8	36	9
Monopolies			
Aluminum	1	2	6
Nickel	1	0	0

Source: G. J. Stigler, "The Kinky Oligopoly Demand Curve and Rigid Prices," *Journal of Political Economy*, v. 55 (1947), p. 443.

One possible objection to Stigler's test is that *inter-industry comparisons* of price changes cannot be made with very much confidence. Customs and conditions of conducting business vary from one industry to another, and it may have just so happened that the "monopolized" sectors in the Table would have had relatively rigid prices regardless of number of firms. Another objection is that what is statistically reported as a *single* industry is often mere convention. Had aluminum and nickel been placed together in a single "non-ferrous metals" category, they would have been classed as an oligopoly rather than as two separate monopolies.

A study by Julian L. Simon[11] employed data that were less vulnerable to these objections. He studied prices quoted for business-magazine advertising, where the magazines had been classified into groups by the Standard Rate and Data Service (SRDS). Since all the groups fell into the business-magazine category, there was relative uniformity in conditions and methods of price quotation. And since the group classification by SRDS was undertaken for the convenience of customers (advertisers), it presumably represented an economically meaningful rather than merely conventional categorization.

The numbers of magazines in the 148 groupings on which data were provided varied from 1 to 29. A magazine without competitors in its grouping could then be considered a monopolist. The data for two different periods, 1955–61 and 1961–64, both suggested that the monopoly groups had *more* rigid prices than the oligopoly groups. Simon's test thus confirmed Stigler's previous negative conclusion as to the kinked-demand hypothesis. (However, the *quantitative* differences found by Simon were by no means as great as those reported by Stigler.)

Comment: One possible explanation of the observations, consistent with assigning at least some degree of validity to the kinked-demand hypothesis for oligopoly, runs in terms of *non-profit goals* of the firm. We saw in Example 11.1 ("Jews and Monopoly") that monopoly firms, sheltered from competition, are in a relatively better position to pursue goals other than economic profit. It might well be that an important non-profit goal for monopoly firms is "the easy life," avoidance of difficult decisions. Changing price, rather than just leaving things as they are, is such a difficult decision. Not only is sheer mental effort required, but "rocking the boat" is more liable to elicit complaint or political scrutiny than simple inaction. We might then expect monopoly and oligopoly prices *both* to be rigid, for different reasons: for oligopolists the kinked-demand hypothesis might be valid, while for monopolists the "easy life" goal might lead to even greater rigidity of prices.

[11]J. L. Simon, "A Further Test of the Kinky Oligopoly Demand Curve," *American Economic Review*, v. 59 (Dec. 1969).

13. C. 3 Variation of Product

In heterogeneous oligopoly, there is another dimension of behavior for the firm to consider: the specification of the product itself. One oligopolist can compete with others not only by raising or lowering price, but by varying the commodity placed on the market.

Product variation was studied in the preceding chapter in the contexts of a number of market structures: monopoly, pure competition, and monopolistic competition. Two main types of product variation were considered: (1) product *assortment* (i.e., the degree to which the range of products offered in the market coincides with the range of subjective consumer preferences), and (2) product *quality* (i.e., the degree to which an objective quality attribute, desired by all consumers, is contained in the market commodity).

We shall not attempt to develop a general theory of oligopoly product variation here. There is one model of oligopolistic product assortment due to Hotelling,[12] however, that has received considerable attention. This model employs a *linear* locational metaphor like that of Figure 12.1 to represent the range of consumer preferences. Specifically, in Figure 13.3 the consumers are supposed to be *uniformly* distributed[13] along a line-segment

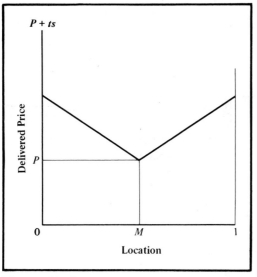

Figure 13. 3
Delivered Price

scaled from 0 to 1, with mid-point $M = \frac{1}{2}$. There is a constant unit transport cost t from the producing location to the consumer. If P is the F.O.B. price for a producing location at M, the diagram shows the delivered price $P + ts$ to consumers as a function of distance s from M.

Assume that there are just two firms (duopoly), with identical costs of producing and delivering the commodity. Under the special assumption of absolutely inelastic consumer demands (!), the model arrives at the conclusion that the duopolists would locate infinitesimally apart at either side of M. In that way, each is closer to half of the market which serves as its "clientele." Thus, the locational metaphor says that the two firms will supply nearly identical products of middling character. First, as neither firm would

---

[12]H. Hotelling, "Stability in Competition," *Economic Journal*, v. 39 (March 1929).
[13]In contrast, Figure 12.1 showed a *bell-shaped* distribution in which middling consumer locations (i.e., preferences) were more common than extreme ones.

permit the other to be closer to more than half the consumers, symmetrical placement on either side of M is dictated. And second, if located anywhere away from M, either firm gains clientele by moving toward the center.[14]

The two-firm outcome under the Hotelling model is *inefficient*. Average distance between the consumer and the nearest producing point is $\frac{1}{4}$, whereas location of the two firms at the quartile points would reduce average distance to $\frac{1}{8}$. That is, it would be possible without additional cost for the industry to meet the range of consumer preferences more closely. In terms of Table 13.1, the Hotelling result is analogous to a Cournot solution; each firm reacts (with respect to location as decision variable) on the presumption that the other firm's decision will remain fixed.

The assumption of absolutely inelastic demand is of course highly unreasonable. Indeed, if this were the case the duopolists' Collusive solution (raise price indefinitely high) would yield infinite revenue and profit regardless of location! Incorporating more reasonable demand assumptions would tend to pull the duopolists away from locations at the mid-point M. If transport charges cannot be passed on to consumers without some loss of sales, the firms will be motivated to locate in such a way as to economize to some degree on these costs.

Another oddity of the Hotelling model is that the whole argument collapses when numbers increase beyond two. A third oligopolist would want to locate an infinitesimal distance on one or the other side of the initial duo. But then one of the firms would be boxed in between two others, leaving it without clientele. This firm would then surely "jump" to the outside, to be followed by the one now left in the middle, and so on in an unending musical-chairs situation. So with more than two firms there cannot be a Cournot-Hotelling *equilibrium*. It is evident that there will be great pressures upon the firms to arrive at some kind of Collusive solution.

13. D OLIGOPOLY AND COLLUSION

The intricacies of strategic models of oligopoly are intellectually challenging, but the results seem unsatisfyingly inconclusive. Another approach[15] has been to assume away all strategic games, and simply treat oligopoly situations as *imperfect collusive arrangements* (i.e., imperfect cartels as described in Section 11.F). Since there is a joint advantage of collusion, all firms under this approach agree upon that aim. However, they all also recognize that each cannot be restrained from "chiselling" (see Figure 11.11) except through a policing mechanism. That is, the assumption is that anyone who can cheat, will. Given that there are costs of trickery on the one hand, and of detection on the other hand, there will be some equilibrium amount of slippage from

---

[14]This model has seemed to many observers to be useful in explaining a seeming tendency of competing political programs in a two-party system to converge toward a centrist position.

[15]Proposed in G. Stigler, "A Theory of Oligopoly," *Journal of Political Economy*, v. 72 (Feb. 1964).

the Collusive solution that represents the ideal for the sellers (though not, of course, for consumers). Thus the parties involved will agree upon forming a cartel with some kind of policing scheme, in the anticipation that it will be tolerably though imperfectly effective.

While models of imperfect oligopolistic collusion are not yet reduced to textbook form, it is possible to derive a number of qualitative implications for real-world behavior. First and most obviously, the fewer the firms involved, the easier it is for them to police one another. And, hence, the more effective the cartel. Second and almost equally obvious, secret price cuts are more likely to be offered to large than to small buyers. To increase business 10% by a chiselling deal with a single customer is one thing; to try to get the same increase of business from ten small customers is stretching secrecy too far. Third, enforcement of collusion should be much easier where the product is homogeneous. Otherwise, price cuts can take the hard-to-penetrate guise of better quality. (Even where the physical commodity is homogeneous, there may be an element of heterogeneity in aspects of the transaction such as credit terms, delivery date, etc.) Fourth, the more unstable the conditions of the industry, the harder it will be to negotiate and enforce agreement on industry adaptation to ever-changing circumstances of supply and demand.

Questions

1. What is strategic behavior? Why are suppliers more likely to engage in strategic behavior when there are only a few of them in the market? What if there is only one supplier (monopoly)?

2. Explain the Cournot solution to the duopoly problem.

3. Under the assumptions of the Cournot model, each duopolist *incorrectly* imagines that the other's output is a fixed constant. Over time, however, each would surely learn that the assumption about the other's behavior is incorrect. What would then be likely to happen?

4. In recent anti-trust cases, the courts appear to believe that small numbers almost inevitably imply cartel-like collusion. Is this inference justified?

5. Some economists have argued that "predatory price cutting" to enforce the Threat solution will almost never be observed. The reason given is that the symmetrical Collusive solution is typically better for both parties. Is this necessarily correct? Is it ever correct? Under what circumstances will predatory price cutting be likely to emerge, if ever?

6. How would the possibility of *entry of new firms* tend to affect the decisions of the oligopolists presently in an industry?

7. Why does a "kinked" demand curve tend to lead to rigid prices? How might a kinked demand curve for any single oligopolist result from the behavior of others designed to enforce a collusive agreement?

Factor Markets, Distribution, and Intertemporal Analysis

Chapter 14
Production and
the Demand for Factors

In the circular flow of economic activity (see Figure 1.1), consumers represent the demand side and firms represent the supply side of the *product market* (the upper portion of the diagram). Previous chapters studied the firms' decisions to supply consumption goods and services in response to consumers' demands. The circular-flow diagram accordingly shows a physical flow of products from firms to consumers, balanced by a financial flow of payments moving in the opposite direction. Now we turn to the *factor market*, the lower portion of the circular-flow diagram. The productive process, taking place *within* the firms, generates products from resources (factors of production). In this chapter we will see how the physical productivity of factors, combined with the valuations that consumers place upon the goods so produced, lead to *factor demand functions* on the part of firm and industry. This gives us a picture of the demand side of the factor market. In the chapter following, we look at the supply side of the factor market—the decisions of resource-owners (who are, ultimately, the consumers themselves) as to the terms on which they offer productive services for use by firms in generating products. The circular flow is thus completed by a physical movement of productive resources from resource-owners to firms, balanced by a financial flow of payments. And, finally, these factor payments become *income* with which consumers can buy products so as to renew the cycle.

In studying the equilibrium of the factor market, *market structure* (degree of competition) continues to play an important role. Indeed, we must take account of market structure not only in the factor market itself but also in the associated product market or markets. A company may be a monopolist of a product like aluminum, and still be only one among many employers (and therefore be a competitive or price-taking buyer) of a productive service like secretarial help in a large city. Conversely, a textile firm may face a highly competitive world market for its product and still be a *monopsonist* [1] employer of labor in a small town.

[1] A monopolist is a sole *seller* in a market; a monopsonist is a sole *buyer*.

The analysis in this chapter proceeds in the following sequence. In Sections 14.A, 14.B, and 14.C the factor market itself is assumed perfectly competitive: both buyers (firms) and sellers (resource-owners) are price-takers. Nevertheless, some or all of the employing firms may have monopoly power in their respective industries (product markets).[2] Section 14.D takes up *monopsony* in the factor market, with or without associated monopoly power in the product market. And note that there is also the possibility of monopoly on the *supply side of the factor market* (i.e., resource-owners with monopoly power). This topic is deferred to the discussion of factor supply in the chapter following.

14. A FIRM'S DEMAND FOR A SINGLE VARIABLE FACTOR

14. A. 1 The Production Function

In full generality, the *production function* of a firm might be written abstractly as:

(14.1)
$$\Phi(x, y, z, \ldots ; a, b, c, \ldots) = 0$$

This says only that there is a technological relationship between the firm's output possibilities $x, y, z, \ldots$ (representing quantities of different possible products $X, Y, Z, \ldots$) that might be produced with alternative combinations of inputs $a, b, c, \ldots$ (representing quantities of different factors $A, B, C, \ldots$). We will be using here simplified versions of firm production functions, with a *single* output commodity X. So the general problem reduces to the analysis of production functions having the form:

(14.2)
$$\Phi(x; a, b, c, \ldots) = 0$$

Such a function can be rewritten to show output as an explicit function of factor quantities:

(14.2')
$$x = \Psi(a, b, c, \ldots)$$

To start with the simplest case, we will assume (in this section only) that the quantities of all factors but one used by the firm are *fixed*. (Thus, this will be a model of an output decision in the "short run" as discussed in Section 9.E.) So we will be dealing with relations between output quantity x of a single product X and input quantity a of a single *variable* factor A. In function form this can be expressed as:

(14.3)
$$x = \psi(a)$$

[2]Firms might also be oligopolists or monopolistic competitors in their respective product markets, but only the polar cases of pure competition and pure monopoly will be examined here.

The quantities of the fixed factors $B, C, \ldots$ no longer appear in equation (14.3) as arguments of the production function. But of course they still have an effect; the amounts of the fixed factors enter into the shape of the $\psi(a)$ function that shows how much X can be obtained per unit of A.

There is a famous technological relation between variable factor input on the one hand, and output quantities on the other. This relation is known as the *Law of Diminishing Returns*. Sometimes, to emphasize the fact that the relation applies where one factor varies in amount *relative* to others, it is called also the *Law of Varying Factor Proportions*.

The Law of Diminishing Returns: If one factor (or group of factors) is increased while another factor (or group of factors) is held fixed, output will at first tend to rise. But, eventually at least, a point will be reached where the rate of increase, the *Marginal* Product[3] $mp_a \equiv \Delta x / \Delta a$ associated with increments of the variable factor, begins to fall; this is the point of diminishing marginal returns. With further increases of the variable factor, the *Average* Product $ap_a \equiv x/a$ will also eventually begin to fall; this is the point of diminishing average returns. As the amount of factor A employed rises still more, A may become actually counterproductive, reducing the *Total* Product x. This is the point of diminishing total returns to factor A.

The Law of Diminishing Returns is illustrated in Figure 14.1. Panel (a) shows the Total Product curve tp_a relating output quantity x and factor input

---

[3] *Mathematical Footnote:* Formally, the Marginal Product is (like all marginal concepts) defined as a limit: $mp_a \equiv \lim\limits_{\Delta a \to 0} \dfrac{\Delta x}{\Delta a} \equiv \dfrac{dx}{da}$. Henceforth in the text note of the translation of marginal concepts into derivative notation will not be taken except where there may be a danger of misunderstanding.

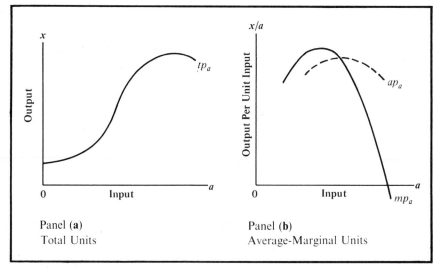

Panel (a)
Total Units

Panel (b)
Average-Marginal Units

Figure 14. 1
The Law of Diminishing Returns

a. Panel (b) shows the corresponding picture in average units (the Average Product curve ap_a showing x/a as a function of factor input a) and in marginal units (the Marginal Product curve mp_a showing $\Delta x/\Delta a$ as a function of factor input a). The relations among the total, average, and marginal magnitudes here are of course consistent with the general laws developed in Section 2.B. As Total Product tp_a is rising or horizontal or falling, Marginal Product mp_a is correspondingly positive or zero or negative (Propositions 2.1a, 2.1b, 2.1c). And the Marginal Product curve mp_a lies above the Average Product curve ap_a when the latter is rising, intersects it when ap_a is horizontal, and lies below it when ap_a is falling (Propositions 2.2a, 2.2b, 2.2c).

The Law of Diminishing Returns is a physical law, taken as a premise by economists; it is not a proposition of economic science. But the common-sense of the Law is understandable in economic terms. There will, in general, tend to be (at any level of output) some most effective *proportion* among the several factors. When we increase the quantity of factor A from a very low level (say, from zero) with other factor quantities held fixed, we are likely to be getting closer to the most effective proportion of factors; hence, Total Product is likely to be increasing at an increasing rate (rising Marginal Product of factor A). When we reach this most effective proportion and push beyond to further augment the quantity of the variable factor A, Total Product will still tend to increase, but at a decreasing rate (declining Marginal Product of factor A). For, while the additional units of factor A are useful, input proportions are increasingly diverging from optimal. Eventually indeed, we may so swamp our productive process with factor A that additional quantities of it actually interfere with production (negative Marginal Product of factor A).

Example 14. 1
Cotton Irrigation
Experiment

In 1960 A. Marani and Y. Fuchs conducted a cotton irrigation experiment in Israel. On April 3 "Pima 32" variety cotton was planted. All plots received 50 mm of water immediately after planting, but none thereafter until July 4. On that date plots were irrigated with varying quantities of water. The following Table shows the results at harvest.

Irrigation Treatment and Yield

Water Applied July 4 (mm)	Growth in Height after July 4 (cm)	Cottonseed Yield (g/m²)	Lint Yield (g/m²)
0	1	58	19
100	8	99	31
150	22	136	42
200	33	131	40

Source: A. Marani and Y. Fuchs, "Effect of Amount of Water Applied as a Single Irrigation on Cotton Grown under Dryland Conditions," *Agronomy Journal*, v. 56 (May/June 1964), p. 282.

In this case there are two outputs of interest: seed and lint. However, the Total Product curves are quite similar for each. The lack of observations at the intermediate 50 mm level unfortunately leaves some doubt as to the shapes of the Total Product curves in the early ranges. But for both products it is evident that for the largest application studied, 200 mm of irrigation water, there are diminishing *total* returns, i.e., Marginal Product is negative. (The plants do actually grow higher at 200 mm than at 150 mm, but the seed and lint yields are both less.) The Average Product and Marginal Product of irrigation water, in terms of both seed and lint, appear to be declining throughout the range of application. Thus, diminishing marginal returns and diminishing average returns seem to hold from the start.

Apart from direct verification of the Law of Diminishing Returns by experiment (as in the example above), there is an indirect verification. Recall that the observation of *diversification in consumption* provided an indirect verification of indifference-curve convexity in Section 4.A.1. Analogous to this is the observation of *factor diversification*—the fact that, normally, firms employ a number of different resources jointly in the production process. For, as we shall see, in the absence of diminishing marginal returns it would be optimal to employ only a *single* factor in production.

14. A. 2 The Factor-Employment Decision

Facing the product market, the firm decides upon the best quantity of output to produce (to supply) in the light of the costs and returns from production. Correspondingly with regard to the factor market, the best quantity of factor for the firm to employ (to demand) varies with the costs and returns of factor employment.

For a price-taking firm in the factor market, whether monopolist or competitor in the product market, the *cost* of hiring factor A is represented by a constant hire-price h_a per unit of A.[4] In Figure 14.2, a horizontal line drawn at the level of the constant hire-price h_a can be regarded as the *factor supply curve* s_a to the firm. (The horizontality of s_a corresponds to the assumption that the firm is too small a demander to noticeably affect factor price.) Denoting the total expenditure on (the total cost of hiring) factor A as $C_a \equiv h_a a$, where a is the quantity of factor A employed by the firm, this supply curve can be interpreted as a curve of *Average Factor Cost* ($afc_a \equiv C_a/a$). And, since the price per unit is constant, it is also a curve of *Marginal Factor Cost* ($mfc_a \equiv \Delta C_a/\Delta a$). Note the analogy: The price-taking firm in the prod-

[4]In some cases a firm may be able either to *hire* or to *buy* a factor. Thus, a business may be able to rent office space or to buy a building for that purpose. We therefore will find it useful to distinguish the *hire-price* h_a of factor A from the price P_a of the factor itself—the source of the productive services used by the firm. But where there is no danger of confusion, we shall sometimes speak of h_a as the "price of the factor" (i.e., of the factor's services).

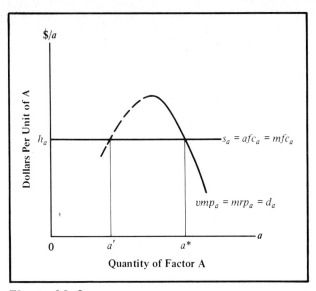

Figure 14. 2
Optimum Factor Employment,
Competitor in Product Market

uct market faces a horizontal *demand* curve d_x for *product X*, while the price-taking firm in the factor market faces a horizontal supply curve s_a for *factor A*. Since Revenue from sales of product X is defined as $R_x \equiv P_x x$, the horizontal demand curve d_x at the given product price P_x is also an Average Revenue function $AR_x \equiv R_x/x$. Analogously, since the Cost of hiring factor A is defined as $C_a \equiv h_a a$, the horizontal supply curve s_a at the given factor hire-price h_a is also an Average Factor Cost function $afc_a \equiv C_a/a$.

What are the *returns* to the firm from employment of a factor? Two elements are involved: (1) the physical productivity of the input, and (2) the value of the commodity produced. In considering hiring another unit of factor it is evident that, so far as physical productivity is concerned, only *Marginal* Product will be relevant. However great the contribution to *Total* Product may have been for earlier units of factor, only the incremental yield from an additional unit will be considered in the hiring decision for that last unit. Combining the elements of physical productivity and value of product leads to the concept called *Value of the Marginal Product* of factor A.

Definition: Value of the Marginal Product vmp_a equals product price P_x times physical Marginal Product mp_a.

(14.4) $$vmp_a \equiv P_x(mp_a)$$.

For a price-taking firm in the product market, product price P_x is constant. Then if the Value of the Marginal Product, $vmp_a \equiv P_x(mp_a)$, exceeds the price

347

h_a of factor A, it will surely pay the firm to employ an additional unit of A. Thus, the optimum condition for employment of factor A by a price-taking firm can be expressed as:

(14.5) $$vmp_a = h_a$$

This equality holds both at employment levels a' and $a*$ in Figure 14.2. However, a subsidiary condition for an optimum is that the vmp_a curve *be falling* relative to the horizontal $afc_a \equiv mfc_a$ curve;[5] and this holds only at $a*$ in the diagram.[6] In terms of economic logic, to employ only a' units of A would be to forego the profitable range where the returns from successively hiring additional units of factor (vmp_a) exceed the costs thereof ($h_a \equiv mfc_a$). The falling vmp_a curve is, of course, a direct reflection of the Law of Diminishing Returns.

Now suppose that the firm employing factor A, while still a price-taker in the factor market, has *monopoly power in the product market*. For such a firm, the returns from increased factor employment will be adversely affected by the falling tendency of price P_x as more output is produced. For a monopolist firm the return on the margin (from the employment of an additional unit of factor A) is not the *value* of the physical Marginal Product but the *revenue increment* achievable by sale of that Marginal Product. This leads to the concept known as *Marginal Revenue Product* of factor A, denoted mrp_a:

(14.6) $$mrp_a \equiv MR(mp_a)$$

Definition: Marginal Revenue Product mrp_a equals product Marginal Revenue MR times physical Marginal Product mp_a.

For a firm that is a competitor in the product market, product price P_x is a constant—in which case (as we know from Section 9.D) Marginal Revenue MR identically equals price P_x. It follows immediately that, *for a competitive firm in the product market, the* vmp_a *and the* mrp_a *curves*—as defined in equations (14.4) and (14.6) respectively—*are identical*. For a firm with monopoly power in the product market, on the other hand, Marginal Revenue MR and product price P_x are both decreasing functions of output. And the

---

[5]This condition corresponds to the technical qualification (in Section 9.D) that the output optimum for the firm occurs at $MC = MR$ *provided that the* MC *curve cuts* MR *from below*. Here the optimum occurs *when* vmp_a *cuts* mfc_a *from above*.

[6]*Mathematical Footnote:* The firm chooses the amout of a to maximize profit $\Pi = R - C = P_x x - h_a a - F$ (where F stands for fixed costs representing expenditures on factors other than A). Differentiating Π and setting the derivative equal to zero, we have as *first-order* condition:

$$P_x \frac{dx}{da} = h_a \quad \text{or} \quad P_x(mp_a) \equiv vmp_a = h_a$$

thus verifying (14.5). Taking the second derivative of Π, the *second-order* condition for a maximum is

$$P_x \frac{d^2x}{da^2} < 0 \quad \text{or simply} \quad \frac{d^2x}{da^2} < 0$$

This means that Marginal Product mp_a (and so the curve vmp_a) must be *falling* to have a profit maximum.

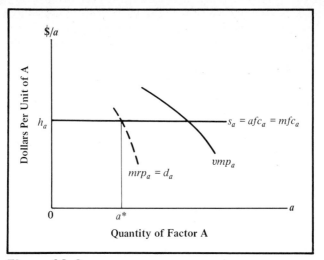

Figure 14. 3
Optimum Factor Employment,
Monopolist in Product Market

MR curve falls faster than the demand or Average Revenue curve—as shown, for example, in Figure 11.1. So *for a monopoly firm, the* mrp_a *curve must lie below and fall faster than the* vmp_a *curve*, as in Figure 14.3. The optimal factor employment a^* for the firm with monopoly power in the product market is determined in this diagram as the intersection of the mrp_a curve with the horizontal factor-supply curve $s_a \equiv afc_a \equiv mfc_a$ at the level h_a.[7]

Since for the competitive firm in the factor market vmp_a and mrp_a are identical, equation (14.5) can be superseded by the following more general Factor Employment Condition that holds for *both* monopolist and pure competitor in the product market:

(14.7) $$mrp_a = h_a$$ Factor Employment Condition, Price-Taking Firm in Factor Market

Again, we have as a technical qualification that the mrp_a curve must cut the horizontal factor-supply curve from *above*.[8]

[7]*Mathematical Footnote:* The firm is maximizing $\Pi = R - C = P_x x - h_a a - F$ as before, but now recognizes that P_x is a decreasing function of output x—and so, indirectly, of input a. Differentiating and setting equal to zero, the first-order condition is:

$$P_x \frac{dx}{da} + x\frac{dP_x}{dx}\frac{dx}{da} = h_a \quad \text{or} \quad \left(P_x + x\frac{dP_x}{dx}\right)\frac{dx}{da} = h_a$$

The element in parentheses on the left is Marginal Revenue, as defined in equation (11.2). So the condition can be expressed as:

$$MR(mp_a) \equiv mrp_a = h_a$$

[8]*Mathematical Footnote:* The second derivative of Π can be written as $d(mrp_a)/da$, which must be negative to satisfy the second-order condition for a maximum. So the mrp_a curve must be falling relative to the horizontal factor-supply curve s_a.

The separate treatments of the firm's *output* decision in Chapters 9 and 11 (for the competitive and monopolist firm, respectively) and of the *factor-employment* decision here might suggest that these are two distinct choices. But, given the production function (14.3), the two decisions are inextricably connected. Having made the factor-employment decision, output is determined; there is no further degree of freedom for the firm to choose a level of output. And, so long as we are dealing with a *single* variable factor, the converse is also true: Choosing output necessarily determines factor employment.[9] Thus, the output solutions of Chapters 9 and 11 and the factor-employment solutions in the present chapter are but different aspects of the firm's single optimizing productive choice.[10]

14. A. 3 Firm's Demand for Factor

The final step in this development is the factor-price-taking firm's *demand function* for the variable factor A. For any given factor hire-price h_a, the Factor Employment Condition (14.7) specifies the amount of A employed by the firm. As h_a varies up or down, the optimal employment of A is that for which $mrp_a = h_a$ (in the downward-sloping range of the mrp_a curve).

Conclusion: The curve of Marginal Revenue Product mrp_a, for any factor-price-taking firm employing a single variable factor A, is (in its downward-sloping range)[11] the firm's demand curve for A.

In Figure 14.2, for a competitor firm in the product market, the factor demand curve d_a coincides with the curve of $vmp_a = mrp_a$. In Figure 14.3,

---

[9]With several variable factors, however, the determination of output still leaves a range of freedom for the selection of the best resource combination to produce that output. This topic is taken up in Section 14.B.

[10]This can be shown without using calculus, by verifying the equivalence of the general optimal Factor Employment Condition (14.7), $mrp_a = h_a$, with the Optimal Output Condition $MC = MR$ of Section 11.B. Marginal Cost MC is by definition $\Delta C/\Delta x$. But with only a single variable factor A, any change in cost ΔC must be due to a variation Δa in the quantity of A. Thus, $\Delta C = \Delta C_a = h_a \, \Delta a$. Marginal Product mp_a is by definition $\Delta x/\Delta a$. Putting these together, we have the string of identities:

$$(14.8) \qquad MC \equiv \frac{\Delta C}{\Delta x} \equiv h_a \frac{\Delta a}{\Delta x} \equiv \frac{h_a}{mp_a}$$

Then, substituting for MC in the Optimal Output Condition $MC = MR$, we obtain:

$$(14.9) \qquad MC \equiv \frac{h_a}{mp_a} = MR \quad \text{or} \quad h_a = MR(mp_a)$$

Since the definition (14.6) tells us that $MR(mp_a) \equiv mrp_a$, the Optimal Output Condition $MC = MR$ is indeed equivalent to the Factor Employment Condition $h_a = mrp_a$. This equivalence holds for *both* monopolist and competitor firm in the product market. In the latter case, the Optimal Output Condition takes on the special form $MC = MR \equiv P_x$, which corresponds to the special form of the Factor Employment Condition $h_a = mrp_a \equiv vmp_a$.

[11]A technical qualification: Strictly speaking, this holds only for that portion of the downward-sloping range where the total expenditure $C_a = h_a a$ on the variable factor A is less than Total Revenue R. (The analogy is with the proviso in Section 10.A that the Marginal Cost curve MC is the firm's *supply curve of product* only over the range where price P_x exceeds Average Variable Cost AVC.)

for a monopolist in the product market, the factor demand curve d_a coincides with mrp_a (and *not* with vmp_a).

*14. B FIRM'S DEMAND FOR SEVERAL VARIABLE FACTORS

The employment decision for a single variable factor, other factors held fixed, corresponds to the firm's output decision in the "short run" (see Section 9.E). In the general or "long run" case all factors are variable. For simplicity here, however, the exposition deals with just *two* variable factors A and B.

14. B. 1 The Production Function

The firm's choice as to the hiring of factors is in some ways analogous to the consumer's decision as to the purchase of consumption goods. Just as consumption goods can be regarded as generating *utility*, so factors as inputs generate *product*. The relation between inputs and output is the production function of the firm. Specifically here, the production function can be written:

(14.10) $$x = \Psi(a, b)$$

Diagrammatically, the production function is the "output hill" of Figure 14.4 which shows output quantity x as a function of input quantities a and b.

*Starred sections represent optional or advanced material.

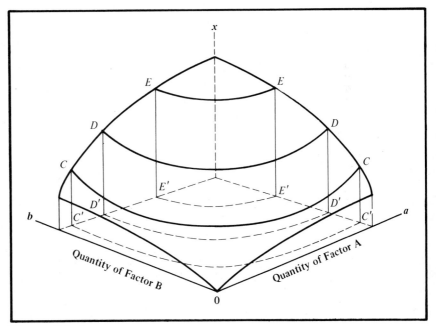

Figure 14. 4
Output as a Function of Two Inputs

There is of course no conceptual problem in quantifying physical output of product, and so no reason to avoid use of a "cardinal" vertical scale for output in a three-dimensional diagram.[12] Nevertheless, the convenience of working in just two dimensions is such that we will make use of the "contour map" of the output hill, as illustrated here in Figure 14.5. But we can always attach some definite numerical output quantity index x to each contour or *isoquant* of the contour map; we are not restricted, as we were in the case of utility, to merely "ordinal" comparisons of higher and lower.

There are two essential aspects of the multi-factor production function: (1) The effect of changes in *relative factor proportions*, and (2) the effect of changes in *scale* (i.e., of proportionate increases or decreases in all factors simultaneously).

With regard to *relative* factor proportions, the Law of Diminishing Returns continues to hold (as a postulated technological fact) in the two-factor case. Consider Figure 14.6. Here, along the surface of the output hill are sketched several curves showing the change in output quantity x as one input varies with the other input held constant. These can be regarded as *Total Product curves*, analogous to the tp_a curve defined for a single variable factor A in the previous section. But there are now Total Product curves for each of the two factors A and B—tp_a and tp_b. Indeed, for each factor there is

---

[12]Whereas, as we saw in Section 3.D, a cardinal scale for quantifying the vertical dimension of the "utility hill" was both doubtful and unnecessary.

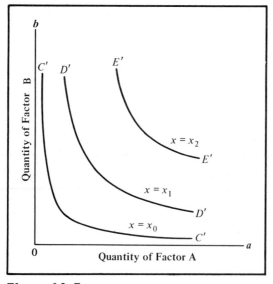

Figure 14. 5
Isoquants of Output

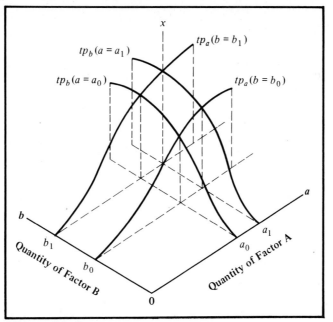

Figure 14. 6
Total Product Functions

an infinite family of such curves, since in general both tp_a and tp_b will depend also upon the specific magnitude at which the *other* factor is held constant. The Total Product curves for factor A are given labels like $tp_a(b = b_0)$ and $tp_a(b = b_1)$. Each such curve shows the variation of Total Product x with changes in the input quantity of factor A, factor B held constant—in the one case at $b = b_0$ and in the other at $b = b_1$. And a set of tp_b curves can correspondingly be defined. It is possible, of course, to associate with any of the Total Product curves of Figure 14.6 an Average Product curve and Marginal Product[13] curve as in Panel (b) of Figure 14.1.

In Figure 14.7 the two families of Total Product curves are shown suggestively on (x, a) and on (x, b) axes, respectively. Each single curve has a form similar to the tp_a curve of Figure 14.1, as dictated by the Law of Diminishing Returns. In Panel (a) the entire tp_a curve is shown as shifting upward as quantities of the other factor B rise from b_0 to b_1 to b_2, and similarly for the other factor in Panel (b). Such an upward shift must occur, if the "other" factor is productive.

With regard to changes in *scale*, the shape of the output hill in Figure 14.4 shows that a kind of diminishing returns *may* obtain even where both factors

---

[13]*Mathematical Footnote:* With two or more variable factors, the Marginal Product of any single factor such as A becomes a *partial* derivative:

$$mp_a \equiv \lim_{\Delta a \to 0} \frac{\Psi(a + \Delta a, b) - \Psi(a, b)}{\Delta a} \equiv \frac{\partial x}{\partial a}$$

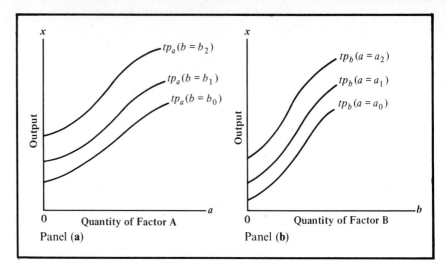

Figure 14. 7
Families of Total Product Curves

increase proportionately. We will assume here that, eventually at least, *diminishing returns to scale* also apply. However, constant or even increasing returns to scale would not be a contradiction of the Law of Diminishing Returns as defined for *varying factor proportions*. Total Product curves can have the normal diminishing-returns shape even on an output hill with constant or increasing returns to scale.

Example 14. 2
Missouri Corn

An agricultural experiment in Missouri reported by J. Ambrosius examined the response of corn yield X (bushels per acre) to variation in two inputs A and B (*number of plants* per acre and *pounds of nitrogen* per acre). Reading horizontally across any single row, the Table shows

Bushels of Corn Per Acre (x)

Pounds of Nitrogen per Acre (b)	Number of Plants per Acre (a)				
	9000	12000	15000	18000	21000
0	50.6	54.2	53.5	48.5	39.2
50	78.7	85.9	88.8	87.5	81.9
100	94.4	105.3	111.9	114.2	112.2
150	97.8	112.4	122.6	128.6	130.3
200	88.9	107.1	121.0	130.6	135.9

Source: John Ambrosius, "The Effects of Experimental Size upon Optimum Rates of Nitrogen and Stand for Corn in Missouri" (1964), quoted in J. P. Doll, V. J. Rhodes, and J. G. West, *Economics of Agricultural Production, Markets, and Policy* (Homewood, Ill.: Richard D. Irwin, Inc., 1968), p. 89.

354

selected points on the Total Product curve tp_a for plants per acre, with b, nitrogen input per acre, held constant along the row. Reading vertically down any column, points are shown on the tp_b curve for nitrogen input b, holding fixed the number of plants per acre, a. The entire tp_a curve tends to shift upward as b increases, and the tp_b curve as a increases.

It is also possible to see that diminishing returns apply here even to *proportionate variation* in both factors together. For example, a doubling of both inputs from the combination $a_0 = 9000$, $b_0 = 50$ to the combination $a_1 = 18000$, $b_1 = 100$ raises output from 78.7 only to 114.2.

Example 14.2 suggests a possible rationale for diminishing returns to scale (i.e., to proportionate variation of factors). In the experiment, nitrogen and number of plants as inputs were varied, but at least one factor—the number of acres—was still held constant. Since in the real world it will not generally be possible to vary literally *all* inputs, we are always in practice dealing still with changes in *relative* factor proportions. The very definition of the firm suggests that some input, to which the label "entrepreneurship" is sometimes applied, remains constant throughout. Even abstracting from this element, certain unchanging aspects of our planet (the gravitational constant or the distribution of minerals, for example) may enter into productive processes. So even though all *marketable* inputs are varied in proportion, the condition wherein some inputs are physically "fixed" is, in some degree, ultimately inescapable.

14. B. 2 The Factor-Employment Decision—Geometry

The factor-employment decision of a firm using two variable factors has, like the production function itself, two aspects: (1) the determination of optimal relative factor *proportions*, and (2) the determination of most profitable *scale*. Following the procedure applied to the consumption decision (in Section 4.A), we shall treat these two aspects first from a geometrical and then from an analytical point of view.

To isolate the aspect of factor proportions, let us hold scale constant by assuming a fixed level of cost $C' = h_a a + h_b b$. We want to determine the a, b input combination, at this given level of cost, that is most advantageous for the firm. Clearly, the best combination is that which maximizes the quantity of output. Geometrically, it will be evident in the contour map or isoquant diagram of Figure 14.8 that the tangency point Q' is optimal. The factor employments at point Q' are a' and b', leading to output level x'. Q' is on the highest output isoquant attainable along the line $C' = h_a a + h_b b$ that represents the given level of cost.

Note the analogy with the optimum of the consumer that was pictured in Figure 4.1. There the consumer was maximizing utility by choice of con-

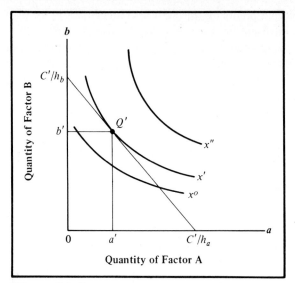

Figure 14. 8
Optimal Factor Balance

sumption quantities x and y, at a specified level of income $I = P_x x + P_y y$. Here the firm maximizes output by choice of factor employments a and b, at a specified level of cost $C' = h_a a + h_b b$.

But of course we want to consider different levels of cost, i.e., of *scale* of output. As cost expands in any proportion, the cost line in the diagram will move out from the origin along both axes in the same proportion. Figure 14.9 pictures a family of cost lines (isoquants of *cost*) $C^\circ, C', C'', \ldots$, as well as a family of production contours (isoquants of *output*) $x^\circ, x', x'', \ldots$. All the cost lines will have the same fixed slope. Since at any level of cost the tangency point represents the optimal proportion or balance of factors, a curve drawn through all such tangency points must contain the overall best position for the firm. This curve may be called the Scale Expansion Path (SEP), in analogy with the consumer's Income Expansion Path (IEP) of Section 4.B.

There are a number of different ways of locating the overall best position of the firm. Perhaps the simplest is to convert the data of the Scale Expansion Path SEP into Total Cost and Total Revenue curves. For any tangency point such as Q' along the SEP in Figure 14.9, there are associated quantities x' of output and C' of cost. With this x, C information for all levels of cost $C^\circ, C', C'', \ldots$, the Total Cost curve $C(x)$ can be plotted as in Figure 14.10. To obtain the Total Revenue curve, the only additional information needed is the *demand function* relating price P_x to the firm's output x. Thus, for each level of x there is a unique P_x. Multiplying the output indexes $x^\circ, x', x'', \ldots$ by the appropriate P_x in each case, we see that isoquants of output x in Figure 14.9 can equally well be regarded as isoquants of Total Revenue $R = P_x x$. (If the firm is a price-taker in the product market, P_x is a constant

356

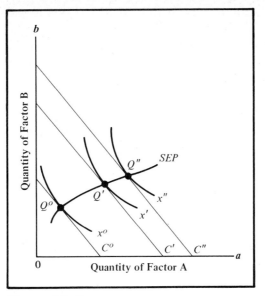

Figure 14. 9
Scale Expansion Path

so that R increases proportionately with output. Then all the different x-contours are multiplied by the *same* P_x to become R-contours. If the firm has a degree of monopoly power, P_x is a declining function of x along the demand curve so that R increases less than proportionately with output.) The x, R information can be plotted as the Total Revenue curve $R(x)$ in Figure 14.10.

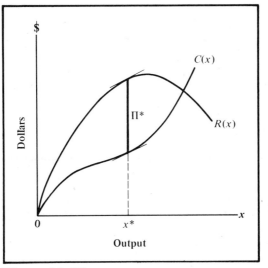

Figure 14. 10

Total Revenue and Total Cost Functions

The best output x^* is that for which profit $\Pi = R - C$, i.e., the vertical distance between the $R(x)$ and $C(x)$ curves in the diagram, is greatest. The optimal x^* tells us the particular x-contour that is best in Figure 14.9. The intersection of this contour with the Scale Expansion Path SEP determines, finally, the optimal factor employments a^* and b^*.

14. B. 3 The Factor-Employment Decision—Analysis

Given diminishing marginal productivity for each of the two factors, at any level of cost the firm will be at an (interior) optimum when the Factor Balance Equation (14.11) holds:[14]

(14.11)
$$\frac{mp_a}{h_a} = \frac{mp_b}{h_b}$$
Factor Balance Equation

That is, at any given scale the relative factor employments are optimal when the Marginal Products *per dollar* spent are equal for each variable factor employed.[15]

MRS_X, the Marginal Rate of Substitution in Production between factors A and B with regard to product X, can be interpreted as the absolute slope at any particular point along an output isoquant. Thus,

$$MRS_X \equiv -\left.\frac{\Delta b}{\Delta a}\right|_X$$

[14] *Mathematical Footnote:* We can use again "the method of Lagrangian multipliers" (see Mathematical Footnote 5 of Chapter 4), to maximize output $x = \Psi(a, b)$ subject to a given level of Cost $C = h_a a + h_b b$.

$$\underset{(a, b, \lambda)}{\text{Max }} L = x - \lambda(h_a a + h_b b - C)$$

The first-order conditions are:

$$\frac{\partial x}{\partial a} - \lambda h_a = 0$$

$$\frac{\partial x}{\partial b} - \lambda h_b = 0$$

$$h_a a + h_b b - C = 0$$

The first two conditions can be written as:

$$\lambda = \frac{\partial x/\partial a}{h_a} = \frac{\partial x/\partial b}{h_b}$$

Thus the first-order conditions correspond to the Factor Balance Equation (14.11). With more than one variable factor, however, diminishing Marginal Product ($\partial^2 x/\partial a^2 < 0$, $\partial^2 x/\partial b^2 < 0$) does not guarantee that the *second-order* conditions for a maximum are met. (Compare the analogous statement about diminishing Marginal *Utility* in footnote 12 of Chapter 4.) An additional required condition is: $\frac{\partial^2 x}{\partial a^2} \frac{\partial^2 x}{\partial b^2} > \left(\frac{\partial^2 x}{\partial a \, \partial b}\right)^2$.

[15] If D is some third factor *not* actually being employed ($d = 0$) at current factor prices, its Marginal Product per dollar is related by an *inequality* condition to the others:

$$\frac{mp_a(a > 0)}{h_a} = \frac{mp_b(b > 0)}{h_b} > \frac{mp_d(d = 0)}{h_d}$$

For the optimal employment of D to be zero, it must be that the Marginal Product per dollar of factor D is less than for other factors, even for the very first unit of D.

(For the analogous concept of the Marginal Rate of Subsitution in Consumption, MRS_C, representing the absolute slope of the consumer's indifference curve, see Section 4.A.2.) And the *Marginal Rate of Substitution in Exchange* between the two factors, MRS_E, is the absolute slope of the Cost isoquant. So the tangency condition of Figure 14.8 representing optimal factor balance can be written simply as:

(14.11')
$$MRS_X = MRS_E$$

Equation (14.11') can be reconciled with the form of the Factor Balance Equation (14.11). The following argument shows that the absolute slope of the output isoquant, MRS_X is equal to the ratio of the marginal products mp_a/mp_b. Suppose a unit decrease in factor A reduces output by 10, then $mp_a = 10$ (approximately). How much of an increment of factor B is required to get back to the same output isoquant? If $mp_b = 5$, then (approximately) 2 units of B will just suffice. So, on the margin, two units of B are the productive equivalent of one unit of A. Then the absolute isoquant slope $MRS_X \equiv -\dfrac{\Delta b}{\Delta a}\Big|_x$ here equals $2 = \frac{10}{5}$. Or, more generally:[16]

$$MRS_X \equiv \frac{mp_a}{mp_b}$$

As for the linear cost isoquant, inspection of Figure 14.8 shows that at cost level C' it has absolute slope $\dfrac{C'/h_b}{C'/h_a}$ or $\dfrac{h_a}{h_b}$. As C' cancels out, for *any* cost isoquant:

$$MRS_E \equiv \frac{h_a}{h_b}$$

Making the appropriate substitutions, it can be seen directly that (14.11') corresponds with (14.11).

The analytical condition for the firm's optimum *scale of output* took the form $MC = MR$ in equation (9.3). We now want to express this same result in terms of employment of factors A and B. First, note the following interpretation of the Factor Balance Equation (14.11):

(14.12)
$$\frac{h_a}{mp_a} = \frac{h_b}{mp_b} = MC$$

That is, Marginal Cost $MC \equiv \Delta C/\Delta x$ equals, for factor A, its hire-price $h_a \equiv \Delta C/\Delta a$ divided by its Marginal Product $mp_a \equiv \Delta x/\Delta a$. Similarly, of

---

[16]*Mathematical Footnote:* Along any output isoquant, x is constant. Thus:

$$dx = \frac{\partial x}{\partial a}da + \frac{\partial x}{\partial b}db = 0$$

Then

$$-\frac{db}{da} = \frac{\partial x/\partial a}{\partial x/\partial b} \quad \text{or} \quad MRS_X = \frac{mp_a}{mp_b}$$

course, for factor B. At the correct factor proportions dictated by the Factor Balance Equation, it is equally costly to expand output by hiring a small increment of A, or of B, or any mixture of the two.[17]

We now employ the Optimum Output Condition $MC = MR$. Multiply all the denominators in (14.12) through by Marginal Revenue MR. In doing this, we can make use of equation (14.6) defining the Marginal Revenue Product as $mrp = MR(mp_a)$. This leads to the Overall Firm Optimality Condition:

(14.13) $$\frac{h_a}{mrp_a} = \frac{h_b}{mrp_b} = \frac{MC}{MR} = 1 \qquad \text{Overall Firm Optimality Condition}$$

It follows immediately that, for each factor separately:

(14.14) $$\begin{cases} mrp_a = h_a \\ mrp_b = h_b \end{cases} \qquad \text{Factor Employment Conditions}$$

Equations (14.14) look, of course, exactly like the single-factor condition in equation (14.7). But we must now keep in mind that mp_a (and therefore mrp_a) depends also upon the quantity of factor B, and similarly for the other factor.

Thus, the scale of factor employments is correct if, for all factors actually employed, Marginal Revenue Product equals factor hire-price. For a firm with no monopoly power in the product market, $MR \equiv P_x$. For such a firm, therefore, equations (14.13) and (14.14) could be written in terms of Value of the Marginal Product vmp (price times Marginal Product) instead of mrp (Marginal Revenue times Marginal Product). The equations in their present general form, however, hold whether the firm is a monopolist or a competitor in the product market.

14. B. 4   Shifts in Factor Prices

We saw in Section 4.C that a change in the price of a consumer good had a *substitution effect* and an *income effect* upon purchases. Analogously here, a change in the price of a factor has a *substitution effect* and a *scale effect* upon factor employment. The substitution effect follows from the change in factor proportions due to the shift in *relative* factor prices h_a/h_b; the scale effect follows from the effect on optimal output due to the implied change in Marginal Cost MC.

---

[17]*Mathematical Footnote:* First, $dx = (\partial x/\partial a)da + (\partial x/\partial b)db$. Since $C = h_a a + h_b b$, $dC = h_a\,da + h_b\,db$. So:

$$MC \equiv \frac{dC}{dx} = \frac{h_a\,da + h_b\,db}{(\partial x/\partial a)\,da + (\partial x/\partial b)\,db}$$

Since $h_a/(\partial x/\partial a) = h_b/(\partial x/\partial b)$ from the Factor Balance Equation, the "Rule of Corresponding Addition" permits us to express MC as:

$$MC = \frac{h_a}{\partial x/\partial a} = \frac{h_b}{\partial x/\partial b}$$

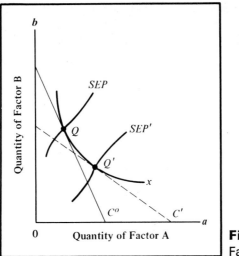

Figure 14. 11
Factor Substitution Effect

The substitution effect is illustrated in Figure 14.11. Here the position Q represents a typical point on the Scale Expansion Path SEP, tangency of a cost isoquant $C°$ and an output isoquant x. A fall in h_a, the price of factor A, necessarily lowers (flattens) the absolute slope h_a/h_b of the cost isoquant. The dashed C' is that member of the family of flatter cost isoquants that is tangent to the initial output isoquant (at position Q'). The new Scale Expansion Path SEP$'$ will therefore be displaced to the right, as indicated in the diagram, illustrating a shift of optimal factor proportions toward the relatively cheapened factor A.

Example 14. 3
Factor Prices
and
Ocean Shipping

Newly constructed ships used by Japanese, continental European, and British shippers during the years 1952–55 were examined by W. Y. Oi in order to compare the relative factor proportions employed. In ocean shipping the important factors of production may be divided into: (a) "capital" (amortization of construction expenses, plus ship maintenance), (b) fuel, and (c) labor (wages plus subsistence at sea). In the period studied, fuel prices were very similar for all shippers. So the essential element was the capital cost versus labor cost comparison. Labor costs were relatively cheapest for the Japanese shippers and most expensive for the continental Europeans, with the British in between.

One consequence of relatively high labor cost (or, equivalently, relatively low capital cost) is the employment of ships with a high designed speed. Faster ships are costlier to construct and maintain, but permit a saving of labor time per voyage. The following Table indicates that, as anticipated, the Japanese chose ships with lowest and the continental Europeans with highest designed speed.

	Small Ships (3000–9000 dwt.)	Large Ships (Over 9000 dwt.)
Japanese shippers	11.46 knots	13.81 knots
British shippers	14.00	14.04
European shippers	14.86	14.93

Source: W. Y. Oi, "The Cost of Ocean Shipping," in A. R. Ferguson *et al.*, *The Economic Value of the United States Merchant Marine* (Evanston, Ill.: The Transportation Center at Northwestern University, 1961), p. 160.

The scale effect is somewhat trickier to illustrate geometrically. Figure 14.12 shows the effect of a fall in h_a alone (from h_a' to h_a'') upon a typical initial cost isoquant. Evidently there is an outward rotation of the cost isoquant, from the position C' to C''. The new tangency will necessarily be on a higher output isoquant x''. Thus, *at any given cost* it will be optimal for the firm to produce more output after a cheapening of a factor.

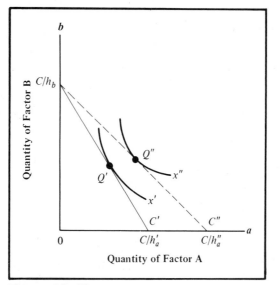

Figure 14. 12
Cheapening of Factor *A*

It seems plausible to expect that a fall in any factor price h_a would surely lead to an expansion of the optimum scale of output. Surprisingly, perhaps, this does *not* necessarily follow. It is true that the Total Cost curve falls with a cheapening of any factor. But the optimal output is determined by the relation between *Marginal* Cost and *Marginal* Revenue ($MC = MR$), i.e., between the *slopes* of the Total Cost and Total Revenue curves. Figure 14.13, Panel (a), shows a normal situation in which the lowering of the Total Cost

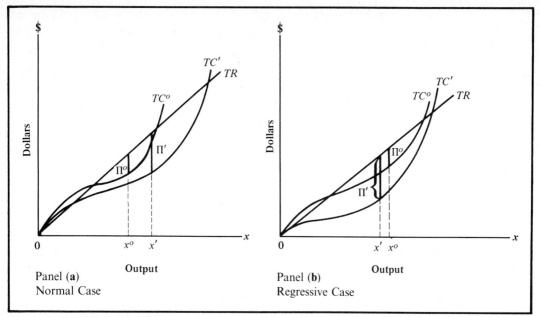

Figure 14. 13 Scale Effect

curve from TC^o to TC' does lead to an expansion of optimal output from x^o to x' (note the location of the profit magnitudes Π^o and Π'). Panel (b) shows the more surprising case in which the lowering from TC^o to TC' is combined with a *steepening* of the slope (thus increasing the MC) in the relevant region, so that the new optimal output x' is less than x^o.

In this latter case, A is called a "regressive factor." It is not difficult to give an economic interpretation of the seemingly paradoxical result, however. Think of A as a factor particularly specialized to and useful for small-scale production, for example, skilled craftsmen. If the price of skilled craftsmen falls, it may pay a firm to shift away from a large-scale mass production technique so as to earn more profit with smaller output—by making better use of the now cheaply available craft skills.

Conclusion: A change in factor price leads to a substitution effect and a scale effect upon factor employment and firm output. The substitution effect is *always* in the normal direction: relatively more of the now relatively cheaper factor will be used. The scale effect of a fall in factor price is normally to increase output, and of a rise in factor price to decrease output. But in the case of a "regressive" factor, the scale effect is reversed.

14. B. 5 Firm's Demand for Factors

In the single-factor situation, the firm's demand curve for the variable factor was given by its Marginal Revenue Product curve *mrp*.[18] In the multi-factor

---

[18]More precisely, by a portion of the downward-sloping branch of the *mrp* curve, as explained in Section 14.A.3.

analysis the firm's demand curve for any of the variable factors still depends upon the Marginal Revenue Product of the factor. However, it is necessary to take account of the *interaction* among the factors that ensues from a change in the price of any single input.

Let us start from an initial position in which the Factor Balance and Optimal Output Conditions are both met, as dictated by equations (14.13) or (14.14). Figure 14.14 shows an initial optimum: $mrp_a (b = b^o) = h^o_a$ at $a = a^o$ (point G), it being understood that the employment $b = b^o$ of the other factor B is

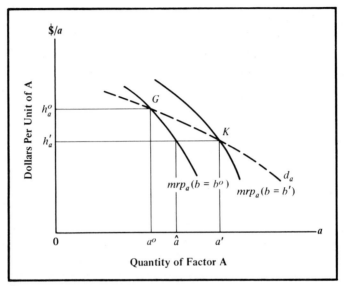

Figure 14. 14
Firm's Demand Curve for Factor

also such that $mrp_b(a = a^o) = h_b$. Now let the hire-pice h_a fall from h^o_a to the level h'_a. If the quantity of the other factor B remained unchanged, the firm would find it advantageous to employ $a = \hat{a}$ units of factor A, since at that level of employment, $mrp_a(b = b^o) = h'_a$. But now we must introduce an interaction associated with the concept of productive *complementarity* among factors.

Two factors are said to be *complementary* if increased employment of one raises the Marginal Product of the other.[19] Complementarity is the normal case, as a firm would rarely wish to employ factors which interfered with one another in production. Executives and secretaries, land and fertilizer, ships and sailors, are all examples of complementary pairs of factors. Two factors are said to be *independent* if increased employment of either has no effect upon the marginal productivity of the other. Handcraftsmen and mass-

[19]Recall that if both factors are productive, increased employment of one will always raise the *Total* Product of the other.

production machines might be an example. If a firm simultaneously produces high-quality hand products and low-quality machine products, it may be that the handcraftsmen work entirely apart from the machines so that there is no interaction one way or the other between them.[20]

Returning to Figure 14.14, suppose that factors A and B are complementary. Analysis of the interaction proceeds as follows. Let price h_a^o fall to h_a', leading to an initial employment expansion from a^o to $\hat{a}$ as just indicated. But this is not the full adjustment. The condition $mrp_b = h_b$ for the *other* factor B is now violated. For the increased employment of A will, assuming complementarity, shift the entire mrp_b curve (not illustrated) upward. This shift dictates more employment of factor B as well. When the secondary adjustment of factor-B employment is made, mrp_a will now in turn shift upward, and so on. This reciprocal interaction must have a limit, however. That is, there must be some increased employment of *both* factors such that the pair of equations (14.14) are restored. The restored equalities can be expressed more explicitly as:

$$\begin{cases} mrp_a(b = b') = h_a' \\ mrp_b(a = a') = h_b \end{cases}$$

Note that h_b is still at its original level; only the price of factor A has changed.

The upshot is that the firm's demand curve for factor A is related in a somewhat more complex way to the mrp_a curves than in the case where A was the only variable factor. In Figure 14.14 the demand curve goes through points like G (showing employment of a^o at price h_a^o) and K (showing employment of a' at price h_a').

Conclusion: Given normal complementarity between factors, the demand curve for any factor is flatter (or more elastic) than the Marginal Revenue Product curves. One implication is that employment of a variable factor tends to be more sensitive to price change in the *long run*, when the amounts of other factors can be varied.

If the factors are independent rather than complementary in production, the interaction effect disappears. Given an initial adjustment from a^o to $\hat{a}$ along the mrp_a curve in response to a fall in price from h_a^o to h_a', the condition $mrp_b = h_b$ for the *other* factor B is in no way disturbed. The initial adjustment is then the full adjustment. The initial mrp_a curve remains the firm's demand curve for factor A, as in the case of a single variable factor. Putting it more generally: In the case of productive *independence* between factors, each

---

[20]If increased employment of one factor actually reduced the Marginal Product of the other, the negative interaction could be called *anti-complementarity*. A possible instance might be the presence of both male and female workers along an assembly line, where the distracting effect of the sex difference overcomes the productive gain from mutual cooperation. Naturally, firms would be expected to avoid the employment of anti-complementary groups of factors.

factor's family of *mrp* curves coalesces into a single *mrp* curve that is not affected by the employment of the other factor.[21]

14. C INDUSTRY DEMAND FOR FACTORS

In proceeding from the *firm's* demand to the *industry's* demand for a factor of production, nothing essential will be lost in returning to the simple case of a single variable factor, as studied in Section 14.A.

First, consider the demand of a *monopolized* industry (i.e., an industry composed of a single seller in the product market) for a factor A. Evidently, the industry demand will be identical with the demand of the monopolist firm itself. The demand curve d_a of Figure 14.3, then becomes without further change the factor demand curve of the monopolized industry.[22]

If the industry consists of a large number of *competitive* producers in the product market, however, there is a complication. The two panels of Figure 14.15 show, respectively, the situations of a typical firm and of the competitive industry as a whole. Suppose an initial equilibrium exists at factor price $h_a = h_a^o$ and product price $P_x = P_x^o$. The firm's demand curve, derived from its curve of Marginal Revenue Product mrp_a (in this competitive case, identical with the firm's Value of Marginal Product vmp_a), is shown in Panel (a) as the curve labelled $d_a(P_x = P_x^o)$. Along the $d_a(P_x = P_x^o)$ curve, a^o is the indicated employment of factor A. For the industry as a whole, we can sum these firm d_a curves horizontally so as to obtain the curve labelled $\sum d_a(P_x = P_x^o)$. At the initial factor price h_a, this horizontal summation curve shows industry employment $A^o = \sum a^o$ of the factor (at point K).

Now let factor price fall to h_a'. In Panel (a) the firm will first move along the initial demand curve, $d_a(P_x = P_x^o)$, to employment level a^* of factor A. The corresponding industry-wide movement in Panel (b) would be to the aggregate employment level A^* (point N). But this is not the full solution. The increased employment of factor A will entail increased firm output of product X.[23] Correspondingly, the industry as a whole will expand aggregate output of X. Given a normally downward-sloping consumers' demand curve for good X, the rise in output will necessitate a fall in product price P_x. And

---

[21]What about "anti-complementary" factors? Intuition might suggest that if the firm's demand curve for factor A is *flatter* than the mrp_a curves in the complementary case and is *the same* as the (unique) mrp_a curve in the intermediate independent case, then it should be *steeper* than the mrp_a curves in the anti-complementary case. *This is incorrect!* In the anti-complementary as in the normal complementary case, the firm's demand curve for factor A is *flatter* than the mrp curves as illustrated in Figure 14.14. The student can verify this, making use of equations (14.14) in parallel with the argument used for the case of complementarity. (*Hint:* After the initial adjustment from a^o to $\hat{a}$, do the mrp_b curves shift up or down? What is the direction of the secondary effect upon the employment of B? How does that secondary effect further react upon the mrp_a curves?)

[22]Where more than one factor is variable, the demand curve d_a of Figure 14.14 becomes relevant.

[23]This is a necessary consequence if A is the only variable factor. With several variable factors, factor A might conceivably be "regressive," however (as explained in Section 14.B.4), in which case output would not expand.

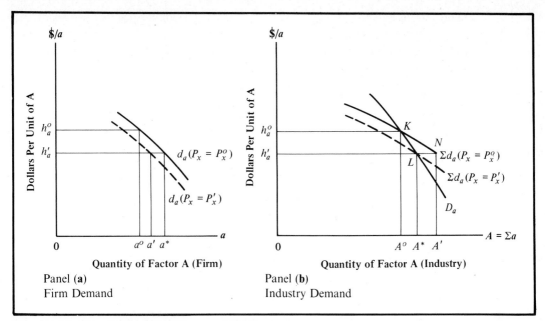

Figure 14. 15   Competitive Demand for Factor

since $vmp_a \equiv P_x(mp_a)$, each firm will observe a downward shift of the overall position of its d_a curve taking place.

After taking the product-price effect into account, the factor demands of the firm and industry at the new factor price h'_a are illustrated by the dashed curves in the two panels of Figure 14.15. Here *product* price P_x has fallen to the level P'_x. The firm operates along the lower (dashed) factor demand curve labelled $d_a(P_x = P'_x)$ to employ a' units of factor A. The industry correspondingly employs A' units in the aggregate, at point L on the horizontal summation curve $\sum d_a(P_x = P'_x)$. The precise amount that product price must fall is determined, of course, by the consumers' demand for the increased output of X generated by the augmented factor employment.[24] The true industry demand curve for factor A is illustrated in Panel (b) by the bold curve D_a that cuts through points K and L on the two different horizontal-summation curves.

Conclusion: The true *industry* demand curve is steeper (less elastic) than the horizontal-summation curves that represent the aggregate of firms' factor demands (under the artificial assumption of constant product price).

An economic analyst, then, might be led astray if he surveyed firms' intentions in attempting to assess the increased *industry* employment that would ensue from a lower factor price. For, the firms are all calculating in terms of the present product price. The analyst should discount firms' inten-

---

[24]With several variable factors, it would also be necessary to take account of possible changes in prices of *other factors*, consequent upon increased employment of factor A.

tions by allowing for the anticipated fall in product price that will result from increased industry output.

Demand for a factor is a *derived* demand. Firms and industries will employ factors only insofar as their employment contributes to the production of *goods* valued by consumers. The elements underlying demand for a particular factor can be summarized under two headings: physical marginal productivity, and value of the goods produced. These are in turn governed by more fundamental forces: (1) Physical marginal productivity of a particular factor *A* is determined, of course, by the laws of technology. But productivity is also affected by the availability and prices of *other* factors complementary to *A* in production. (2) The values placed by consumers, upon the goods to whose production factor *A* contributes, depend upon the demand-determining conditions studied in Part II: tastes, consumer incomes, etc. An additional element affecting factor demand is *market structure in the product market*. Specifically, we have seen that a monopolized industry will demand less of a factor than a competitive industry would ($mrp_a < vmp_a$).

Another question of importance concerns the determinants not of the *level* of factor demand but of its *elasticity*, i.e., its responsiveness to changes in factor price. Three propositions will be asserted without proof here: Demand for factor *A* will be more elastic: (1) the more elastic are the consumer demands for the goods produced by *A*; (2) the slower and less powerful is the operation of the Law of Diminishing Returns; and (3) the more elastic is the *supply* of factors complementary to *A* in production. These propositions are left for the student to verify.

14. D MONOPSONY IN THE FACTOR MARKET

The analysis so far in the current chapter has allowed for the possibility of monopoly power in the *product* market, while assuming competitive conditions (price-taking behavior) on both sides of the *factor* market. The possibility of monopoly *on the supply side* of the factor market will be considered in the next chapter. Here we turn to the analysis of a single buyer or "monopsonist" *on the demand side* of the factor market.

The situation of such a monopsonist is illustrated in Figure 14.16. The worth of incremental units of factor *A* to the firm is indicated, as before, by the curve of Marginal Revenue Product mrp_a. But the monopsonist firm recognizes that the supply curve of factor that it faces is upward-sloping (rather than effectively horizontal as in Figures 14.2 and 14.3). The firm is so large an employer of factor *A* that its own decisions to hire more or fewer units drive the price h_a up or down.

Recall that $C_a \equiv h_a a$ is the total expenditure of the firm in hiring factor *A*. With regard to C_a as a total, the supply curve s_a is a curve of Average Factor Cost afc_a, as $h_a \equiv C_a/a$ is the average amount that must be paid to hire any specified number of units of factor *A*. The *additional* expense incurred by the firm in hiring an incremental unit of factor *A* is its *Marginal* Factor Cost $mfc_a \equiv \Delta C_a/\Delta a$.

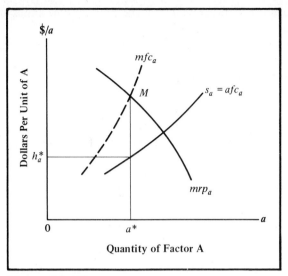

Figure 14. 16
Monopsony in the Factor Market

When the supply curve $s_a = afc_a$ is horizontal (as in Figures 14.2 and 14.3) the curve of Marginal Factor Cost mfc_a coincides with it at the level of the given market hire-price h_a. But here the afc_a curve is a rising function of factor quantity. Therefore the mfc_a curve must lie above it (Proposition 2.2b).

More explicitly, the increment of expense due to hiring an additional unit of factor is the sum of two elements: h_a is the payment to the additional unit of factor itself, and $a\Delta h_a$ is the expense due to the increased price paid to all units previously employed. Thus:

(14.15)
$$mfc_a \equiv \frac{\Delta C_a}{\Delta a} \equiv h_a + a\frac{\Delta h_a}{\Delta a}$$

Here the rising supply curve means that $\Delta h_a/\Delta a$ is positive in sign, thus verifying that $mfc_a > h_a \equiv afc_a$.

The optimality condition for the monopsonist firm is equality between the marginal benefit and the marginal expense of hiring factor A. Thus:

(14.16) $mrp_a = mfc_a$ Factor Employment Condition, Monopsony Firm

In Figure 14.16, this equality obtains at employment level a^*. The firm will then pay the factor price h_a^* required to elicit this quantity of factor, as indicated by the height of the supply curve s_a at $a = a^*$. Note that h_a^* lies *below* the intersection of mrp_a and mfc_a at point M in the diagram.

The analogy between the monopsonist solution in the factor market and the monopolist solution in the product market will not have escaped the reader. Geometrically, the factor-unit monopsony picture of Figure 14.16

is a kind of inverted analog of the product-unit monopoly picture in Figure 11.4.

With the alternative polar assumptions of price-taking versus monopolist behavior in the product market, and price-taking versus monopsonist behavior in the factor market, there are *four* basic cases to consider. The corresponding forms of the Factor Employment Condition (best amount of factor to hire) and the Optimum Output Condition (best amount of output to produce) are given in Table 14.1. The *general* result is that shown for the Monopolist-Monopsonist in the upper-left corner. But with price-taking behavior on one or both sides of the market, special cases are obtained: (1) price-taking behavior in the product market (in which case $MR \equiv AR \equiv P$); (2) price-taking behavior in the factor market (in which case $mfc_a \equiv afc_a \equiv h_a$); and (3) price-taking behavior in both markets, in which case both simplifying conditions apply. (Questions for the student: Which special case corresponds to the Conditions shown in the upper-right corner of the Table? Lower-left corner? Lower-right corner?)

Of course, the Factor Employment Condition and the Optimal Output Condition must be equivalent: The best amount of factors to employ must generate the most profitable level of output. In the footnote, this equivalence is shown for the Monopolist-Monopsonist optimality conditions which, being the most general, include all the others.[25]

[25]Algebraically, equations (14.15) and (14.16) can be combined and juxtaposed for comparison with equation (11.2):

(14.17)
$$mfc_a \equiv h_a + a\frac{\Delta h_a}{\Delta a} = mrp_a$$
$$MC = MR \equiv P_x + x\frac{\Delta P_x}{\Delta x}$$

The upper equation of (14.17) yields the solution for the optimal number of factor units to employ, and the lower for the optimal number of output units to produce.

If A is the only variable factor, we can write the following string of identities for Marginal Cost MC:

(14.18)
$$MC \equiv \frac{\Delta C}{\Delta x} \equiv \frac{\Delta C_a}{\Delta x} \equiv \frac{\Delta C_a}{\Delta a}\frac{\Delta a}{\Delta x}$$
$$\equiv \frac{mfc_a}{mp_a}$$

Now recall the familiar identity:

$$mrp_a \equiv MR(mp_a)$$

So the Factor Employment Condition $mfc_a = mrp_a$ can be written as:

$$MC(mp_a) = MR(mp_a)$$

Cancelling out mp_a, we have $MC = MR$, the Optimal Output Condition represented by the second equation of (14.17). As in the corresponding development in Section 14.A.2, determining the optimal number of factor units to employ is equivalent to fixing the optimal output to produce.

If there is more than one variable factor, an extension of the analysis in Section 14.B.3 will show that the Overall Firm Optimality Condition (14.13) becomes:

(14.19)
$$\frac{mrp_a}{mfc_a} = \frac{mrp_b}{mfc_b} = \frac{MR}{MC} = 1$$

Table 14. 1

Factor Employment and Optimal Output Conditions

Factor Market Structure	*Product Market Structure*	
	Monopolist	Price-taker
Monopsonist	$\begin{cases} mfc_a = mrp_a \\ MC = MR \end{cases}$	$\begin{cases} mfc_a = mrp_a \equiv vmp_a \\ MC = MR \equiv P \end{cases}$
Price-taker	$\begin{cases} h_a \equiv mfc_a = mrp_a \\ MC = MR \end{cases}$	$\begin{cases} h_a \equiv mfc_a = mrp_a \equiv vmp_a \\ MC = MR \equiv P \end{cases}$

Example 14. 4
Monopsony in
Professional
Baseball

The leading (and perhaps the only important) example of labor-market monopsony exists in the realm of professional sports. Here a legal quirk, perhaps based upon the idea that sports are play (a "pastime") rather than a business, has permitted the organization of buyers' cartels with respect to employment of players. The most important cartel instrument is the "reserve clause," which makes the player the exclusive property of the team that first signs him up, or to which he is "traded" thereafter. Should a player refuse to accept the wage offer of the team whose property he is, he cannot play for any other team in the cartel.

Gerald W. Scully investigated the effect of the reserve clause in major league baseball. He anticipated that the buyers' cartel would cause a divergence between Marginal Revenue Product *mrp* and wage (see Figure 14.16).

But first, differences in player *quality* (i.e., in *mrp*) had to be allowed for. Using 1968 and 1969 data, Scully estimated "gross" *mrp* in terms of the player's effect on gate receipts and broadcast revenues. Deducting related expenses, and in particular player development costs, led to estimates of "net" *mrp* for players of different qualities. (Since substantial player development costs, on the order of $300,000, are incurred before it is known how successful the athlete will be, it sometimes happens that net *mrp* turns out to be negative.) *On the average*, in a competitive situation wages would be equal to net *mrp*. If the actual structure is one of monopsony, however, wages on the average would fall short of net *mrp*.

The Table below shows some of Scully's results. For batters and pitchers falling into different quality groups, net *mrp* and average salary are compared. While for "mediocre" players salary is above net *mrp*—and indeed, the latter is actually negative—for "average" and "star" players, net *mrp* far exceeds salary. Thus, on balance there is considerable evidence of monopsony power.

Quality versus Pay of Baseball Players

	Quality Group	Net mrp	Salary
Hitters	Mediocre	$-30,000	$17,200
	Average	128,300	29,100
	Star	319,000	52,100
Pitchers	Mediocre	-10,600	15,700
	Average	159,600	33,000
	Star	405,300	66,800

Source: G. W. Scully, "Pay and Performance in Major League Baseball," *American Economic Review*, v. 64 (Dec. 1964), p. 928.

Comment: Contrary to common opinion among fans and sports writers, star players are not "overpaid." In fact, they receive far less than their economic worth.

14. E AN APPLICATION: MINIMUM-WAGE LAWS

Two economic models are in contention for explaining or predicting the consequences of minimum-wage legislation. For the *competitive-market model*, the effects of price floors or ceilings are as previously discussed in Section 2.A. The alternative *monopsony-market model* is based on the analysis of the preceding section 14.D.

The competitive model is illustrated in Figure 14.17. The commodity is labor L, whose hire-price is the wage rate w. An initial competitive equilibrium

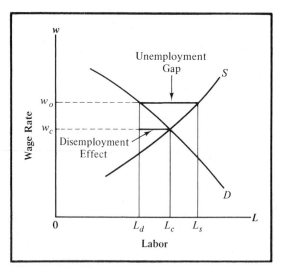

Figure 14. 17
Minimum Wage, Competitive Model

exists at wage w_c and employment L_c. Now a minimum wage is imposed, at a level w_o higher than w_c.[26] At wage w_o the labor offered on the market is the quantity L_s but the labor demanded is only L_d. The perceived *unemployment gap* at the legal wage is $L_s - L_d$. However, the *disemployment effect* actually due to the floor is the somewhat lesser quantity $L_c - L_d$. Analysts using the competitive-market model would clearly predict some degree of disemployment and a larger degree of unemployment, as a result of imposition of a minimum wage higher than the pre-existing market equilibrium wage.

The monopsony model leads to rather different implications, illustrated in Figure 14.18. The pre-existing situation has employment L_m (at the inter-

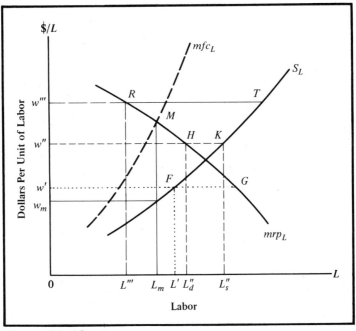

Figure 14. 18
Minimum Wage, Monopsony Model

section of the mrp_L and mfc_L curves); the wage $w_m < mrp_L$ is determined along the labor supply curve S_L (as in Figure 14.16). With the introduction of an effective minimum-wage law, *the market supply curve is replaced by a horizontal line at the level of the imposed minimum wage* (in the range where the market supply curve S_L lies below the level of the minimum wage). That is, the monopsonist employer is *forced to be a price-taker* at the minimum wage, wherever the market supply conditions would otherwise have permitted establishing a monopsony hire-price lower than the legally imposed wage.

Three classes of possibilities are illustrated in Figure 14.18. First, suppose that the minimum wage is only a little higher than w_m, for example, w' in the diagram. Then the *effective* supply curve to the firm is horizontal at the level

[26]A minimum wage *lower* than w_c would clearly be without effect.

w' until the S_L curve is reached at point F. In this range the Marginal Factor Cost mfc also equals w'. The firm would actually want to employ the quantity associated with point G, where $w' = mrp_L$. However, this solution is not possible on supply grounds. The laborers would not supply more than L' units at wage w'; if more than this amount of labor supply is to be elicited, the wage would have to rise above w'. Consequently, the employment level would be L'. Note that, relative to L_m, the minimum-wage law here has *increased* employment! Nor is there any perceived unemployment at the legally imposed wage.

Now consider a somewhat higher minimum wage indicated by w'' in Figure 14.18. At this wage the firm would again be forced to be a price-taker, and would not want to employ more than L_d'' units (at point H), using the condition $w'' = mrp_L$. This employment is also greater than the L_m of the unregulated monopsony solution; no *disemployment* takes place. However, since w'' is a wage higher than the intersection of the S_L and mrp_L curves, some *unemployment* will be perceived. At the w'' wage, the offered labor supply would be L_s'' which is more than the firm wants to hire. The resulting unemployment gap is indicated by the distance HK in the diagram.

Finally, w''' represents a still higher minimum wage, higher than the level at which the mrp_L and mfc_L curves intersect. Here the effective employment would be reduced to L'''. Thus, a minimum wage as high as w''' would lead to the same qualitative implications as in the competitive-market model. With this high wage there would be some *disemployment* as compared with L_m, and a large *unemployment* gap represented by the distance RT in the diagram.

Conclusion: The competitive-market model unambiguously implies both disemployment (less L employed) and unemployment (a supply-demand gap) as a result of any minimum wage higher than the unregulated equilibrium. The monopsony-market model has three possible outcomes: (1) At a relatively low minimum wage w', employment actually increases; there is no disemployment or unemployment. (2) At an intermediate minimum wage w'', employment increases but there is some unemployment. (3) At a relatively high minimum wage w''', there is both disemployment and considerable unemployment.

Which of these models is the more relevant? That is an empirical question that has been subjected to investigation by a number of economists.

Example 14. 5
Minimum-Wage
Legislation

In determining the effects of minimum-wage legislation upon wages and employment, it is essential to appreciate that labor is not homogeneous. There is a spectrum of labor skill and quality. At the moment of imposition of a new or increased legal minimum wage, some workers will already be earning more than the imposed minimum and others less. Under any market model, minimum-wage laws will have quite different impacts upon high-wage and low-wage workers.

Using the competitive model, low-skilled (low-wage) workers would be affected as in Figure 14.17: Their wage rates would rise, but some of them would suffer substantial disemployment. There would be no *direct* impact upon high-skilled workers already earning more than the minimum wage. (However, there may be an *indirect* effect on them due to the higher wage imposed upon employers of low-skilled workers.) If the monopsony model of Figure 14.18 were valid, on the other hand, we would expect to observe one important difference: there should be medium-skilled workers for whom the increased minimum wage causes both a higher wage rate and *higher* employment. (These would be workers initially earning a wage somewhat less than, but not too far below, the new minimum wage.)

An early study by A. F. Hinrichs[27] classified plants in the seamless hosiery industry by wage group. It was found that, after imposition of the 25-cent minimum wage in October 1938, low-wage plants had a relatively greater loss in employment (and a relatively greater rise in average hourly earnings) than high-wage plants. Indeed, despite generally improving business conditions, the lowest-wage plants suffered an *absolute* loss in employment. A more extensive study by J. M. Peterson[28] confirmed Hinrichs' results as to the seamless hosiery industry, and showed a similar picture for Southern sawmills and for men's cotton garments, over several steps of minimum-wage increases between 1938 and 1950. The pattern was consistent, in that in each case low-wage plants lost relatively more in employment while paying a relatively greater wage increment. In addition, Peterson showed a relative loss in employment position for low-wage versus high-wage *cities*, and a *regional* tendency of industry to shift away from the low-wage South. The regional effect was emphasized in a study by M. R. Colberg,[29] who examined the impact of the 1957 $1.00 minimum-wage law upon high-wage and low-wage *counties* in Florida. The law was found to have caused a relative decrease in employment in low-wage counties.

A number of recent studies have directed attention specifically to low-wage *workers*, and particularly to the effects of minimum-wage laws on *teenagers*. In general, teenagers are relatively lacking in the skills and experience necessary to earn high wages. Hence a large fraction of them are likely to be in the position where a uniform legal minimum

[27]A. F. Hinrichs, "Effects of the 25-Cent Minimum Wage on Employment in the Seamless Hosiery Industry," *Journal of the American Statistical Association*, v. 35 (March 1940).
[28]J. M. Peterson, "Employment Effects of Minimum Wages, 1938–50," *Journal of Political Economy*, v. 65 (Oct. 1957).
[29]M. R. Colberg, "Minimum Wage Effects on Florida's Economic Development," *Journal of Law and Economics*, v. 3 (Oct. 1960).

wage is higher than their equilibrium market wage. Under the competitive model, in consequence, a relatively large disemployment effect upon teenagers would be anticipated. A study by Y. Brozen[30] found that successive increases in the legal minimum wage were indeed reflected by rises in the teenage unemployment rate. But as productivity and inflation progressed over time, the equilibrium wage for teenagers tended to "catch up" with the legally fixed minimum so as to erode the disemployment effect, until the next round of minimum-wage legislation began the cycle over again.

A sophisticated statistical regression analysis over the period 1954–1968 by T. G. Moore allowed not only for the *level* of the minimum wage but for its *coverage* of the labor force (since, over time, not only level but coverage has tended to increase). A portion of Moore's results are shown in the following Table.

Relation of Younger Age-Group Unemployment
to Minimum Wage

| | Determining Variables | | |
| | *Employed* | |
Unemployment Rate of:	*Unemployment Rate, Males 25 and Older (%)*	*Workers Covered by Minimum Wage (%)*	*Minimum Wage as Proportion of Hourly Earnings*
Nonwhites, 16–19	1.428	.2549	1.75927
Whites, 16–19	1.2628	.077	.58461
Males, 16–19	1.779	.080	.61649
Females, 16–19	.915	.171	.73988
Males, 20–24	1.586	−.063	.05346

Source: T. G. Moore, "The Effect of Minimum Wages on Teenage Unemployment Rates," *Journal of Political Economy*, v. 79 (July/Aug. 1971), p. 901.

The data in the Table may be interpreted as follows, using the first row as an example. The unemployment rate of Nonwhites aged 16–19: (1) Increased 1.428% for each percent rise in the unemployment rate of males 25 and older. (This reflects the high sensitivity of the teenage unemployment rate to changes in *general* business conditions and levels of unemployment.) (2) Increased .2549% for each percent rise in the *coverage* of the minimum-wage law. And (3) Increased 1.75927% for each percent increase in the *ratio* of the legal minimum wage to the average hourly earnings of production workers in private nonagricultural employment. Note that males 20–24, above the teenage category, were *not* substantially affected by the minimum-wage legislation (bottom row).

[30] Y. Brozen, "The Effect of Statutory Minimum Wage Increases on Teen-Age Unemployment," *Journal of Law & Economics*, v. 12 (April 1969).

Comment: All these studies provide solid confirmation for the predictions of the competitive model of Figure 14.17. The monopsony model of Figure 14.18, being consistent with a variety of outcomes, is not conclusively refuted by these results. However, none of the studies show any hint of the *favorable* effect of a minimum-wage law on employment of some middle-quality workers, that is predicted by the monopsony model.

Regardless of economic impact, it appears that minimum-wage legislation must have satisfied some criteria of *political* effectiveness to have become so important a feature of the economic situation. The supposed "beneficiaries"—those directly impacted low-wage workers receiving less than the minimum wage (largely teenagers and "minorities")—have mixed incentives with regard to such legislation. While most of the directly impacted group will indeed receive a wage increase, a good proportion are likely to find themselves disemployed. The most significant political pressure for higher minimum wages seems to come from organized labor, in particular the AFL-CIO. Few of the relatively high-paid workers represented by the AFL-CIO are in the directly impacted group receiving less than the minimum wage. It is for such skilled, high-wage workers that an increased minimum wage represents an unalloyed (though indirect) benefit! A higher minimum wage raises the cost of unskilled relative to skilled workers. The consequence is to induce firms to employ fewer of the unskilled workers, raising demand for the skilled workers represented by the AFL-CIO.

Questions

1. Draw a typical Total Product curve tp_a for a factor of production A. Compare the implications for the Average Product and Marginal Product curves if tp_a has a positive or has a zero intercept on the output axis. Compare the implications if tp_a is increasing at an increasing rate in the initial portion of the curve or if tp_a is increasing at a decreasing rate from the very beginning.

2. As the quantity of factor A increases, explain why the point of diminishing *marginal* returns is reached first, then the point of diminishing *average* returns, and finally the point of diminishing *total* returns.

3. What is the empirical justification for the Law of Diminishing Returns?

4. Does the curve of Marginal Revenue Product for factor A, mrp_a, necessarily lie below (to the left of) the curve of Value of the Marginal Product, vmp_a? Explain. Which is the firm's demand curve for factor A?

5. Why is $mrp_a = h_a$ the Factor Employment Condition for a price-taking firm in the *factor* market? What if the firm is not a price-taker in the *product* market? Is this condition sufficient, or are there other subsidiary conditions that must be met?

6. Is it ever rational to employ so much of a factor as to be in the region of diminishing marginal returns? In the region of diminishing average returns? In the region of diminishing total returns?

7. If there is only one factor capable of being varied, does the Law of Diminishing Returns rule out the possibility of constant or increasing returns to scale? What if there is more than one variable factor?

8. With two factors A and B, explain why the conditions $mrp_a = h_a$ and $mrp_b = h_b$ lead not only to the choice of optimal factor proportions but also to the optimal *scale* of output.

9. Do firms tend to "specialize" or to "diversify" in the employment of factors? Explain why *convex* output isoquants are consistent with observation. What would be observed if output isoquants were *concave* to the origin?

10. With two factors of production, is the slope of the output isoquant equal (in absolute value) to the ratio of the Marginal Products? Explain. Interpret the absolute slope of the *cost* isoquant as a ratio.

11. If the price of one of two variable factors declines, show in terms of the Scale Expansion Path that the firm will necessarily use *relatively* more of the cheapened factor than before. Will the firm's *output* necessarily increase? Will the firm necessarily employ *absolutely* more of the cheapened factor?

12. Why will the demand curve of a competitive industry for a factor of production be less elastic than the summation of the demand curves of the separate firms? What if the industry is monopolized rather than competitive?

13. True or false? Explain in each case. The economy-wide demand curve for factor A will be more elastic:
   a. The more inelastic the consumer demand for goods in the production of which A is employed.
   b. The weaker the operation of the Law of Diminishing Returns as employment of A is varied.
   c. The more elastic is the *supply* of factors complementary to A.

14. Can a demand curve for factor A be derived if the employer of A is a *monopsonist*? That is, is there a relation that shows the quantity employed as a function of price? Why or why not?

15. With regard to Table 14.1, the monopolist–monopsonist Factor Employment Condition $mfc_a = mrp_a$ is said to be the "most general." Show that this condition also covers the case of a firm that is a price-taker in both product and factor markets.

16. Show how, upon imposition of a minimum-wage law, the monopsony model might predict *increased* employment. Given an initial dispersion of wage rates (high-skilled, mid-skilled, and low-skilled workers) under this model, which groups would tend to find employment decreasing and which increasing? Compare the predictions with the competitive model. Apart from the studies reviewed in the text, what other data might shed light as to the comparative validity of the monopsony versus the competitive models?

Chapter 15
Factor Supply, Factor-Market Equilibrium, and Income Distribution

In this chapter, *the supply side of the factor market* completes the round of the circular flow of economic activity first pictured in Figure 1.1. Factor supplies derive ultimately from the choices of resource-owners between two alternatives: market versus non-market uses ("reservation uses") of the factors under their control. These choices constitute the topic of the first two sections. The interaction of factor supply and demand, leading to the determination of competitive equilibrium in the factor markets, is taken up in Section C, together with the analysis of forces disturbing or modifying this equilibrium. Monopoly on the supply side of the factor market is considered in Section D (monopoly on the demand side, or *monopsony*, having been studied in the previous chapter). The distribution of income, i.e., the division of the national product among various categories and classes of resource-owners, is the next subject. This leads finally into the topic of "capital," or more generally, the intertemporal choice process that generates changes in resource supplies over time.

15. A THE OPTIMUM OF THE RESOURCE-OWNER

In the analysis of consumption and demand in Chapter 4, the individual was postulated to be already in possession of a given income I out of which he could purchase desired consumption goods. But of course this income does not come out of thin air; *income consists of earnings received from the employment of resources (factors) owned.* Thus the consumer, viewed from another aspect, is the resource-owner.

In his resource-owning role, as in his consumptive role, everyone has a decision problem. He must decide how much to supply on the market, as against the alternative of reserving some or all of his owned resources for his own non-market use. For concreteness, let us think in terms of an owner of

381

Chapter 15
Factor Supply,
Factor-Market
Equilibrium, and
Income Distribution

his own labor capacity. Then the decision problem is *between labor income and "leisure."*[1]

Figure 15.1 shows an individual's preference map in terms of indifference curves between *income I* (which stands here as a proxy for the consumption goods purchasable out of income) and *leisure R* (i.e., reservation uses of his time). The arrows showing preference directions indicate that income and leisure are both "goods" rather than "bads." Before any exchange takes place, the individual at his *endowment* position E has R^t units of leisure at his disposal (24 hours per day, let us say) and I^t units of endowed or non-labor income from property earnings. The diagram is bounded both on the right and on the left. The bound on the right at R^t says that, no matter what, the individual cannot "buy" more than 24 hours of leisure per day; the bound on the left says that he cannot sell more than 24 hours of his labor per day!

The opportunity set is indicated by the shaded area lying below the budget line EK. Starting from E, as the person sells an hour of labor (i.e., sacrifices an hour of leisure) he receives in exchange the hourly *wage rate* h_L, where h_L is the "hire-price" of labor. If the individual is a price-taker with respect to the wage rate, the budget line has constant slope $\Delta I/\Delta R = -h_L$.[2] The wage

---

[1]"Leisure" perhaps suggests a mere lazing away of one's time. But the term as used here covers time devoted also to productive activities, so long as these are outside the market context. An obvious and enormously important example is home-making: the housewife provides productive services that would be extremely costly to procure on the market. (Even husbands provide labor inputs into household productive activity.)

[2]More explicitly, the slope of the budget line might be expressed as $-h_L/P_I$, where P_I is the "price" of a unit of income. But P_I is by definition unity, since income is measured in units of "numeraire," in this case dollars.

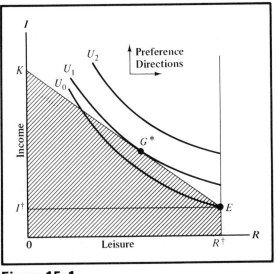

Figure 15. 1
Optimum of the Resource-Owner

382

Chapter 15
Factor Supply,
Factor-Market
Equilibrium, and
Income Distribution

rate h_L can be regarded equivalently as the price of an hour *of labor* or of an hour *of leisure*. The equation of the budget line is:

(15.1) $$h_L R + I = h_L R^\dagger + I^\dagger$$

This equation tells us that the value of the individual's endowment, shown on the right-hand side as his non-labor income $I^\dagger$ plus the market value $h_L R^\dagger$ of his endowed time, must equal his achieved income I plus the market value $h_L R$ of the leisure that he in effect "purchases" (by not working). Alternatively, this same relation can be formulated in terms of *labor or working hours* L rather than leisure hours R, where by definition $L \equiv R^\dagger - R$. Then (15.1) can be rewritten:

(15.1') $$I^\dagger + h_L L = I$$

In this form, the budget equation tells us that the person's achieved income I is composed of his endowed or property income $I^\dagger$ plus his labor earnings $h_L L$.

The individual's *resource-employment optimum* (balance between market and reservation uses of his labor-time resource) is at the tangency position G^* in Figure 15.1. The logic is entirely parallel to that used in finding the *consumptive optimum* in Section 4.A (compare Figure 4.1). That is, G^* is the point on the highest indifference curve attainable within the opportunity set.

Analytically, the tangency condition can be expressed as a Substitution Equivalence Equation between two Marginal Rates of Substitution:

(15.2) $$MRS_R = MRS_E \equiv h_L$$

This equation, in exactly the same form as equation (4.4), says: At a tangency optimum the *Marginal Rate of Substitution in Resource Supply* (i.e., the ratio $\left.\dfrac{\Delta I}{\Delta R}\right|_U$ representing the amount of additional income ΔI for which the individual is just *willing* to sacrifice another unit of leisure ΔR) must be equal to the *Marginal Rate of Substitution in Exchange* between income and leisure (i.e., the ratio $\left.\dfrac{\Delta I}{\Delta R}\right|_E$ representing the income increment h_L which the market *permits* him to acquire in exchange for another hour of leisure). MRS_R is the absolute value of the indifference-curve slope in Figure 15.1; following the argument of Section 4.A, MRS_R can also be interpreted as the ratio of the *Marginal Utilities* of leisure and income—$MRS_R \equiv MU_R/MU_I$. MRS_E is the absolute slope of the budget line, or in this case simply the wage rate h_L. So (15.2) can equivalently be written:[3]

(15.2') $$\frac{MU_R}{MU_I} = h_L$$

---

[3]*Mathematical Footnote:* Using the method of Lagrangian multipliers, the optimization problem of the resource-owner can be expressed as:

$$\operatorname*{Max}_{(I, R, \lambda)} L = U(I, R) - \lambda(h_L R + I - h_L R^\dagger - I^\dagger)$$

383

Chapter 15
Factor Supply,
Factor-Market
Equilibrium, and
Income Distribution

As in Chapter 4, *convexity* of the indifference curves here is justified by the observation of "diversification" between income and leisure. (People normally work somewhere between zero and 24 hours per day!) Of course, an individual very well endowed with property income (very large $I^\dagger$) might choose not to work at all. In terms of the geometry, such a "corner solution" would be preferred if the indifference curve U_0 in Figure 15.1 were steeper than the budget line EK at the endowment position E.[4]

Continuing to pursue the analogy with the consumptive optimum of Chapter 4, let us now consider what happens: (1) when endowed (non-labor) income $I^\dagger$ varies, and (2) when price h_L changes.

Variation of income is illustrated in Figure 15.2, where the budget line takes successively higher positions from $E°K°$ to $E'K'$ to $E''K''$. Both income I and leisure R are by assumption "normal" goods. That is, an upward shift of the budget line due to a rise in endowed non-labor income $I^\dagger$ would be expected to lead to increased consumptive income I *and* increased leisure R. The consequence is a positively-sloped *Income Expansion Path* (IEP). The individual takes only part of the benefit of any increment of endowed income in the form of consumption goods; the remainder of the gain is taken in the form of increased leisure.

Figure 15.3 shows the consequence of variation in h_L, the wage rate or "price of leisure." As the wage rate rises, the budget line rotates around the endowment position E so as to become increasingly steep. The *Price Expansion Path* (PEP) goes through all the tangency-optimum positions along these steepening budget lines $EK°$, EK', EK'', ... For relatively low wage rates the negative slope of PEP indicates that more labor L will be offered (i.e., less leisure R "purchased") as the wage rises. But for sufficiently high wage rates, it is quite possible for PEP to enter a range of positive slope (in the diagram, the range above G') where a higher wage will lead to a *lesser* quantity of labor offered.

Then:

$$\frac{\partial L}{\partial I} = \frac{\partial U}{\partial I} - \lambda \quad = 0$$

$$\frac{\partial L}{\partial R} = \frac{\partial U}{\partial R} - \lambda h_L = 0$$

$$h_L R + I - h_L R^\dagger - I^\dagger = 0$$

Eliminating λ in the first two equations:

$$\frac{\partial U/\partial R}{\partial U/\partial I} = h_L$$

This is the form of (15.2′).

The form (15.2) follows directly from the equivalences:

$$-\frac{dI}{dR}\bigg|_U \equiv \frac{\partial U/\partial R}{\partial U/\partial I} \equiv MRS_R \quad \text{and} \quad -\frac{dI}{dR}\bigg|_E \equiv h_L \equiv MRS_E$$

[4]The analytical condition for this corner solution is that at $R = R^\dagger$, $MRS_R > MRS_E$.

384

Chapter 15
Factor Supply,
Factor-Market
Equilibrium, and
Income Distribution

This seemingly puzzling situation is due to the interaction of the *income effect* and the *substitution effect* of the change in h_L. As explained in Section 4.C, when the substitution effect alone of a price change is considered (i.e., when real income is held constant) a *rise* in price must lead to a *fall* in quantity purchased. In this case, an increase in the wage rate h_L means a rise in the price of leisure and so less leisure will be "purchased." And since choice of a smaller amount of leisure means that labor supplied must be larger, the *pure substitution effect dictates that the higher the wage* h_L *the greater the hours worked* L.

But an increase in wage is not a pure substitution phenomenon. As the individual here is a *seller of labor*, he is effectively enriched by any increase in the wage rate. And since leisure is a normal good, the income or enrichment effect considered in isolation would lead to *greater* "purchases" of leisure as the wage rises. Thus, the income and substitution effects of a wage change act in opposite directions. This contrasts with the situation in the theory of consumption, where, for a "normal" superior good, the substitution effect and the income effect of a price change are *reinforcing*.

Not only does the income effect act in opposition to the substitution effect in the labor-supply decision, but the *magnitude* of the income effect is relatively large. The reason is the contrast between "diversification in consumption" and "specialization in production." Since the consumer generally buys a wide variety of products, a rise in the price of any single commodity is not likely to improverish him substantially. But in terms of factor-supply, there is one single price that will be *very* important for the resource-owner,

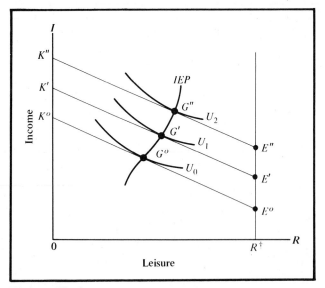

Figure 15. 2
Income Expansion Path

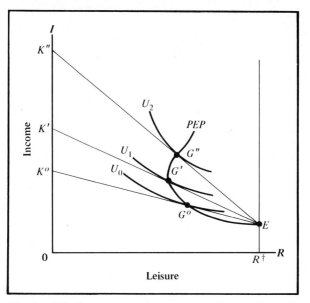

Figure 15. 3
Price Expansion Path

namely, the wage of the particular type of labor service in which he special-izes. Changes in this wage will normally mean a very considerable shift in real income.

Despite the importance of the income effect, *the substitution effect must nevertheless dominate the labor-supply decision at very low wage rates.* This may be seen as follows. Since the indifference-curve slope is negative at the endowment position E, there is some wage rate so low (corresponding to this slope) that it would elicit from the person a zero offer of labor.[5] If we con-sider wage rates only slightly above this, any income or enrichment effect must be very small. The magnitude of enrichment due to a wage increase is on the order of $L(\Delta h_L)$, where Δh_L is the wage increment and L is the hours worked. If L is close to zero hours, the person cannot be *substantially* enriched by a wage-rate change. It is only in the upper regions of the PEP curve that enough hours are worked to make the enrichment $L(\Delta h_L)$ substantial, in which case it might overcome the substitution effect so as to cause the PEP curve to enter a range of reversed slope as shown in Figure 15.3.

Conclusion: In the resource-employment decision, the income and sub-stitution effects of changes in hire-price h_L work in opposite directions. The substitution effect must dominate (more employment will be chosen as h_L rises) at low hire-prices; the income effect may dominate, however, for suffi-ciently high h_L.

385

[5]As would, of course, any still lower wage.

Existing relief or "welfare" arrangements for support of the unemployed have a strongly adverse effect upon the incentive to work. The Negative Income Tax proposal is an attempt to overcome this adverse effect.

With some oversimplification, the current welfare-relief arrangement may be pictured as in Figure 15.4. The individual here is assumed to have no

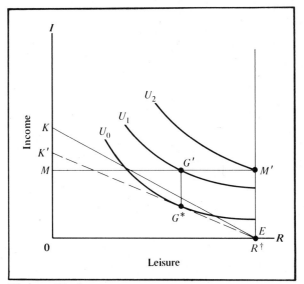

Figure 15. 4
Employment versus Welfare, I

property income, and so his endowment position E lies along the horizontal axis at $R = R^\dagger$ (24 hours of leisure per day). The pre-tax wage rate at which he could work is reflected in the slope of the solid budget line EK; in the absence of taxes or a welfare system, he would find a tangency optimum (not shown) along EK. But in actuality he would have to pay income and social security taxes on his labor earnings, so that his effective or post-tax budget line is the dashed EK'.[6] Along EK', his employment optimum is indicated by the tangency with indifference curve U_0 at G^*.

Now suppose that the welfare system provides a level of *minimal income maintenance* represented by the horizontal line MM'. This means that, should earnings from employment be less than the amount $OM = EM'$, they will be supplemented to bring income I up to that level. A person who attains G^* by working would therefore receive a cash payment bringing him up to posi-

---

*Starred sections represent optional or advanced material.
[6]The diagram assumes that taxes on income are a simple proportion of earnings. Ideally, we should allow for exemptions, progressivity, and other complex features of the tax structure. But doing so is not essential for our purposes.

387

Chapter 15
Factor Supply,
Factor-Market
Equilibrium, and
Income Distribution

tion G' on MM'. But if leisure is always a good, the position M' on indifference curve U_2, attainable without working at all, is clearly preferred to G' on indifference curve U_1. Subject to the proviso that income and leisure are both *goods* (preference directions are north and east), no one will work at all if his employment optimum G^* along EK' lies below MM'.[7]

Furthermore, even for some individuals whose employment optimum G^* would otherwise lie *well above* MM', the no-work position M' available under welfare may still be preferable. In Figure 15.5, indifference curve U_1

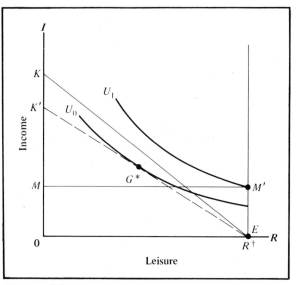

Figure 15. 5
Employment versus Welfare, II

through M' again represents a higher level of satisfaction than can be achieved at the employment optimum G^*. Even though G^* would generate more spendable income I than received under the dole, the increased leisure at point M' may be valued more highly by the individual.

The Negative Income Tax (NIT), as an alternative to the existing welfare system, is pictured in Figure 15.6. We see once again the pre-tax (solid) budget line EK and the after-tax (dashed) budget line of the previous diagram, with an employment optimum G^* that is inferior (in the eyes of the individual) to the unemployment position at M' attainable under the welfare system. The NIT alternative is based upon the following considerations: (1) The income maintenance level MM' is still guaranteed to the individual, whether or not he works. (2) A "breakeven level" of income is established, represented by the horizontal line BB' in the diagram, that is *higher* than

---

[7]Welfare administrators sometimes attempt to require that those capable of working do so. But, *de facto*, effective control is very limited. An unwilling worker can easily arrange to be discharged by his employer.

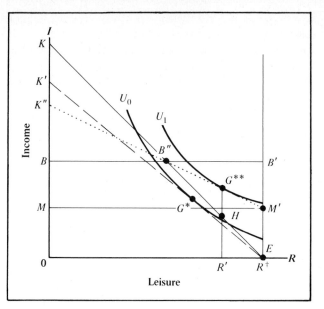

Figure 15. 6
NIT versus Welfare, I

MM'. (3) Above the breakeven level, the individual is a payer of (positive) taxes; below, he is a recipient of (negative) taxes.

The effect is to make a different NIT budget line, represented in Figure 15.6 by the dotted $M'K''$, relevant for the individual's employment decision. $M'K''$ incorporates the effect of positive or negative taxes. It intersects the horizontal breakeven line BB' at the point B'' which also lies on the pre-tax (solid) budget line EK. If the person supplied so much labor as to attain the position B'', he would neither pay taxes nor receive any supplementary income. Beyond B'', he would be a net payer of taxes,[8] but short of B'' he would be a net recipient of income supplement.[9] In the case illustrated in the diagram, he chooses the position G^{**}, offering $L = R^\dagger - R'$ hours of labor. His pre-tax earnings are $R'H$ in the diagram, and his income supplement is HG^{**}. He is working (at least some hours) under the NIT, and there is to that extent a social gain over the welfare system that led him to prefer total unemployment.

Defenders of NIT point to the psychologically corrosive effect of welfare-induced unemployment upon the worker's sense of independence and self-esteem. Opponents point out, on the other hand, that the NIT may itself constitute a source of psychological corrosion for a *much larger* number of workers who will now be receiving "unearned" income supplements from government, even though remaining (to some extent, at any rate) employed. Furthermore, the higher *marginal* tax rate under NIT (flatter slope of $M'K''$

[8]That is, the pre-tax budget line EK is *higher* than the NIT budget line $M'K''$ in this range.
[9]That is, in this range EK is lower than $M'K''$.

388

389

Chapter 15
Factor Supply,
Factor-Market
Equilibrium, and
Income Distribution

as compared with *EK'* in Figure 15.6) is likely to induce working individuals to choose a lesser *degree* of employment.

Both of these adverse effects are illustrated in Figure 15.7. This diagram again compares the welfare after-tax budget line *EK'* (dashed) with the NIT after-tax budget line *M'K''* (dotted). (The *pre-tax* budget line *EK* of the previous diagram is not needed here, and so has been omitted.) But the individual's preferences and opportunities are now such that under the welfare system his preferred position along *EK'* is at *G** on indifference curve U_0; he does not accept relief, but on the contrary shows a relatively great willingness to work. Along *M'K''*, however, his preferred position is *G*** along indifference curve U_1. As is evident, under NIT the individual will work far fewer hours. Furthermore, he has also been induced to abandon a position of sturdy tax-paying independence at *G** in favor of a socially dependent role below the breakeven income level *BB'*.

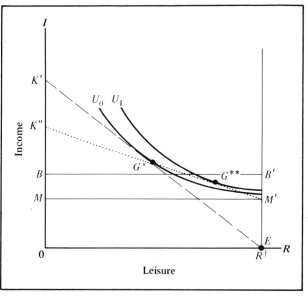

Figure 15. 7
NIT versus Welfare, II

It is even possible that an individual who would have chosen employment under the welfare-relief system could turn to unemployment under the NIT! Such a situation is illustrated in Figure 15.8. The analysis (showing that *G** along *EK'* would have been preferred to the welfare-unemployment position *M'*, but that unemployment at *M'* is superior to any other attainable position along the NIT budget line *M'K''*) is left to the student as an exercise.

Whether the NIT proposal is on balance a desirable one depends, at least in part, upon the frequency with which the various types of situations described in these diagrams will be encountered. A number of experiments are now being conducted to cast light upon this question.

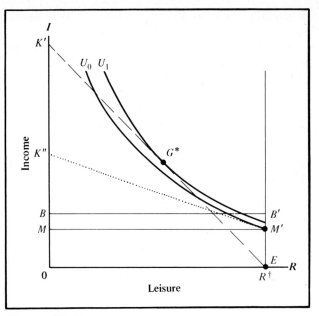

Figure 15. 8
NIT versus Welfare, III

15. C RESOURCE SUPPLY TO THE MARKET, AND FACTOR-MARKET EQUILIBRIUM

The data represented by a person's Price Expansion Path PEP of Figure 15.3 could be plotted in a separate diagram on R, h_L axes as his "demand curve for leisure R." It is more usual, however, to present the data on L, h_L axes as his *supply curve for labor L*, where by definition $L \equiv R^\dagger - R$ as before. Figure 15.9 shows such an individual supply curve s_L. Along s_L, as argued in Section 15.A, the slope is surely positive in the lower range: At very low wage

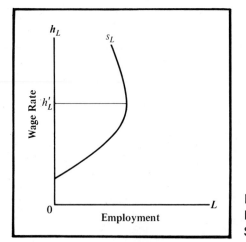

Figure 15. 9
Backward-Bending
Supply Curve of Labor

391

Chapter 15
Factor Supply,
Factor-Market
Equilibrium, and
Income Distribution

rates, an increased wage will elicit increased offers of labor hours. It *may* be the case, however, that above some particular wage rate h'_L any further wage augmentation will lead to a decreased labor offer; should that occur, the labor-supply curve is said to be "backward-bending" in the range above h'_L.

When individual supply curves are aggregated (summed horizontally), the overall factor-market supply curve S_L is obtained as in Figure 15.10. The aggregate S_L is likely to have a normal positive slope even if some of the component individual supply curves have backward-bending ranges, since the various individuals' h'_L points as in Figure 15.9 will differ. But it is possible that even the aggregate supply curve may be found to be backward-bending at high wage rates.

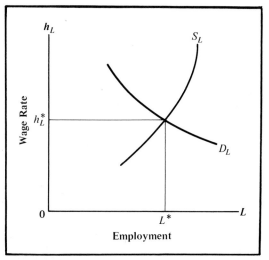

Figure 15. 10
Equilibrium in the Factor Market

Market equilibrium under conditions of competition is of course determined by the intersection (as shown in Figure 15.10) of the aggregate supply curve just discussed and the aggregate demand curve derived in the previous chapter. Changes in equilibrium price and quantity, as always, come about as a result of shifts in supply or demand functions, or both.

In terms of the discussion of determinants of factor demand in Section 14.C, we know that the forces that may shift *demand* functions for factors include:

1. *Technological change:* Technical progress tends to shift Marginal Product (*mp*) upward, and hence to increase $mrp \equiv MR(mp)$ that determines firms' demand for factors.[10]

---

[10]It is possible (though not very likely) for technical progress to have a favorable effect on Average Product *ap* while reducing Marginal Product *mp* (for some or all factors) in the relevant range. Since factor demand is related to the *Marginal* Product, such a change would, at least in the neighborhood of the previous equilibrium, tend to shift the factor demand curve *downward*.

392

Chapter 15
Factor Supply,
Factor-Market
Equilibrium, and
Income Distribution

2. *Demand for final products:* Similarly, an increase in the demand for some product, leading to a rise in its price and associated Marginal Revenue, raises the demand for any factor used in its production.

3. *Supply of cooperating or competing factors:* As the Marginal Products of different factors are interrelated (as discussed in Section 14.B), the demand for any one will be affected by changes in the availability of other factors that can complement it or substitute for it. In particular, an increase in the *supply* of one of a pair of complementary factors will raise the *demand* for the other.

Some of the important influences operating to shift *factor supply* functions are:

1. *Wealth:* Higher endowed wealth increases the ability to "purchase" *reservation uses* of owned factors, and hence tends to diminish the supply offered on the market.

2. *Social trends and legal context:* Social and legal forces may at times encourage, at other times discourage, market availability of factors. In some societies women may be secluded from employment except for domestic activity. In other communities there have been severe restrictions upon the permitted market uses of land or other resources.

3. *Investment and accumulation:* In recent centuries in the Western world, stocks of produced resources ("capital goods") have accumulated enormously over time. Each generation has so arranged its affairs as to leave its successor generation better endowed with these man-made resources. (The process of intertemporal choice leading to this result will be considered in Chapter 16.)

4. *Demography:* The growth of the human stock has paralleled the accumulation of goods over time. (Of course, human beings are also a kind of "produced resource," though generated in response to somewhat different motivations.) The aggregate size of the human population and its detailed age-sex composition obviously affect the supply of labor available to the market.

Example 15.1
The Black
Death[11]

The Black Death (1348–50) is generally believed to have carried off between a quarter and a third of the population of Western Europe. Later recurrences of plague in 1360–61, 1369, and 1374 may each have accounted for perhaps 5% of the populations remaining. There was a drastic reduction in labor supply with an immediate effect on wages: "The increase due to the plague is 32% for the threshing of wheat, 38% for barley, 111% for oats in the eastern counties. In the middle counties

[11]Discussion based upon J. Hirshleifer, "Disaster and Recovery: The Black Death in Western Europe," RAND Corporation Memorandum RM-4700-TAB (Feb. 1966).

393

Chapter 15
Factor Supply,
Factor-Market
Equilibrium, and
Income Distribution

the percentages of rise are 40, 69, 111; in the south, 33, 38, 75; in the west, 26, 41, 44; in the north, 32, 43, and 100."[12]

The English government responded to this shock with what we would now call a "wage freeze," eventually formalized as the Statute of Laborers (1351). This decree not only froze wages but forbade idleness and required reasonable prices for necessities. Another ordinance in the same year prohibited emigration. Efforts were made for some years to enforce these regulations, though a similar Statute of Laborers in France seems to have been largely a dead letter.

Despite governmental interventions and the inherent rigidities of the feudal-manorial system, the economic logic of the situation (the increased scarcity of labor relative to other resources and, in particular, relative to land) dictated a rise in wages and in per capita incomes of the laboring classes. This is evidenced by innumerable reports of individuals stepping up to fill vacant higher places in the manorial economy, by records of remissions and recontracts of feudal dues owed the lords, as well as by loud complaints against unwontedly lavish living by the lower orders. (For example, a Statute of Dress of 1363 forbade the lower classes to imitate upper-class attire.)

Comment: The feudal system was about as far removed from the economists' competitive model as can be imagined. Feudal economic relationships are in principle dictated solely by custom and status. Nevertheless, competitive forces could not be denied. The system could not withstand the pressure of such a drastic and sudden change in factor availabilities as represented by the Black Death; hence the complaints about flight of labor, vagrancy, "wasting," etc., and calls upon the government to cancel the market concessions granted to the upstart tenants. A concerted governmental attempt early in the reign of Richard II to reverse the clock and enforce feudal dues and status relationships led to the Peasants' Revolt of 1381. This came within a hair of overturning the monarchy. Among the peasants' demands were the abolition of serfdom, of feudal dues and services, of governmental monopolies, and of restrictions on buying and selling. In short, the peasants anticipated Adam Smith in wanting *laissez faire*, so that market-place revisions of economic status could proceed in their favor.

[12]H. Robbins, "A Comparison of the Effects of the Black Death on the Economic Organization of France and England," *Journal of Political Economy*, v. 36 (Aug. 1928), p. 463.

15. D MONOPOLIES AND CARTELS IN FACTOR SUPPLY

Monopoly on the *demand* side of factor markets—monopsony—was studied in Section 14.D. Monopoly on the *supply* side of the factor market is the subject here.

394

Chapter 15
Factor Supply,
Factor-Market
Equilibrium, and
Income Distribution

As every firm's product is in some respects unique, every firm has *some* degree of monopoly power in the product market. Similarly for resources: Every resource has some degree of uniqueness and therefore every resource-owner has some monopoly power in the factor market. But if a sufficient range of close substitutes is available, the competitive model, which postulates price-taking behavior of market participants, will nevertheless be a satisfactory approximation of reality. Ownership of resources is, in actuality, very widely diffused in modern economies of the Western world. Hence *monopoly* power is likely to be significant only in very unusual cases. Motion picture stars and athletic champions are possible examples of highly unique resources for which a substantial degree of monopoly power exists. On the other hand, more or less successful *cartels* of resource-suppliers (e.g., trade unions) are very common.

15. D. 1   Optimum of the Monopolist Resource-Owner

The formal solution for the resource-monopolist is very simple in the special case where there are no reservation uses for the factor. Then the monopolist will merely seek to maximize his "Total Revenue" or, we shall say, his *Total Factor Income (TFI)*. TFI is equal to the factor earnings $h_L L$ from his given quantum $R^\dagger$ of resources. This maximization *may* dictate holding some units of the resource off the market, not for reservation uses (as, by assumption, there are none) but simply in the interests of obtaining a higher price through monopoly power. Figure 15.11 illustrates such a situation, in terms of a "total" function in Panel (a) and "average-marginal" functions in Panel (b). The monopolist's earnings-maximizing employment L^* occurs at the maximum of the TFI curve in Panel (a); Panel (b) shows, equivalently, how L^*

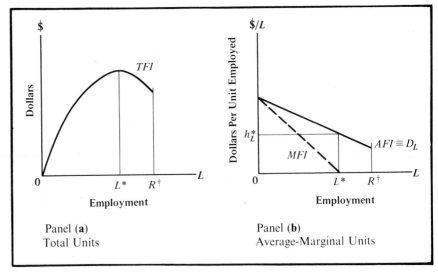

Figure 15. 11
Factor Monopoly—No Reservation Uses

395

Chapter 15
Factor Supply,
Factor-Market
Equilibrium, and
Income Distribution

is determined at the point where *Marginal Factor Income MFI* $\equiv \Delta I/\Delta L$ falls to zero. The wage set by the monopolist will be h_L^*, the height of the factor demand curve D_L at $L = L^*$. (Since $h_L \equiv TFI/L$, the factor demand curve can be identified with the *Average Factor Income* function *AFI*.)

If, on the other hand, the curve of Total Factor Income *TFI* is rising throughout the relevant range of $L \leq R^\dagger$ (equivalent to a factor demand curve that is *elastic* throughout this range), the resource-monopolist without reservation uses will *not* find it to his interest to hold any units off the market. In that case *MFI* remains greater than zero at $L = R^\dagger$, where all of the resource available is employed.

If there are *reservation* uses of the factor, the monopolist would have to balance these uses against increased factor earnings in the market. His decision may be illustrated in terms of the preference diagram of Figure 15.12.

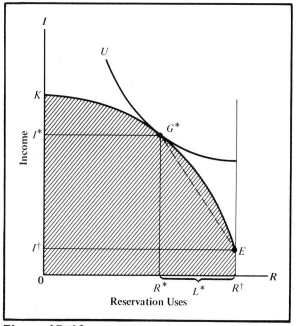

Figure 15. 12
Factor Monopolist with Reservation Uses, I

This differs from Figure 15.1 in that the shaded opportunity set is now bounded by a concave curve rather than a straight line. The concave "budget curve" represents the fact that the wage h_L is *not* constant, but rather is a decreasing function of employment $L = R^\dagger - R$. The monopolist's optimum position is of course at the indifference-curve tangency G^*; his reservation quantity is R^*, and corresponding employment quantity L^*.

This solution is translated to a price-quantity diagram on L, h_L axes in Figure 15.13. The Marginal Factor Income $MFI \equiv \Delta I/\Delta L$ for any employment level L corresponds to the absolute slope $-\Delta I/\Delta R$ (since $\Delta L = -\Delta R$)

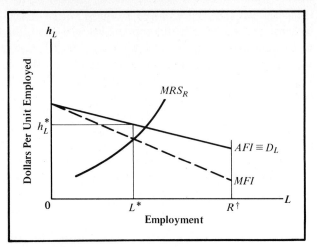

Figure 15. 13
Factor Monopolist with Reservation Uses, II

of the concave budget curve in Figure 15.12. This is the "Marginal Revenue" in income units of sacrificing an hour of leisure. What corresponds to "Marginal Cost" for the factor-monopolist is the *marginal value of the reservation uses*, which is nothing but his Marginal Rate of Substitution MRS_R between income and the reservation uses of his resource analyzed in Section 15.A. As indicated there, MRS_R corresponds to the absolute indifference-curve slope $\frac{\Delta I}{\Delta R}\Big|_U$. The rising curve MRS_R in Figure 15.13 shows increasing "Marginal Cost" of accepting income in place of leisure. So the tangency at G^* in Figure 15.12 (equality of the budget-curve slope and indifference-curve slope) corresponds to the intersection of MFI and MRS_R in Figure 15.13. (The monopoly optimum wage h_L^* in the price-quantity diagram, corresponding to the Average Factor Income $AFI \equiv (I^* - I^\dagger)/L^*$, is shown by the absolute slope of the dashed EG^* in the earlier indifference-curve diagram.)

Conclusion: The monopolist supplier of a resource, like the monopolist supplier of a product, will set Marginal Revenue equal to Marginal Cost. In the factor market, Marginal Revenue corresponds to Marginal Factor Income MFI. Marginal Cost corresponds to MRS_R, the Marginal Rate of Substitution between income and reservation uses of the resource.

15. D. 2   Resource Cartels

Trade unions of employees are often accused of being labor monopolies. Technically, they are *cartels*, associations or coalitions of resource-suppliers. Their members have little or no monopoly power individually, but as a collective group may be able to influence the ruling price-quantity outcome of the market process.

As explained in Section 11.F, all cartels have an Achilles heel. Given that

397

Chapter 15
Factor Supply,
Factor-Market
Equilibrium, and
Income Distribution

the other members are loyally abiding by the agreement, it pays any single member to "chisel" and undercut the standard terms. All cartels therefore require enforcement devices, most commonly achieved through use of government power. In the case of trade unions in the United States, an election is normally held under the terms of the National Labor Relations Act to determine "collective-bargaining representation." Whichever union wins a majority of the vote cast in the final round becomes the exclusive bargaining agent for *all* workers in the collective-bargaining unit.[13] ("No union" is also one of the options.) When a collective-bargaining agent has been officially certified, individual bargaining is prohibited—thus ruling out, or at any rate minimizing, the possibility of the worker "chiselling" by accepting less than the standard pay for the given work or offering more work at the standard pay.

[13] The administrative-legal process that determines just what is the appropriate "bargaining unit" may be quite crucial for the final outcome of the election.

Example 15. 2
Unionization
and Hotel
Workers[14]

Before 1929, there was very little unionization of hotel workers. In the two decades after 1929, the Hotel and Restaurant Employees and Bartenders International Union was able to organize in a number of cities. As may be seen in the following Table, wage rates rose somewhat faster in the unionized cities.

Average Hourly Earnings of Hotel Employees (1929 = 100)

	1929	1935	1939	1948
Weighted mean index, 19 union cities[a]	100	81	88.4	188
Weighted mean index, 12 non-union cities[b]	100	76	80	168
Ratio (union/non-union)	100	1.06	1.10	1.12

Source: Joseph Scherer, "Collective Bargaining in Service Industries: A Study of the Year-Round Hotels," Ph.D. dissertation, University of Chicago, 1951.
[a] More than 35% of hotel workers organized in 1948.
[b] Less than 10% of hotel workers organized in 1948.

After adjustment of the data to eliminate regional wage effects (since unionized cities tended to be Northern and non-unionized cities Southern), the ratio of union to non-union wage indexes was found to be 1.06. That is, wages in the union cities grew about 6% more, in the course of twenty years, as compared with non-union cities.

Note, however, that the union versus non-union differential is small in comparison with the overall wage swings over the twenty years covered by the Table.

[14] Discussion based on H. Gregg Lewis, *Unionism and Relative Wages in the United States* (Chicago: University of Chicago Press, 1963), p. 58.

398

Chapter 15
Factor Supply,
Factor-Market
Equilibrium, and
Income Distribution

Since different interests must be reconciled in collective decisions, the determination of the market policy of any cartel creates internal political conflict. In the case of trade unions, elaborate internal machinery often exists to solve this "problem of collective action."[15]

But trade unions are by no means the only cartels effective in resource supply. Professional associations, such as the American Medical Association (see Example 15.5, "Returns to Medical Education," below) are frequently charged with cartel-like behavior. In general, loosely organized resource-supply cartels find it easier to achieve their ends by *restricting entry* to the trade than by *fixing prices*. Entry is relatively visible, where price-chiselling may be secret. A sufficiently tight lid on supply, through control of entry, will inevitably force up the market price even though market behavior remains competitive for those actually in the trade. In a supply-demand equilibrium like that of Figure 15.10, entry control may have shifted the supply curve S_L so far to the left as to essentially achieve a monopoly-like price-quantity outcome.

[5]See Section 18.C.

Example 15. 3
Barbers

As of the date of a study by Simon Rottenberg,[16] 47 of the old 48 states had laws licensing barbers. The main impetus for the legislation was lobbying by barbering associations. Educational requirements for securing a barber's license are an important barrier to entry. The Illinois law, for example, requires (among other things) 1,872 study hours in a recognized barber school as well as passing an examination covering topics related to the theory and practice of barber science and art. These include anatomy and physiology, hygiene and sanitation, barber history and law, pharmacology, electricity and light, and even haircutting, shaving, etc. Apprenticeship rules may be an even more important restriction on entry: A minimum apprenticeship of $2\frac{1}{4}$ years must be served, and no shop may employ more than one apprentice for each registered barber. The barber associations also oppose licensing reciprocity among states (for then students would acquire licenses in the less restrictive jurisdictions).

While the barbering associations have also pressed for minimum price-fixing, only fourteen states had such laws.

Comment: Non-legal methods were at one time a significant deterrent to price "chisellers." A disproportionately large number of unexplained fires used to occur, from time to time, on the premises of price-cutting barbers.

[16]Simon Rottenberg, "The Economics of Occupational Licensing," in H. Gregg Lewis *et al.*, *Aspects of Labor Economics* (Princeton, N.J.: Princeton University Press, 1962).

399

Chapter 15
Factor Supply,
Factor-Market
Equilibrium, and
Income Distribution

One curious exception to tight control over occupational entry is the legal profession. A very large increase in the capacity of law schools and in their throughput of students into the profession has occurred in the United States recently, without apparent objection on the part of those in the trade. This exception is, however, understandable and in a sense "proves the rule." Each additional barber or doctor or accountant competes with his fellows and takes business away from them. But the legal process is such that each additional practitioner, by adding to the number of lawsuits, presentments, hearings, trials, pleadings, appeals, writs, demurrers, rebuttals, rejoinders, etc., makes *more* business for his colleagues.

Of course, cartels may be effective over non-labor resources as well.

Example 15. 4
Tobacco
Allotments

Under the market order[17] regulating the supply of tobacco, certain specific acres of farmland carry "allotments" permitting tobacco to be grown thereon. Anyone may grow tobacco, but he must compete with all other growers to buy or rent some "allotted" acres on which to do so. Thus, the government-sponsored cartel works in behalf of owners of the resource of "allotted" land, not of growers as such. One study has estimated the *premium* paid by growers for land with an allotment (over equivalent land without allotment) as between $962 and $2500 per acre (for land suitable for growing flue-cured tobacco in North Carolina and Virginia counties in the period 1954–57).[18]

[17]See also Example 11.5, "Agricultural Marketing Orders."
[18]F. H. Maier, J. L. Hedrick, and W. L. Givson, Jr., "The Sale Value of Flue-Cured Tobacco Allotments," Agricultural Experiment Station, Virginia Polytechnic Institute, Technical Bulletin No. 148 (April 1960), p. 40.

15. E   THE "FUNCTIONAL" DISTRIBUTION OF INCOME

15. E. 1   The Problem of Classification

Factors of production have traditionally been classified under the headings of *labor*, *land*, and *capital*. To these were supposed to correspond three categories of "functional" factor returns, namely: *wages* to labor, *rent* to land, and *interest* to capital. In the emerging period of economic thought, most particularly in England in the late eighteenth and early nineteenth centuries, this categorization had political and sociological relevance. The three factor groupings corresponded to major social classes of the time. Land was owned by the old aristocracy, capital (material assets other than land) by the rising bourgeoisie, while the working classes could be regarded as owning their labor power. Even sociologically speaking, this classification was never very useful for societies (like America) lacking a feudally-based aristocracy; with

400

Chapter 15
Factor Supply,
Factor-Market
Equilibrium, and
Income Distribution

changes in economic circumstances it hardly remains interesting today.[19] And in any case, the claim that these three factor returns are "functionally" distinct in economic terms is analytically indefensible.

Land versus capital: *Land* is traditionally defined as the "natural and inexhaustible productive powers of the soil," i.e., its native fertility, mineral content, topographical features, and location. *Capital* in contrast with land is thought of as "produced means of production." Thus, capital is supposed to be man-made resources (e.g., buildings or machines), created and accumulated by human forethoughted sacrifice of present consumption for future production. But the distinction collapses once it is realized that the actual powers of the soil are as much a human creation as any building or machine. Human effort went into the discovery of the vast new lands of America, and, for that matter, into the draining of marshes and clearing of wasteland in the Old World. Nor can the fertility of land be maintained except by continuing human effort and sacrifice. Most important of all, the original *source* of any productive power is only of historical, not of economic or functional, significance.

It is sometimes claimed that a useful distinction between land and capital can be made in terms of supply curves. Supposedly, the supply of land is absolutely fixed by nature (a vertical supply curve) while the supply of man-made resources is responsive to price (a positively-sloping curve). But more land *will* be provided at a price (if necessary, reclaimed from the ocean), while existing land will be permitted to erode away if the reward for maintaining it is insufficient. Furthermore, as long as there are any reservation uses of land, its supply *to the market* will not in general be "fixed" (independent of price).[20]

Labor versus capital: Nor is it possible in the last analysis to distinguish between *labor power* (the source of human services) and capital. In modern society a worker does not sell raw labor power, but rather his trained and educated capacity to apply effort. Training is part of his capital, his "human capital," just as a tool he owns is a part of his capital. There is no functional difference between the worker sacrificing his time and trouble to equip himself with training (to invest in professional education) on the one hand, or to equip himself with a set of tools on the other.[21]

---

[19]Ditch-diggers and corporate presidents both appear within the category of "labor," while the category of "land-owners" includes impoverished Southern Negroes together with the descendants of John Jacob Astor.

[20]The supply curve of land to *all* uses (including reservation uses) will indeed be a vertical line independent of price. But this is true for any resource, including labor. (If "leisure" is counted as a use of labor, the supply of labor is necessarily the entire quantum in existence.) Meaningful supply curves always refer to quantities offered for *market* use, excluding reservation uses.

[21]There remain, of course, important differences between human capital and material capital. For one thing, training is less subject than material property to confiscation. (It is said that the emphasis of the Jews upon education is based upon the "portability" of this form of capital.) On the other hand, human capital perishes instantly with the death of its possessor, and can only with difficulty be transferred to others.

15. E. 2   An Application: Investment in Human Capital

There is an interesting interaction between the returns from investment in human capital and the income-versus-leisure choice (the resource-employment decision) discussed in Section 15.A.

Figure 15.14 shows a situation in which an individual is *indifferent* between two situations G^* and D^* on indifference curve U. His endowment E, con-

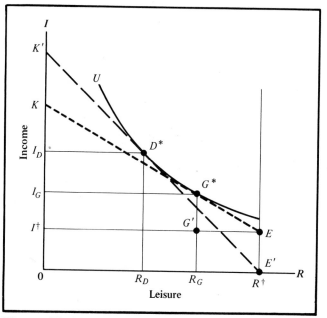

Figure 15. 14
Returns to Education

sisting of $R^\dagger$ of labor capacity and $I^\dagger$ of property income, lies on budget line EK. At the resource-employment optimum G^* he has labor earnings equal to G^*G', summing to an income of I_G. But now suppose he has another alternative—adding to "human capital" by investing in education. Let us assume he must give up all his property income $I^\dagger$ (sacrifice all his non-human capital) to acquire this training; his effective endowment position afterward therefore becomes E' on the horizontal axis. But as a result of the education he earns a higher wage, so that his new budget line $E'K'$ is steeper than EK.

Although position D^* is by hypothesis indifferent to G^*, *the income I_D achieved at D^* is much greater* than I_G. The circumstances faced by the educated person, after having invested so heavily in acquiring human capital, lead him to select a resource-employment optimum with relatively little leisure R_D and relatively high achieved income I_D. Those who become educated should rationally work harder ever after!

Example 15. 5
Returns to
Medical
Education

The professional medical associations, in particular the AMA, have been accused of functioning as an entry-restricting cartel. Evidence has been brought forward showing that, *in terms of income achieved*, there seems to be an "excess" return to investment in medical education. That is, medical education seems to be more profitable than is normal for investment in material capital, suggesting that there may be a cartel at work effectively limiting entry into this profitable form of training.

C. M. Lindsay[22] has contended, however, that this comparison in terms of *additional income* achieved fails to allow properly for the *lesser leisure* typically associated with the resource-employment decisions made after human-capital investments, and after medical training in particular. A true comparison should adjust for this lesser leisure.

In the Table, the "unadjusted" MD returns represent the seeming excess value of medical education ($24,376) in comparison with college graduates generally. This measures the net balance of additional income achieved against the cost of medical training, but *without* any offset for additional working hours. There are two ways of allowing for the difference in working hours: Adjusting college-graduate hours worked *up*, or adjusting MD hours worked *down*. (The true comparison must lie between the results of these two alternative adjustments.)

Reportedly, MD's worked 62 hours per week on the average. For the sake of comparison, alternative assumptions of a 40- and a 45-hour average workweek were used for college graduates. If college graduates are working 45 hours per week, the Table shows that a differential or excess net return to medical education persists, the true number lying somewhere between the alternative adjusted excess-return figures of $10,830 and $1,950. On the 40-hour assumption, however, the two adjustments average out very close to zero. So if college graduates generally are working close to 40 hours per week, there is no evidence of an excess return to medical education *once the MDs' loss of leisure is properly taken into account.*

Excess Returns to Medical Education

	40-Hour Week	*45-Hour Week*
Unadjusted MD excess returns	$24,376	$24,376
Adjusted by raising college graduate hours (to 62)	4,660	10,830
Adjusted by lowering MD hours	−4,580	1,950

Source: C. M. Lindsay, "Real Returns to Medical Education," *Journal of Human Resources*, v. 8 (Summer 1973), p. 338. An interest rate of 10% was used to represent the "normal" return from which the "excess" was calculated. (The original source shows the computation in terms of interest rates of both 5% and 10%.)

[22]C. M. Lindsay, "Real Returns to Medical Education," *Journal of Human Resources*, v. 8 (Summer 1973).

> **Comment:** The 62-hour figure for MDs is suspect, however. Doctors are likely to report themselves as working harder than they really are. If doctors do not in fact work as many as 62 hours per week, the evidence here would tend to support the hypothesis of an excess (cartel-like) return to medical education.

15. E. 3 Capital versus Income—Sources and Services—
The Rate of Interest

The key to understanding the nature of "capital" lies not in the distinction between capital and land or labor, but in the *contrast between capital and income*. This contrast rests upon the difference between a *source* of productive services and the productive services themselves. The human being is the source of labor services, but the labor service proper is the "man-hour" (or other such unit representing the employment of a worker over some defined period of time). Similarly, land is a source of productive services, but the service itself is measured in units like acre-years. And again, it is necessary to distinguish buildings and machines (both sources) from the services of building and machines.

Sources and their services may both be traded in markets. There is a price for an acre of land, and a price for a year's use of an acre of land (the hire-price or rental). There is a price for a building, and a rental for use of the building over some period of time. In a non-slave economy, in contrast, the *sources* of labor services (the human beings themselves) may not be sold, though labor still can be hired for a periodic wage (the hire-price per man-hour). The "factor prices" discussed in this and previous chapters have been the *hire or rental prices of the productive services*, the "wage rates" per unit of time for the use of the resources, and not the prices of the resources themselves.

The sources of factor services constitute an individual's or a nation's "capital." Land is capital, machines and buildings are capital, and the human being's training, strength, and skill, as sources of labor power, are capital.

Example 15. 6
Capital in the
Slave-Owning
South[23]

> The following Table summarizes the value in 1860 of various categories of property (capital) in the 15 states where slaves were emancipated by President Lincoln's proclamation. Slave values varied of course with age and other characteristics; the mean was $933. Emancipation constituted an enormous loss to the slave-owners but there was, of course, a corresponding gain to the slaves in the form of the transferred ownership of their own persons. (Indeed, since free labor is certainly more
>
> [23]Discussion based on L. Rose, "Capital Losses of Southern Slaveholders Due to Emancipation," *Western Economic Journal*, v. 3 (Fall 1964).

404

Chapter 15
Factor Supply,
Factor-Market
Equilibrium, and
Income Distribution

productive, the economic value of the gain to the former slaves exceeded the loss to the slave-owners.)

Wealth Data, 15 Southern States, 1860 (*millions of dollars*)

Value of real estate and personal property	$8644
Value of land in farms	2550
Value of implements and machinery in use	104
Value of livestock	515
Value of slaves emancipated	3685

Source: L. Rose, "Capital Losses of Southern Slaveholders Due to Emancipation," *Western Economic Journal*, v. 3 (Fall 1964), pp. 43, 49.

Comment: A complete tabulation of the capital of the South would also have to include the labor-power value of the *free* population.

Two important senses of the word "capital" must be carefully distinguished: *real-capital* versus *capital-value*. Real-capital refers to the sources themselves: buildings, land, labor power, etc. Capital-value is the market valuation of these sources. (To avoid the ambiguity of the word "capital" standing alone, it is good practice always to specify whether it is real-capital or capital-value that is meant.) There are two corresponding senses of the word "income." The services of land generate a flow of *real-income* (e.g., bushels of wheat per year). But if the prefix "real" is omitted, the word "income" standing alone is commonly understood to be in value terms. Thus, an acre of land yields a rental income (dollars per year) to the owner, corresponding to the dollar value of the real-income in bushels per year actually produced.

In the Factor Employment Condition, equation (14.7)—$h_a = mrp_a \equiv MR(mp_a)$—the physical Marginal Product mp_a is the real-income produced by the land, in units of commodity X per acre per year. The Marginal Revenue Product, mrp_a, is in units of dollars per acre per year. Factor price h_a therefore, the hire-price or "wage" of factor A (land), is also in units of dollars per acre per year.

For those productive resources that are marketable, there will be some market-determined *ratio between the annual value of the service and the market value of the source*, i.e., ratio between the income and the capital-value. This ratio, the proportionate *yield* on the capital-value of the source, corresponds to the *rate of interest* earned from ownership of the resource. Suppose an acre of land is valued at $1000 and generates real-income (has a Marginal Product) of 50 bushels of wheat per year. If the price of wheat is $2 per bushel, the income is $100 per year. Then the rate of interest r earned upon the investment in land is $100/$1000 or 10% per annum. More generally, for any factor:

(15.3) $$\text{Rate of interest } r \equiv \frac{\text{Annual income}}{\text{Value of source}}$$

405

Chapter 15
Factor Supply,
Factor-Market
Equilibrium, and
Income Distribution

In performing this calculation, however, it is important to account for all aspects, both positive and negative, of "income." For example, suppose the asset *depreciates* in value during the year because of wear-and-tear or obsolescence. Then the loss due to the depreciation during the year must be taken into account as an offset in calculating the "net" income from the source.

With income properly accounted for, there is a fundamental proposition that governs the relation between income and capital-value:

Proposition: The proportionate yield (rate of interest earned) on all assets tends to come into equality.

If the yield on asset T were lower than on another asset S, holders of T would be trying to sell out in order to buy S instead. This would drive down the price P_T (capital-value) of T and drive up the price P_S (capital-value) of S. As may be seen from equation (15.3), as the dollar value of source T falls its percent yield must rise, while as the dollar value of source S rises its percent yield must fall. In this way the incentives of individuals to achieve the maximum returns on their asset-holdings tends to bring the rate of interest earned on all assets into equality.

We can now see more clearly into the relation between interest and the traditional "functional" categories: rent as the return to land and wages as the return to labor. Since rent is the hire-price of land, *annual rent on land will (in equilibrium) be equal to the interest yield on the capital-value of the land. In a slave economy, annual wages as the hire-price of labor would tend to equal the interest yield on the capital-value of the slave.* And even in a free economy, the additional income due to investment in training would, allowing for loss of leisure, tend to equal the interest yield on the cost of acquiring that training (see Example 15.5, "Returns to Medical Education").

In equation (15.3), dollars/year of income from the services of factor A must equal the hire-price h_a. Dollar value of the source, the price of factor A itself, is P_a. For factor A, then (and for any factor):

(15.4)
$$h_a = rP_a$$

Conclusion: Interest is best regarded not as a subdivision or portion of income. Rather, *all* factor incomes can be regarded as the interest yields on the capital-values of the sources of factor services. Or put another way: The interest rate is, for any factor, the ratio between the hire-price and the value of the factor itself.

15. F ECONOMIC RENT AND PRODUCER SURPLUS

A portion of the income earned by any factor may constitute what is known as "economic rent," to wit, that part of the return to the factor in excess of the amount required to call it into employment.

Consider Figure 15.15. Here, for some factor or resource A, the supply curve S_a is vertical; i.e., there are no reservation uses. It follows that the

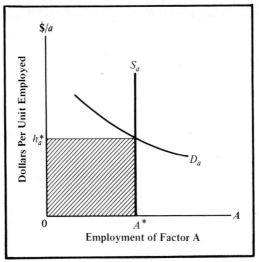

Figure 15. 15
Resource-Owners' Surplus, I

entire income payment for the hire of that resource, the shaded rectangle $h_a^* A^*$ in the diagram, is an "excess" payment and therefore economic rent. This is so since the vertical supply curve shows that the quantity A^* would be forthcoming even at an infinitesimal wage. With an upward-sloping factor supply curve as in Figure 15.16, however, the region of "excess" payment is the shaded area lying above S_a but below the market price h_a^*. Here not all of factor income is economic rent, because of the existence of reservation uses (compare the upward-sloping MRS_R curve of Figure 15.13).

Economic rent as pictured in Figure 15.16 looks very similar to the representation of *Producer Surplus* in Figure 7.10. And indeed, economic rent is the analog of Producer Surplus. Producer Surplus measures a selling indi-

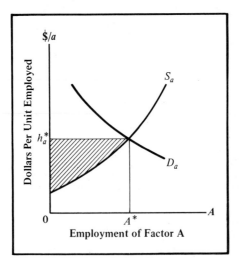

Figure 15. 16
Resource-Owners' Surplus, II

407

Chapter 15
Factor Supply,
Factor-Market
Equilibrium, and
Income Distribution

vidual's net gain from trade *in the product market*; economic rent measures his net gain from trade *in the factor market*, i.e., from market employment (as opposed to nonmarket or reservation uses) of the resources he owns.

Sometimes it is useful to take a narrower point of view. We can speak of the economic rent from employment versus non-employment (market returns versus reservation uses) of a resource. Or we can speak of the economic rent in the *best* (versus the second-best) market employment of a resource. For a male opera singer it may be that his next-best alternative is not leisure but driving a truck. Then the difference between his incomes as opera-singer and as truck-driver is the economic rent attaching to his best employment.

Example 15. 7
Economic Rent
and the Military
Draft

Until recently, a sizeable portion of the human resources employed by the Department of Defense was acquired by conscription. Wages to enlistees were low, and military "requirements" were met by supplementing volunteers with draftees.

In 1967, Walter Oi[24] analyzed the losses in economic rents that would be suffered, given a continuation of conscription, by suppliers of labor services to the armed forces. At the low rates of military pay being contemplated, intake of 472,000 recruits annually would consist of 263,000 "true volunteers" and 209,000 "reluctant enlistees." (Reluctant enlistees include both those drafted and those induced to enlist by the prospect of the draft.)

The draft "tax" on economic rent affects both these groups. The true volunteers are those already willing to serve at the existing pay rates. But if military salaries were raised high enough to eliminate any need for reluctant enlistees, the true volunteers would also be paid more. The loss of this benefit (economic rent that would otherwise be received) was estimated as $3400 per volunteer, on the average. Furthermore, since the same wage increment would be received by the reluctant enlistees as well, their loss comes *at least* to the same $3400 per person. (It would be exactly $3400 only if those chosen to be drafted were those with the poorest alternative employments.)[25] On this minimal assumption, the $3400 loss per reluctant draftee was estimated to consist of an $1888 loss of civilian opportunities and a $1512 loss due to the low military pay.

[24]W. Y. Oi, "The Economic Cost of the Draft," *American Economic Review*, v. 57, (May 1967), pp. 39–62. The figures quoted here are attributed by Oi to R. C. Amacher *et al.*, "The Economics of the Military Draft" (Morristown, N. J.: General Learning Press, 1973).
[25]This is the analog of the "ideal" assignment of ration tickets, described in Section 7.E.2, that minimizes the loss of Consumer Surplus under rationing.

We have now taken account of the individual in his two decision-making aspects of *consumer* and *resource-owner*. But there remains for him at any moment of time a third dimension of choice: *between consumption and increased resource-ownership*. The person not only has to make decisions as to how to employ his currently-owned resources and how to consume his income, but also whether and to what extent to refrain from consuming (to save) so as to build up his real-capital. Having chosen to save, he can increase his resource-ownership by purchasing already-existing sources of factor services (land, machines, buildings, etc.) from someone else. Over the economy as a whole, of course, such transactions cancel out as there must be a seller for each buyer. But a firm or an individual might also physically *produce* a social increment of real-capital by manufacturing new resources not previously in existence, or, for that matter, by "manufacturing" new human capital through undergoing training. The process of refraining from consumption is called *saving*; the process of actually building new real-capital is called *investment*.

From the individual's point of view, today's consumption-versus-saving decision can be reinterpreted as an intertemporal choice between *present* consumption and *future* consumption. By not consuming today and saving instead, the person builds up his stock of owned resources so as to augment his future income—convertible into consumption at later dates. Eventually, in his later years perhaps, he is likely to "dis-save" by gradually drawing down or selling his remaining real-capital. (He may, however, plan to leave a legacy to his descendants, thereby participating by proxy in consumption activities beyond his own death.) We are thus led to the topic of *intertemporal* choice, which will constitute the subject of Chapter 16.

The familiar picture in Figure 1.1 of the circular flow of economic activity can now be made a degree more realistic by separating consumption and saving flows, as suggested in Figure 15.17. We now imagine that there are two types of firms: those producing consumption goods and those producing real-capital or "investment goods" (buildings, land, machines, etc.). In the upper portion of the diagram (the product market) the two types of products are purchased by the consumers' consumption expenditures and savings expenditures, respectively. In the lower part of the diagram (the factor market), resource-owning individuals supply factor-services to the employing firms. An individual's decision to save rather than consume will involve the acquisition of an augmented stock of resources, permitting him at some later date to supply a larger quantity of productive services and thereby earn more future income.[26]

---

[26]The implicit assumption underlying the diagram is that all resources are *owned* by individuals and *rented* to firms for productive employment. In actuality firms themselves may legally *own* as well as hire resources. But resource-ownership on the part of firms can be regarded merely as a convenient fiction, since ultimately all firms are themselves owned by individuals.

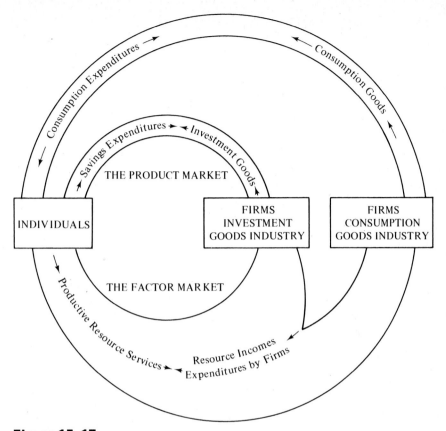

Figure 15. 17
The Circular Flow: Consumption and Investment

Questions

1. If a resource-owner had no interest whatsoever in "reservation uses," what would be the shape of his preference function between income I and reservation uses R? What would be the shape of the preference function if, in the case of a labor-supplier, there was actually a positive taste for working within a certain initial range of employment (i.e., a range in which leisure is a "bad" rather than a "good")?

2. Apart from leisure as a reservation use of labor, what other resources are likely to have nonmarket reservation uses yielding utility to their owners?

3. Diagram a situation in which a resource-owner chooses a "corner solution" so as to devote all of his resource to reservation uses. Does this necessarily imply that income I must be a "bad" or a "neuter" commodity at the solution point? Diagram a situation in which the resource-owner's optimum is such that no reservation uses R are retained. Does this imply that R must be a "bad" or a "neuter" commodity at the solution point? Explain.

410

Chapter 15
Factor Supply,
Factor-Market
Equilibrium, and
Income Distribution

4. With the advent of the women's liberation movement, there is reason to believe that women's preferences may be changing so as to make reservation uses of their time less attractive than before in comparison with market employment. What effect would such a taste change have upon the supply curve of female labor? Upon the relative market wages of male and female workers?

5. Explain why the Price Expansion Path (*PEP*) on *I,R* axes is normally negatively sloped, but may become positive sloped at sufficiently high wage rates. What is the implication for the shape of the supply curve of labor? Could there be such a slope reversal if leisure were an inferior good?

6. In modern times, real wealth and real wage rates have steadily increased throughout the western world. But average working hours in market employment have steadily fallen. Would the pure "income effect" (due to rising per-capita wealth) tend to lead to lesser market employment? Would the pure "substitution effect" (due to the relative price shift represented by the rising wage rate) tend to have this effect? Comment upon the relative importance of the two in the light of the evidence.

7. In what way does the market opportunity set of a factor-monopolist differ from that of a competitive supplier of factor services? How will the optimum of the resource-owner be affected?

8. Consider the situation of a slave who has no market opportunity set for disposition of his labor power. Suppose the master simply provided a fixed "income" *I* (in the form of consumption rations) to the slave. What would be the optimum *I,R* position from the point of view of the slave? What position would the master prefer? How is the divergence likely to be resolved? Might it be in the interests of the master to free his slave and pay him wages? Might it not?

9. An individual who invests heavily in developing his labor skills will afterward earn a higher wage. But he is also likely to work more hours than he otherwise would have. Explain why.

10. Suppose that entry into a particular field of employment for a resource like labor or land is restricted by the requirement to obtain a special license, but that the license is traded in the market. Assuming a fixed number of licenses, use supply-demand analysis to determine the equilibrium price of a license. How is the market demand curve for licenses derived from the demand curve and supply curve for the resource service?

11. Explain the traditional "functional" classification of factors of production.

12. In some nations, higher income taxes are imposed upon "unearned" as opposed to "earned" income (i.e., higher taxes upon income from property as opposed to income from labor services). What are the likely effects upon investment in human capital as opposed to investment in physical capital? On the other hand, it has been maintained that most income taxes are biased against labor income by failing to allow any deductions for *depreciation* of

411

Chapter 15
Factor Supply,
Factor-Market
Equilibrium, and
Income Distribution

the worker's labor power over time. What would be the consequence of allowing such deductions?

13. According to the "single tax" movement, a tax on land is likely to be particularly effective. As the supply curve of land is vertical, its availability to society will allegedly not be affected by any reduction in after-tax returns. If a land tax is levied upon *market uses* of the resource (income tax), would the market availability of land be affected? If the tax were levied instead upon *ownership* of the resource (wealth tax), would the market availability of land be affected? Explain in terms of an indifference-curve map and market opportunity set on I,R axes. Then make an analogous comparison, in terms of the market availability of labor, of an *income* tax upon labor earnings versus a *wealth* tax upon labor capacity. (The latter is a so-called "facultative" tax, a fixed sum proportioned to a person's *ability* to earn rather than to his actual market earnings.)

14. What is the relationship between the hire-price of a factor and the purchase price of that factor?

15. What is economic rent? What is its relation to Producer Surplus?

Chapter 16
Intertemporal Choice: Saving, Investment, and Interest

In the preceding chapter, it was noted that individuals had to make choices not only (1) as to purchase of consumption goods out of income and (2) as to the supply of resource services to the market so as to generate income, but also (3) between devoting income to current consumption or to the acquisition of *additional* amounts of resources or "real-capital." This last is commonly described as the choice between consumption and *saving* or *investment*. ("Saving" denotes refraining from consumption, whereas "investment" indicates the actual formation of new capital assets. The market process, as we shall see, brings the aggregate of saving and the aggregate of investment into equality.)

In this chapter we will emphasize, as the motive underlying the choices between consumption on the one hand and saving or investment on the other, desires on the part of individuals to *achieve a preferred intertemporal balance of consumption* between present and future. An individual may buy or build a house to provide himself with future shelter; a farmer may hold back corn from current use to plant seed for next year's crop; and a business firm maintains or replaces its machinery and equipment in order to provide for productive capacity in coming years. In each case capital assets are being acquired, at the sacrifice of current consumption, as a way of providing for future income and consumption.

Section 16.A will review the processes of individual decision and market equilibrium in the disposition of income claims of different dates. Section 16.B takes up the criteria for investment decision used or proposed for use by business firms or branches of government. Later on the very important distinction between *real* interest and *money* interest will be introduced and analyzed. The concluding section reviews the forces determining the magnitudes of real and money rates of interest.

16. A CONSUMPTION AND PRODUCTION OVER TIME

In the analysis of intertemporal choice, the fruitful simplification will be adopted of assuming that there is a *single consumptive commodity C* differ-

414

Chapter 16
Intertemporal
Choice:
Saving, Investment,
and Interest

entiated only by date. Specifically, individuals will be regarded as making choices among *this year's consumption* C_0, *consumption one time-period in the future* C_1, *two time-periods from now* C_2, etc. Here the subscript 0 represents "now," and the other numbered subscripts are time-units (years) from the present period. For utmost simplicity, however, in this section a two-period model will be analyzed: choice between *this year's consumption* C_0 and *next year's consumption* C_1. As in the case of ordinary consumption choices, the optimum position for an individual will depend upon his preferences and his opportunities. And the equilibrium in the market, determining the relative prices of claims to current consumption C_0 and future consumption C_1, will integrate and balance the separate choices of all the individuals in the economy.

16. A. 1   Borrowing-Lending Equilibrium

In the light of the above, we can see that the problems of individual intertemporal decision and overall market equilibrium are in principle no different from the corresponding problems for ordinary consumption commodities X and Y within a single period of time. And specifically, on the level of the individual the intertemporal optimization that is pictured in Figure 16.1 looks almost exactly like the "optimum of the consumer" shown originally in Figure 4.1. In Figure 16.1 here we once again have an individual's *preference map* (indifference curves U', U'', U''', . . .), and a consumption *opportunity set* bounded on the northeast by a *budget line KL*. The optimum of the

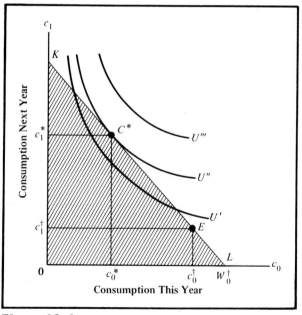

Figure 16. 1
Intertemporal Consumptive Optimum

415

Chapter 16
Intertemporal
Choice:
Saving, Investment,
and Interest

consumer will of course again be at the tangency C^*—a consumption "basket" that takes the form of an intertemporal income stream, consisting of the amounts c_0^* of current consumption and c_1^* of future consumption.

A special terminology is employed for the analysis of intertemporal choice, however, and we need to translate this familiar solution into that terminology. First, note that in Figure 16.1 the budget line KL goes through an intertemporal *endowment* position E (compare the analysis of Chapter 7, Section C) representing given quantities $c_0^\dagger$ and $c_1^\dagger$ of anticipated current and future income available to the individual before entering into exchange.[1] When the individual moves northwest along the budget line from his endowment position E, he is said to be "lending," i.e., sacrificing some units of current consumption C_0 in exchange for future consumption C_1. Should he move southeast, obtaining more C_0 at the expense of C_1, he is said to be "borrowing." The individual pictured in Figure 16.1 chooses to be a lender in the amount of $c_0^\dagger - c_0^*$, his anticipated repayment next year being $c_1^* - c_1^\dagger$. Had his endowment position E lain to the northwest of his intertemporal optimum C^* along the budget line, on the other hand, he would have been a borrower. This is the traditional situation of an "heir with great expectations," as in Charles Dickens' novel, i.e., someone poor today, but with rich prospects for the future.

What is the rate of exchange at which the market will permit the trading of current consumption entitlements C_0 against future entitlements C_1 (by lending or borrowing)? This rate corresponds geometrically to the slope of the budget line. Following our previous terminology and notation, we could write the price of C_0-claims as P_0, and of C_1-claims as P_1. Then the budget-line slope would be denoted $-P_0/P_1$. Assuming that current claims C_0 serve as "numeraire" ($P_0 \equiv 1$), the ratio becomes simply $-1/P_1$. But in the special terminology of intertemporal exchange, the concept of "the rate of interest" r is introduced. Specifically, we shall define the annual rate of interest r here as the *premium* on the relative value of current over one-year-in-the-future consumption claims. Looking at it the other way, $1 + r$ of future claims C_1 is what the market will return for each unit of current claims C_0 sacrificed. Thus:

(16.1)
$$1 + r \equiv \frac{P_0}{P_1} \equiv \frac{1}{P_1} \equiv -\frac{\Delta c_1}{\Delta c_0}$$

Consequently, the slope of the budget line in Figure 16.1 is $-(1 + r)$.

One other point of great importance concerns the *nature of the constraint* fixing the distance of the budget line from the origin, and thereby determining the magnitude of the individual's consumption opportunities. In the previous analysis of consumption in a single period (in Section 4.A), it was the individual's *income I* that constrained his choices according to equation (4.1), $P_x x + P_y y = I$. This equation was employed as a simplification in

---

[1] Throughout our analysis, *uncertainty* will be ruled out. Thus, anticipations as to the future are sure to be realized.

416

Chapter 16
Intertemporal
Choice:
Saving, Investment,
and Interest

Chapter 4, while admitting the known fact that people often spend less than their current income on consumption (they save) or more than their income on consumption (they borrow). We are now in a position to correct this flaw in the preceding analysis. It is not the individual's *income I* that limits his consumption choices over time but rather his endowed *wealth* $W_0^\dagger$:

Definition: Endowed wealth $W_0^\dagger$ is the market value of an individual's intertemporal endowment of present and future claims.

In terms of the conventional "price" terminology, endowed wealth would be expressed in terms of the values of the endowment elements $(c_0^\dagger, c_1^\dagger)$ as follows:

(16.2) $$W_0^\dagger \equiv P_0 c_0^\dagger + P_1 c_1^\dagger \equiv c_0^\dagger + P_1 c_1^\dagger$$

And in terms of the alternative "interest" terminology, since $P_0 \equiv 1$ and $P_1 \equiv 1/(1+r)$ follows from equation (16.1), endowed wealth is:

(16.2′) $$W_0^\dagger \equiv c_0^\dagger + \frac{c_1^\dagger}{1+r}$$

Geometrically, if $P_0 \equiv 1$ then the endowed wealth is the horizontal intercept of the budget line *KL*. Note that the subscript 0 is attached to the symbol for wealth. The reason is that what wealth signifies is a *present market value*, a worth today in numeraire or C_0-units of the specified endowment combination or time-stream.

The constraint itself, the budget line *KL* of Figure 16.1, can similarly be expressed in two ways:

(16.3) $$c_0 + P_1 c_1 = W_0^\dagger$$

(16.3′) $$c_0 + \frac{c_1}{1+r} = W_0^\dagger$$

The borrowing-lending equilibrium in terms of commodities C_0 and C_1 is entirely analogous to the market equilibrium involving commodities X and Y discussed in Section 7.C. By imagining different prices P_1 (or interest rates r) determining different budget lines through each individual's endowment position E, Price Expansion Paths can be derived as in Figure 7.3. And these can then be translated into supply and demand curves for the separate individuals, and for the market as a whole, as in Figures 7.4 and 7.5. The successive steps in the development will not be recapitulated here. However, the final result is pictured in Figure 16.2, which corresponds to Panel (a) of Figure 7.5. On the horizontal axis here are measured aggregate amounts of market borrowing or lending. The L^t curve is the market supply of lending, and the B^t curve the market demand for borrowing of current consumption claims C_0. The L^t curve represents the aggregate responses (desired transactions at different market prices) of individuals like the net lender pictured in

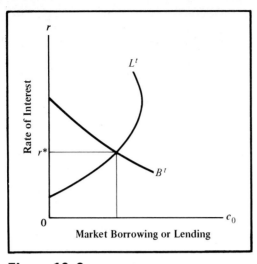

Figure 16. 2
Intertemporal Borrowing-
Lending Equilibrium

Figure 16.1, and the B^t curve the responses of borrowers, i.e., of persons for whom the endowment position E lies to the northwest rather than to the southeast of the preferred intertemporal optimum position $C*$.[2] On the vertical axis of the borrowing-lending diagram it is usual to put the interest rate r, so that the supply-demand intersection determines the equilibrium rate of interest $r*$. The height of the rate of interest is an indication of the *relative price* of current in terms of future consumption claims. More precisely, this relative price was given in equation (16.1) as $1 + r = P_0/P_1$. But the constant 1 can be shifted to the other side, so that $r = P_0/P_1 - 1$ does indeed represent the relative value (more specifically, the *premium* component of the value) of current in comparison with future consumption entitlements.

The analysis so far has been of a pure borrowing-lending equilibrium. Lending corresponds to *saving* (refraining from consumption) on the part of some persons in the economy, necessarily balanced by the borrowing or *dis-saving* of others. In this model no actual new formation of real-capital (no *investment*) is taking place. The pure borrowing-lending model corresponds, therefore, to the discussion of "Supply and Demand in Pure Exchange" in Section 7.C. But the process of the formation of real-capital is a species of *intertemporal productive transformation*, as when current corn is transformed into future corn by the physical planting of seed. Consequently, dealing with real investment will correspond with the model of productive transformation analyzed under the heading of "Exchange and Production" in Section 7.D.

[2]It should be realized, however, that for a sufficiently high rate of interest someone previously a borrower might shift over and become a lender, while for a sufficiently low rate of interest someone previously a lender might become a borrower.

417

16. A. 2   Saving-Investment Equilibrium

Figure 16.3, analogous to Figure 7.6, shows the intertemporal productive-consumptive situation of a Robinson Crusoe isolated from all trade. Starting from an intertemporal endowment combination $E = (c_0^\dagger, c_1^\dagger)$, Robinson's

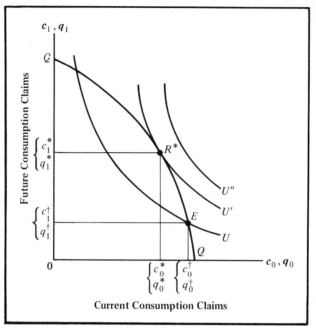

Figure 16. 3
Intertemporal Productive-Consumptive Optimum
Robinson Crusoe

productive transformation opportunities are indicated by the his Production-Possibility Curve QQ. The QQ curve is the locus of possible productive combinations (q_0, q_1). Since the endowment combination is one point on the curve, we can also write $E \equiv (q_0^\dagger, q_1^\dagger)$. The concave shape of QQ represents a kind of diminishing returns in intertemporal transformation. For example, doubling the consumptive sacrifice (input of seed) will not generally double the return (output of next year's corn). Evidently, the optimum position for Robinson is the tangency point R^* in the diagram. This is a joint productive-consumptive optimum: $R^* \equiv (c_0^*, c_1^*) = (q_0^*, q_1^*)$.

We can now interpret the Crusoe or "autarky" solution in terms of the special terminology of intertemporal choice. Robinson's *saving* (refraining from consumption) is, as before, the horizontal distance $c_0^\dagger - c_0^*$. But here no lending occurs, as there is no other person with whom an exchange of current for future consumption claims can take place. Rather, Robinson's saving is used solely for physical *investment* (planting seed): $c_0^\dagger - c_0^* = q_0^\dagger - q_0^*$. The yield in terms of future corn is shown in the diagram by the

418

419

Chapter 16
Intertemporal
Choice:
Saving, Investment,
and Interest

vertical distance $q_1^* - q_1^\dagger = c_1^* - c_1^\dagger$. For an isolated Robinson Crusoe, therefore, plantings of seed (investing) exactly equal non-consumption of corn (saving).

Given the possibility of exchange with other persons, however, the saving-investment equality need no longer obtain for any single person separately. Figure 16.4 pictures an individual possessing *both* productive opportunities and market opportunities. The productive opportunities are represented, as before, by the Production-Possibility Curve QQ. The market opportunities

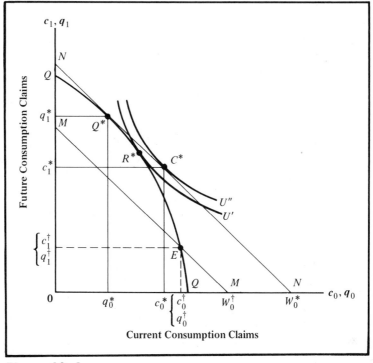

Figure 16. 4
Intertemporal Productive-Consumptive Optimum
with Exchange

can be represented by straight market lines of slope $-P_0/P_1 = -(1 + r)$ through attainable points on QQ. Each market line is associated with a particular magnitude of attained wealth according to the equation:

(16.4)
$$W_0 = q_0 + \frac{q_1}{1 + r}$$

One such line, MM, shows the possibilities for market exchange from the endowment position E—the associated wealth being $W_0^\dagger$ as before. But it is obviously superior for the individual here first to attain a productive opti-

420

Chapter 16
Intertemporal
Choice:
Saving, Investment,
and Interest

mum at Q^*, where QQ is tangent to the *highest* attainable market line. This line NN is associated with the maximum attainable level of wealth, W_0^*.

(16.5)
$$W_0^* = q_0^* + \frac{q_1^*}{1+r}$$

He can *then* engage in market exchange along the line NN, attaining a consumptive optimum at C^* far superior to what he could achieve by isolated production. The attained wealth W_0^* represents the level of *constraint* for the consumptive optimization decision:

(16.6)
$$c_0 + \frac{c_1}{1+r} = W_0^*$$

In terms of the special intertemporal terminology, the individual pictured in Figure 16.4 is engaging in physical *investment* (planting of seed corn) to the extent of the horizontal distance $q_0^\dagger - q_0^*$. But his *saving* is a lesser amount, indicated by the horizontal distance $c_0^\dagger - c_0^*$. That is, the individual does save a portion of his endowed current income, but *not* enough to fully "finance" the investment. It follows that some other members of the society must be saving enough to make up the deficiency, i.e., to provide the remainder of the needed seed corn for the individual of Figure 16.4 to plant. *In the aggregate,* saving (e.g., refraining from current consumption to provide seed corn) must equal investment (e.g., physical sacrifice of current consumption

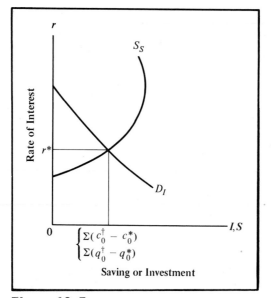

Figure 16. 5
Intertemporal Productive-Consumptive
Equilibrium

421

Chapter 16

Intertemporal
Choice:
Saving, Investment,
and Interest

via the planting of seed corn). The condition of market equilibrium is precisely that this equality must hold.

Market equilibrium is shown in Figure 16.5, which corresponds to Figure 7.8 earlier. On the horizontal axis are represented aggregate saving and investment quantities. The curve S_S shows the overall "supply of saving," i.e., the sum of the individual $c_0^\dagger - c_0^*$ magnitudes. The curve D_I shows correspondingly the overall "demand for investment," i.e., the sum of the individual $q_0^\dagger - q_0^*$ magnitudes. The supply of saving and demand for investment are both functions of the interest rate $r \equiv P_0/P_1 - 1$. The derivation of these curves, proceeding from the individual optimization diagram to individual supply and demand curves and then to market-wide aggregates, follows Section 7.D in all essentials and so is omitted here.

Conclusion: The equilibrium interest rate r^* is that at which the aggregate supply of saving in the economy balances the aggregate demand for productive investment.

16. B INVESTMENT DECISIONS AND THE PRESENT-VALUE RULE

The analysis of the processes of choice of consumption and production patterns over time is widely regarded as constituting one of the more difficult branches of economic theory. On the other hand, this is also a branch of economics that is of intense and immediate concern for practical men of affairs. Decision-makers in government and business continually face such choices as: What investment projects to adopt? How to finance the set of chosen projects? Over what time frame to pay out the benefits? In this section and the one following, the theoretical results derived in Section 16.A will be applied to certain aspects of the investment decision problem arising in the world of affairs.

16. B. 1 The Separation Theorem

An essential feature of productive-consumptive optimization as pictured in Figure 16.4 is the fact that *the productive optimum position is entirely independent of the individual's preferences.* No matter how the indifference curves may shift around, the productive optimum Q^* is unchanged. For, the location of Q^* depends only on the Production-Possibility Curve QQ and the slope of the market lines. This independence, called the *Separation Theorem*, follows from the assumption of perfect and costless markets (see Chapter 8). Suppose that market transactions were instead costly, that an individual could only borrow at a much higher rate of interest than that at which he could lend.[3] The amount that such a person would physically invest, his choice of Q^* on the Production-Possibility Curve, would then depend in part

---

[3] This difference might be due to "proportional transaction costs" as discussed in Section 8.B.

422

Chapter 16
Intertemporal
Choice:
Saving, Investment,
and Interest

upon his preferences, i.e., upon how much he was willing to self-finance (save). Then his productive and consumptive decisions would not be entirely separated. In the extreme case of an isolated Robinson Crusoe, where costs of transacting are infinite, there are *no* market opportunities at all. For Robinson Crusoe, the productive and consumptive decisions must be entirely identical; *all* his physical investment must be self-financed.

If the conditions underlying the Separation Theorem can be regarded as approximately applicable, there is a very important practical implication. Suppose that one individual (the "principal") were to delegate his productive decisions to another (the "agent"). *The agent would not have to know anything about the personal time-preferences of his principal.* If the agent maximizes attained wealth W_0^*, an objective market magnitude, this suffices to assure that his principal is made as well off as is possible.

Even more important, an agent could work simultaneously for a number of *different* principals with diverging time-preferences. These principals might be in a position to advantageously combine their productive opportunities by forming a *firm* (see Chapter 9), agreeing first upon some appropriate fractional division of ownership of the firm. Then the agent's maximizing the wealth of the firm suffices to maximize the wealth increments going to each and every one of the owners, regardless of divergences in their intertemporal consumption desires. So the types of investments a firm could advantageously undertake need not take into account whether the owners are "heirs with great expectations," or forethoughted savers, or any mixture thereof.[4]

16. B. 2 The Present-Value Rule for Investment Decision

Suppose that a "project," i.e., an investment (or disinvestment) opportunity, is under consideration for adoption. What is the appropriate *Investment Decision Rule*?

A project can be regarded, in the simple two-period model so far assumed, as characterized by a sequence of dated "payments," i.e., income increments (or income decrements) z_0 and z_1. If z_0 is negative and z_1 is positive, present income is being sacrificed for future income and we have an *investment* project. If z_0 is positive and z_1 negative, it would be a *disinvestment* project.

No matter what the pattern of positive or negative elements, the *Present Value V_0* of a project is defined as:

(16.7)
$$V_0 \equiv z_0 + \frac{z_1}{1+r}$$

Comparison with the definition of wealth in equation (16.4) shows that Present Value can be regarded as a *wealth increment* (to the decision-making unit) associated with adoption of the project in question. *Given the Separa-*

---

[4]When the Separation Theorem is *inapplicable*, there is said to be a "clientele effect" in the decisions of the firm. We would expect principals of different tastes to sort themselves out, becoming owners of different types of firms, each of which could cater to the particular time-preferences of its owners.

423

Chapter 16
Intertemporal
Choice:
Saving, Investment,
and Interest

tion Theorem, wealth-maximization is the object of all productive decisions. Then positive wealth increments are unambiguously desirable and negative wealth increments undesirable. These considerations lead to:

Present-Value Rule #1: Adopt any incremental project for which Present Value V_0 is positive; reject any project for which Present Value V_0 is negative. (Note that this rule has the same form for investment and disinvestment projects.)

There are possibilities of complications where projects are *interdependent*. Conceivably, adoption of any one project might change the z_0, z_1 sequence associated with another. The obvious implication for these cases is to adopt that *set* of projects whose combined payment stream has maximum Present Value. We shall not go through all the interdependence possibilities here, but rather state the rule applicable when projects or combinations of projects are *mutually exclusive*:[5]

Present-Value Rule #2: If two projects (or combinations of projects) are mutually exclusive, adopt that which has the higher Present Value V_0.

16. C MULTI-PERIOD ANALYSIS

The discussion to this point has been limited to consumption and investment choices over two dates: "now" (time-0) and "one year from now" (time-1). But the same general principles apply to more complex multitemporal decisions. We can think of individuals as attempting to attain preferred consumption combinations over any number of dates from "now" to an "economic horizon" at some future date T. Thus, the ultimate objects of choice are consumption sequences $c_0, c_1, c_2, \ldots, c_T$. In proceeding from an initial income-endowment sequence $c_0^\dagger, c_1^\dagger, \ldots, c_T^\dagger$ to his preferred consumption sequence, the individual will be making a variety of intertemporal productive transformations and market exchanges. But as before, if the Separation Theorem is applicable, then determination of the productive optimum $Q^* = (q_0^*, q_1^*, q_2^*, \ldots, q_T^*)$ can be guided solely by the goal of *wealth-maximization* independent of preferences. Thus, the Present-Value Rule continues to apply. However, we must generalize the concept of Present Value to a multi-period form.

In terms of market equilibrium, the interaction of individuals' supplies and demands today for consumption claims at different dates will determine prices $P_0, P_1, P_2, \ldots, P_T$.[6] We can fix $P_0 \equiv 1$, letting current claims continue

---

[5] Any list of alternative projects, interdependent or not, can be grouped into mutually exclusive combinations. Thus, three projects A, B, C can be sorted into the eight mutually exclusive combinations 0, A, B, C, AB, AC, BC, and ABC (where 0 represents adopting *no* project at all).

[6] It is important to note that while the claims represent rights to income at different dates, the prices are those quoted in the trading that takes place now. P_1 is the price *today* of a claim to income payable one year in the future, P_2 is the price *today* of a claim payable two years in the future, etc.

424

Chapter 16
Intertemporal
Choice:
Saving, Investment,
and Interest

to serve as "numeraire." The ratios of the prices ruling at different dates will depend, of course, upon the interaction of all the separate individuals' time-endowments, productive opportunities, and time-preferences.

In translating from *prices* to *interest rates*, there are two different formulations in common use.

Consider the successive one-year price ratios $P_1/P_0, P_2/P_1, \ldots, P_T/P_{T-1}$. These can be used to define the successive one-year "forward" interest rates $r_1, r_2, \ldots, r_T$ on the left side of the Table of Interest-Rate Equivalents below. Here r_1 is the rate appropriate in converting or discounting time-1 claims into their present or time-0 equivalents, r_2 the rate for discounting time-2 claims into time-1 equivalents, etc.

Alternatively, we can consider the ratios $P_1/P_0, P_2/P_0, \ldots, P_T/P_0$—defined so that P_0 appears in all the denominators. These can be used, as on the right side of the Table, to define the "long term" interest rates $R_1, R_2, \ldots, R_T$. These rates are appropriate for discounting the claims of any date *directly* into current (time-0) equivalents.

Table of Interest-Rate Equivalents

$$\frac{P_1}{P_0} = \frac{1}{1 + r_1} \qquad\qquad \frac{P_1}{P_0} = \frac{1}{1 + R_1}$$

$$\frac{P_2}{P_1} = \frac{1}{1 + r_2} \qquad\qquad \frac{P_2}{P_0} = \frac{1}{(1 + R_2)^2}$$

$$\cdots \qquad\qquad \cdots$$

$$\frac{P_T}{P_{T-1}} = \frac{1}{1 + r_T} \qquad\qquad \frac{P_T}{P_0} = \frac{1}{(1 + R_T)^T}$$

The Present Value of a multi-period sequence of income increments (or decrements) can be correspondingly expressed in two different forms:

(16.8) $$V_0 \equiv z_0 + \frac{z_1}{1 + R_1} + \frac{z_2}{(1 + R_2)^2} + \cdots + \frac{z_T}{(1 + R_T)^T}$$

(16.9) $$V_0 \equiv z_0 + \frac{z_1}{1 + r_1} + \frac{z_2}{(1 + r_2)(1 + r_1)}$$

$$+ \cdots + \frac{z_T}{(1 + r_T)\cdots(1 + r_2)(1 + r_1)}$$

For some purposes the first formulation is the more convenient, for other purposes the second. There is no ultimate difference between them. The "long term" rate R_t applicable for discounting claims dated t years from now is obviously a kind of average of the forward rates $r_1, r_2, \ldots, r_t$ between now and that date.

While there are some phenomena of economic interest leading to systematic patterns in the "term structure" of the r_t or R_t interest rates, in most practical investment-decision applications it is customary to assume that the currently applicable rate will maintain itself into the future. Of course, if the

r_t are all equal to some common value r then all the R_t will also be equal to r, so that the two formulations of (16.8) and (16.9) become identical in the form:

$$(16.10) \qquad V_0 \equiv z_0 + \frac{z_1}{1+r} + \frac{z_2}{(1+r)^2} + \cdots + \frac{z_T}{(1+r)^T}$$

Example 16. 1
Present Values
of the Feather
River Project

The Feather River Project is an enormous undertaking of the State of California, designed to convey water from a dam and reservoir in the northern part of the state to numerous delivery points in the central and southern portions. The following Table shows the results of an independent assessment (made prior to construction) of the prospective Costs and Receipts of the project and of the net balance of the two, all calculated in terms of present values. Three alternative routes then under consideration were evaluated; the present-value calculation considered two alternative interest rates, 2.7% and 5%.

While all the Present Values were negative, the higher 5% interest rate was associated with relatively lower present values of both Costs and Receipts. Since the Cost sequence is a series of positive payments at each date, and the Receipts sequence also a series of positive elements, the larger the r the smaller the discounted sum for each, as may be seen from equation (16.10). But the Table shows that the impact of a higher r upon Receipts is greater than upon Costs. The reason is that Costs are typically incurred *earlier* in time than Receipts are received, so that a rise in the discount factor $(1 + r)$ operates more powerfully to reduce the latter. It often happens that a project will show a favorable balance of Receipts over Costs when *undiscounted*, i.e., when calculated in

Present Values of the Feather River Project (millions of dollars)

Interest Rate	Costs	Receipts	Net Present Value	Net Present Value, Adjusted[a]
2.7%				
Route 1	$1,241	$1,079	$−162	$− 97
Route 8A	1,123	1,012	−111	− 46
Route 10A	1,029	919	−110	− 46
5%				
Route 1	1,035	515	−520	−502
Route 8A	860	445	−415	−397
Route 10A	799	409	−391	−372

Source: J. C. DeHaven and J. Hirshleifer, "Feather River Water for Southern California," *Land Economics*, v. 33 (Aug. 1957), p. 201. (Some technical footnotes omitted.)

[a]Adjustment credits an allowance for flood-control benefit and salvage value.

426

Chapter 16
Intertemporal
Choice:
Saving, Investment,
and Interest

terms of $r = 0$ in the discounting equation. *The higher the* r, *the less attractive the project* is a reliable general rule.[7]

Comment: The Feather River Project was adopted, despite the showing of negative net Present Value. Thus, the investment decision rule of this chapter was violated. Indeed, the route adopted was that which had the *most unfavorable* Receipts-Cost balance. (Reasons why this might have occurred are suggested in the analysis of the political process in Chapter 18.)

[7]Which is the *correct* discount rate r to use? For a private profit-maximizing individual or firm, r is determined in the market. But since a government agency need not show a profit, it might calculate in terms of any r it thinks appropriate. Whether a government investment *should* face a market test of adoptability is a controversial issue in "Welfare Economics" (see Chapter 17).

Let us now modify equation (16.10), which defined the Present Value V_0 of a project at some constant intertemporal interest rate r, in the following ways. First, assume that the "economic horizon" T is infinite. Second, let any current payment element z_0 be directly incorporated into V_0 as part of the Present Value. And third, assume that the future receipts $z_1, z_2, \ldots$ extending out to infinity remain at some constant level z. Then (16.10) reduces to the simple form:[8]

(16.10′)
$$V_0 \equiv \frac{z}{r} \quad \text{or} \quad r \equiv \frac{z}{V_0}$$

This formulation is equivalent to equation (15.3) of the previous chapter that expressed the relation between annual income from any source of productive services and the value of the source itself. Our derivation shows how the rate of interest r can be interpreted in two different ways: (1) as the *time-premium*, the extra market value of an earlier over a later-dated claim and (2) as the relation that must hold in equilibrium between an *income flow* z in comparison with the *value of its source* V_0. We sometimes say that V_0 in equation (16.10′) is the "capitalized" value of the annual income z, or that z

[8]The derivation proceeds from (16.10), under the special assumption above, as follows:

$$V_0 = z\left[\frac{1}{1+r} + \frac{1}{(1+r)^2} + \cdots\right]$$

Let $1/(1 + r)$ be denoted as k. Then:

$$V_0 = z(1 + k + k^2 + \cdots) - z = \frac{z}{1-k} - z$$

But

$$1 - k = 1 - \frac{1}{1+r} = \frac{r}{1+r}$$

So

$$V_0 = \frac{1+r}{r} - z = \frac{z}{r}$$

is the annual yield of V_0 as "principal sum." These statements are all correct, under the special assumptions that led to the expression of (16.10) in the special form (16.10′).

Example 16. 2
Fire Yours,
Hire Ours!

Errors in economic reasoning involving time often stem from an elementary fallacy: failing to appreciate that a dollar in the distant future is worth less today (has lower Present Value) than a dollar in the relatively near future. The following is an extract from a letter to Consumers Union (the well-known consumer advice organization).

Dear Editor:

I have just read your "Economics for consumers: Notes to home buyers" in the April 1972 issue. As it happens, I am in charge of job placement for the fledgling economists trained here at _____ University. Putting these two together, I can say in short: FIRE YOURS, HIRE OURS.

Your consumer economist compares the same appliances, available at $675 from a store but at $450 through the builder. The store's financing arrangement is a 2-year contract at 15% interest. The builder's is a mortgage add-on, 27-year contract at $7\frac{3}{4}\%$. Your economist assures CU's readers that the store offers the better deal! He arrives at this conclusion by adding up all the interest payments and tacking them onto the purchase price—making the totals $785 for the store deal and $1075 for the builder deal. One's mind reels at the enormity of the error here, flying as it does in the face of both formal economics and common sense. Formally speaking, it suffices to point out that a dollar payment deferred 27 years has a present worth of only 13 cents (at $7\frac{3}{4}\%$ interest, a reasonable current rate). Payments at different dates cannot be aggregated meaningfully without allowing for the time-value of money.

Returning to common sense, I don't suppose many of your readers could really have been fooled into thinking that it's better to buy at $675 than at $450, or better to pay 15% than $7\frac{3}{4}\%$ interest.

Sincerely,
Professor X

16. D REAL INTEREST AND MONEY INTEREST

What we have been referring to as the rate of interest so far in this chapter is more specifically known as the *real* rate of interest. Following the usual practice in price theory, we have looked behind the "veil of money" so as to

428

Chapter 16
Intertemporal
Choice:
Saving, Investment,
and Interest

gain an understanding of how the concept of interest is related to the rate of market exchange between current real consumption claims and future real consumption claims. Returning for simplicity to a two-date model (time-0 and time-1), the real rate of interest is the proportionate market premium on current real claims C_0 relative to real claims C_1 to be received one year in the future. Denoting quantities exchanged in markets as Δc_0 and Δc_1, we have seen that (in absolute values) the exchange ratio must satisfy:

(16.11)
$$\frac{\Delta c_1}{\Delta c_0} = 1 + r$$

But, in common parlance, the expression "the rate of interest" is ordinarily understood to be associated with the lending and borrowing of *money*. The *money rate of interest*, which can be symbolized as r', need not in general be exactly equal to the real rate of interest r. The money rate of interest is the premium on *current money* m_0 relative to *future money* m_1. That is, if current money is exchanged in the loan markets against future money in the amounts Δm_0 and Δm_1, the exchange ratio (in absolute terms) defines the *money* rate of interest in the expression:

(16.12)
$$\frac{\Delta m_1}{\Delta m_0} = 1 + r'$$

What is the relation between the real rate of interest r and the money rate of interest r'? This is connected with movements of the "price level," that is, with changes in the prices (in contemporaneous *money* units) of *real* goods. At time-0 and time-1, money is traded for real goods in exchange ratios $\Delta m_0/\Delta c_0$ and $\Delta m_1/\Delta c_1$. These exchange ratios (in absolute values) define the current and future money *price levels* P_0^m and P_1^m:

(16.13)
$$P_0^m = \frac{\Delta m_0}{\Delta c_0} \quad \text{and} \quad P_1^m = \frac{\Delta m_1}{\Delta c_1}$$

These imply:

$$\frac{\Delta m_1}{\Delta m_0} = \frac{P_1^m(\Delta c_1)}{P_0^m(\Delta c_0)}$$

This can be rewritten, using equations (16.11) and (16.12):

(16.14)
$$1 + r' = (1 + r)\frac{P_1^m}{P_0^m}$$

In terms of economic logic, equation (16.14) is readily understandable. The left-hand side, $1 + r'$, is what a lender receives in future money in return for giving up one unit of current money. The amount so received must depend, in part, upon the *real* future return $1 + r$ per unit of current *real* claims sacrificed. But money may rise or fall in value relative to the underlying real claims. Hence, the rate of money interest r' must be sufficiently high

429

Chapter 16
Intertemporal
Choice:
Saving, Investment,
and Interest

to make up for any increase in the price level that makes future real claims more expensive relative to future money.

It is convenient to express the ratio of money price levels, P_1^m/P_0^m, as $1 + a$, where a is the *anticipated rate of price-level inflation*. Then:

(16.15) $$1 + r' = (1 + r)(1 + a)$$

or

(16.16) $$r' = r + a + ra$$

This says that the money rate of interest equals the real rate of interest plus the anticipated rate of price inflation, plus the cross-product of the latter two. When r and a remain in their usual range of percentage points, the cross-product term can to a fair approximation be ignored. With *compound* interest, the shorter the period of compounding the more correct it is to drop the cross-product. For continuously-compounded interest, the cross-product drops out entirely and we have exactly:

(16.17) $$r' = r + a$$

It is in this simple form (16.17) that the relation between real and money interest rates is usually expressed.

Proposition: The money rate of interest equals the real rate of interest plus the anticipated rate of price inflation.

Example 16. 3
Real and
Money Rates
of Interest

William E. Gibson[9] examined the effects of inflationary expectations upon the "nominal" (money) rates of interest paid on U.S. Treasury securities in the period 1962 to 1970. In all such studies, the practical problem is to find a measure of "inflationary anticipations," which are not a directly visible magnitude. The measure used by Gibson was derived from a semi-annual survey of economists conducted by Joseph Livingston, a nationally syndicated financial columnist.

Using this information as an estimate of anticipations a, and the recorded interest rates as the measure of the money rate r', Gibson estimated statistically an equation in the form:

$$r' = H + Ka$$

Here H and K were the parameters of the line of best fit to the observed data. On the assumption that the *real* rate of interest r was constant over this period, comparison with equation (16.17) above shows that the

[9] William E. Gibson, "Interest Rates and Inflationary Expectations: New Evidence," *American Economic Review*, v. 62 (Dec. 1972).

430

Chapter 16
Intertemporal
Choice:
Saving, Investment,
and Interest

fitted parameter H is an estimate of the real rate r. Also, the fitted parameter K should be simply equal to unity.

The statistical evidence varied somewhat according to the type of security considered. But the H figures obtained suggested a *real* rate of interest between 2% and 3% (much lower than the nominal interest rates in this period, of course). And the K estimates were not far from unity (for example, .9300 for 3-month Treasury bills, .8959 for 3-year to 5-year Treasury notes).

One interesting point is that the K estimates were closer to unity in the latter than in the earlier portion of the period. The suggestion is that the general public was gradually "learning" to adjust its investments to the prospect of continuing inflation.

Equation (16.17) is connected with important issues of *macro*economic policy. Suppose the government desires, for reasons that do not concern us here, to reduce the money interest rate r'. One thing the government can do is to increase the aggregate money balances in the economy (for example, by paying its bills with newly printed money). In the short run, as the aggregate amount of current money m_0 rises, this does tend to lower the money rate of interest. For, if people have more m_0 in their hands they are more inclined to make market exchanges Δm_0 of current money against future money, i.e., they are more inclined to *lend* money for future return. As we can see in equation (16.12), when the denominator Δm_0 on the left-hand side rises then r' on the right-hand side falls. However, there is an important after-effect to consider. When government increases the aggregate of current money m_0, equation (16.13) tells us that the current money price-level P_0^m also tends to rise ("more money chasing the same amount of goods"). It *may* happen that this process tends to generate public anticipations of further future price inflation. People may think that if the government has found it convenient to print more money forcing up the current price-level P_0^m, they will find it convenient to do so again in the future. Should these anticipations become general, a rises in equation (16.17), so that the money rate of interest r' must rise! Hence, a successful attempt to lower r' *in the short run* may only serve to raise it higher *in the long run*.

16. E DETERMINANTS OF INTEREST AND INVESTMENT

What are the underlying forces tending to cause interest rates to be high in some countries and low in others, high in some eras and low in others? It is possible, in line with the analysis here, to classify the determinants of *real* interest rates under the headings: (1) time-preference, (2) time-endowment, and (3) time-productivity. Given these determinants of *real* interest, the *money* interest rate is accounted for by incorporating the anticipations of

431

Chapter 16
Intertemporal
Choice:
Saving, Investment,
and Interest

price-level inflation as shown by equation (16.17). And in fact, countries with established patterns of ongoing price inflation do have correspondingly high money rates of interest.

1. Time-preference: The higher the general pattern of preference in a community for *current* as against *future* consumption, the steeper the indifference curves on c_0, c_1 axes (as in Figure 16.1) tend to be. The market price ratio $P_0/P_1 = 1 + r$ (the absolute slope of the market lines) must to a greater or lesser extent reflect this, so that *high time-preference causes high interest.* Low time-preference is associated with personal characteristics such as fore-thoughtedness, strong family ties, willingness to defer enjoyment, etc. The later years of the Roman Empire were characterized by a decline in such "Puritanical" attitudes, and interest rates were accordingly high. A similar shift in values appears to be taking place in the Western world today, which might help explain the recent tendency of Western interest rates to rise.

2. Time-endowment: As we have seen, an "heir with great expectations," whose personal income-endowment lies mainly in the future, tends to be a borrower. In Figure 16.1 the endowment position E for such an heir would lie toward the northwest, in the region where the indifference curves are steep. If an entire society were in the situation of expecting future income to be much greater than current income, the interest rate (reflecting the absolute slope of the market lines) would correspondingly tend to be high. An interesting example is a community struck by a disaster. It is usually the case that a catastrophe damages goods relatively close to consumption more drastically than it impairs the basic productive powers of the economy. A drought or a hurricane, for example, will commonly destroy growing crops to a greater degree than fundamentals such as fertility of the land, capacity and training of the population, etc. It follows that present or near-future income-endowments are affected more seriously than far-future endowments, so that interest rates tend to rise when disaster strikes.

3. Time-productivity: Higher time-productivity tends to be reflected in higher ratios $\Delta q_1/\Delta q_0$, i.e., higher absolute slopes of individuals' intertemporal Production-Possibility Curves QQ. Again, if this relation is typical of a community the market interest rate must to a greater or lesser extent reflect this. Thus interest rates have tended to be high in newer and more productive communities, e.g., higher in America than in England, and higher in California than in Massachusetts.

Finally, a very important consideration is the *degree of isolation* of a community. There may be a very special or idiosyncratic situation as to time-preference, time-endowment, or time-productivity in a small local area. Nevertheless, unless that region is isolated from commerce the interest rates there cannot diverge too far from the more normal rates representing the typical picture in the outside world. For the process of exchange will lead to a flow of investments and loans (in the form of money and real claims) from the low-interest area to the high-interest area of any integrated market. The differences historically observed between interest rates in England and America, or between Massachusetts and California, have therefore been much smaller than would have been the case had the communities in question been isolated from one another.

Example 16. 4
Interest and
the Gold Rush[10]

Gold was struck in California in 1848, and the gold rush was on. The gold miners (and most other Californians as well) typically thought of themselves as having little current endowed income, but as prospectively very rich. Thus, they were in a situation comparable to that of "heirs with great expectations," and would be expected to be borrowers.

However, until the completion of the first transcontinental railroad in 1869 California was largely isolated from the rest of the world. Hence, Californians for the most part had to borrow from one another. Consequently, the interest rate during the period of the gold rush was generally very high, 24% per annum being a typical figure. This was far higher than the rate then ruling in the East. In the decade following the completion of the transcontinental railroad, it became much more feasible to transfer real resources in the form of loans from the East, and the interest rate in California dropped to around 6%.

[10]See Irving Fisher, *The Theory of Interest* (New York: The Macmillan Company, 1930; reprinted [Augustus M. Kelley] 1955), Chap. 18.

Questions

1. Explain the analogy between the intertemporal optimum of the consumer (choice between current consumption C_0 and future consumption C_1) and the optimum of the consumer at a moment of time (choice between consumption of commodity X and commodity Y). What determines the shape of the intertemporal market opportunity set?

2. Which is correct: (a) The annual rate of interest is the ratio P_0/P_1 of the price of a current consumption claim over the price of a consumption claim dated one year in the future; (b) The annual rate of interest is the *premium* on the value of current relative to one-year future claims, as given by the expression $P_0/P_1 - 1$? Explain.

3. In a two-period preference diagram, illustrate plausible endowment positions in the following cases. Indicate whether each person is likely to be a borrower or a lender.

    a. A young man with an elderly, wealthy, loving uncle in Australia.

    b. A farm-owner whose crop has been destroyed by hurricane.

433

Chapter 16
Intertemporal
Choice:
Saving, Investment,
and Interest

c. A sugar-*beet* farmer who has just learned that this year's sugar-*cane* crop has been destroyed by hurricane.

d. A 35-year-old star baseball player.

4. What is *wealth*? How is it related to current and future *incomes*?

5. In a pure-exchange situation, at market equilibrium the total of borrowing equals the total of lending. What can be said about saving and investment?

6. In a productive situation, at market equilibrium the total of saving equals the total of investment. What can be said about borrowing and lending?

7. "Saving need not equal investment for any single individual, but the two must be equal for the market as a whole." Is this necessarily true in equilibrium? Would it be true in a disequilibrium situation, as might result from a floor or ceiling upon interest rates?

8. What is the Separation Theorem? What is its importance? What would tend to happen if it were not applicable?

9. What is the Present Value Rule? Will this rule always lead decision-makers to correct choices of projects when the Separation Theorem holds? What if the Separation Theorem does not hold?

10. For a particular project M, the time sequence of payments is $z_0 = -100$, $z_1 = 125$. Is this an investment or a disinvestment? What is its Present Value V_0 when the interest rate r is 10%? At $r = 20\%$? At $r = 30\%$? What is the highest rate of interest at which the project should be adopted?

11. The Table here shows alternative payments sequences for two *interdependent* projects M and N. The columns headed "Alone" show the payments associated with each if it were adopted *separately*. The other columns show the payments associated with each if the other were *also* to be adopted. If the interest rate r were 20% and you were required to adopt no more than one project, which (if any) should be adopted? If you could adopt both together, would you want to do so?

Project	Alone		With the Other Project	
	z_0	z_1	z_0	z_1
M	-100	125	-90	110
N	-50	90	-60	95

12. Explain the relation between the rate of interest r as defined in the equation $r = P_0/P_1 - 1$ and as defined in the equation $r = z/V_0$.

13. In a newly settled country, resources are likely to have great potential but are as yet undeveloped. Would you expect the interest rate to be high or low? Comparing situations in which the new country is or is not in close contact with the rest of the world, in which situation will the interest rate be higher? In which will more investment take place? Explain.

14. One country is "stagnant" (i.e., little investment and economic growth is taking place) because productive opportunities yielding a good return on

434

Chapter 16
Intertemporal
Choice:
Saving, Investment,
and Interest

investment are lacking. Another country has excellent investment opportunities, but little investment because time-preferences are very high. Which country would tend to have a high, and which a low, interest rate? Explain.

15. What is the *money* rate of interest, and how is it related to the *real* rate of interest? In the two preceding questions, was the interest rate referred to the money rate or the real rate of interest?

16. Money interest rates have been on a sharply rising trend over the past thirty years throughout the world. Which of the following might provide part of the explanation, and analyze:

    a. Higher rates of time-preference (changes in tastes).

    b. Higher rates of time-productivity (changes in investment opportunities).

    c. Lower ratios of current to anticipated future incomes (increased relative scarcity of current endowments).

    d. Higher rates of inflation (changes in anticipations as to monetary policies of governments).

Six

Political Economy

Chapter 17

Welfare Economics: The Theory of Economic Policy

This chapter is devoted to the problem of *how economists address questions of policy*—the topic traditionally called "political economy." While the emphasis in this text has been upon positive economic science, the normative analysis of policy issues has played a crucial role in the development of economic thought. As mentioned in Chapter 1, in laying the foundation of modern economics in *The Wealth of Nations* Adam Smith was motivated largely by a desire to recommend very definite economic policies. Or perhaps we should say *non*-policies since, for the most part, he urged *laissez faire*. And economists to this day remain active in criticism or in defense of alternative plans, programs, institutions, or legislation designed to cope with social problems. The title "welfare economics" is currently given to study of the theoretical underpinnings of economic policy.

The first section of the chapter considers the *goals* of policy. Section 17.B reviews what might be called Adam Smith's "Theorem of the Invisible Hand," which asserts a kind of optimality of the laissez-faire economy. Following this in Section 17.C we take up the flies in the ointment, the various reasons that have been adduced to explain why Smith's theorem fails (or is, perhaps, irrelevant whether it fails or not). Section 17.D considers the ever-challenging issue of economic equality.

17. A GOALS OF ECONOMIC POLICY

Economic theorists have concentrated attention almost entirely upon two of the many possible goals of policy: (1) efficiency, and (2) distributive equity. Roughly speaking, these two criteria represent the *size* of the economic pie and the *distribution* of slices among the possible claimants.

17. A. 1 Efficiency versus Equity

To begin with, suppose that an individual's well-being can be summarized simply by the amount of income I he has available for consumption. Then, as

438

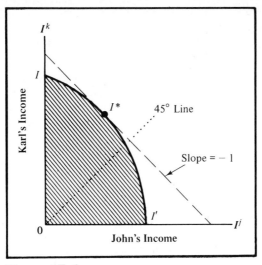

Figure 17. 1
Social Allocations of Income

between two persons John and Karl constituting a community, the alternative social allocations of income might be represented on I^j, I^k axes as in Figure 17.1. The shaded area shows the set of I^j, I^k combinations potentially available to this two-person community, i.e., the "social opportunity set," as a result of the social processes governing the production of goods and the assignment of income claims to individuals.

The curve II' that bounds the social opportunity set on the northeast, the Social Opportunity Frontier, might have any of a variety of shapes. As drawn, it is concave to the origin suggesting that a greater *aggregate* social income $I^T = I^j + I^k$ could be attained toward the middle of II' rather than at the corners. This might be plausibly justified as follows. At the lower right corner John is totally dominant; I^j is as high as it can be, while Karl receives literally nothing—$I^k = 0$. But then Karl will surely exit from the community (by death or emigration), in which case his productive powers will no longer be available to augment the aggregate social product I^T. If production is a cooperative process, providing Karl with some incentive in the way of income I^k will, up to a point at least, make the aggregate I^T larger than it would otherwise be. In a different terminology, the social mechanism that generates and distributes income is not a "constant-sum game." If Karl is induced to produce more as a result of receiving more, John will not lose the entire amount that Karl gains.

Efficiency in terms of incomes can simply be defined as achieving the maximum aggregate income $I^j + I^k = I^T$. Geometrically, this maximum is shown as $I*$ in Figure 17.1. It is located at the point of contact of II' with the highest possible line of slope -1 (i.e., of angle 135° to the horizontal), the dashed line in the diagram. A somewhat weaker concept of efficiency does not require that aggregate income be maximized, but only that the parties end up

439

somewhere on the Social Opportunity Frontier *II'* rather than in the interior of the shaded region.

We know, however, that money income, or even "real" income, is not an adequate index of an individual's well-being. First of all, a person may derive satisfaction from *reservation uses* of his resources (e.g., leisure) as an alternative to maximizing his market income. Second, how the individual *spends* his income over the many different consumption goods will clearly affect his achieved level of satisfaction. Perhaps most important, markets might be imperfect or even non-existent, as in a feudal or a communist society. In such an environment, "income" defined as the market earnings from owned resources would be a defective or even entirely meaningless measure of well-being.

We can get around this problem by using the familiar concept of *utility U* as index of the degree of satisfaction. Figure 17.2 shows the social oppor-

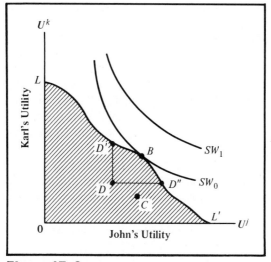

Figure 17. 2
Social Allocations of Utility

tunity set in terms of achievable utilities U^j and U^k of the two individuals. Because of the *non-cardinality* of utility and its *incommensurability* between individuals,[1] U^j and U^k cannot be added to form a meaningful total or social aggregate U^T. Consequently, the particular shape assigned to *LL'*, the Social Opportunity Frontier in terms of utilities, is irrelevant aside from *ordinal* properties. These are summarized by the negative slope of *LL'*, which tells us that one party cannot be made better off without making the other worse off. (In utility terms the only meaningful question is whether one or the other or both parties are better off; *how much* better off cannot be measured.)

[1]See Section 3.D.

Definition: An allocation of goods in an economy is said to be "Pareto-preferred"[2] if, in comparison with another, all parties concerned are *at least* as well off and one or more of the parties is actually better off.

Consider the allocation D in the interior of the social opportunity set of Figure 17.2. Comparing D' with D, Karl is better off and John is no worse off, so D' is Pareto-preferred to D. At D'' John is better off and Karl is no worse off, so the allocation D'' is also Pareto-preferred to D. And for any point *between* D' and D'' along the boundary LL', *both* parties are better off so that any such point is Pareto-preferred to D.

Generalizing this reasoning, for any point like D in the interior of the social opportunity set there will be points on the frontier LL' that are Pareto-preferred to it. But comparing any two allocations along the boundary LL' itself, the utility gain to one party will necessarily be associated with a utility loss to the other. Hence, for no point on the frontier will there be any other allocation Pareto-preferred to it.

The set of boundary points, the Social Opportunity Frontier, is called the set of *Pareto-optimal* allocations. Any of these points can be said to "maximize the size of the economic pie," in the weak sense represented by the absence of any allocation Pareto-preferred to it. And so *in utility terms, the efficient set is the Pareto-optimal set.*

What about the goal of distributive equity? Here we lack any principle with as compelling appeal as Pareto-optimality.[3] *Equality* as a goal receives a great deal of support, but because of non-cardinality and incommensurability the "equality of utilities" is meaningless. In practice, something like *equality of incomes* is often taken as an important goal. This question is considered further in Section 17.D.

One tradition in welfare economics "solves" the social optimality problem by imagining a special kind of interpersonal utility measure summarized in a so-called *social welfare function.* In Figure 17.2 we might lay down indifference contours of interpersonal utility or "welfare" (SW_0 and SW_1 in the diagram) and declare that the social optimum of perfect bliss occurs at point B where the boundary LL' touches the highest attainable welfare-indifference contour. The "only" difficulty is the absence of any agreement as to what the content of such a social welfare function might be!

Unfortunately, inability to say anything useful about distributive equity impairs the applicability even of the efficiency criterion. In Figure 17.2, suppose that a social choice is to be made between the alternative allocations D' and C. D' is in the Pareto-optimal or efficient set, and C is not. But the distribution between the parties concerned is such that D' is not Pareto-preferred *to* C; Karl is better off at D', but John is worse off.

---

[2]Vilfredo Pareto (1848–1923), Italian economist and sociologist (mentioned in Section 3.D above).

[3]Not everyone would agree that Pareto-optimality is a very compelling principle! (See below.)

Turning to somewhat deeper issues, the narrowness of the two criteria traditionally recognized by economists has been the object of some criticism. The philosophy underlying welfare economics is called *utilitarianism*.[4] The main themes of utilitarianism may be summarized in the two-fold assertion: (1) Social policies, rules, and institutions are to be judged solely in terms of their *consequences*; and (2) the only relevant consequences are the degrees of satisfaction of the *wants of individuals* ("pleasures and pains").

The first assertion represents a kind of social pragmatism. For utilitarians all social practices or arrangements, e.g., monarchy or voting or the market or capital punishment or the family or the nation, are merely means or instruments. They should not be adopted or rejected because they agree or disagree with the word of the Bible, or with natural law, or with the dictates of ethical principles, or with historical tradition or timeless custom. Instead, the only criterion is: Do they give rise to desirable social outcomes? Where others might say "The ends do not justify the means," the utilitarian replies: "What can justify means except the ends attained?"

The second assertion represents a radical individualism. Policies may or may not serve the purposes of God, may or may not advance science and learning, may or may not promote the survival of the race or nation or the gene pool; none of this is relevant for the utilitarian. What counts is whether the results comport with the desires of individuals. President John F. Kennedy once declared, "Ask not what your country can do for you, ask what you can do for your country!" To which a utilitarian might reply, "Why have a country except for what it can do for you?"

A somewhat separate question turns on the issue of *hedonism*. Are the individual consequences entering into the utilitarian calculus of social well-being limited exclusively to sensate satisfactions, as the hedonists would have it? What about "higher wants," for example benevolent desires to help others? The economic utilitarians generally answer this question by saying that it is the satisfaction of factually observable wants, whether sensate or "higher," that should govern policy. On this approach, benevolent desires are counted as well as hedonistic ones, but of course only to the extent that they are actually present—as measured, for example, by individuals' willingness to sacrifice sensate for higher goals.

Upon departing from utilitarian premises, *both* efficiency and equity as goals lose much of their force. Non-utilitarians might make any of the following arguments.

1.   Social policy should be directed not at giving individuals what they *want*, but what they *ought to have*. As the great moralists and our sacred texts have told us, as observation of others and candid self-examination reveal, and as history demonstrates, most of what people want most of the time they would be better off not getting. Efficiency is

---

[4]The similarity between the words "utility" and "utilitarianism" is not accidental. Both are due to Jeremy Bentham.

a goal for raising pigs, not for the social life of a community of people. Even the "equity" goal means little more than fair division among pigs at the trough.

2. Even admitting that an efficient and equitable distribution of satisfactions of individual wants might to some extent be a legitimate social goal, it is absurd to assert that this is the only relevant goal. Liberty, justice, order, community—all express goals of policy that transcend the satisfaction of individual wants.

3. More important than the social allocation of *outcomes*, the attainment of goals, is the question of the *means* by which these social outcomes are achieved. Far better is an allocation of goods and services that is both inefficient and inequitable, but arrived at in a spirit of voluntary cooperation under law, than a perfectly ideal allocation established by dictatorial decree or political trickery.

4. Recognition of the social provenance of individual "wants" exposes the emptiness of utilitarian criteria. What individuals desire is very largely a result of their social conditioning. Much more important than the *want-satisaction* process is the *want-creation* process. The main goal of policy should be to affect the formation of the proper wants.

No resolution of these difficult philosophical questions can be provided here. It is clear that utilitarianism can be criticized from many different points of view: dictatorial or democratic, radical or conservative, ethical or cynical. In any case economics is the science of the *instrumental*, of the choice of proper means for given ends. However defective utilitarian ends may be, they do carry a great deal of force in modern value systems and therefore must be reckoned with in the analysis of economic policy.

Most of the debates among economists—over monetarism vs. fiscalism, minimum wages or price controls, depletion allowances or import quotas—are carried on within utilitarian ground rules. But for a second class of issues, e.g., racial discrimination, capital punishment and abortion, the proper extent and scope of government activities, individual liberty versus civic order, questions are raised that go beyond the utilitarian. The progress of economic science, the development of more accurate data and more fruitful and rigorous theories, can be expected to go far toward resolving the former class of disagreements. But if one economist prefers Maoism and another capitalism, or one prefers to exterminate and the other to tolerate an inconvenient minority group, the fundamental sources of contention are almost surely divergences in values not capturable within the utilitarian framework. Such divergences will not be eliminated by advances in scientific economics.

17. B   THE THEOREM OF THE INVISIBLE HAND

Adam Smith asserted that the invisible hand of self-interest "frequently" leads men to effectually promote the interests of society. Economists in modern times have refined this idea into a more precise theorem that can be worded as follows: *Given a number of ideal conditions, optimizing behavior on the part of individuals and firms under pure competition leads to an efficient* (*Pareto-optimal*) *social outcome.* In this section we shall go through the meaning of this "Theorem of the Invisible Hand." The ideal conditions, and the consequences of their separate or combined violation, are discussed further in Section 17.C. But note that the theorem relates solely to the social goal of *efficiency*. The question of distributive *equity* will be considered further in Section 17.D.

A formal demonstration of the Theorem of the Invisible Hand would make use of the equations of general equilibrium derived and discussed in the Appendix. An intuitive treatment will suffice here, however. It will be shown that competitive equilibrium implies: (1) efficiency as among consumers (in the allocation of consumption goods), (2) efficiency as among resource-owners (in the provision of resources for productive uses), and (3) efficiency as among firms (in the conversion of resources into consumable goods).

To isolate the question of *efficiency among consumers*, we can return to the analysis of Section 7.B. Equation (7.1) can be repeated in slightly changed notation here:

(17.1)
$$MRSC_{XY}^{j} = \frac{P_x}{P_y} = MRSC_{XY}^{k}$$

This says that, for any pair of individuals John and Karl, as a condition of competitive equilibrium each person's *Marginal Rate of Substitution in Consumption*, here denoted $MRSC_{XY}$ (the absolute slope $-\dfrac{\Delta y}{\Delta x}\bigg|_U$ along his indifference curve between commodities X and Y), must equal the price ratio P_x/P_y (the absolute slope of the budget line). In this discussion, it will be convenient once again to pierce the veil of money and think in terms of real commodities only. One of the consumption goods, in particular Y, can be chosen as the "numeraire" or basis of pricing. Then P_y is necessarily unity (the price of Y, in units of Y, must be 1) so that P_x/P_y reduces to P_x. With this understood, the condition of efficiency among consumers can be expressed more simply as:

(17.1′) $MRSC_{XY}^{j} = P_x = MRSC_{XY}^{k}$ Efficiency among Consumers

It is the equality $MRSC_{XY}^{j} = MRSC_{XY}^{k}$ that represents the condition of efficiency. Its meaning is that, on the margin, John is no more willing to sacrifice a unit of Y (to obtain more X) than is Karl. A discrepancy between these Marginal Rates of Substitution would imply inefficiency, since then the two parties could mutually benefit from trade. (The one more willing to give up Y in exchange for X would do so, receiving in payment some X from the one more anxious to acquire Y.) A benevolent and omniscient dictator might directly impose such an equality between $MRSC_{XY}^{j}$ and $MRSC_{XY}^{k}$ without the aid of any market system. In a regime of competitive markets, however, *the equality emerges from the self-regarding actions of each trader in setting his own* $MRSC_{XY}$ *equal to the market exchange rate between* X *and* Y, i.e., to the price P_x. Thus, the market price P_x *mediates* the efficient equality of the individuals' Marginal Rates of Substitution in Consumption.

For *efficiency among resource-owners*, an exactly corresponding argument leads to the condition that can be expressed as:

$$\textbf{(17.2)} \qquad MRSR_{AI}^j = h_a = MRSR_{AI}^k \qquad \text{Efficiency among Resource-Owners}$$

This equation follows, again with slightly changed notation, from equation (15.2). As described in Section 15.A, each separate owner of a resource A sets $MRSR_{AI}$, his *Marginal Rate of Substitution between reservation uses of A and income I*, equal to the hire-price h_a of factor A. Geometrically, the equality is between the absolute slope $-\dfrac{\Delta I}{\Delta R_a}\bigg|_U$ of his indifference curve (between income I and "leisure" or reservation uses R_a) and the absolute slope h_a of the budget line. Since Y is the numeraire commodity in which real income is measured, $MRSR_{AI}$ is equivalent to $MRSR_{AY}$, that is, to the Marginal Rate of Substitution between reservation uses of A and consumption of the numeraire commodity Y. Again, the individuals' separate Marginal Rates of Substitution are not equated directly, as might be done by a dictator. Rather, in a regime of competitive markets the separate optimizations are mediated and brought into efficient equality by the hire-price h_a of factor A.

With regard to *efficiency among firms*, think of production as the process of converting resource A into good X. We know from Section 14.A that the competitive (price-taking) firm sets vmp_a, the Value of the Marginal Product of factor A, equal to the hire-price h_a. Specifically, equation (14.5) implies that for any two price-taking firms f and g:

$$\textbf{(17.3)} \qquad vmp_a^f = h_a = vmp_a^g \qquad \text{Efficiency among Firms}$$

That this is an efficiency condition is immediately evident. If the equality did not hold, on the margin one firm could convert a unit of resource A into greater product value than the other. Furthermore, since by definition $vmp_a \equiv P_x(mp_a)$, and since P_x will be the same as among all firms in a given market, the inequality would have to be between the physical Marginal products mp_a^f and mp_a^g. It would then be socially more efficient to shift some units of resource A away from the firm with lower mp_a and to the firm with higher mp_a. Once again, the efficient equality condition is not imposed by dictation but rather emerges from the mediating role of competitive price.

An alternative version of the efficiency condition as among firms takes the familiar form:

$$\textbf{(17.3')} \qquad MC_x^f = P_x = MC_x^g$$

This condition differs from (17.3) only in being expressed in units of output X rather than units of input A.[5]

Formally speaking, these results should be generalized to deal with any numbers of individuals, of firms, of products, and of resources. But the generalization would merely be a complication; the essence of the efficiency conditions is epitomized in what has already been set down.

17. C WHAT CAN GO WRONG? ALMOST EVERYTHING!

The trouble is, the Theorem of the Invisible Hand is too good to be true! There are many ways in which things can go wrong. Indeed, a large portion of modern economic analysis has taken the form of exploration of conditions leading to failure of the theorem.

17. C. 1 Monopoly

The most obvious real-world feature limiting the applicability of the Theorem of the Invisible Hand is *monopoly*. Monopoly can and does exist, to some degree at least, on both sides of the various product and factor markets in the economy. Firms might be monopolist sellers of product or monopsonist employers of resources, while individuals might be monopolist sellers of resources or monopsonist buyers of products. And it is not necessarily monopoly or monopsony in the strict sense that lead to failure of the theorem. Any non-price-taking behavior, whether due to cartels, oligopoly, or any of the situations analyzed in Chapters 11 through 13, implies violation of the efficiency conditions of the previous section.

An important policy distinction has been made between *natural* and *contrived* monopoly. In "natural" monopoly, economies of scale are so great that one firm can always produce more cheaply than can a larger number. Public utilities (electricity, telephone, gas, etc.) are commonly believed to fit into this category. Traditional policy with regard to natural monopoly has been to retain the single large firm but to prevent monopolistic exploitation through a regulatory process (see Section 11.D). "Contrived" monopoly is said to arise when the economies of scale are not a dominant feature; certain other circumstances have somehow blunted competitive forces. Here the traditional "trust-busting" policy has attempted to break up monopolistic concentrations. Despite this supposed dedication to competition, however, government policy has in many ways tended to support the monopolization, or at any rate the cartelization, of sectors of the economy.[6]

Given either natural or contrived monopoly, the Invisible Hand does not

---

[5]The equivalence of the two formulations follows immediately from the identity explained in the derivation of equation (14.8):

$$MC_x = \frac{h_a}{mp_a}$$

Since $vmp_a \equiv P_x(mp_a)$, simple algebra converts (17.3′) into the form (17.3).

[6]See, for instance, Examples 11.5 ("Agricultural Marketing Orders") or 15.3 ("Barbers").

induce behavior that serves the interests of others, at least not to the optimal degree. The profit-maximizing monopoly firm is motivated to set $MC_x = MR_x$ rather than $MC_x = P_x$ (see Section 11.B.2), thus violating the condition in equation (17.3′). Since $MR_x < P_x$, the monopolist ordinarily produces "too little" output of X. In terms of factor units, it is equation (17.3) that is violated. As shown in Section 14.A, the profit-maximizing factor-employment condition for the firm is $mrp_a \equiv MR_x(mp_a) = h_a$ whereas the efficiency condition (17.3) is $vmp_a \equiv P_x(mp_a) = h_a$. Then $MR_x < P_x$ implies $mrp_a < vmp_a$. So "too little" of factor A will be hired by the monopolist firm. By corresponding arguments, it can be shown that a monopsonist employer of factor, or a monopolist supplier of factors, or even a monopsonist consumer of a product (should that case ever arise) will all violate one or more of the efficiency conditions of the preceding section.

Conclusion: Under monopoly there is "too little" market exchange. And in consequence, there will also be "too little" productive specialization and "too little" market employment of factors.

In effect, monopoly deprives society of some of the mutual benefits of trade. Although the economic agent possessing monopoly power derives advantages therefrom, in principle it would be possible to improve matters by achieving a Pareto-preferred solution. If price-taking behavior were substituted for monopolistic exploitation, the gain would be great enough to permit compensating the monopolist while still leaving something over for the rest of society.[7]

17. C. 2 Disequilibrium

In the case of monopoly or monopsony, failure of efficiency is due to non-price-taking behavior on the part of economic agents. But violations of the efficiency conditions may remain even if all agents are price-takers.

One extremely important source of difficulty is *market disequilibrium*. In Section 17.B great emphasis was placed upon the mediating role of prices in bringing the separate optimizing decisions of individuals and firms into accord. But what if the currently quoted price is not the right one for clearing a market? It is true that there will then surely be corrective forces at work tending to bring about equilibrium (as explained in Section 2.A). But given a world in which the determining conditions are ever-changing, the chances are that prices will always be some distance from and scarcely ever at their equilibrium values. Disequilibrium is therefore the prevalent state of affairs.

Since prices will sometimes be too high and at other times too low, it might be thought that the effects of disequilibrium would tend more or less to cancel out over the economy. That, however, is not the case. Prices that diverge from disequilibrium levels, whether too high or too low, tend to *reduce* quantities

---

[7]These gains and losses were discussed in terms of the concepts of Consumer Surplus and Producer Surplus in Section 11.C (see especially Figure 11.4).

exchanged in markets and therefore limit the economy's ability to derive the advantages of specialization in production. Like monopoly, disequilibrium wipes out some of the potential gains from trade.

This is easy to see in Figure 17.3, which pictures a market with normally sloping supply and demand curves. The price P^+ is too high to equate supply and demand. At that price the effective quantity exchanged Q^+ is the *lesser* of the supply and demand quantities, in this case, the demand quantity. It is true that at the high price P^+ there are unsatisfied sellers, but they cannot find

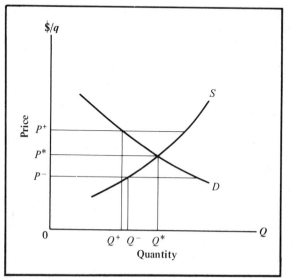

Figure 17. 3
Disequilibrium

customers ("It takes two to tango!"). The price P^- on the other hand is too low to clear the market, but again here it is the *lesser* (offered) quantity Q^- that governs; there are now unsatisfied buyers, but they cannot find willing suppliers. While price is in the one case above and in the other case below the equilibrium P^*, in both situations the quantity exchanged is *less* than the equilibrium Q^*.[8]

Conclusion: Disequilibrium, like monopoly, leads to non-Pareto-optimal outcomes because of reduced volumes of trade.

Disequilibrium in one or more particular markets may have significant *macroeconomic* consequences. The incomes that consumers have available for spending on goods do not come out of the air; they derive from earnings received as resource-owners. A market disequilibrium reducing the scale of production, in one or more markets, must adversely affect individuals' real

---

[8]The consequent efficiency loss can be analyzed in terms of Consumer and Producer Surplus, in the same way as the losses due to the *artificial* government-imposed disequilibria (price ceilings or price floors) that were studied under the heading of "Hindrances to Trade" in Section 7.E.2.

incomes. Factor suppliers will have to select less remunerative alternative employments or less desired reservation uses of the resources they own. The reduction in real incomes will in turn affect consumers' demand functions for goods, in accordance with the "Engel curve" analysis in Section 4.B.1. Thus, disequilibrium in *one* market will tend to reduce demand (shift demand curves to the left) *in all other* markets. A second-order adjustment in these other markets will then carry the process further. A self-reinforcing process may thus ensue in which an initial disequilibrium has a multiplied negative effect upon resource employment and real incomes. Some macroeconomic theories place this "multiplier" process in a central role as explaining the movements of the so-called business cycle.

17. C. 3   Externalities and Coase's Theorem

"Externalities" are said to arise when the voluntary economic activities of economic agents—in production, consumption, or exchange—affect the interests of other economic agents in a way *not* setting up legally recognized rights of compensation or redress. But this definition is too broad for present purposes. Each individual person is affected by the infinitely varied actions of other people all over the globe that may tend to raise or lower the prices of commodities he either consumes or produces. We here rule out these merely "pecuniary" externalities that take effect only through market prices. Rather, we will be concerned with the *direct* externalities, whose impact upon other parties operates not through price shifts but immediately upon technological opportunities or preference functions.

Consider the problem of *pollution*. A firm using river water, let us say, discharges the effluent back to the river after degrading its quality. The upstream use may adversely affect the operations of another firm downstream; for example, the polluted river water may no longer be productively usable downstream, at least not without further input of resources for purification. Or residential consumers downstream may suffer a loss of consumptive satisfaction (utility) from having to use lower-quality water for drinking and other domestic purposes.

Pollution is an example of a direct externality that is harmful. But such an externality might also be beneficial. An upstream user's activities may actually improve the quality of the river water from the point of view of some or all downstream users.

Conclusion: Direct externalities, beneficial or harmful, lead the Invisible Hand astray. In the interests of efficiency, the agent generating the externality ought, if the externality is beneficial, to be induced to engage in the process even more than his private self-interest would dictate. If the externality is harmful, of course, the generating agent ought to be induced to diminish the scale of his polluting activity in comparison with what his self-interest would dictate.

Externalities, therefore, represent sources of social gain or loss that do not get translated into the market signals that constitute the Invisible Hand.

Traditional policy analysis has recognized a number of alternative remedies for this problem.

1. Tax-subsidy Adjustments: A tax placed on the generation of a harmful externality will tend to reduce the amount of externality imposed on others. An ideal corrective tax would add to the private Marginal Cost, the cost recognized by the polluting producer in his own self-interest, a penalty that is just enough to balance the harm suffered, on the margin, by others. Thus the sum of the tax and the private Marginal Cost would bring home to the generating agent the total true social Marginal Cost of carrying on the polluting activity. For a beneficial externality, correspondingly, a corrective *subsidy* would be called for to induce an ideal (greater) level of the externality-generating activity.

2. Unitization: If the upstream and the downstream productive processes using the river water were merged or "unitized" under the control of a single economic agent, what was previously an externality would be *internalized*. The single integrated water-using enterprise would now carry on the polluting activity at a socially efficient level, i.e., it would pollute only so long as the marginal upstream gain exceeded the marginal downstream loss. A particularly important instance of unitization occurs in oilfield operations. The externality here is the fact that pumping at any well adversely affects the output of other wells in the same field (by drawing away the fugitive oil, and by reducing gas pressure). Under diversified ownership, the consequence is inefficient over-drilling and over-pumping. At any given well the owner is motivated to pump faster than he otherwise would, to capture oil under others' land and to prevent others from capturing the oil under his land. And in any given land tract, the owner is similarly induced to drill more wells than he otherwise would—locating wells all along his boundaries so as to minimize oil loss to others. With unitization, the sole ownerships of individual wells are exchanged for *pro rata* shares in the overall operations of the oilfield. This eliminates the motivation to over-pump or to over-drill; the unitized incentive is simply to produce most efficiently from the integrated field, as it no longer makes any difference on whose land the oil is brought to the surface.

3. Property Reassignment: The fundamental source of the externality phenomenon is an inappropriate assignment of property rights. If the span of actual effect always coincided with the span of legally-recognized control, externalities would not occur. In the river-water example, the downstream user should ideally be assigned a property right to receive water of some specified quality from the hands of the upstream user. If the first user degrades the quality below this level, he should be liable for the damages suffered by later users. Conversely, if the upstream user leaves the water in better condition than legally required, he should in principle be entitled to compensation from later users. Such a definite assignment of property in water quality would not, as might first be thought, simply freeze the pattern of uses in accordance with the legally defined rights. Should some other arrangement be mutually preferred, the parties concerned could negotiate an exchange of property rights. If the downstream user was initially entitled to absolutely pure water, for example, the upstream producer could nevertheless buy from him the right to pollute the river to some specified degree.

This last concept has been generalized into what is known as *Coase's Theorem.*[9] The thrust of Coase's Theorem is that the Invisible Hand is really much more effective than the argument about externalities at first suggests. For there are natural market forces at work tending to bring the "external" effects into the calculations of the responsible parties. If a producer initially owns the right to generate a harmful externality, those adversely affected can offer him a financial reward for *not* exercising that right. Or if the other parties are initially entitled to be safe from the externality, it is up to the producer to offer terms of compensation at which they will accept a degree of harm. (In the case of a beneficial externality, of course, the argument applies in reverse.) So long as the legal rights are well-defined and marketable, the Invisible Hand will tend to lead the parties to an efficient outcome, i.e., to a result that exhausts all possibilities for further mutual gain.

[9]R. H. Coase, "The Problem of Social Cost," *The Journal of Law & Economics*, v. 3 (Oct. 1960).

Example 17. 1
**The Apples
and the Bees**

One of the classical illustrations used in economists' discussions of externalities has been a tale of the apples and the bees. The apple-grower's orchard provides the beneficial externality of nectar for his neighbor's bees, a contribution to the production of honey for which the orchardist receives no reward. And the bees return the compliment by pollinating the apple blossoms *gratis*, thus contributing to the output of the orchard. These interacting externalities were assumed to represent a clear case of inadequate guidance by the Invisible Hand. Government action was supposed to be necessary to induce the orchardist to optimally cooperate with the beekeeper, i.e., to grow *more* nectar-yielding apple blossoms than the orchardist's self-interested calculation would dictate. And similarly, it was supposed, something had to be done to induce the beekeeper to provide *more* pollination benefits to his apple-growing neighbor than would ensue as a merely incidental side-effect of profitable honey production.

Upon looking into beekeeping in the state of Washington, however, Steven N. S. Cheung found the Invisible Hand alive and well! In actual fact, beekeepers and orchardists do not produce beneficial externalities for one another in a state of ignorance. On the contrary, active market dealings govern the placement of hives. The market terms depend upon the relative values of the two interacting "external" benefits: the honey yield to the beekeeper, as against the pollination services gained by the grower. The Table below illustrates that where honey yield is great, the beekeeper ordinarily pays an "apiary rent" for the right to place his hive on the grower's land. Where the honey yield is small, the grower pays pollination fees for the privilege of having hives placed on his land. Far from the process being an accidental one, Washington bees are even exported to California to help pollinate the early-season almond crop. Evidently, market processes are at work to bring "externalities" into private economic calculations.

Honey Yields and Pricing Arrangements, Washington (1970–71)

Season	Crop	Surplus Honey (Pounds per Hive)	Pollination Fees	Apiary Rent per Hive
Early Spring	Almond (Calif.)	0	$5–$8	—
	Cherry	0	$6–$8	—
Late Spring (major pollination season)	Apples and Soft Fruits	0	$9–$10	—
	Blueberry (with maple)	40	$5	—
	Cabbage	15	$8	—
	Cherry	0	$9–$10	—
	Cranberry	5	$9	—
Summer and Early Fall (major honey season)	Alfalfa	60	—	13¢–60¢
	Alfalfa (with pollination)	25–35	$3–$5	—
	Fireweed	60	—	25¢–63¢
	Mint	70–75	—	15¢–65¢
	Pasture	60	—	15¢–65¢
	Red Clover	60	—	65¢
	Red Clover (with pollination)	0–35	$3–$6	—
	Sweet Clover	60	—	20¢–25¢

Source: Steven N. S. Cheung, "The Fable of the Bees: An Economic Investigation," *The Journal of Law & Economics*, v. 16 (April 1973), p. 23.

Alas for the economists' fable, apple growing yields little or no honey! (The "apple honey" sold in markets seems to be an instance of imaginative labelling.)

So far so good. But Coase's Theorem proves too much! Consider the case of simple monopoly, which (by the standard analysis) leads to an inefficient outcome—underproduction of the monopolized good. But wherever there is inefficiency there must be a mutual advantage of trade. Then, according to

Coase's Theorem, the Invisible Hand should lead the monopolist and his customers to get together in some efficient arrangement; the monopolist can be made at least as well off as before, while the customers will do better. So monopoly should disappear, along with externalities!

The problem with the application of Coase's Theorem to "solve" the problem of monopoly, as in its application to "solve" the problem of externalities, is that the negotiations required may be impracticable. Where large numbers are involved, it may be unfeasible to secure a sufficient degree of unanimity. *Unitization*, for example, as an efficient solution of the externality problem in oilfields should, according to Coase's Theorem, tend to come about simply in response to the Invisible Hand. But in practice it has been necessary to pass special legislation whereby hold-out minority tract-owners in an oilfield are compelled to comply with a unitization agreement favored by a sufficiently large majority. It is the "free rider" problem that makes unanimity almost impossible. If the majority agree to cease overpumping their wells, it pays to be a member of the non-complying minority. The latter secure the advantage of others' pumping reductions, while still pumping as hard as they wish themselves.[10]

If the numbers involved are small, on the other hand, the problem becomes one of *strategic behavior* (as discussed in Chapter 13). When a small number of bargainers face each other, the mere possibility of a mutually advantageous agreement does not guarantee that such an agreement will be reached.

Nevertheless, Coase's Theorem does clarify our ideas as to the fundamental meaning of so-called "externalities." From a policy point of view, it suggests *that the unambiguous assignment of exchangeable property rights*, whatever the specific nature of the assignment may be, might be an important step in promoting the achievement of efficiency.

[10]The motivation is essentially the same as that of the "chisellers" in a cartel situation (see Section 11.F). But, it should be noted, absolutely unanimous cooperation is not strictly necessary for a workable degree of agreement in either the unitization or cartel contexts.

Example 17. 2
Water Law[11]

In the eastern states, the law governing the use of flowing streams is based mainly upon the "riparian" doctrine; in the West, the "appropriation" doctrine dominates.

While the legislation of each state has unique features, the basic idea of the riparian principle is that every owner of land bordering a stream has an equal right to reasonable use of the flow. The riparian doctrine of property rights in water is defective *both* in terms of ambiguity and exchangeability. What is a "reasonable" use for one party relative to others is a subject of continual contention before administrative agencies and law courts. Water-users are deterred from making costly invest-

[11]Discussion based upon J. Hirshleifer, J. C. DeHaven and J. W. Milliman, *Water Supply: Economics, Technology, and Policy* (Chicago: University of Chicago Press, 1960), Chap. 9.

ments, however efficient, for fear that a judicial or administrative redetermination of "reasonable" uses may later deprive them of supply. Nor can any user buy another's water right, since all are equally entitled to the flow. In particular, it is generally impossible to buy the right to transfer water away from the stream onto "*non*-riparian" land, however productive such a transfer may be.

In the relatively arid western states, scarcity of water made the riparian doctrine intolerable. The appropriation doctrine that tended to be adopted instead is based upon the concept that "first in time is first in right." Subject to qualifications and conditions that vary from state to state, first users were given the right to appropriate specified quantities of flow, sometimes limited also as to time, place, or manner of diversion. In particular, appropriated water was no longer tied to "riparian" uses but could be transferred away from the stream. The appropriation doctrine represented a considerable improvement from the point of view of *certainty* of rights. However, the *exchangeability* of rights has remained subject to erratic legal intervention.

In recent years there has been a tendency, even in the western states, to empower administrative agencies or courts to determine what constitutes "reasonable" use for the award or deprivation of water rights. In consequence, the ambiguity of rights to water use has been increasing rather than decreasing. Recent legislation has also tended to be increasingly hostile to market exchanges of water rights. Under the statutes of Colorado, for example, it is illegal to sell water found in the state outside its boundaries. Colorado legislators seem to lack confidence in the ability of naive Coloradans to exact an appropriate price for their water from wily out-of-staters.

17. C. 4   Public Goods

A commodity is called a "public good" if its consumption by any one economic agent does not reduce the amount available for others in the community. Or putting it another way, if providing the good for *anyone* makes it possible to provide it for *everyone*, without additional cost. Public goods thus represent a particular type of beneficial externality. A private good (e.g., a banana) is used or consumed *exclusively*; a public good is (or may be) used *concurrently* by many economic agents.

The traditional example is the lighthouse. If one ship receives the benefit of the warning signal, that in no way deprives others from doing so. Or in radio or television, a broadcast program is available non-exclusively to any and all persons equipped with suitable receivers.[12]

---

[12]Since there are *some* costs to users (stationing a lookout to watch for the lighthouse, buying a receiving set for the broadcasts), the goods mentioned are not absolutely "pure" public goods. This qualification is minor in the cases instanced. But many goods lie in the

If Z is a public good, with the numeraire commodity Y remaining a private good, the efficiency condition as between a producing firm f and two consumers John (j) and Karl (k) can be expressed as:

(17.4)
$$MC_z^f = MRSC_{ZY}^j + MRSC_{ZY}^k$$

That is, the Marginal Cost of the producing firm must be set equal to the *sum* of the consumers' marginal valuations of the public good. Geometrically, the picture is as in Figure 17.4. The two individuals' separate demand curves (each showing the quantity of Z that would be purchased by that consumer, as a function of the real price of Z in units of numeraire Y) are shown as d^j and d^k. The demand curves are derived by the same logic as in the case of private goods (see Section 4.B); from the point of view of any one individual, the "publicness" of the commodity is irrelevant. At any given price P_z quoted to him, the consumer will purchase additional units until his Marginal Rate of Substitution in Consumption $MRSC_{ZY}$ falls to equality with P_z. Thus, the demand curve d^j can be regarded as a schedule of John's $MRSC_{ZY}^j$, and d^k as a corresponding schedule for Karl. The aggregate value of any additional unit of Z, produced for concurrent consumption by the two consumers together, is then shown in the diagram by the social valuation function Σ—the *vertical* summation[13] of d^j and d^k. The intersection of the MC_z and Σ

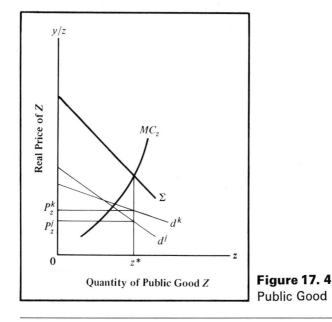

Quantity of Public Good Z

Figure 17. 4
Public Good

---

intermediate range of the spectrum between wholly private and wholly public. A stage performance, for example, is "public" as among the members of a given audience. But the capacity of the theater sets a limit on the number who can be concurrently served, all others being excluded. In this discussion only "pure" public goods will be considered.
[13]The familiar market demand curve applicable to private goods is the *horizontal* summation of the individual demand curves (see Section 4.D). The curve Σ is *not* a market demand curve in this usual sense.

curves represents the satisfaction of condition (17.4) above, so that $z*$ is the efficient level of output.[14]

The problem for the Theorem of the Invisible Hand is: Can achievement of the efficiency condition (17.4) be mediated by market prices? First of all let us assume that, in principle at least, it is possible to charge for the use of the public good and to *exclude* those who do not pay. In television, for example, a coded or "scrambled" message could be broadcast that is only interpretable with the aid of a paid descrambling device.[15] Then private firms can contemplate producing public goods for market sale.[16] The market prices that would serve the needs of mediation are P_z^j and P_z^k in Figure 17.4, each price being equal to the respective consumer's separate $MRSC_{ZY}$ at the efficient output level $z*$. The price-mediating conditions are:

(17.5) $$\begin{cases} MRSC_{ZY}^j = P_z^j \\ MRSC_{ZY}^k = P_z^k \end{cases} \quad \text{and} \quad MC_z = P_z^j + P_z^k$$

It is evident that the three equations (17.5) imply satisfaction of the efficiency condition (17.4).

So there is a set of prices that would fill the bill. But could these prices be arrived at by a market-equilibrium process?

Note, first, that *price discrimination* is required since, in general, $P_z^j \neq P_z^k$. It was shown above (in Section 11.E), that a monopolist seller could—where resale of the good between consumers is impossible—segment his market so as to be able to charge different prices to different consumers. In the case of public goods, it may again be possible to segment the market (prevent resale). Then a monopolist *could* arrive at the solution (17.5), corresponding to the intersection of MC_z and Σ in Figure 17.4. But he would not be motivated to do so! The monopolist would want to choose an output such that Marginal Cost MC_z equals the sum of the *Marginal Revenues* mr_z^j and mr_z^k in the segmented markets represented by the two individuals, rather than the sum of the prices P_z^j and P_z^k. Each person's Marginal Revenue curve mr would of course lie below his associated demand (Average Revenue) curve d, so that

[14]If one individual's d schedule were such as to make his $MRSC_{ZY}$ actually negative for sufficiently great public-good output, on the margin Z would be for him a *bad* rather than a good. Given a "free disposal" possibility (as in the case of broadcasting, where one can simply turn off his receiver), any negative $MRSC_{ZY}$ need not be suffered, so that the social valuation function Σ would be a summation only of the *positive* ranges of the individual d curves. But if it were not possible for an individual to evade consumption of a public good, even after it becomes for him a bad, the Σ curve would be the *algebraic* sum of both positive and negative values along the individual d curves. (A possible example is national defense. This may be a public good for the majority, but a public bad for a minority of traitors who favor the enemy!) In what follows, it will be assumed that public goods do not ever become bads.

[15]Sometimes, however, this may be impracticable. Consider mosquito abatement. This is clearly a public good. But to exclude non-payers from the benefit, it would be necessary to somehow train or signal the mosquitoes that some targets were permissible.

[16]Radio and television broadcasts are provided privately even *without* explicit charge to the consumer. But of course the listeners are really paying something, in being willing to have their time and attention captured by commercial messages. (See the discussion of "time-prices" of goods in Section 6.D.)

the vertical sum $mr_z^j + mr_z^k$ would lie below the vertical sum of the prices represented by the Σ curve. It follows that the monopolist, as we would expect, chooses an output *smaller* than that required by the efficiency condition (17.5).

Suppose, on the other hand, that the monopolist were somehow induced to act as a price-taker,[17] calculating in terms of $P_z^j + P_z^k$ rather than $mr_z^j + mr_z^k$, *but that price discrimination was barred.* (Even if discrimination were technically and legally feasible, the monopolist might not be able to secure the information as to individual demand functions necessary for doing so.) Then the effective vertical summation curve Σ' from a revenue point of view (not shown in the diagram) would lie *below* the true Σ. The consequence, as before, would be a less than efficient output of the public good.

A public good might, conceivably at least, be provided *competitively* rather than monopolistically. Television broadcasting is a case where we see hot competition among firms (channels). However, the product differentiation as among competing broadcasters makes the instance closer to "monopolistic competition" (see Section 12.B) than to pure competition. As in the case of a monopolist supplier, the information necessary for effective price discrimination, even apart from legal or technical difficulties, poses a serious obstacle. So even a hypothetical competitively supplied public good is likely to be "under-produced."

Conclusion: The efficiency conditions for public goods require price discrimination in accordance with consumers' Marginal Rates of Substitution in Consumption. Because of the difficulty and costs of excluding non-payers, and of charging correct discriminatory prices, public goods are likely to be under-supplied by private firms.

One other consideration reinforcing this conclusion is the existence of *transaction costs* associated with the conversion of a public good into excludable private property. If a television broadcast is "scrambled" to permit charging a fee for receiving the program, society is bearing a cost in terms of the resources used for scrambling and descrambling, as well as for the efforts involved in negotiating over price, billing, and all other costs of the market-exchange process. Again, these costs lead to under-production.

According to some welfare theorists, the various difficulties in private supply of public goods dictate that they be "publicly" (i.e., governmentally) provided instead. Indeed, some have thought that the concept of public goods serves to define the proper scope of government: "Private goods" ought to be privately supplied, and "public goods" ought to be publicly supplied. But in fact we do observe private firms supplying public goods. Television broadcasting is the obvious example, but even lighthouse services have at times been privately provided! And on the other hand government agencies, while supplying public goods like national defense, are also in the business of

---

[17]In Section 11.G we saw that the presence of alternative claimants for the *right* to be a sole seller may effectively eliminate monopoly power. And indeed, this commonly occurs in the case of cable transmission of television programs—a public good.

producing a vast range of private goods. Among the many examples are electric power (TVA), irrigation water (the U.S. Bureau of Reclamation), insurance (Social Security), education (public schools), and of course postal services (the U.S. Mail).

Government provision is inevitable only for those public goods for which *exclusion* of non-payers is unfeasible. Here the same "free rider" problem arises as already discussed under the heading of "Externalities" in Section C.3. If a non-payer can derive benefits on essentially the same terms as someone who does pay, each and every person will be motivated to let the others foot the bill. In such circumstances provision of the public good by private firms may be impossible. But the difficulty is due to the *non-exclusionary* aspect rather than to the *public-good* aspect. Even a perfectly ordinary private good, not collectively consumed (e.g., food service in a restaurant) could not be profitably provided on a private basis—if non-payers could invade the premises and enjoy the benefit on the same basis as the paying customers!

17. D THE PROBLEM OF EQUALITY

Equality of income carries great weight as a political objective, especially in democratically governed societies. Attempts have been made to defend equality on utilitarian grounds. Suppose that individuals had cardinal and interpersonally comparable utility functions, characterized by diminishing Marginal Utility, and furthermore that *all these utility functions were essentially identical*. Then the total social aggregate of utility would be maximized by dividing income equally. This argument involves strong assumptions, of course, over and above acceptance of the philosophical premises of utilitarianism.

Alternatively, equality of income might be proclaimed as an "ethical" postulate in its own right, free of any utilitarian underpinnings. (But note that what some commend as high ethics, others would disparage as low envy.)

17. D. 1 An Application: Rawls' Concept of "Justice"

The philosopher John Rawls has recently proposed a strongly egalitarian criterion of "social justice."[18] The criterion deals primarily with distribution of the measurable goods of society, and so can best be regarded as mappable on the objective income axes I^j, I^k of Figure 17.1 rather than the subjective utility axes U^j, U^k of Figure 17.2.

Rawls' key concept is what he calls "the difference principle": Inequality in a society, he asserts, is justified *only* to the extent that it benefits the *least* advantaged. In Figure 17.5, the 45° line shows all the conceivable income allocations I^j, I^k for which equality holds, i.e., for which $I^j = I^k$. Now consider the shaded social opportunity set bounded by the curve II'. The best attainable point on the 45° line is evidently the point F; this is the equality

[18]John Rawls, *A Theory of Justice* (Cambridge, Mass.: Harvard University Press, 1971).

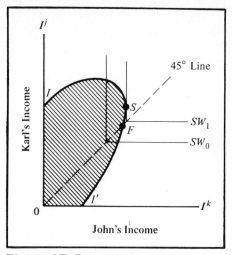

Figure 17. 5
Rawls' Social Optimum

optimum. In moving from F toward the point S along the Social Opportunity Frontier II', a degree of inequality is being created (since, northwest of the 45° line, John's income I^j exceeds Karl's income I^k). But this is *justified*, according to Rawls, in that even the poorer individual (Karl) is thereby made better off.

It will be evident that the application of Rawls' difference principle leads to selection of the point S as the social optimum in Figure 17.5. More generally, his rule is equivalent to asserting a particular shape for the interpersonal or social "welfare" function. Specifically, the isoquants of social welfare or of Rawlsian "justice"[19] are rectangular with corners on the 45° line, as exemplified by SW_0 and SW_1 in the diagram.

Now consider instead a social opportunity set like that portrayed in Figure 17.1, where the frontier II' has negative slope throughout (i.e., where John cannot gain unless Karl loses, and vice versa). Under these circumstances the Rawlsian optimum always requires *absolute equality of income*.

17. D. 2   Equality and Pareto-Optimality

A different approach to the problem of equality emphasizes that purely private motivation, in a world of individuals who are not completely selfish, will suffice to bring about a certain degree of equality. And indeed, the equality thus voluntarily achieved will represent an efficient (Pareto-optimal) allocation of incomes.

In Section 6.A.1, the "demand for charity" was studied. Apart from minor

[19] Rawls' identification of the word "justice" with "equality" is questionable terminology. Our ordinary understanding of "justice" is as a proper *relationship between a man's actions and his rewards*. The Biblical "eye for an eye" may be a primitive concept of justice, but it is the sort of thing that we mean by justice. In contrast, Rawls' concept concerns the distribution of rewards to individuals *independent of any actions on their part*. This is not justice, but bounty.

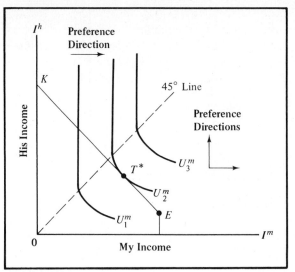

Figure 17. 6
The Economics of Charity

changes in notation, Figure 17.6 here is essentially equivalent to Figure 6.1 in the earlier chapter. I have preferences as between "My income" I^m and "His income" I^h, such that *both* I^h and I^m are "goods" for me when $I^h < I^m$ (i.e., I am benevolent to someone poorer than myself). Given an initial endowment allocation E of incomes such that $I^h < I^m$, the opportunity locus or "budget line" EK shows the allocations I can attain by unilaterally transferring my income to him.[20]

In the situation of Figure 17.6, my transfer optimum is the tangency T^*. Furthermore, if his preference function is like mine, the circumstances that impel me to donate to him (I am richer than he) also motivate him to accept the gift (he is poorer than I). Being mutually desired, the transfer is Pareto-optimal.

17. D. 3 Equality as a Public Good

Still another approach emphasizes that equality can be regarded as a "public good," in the sense of Section 17.C.4. For, an increased degree of equality that satisfies the benevolent desires of any one individual will, without additional cost, also increase utility for any other person who is similarly situated and has similar benevolent preferences.

Returning to Figure 17.6, suppose that, before I make my individual voluntary transfer changing the income allocation from the endowment position E to the optimum T^*, some third party G were to make a gift to my

---

[20]As explained in Chapter 6, in the absence of taxes EK would have a slope of -1, an angle of 135° with the horizontal. But if charitable donations are tax-deductible, I can transfer a dollar to him at a cost to me of somewhat less than a dollar, making the slope of EK steeper than 135°.

prospective beneficiary *H*. My opportunity locus *EK* in the diagram would then shift upward by the amount of *G*'s gift, without any action on my part. Thus I could clearly attain a higher level of satisfaction (tangency with a higher indifference curve on I^m, I^h axes) than before. *G*'s gift has, to some degree, enabled me to satisfy my taste for benevolence without cost to myself.

Furthermore, this is an example of a *non-excludable* public good. Having made the gift to *H*, the third party *G* is in no way able to prevent me from enjoying his having done so. The consequence is, once again, a "free rider" problem. Following the familiar free-rider theme, it follows that a less-than-efficient amount of income transfers would be undertaken by private individuals. This analysis therefore provides a rationale for government intervention via *fiscal redistribution*, whereby taxes levied on the wealthier classes are collected for transfer to poorer groups.

To fit ideally into the model of benevolence as a public good, however, the redistributive taxes would have to be voluntarily levied upon themselves by the wealthier groups! A more cynical explanation of the phenomenon of fiscal redistribution would not make any use of benevolence as a motive, but would run simply in terms of political realities. This topic is considered further in Chapter 18.

But in any case, private charity is an important phenomenon. Hence, benevolent preferences surely do exist, and so cannot be entirely dismissed as motivation for fiscal redistribution.

17. E WELFARE ECONOMICS—CONCLUSION

Welfare economics has been primarily preoccupied with the problem of *efficiency*, i.e., with the determination of the conditions leading to allocations on the Social Opportunity Frontier (as shown, for example, by the curve *LL'* in Figure 17.2). Any such allocation is characterized by the condition that there exists no other Pareto-preferred to it.

Achievement of efficiency is, however, neither necessary nor sufficient as a criterion of ideal social policy. The *distribution* of income as among individuals and social classes is another important criterion. Even granting the appropriateness of a certain tilt toward *equality* of income, the question remains as to how far to go in sacrificing efficiency for equality. And there are, of course, many other criteria with some claim to be considered in social policy: liberty to retain and use lawfully acquired talents or property, communitarian versus individualistic values, and other non-utilitarian considerations.

Nevertheless, economists' emphasis upon the efficiency criterion has probably played a useful social role. The political processes that determine social policy tend almost entirely to overlook considerations of efficiency. Whether the issue be the progressive income tax, the protection of some industries by tariffs and quotas, the penalization of others for "excessive" profits, the existence of monopoly, or the proper scale of government, it has become a function of the economist to point out that there are efficiency implications that need to be evaluated as one input into the social decision process.

An older generation of welfare economists tended to think in terms of a policy shotgun with two barrels: (1) a presumption in favor of *laissez faire*, based on the Theorem of the Invisible Hand as discussed in Section 17.B above, but modified by (2) a presumption in favor of government intervention, to remedy the specific failures and distortions of the Invisible Hand reviewed in Section 17.C. Neither barrel of the shotgun quite hits the target! The efficiency even ideally attainable by the Invisible Hand is, as we have seen, not a fully satisfactory guide to policy. On the other hand, a failure of the Invisible Hand to achieve efficiency does not of itself provide any warrant for belief that the alternative of government intervention will improve matters.

To gain some understanding of this last question, it would be desirable to subject the process of political or governmental decision-making to an analytic investigation that parallels our treatment of the market process. Economists have indeed, though only very recently, turned to serious *positive* analysis of government, i.e., to the economic consequences of what government actually does as opposed to what in some ideal sense it "ought" to do. Recent developments in this field of inquiry will be examined in the following chapter.

Questions

1. Explain and justify the normally "concave" shape of the Social Opportunity Frontier in income terms (Figure 17.1). What can be said about the shape of the Social Opportunity Frontier in utility terms (Figure 17.2)?

2. Show how a Social Opportunity Frontier in utility terms for two individuals may be derived from the *contract curve* of the Edgeworth box diagram (discussed in Section 7.B).

3. What meaning, if any, can be given to the concept of a "social optimum"? How valid is "efficiency" or Pareto-optimality as a criterion of social optimality?

4. What is the Theorem of the Invisible Hand?

5. What are the conditions of "efficiency" reached under ideal conditions by the unregulated market process? Can the conditions be achieved, in principle, without use of the market? What are the major considerations bearing upon market versus nonmarket means of achieving efficiency?

6. Explain why a firm that is a monopolist in the product market is said to hire "too little" of the factors it uses for production. Explain why a firm that is a monopsonist in the factor market is also said to hire "too little." Given these effects, does it follow that too large a proportion of the community's resources are employed by competitive firms, or are retained for reservation uses by resource-owners, or both?

7. What are public goods? What are externalities? Is a public good a special case of an externality?

8. What is the efficiency condition for optimal provision of a public good? In what sense is it appropriate in the case of public goods to sum individual demand curves *vertically*, whereas for private goods the summation takes place *horizontally*?

9. What limits the possibility of private supply of public goods? Will public provision mean that a more nearly optimal amount will be supplied?

10. In the apples-bees example in the text, the externality is mutually beneficial. Provide an example of a reciprocal relation in which the mutually imposed externalities are harmful. Can there be a case in which in one direction the effect is beneficial but in the other direction harmful?

11. What is the Coase Theorem? Explain the relevance of each of the following conditions for the actual empirical applicability of the theorem: (a) Well-defined property rights, and (b) Low costs of negotiating and enforcing agreements. What sorts of real-world considerations tend to make property rights ambiguous and uncertain? What considerations tend to make the costs of negotiating and enforcing agreements high?

Chapter 18
Government and the Economy: A Positive Analysis

It is sometimes thought that the difference between human actions in the economic and political spheres lies in the realm of *motives:* Self-interest is expected to be the governing force in economic decisions, while in their political decisions people are supposedly concerned primarily with the public interest. This naive view is rejected here. The individuals who interact in their economic decisions are the same people, with the same motives, as those engaging in or subject to political decisions. To compare and contrast political and economic behavior we must look not to differences of motives but to differences in the *processes of human interaction*—differences in "the rules of the game."

In the economic sphere individuals interact primarily through the market, whose key feature is *contract*. One party agrees to sell, and the other to buy. In the political sphere the mode of human interaction is primarily through *government*. What is the difference? You *contract* with your bank, your employer, your grocer. But parents *govern* their minor children. The warden *governs* his prisoners. And all of us *are governed by* legislators, judges, and others in positions of political authority. Contractual association, being voluntary, is a relation of equality. But the essence of government is *subordination*: some persons are empowered, with the ultimate sanction of force, to impose their will upon others.

Political theorists have been at pains to justify, or at any rate to explain, why human societies must have or do have such subordination. Some of the leading theories are reviewed in Section 18.A. Section 18.B turns to the fundamental logic of *voluntary (contractual) political associations*, which come closest to the economic model in that subordination occurs "with the consent of the governed." Afterward, we will use the results obtained to examine a number of the ways in which economic and political decisions interact.

18. A THEORIES OF THE STATE

Government, in the most general sense of the word, arises (as has been noted) in many contexts, including families, prisons, universities, and monasteries.

But when we speak of "the" government we specifically mean the *state*. The state is a system of subordination that organizes *all* the individuals in a given geographical area, within which it possesses an effective monopoly of physical force. The all-inclusiveness of the state means that the political association is an *involuntary* one; a disaffected individual can escape it only by becoming an exile or outlaw. The edicts of those in state authority are enforced (where not voluntarily accepted) by coercion, i.e., by the threat of violence. It is the effectiveness of the *threat* that characterizes the functioning state. If *actual* violence must be continually used we have either war (between contending governments) or anarchy (the absence of government).

In the history of political thought the "positive" question of what the state *is* has often been confused with the "normative" issue of what it *should be*. Our interest here is solely in the positive or scientific aspect. Why do individuals accept a role of subordination in the political system (the "polity")? What functions does the state perform that promote the interests of the governed individuals? These two questions, which are at bottom the same, can be approached in terms of alternative "theories of the state."

1. Divine ordinance: If the authority of kings (or other rulers) over lesser mortals is generally believed to be divinely ordained, there is no problem explaining why the governed accept subordination. The divine-right doctrine seems a handy one for rulers, but there is another side of the coin. Under this theory the *function* of the governor can only be to carry out God's will, not his own will. Should the ruler fail to carry out God's will, it seems plausible that he forfeits his authority, for which there is good Biblical precedent beginning with the story of Saul. So even kings may have been uncomfortable with a theory in which their credential for power is the debatable matter of God's will.

For our purposes, the point is that the divinely ordained state (whether monarchy or republic or other) exists to serve *neither* the purposes of the ruler nor of the ruled, but rather those of God. However out of fashion intellectually, this belief is still ingrained to some degree in popular thinking. Our modern rulers still retain some useful shreds of the mystic aura once attached to sanctified leadership. Hence our shock when we learn of their all too human failings.

2. Naked power: At the other extreme from divine ordinance lies the view that government represents nothing but ability to seize and hold power—to coerce others into obedience. Dominance among men, on this view, is not fundamentally different from the dominance observable in a pack of wolves. What limits any human ruler's domain is, ultimately, the fact of diminishing returns to the activity of organizing a system of coercion. Even Alexander's Macedonians eventually mutinied, forcing him to set a limit to his empire; it was Napoleon's refusal to accept any limit that led to his downfall.

A system of government based on naked power may still gain wide support, simply by being profitable to enough participants. The Third Reich promised the Germans the role of master race in a conquered world. But as there will necessarily be large numbers of individuals assigned the role of slaves or victims, the military burden on the masters may be more than they can bear.

3. Instinctual-biological: According to Aristotle, man is by nature a "political animal," a creature for whom society and government are not an incidental but an essential aspect. In extreme form this becomes the "organic" conception, which says that the individual is unimportant and only the community counts. The organic position is that the function of the state is to promote *community* survival and growth, not individual interests. People allow themselves to be ruled by the state because their individual lives are purposeless apart from the interests of the community.

A more moderate view strikes a balance between individual and community objectives. People have individual goals, but a social instinct is a part of the human make-up. Evolution has selected such a social instinct for survival just as it has selected the social characteristics of ants, bees, wolves, and monkeys. The inbred human social traits go beyond the mere tendency to associate in company; they include also the willingness to lead and to be led, i.e., the principle of subordination (also observed, of course, in many animal species).

The main selective pressure upon the social organization of human communities has surely been *war*. With only minor exceptions, those races or strains of humanity have survived that were efficient at war. Leadership is critical for success in war, as is the willingness of the individual to sacrifice himself, even to give his life, for the group. Thus, subordination and a degree of unselfishness are grounded on instincts formed by an evolutionary process. Leaders, so long as their behavior seems consistent with group survival, can count on the self-sacrificing instincts of followers.

4. Voluntary contract: One way of explaining the existence of government, without departing from individualistic premises, is to deny that there is any ultimate difference between voluntary contractual association and the state. This leads to the contention that the state itself is founded upon a *social contract*. Even where such contracts historically occurred (the Mayflower Compact is the leading example), this cannot mean that the present-day descendants of the signers remain bound thereby. Rather, as Socrates declared in rejecting the opportunity to flee from the death sentence imposed on him by the Athenians, the contention is that any individual is bound to accept the obligations and penalties of citizenship if he has partaken of the benefits thereof.

Social-contract theorists have usually pitched their arguments in normative terms: How "ought" the citizens or the rulers behave? But the underlying hypothesis can also be regarded as a positive theory. It asserts that rational individuals, to escape anarchy, combine to subject themselves to a system of subordination in the form of a "constitution." Even though some actions adverse to their interests are bound to be adopted, they will support the constitution on the basis of an *overall* comparison of costs and benefits.[1] The social-contract or voluntary-association theory of government, in its democratic version, fits most naturally into the approach of the economist. Since the economist understands contracts, he is already tooled up for dealing with the contractual state! Without passing judgment on the scientific merits of this explanation of government and subordination, the next section studies how the desires of individuals can be mediated and integrated through a government mechanism (a polity) of the voluntarist type.

18. B THE VOLUNTARIST POLITY AND ITS IMPERFECTIONS

The essence of the voluntarist view of the state can be grasped by thinking of *political parties* as akin to *business firms*. Business firms offer goods and services, at specified prices, to the consumers. Political parties offer packages of government policies, at certain costs in the form of taxes and other burdens, to the citizens. Firms are groupings of individuals trying to make a profit by providing *consumers* with what they want. Political parties are groupings of individuals trying to make a "profit" (which might, in some degree, represent satisfactions like power or glory apart from pecuniary remuneration) by providing *citizens* with what they want.

Indeed, ideal *laissez faire* in the economy corresponds to ideal democracy in the polity.[2] In each case, the enforcement mechanism is *competition*. In the ideal market economy, perfect competition among firms drives profits to zero in long run equilibrium (see Section 10.D). Then firms have no power to do anything other than what consumers want, since any firm that fails to satisfy consumers will be driven out of business by other firms. In the ideal polity, perfect competition among parties similarly drives political "profit" to zero. Parties have no power to do anything other than what citizens want, since any party that fails to satisfy citizens will be voted out of office. Thus, Adam Smith's Invisible Hand is operative, to some degree at least, in the political as well as in the economic arena.

In the chapter preceding, we reviewed (under the heading of "Welfare Economics") the various imperfections of real-world market economies—monopoly, disequilibrium, externalities, etc.—that lead to results falling short of the ideal. It was emphasized that these imperfections of markets do not imply the conclusion that government necessarily "ought" to intervene. For one thing, one has to know something first about possible imperfections of the political process. We now take up this topic, the imperfections of

[1]See, especially, J. M. Buchanan and G. Tullock, *The Calculus of Consent* (Ann Arbor: University of Michigan Press, 1962).
[2]See Gary S. Becker, "Competition and Democracy," *Journal of Law and Economics*, v. 1 (Oct. 1958).

political mechanisms when viewed as systems by which citizens voluntarily associate to achieve desired ends.

18. B. 1   The Problem of Delegation

The political process does allow citizens to choose policies, in a sense, but only under severe restrictions. Except to a small degree, citizens do not vote directly on policies. They vote only (and possibly at one or more removes) for *delegates* in the legislative, executive, and judicial branches of government; it is these delegates who make the actual policy choices. But elections of delegates are relatively infrequent. Whereas individuals make a host of market decisions every single day, they can only choose or recall their political delegates over election intervals measured in years. Some of the most important political officeholders, such as U.S. Supreme Court justices, are only indirectly "elected" at all, and are beyond effective control thereafter. So delegates may have a considerable degree of "power" (i.e., of leeway to violate the preferences of their constituents) before having to face a day of reckoning.

The *limited options* available further erode the control that citizens have over their delegates. First of all, there is the "bundling" of issues in the election process. A voter may prefer the position of one candidate for office on one question, of a competing candidate on a second issue, and so forth. But the delegate elected will be representing (or misrepresenting) the voter in *all* decisions to be made during his term of office.

Third, political competition is highly imperfect. There appear to be strong economies of scale in the political process, so that candidates rarely stand for office independently. Instead, they are almost always tied in with organized political parties. In some democratic countries, there are only two effective parties, a situation that would be called "duopoly" in the economic sphere (see Section 13.A), where it is considered a serious imperfection of markets.

A number of political devices may provide citizens with a somewhat greater range of options of governmental choice: (1) In some countries, political competition is more varied in that multi-party systems exist. (2) Some states permit citizens to propose laws outside the legislature (the *initiative*), and to *recall* elected officers between scheduled elections. (3) Within parties, the "primary" and other techniques of participation provide ways for citizens to influence final choices offered the voters in the actual election. (4) Under a federal system, the citizen may support one party for national office and a different one for local office. (5) Similarly, where there is separation of powers the voter may choose different parties to represent him in the legislative and executive branches of government.

But these are all highly imperfect devices. Indeed, while improvements from the single point of view of *representation* of citizen preferences, some or all of the devices may be objectionable on other grounds. They may be inconsistent, for example, with effectiveness of government—with simply getting things done. In any case, the scope of individual choice remains drastically less in the political arena than in the market-place.

Modern democratic political systems operate (with some qualifications) on the principle of *majority rule*. The necessity of making decisions through delegates poses a problem, as we have seen, since the delegate may not faithfully serve his constituents' interests. But what if the constituents differ among themselves? Then, to be elected, the delegate need only serve the majority interest; he must please only 50%-plus-one of those who turn out to vote.

This obviously puts the minority at a grave disadvantage. Conceivably, even their most vital interests may be at the mercy of the majority. If on some policy issue 75% of his constituency prefer alternative #1 and 25% prefer alternative #2, the delegate will be unlikely to divide his support in this proportion. Rather, his incentives are to give full support to the group capable of reelecting him, those favoring alternative #1. In contrast, majority and minority preferences are normally *both* provided for, in due proportion, in a market economy. If 75% of consumers prefer chocolate and 25% prefer vanilla, chocolate and vanilla flavors will tend, other things equal, to be provided in just about these proportions.

The majority-minority problem repeats itself at a higher level, since the delegates themselves normally decide policies by majority voting in the legislative process. It is therefore conceivable that the "majority" position may represent only a bare 50% of the voters in a bare 50% of the election districts, so that the "majority" may be the 25% and the "minority" the 75% of the national constituency! This is of course only a very remote possibility.

Devices have emerged tending to provide partial remedies for the majority-minority problem. *Constitutional protection* limits the types of laws a majority can pass, thus affording some minimal security for minority rights. A very interesting phenomenon, that arises most visibly on the higher or legislative level, is called "log-rolling." Suppose that the minority legislators feel very strongly on a particular issue *A*. Then to swing over votes on issue *A*, they may promise other legislators to support *their* positions on separate issues *B, C, D*, etc., to be voted on at later dates. In this way the *intensity* of minority preferences is registered, to some degree, as a counterweight to the mere numbers of the majority.

The process of log-rolling can be regarded as a partial injection of market considerations into the political process. Through "political market exchange," delegates' votes on some issues are "bought," to be "paid for" by votes on other issues. Log-rolling, though generally considered an evil,[3] reminds us of the Fundamental Theorem of Exchange (Section 7.A)—the *mutual advantage of trade*. Indeed, efficiency in the sense of a *Pareto-optimal* outcome—a result in which it is no longer possible to achieve any further gains to anyone without hurting others (see Section 17.A)—would be achieved if legislators' votes on issues could be openly purchased for money!

The underlying logic is this. Setting aside problems of transaction costs and strategic behavior, an ideal system of political market exchange would

[3]Not without reason, as indicated in Section 18.C.

be one requiring *unanimous* consent for every action. To achieve concurrence, every dissenter's vote would have to be "bought" by the winning side. This would guarantee that all political actions undertaken are actually Pareto-preferred over the initial situation (i.e., constitute an improvement for some, and an injury for none). Those who suffer from the chosen action are compensated by the purchase of their votes. With majority rule and log-rolling, it is true that compensation is not paid to all those affected—only to a number sufficient to comprise a voting majority. Nevertheless, since *both* sides will be trying to buy votes, the winning side will be the one able to bid higher. Hence under a bought-vote system the more highly-valued alternative would always be chosen. The result is Pareto-*optimal*, though not in general unanimously preferred (Pareto-*preferred*)[4] over the status quo.

That the purchase of votes seems offensive appears to be due to the problem of *delegation* discussed above. In a *direct* democracy, offering compensation, to win the approval of those adversely affected by a proposed policy alternative, would surely be quite reasonable. But our knowledge of the world leads us to suspect that any compensation privately paid to the delegate in a *representative* democracy will not be perfectly translated into benefits for his constituents! That is true enough, but we should realize where the real objection lies: in the delegation of decision-making power, not in the process of offering compensation to win the approval (buy the votes) of those injured by proposed public decisions.

18. B. 3   The Problem of Voting

It is the *vote* that represents the ultimate discipline that an individual citizen can exercise upon his delegate. But the effectiveness of a single vote is so minuscule that the citizen is scarcely motivated to go to the polls at all! Even if the election of his preferred candidate were worth an enormous sum to the voter, *his* voting will actually have an effect upon the outcome only in a fantastically improbable situation, i.e., the case where his own ballot gives his candidate a majority of one. Or if the citizen is not so interested in electing his candidate as in swelling the poll for a particular ideological position, again one vote more or less would scarcely ever be noticeable. And even if the voter has no selfish aims at all but intends to cast a purely public-spirited ballot, his single vote will no more measurably serve the *public* interest than it would his own *selfish* interest.

If it were possible and legal for a candidate to *buy* votes, there would be no problem of motivating the voter. Parallel to the argument for log-rolling, a surprisingly good case can be made for buying citizens' votes at election

---

[4]It was shown in Section 17.A that a *Pareto-optimal* outcome is not necessarily *Pareto-preferred* to any given initial situation. In Figure 17.2, the Social Opportunity Frontier LL' is the set of Pareto-optimal outcomes. Starting from position C in Figure 17.2 as status quo, under the unanimity rule Pareto-preferred improvements would be adopted until an outcome like B on the Frontier—both Pareto-optimal, and Pareto-preferred to C—was attained. With bought votes under *majority* rule, however, the tendency is to attain a point like D'. Position D' is Pareto-optimal, but *not* Pareto-preferred to the starting position C (because a dissenting minority may have been victimized).

time! For this means that the political parties would be repaying the constituents in advance for the gains to be reaped in office. "Competition for the field" (see Section 11.G) before election would compensate for the scarcely controllable power granted the delegates after their election.

If votes are not paid for, and if the chance of affecting the outcome is negligible, why are so many votes actually cast in elections? If citizens are rational, it can only be that the *costs of casting a ballot are low*. And indeed, at least for city-dwellers and when the weather is good, the cost is small. Voting may actually be fun; it provides sociability and a feeling of civic accomplishment to offset the small travel and time cost involved.

Another somewhat subtler consequence of the imperfections of the political representation process enters here. In the market-place you "get what you pay for." In the political arena, it is all too easy to vote in a candidate and not get desired results out. (The main cost to the individual of such an outcome is not the trivial effort of wasted voting, of course, but the taxes and other burdens of undesired policies.) In view of the problems of electing a candidate supporting the whole bundle of one's preferred policies, and of ensuring that he abides by the platform upon which he was elected, it simply is not worthwhile for the rational citizen to invest large resources in determining what *are* the best policies. Voting is cheap, but voting *intelligently* may be quite costly. And so citizens typically find themselves ill-informed on the issues about which they are casting ballots.

Example 18. 1
Determinants
of Voter Turnout

If a citizen rationally considers whether to turn out and vote, his decision to incur the costs thereof should depend in part upon (1) the importance of the election, and (2) the probability of affecting the outcome. Y. Barzel and E. Silverberg[5] investigated the impact of these determinants upon the proportion of citizens actually casting ballots in U.S. gubernatorial elections in the years 1962, 1964, 1966 and 1968 (122 elections).

Among other findings, they obtained the results that:

1. *The larger the population, the smaller the percent of turnout.* This represents rational behavior, since the larger the population the smaller is the probability of a *single* vote determining the election. An *increase* of 1,000,000 in voting-age population of the state was associated with a 6% *decline* in the percent voting.

2. *The more one-sided the election, the smaller the turnout.* Again rational, since if voters had some inkling in advance of the one-sidedness they would place lower credence upon their own single ballot affecting the outcome. Statistically a 10% *increase* in the majority fraction was associated with a 7.7% *decline* in percentage voting.

[5] Y. Barzel and E. Silverberg, "Is the Act of Voting Rational?" *Public Choice*, v. 16 (Fall 1973).

3. *Coincidence of non-gubernatorial with gubernatorial elections increased turnout.* Statistically, a Presidential candidacy raised the fraction voting by 11.1%; a Senatorial candidacy by 5.5%. Obviously, it is more rational to vote, the more important is the election.

Comment: It would have been of interest to see if the difficulty and cost of voting significantly affected turnout. One would anticipate a larger fraction voting, the better the weather, the less the average distance to the polls, the more convenient the voting hours, etc. As another point, it is also reasonable to expect a larger turnout on the part of those who expect to be able to cast *intelligent* ballots. (College graduates? Economics students?)

18. C COLLECTIVE ACTION, FREE RIDERS, AND PRESSURE GROUPS

The traditional "welfare-economics" view was that a showing of imperfections of the market process was already a presumptive justification for government remedial action. But surveying the drastic imperfections of the representation process in the democratic polity (when that process is regarded as a voluntaristic way of achieving individual ends) may tempt one to swing to the other extreme. So the question arises: Can an affirmative case be made for decision-making through the institution of government, to explain why at least a *portion* of economic activity is channeled through the state rather than through the market?

The usual economic answer is connected most fundamentally with the existence of *public goods*, i.e., of goods such that provision for any one person in the community means provision for all.[6] It was already explained in Section 17.C.4 why and how the market tends to "under-provide" public goods. This topic will be briefly reviewed here, with emphasis upon the *free-rider* problem.

We have already encountered the free-rider problem in several different contexts. In the case of a *cartel* (see Section 11.F), all members gain if they can stick together, holding down output so as to be able to impose a higher price on consumers. But granted that all other sellers are cooperating, any single member of the cartel is motivated to "chisel"; he is tempted to take advantage of the high price in order to produce more than his assigned share. Similarly in the case of a *productive externality*, as when oil is pumped from a pool underlying the lands of several owners (Section 17.C.3). Here again it is in the interests of all jointly to hold back output, but in the interests of any single producer to expand output once the others are holding back. In each

[6]This defines the limiting case of a "pure" public good; more generally, a commodity might partake of publicness to some partial degree.

case, the economic agent calculating in his own self-interest is tempted to be a *free rider* upon others who are subordinating self-interest to the group-interest. The paradox here is that all lose when all pursue their sole self-interest, and yet each has no guarantee that his own restraint will be matched by the restraint of others.

The essence of the free-rider problem is that private costs must be incurred for group benefits. Where numbers are *small* enough, it may nevertheless be rational for self-interested individuals to generate positive quantities of public goods of benefit to others. But two theorems are of importance here: (1) A less than Pareto-optimal quantity will be so supplied, and (2) those with larger stakes in the outcome (e.g., those endowed with larger proportions of the aggregate wealth) will tend to supply *more* than proportionately larger quantities of the public good.

While these theorems can be formally proved, a common-sense justification will suffice here. An individual Robinson Crusoe alone on an island would choose a preferred balance between two goods—say, between fish and mosquito-abatement. Both of these must necessarily be private goods so long as Robinson is isolated. But now suppose that Robinson is joined by Friday. Any effort at all on Friday's part in the way of mosquito-abatement provides Robinson with some "free" amount of the latter good. Counting on Friday to do something in this direction, Robinson will rationally redirect his efforts, striking a new balance so as to self-provide more fish (private good) and less mosquito-abatement (public good). The argument applies reciprocally to Friday's decision, of course. Each cuts back on provision of the public good, since he suffers the full marginal cost of his own efforts but does not receive the full marginal benefits thereof, some of which "spill over" to the other party. Hence an amount of the public good is produced that is less than what an omniscient and benevolent government would arrive at.

As to the second theorem, suppose that Robinson owns 80% of the resources on the island and Friday only 20%. Then Robinson knows that whatever mosquito-abatement takes place will have to be pretty much his own doing. He will therefore act *almost* as if he were alone on the island. Friday knows that Robinson will in any case be providing relatively ample amounts of the public good, perhaps far more than Friday would ever be interested in or could afford to provide himself with. Hence Friday will cut back his mosquito-abatement efforts to little or nothing. Thus, Robinson will be supplying *more* than his proportionate 80% and Friday *less* than his proportionate 20% of whatever public good is provided.

Example 18. 2
The Economics
of Alliance

An *alliance* between independent nations is generally undertaken in the interests of mutual defense. But defense is, to an important degree at least, a "public good" for the allied powers. Destruction of an enemy's bombers, for example, reduces the threat against each and all of the possible target nations. Since each participating nation receives only a portion of the benefit of any marginal increment of expenditure, all are tempted to "free ride" on the efforts of the others. But the larger nations are not in a position to "free ride" to nearly the same degree as the smaller allies.

A study of the North Atlantic Treaty Organization (NATO) defense expenditures in 1964 verified the differential expenditures of larger and smaller participants. The following Table compares the rankings of NATO nations as to size (measured by GNP) and as to proportion of budget devoted to defense expenditures. The association is evident to the eye, and statistical testing indicates a high degree of significance.[7]

NATO Statistics

	GNP, 1964		Defense Budget as % of GNP	
	$ Billion	*Rank*	*Percent*	*Rank*
United States	569.03	1	9.0	1
Germany	88.87	2	5.5	6
United Kingdom	79.46	3	7.0	3
France	73.40	4	6.7	4
Italy	43.63	5	4.1	10
Canada	38.14	6	4.4	8
Netherlands	15.00	7	4.9	7
Belgium	13.43	8	3.7	12
Denmark	7.73	9	3.3	13
Turkey	6.69	10	5.8	5
Norway	5.64	11	3.9	11
Greece	4.31	12	4.2	9
Portugal	2.88	13	7.7	2
Luxembourg	.53	14	1.7	14

Source: M. Olson, Jr., and R. Zeckhauser, "An Economic Theory of Alliances," *Review of Economics and Statistics*, v. 48 (August 1966), p. 267.

[7]The most conspicuous exception, Portugal, is explainable on other grounds. This nation, tiny in GNP, supported a large defense budget because of its colonial commitments in Africa rather than its participation in NATO.

It is conceivable, then, that collective wants can be provided for, given small numbers, even without a government. NATO may be performing adequately, for example, without being in any way a super-government capable of coercing its members. But where numbers are quite large, and no single agent is in a position to derive a significant portion of the benefit from private action in the group interest, little or none of the public good will be supplied on self-interested grounds. Hence, waiving the possibility of large-scale benevolence,[8] if *any* of the public good is to be supplied a collectivist institution will have to provide it. The free-rider problem is overcome because in voting (if only indirectly, through election of delegates) for the supply of certain public goods, each citizen is also voting to impose the burden of the costs thereof *upon others as well as upon himself.*

The difference between the effectiveness of large and small groups in achieving collective ends has an important implication for observed political behavior. The members of a compact "special interest" (for example, businessmen and workers in a particular industry) are few in number compared to the population at large. Nevertheless, they are often successful in achieving political favors like tariffs or subsidies at the expense of the general consuming public. The reason is that the effective influence of the individual citizen-voter upon government is, for the reasons outlined in Section 18.B, extremely weak. Filling the vacuum are "pressure groups," which are sub-collectives of individuals interested in pushing particular policies or points of view upon the delegated representatives of the voters. Special interests have two factors on their side in forming pressure groups. First, their motivation is stronger. Since their financial interest is concentrated (as in the case of a single industry), they will gain far more from appropriate political action than any comparably sized group of the general public stand to lose, even though the *entire* public may suffer in the aggregate a much greater loss than the gain to the special interest. Second, being small in number they are more able to overcome the free-rider problem in forming their pressure group.

[8]Public-interested benevolence is not entirely unknown, of course. In ancient Greece, the civic institution of the drama was largely supported by individual donors, and of course analogous modern examples can be cited. (A reputation for unselfish benevolence may, in some people's preference functions, be a private good worth buying!)

Example 18. 3
Regulated
Electricity Rates

Electricity, as a "natural monopoly," is now governmentally regulated in almost all states. The problem of collective action suggests the hypothesis that the relatively small numbers of *large* consumers of electricity will have an advantage over the multitude of *small* consumers of electricity in forming a pressure group that can influence the decisions of the political agencies responsible for regulating rates.

This hypothesis was tested by George Stigler and Claire Friedland, making use of data from earlier years when there were still a considerable number of unregulated states. Since it can be presumed that *industrial* users of electricity are relatively large in scale (and small in number) in comparison with *residential* users, the ratio of the residential price to the industrial price is a relevant measure of the hypothesis that large users are favored over small. This ratio alone is not a satisfactory criterion, however, since there may well be differences in the cost of service that would warrant some degree of rate inequality between industrial and residential users. But there is no obvious reason *for the ratio to differ as between regulated and unregulated states.*

The data showed that the ratio was indeed substantially higher for the regulated states, consistent with the hypothesis that regulation works to the comparative advantage of large consumers over small consumers.

Average Ratio $\dfrac{\text{Residential Price}}{\text{Industrial Price}}$ for Electricity

	1917	1937
Regulated states	1.616	2.459
Unregulated states	1.445	2.047

Source: G. J. Stigler and C. Friedland, "What Can Regulators Regulate? The Case of Electricity," *Journal of Law and Economics*, v. 5 (Oct. 1962), p. 9.

To some extent, the "pressure group" phenomenon counterbalances the tendency of the democratic polity to over-ride the interest of minorities (see Section 18.B.2). But it does so in a rather capricious way, protecting only those minorities strategically positioned (by reason of concentration) to influence the political process. One point of interest is that since production is generally a *specialized* activity and consumption an *unspecialized* one, government interventions have historically tended to favor producers over consumers. As we are all *both* producers and consumers, it might be thought that the effects cancel out. But the political measures that favor producers (for example, permitting formation of a cartel) tend to be anti-competitive. This leads to a loss of economic efficiency, apart from possibly objectionable distribution effects.

18.D BUREAUCRACY

The classes of political decision-making agents considered to this point include citizen-voters, political parties, elected representatives or delegates, and pressure groups. But another important element of the picture, the governmental bureaucracy, has not yet been referred to.

The bureaucracy consists of that class of government personnel not responsible for *making* policy decisions but for *implementing* them. Supposedly impartial and neutral, bureaucrats are not subject to election or recall at the hands of the voters. It follows that if bureaucrats really do determine the actual outcomes of decisions, the ability of citizens to achieve their desires through the political mechanism (i.e., through their control over elected delegates) is even weaker than has previously been indicated.

Now it is an obvious fact of common knowledge that implementation is as important as decision. Or, for all practical purposes, implementation *is* the actual decision. Hence the bureaucracy surely does have substantial power. We would expect leading bureaucrats, from their positions of strength, to negotiate with the other powerful actors on the political scene so as to participate importantly in actual governmental choices.

What are the interests of the bureaucracy? Apart from high wages for small effort, a critical aim is *tenure of office*. If a bureaucrat could be easily dismissed, he would not long survive any battle with powerful elected delegates or pressure groups. Hence a prime goal is the strengthening of civil service regulations so as to permit dismissal only "for cause," strictly interpreted. This aim has been very satisfactorily achieved; the spoils system is to a large degree a thing of the past.

A second plausible bureaucratic aim is *agency growth*: Office holders in a position to influence decisions are motivated to build empires by increasing the size of the resources under their control. As has been shown first by Professor Parkinson,[9] this works out in a remarkably regular fashion. The British Admiralty bureaucracy grows although the Royal Navy diminishes; let the colonies declare their independence, Her Majesty's Colonial Office continues to expand; and the U.S. Department of Agriculture goes on growing in budget and employment while the number of farmers shrinks.

[9]C. Northcote Parkinson, *Parkinson's Law* (1957).

Example 18. 4
Taxicab
Regulation

The taxicab industry in different cities tends to be regulated under one of two alternative systems: (1) municipal agency, or (2) independent commission. In a study of 33 cities, Ross D. Eckert argued that these modes of regulation are associated with different incentive structures for the regulators.

The decision-making officeholders in a municipal agency have, one would expect, the typical motivations of bureaucrats. As the degree of detailed supervision of the taxicab industry increases, larger budgets and staffs will be "needed," with correspondingly higher salaries for the directors of such a massive and important regulatory activity. Independent commissioners, however, are in quite a different position. They generally engage in other public or private activity; their commission service is only a part-time occupation. Complex and detailed taxicab regulation, with consequent need to supervise large staffs, hear complaints, grant exceptions, etc., would require costly sacrifice of their time and effort. And since commissioners normally hold office only for a limited term of years, any long-run return (e.g., an upward trend in salaries for commissioners) that may result from more energetic regulatory activity may go only to benefit their successors in office.

One way of *reducing* the level of regulatory effort is to have a single "responsible" operator of all the taxicabs in a city. Outright monopoly situations are indeed more common in commission-regulated than in agency-regulated cities. But for a variety of reasons literal monopoly is rare. Many cities, however, have partial degrees of regulation-imposed monopoly effected through division of the market by quotas, territory assignments, or exclusive taxistands. The hypothesis is that commissioners would prefer this situation, whereas agency bureaucrats would welcome the necessity for elaborate and detailed regulatory dealings with a multiplicity of small operators. The data below show that the hypothesis was verified.

Taxicab Regulatory Status, 33 U.S. Cities

	Monopoly or Market Division (number of cities)	Neither Monopoly nor Market Division (number of cities)
Commissions	5	1
Agencies	5	22

Source: Ross D. Eckert, "On the Incentives of Regulators: The Case of Taxicabs," *Public Choice*, v. 14 (Spring 1973), p. 90.

18. E THE SCOPE OF GOVERNMENT

Perhaps the key scientific questions in political economy are: What determines the *types* of activities carried on through government, and the *scale* on which those activities are conducted? The economic approach suggests that observed behavior reflects the goals and the relative strengths of the groups participating in the day-to-day decisions of government, interacting according to the constitutional "rules of the game" in the political sphere.

As we have seen, among the groups exercising political power are political parties, elected delegates, pressure groups furthering special interests, and bureaucrats. In a democratic system the "will of the people" (enforced ultimately by delegates' desire to be reelected) also plays an important role, but only as one element in the picture. Thus, the problem for *positive* political economy is to work out the logic of the interaction of these groups, under alternative constitutional structures, so as to be able to predict and understand the actual functioning of the political mechanism.

18. E. 1 Functions of Government

Standard statistical classifications of the expenditures of Federal, state, and local government units in the United States do not always permit an entirely satisfactory breakdown by function. Table 18.1 is condensed from official statistical data.

As a first step to understanding, we can classify the various types of observed government activity under four main functions: (1) defense, (2) law, (3) production, and (4) distribution.

Table 18. 1

Direct General Expenditure by Function,
by Level of Government, 1971–72
(in Millions of Dollars)

	Federal	State	Local	All Governments	% of Total
Total	154516	62051	104822	321389	100.00
National Defense and International Relations	79258	—	—	79258	24.66
Postal Service	9366	—	—	9366	2.91
Space Research and Technology	3369	—	—	3369	1.05
Transportation					
Highways	432	12747	6263	19442	6.05
Other	4141	303	1551	5995	1.87
Sewerage and Sanitation	—	—	4729	4729	1.47
Police, Fire, and Correction	665	2209	8453	11326	3.52
Education and Human Resources					
Education	5104	17153	47734	69990	21.78
Health and Hospitals	4166	6008	6858	17033	5.30
Housing and Urban Renewal	2630	34	2747	5411	1.68
Other	—	63	3074	3137	.98
Natural Resources	11105	2470	640	14215	4.42
Public Welfare	2488	12247	8822	23558	7.33
Administration	3400	3675	4897	11971	3.72
Interest on Public Debt	17114	2135	3827	23077	7.18
Other and Unallocable	11278	3008	5228	19514	6.07

Source: U.S. Bureau of the Census, *Governmental Finances in 1971–72*, Series GF 72-No. 5, U.S. Government Printing Office, Washington, D.C., 1973, p. 23.

1. Defense: The absolutely essential minimal function that government must provide for any society is protection against external and internal enemies. The government *is* the group exercising dominant force; if the existing government group fails to provide protection in a trial of strength, the newcomers will then constitute the government. The data of Table 18.1 show that National Defense and International Relations accounted for about 25% of government general expenditures in 1971–72. To this should be added the bulk of expenses under the category Police, Fire, and Correction; also, Interest on Public Debt in large part represents past military expenditures; and finally, shares of Administration and Other might well be attributed to Defense. Overall, some 35% of government expenditures in 1971–72 can be regarded as accounted for by the Defense function.

2. Law: To operate at any level of effectiveness, members of a society cannot live completely at the whim of the governors. Rather, there must be some system of rights or property defining how individuals are permitted to act, alone or in association with others. This system of rights, with correlative duties thus placed on others not to interfere with those rights, is *law*. Since law must be enforced to be useful, it cannot exist without government. Hence the nullity of so-called *international law*, in the absence of a super-government prepared to coerce those regimes that tear up the "scraps of paper" (treaties) that represent contracts among nations.

Apart from the expenditures already accounted for under the heading of Defense, the budgetary burden of the legal system (legislatures, courts, etc.) is not large. The costs constitute only some fractions of relatively small categories like Police, Fire, and Correction and Administration in the Table. (In early times, law was actually dispensed at a profit by royal courts, the fees serving as an important source of government revenue.)

Provision of a system of defense, and the administration of justice, are universally recognized as *essential* functions of government. Beyond this, however, governments may take a more or less activist role in guiding the economic performance of society—the production and distribution of goods and services.

3. Production: Government is, as explained in Section 18.C above, uniquely able to make the collective choices involved in the provision of non-excludable *public goods*. Individuals can be regarded as voluntarily demanding public goods through the institution of government, thus avoiding the free-rider problem that would otherwise lead to under-provision of these goods. (It is possible to consider Defense and Law also as types of public goods, but for our purposes they are kept separate.) In Table 18.1, the expenditures (apart from those already listed under Defense and Law) that contain important public-good elements include Education, Transportation, and Space Research and Technology. Even if all the expenditures so categorized could be regarded as going to the purchase of public goods, the total is only around 31% of the aggregate of government spending.

Evidently, government is also in the business of providing a vast range of ordinary *private* goods. Postal Service, Social Insurance,[10] and Housing all represent goods that are essentially similar to commodities or services that are also provided privately—or surely would be so provided were it not (as in the case of the government's postal monopoly) illegal to do so. Health and Hospitals contains a small public-good component (preventing epidemics), but for the most part the expenditure represents provision of a private good—personal medical care. Even Education (though counted above within the public-good category) is much more importantly a private than a public good; the benefits of governmental expenditures for education go *primarily* to the educated person, and only secondarily to the remainder of society.

Apart from the actual provision of public or private goods, modern governments affect the productive efficiency of the economy in a variety of

[10]Social Security and other social insurance arrangements are not included in the data of Table 18.1. The receipts and expenditures for these activities are regarded as going into or coming out of "trust funds" rather than the regular government accounts.

important ways. The provision and control of *money* facilitates the process of exchange (see Chapter 8).[11] The *stabilization of economic activity*—prevention of depressions, inflations, etc.—is also generally recognized as an appropriate function of modern government.[12] Anti-monopoly activities of agencies like the Anti-Trust Division of the Department of Justice, and the regulation of "natural monopolies" through governmental commissions, are designed to or can be defended as tending to improve efficiency in the allocation of resources.

Government policy toward monopoly provides an interesting test case for observing the interaction of politically powerful groups. To the extent that the political process tends (as remarked above) to give more weight to *producer* than to *consumer* interests, we might well doubt the effectiveness of government in controlling monopoly. And indeed, the charge has been made that regulatory agencies are often captured by the special interests they are supposed to be guarding against. On the Federal level the Interstate Commerce Commission (regulating surface transportation), the Civil Aeronautics Board (regulating the airlines), and the Federal Communications Commission (regulating radio and television) have all been the targets of such charges. And in cases like the cartelization of many sectors of agricultural marketing (see Example 11.5), that the aim of government action was achieving higher prices for producers at the expense of consumers is scarcely a secret. On the other hand, whatever the wisdom of the "trust-busting" activity of the Department of Justice and the Federal Trade Commission, these agencies are generally regarded as independent of producer control. How the observed differences of behavior stem from the motivations, legal status, and incentives of the participants is a topic largely remaining to be explained.

4. Distribution: An important activity of modern government is redistribution of income or wealth—in democratic countries at least, primarily from richer to poorer classes. In Table 18.1, the category of Public Welfare (7.3% of aggregate expenditures) is explicitly redistributive. But redistribution is also an important aspect of other categories, and indeed helps explain what might otherwise be regarded as anomalies. Consider the expenditures under the heading of Health and Hospitals. A typical procedure here is for government agencies to provide a relatively low quality of hospital or medical care, at zero price or at a very low price, to all who choose to use that service. But since the rich can afford and generally will prefer to buy somewhat better health care privately, only the poor choose the government service. The effect is a redistribution of income "in kind" to the poor. To greater or lesser degree, this analysis applies to public housing (all but the very poor will prefer private

---

[11]It is an interesting topic of monetary theory whether the government role is inherent in the existence of money. Privately-produced moneys, it might be argued, could serve as well as or better than government money.

[12]Unfortunately, it is easier to recognize this function than to achieve it! It remains subject to controversy whether governmental attempts to stabilize the economy have actually made things better rather than worse.

housing), to public education (the rich can afford private schools), to subsidized public transit (the rich travel by private car), etc.

Example 18. 5
Tax-Expenditure
Redistribution

The Tax Foundation attempted, for the year 1961, to assess the overall redistributive effect of the tax-expenditure system (Federal, state, and local). Making a number of rather heroic assumptions about the burden of taxes collected and the benefits of expenditures on behalf of the different income classes, the researchers were able to summarize the results as shown in the following Table.

Redistributive Effect of Government Budgets, 1961

Income Class (after personal taxes)	Ratio of Government Benefits to Taxes
Under $2000	4.1
$2000–2999	2.6
$3000–3999	1.7
$4000–4999	1.2
$5000–5999	1.1
$6000–7499	.9
$7500–9999	.8
$10,000–14,999	.7
$15,000 and over	.4

Source: Tax Foundation, Inc., *Allocating Tax Burdens and Government Benefits by Income Class*, Government Brief No. 8, 1967, p. 2.

Comment: As government expenditures in the aggregate were more than 30% of GNP in 1961, a very significant amount of redistribution from the rich to the poor evidently took place through the tax-expenditure system in that year. And, more recently, both the proportionate level of government spending in relation to GNP and the fraction of that spending directed toward the redistribution function have been increasing.

The redistributive activity of the preceding example does suggest that the power of the vote is not as close to a nullity as might have been inferred from the discussion in Section 18.B. It is surely conceivable, as has indeed occurred through much of history, that government might serve as agent of the rich, grinding the faces of the poor to produce luxury for the powerful. But if the vote does have real power, then in a democratic polity this power will be distributed more equally than income. Hence the poor will be able to use the governmental process to convert some of their comparatively greater political strength into money income. And the higher the income bracket, the greater the weight of numbers and political power in the hands of those lower down on the ladder; hence the more punitive the burden of fiscal redistribution that can be expected.

It ought to be remembered, however, that expenditures *on behalf of* the poor are not necessarily payments *to* the poor. In a program like Federally funded job training, for example, the bulk of the actual payments may go to middle-class bureaucrats—specifically, to teachers and administrators. The benefits to poor trainees are "in kind," and may or may not be translatable by them into higher future cash incomes. Hence the interests of the poor and of the bureaucratic class in the redistributive process are intertwined.

18. E. 2 Instruments of Government Policy

Government can carry out its functions either directly or indirectly. Given the objective of achieving a higher level of education of the population, for example, there are still policy choices to be made. Government might subsidize education (in the limit, make it free) thus *inducing* consumers to choose more education voluntarily. Or government might declare education compulsory, thus *forcing* consumers to buy more—or accept more, if free. Current practice in the United States is to have education both free and compulsory up to a certain school-leaving age, and optional (but still more or less subsidized) thereafter.

Perhaps an even more important policy choice is whether or not government is actually to *provide* the service. Education might be made free and compulsory, and yet provided entirely through a system of private schools (see the discussion of subsidies versus vouchers in Section 4.E). The government could reimburse private schools for students enrolled, setting standards and monitoring performance, without actually being in the business of hiring teachers, erecting buildings, etc. Even pure public goods like lighthouse services could be provided privately, on contract with government.

At various times and places, a surprising variety of what we customarily think of as government-provided goods have actually been produced privately, sometimes at state expense, sometimes not. The bounty-hunters of the pioneer West tracked down criminals. Toll roads and canals can be and have been private businesses. There are private arbitration courts today that reduce the need to use public justice. There is one single service that, one would suppose, *must* be provided by government itself if it is to remain government—defense. Yet even this service has at times been provided commercially, by firms supplying mercenary soldiers. (Experience on this score has been largely unfavorable, however; a mercenary chief strong enough to be useful in defense is all too inclined to take over the government himself.)[13] Still, at least military *research* today is largely produced privately, on government contract.

The interests of the bureaucracy, it is clear, lie in the larger scale of agency

[13]Machiavelli, *The Prince*, Chap. 12.

activity made possible by *direct* government provision of goods and services. The incentives of the other major actors on the political scene are mixed, however. The choice between direct and indirect instruments for carrying out government functions, like the scope of the functions themselves, remains a largely unexplored scientific question.

18. E. 3 A Scientific Issue in Political Economy:
Growth of Government

One of the most striking phenomena of modern times has been the steady growth of the government sector. Despite the hot political debates that have greeted the successive steps of government expansion, there is surprisingly little scientific understanding of the forces tending to bring it about.

The first and most obvious explanation is the increasing burden of the Defense function. As the technology of attack and destruction has improved so fantastically (nuclear bombs, intercontinental missiles, etc.), the difficulty and cost of defense have grown correspondingly. But suppose we entirely exclude the Defense function. The scope of government has grown enormously in the non-defense sector as well.

Example 18. 6
Growth of
Government

Various stages in the expansion of the overall government sector in the United States are shown in the following Table.

Growth of Government in the United States

Date	Total Expenditures		Civilian Expenditures	
	$ Billions	% of GNP	$ Billions	% of GNP
1890	$ 0.8	6.5%	$ 0.7	5.0%
1902	1.5	7.3	1.2	5.8
1913	3.2	7.8	2.8	6.8
1922	9.3	12.6	7.9	10.7
1929	10.7	10.4	9.5	9.2
1940	17.6	17.6	15.5	15.5
1950	65.9	23.1	42.2	14.8
1960	136.1	27.0	84.4	16.7
1970	313.0	32.2	225.1	23.1

Source: R. A. Musgrave and P. B. Musgrave, *Public Finance in Theory and Practice* (New York: McGraw-Hill, 1973), p. 118.

As may be seen, government expenditures have more than kept up with both the real growth of the economy and the inflation of prices, so as to constitute a steadily increasing fraction of GNP. Despite the fact that big jumps in expenditures have typically taken place in wartime, civilian expenditures as percent of GNP have also grown steadily.

Basically, there are two possible lines of explanation for the phenomenon of expansion of government. The first gives primary weight to the *voluntarist* aspect of political decision. On this view, government has expanded in response to desires on the part of the community for the types of services government can best provide. The second approach emphasizes, in contrast, *changes in the balance of political power* possessed by organized groups on the political scene.

Voluntaristic explanations might run in terms of some or all of the following points: (1) Public goods, in contrast with private goods, might have income elasticity greater than unity (see Section 5.A). Then with rising national income over time, citizen-voters have desired more of the public goods that government characteristically provides. (2) With increasing wealth and population, the limited geographical space we inhabit has become more and more crowded. In our daily lives we are therefore increasingly imposing *externalities* (see Section 17.C.3) upon one another. Hence the need for more government control of activities that could have safely been left private in a more dispersed and isolated society. (3) The technical efficiency of government may have grown relative to the private sector. With advances like computers, it has become possible to conduct enterprises on a much larger scale than previously. Government, as the largest-scale enterprise in society, may have gained in relative effectiveness.

Explanations that run in terms of political power, on the other hand, might point to considerations like the following: (1) The government bureaucracy, as it grows in numbers, becomes an increasingly potent political force. Wars and defense crises that require gigantic budgetary expansions leave in their wake a mass of officeholders, with sufficient political clout to resist budgetary contraction when the crises pass. (2) An important sociological development with consequences for the political structure has been the growth of the *educated class* in the population (say, those with college degrees). Educated persons are *relatively* better equipped to achieve positions of status and power in government rather than in business. Legislators, bureaucrats, and other important actors on the political scene are themselves members of the educated class and inclined to be responsive to its interests, especially as the educated are much more politically active than the population at large. (3) A related point is connected with a cultural change that has brought about an increasing gap between the *values* of the more and less educated classes. On problems like racial equality, on issues such as the proportions of national resources to be devoted to the advancement of arts and sciences, on matters of social relations such as the relative status of businessmen versus professors, the educated classes may hold views divergent from those of the remainder of the population. With their increasing and disproportionately important influence in government, the educated groups have been able to use the political mechanism to achieve aims that are less fully attained in private decisions.

The degree of truth in each of these points, and the comparative explanatory values of the voluntarist and the political-power approaches, unfortunately cannot be explored here. Indeed, the state of our knowledge as to major issues of political economy hardly goes beyond the formulation of hypotheses such as those outlined.

Questions

1.   Why is the "voluntarist" approach to the problem of political behavior particularly amenable to economic analysis? What other approaches are there?

2.   What are some of the major obstacles preventing the expression of the "will of the people" through the political process? How are these analogous to, and how different from, the difficulties of the market process?

3.   How may *delegation* of decision-making power to political representatives lead to decisions diverging from the desires of constituents? Considering the corporation as a kind of political system, what protections and escape hatches do stockholders have that may not be available to members of the polity?

4.   Under what circumstances does the "free rider" problem emerge? How valid is the assertion that all government is fundamentally a response to the free-rider problem?

5.   Services that are *financed* by government need not actually be *produced* in the government sector. Under what circumstances is government likely to contract with private enterprise for production of government-financed services? Under what circumstances are there activities financed by the private sector but actually produced by government?

6.   How do the opportunities and incentives of bureaucrats differ from those of elected officials? How do they differ from managers of private firms?

7.   Would the fidelity of the political system to citizen desires be improved by any or all of the following: more frequent elections, more numerous legislatures, elected rather than appointed judges, the spoils system rather than the merit system in civil service? Comment.

8.   Is a unanimous consent rule, with buying of dissident votes, an ideal political system—apart from transaction costs? Does the process of "logrolling" provide some approximation of this result? What are some of the objections to log-rolling?

9.   Under what political mechanisms or situations do majorities tend to exploit minorities? Under what mechanisms or situations is it the other way around?

10.   If votes could be bought for money, would *both* the rich and the poor be better off in accordance with the mutual advantage of trade? What is the objection to buying votes for money?

11. What explains the steady growth of the government sector relative to the private sector in the past century? Why was there a relative decline in the government sector during the era of industrialization in Great Britain?

12. Suppose there were a sudden unexpected increase in demand for a product now provided through the government sector. Would you expect any systematic differences in the price-quantity response as compared with a product provided through the private sector? What about the response to a decrease in demand? What about responses to increases or decreases in cost of production?

Appendix
Equations of
General Equilibrium

The more advanced or more mathematically-equipped student can gain additional insight into the inter-relationships that comprise the economic system from study of the equations that hold in general equilibrium. These equations form what is called a *choice-theoretic structure*. Prior to the equations themselves must come the specification of:

The objects of choice: The goods (or bads) whose production, transformation, or exchange the system is to explain. We will consider here as objects of choice only consumption goods and productive services—omitting, among other things, money.

The decision-making agents: Only individuals and firms will be considered here, omitting, among other things, governments.

The goals of and constraints on behavior: Utility-maximization for individuals and profit-maximization for firms are the goals postulated. Constraints reflect the fact that market and productive opportunities are always limited.

The modes of interaction: Only market interactions are allowed for (ruling out force, fraud, charity, etc.). In addition, perfect competition is assumed; all participants behave as *price-takers*.

The equations themselves can be usefully classified into: (1) those on the level of the decision-making agents, expressing the principle of *optimization*, i.e., maximization subject to constraint, and (2) those on the level of the market interaction, expressing the principle of *equilibrium*.

Three different equation systems are formulated in the sections that follow. Section A.1 has only *individuals* as decision-making agents in a world of pure exchange: *consumption goods* are the sole objects of choice, and there are *market opportunities* only. Section A.2 extends the individuals' opportunities to incorporate *opportunities for productive transformations among consumption goods*. Section A.3 incorporates *productive services* as additional objects of choice and introduces *firms as specialized productive decision-making agents.*

In this Appendix, calculus notation is used where appropriate.

A.1 INDIVIDUALS AS DECISION-MAKING AGENTS: PURE EXCHANGE

We will assume a world of J individuals as decision-making agents, indexed by the running symbol $j = 1, \ldots, J$. But to avoid needless generality, we can assume just two consumption goods, X and Y, as the objects of choice. For the typical individual j, the utility function can be expressed as:

$$\text{(A.1)} \qquad U_j \equiv \Phi_j(x_j, y_j)$$

The individuals' utility functions are not actually part of the set of relations determining the equilibrium. That is, there is no need to know the "cardinal" utility magnitudes associated with the equilibrium state of the economic system. Only the Marginal Rates of Substitution in Consumption, the MRS_C^j, are actually involved. MRS_C^j is the absolute value of the derivative that can be defined:

$$\text{(A.2)} \qquad \left. \frac{dy_j}{dx_j} \right|_U \equiv \phi_j(x_j, y_j)$$

The assertion here is that each individual's MRS_C is determined as a function ϕ_j of his own commodity consumptions x_j and y_j. The individual-identifier symbol j will usually be suppressed (where not needed for purposes of clarity or emphasis), so that (A.2) can be rewritten:

$$\text{(A.2')} \qquad \left. \frac{dy}{dx} \right|_U \equiv \phi(x, y) \qquad \begin{array}{l} MRS_C \text{ Function} \\ (J \text{ equations}) \end{array}$$

Geometrically, this specifies the slope of the indifference curve for any x, y point in a diagram like Figure 4.1; consequently, the equation can be taken as corresponding to the preference map.

Each person as decision-making agent in pure exchange faces only market opportunities:

$$\text{(A.3)} \qquad P_x x + P_y y = I \qquad \begin{array}{l} \text{Budget Constraint} \\ (J \text{ equations}) \end{array}$$

Here P_x and P_y are the market prices, and I his given level of income. The equation represents the *use* or disposition of income. The *source* of income in pure exchange is the market value of the individual's endowed quantities $x^\dagger, y^\dagger$ in his possession before the opening of trading.

$$\text{(A.4)} \qquad I \equiv P_x x^\dagger + P_y y^\dagger \qquad \begin{array}{l} \text{Source of Income} \\ (J \text{ equations}) \end{array}$$

Equations (A.3) and (A.4) correspond geometrically to the individual's budget line in Figure 4.1.

The consumptive optimum condition (derived as shown in Mathematical Footnotes 5 and 11 of Chapter 4) is:

(A.5)
$$-\frac{dy}{dx}\bigg|_U = \frac{P_x}{P_y}$$
Consumptive Optimum
(J equations)

This condition, together with (A.3), corresponds to the geometrical tangency position C^* in Figure 4.1.

Equations (A.2), (A.3), and (A.4) determine the consumptive optimum for each single individual *given* the market prices P_x and P_y. But in the analysis of market equilibrium, prices are variables to be determined. The determining condition is, of course, the equilibrium of overall supply and demand. For commodity X, this equilibrium could be expressed as the condition that the sum over all the individual's *net* market quantities demanded, $\sum_{j=1}^{J} x_j^n$ (where $x_j^n = x_j - x_j^\dagger$), be zero. But it is more convenient to express the supply-demand equality in terms of "conservation conditions" for the aggregate sum of the *gross* magnitudes consumed x_j and the quantities endowed $x_j^\dagger$. That is, for each commodity in pure exchange the sum of the consumptions must equal the sum of the endowments.

(A.6)
$$\begin{cases} \sum_{j=1}^{J} x_j = \sum_{j=1}^{J} x_j^\dagger \\ \sum_{j=1}^{J} y_j = \sum_{j=1}^{J} y_j^\dagger \end{cases}$$
Conservation Conditions
(2 equations, of which
only 1 is independent)

This equality corresponds geometrically to the supply-demand intersection of Figure 7.5, Panel (b).

It is customary in general-equilibrium models to show that the number of independent and consistent equations is equal to the number of variables. Such an equality would guarantee existence of a unique solution in a system of *linear* equations. Our general-equilibrium conditions are not ordinarily linear, but in certain circumstances may be regarded as approximately so in the neighborhood of a possible equilibrium.

We appear to have, omitting the unneeded utility function (A.1), $4J + 2$ equations, corresponding in number to the individual variables $x_j, y_j,$ $\frac{dy_j}{dx_j}\big|_U$, I_j plus the two market prices P_x and P_y. However, we do not really have two independent conservation conditions. One follows from the other, given the rest of the system.[1] That leaves only $4J + 1$ equations for the $4J + 2$ variables. And in fact the equation system does *not* suffice to determine the two market variables P_x and P_y in addition to the $4J$ individual

---

[1] If the budget equation (A.3) and the definition (A.4) are summed over the J individuals we have:
$$P_x \sum x + P_y \sum y = P_x \sum x^\dagger + P_y \sum y^\dagger$$
Then if $\sum x = \sum x^\dagger$, as specified by the first equation of (A.6), the second equation of (A.6) follows immediately.

variables. What it does determine is the price *ratio* P_x/P_y, which is all that is needed. This could be shown by dividing both sides of (A.3) and (A.4) by P_y, in which case only the price ratio P_x/P_y would appear in the equation system at all. Or alternatively, if Y were chosen as "numeraire" so as to fix $P_y \equiv 1$, only the numerator P_x of the price ratio would appear as a variable.

We can easily generalize the objects of choice from only two goods to any number of goods G, indexed by the running symbol $g = 1, \ldots, G$. In setting forth the generalized equations, individual consumption quantities would be expressed in the form x^g_j, the (usually suppressed) subscript identifying the individual and the superscript the good. One of the commodities, say the last or Gth, can be selected to serve as the basis of comparison for defining all the MRS_C, the Marginal Rates of Substitution in Consumption, as absolute values of the partial derivatives $\left.\dfrac{\partial x^G}{\partial x^1}\right|_U, \left.\dfrac{\partial x^G}{\partial x^2}\right|_U, \ldots, \left.\dfrac{\partial x^G}{\partial x^{G-1}}\right|_U.$[2] Choosing this same commodity G as numeraire, so that $P_G \equiv 1$, the system will determine the equilibrium price ratios $P_1/P_G, P_2/P_G, \ldots, P_{G-1}/P_G$ as well as the GJ quantity variables (the x^g_j quantities, each representing consumption of a particular good by a particular individual) and the $J(G-1)$ Marginal Rates of Substitution in Consumption.

The student may write out the set of equations for the G-good case as an exercise, verifying that the number of independent equations corresponds to the number of variables to be determined.

A. 2 INDIVIDUALS AS DECISION-MAKING AGENTS: PRODUCTIVE TRANSFORMATION AND EXCHANGE

In the choice-theoretic structure of this section, individuals can engage in productive transformations of their commodity endowments (dealings with Nature, so to speak) as well as market exchanges (dealing with other individuals).

For the typical individual, the utility function U is again defined as in equation (A.1). However, we can proceed directly here to the specification of the Marginal Rate of Substitution in Consumption, in the same form as before:

(A.7)
$$\left.\frac{dy}{dx}\right|_U = \phi(x, y)$$

MRS_C Function
(J equations)

The budget constraint and consumptive optimum equations are also unchanged in form.

[2]Partial derivative notation is appropriate here because all other variables are held constant. Thus, $\left.\dfrac{\partial x^G}{\partial x^1}\right|_U$ holds constant the quantities consumed of commodities $2, \ldots, G-1$ (as well as the level of utility) so as to accord with the definition of Marginal Rate of Substitution in Consumption between commodities 1 and G. To wit, as the amount of commodity G that the individual (in terms of his preferences) is just willing to substitute on the margin for a unit of commodity 1.

(A.8) $$P_x x + P_y y = I$$ Budget Constraint
(J equations)

(A.9) $$-\frac{dy}{dx}\bigg|_U = \frac{P_x}{P_y}$$ Consumptive Optimum
(J equations)

The first change encountered, as compared with the pure-exchange model, occurs in the specification of the *source* of income. The magnitude of income constraining consumption is not now given by the market value of a fixed endowment basket x^t, y^t but rather by the value of the basket defined by the elements x^q, y^q of the individual's productive optimum position Q^*.

(A.10) $$I = P_x x^q + P_y y^q$$ Source of income
(J equations)

Equations (A.8) and (A.10) correspond geometrically to the market line MM in Figure 7.6.

In the regime of productive transformation and exchange, the individual's income is not a constant but is itself found by a process of *maximization* subject to the constraint of the productive transformation opportunities.

(A.11) $$\Omega(x^q, y^q) \equiv 0$$ Productive Constraint
(J equations)

(A.12) $$\frac{dy^q}{dx^q}\bigg|_Q \equiv \omega(x^q, y^q)$$ MRS_T Function
(J equations)

(A.13) $$-\frac{dy^q}{dx^q}\bigg|_Q = \frac{P_x}{P_y}$$ Productive Optimum
(J equations)

Equation (A.11) expresses the productive constraint itself, corresponding geometrically to the Production-Possibility Curve QQ in Figure 7.6. MRS_T, the Marginal Rate of Substitution in Productive Transformation, is the absolute value of the derivative defined in (A.13), corresponding to the absolute slope along the QQ locus. And the optimization condition (A.13) corresponds to the tangency Q^* along QQ that determines the position of the market line MM of highest attained income.

Finally, to close the system we have the supply-demand equilibrium conditions, expressed as conservation conditions:

(A.14) $$\begin{cases} \sum_{j=1}^{J} x_j = \sum_{j=1}^{J} x_j^q \\ \sum_{j=1}^{J} y_j = \sum_{j=1}^{J} y_j^q \end{cases}$$ Conservation Conditions
(2 equations, of which
only 1 is independent)

For each commodity, the equations say that the sum of the individuals' consumptions must equal the aggregate of the quantities generated by productive transformations. This corresponds geometrically to the supply-demand intersection determining the X^* magnitude in Figure 7.8.

We have here $7J + 2$ equations. As to the variables, there are J each of the individual variables $x, y, x^q, y^q, I, \dfrac{dy}{dx}\Big|_U$, and $\dfrac{dy^q}{dx^q}\Big|_Q$, plus the two market prices P_x and P_y. As in the pure-exchange system of the previous section, one of the two conservation equations is not independent.[3] A similar conclusion follows, that the equation system does not suffice to determine the absolute market prices P_x and P_y but only their ratio P_x/P_y, i.e., the price of X in terms of Y as numeraire.

The extension from only two goods X and Y to any number of desired goods $g = 1, \dots, G$ is left as an exercise for the student to carry out, following the corresponding discussion of the pure-exchange system in the previous section.

A. 3 INDIVIDUALS AND FIRMS: CONSUMPTION, PRODUCTION, AND EXCHANGE

The equation system of this section introduces *firms* as decision-making agents. Firms are artificial entities specialized to the process of production; they do not consume, have no endowments, but are here assumed to possess all the productive opportunities of the economy. Ultimately, all firms are owned by individuals and distribute their profits back to owners. *Production* in this section is no longer a process of transformation between alternative combinations of consumption goods. Rather a new class of commodities (objects of choice) is introduced in the form of *resources* (more specifically, the *services* of resources). Firms engage in productive processes that convert resource services into consumption goods. A new and important feature is that individuals generally attach utility to *reservation uses* (leisure or non-market uses) of the resources they own.

For simplicity here, the equation system will incorporate only two consumption goods X and Y and two resources A and B. There are J individuals $(j = 1, \dots, J)$ and F firms $(f = 1, \dots, F)$.

The utility function for a typical individual j can be expressed in the form:

(A.15) $$U_j = \Phi_j(x_j, y_j, a_j, b_j)$$

Once again, the individual identifier symbol j will ordinarily be suppressed except as a point of emphasis. It is important to note that a and b in (A.15) represent the *reservation* quantities. The relations between the reservation quantities and the *net* quantities a^n and b^n offered for hire in the factor markets are simply:

(A.16) $$\begin{cases} a + a^n = a^\dagger \\ b + b^n = b^\dagger \end{cases} \quad \begin{array}{l}\text{Resource-Use Identities}\\ (2J \text{ equations})\end{array}$$

[3] If the equations (A.8) and (A.10) are summed over the J individuals, we have
$$P_x \sum x + P_y \sum y = P_x \sum x^q + P_y \sum y^q$$
Then if $\sum x = \sum x^q$ as asserted by the first conservation equation, the second is directly implied.

That is, for each factor the reserved quantity and the hired quantity sum to the individual's given resource-endowment.

As was the case previously, the "cardinal" utilities U_j are not actually needed for determination of equilibrium, so that (A.15) does not enter the equation system. What do enter are the Marginal Rates of Substitution in Consumption (thinking of the *reservation uses* of resources as a kind of consumption). The MRS_C here correspond to absolute values of partial derivatives of (A.15):

(A.17)
$$\begin{cases} \left.\dfrac{\partial y}{\partial x}\right|_U = \phi_{xy}(x, y, a, b) \\[2mm] \left.\dfrac{\partial y}{\partial a}\right|_U = \phi_{ay}(x, y, a, b) \qquad \begin{array}{l} MRS_C \text{ Functions}[4] \\ (3J \text{ equations}) \end{array} \\[2mm] \left.\dfrac{\partial y}{\partial b}\right|_U = \phi_{by}(x, y, a, b) \end{cases}$$

We now must introduce the budget condition. As before, we have two equations, one representing the *spending* of income I and the other the *earning* thereof.

(A.18) $$P_x x + P_y y = I \qquad \begin{array}{l} \text{Budget Constraint} \\ (J \text{ equations}) \end{array}$$

(A.19) $$I = h_a a^n + h_b b^n + \sum_{f=1}^{F} \sigma_f \Pi_f \qquad \begin{array}{l} \text{Source of Income} \\ (J \text{ equations}) \end{array}$$

Equation (A.18) is in the familiar form of the budget constraint. Equation (A.19) shows that the income available for an individual's consumption derives from earnings from market employment of his owned resources (h_a and h_b being the hire-prices of factors A and B respectively) plus the individual's share in the profits of firms. Here Π_f is the profit of the fth firm and σ_f is the individual's fractional ownership of that firm.

The usual optimization procedure, maximizing utility subject to (A.18) as constraint, leads to the consumptive optimum conditions in the form of equalities of the MRS_C magnitudes with corresponding price ratios:

(A.20)
$$\begin{cases} -\left.\dfrac{\partial y}{\partial x}\right|_U = \dfrac{P_x}{P_y} \\[2mm] -\left.\dfrac{\partial y}{\partial a}\right|_U = \dfrac{h_a}{P_y} \qquad \begin{array}{l} \text{Consumptive} \\ \text{Optimum Conditions} \\ (3J \text{ equations}) \end{array} \\[2mm] -\left.\dfrac{\partial y}{\partial b}\right|_U = \dfrac{h_b}{P_y} \end{cases}$$

The first equation of (A.20) expresses the familiar optimum conditions relating the MRS_C to the price ratio between the two consumption goods X and Y.

---

[4] It is possible to define three additional MRS_C functions: $\left.\dfrac{\partial x}{\partial a}\right|_U$, $\left.\dfrac{\partial x}{\partial b}\right|_U$, and $\left.\dfrac{\partial b}{\partial a}\right|_U$. However, these are not independent of the three already specified in (A.17); there are only three independent slopes in a four-dimensional space.

In the other two equations, the reservation uses of resources A and B are treated exactly like consumption goods. Thus, the hire-price h_a received on the market for *employment* of A can be regarded as the price of choosing reservation uses instead of earning income through employment.

We now consider the decisions of the firms. Each firm is postulated to maximize *profit* Π_f defined in:

(A.21) $$\Pi_f = P_x x_f + P_y y_f - h_a a_f - h_b b_f$$

Definition of Profit
(F equations)

Profit is, of course, the difference between revenues from sale of produced goods X, Y and costs incurred in the hiring of resources A, B.

Each firm has a production opportunity with associated MRS_T functions, the Marginal Rates of Substitution in Transformation between inputs and outputs.

(A.22) $$\Omega_f(x_f, y_f, a_f, b_f) \equiv 0$$

Production Function
(F equations)

Equation (A.22) is analogous to the production function of (A.11), except of course that the resource inputs are made explicit.

(A.23) $$\begin{cases} \left.\frac{\partial y_f}{\partial x_f}\right|_\Omega \equiv \omega_{xy}(x_f, y_f, a_f, b_f) \\ \left.\frac{\partial y_f}{\partial a_f}\right|_\Omega \equiv \omega_{ay}(x_f, y_f, a_f, b_f) \\ \left.\frac{\partial y_f}{\partial b_f}\right|_\Omega \equiv \omega_{ab}(x_f, y_f, a_f, b_f) \end{cases}$$

MRS_T functions[5]
($3F$ equations)

The first of these expressions defines the MRS_T relevant for the transformation opportunities between the consumption goods X and Y. The partial derivative is of the usual negative sign. The other two refer to transformation opportunities between inputs and output. Here the partial derivatives have positive sign. In particular, $\left.\frac{\partial y_f}{\partial a_f}\right|_\Omega$ is the *Marginal Product of factor* A *with respect to output* Y. Similarly, $\left.\frac{\partial y_f}{\partial b_f}\right|_\Omega$ is the *Marginal Product of factor* B *with respect to output* Y.

The productive optimum conditions are:

(A.24) $$\begin{cases} \left.\frac{-\partial y_f}{\partial x_f}\right|_\Omega = \frac{P_x}{P_y} \\ \left.\frac{\partial y_f}{\partial a_f}\right|_\Omega = \frac{h_a}{P_y} \\ \left.\frac{\partial y_f}{\partial b_f}\right|_\Omega = \frac{h_b}{P_y} \end{cases}$$

Productive Optimum
($3F$ equations)

[5]Again, it would be possible to define three additional MRS_T functions, but the three given suffice to determine all the possible slopes in this four-dimensional space.

The first of these, involving only transformation between consumption-good outputs, is the analog of (A.13). The second and third expressions involve the Marginal Products of factors A and B; they correspond to the Factor Employment Conditions of Section 14.B. $P_y \dfrac{\partial y_f}{\partial a_c}\bigg|_\Omega$ defines the Value of the Marginal Product of factor A (with respect to output Y), so the second condition can be expressed as $vmp_a = h_a$ in the notation of Chapter 14. A similar translation leads to expression of the third condition as $vmp_b = h_b$.

Finally, there are the conservation conditions:

(A.25)
$$
\begin{cases}
\sum_{j=1}^{J} a^n = \sum_{f=1}^{F} a_f \\
\sum_{j=1}^{J} b^n = \sum_{f=1}^{F} b_f \\
\sum_{j=1}^{J} x = \sum_{f=1}^{F} x_f \\
\sum_{j=1}^{J} y = \sum_{f=1}^{F} y_f
\end{cases}
\qquad
\begin{array}{l}
\text{Conservation Conditions} \\
\text{(4 equations, of which} \\
\text{only 3 are independent)}
\end{array}
$$

In each case, individual magnitudes are summed on the left-hand side and firm magnitudes on the right-hand side. The first two equations express, for each productive resource, equality of the total of the net (non-reserved) quantities *supplied* by individuals with the aggregate of inputs *employed* by firms. The remaining two conditions equate, for each consumption good, the aggregate of individuals' consumption with the aggregate of firms' production.

Omitting the utility functions (A.15), there are a total of $10J + 8F + 4$ equations. The variables may be classified as:

Individual variables: $x, y, a, b, a^n, b^n, \dfrac{\partial y}{\partial x}\bigg|_U, \dfrac{\partial y}{\partial a}\bigg|_U, \dfrac{\partial y}{\partial b}\bigg|_U, I$

Firm variables: $x_f, y_f, a_f, b_f, \dfrac{\partial y_f}{\partial x_f}\bigg|_\Omega, \dfrac{\partial y_f}{\partial a_f}\bigg|_\Omega, \dfrac{\partial y_f}{\partial b_f}\bigg|_\Omega, \Pi$

Market variables: P_x, P_y, h_a, h_b

The numbers correspond. As usual, however, not all the conservation conditions are independent; one can be shown to follow from the other three. This tells us that, again, the absolute prices are not determined. What are determined are the *price ratios*. And indeed, the entire system could have been written out using only the price ratios P_x/P_y, h_a/P_y, and h_b/P_y instead of the absolute prices.

Once again, the extension to any number of consumption goods and any number of productive resources is left as an exercise for the student.

Index

500

502

503